THE UNIVERSITY OF
WINCHESTER

Heidegger

EMMANUEL FAYE

Heidegger

THE INTRODUCTION OF NAZISM
INTO PHILOSOPHY IN LIGHT OF
THE UNPUBLISHED SEMINARS
OF 1933–1935

Translated by Michael B. Smith
Foreword by Tom Rockmore

Yale University Press
New Haven
& London

Published with assistance from the Ernst Cassirer Publications Fund.

Set in Sabon type by Keystone Typesetting, Inc.
Printed in the United States of America.

Library of Congress Cataloging-in-Publication Data
Faye, Emmanuel.
  [Heidegger, l'introduction du nazisme dans la philosophie. English]
  Heidegger: the introduction of Nazism into philosophy in light of the
unpublished seminars of 1933–1935 / Emmanuel Faye ; translated by Michael B.
Smith ; foreword by Tom Rockmore.
     p. cm.
  Includes bibliographical references and index.
  ISBN 978-0-300-12086-8 (cloth : alk. paper)
  1. Heidegger, Martin, 1889–1976 — Political and social views. 2. National
socialism and philosophy. I. Title.
B3279.H49F34513   2010
193 — dc22
2009014302

A catalogue record for this book is available from the British Library.

This paper meets the requirements of ANSI/NISO Z39.48-1992 (Permanence of
Paper).

10 9 8 7 6 5 4 3 2 1

Contents

Foreword to the English Edition

The causes, the extent, and the philosophical consequences of all kinds for Heidegger's involvement with National Socialism have been discussed in a large and growing debate, which has not so far arrived at anything resembling a consensus. There are a number of reasons why it has been so difficult to clarify Heidegger's relation to Nazism. One is that there has never been unrestricted scholarly access to all the documentation in the Heidegger archives in Marbach. Another is the sheer unwillingness, despite contrary evidence, of so many observers to detect more than a momentary, contingent link between Heidegger and National Socialism, a link supposedly unrelated to his philosophical position. This strangely complacent view of Heidegger's Nazism, which is widespread in the debate, is contradicted by his former student, one of his main German defenders, Hans-Georg Gadamer, who wrote: "Sometimes, in admiration for the great thinker, Heidegger's defenders declared that his political error had nothing to do with his philosophy. That they could pacify themselves with such an argument! They did not notice how insulting such a defense of such an important thinker was."[1]

In France, the problem of the relation between Heidegger's thought and his politics is a familiar topic that has been debated, often hotly debated, for more than half a century. Emmanuel Faye's book, *Heidegger: The Introduction of Nazism into Philosophy in Light of the Unpublished Seminars of 1933–1935,* caused an enormous stir in France when it was published in 2005. As an aid in understanding Faye's book, it will be helpful to situate it against the ongoing French Heidegger debate.

Hegel was already known in France during his lifetime, but Edmund Husserl was not introduced to French readers until the late 1920s. As part of a general French turn to phenomenology, Heidegger began to be translated in the early 1930s. Soon after the end of World War II, when Heidegger's Nazism became known, a debate began that has since never ended. Before Faye's book appeared, the French Heidegger debate occurred in a series of three identifiable waves.

The initial phase of the debate began in the pages of *Les Temps Modernes,* Jean-Paul Sartre's journal, in the late 1940s. It featured articles by Karl Löwith, Maurice de Gandillac, and Alfred de Towarnicki, which were followed some time later by articles by Eric Weil and Alphonse de Waelhens, ending with responses by Löwith and de Waelhens. When National Socialism came to power in Germany, Löwith, a German Jew who was Heidegger's first graduate student, went into exile, finally ending up in the United States.[2] Weil, another German Jew, was Ernst Cassirer's assistant before fleeing to France. De Waelhens was a Belgian phenomenologist. Alfred de Towarnicki was a French journalist devoted to defending Heidegger over many years. Maurice de Gandillac was a well-known French philosopher.

In his contribution, Löwith focused on the political implications of Heidegger's philosophy.[3] He brought to the attention of the scholarly public a problem that until then was little known, especially in France, which had opposed Nazism but unknowingly adopted a thinker with a Nazi past as a central philosophical reference. Löwith's article created a debate that has since never ceased.

The French debate immediately raised two basic ways of understanding the relation between Heidegger's philosophy and his Nazism: as either "contingent," a mere passing moment without particular significance in the evolution of an important thinker, or, on the contrary, in a sense "necessary," since it provides an interpretive framework for all further debate. These views are obviously incompatible. Löwith sees Heidegger's turn to National Socialism as deriving directly from his philosophical position. He criticizes Towarnicki, who treats Heidegger's link to National Socialism as merely temporary, regrettable, and unmotivated by his underlying philosophical position, and he rejects de Gandillac's assertion that Heidegger was unaware of what he did.

As befits a scholarly discussion, the initial phase of the French discussion of Heidegger's relation to Nazism was compact, sharply delimited, calm, and scholarly. The second phase, which was less compact and more difficult to delimit, ran roughly from 1948, when the first French edition of Georg Lukács's study of existentialism and Marxism appeared,[4] to the publication of Jean-Michel Palmier's study of Heidegger's political writings in 1968,[5] the year of the French student uprising. Participants in this phase of the debate, which was often very heated, even strident, include François Fédier, Jean-Pierre Faye (Emmanuel Faye's father), François Bondy, Alfred Grosser, Robert Minder, Aimé Patri, and others writing in such journals as *Médiations* and *Critique*. The frequently excited character of the French debate reflects the political stakes in the critique or defense of Heidegger's theories in a country that went to war to oppose Nazism.

The remarkable change in tone is due to a variety of factors. Sartre brought out *Being and Nothingness* in 1943 to worldwide acclaim. At the end of World War II, conservative French thinkers rallied around Heidegger in distancing themselves from Sartre, who was then close to the French Communist Party. As Heidegger displaced Sartre in the French philosophical pantheon, French scholars sometimes acted as if they were as much engaged in defending French thought as in defending Heidegger's position. At the time, publications by Guido Schneeberger, Theodor Adorno, Paul Hühnerfeld, and others calling attention to Heidegger's Nazi turning meant that Heidegger's philosophy, not only his personal reputation, was now at risk. Finally, France was approaching a political crisis that would nearly paralyze the country for a number of months beginning in March 1968.

The entire translation of *Being and Time* did not appear in France until the mid-1980s; until that time, the French Heidegger discussion revolved mainly around the "Letter on Humanism" (1947). This text is Heidegger's response to a letter addressed to him on 10 November 1946 by Jean Beaufret. Beaufret was at the time a young, nearly unknown philosopher, interested in existentialism, who later turned from Sartre to become Heidegger's staunchest French defender. Heidegger replied in December of that year and then reworked his response for publication. His response, which took the form of an open letter to a figure on the French philosophical scene, just when Heidegger was in eclipse because of his association with the Nazis, is both philosophical and strategic in character. For instance, there was an obvious strategic value in Heidegger's claim of a turning (*Kehre*) in his position, by implication a turning away from his earlier view (perhaps even by implication a turning away from Nazism). The concept of the turning seemed a tacit, even graceful admission of an earlier complicity, combined with a suggestion of a fresh start. It also suggested a reasonable alternative to Sartre, to many observers an objectionable French guru.

In his "Letter," Heidegger can be read as stating his desire to turn over a new leaf in abandoning philosophy for thought (*Denken*). This can be taken as an implicit admission of culpability. It can also be read as a continuing radicalization of the same position without any inflection. Beaufret, who quickly became Heidegger's defender, took a more extreme line, which developed only slowly as he also turned increasingly, as is common among French Heidegger apologists, to extreme right-wing politics. In his letter to Heidegger, he mentions his concern with the relation of ontology to ethics. He later provided a curious answer to his own question in two ways. On the one hand, he steadfastly denied a more than casual relation between Heidegger and National Socialism, a denial he maintained in different forms and over many years. On the other, it was discovered after he died that he had rallied to the French version of the "revisionist" view of history, a version attributed to Robert Faurisson that simply denies the Holocaust as well as the existence of gas chambers in the Nazi concentration camps.[6]

The works by Lukács, the great Marxist philosopher and literary critic, and by Palmier, the specialist in German literature, were unrelated. Lukács's study of Marxism and existentialism, a polemical work written during his Stalinist phase, dismisses existentialism from an orthodox Marxist perspective. In passing, he attacks Heidegger's position as prefascist. He develops this criticism at length in an appendix entitled "Heidegger Redivivus" — in response to Heidegger's "Letter on Humanism," the document that cemented Heidegger's relation to French philosophy — which was added to the German edition of his book.

Lukács's work affected the French discussion of Heidegger only marginally, through its influence on Merleau-Ponty and Sartre. Palmier defends Heidegger against the various attacks, perhaps for the first time in the French discussion, through detailed textual analysis. Palmier's study, which appeared after a sharp exchange between François Fédier and Jean-Pierre Faye, was intended as an initial approach to Heidegger's writings from April 1933 to April 1934 — that is, during Heidegger's period as rector of the University of Freiburg.

We do well, to characterize this phase of the discussion, to turn to the polemic between François Fédier and Jean-Pierre Faye. Most of the French critics of and apologists for Heidegger did not read German, and few of the relevant documents were available in French translation. Roughly until the beginning of the 1960s, the battle around Heidegger and Nazism was mainly waged in ignorance of the historical record.

The second battle of the ongoing French conceptual "war" concerning Heidegger was launched by J.-P. Faye in 1961 through the publication of French translations of certain Heideggerian texts, including the infamous rectoral address ("Rektoratsrede") and the homage to Albert Leo Schlageter, a German terrorist who was executed for his crimes, a homage already cited by Löwith, and above all Heidegger's personal profession of loyalty to Adolf Hitler and the National Socialist state.[7] The main contribution of J.-P. Faye's various articles was to cast doubt on the very idea that Heidegger's Nazi turning was unrelated to his philosophy. Fédier's initial intervention in the discussion occurred some five years after Faye's articles. He turns to Faye only when the latter responded to his impassioned defense of Heidegger against all comers. Since that time, Fédier has maintained his visible role — which now, after the death of Beaufret, his former teacher, is his alone — as the self-appointed "official" spokesman for the view that Heidegger's Nazi turning was short, unwitting, and unrelated to his thought, determined to "deconstruct" any and all stronger claims.

Fédier's self-described intent was not to answer a polemic but to examine the presuppositions of hostile arguments. In each instance, Fédier "proves" to his own satisfaction that the critic is methodologically incapable of comprehending Heidegger's Nazism without acknowledging the "main facts" of the case. Fédier, who is not content with demonstrating there is no significant relation between Heidegger's thought and his politics, further argues that an analysis of Heidegger's courses between 1934 and 1944 clearly demonstrates Heidegger's opposition to Nazism.

The third phase of the French debate began when Victor Farías's study of Heidegger and Nazism flared up like an intellectual supernova in the fall of 1987.[8] The amplitude of the reaction to a study of the relation between philosophy and National Socialism in an obscure German thinker by a Chilean professor of Spanish literature teaching in Berlin is explicable only because Farías for the first time revealed this relation to the wider, nonspecialized public. Suddenly everyone in France knew what until then only a few specialists had known — that is, that Heidegger's thought was linked, perhaps even deeply so, to the very same Nazi ideology France had gone to war to combat.

One must distinguish between the immediate, violent reaction to this book in French circles and the more measured later discussion. Obviously, the quick French reaction to Farías's work was part of an almost instant response that, it is fair to say, swept over Western Europe. The major newspapers and many magazines in all the main European countries carried articles concerning this study, often with a kind of concealed amusement directed at its French reception.

The immediate reaction, what in French is aptly called "une réaction à chaud," was precisely that — namely, heated, often overheated to a degree unusual even in hothouse French intellectual circles. This phase of the controversy, more symptomatic of the depth of feeling than any depth of insight into the problem, was played out in the pages of the daily papers, in the weekly magazines, in art and literary journals, on television, and so on, in short, through forms of communication not often associated with the measured tread, over the centuries, of austere philosophical debate. What had earlier been a disagreement among scholars concerning a well-known but obscure German thinker quickly became an intellectual free-for-all in which opinions, even frank accusations, were voiced in rapid fashion. This guaranteed a "succès de scandale" for a book that rapidly became a "cause célèbre."

The amplitude of the immediate reaction, which lasted for weeks in certain cases, may be indicated through a simple list, in no particular order, of some newspapers and journals that ran articles, sometimes numerous articles, on the topic: *Art Press, La Quinzaine Littéraire, Le Monde, Le Matin, Libération, La Croix, Le Quotidien de Paris, Le Figaro, Le Magazine Littéraire,* and *Le Canard Enchaîné.* Christian Jambet, a former "nouveau philosophe," set the tone in his preface to the French edition of Farías's work. His sharply worded preface begins with a reference to the traditional belief in the virtue of philosophy for life before moving on to Heidegger's identification of authentic existence with a mere semblance, a mere representative of the politics of extermination. Jambet ends with a statement intended to sum up Heidegger's thought in a reference to a well-known film, *Night and Fog (Nuit et brouillard)*, on the Nazi concentration camps: "Heidegger has the merit of making ontology the question of our time. But how can we accept that philosophy, born of Socrates' trial for leading a just life, ends in the twilight where Heidegger wanted to see the end of the gods, but which was only the time of Night and Fog?"[9]

In his preface, opposing Heidegger to the entire philosophical tradition, Jambet raises the question of the specific difference between them, in the treatment of the relation between thought and absolute evil. But he does not address the theme, highly relevant in the French context, of the specific link between Heidegger's philosophy and French thought. Certainly, this topic is partially responsible for the inflamed, passionate character of the immediate French reaction. Freiburg historian Hugo Ott caught the mood extremely well in the opening comment of his review of Farías's book: "In France a sky has fallen in — the sky of the philosophers."[10]

In philosophy in general, because of the length of the gestation period required, debates normally unfold slowly, over periods measured in years, more often in decades or centuries. In French circles, where the half-life of a theory is always short, debate unfolds more quickly since to publish slowly is to risk commenting on a topic only as it disappears into history. Until the publication of Farías's work, with the exception of Palmier's study, no book wholly or even mainly centered on the theme of Heidegger and Nazism had ever appeared in France. After Farías, this lacuna was filled at a speed extraordinary even by the standards of the French intellectual discussion.

Farías's book was published in October 1987. From that period until the following May, a steady, even if steadily diminishing, stream of articles continued to pour out. In an extraordinary burst of scholarly creativity, no less than seven book-length studies devoted to Heidegger's thought and politics appeared in less than a year.[11] In most cases, these books reflected the new consensus that there was a problem, but they differed widely on its description and analysis.

A striking example is offered by Jacques Derrida. The same important philosopher who was for many years the central student of Heidegger's writings in France, someone who more than anyone else called attention to the genuine complexities of Heidegger's thought, was also caught in a kind of tension, even a performative contradiction, in defending someone who opposed many of his own values. This tension was clear in a book in which he examines Heidegger's Nazi proclivities, which he attributes to Heidegger's continued attachment to metaphysics! As a confirmed defender of the faith, Derrida, in an interview, harshly condemned Farías's book but also at the same time confirmed its main thesis. In conceding the inextricable connection between Heidegger's Nazism and philosophy, he insisted on the need to show the deep link between Heidegger's thought and actions to the possibility and reality of what Derrida, using the plural, refers to as all the Nazisms.[12]

Faye's book, which also led to an enormous, confused polemic in the overheated French intellectual environment, constitutes the fourth wave of the French debate about Heidegger and Nazism. In the roughly two decades between the end of the polemic about Farías's work and the appearance of Faye's study, the debate concerning Heidegger and Nazism has continued to simmer, mainly in France and Germany. Faye's book constitutes a turning point in this debate. Until Faye, much of the discussion was carried on between French participants about French views of Heidegger. Faye's intervention changed that. His work is arguably the first French study of Heidegger and National Socialism that surpasses the narrow limits of the French debate and the French reception of Heidegger to discuss the more general problems.

In this interval, publications about Heidegger and Nazism continued to emerge from the press. Dominique Janicaud, who had earlier responded to Farías, brought out an exhaustive study of the French Heidegger debate in two volumes, of which the second contains interviews with leading French contemporary philosophers.[13] Christian Tilitzki published an extremely detailed but controversial study of German academic philosophy in the Weimar Republic and the Third Reich.[14] Marion Heinz and Goran Gretić edited a collection of papers that were originally presented in colloquia on philosophy and National Socialism.[15] Antonia Grunenberg wrote a comparative study of

Hannah Arendt and Martin Heidegger that described their love affair as well as ways in which Heidegger later sought to manipulate her.[16] Yves Charles Zarka drew attention to Carl Schmitt's effort to link his anti-Semitism to his Catholicism.[17]

With the exception of Zarka's book, which evoked a strong, but brief reaction, the debate between the close of the polemic surrounding Farías's book and the appearance of Faye's study was relatively calm, even in France. This suddenly changed when Faye's work appeared. In France, Heidegger has long been a central intellectual presence. Over decades Heidegger has continued to influence a long series of important French intellectuals, from Sartre to Michel Foucault, Derrida, Paul Ricoeur, Michel Henry, the psychoanalyst Jacques Lacan, the poet Paul Celan, the philosopher Emmanuel Levinas, and so on. Yet there is a growing realization that, as Roger-Pol Droit already said in his review of the Farías book when it appeared two decades ago, it is not possible to continue as if nothing had happened.[18]

Faye detects a deep continuity between extreme right-wing politics and extreme right-wing contributions to the intellectual debate. He believes that the struggle against Nazism that ended militarily at the end of World War II still continues in the ongoing battle against the principles underlying German fascism in the views of Heidegger, German historian Ernst Nolte, German legal theoretician Carl Schmitt, and others. According to Faye, the edition of Heidegger's *Collected Works* now being published simply "banalizes" theories that are inseparable from the same social context that produced National Socialism. Faye strongly opposes an effort to subordinate or otherwise "instrumentalize" philosophy for such goals.

Faye's thesis, which some observers may discount as extreme, is that from very early in his career, before he wrote *Being and Time*, Heidegger was committed to principles in the air at the time, principles that were also basic to then nascent Nazism. In a single sentence, the main idea seems to be Heidegger's absolute disrespect of the human individual, who is entirely subordinated to the state, hence evacuating any hint of the possibility of morality in the ordinary sense of the term. Faye develops this thesis in great detail, in what is the fullest review so far in the literature in any language of the relation between Heidegger and National Socialism, with special attention to so far unpublished writings from the early 1930s, particularly during the crucial period of 1933–1935.

The result is a kind of very "thick" contextual reading of Heidegger in the conceptual matrix of his epoch, which Faye carries out very well. His discussion is based on extremely detailed readings of previously unavailable texts and rereadings of texts that are already available. He argues that when we see the often hidden agenda linking Heidegger to other Nazi "thinkers" of the period, his published texts take on a very different, extremely dark, deeply troubling hue. According to Faye, Heidegger's early and later writings reveal a continuous, unmodified commitment to what one might call a deep anti-humanism featuring a strong commitment to some of the darkest sides of the human soul. He shows in arguing against various Heidegger apologists that Heidegger's turning to Nazism is neither an accident due to a lack of aware-ness of the aims of that "movement" nor a passing moment in his career, but a deep and abiding thread running throughout his entire career. It is then not the case that Heidegger's "philosophy" had already taken shape before he encoun-tered Nazism. On the contrary, his position is based on a conception of histor-ical existence and its surroundings comparable to the racial doctrine of Na-tional Socialism that at the time was spreading throughout the intellectual context in different ways.

Others have already examined such issues as Heidegger's Nazi turning, the relation between his political choices and his "philosophy," the relation of his position to the surrounding context, and so on. These various dimensions are related to, but in each case different from, the aim of Faye's text. Faye, who frames his investigation in different terms, proposes to study the very founda-tions of Heidegger's work in general. One of Faye's conclusions is that in Heidegger's writings Nazism is present not only in his terminology but even in the very roots of his work that simply cannot be dissociated from his political choices. To put the point simply, Heidegger's philosophical theories and politi-cal practice are indissociably linked.

It is not possible here to explore the arguments Faye advances to support his conclusions. Suffice it to say that Faye usefully draws a series of distinctions around the concept of racism. One of the strategies employed by Heidegger apologists consists in pointing out that since Heidegger did not favor Nazi biologism, he could not have been a Nazi. In response, Faye shows there were different kinds of Nazi racism based on biology as well as on the concept of spirit (*Geist*). Since Hitler himself employed both kinds of racism, there is, as Faye notes, no saving grace in opposing biologism but in favoring racism based on *Geist*. The one is fully as bad as the other, and, as Faye shows, many writers in the period, including, say, Erik Wolf, favored both kinds of racism. This part of the argument coincides in part with an analysis earlier worked out independently by Hans Sluga.[19]

Faye is unusually well informed not only about Heidegger, whose texts he knows extremely well, but also about the full range of Heidegger studies as they bear on his theme in a variety of languages. Since a number of the texts crucial to understanding the interrelation between Heidegger's Nazism and his

philosophy have never appeared, it is still very difficult to analyze this period
in his evolution in depth. Faye makes a vitally important contribution toward
the detailed analysis of specific texts. These include the lecture courses from
1933 to 1934, published in Heidegger's collected works (GA 38) in 1998 and
in 2001 (GA 36–37), as well as the notes on Ernst Jünger, which appeared in
GA 90 in 2004, and parts, but only parts, of two as yet unpublished seminars:
On the Essence and Concepts of Nature, History, and State (winter semester
1933–1934) and *Hegel, on the State* (winter semester 1934–1935).

The book is brimming with useful insights. Faye argues that Heidegger's
rejection of humanism entails the rejection of a concept that arises in the
Renaissance. He claims that in virtue of his turn away from the individual,
authenticity is for Heidegger always the authenticity of the German people
(*Volk*) understood as an organic totality. This conception, which in *Being and
Time* refers to the people, later allows for a seamless adoption of the Nazi idea
of the *Volksgemeinschaft* rooted in blood, soil, and spirit. This explains the
strength of his repeated rejection of Descartes in *Being and Time* and elsewhere. In a seminar given in summer semester 1933, almost immediately after
he became rector of the University of Freiburg, Heidegger violently rejects
Descartes's effort to think of human being on the basis of individual consciousness as distinguished from the individual's existence in the historical community of the people (*Volk*). This critique is consistent with Heidegger's adoption
in both public and private during the 1930s of the infamous so-called leadership principle (*Führerprinzip*), or the view that Hitler's every whim or desire
must be accorded the value of law binding on everyone. Faye argues convincingly that Heidegger did not, as Farías thinks, try to "found" or "ground"
Nazism in his theories, or Nazi politics in phenomenological ontology. Rather,
he constructed his theories on his belief in the basic principles of what became
Hitlerism and Nazism. It follows, as Faye suggests, that the failure of Nazism
represents the failure of Heidegger's philosophical theories that were constructed on what was in effect a Nazi basis. Faye further points out the way in
which Heidegger repeatedly tried, especially in his seminars during the early
1930s, to create the conditions for Nazism to endure beyond the person of
Hitler.

One of the most impressive features of this book is Faye's accounts of the
relation of Heidegger to the full panoply of Nazi "philosophers," including
Carl Schmitt, the Nazi legal theoretician who later became an important intellectual figure in both Western liberal as well as conservative thought. Others
include such lesser lights as Erik Wolf, Alfred Baeumler, Ernst Krieck, Ludwig
Ferdinand Clauß, Erich Rothacker, and Hans Heyse. Faye can be said to break
new ground in this respect since these interactions, which are crucial for grasp-

ing what Heidegger thought he was doing at the time, are not well understood. To take an example, Faye studies the close relation between Heidegger and Schmitt in great detail. The result reflects on both of them, especially Schmitt, who, though he appeals to the liberal intelligentsia in Europe and the United States despite his Nazi past, appears to be considerably more compromised by his association with Nazism than is often acknowledged. The differences between their views are more often differences as concerns their own conceptions of Nazism as distinguished from doctrinal differences in theories unrelated to the politics of the period. Faye further documents the little-known link between Heidegger and Wolf in great detail. He argues cogently that Heidegger's decision to resign as rector had nothing to do with a fictitious discouragement about Nazism, about which he continued to remain enthusiastic even after he left the rectorate, but everything to do with frustration about his own efforts to "Nazify" the German university. Faye points out, for those who think Heidegger then simply turned away from Nazism, that, on the contrary, he continued to work, in the Nazi Archives in Weimar and elsewhere, to perfect his vision of Nazism in "instrumentalizing" his own view of philosophy, so to speak.

Both the dismissal of Heidegger as a philosopher worth taking seriously qua philosopher and the exposure of the very dark side of Heidegger's "instrumentalization" of philosophy in the service of National Socialism are likely to appear controversial. Apologists such as Fédier and on occasion more neutral observers suggest that Faye's claims about Heidegger are literally false and that finally the whole Heidegger affair is finally based on nothing at all. It is obvious that this book will shock many readers. It is so far the best researched and the most "damaging" of the books on Heidegger and National Socialism. Faye, who has certainly done his homework, shows in exquisite detail that the situation is much worse than has so far been known. It will be hard to continue to practice damage control in merely explaining everything away. The Heidegger *Nachlaß* is controlled by his family, and access to it is restricted to those likely to be friendly to Heidegger as the orthodox Heideggerians understand the man and his theories. It is clear there are still a lot of damaging materials in the *Nachlaß*. Faye makes a major contribution to showing why we should now have a very different view of Heidegger's philosophical contribution. Faye shows convincingly the nature and extent of Heidegger's continued implication in National Socialism, both before and after his period as rector of the University of Freiburg im Breisgau, at a time in which he supposedly had already broken with Nazism.

Faye's book evoked reactions throughout the old continent. One must distinguish between the reviews of Faye's book in the European daily press, which was positive, and reactions over the longer term — reactions that at this time are still unfolding. In a detailed review, Kurt Flasch, a well-known German philosopher, said that on the basis of the serious and documented nature of Faye's study, all the claims about what we thought we knew concerning the relation of Heidegger's thought and his Nazism need to be reexamined.[20] In France, the immediate reaction to Faye's book reflected the continual French love-hate relation with Heidegger. The same Roger-Pol Droit who detected the importance of Farías's book was very positive with respect to Faye's contribution in stressing the need, as part of the war against Nazism, to examine the relation between Heidegger's thought and his politics in detail.[21]

Not surprisingly, in the French context as well as abroad Faye has his defenders as well as his detractors. The French detractors include a whole range of younger Heideggerians, who find reasons to justify rejecting the views expressed in Faye's book without reading it.[22] In their ranks, there is Maxence Caron, the author of a lengthy study of Heidegger's concepts of being and subjectivity,[23] who distinguishes between Heidegger the individual, who is compromised by his political choices, and the philosopher whose thought is, he asserts, politically innocuous.[24] One can note that the same Caron who denies the political character of Heidegger's thought is not himself neutral. He was not averse to presenting a paper on Heidegger and rootedness (*Bodenständigkeit*) in April 2007 to the student branch of Action Française.[25] And then there is the indefatigable Fédier, the tireless defender over decades of the master thinker, who has spent his whole career denying anything and everything that casts doubt of any kind on either Heidegger or his work. As soon as Faye's book appeared, Fédier immediately took steps to publish a public refutation of it in the form of a thick collection of articles by staunch Heideggerians. Heidegger's works are published in France by Gallimard. Yet Fédier's response, which was judged too indulgent with respect to Beaufret's link to French negationism, as well as possibly defamatory, was rejected by Gallimard and published only by another editor.[26]

More recently, a special issue of *Les Temps Modernes* (no. 650, July–October 2008) devoted to Heidegger appeared. Its introduction states that it is aimed at restoring the whole extent of Heidegger's thinking in reaction to those who (like Emmanuel Faye, who is not named) would withdraw his books from the library and his position from the French teaching program. This special issue, entitled "Heidegger: Qu'appelle-t-on le Lieu?" (Heidegger: What Is Called Place?), raises questions about Heidegger's political attitude on the basis of his understanding of place (lieu). After noting that Sartre, who founded this review, was already interested in the relation of philosophy and

politics in Heidegger's thinking, it reproduces articles by Löwith and de Waelhens noted above, an unrelated piece by Heidegger, and fourteen papers written for the occasion. In a short article entitled "Heidegger and the Question of
Place," Joseph Cohen and Raphael Zagury-Orly propose shifting the focus
from a confrontation among Heidegger's critics and defenders to "the place
from which his thought comes and from which man can emerge" (p. 5) to
resituating the debate on what is deepest in his own thought. In other words,
they concede Gadamer's point that Heidegger's Nazi turning is inseparable
from his overall philosophical position.

This special issue of *Les Temps Modernes* is significant in two ways. On the
one hand, it indicates the desire of Sartre's heirs to show that he was not in any
sense incorrect in his judgment of the relation of Heidegger's thought and
politics. On the other, it clearly signals after Faye's intervention in the debate,
while publicly resisting his view, the need once again to examine the relation of
Heidegger and Nazism, but this time on the basis of a full grasp of Heidegger's
seminars from 1933 to 1945, which is the thrust of Faye's own contribution.

This "gesture" in *Les Temps Modernes* is perhaps the start of a new chapter
in the French infatuation with Heidegger where, in one sense, nothing has
changed. As in the past, and even though Faye shows in detail the degree to
which Heidegger's thought is infected by Nazism, Fédier and his colleagues
steadfastly admit nothing while continuing to deny everything, any blemish on
the thought of this important thinker. Yet in another sense, much has changed
and is still changing. Heidegger, who after the war appeared to offer a genuine
alternative to Marxism and who was for many years, roughly throughout the
second part of the twentieth century, the central pole of French philosophy, is
still a central reference in French philosophy. However, the situation is evolving since analytic philosophy is becoming more important in France and
younger philosophers are increasingly interested in arguments in place of or-
acular statements about Being (*das Sein*) and the event (*das Ereignis*).

But, one might object, all of this is anecdotal. It concerns only Heidegger's
life and times, but not his thought, certainly not philosophy in any general
way. Yet it would be wrong to infer that examination of the relation of Heidegger and National Socialism is of merely anecdotal interest, not worthy of
serious philosophical discussion. We see the philosophical relevance of understanding the relation between thought and its surroundings in relation to the
venerable question of the relation of philosophy and the good life.

The Socratic claim that the unexamined life is not worth living led quickly
to the Platonic view that philosophy is indispensable to the good life, however
understood. In his vision of the ideal state, Plato subordinates politics to

philosophy. The inverse subordination of philosophy to politics during the twentieth century raises doubts about the ancient link between philosophy and the good life, philosophy and ethics.

The venerable claim for the relation of philosophy and the good life is stated in different ways in the twentieth century. Marxist Georg Lukács accepted Stalinism in putting reason in the service of dogma, thereby disgracing reason.[27] Philosophical reason in the form of the ancient distinction between science and opinion was invoked in the 1930s by Edmund Husserl as the only bulwark against the rising tide of Nazism.[28] Heidegger in turn linked his interest in the obscure question of the meaning of Being with the venerable concern with understanding human being, or what in his language is called *Dasein*.[29] At the end of World War II, he clarified his view in the "Letter on Humanism" in posing a stark alternative. On the one hand, there is what he calls "homeless-ness" supposedly due to "the abandonment of Being by [human] beings."[30] And on the other, as he says, there are "those young Germans," who "when confronted by death"[31] were sustained by Friedrich Hölderlin in a different attitude, described as "a humanism that thinks the humanity of man from nearness to Being."[32]

Through the actions of Lukács, Heidegger, and others, the link between philosophy and ethics that was forged early in the Greek tradition is now under attack. Once upon a time it was said and may even have been believed that philosophy was the minimum condition of the good life. That assertion seems harder to accept now. Philosophers need to scrutinize their craft to make the case in new and different ways. In examining what philosophy has been, Faye makes a useful contribution to that task.

A related difficulty consists in the relation of thought to context, hence the important difference between philosophy and *Weltanschauung, Zeitgeist,* or any of the many near synonyms. At stake is whether, as Husserl clearly says, the distinction can validly be drawn between philosophy that claims eternal, timeless validity and status as universal science and the historical moment.[33] The answer is that the distinction between thought and its surroundings is never absolute. No philosophical theory can ever be wholly reduced to its surroundings, from which none can ever be wholly isolated. There is always some kind of interaction, hence inevitably a "contamination." If only because each philosopher reacts to predecessors, it seems unlikely that any philosophi-cal theory is ever wholly unrelated to time and place. Yet there are limits to observe. Any position that could be understood as "genuine" thought as op-posed to mere ideology, even philosophy as such, is clearly at risk when for whatever reason philosophers voluntarily reduce the conceptual distance be-tween themselves and their surroundings by lending uncritical support to current political imperatives. The relation of philosophy and philosophers to the surrounding world is obviously different in different cases. Yet on inspection it is arguable, as Faye brings out, that Heidegger's theories lend philosophical cover to some of the darkest human impulses in the intellectual context in the early twentieth century, impulses that later led to Nazism, World War II, and the Holocaust. Heidegger's difficulty does not lie in getting too close to Being. It rather lies in being dazzled or even blinded by a political sun from which he never later averted his gaze during and arguably even before he set out on his philosophical journey.

Tom Rockmore

Preface

We have not yet grasped the full significance of the propagation of Nazism and Hitlerism in the domain of thought and ideas — that mounting tidal wave that sweeps up minds, dominates them, possesses them, and eventually overcomes all resistance. Against it, the military victory was but the winning of a first battle — a vital one, to be sure, and a costly one for humanity, since it took a world war. Today a different battle, more protracted and sinister, is unfolding: a contest in which the future of the human race is at stake. It calls for a heightened awareness in all areas of thought, from philosophy to law and history.

Whether we are considering the case of Heidegger, Schmitt, Jünger (in many respects), or Nolte, these main propagators of Nazism in the life of letters have taken the time to refine their strategy of reconquest after the defeat of the armies of Hitler's Reich. By an interplay of the obfuscation of real causes, the dilution of responsibilities in a globalization of approaches, the disqualification of humanistic thought and universal values, the mythologizing of self in the figure of the "shepherd of being," the "Christian Epimetheus," the "anarch," the theoretician of the "historical right," these authors have scripted the roles of philosophy, law, letters, and history, enlisting them in the service of the "revision" and ultimately of the rehabilitation of the foundations of Nazism. Some have progressively conquered a planetary audience with a public that most often does not realize what is at stake, in the long run, in this conquest of minds. It is true that the front lines of the invasion are not found on any map. There is no geopolitics of the mind, although the increasing number of apologetic or too complacent works is an indication of the magnitude of its propagation.

Nevertheless, centers of criticism and resistance have sprung up progressively in many countries. For Heidegger, the subject of this work, very incisive criticisms have been raised, both in Europe and on the American continent, since Karl Löwith perceived and reported as early as 1947 that he was "more radical than Mr. Krieck and Mr. Rosenberg," two pillars of the Nazi regime, but who, being less adroit and more trivial, did not see their reputations survive the defeat of the Third Reich. Furthermore, new documents and deeper research allow us today to see to what extent Heidegger devoted himself to putting philosophy at the service of legitimizing and diffusing the very bases of Nazism and Hitlerism. That is why I want to make available to the public some of the most significant moments of the seminars taught between 1933 and 1935, taken from the archives of Heidegger's unpublished manuscripts. A few of these texts, known to only a handful of researchers, are in fact political education courses at the service of Hitler's state and go so far as to identify the ontological difference between being and individual entities with the political relationship between the state and the people, while other texts explicitly explore the means of perpetuating the "spirit" of Nazism. In making these excerpts public, my intention has been simply to exercise the right to historical and philosophical truth. I have also based my work on the speeches, lectures, and courses over these same years that have recently appeared in Germany and can be consulted only by readers of German. These texts, published in volumes 16, 36/37, and 38 of the so-called complete works, are every bit as racist and virulently National Socialist as those of the official "philosophers" of Nazism, such as Alfred Baeumler or Hans Heyse. They surpass the others by the virulence of their Hitlerism, which no other "philosopher" of the regime has equaled. Despite that, these Hitlerian and Nazi texts of Heidegger are to be found on the philosophy shelves of public libraries. The seriousness of that situation calls for a new and heightened awareness. Without ever dissociating philosophical reflection from indispensable historical investigation, I have tried to bring together the establishment and analysis of historical and textual sources, as the historians Hugo Ott and Bernd Martin (as well as Guido Schneeberger and Victor Farías), with the philosophical critique, which has been developed by a series of authors as varied as Ernst Cassirer, Benedetto Croce, Karl Löwith, Theodor Adorno, Günther Anders, Hans Blumenberg, Jürgen Habermas, Ernst Tugendhat, Éric Weil, Rainer Marten, Nicolas Tertulian, Jeffrey Barash, Domenico Losurdo, Arno Münster, Richard Wolin,

Tom Rockmore, Thomas Sheehan, Herman Philipse, Hassan Givsan, Reinhard Linde, and Julio Quesada, to mention but a few of the most important names.

But this book proposes a new understanding of what Heidegger brought about. With the help of texts little known outside the German-speaking world, some not even published, and taking into account those individuals with whom he chose to surround himself — the "philosopher" Erich Rothacker, the historian Rudolf Stadelmann, and the legal scholar Erik Wolf — I intend to prove that the question of the relationship between Heidegger and National Socialism is not that of the relationship between the personal commitment of a man temporarily gone astray and a philosophical work that remains almost unaffected, but rather that of the deliberate introduction of the foundations of Nazism and Hitlerism into philosophy and its teaching.

In showing this, it is not my desire to add to Heidegger's renown by making it even more diabolical. I do not subscribe to the theory of a Heidegger "thinker" of Nazism, because rather than enlightening us, he has done nothing but blend the characteristic opacity of his teaching with the darkness of the phenomenon. Far from furthering the progress of thought, Heidegger has helped to conceal the deeply destructive nature of the Hitlerian undertaking by exalting its "grandeur." Far from enriching philosophy, he has worked to destroy it, by making it subservient to a movement that, by the murderous discrimination underlying it and the project of collective annihilation to which it leads, constitutes the radical negation of all humanity and all thought.

After the paroxysm of the Nazi and Hitlerian period, long elaborated in Heidegger's writings even before 1933, and after the toxic spite often characterizing his courses taught in 1933–1934, the diffusion of Heidegger's works after the war slowly descends like ashes after an explosion — a gray cloud slowly suffocating and extinguishing minds. Soon the 102 volumes of the so-called complete work (sixty-six volumes have appeared to date), in which the same assertions are repeated over and over through thousands of pages, will encumber by their sheer bulk the shelves reserved for twentieth-century philosophy and continue to spread the fundamental tenets of Nazism on a worldwide scale.

It is therefore of the utmost importance to see clearly into that undertaking, to react and resist its influence before it is too late. Such heightened awareness is indispensable if we are to return to what philosophy truly has to contribute to the thought, overall evolution, and achievements of mankind.

Acknowledgments

The research carried out in this work is based on unpublished manuscripts and documents deposited in the Deutsche Literatur Archiv of Marbach am Neckar, in the Bundesarchiv of Berlin, in the archives of the University of Freiburg im Breisgau, and at the Ministry of Foreign Affairs (Colmar Bureau); and on the special collections available at the Bibliothèque Nationale de France, the British Library, the libraries of the University of Strasbourg, of Freiburg im Breisgau (especially the library of the Institut für Staatswissenschaft und Rechtsphilosophie), of Paris IV (Malesherbes Center), and at the Bibliothèque de documentation internationale contemporaine (German collection) of Paris X-Nanterre. I wish to thank the individual personnel of those institutions.

Among all those with whom I have had contact and who have enlightened and spurred on my work, I would like to thank in particular Jeffrey Barash, Jean Bollack, Ruedi Imbach, Hugo Ott, Bruno Pinchard, Nicolas Tertulian, Roseline Thiberge, Denis Trierweiler, and Richard Wolin. The discussions on Heidegger occasioned by various colloquia at the Warburg Institute of London, the Universities of Tours, Lyons, Poitiers Nancy, Nice, Urbino, New York (NYU and CUNY), Saarbrücken, Bremen, the Académie Catholique de Trèces, the Fritz Bauer Institut and the Institute of Philosophy of the Goethe-Universität of Frankfurt, the Instituto de Cultura of Barcelona, and with the participants in my seminar on Descartes and Heidegger at the University of Paris Ouest–Nanterre La Défense have also enriched my reflections.

My thanks as well to Michael Smith, whose fine translation truly recreated my analyses in English, to Tom Rockmore for his well-informed preface, and to the various members of Yale University Press who have expressed their confidence in this work by taking on its publication, as well as all those who have taken part with such professionalism to bring this work to its final form, including Sarah Miller, Ann-Marie Imbornoni, and Joyce Ippolito.

The translator would like to express his gratitude to research librarian Xiaojing Zu of Berry College for her technical assistance.

Introduction

We have come to a decisive moment in the understanding and thorough-
going assessment of Heidegger's work. After the publication of the well-
informed critiques of Karl Löwith and Eric Weil in France after the Liberation,
followed by the re-publication of several political speeches at the beginning of
the 1960s by Guido Schneeberger, the research of Hugo Ott and Victor Farías
brought a major body of revelations and historical clarifications in the late
1980s, enabling us to appreciate the radical nature of the rector of Freiburg im
Breisgau's National Socialist commitment. But since these last works were
based almost exclusively on facts and speeches and not much on Heidegger's
teaching itself, it still seemed possible, with a lot of self-delusion, to separate
the man from the work, or to distinguish the political from the "philosophical." Today the situation is completely different. We now have available to us
(in German) nearly all the courses he taught. (The only course not yet published is that of the summer semester of 1932.) Furthermore, it is now possible, thanks to summaries and quotations published in a number of studies, to
form an idea of some of the unpublished seminars, for which outlines and
notes taken by his students have been kept in the Heidegger archives of Marbach. Being intended for a select public, the seminars offer a different perspective than the courses.

Despite this, the current situation remains fundamentally unsatisfactory for the reader legitimately desirous of getting at the truth. The "complete" edition, or *Gesamtausgabe,* which is not a critical edition, gives no guarantee of philosophical exactitude, as several well-informed critics have shown. And the consultation of the unpublished seminars (let alone the correspondence) is permitted only sparingly by Hermann, Martin Heidegger's son, to a few university professors with all the right credentials. Thus, almost three decades after Martin Heidegger's death, a large portion of his writings remains inaccessible not only to the public but to the best-informed researchers, the moment they undertake to subject his life and work to uncompromising scrutiny.

Despite all these obstacles, what we are in a position to know today — either about the courses, from the "complete" edition, or about the unpublished seminars, from certain transcripts circulating among the specialists — completely overturns the perception we have long had of Heidegger. In these documents we discover the reality of what he taught his Freiburg students week after week during the years 1933–1935. Not only do the classes and seminars of these years confirm the radical nature of his allegiance to Hitler, they reveal the degree to which the "philosophical" and the political become one in his mind and the fact that it is at the very heart of the "philosophical" that Heidegger situates the political, understood in its most radically Nazi sense. In his unpublished political education seminar of the winter of 1933–1934, he unreservedly assimilates the relation between being and entities to the relation uniting the state and the racial community of the people of the Hitlerian *Führerstaat.* Moreover, in his classes Heidegger takes up the question inherited from Kant, "What is man?" only to reduce it to the question "Who are we?" — this "we" designating precisely the *völkisch* existence of the German people beneath the Hitlerian yoke. The only answer Heidegger gives to the question is his affirmation that "we are the people" (*wir sind das Volk*), the only people that still have, according to him, a history and a destiny, the only "metaphysical" people . . .

Thus we witness, in the courses and seminars that are ostensibly presented as "philosophical," a progressive dissolving of the human being, whose individual worth is expressly denied, into a community of people rooted in the land and united by blood. The unpublished seminar of 1933–1934 goes so far as to identify the people with a "community of biological stock and race" (*Stammesgemeinschaft und Rasse*). Thus, through Heidegger's teaching, the racial conceptions of Nazism enter philosophy. This radical perversion of philosophy is not limited to some occasional speeches: it is confirmed in thousands of pages and even in the totality of a work in which everything hangs together, as is demonstrated, for example, by the references to the rectoral address and the racist course of 1934 titled *Logic,* which appear in the *Contri-*

butions to Philosophy from the years 1936–1938. Nor is it the case that the most openly Hitlerian and Nazi writings of the years 1933–1935 constitute an exceptional moment that nothing would have led one to foresee and that was soon foresworn. The fact is that these writings cannot be isolated from the rest of the work. They appear as revelatory moments of the dark inner sanctum of his "doctrine," to which he remained faithful to the end; and the examination of the unpublished or untranslated texts reveals that doctrine's identity with the very foundations of National Socialism.

That is why today we must grasp the full significance of Heidegger's introduction of Nazism into philosophy. National Socialism not only took over German political and military life: it systematically attacked every area of social, intellectual, and cultural life. It invaded law, history, biology, medicine — but also architecture, music, and poetry, not to mention religion. Philosophy was not spared. That is the area in which the danger has proved greatest, for by taking on philosophy, Nazism has attempted to subvert the bases of thought and spirit. If we do not heed this danger and resist it, the principles of racism and the attempted destruction of humankind that are synonymous with Nazism and Hitlerism will continue to spread and exert their influence by means of that same "movement."

Heidegger's case is not just one among others. If the Third Reich won the enthusiastic allegiance of many of the "philosophers" or so-called philosophers such as Alfred Baeumler, Ernst Krieck, Hans Heyse, and Oskar Becker (the last two were Heidegger's students), he alone succeeded in having his work, which had participated in all the phases of the Third Reich from 1933 to 1944 and ended in 1945 with the defeat of Nazism, continue to be read after the war and enjoy worldwide dissemination.

What is particularly serious is that the writings that are the most subservient to Hitler — such as the speeches, lectures, and courses of 1933–1935, or those that legitimate racial selection, such as the development of that theme in 1939–1940 titled *Koinon,* the course on Nietzsche taught in 1941–1942, or the recently published reflections on Ernst Jünger — are today included in the so-called complete works, or *Gesamtausgabe,* without Heidegger's having arranged for their publication's being accompanied by the slightest expression of regret. (In his last letter written to his publisher Vittorio Klostermann on 29 January 1976 [Deutsches Literaturarchiv, Marbach], he settles the distribution of royalties between himself and the editor of each volume down to the last detail but never expresses the least reservation about the fact of publishing and disseminating the most openly Nazi courses of the years 1933–1944.) And yet these writings, an apology for a murderous discrimination, radically negate the human truths that are the underlying principle of philosophy.

The situation calls for an awakening of consciousness commensurate with the dimensions of the problem. It is with this goal that the present book was written. It constitutes the result of three decades of reflection and years of research carried out not only in studying Heidegger's works published in German and not yet available in French but also in consulting several archives and manuscripts preserved in Germany and France. Moreover, out of a determination to affirm nothing not supported by texts and testimonies, I have, in the name of what legal scholars have called our right to history, quoted as much material as possible, with the intention of providing readers with texts either difficult to access or even previously unpublished. In most cases, the German specialist will find the original German for the translation I propose in the notes.

I analyze writings not only by Heidegger but also by some of the intellectual figures most involved in National Socialism with whom he corresponded or to whom he was particularly close. I have, for example, entirely reconsidered the question of the intellectual relationship between Martin Heidegger and Carl Schmitt and their reciprocal influence, based on explicit references to Schmitt discovered in Heidegger's unpublished seminars. I have also brought to bear their respective conceptions of the *polemos* and "combat" (*Kampf*)—to which I must add Alfred Baeumler's conception of the interpretation of fragment 53 of Heraclitus. Additionally, I have studied the writings of figures hitherto left in the shadows, such as Erich Rothacker, Rudolf Stadelmann, Erik Wolf, and Oskar Becker. By the very close relations the authors of these writings sometimes had with Heidegger, their texts bring critical clarifications to the racial dimension that is the basis of the latter's ideas. Indeed, when we observe everything that—from the 1920s on, and against a background of racial doctrine that was expressed at the time jointly with the concept of "surrounding world" (*Umwelt*)—connects such authors as Heidegger, Rothacker, Becker, and Clauß, we understand that Heidegger's work is not at all a "philosophy" he formed before happening upon Nazism but a doctrine that as early as the 1920s is founded on a conception of "historical existence" and "surrounding world," which are closely allied to the racial doctrine of National Socialism as it spread through and colonized intellectual life, in forms partially transposed or disguised.

I also wanted to show the importance of certain essential documents, such as the two excerpts republished in 1938 and 1943, of the "rectoral address" by the Schmittian jurist Ernst Forsthoff. Forsthoff published Heidegger's text alongside an anti-Semitic public bill written in April 1933 by the Association of Nazi Students, or DSt (Deutsche Studentenschaft), whose actions Heidegger, then rector of Freiburg, supported and with whose leaders he had cultivated close relations. (See below, Chapter 2, 53–57, and the appendixes, 331–333). These two republished excerpts are mentioned neither by his defenders nor by his son, who subsequently had occasion to edit the address in question. Lastly, as the subtitle indicates, this book derives its raison d'être from an effort to delve deeper, which was made possible by two unpublished seminars. The first, taught during the winter semester of 1933–1934, is titled *On the Essence and Concepts of Nature, History, and State.* There we discover that Heidegger devoted himself entirely to implanting in the hearts and minds of his interlocutors the figure, or *Gestalt,* of Hitler, and to spreading the eros of the people for their *Führer.* The course outline of the seminar reveals that behind the terms central to his "doctrine," such as "being" and "entities," it was in reality the relation between the Hitlerian state and the people, understood as a community of biological stock and race, that was intended. And his unqualified defense of speeches by Hitler and of the *Führerstaat* show to what degree Hitlerism, with its relation of dominance of the *Führung* over *Gefolgschaft* — that is, of the leader over his adherents or "following" — preoccupies his thoughts at that time.

The second seminar, the title of which is *Hegel, on the State* and which was team taught with Erik Wolf during the winter semester of 1934–1935, exposes his conception of the political as the self-affirmation (*Selbstbehauptung*) of a people or race, presented by him as more originary than Schmitt's discrimination between friend and enemy. Heidegger's thematic developments reveal his personal ambition to be the one who prepares the most long-term future of the Nazi state. Neither his resignation from the rectorship nor the Night of the Long Knives (*Nacht der langen Messer*) diminished his commitment to National Socialism. The examination of the writings and courses from the years 1939–1942, with their defense of racial selection, confirms this in the most definitive manner.

Today, these various texts confirm the correctness of what Hugo Ott and Victor Farías independently showed in the 1980s — namely, the intensity of Heidegger's National Socialist commitment. We must gratefully acknowledge, in this connection, the tenacity and courage with which Farías, the author of *Heidegger and Nazism,* successfully carried out and published his research, without fearing the most excessive attacks from Heidegger's defenders, who themselves had not, for the most part, carried out any research worthy of the name on the question. A few years later, Farías published a second book in Spain, in which he included the course of 1934 titled *Logic,* in the form of a manuscript left by Helene Weiss. But the existence of that work has been so well hidden that it is not to be found in any library in France. Those very individuals who unjustly accused Farías of not having taken the time to read

Heidegger have refrained from revealing the existence of his course and from learning its lessons. (The only serious allusion that has been made to it is by Richard Wolin, in *Heidegger's Children*.)

I also want to pay homage to the levelheadedness and accuracy of the work of Hugo Ott, who, in a series of articles followed by an epoch-making monograph, undertook extensive investigations on Heidegger's rectorship, even as Heidegger's son, in 1983 (exactly fifty years after Hitler's rise to power), was publishing an apology for the rectoral address. Hugo Ott also published a profoundly moving story, inspired by the deportation of the Jews of Freiburg, in which he refers to the anti-Semitic declarations of Heidegger and Jünger. While the research of Victor Farías and Hugo Ott have taught me a great deal by their very difference — the first accumulating a considerable number of documents and facts, the second concentrating on a few essential moments, such as the period of the rectorate — my book stands on difference, and its objective is not the same. It is not Martin Heidegger's political commitment as such that I have undertaken to study but the question of the foundation underlying his work as a whole. This inquiry is linked to the new situation created by the advancing publication of the *Gesamtausgabe* and the discovery of seminars and documents either unpublished or left in the shadows.

For a philosopher, the essential question remains the following. What is the basis of a work in which the most extreme principles of Hitlerism — not in a few isolated texts dictated by circumstance but through thousands of pages of speeches, lectures, courses, seminars, and personal fragments — are expressed? Heidegger constantly uses the words most operative among the National Socialists, such as "combat" (*Kampf*), "sacrifice" (*Opfer*), "destiny" (*Schicksal*), and "community of people" (*Volksgemeinschaft*). The most untranslatable Nazi terms — because they are so politically charged — such as *völkisch, Volksgenosse, Führung,* and so on, are just as familiar to him. (The word *völkisch* expresses a conception of the people understood as a racial community, "with a strong anti-Semitic connotation," according to *Grimms Wörterbuch*.) Furthermore, he does not hesitate to adopt words that bear the strongest connotations in racial doctrine and Nazi mythology, such as "blood" (*Blut*), "soil" (*Boden*), "rearing" (*Zucht*), and "race" (*Stamm, Geschlecht, Rasse*). Finally — and this is what is of most concern for philosophy — these terms are often associated, and even sometimes identified, with the central ideas of his "doctrine," such as "being," "entities," "historical existence," "metaphysics," the "essence" and "truth" of being.

The in-depth study of his writings has progressively revealed to me that the reality of Nazism with which I was confronted in reading Heidegger, far from merely marking his language, inspired his works in their entirety and nourished them at the root level—so much so that it was impossible to dissociate them from his political commitment. That is why, by the texts I have brought to light and the demonstrations I propose, I wanted to show the reality of the undertaking to which he dedicated himself—namely, the introduction into philosophy of the very content of Nazism and Hitlerism. Only on the condition that we recognize that reality can we become fully cognizant of the dangers to humanity and to thought involved in any attempt to further the acceptance or legitimation of those works.

I

Before 1933: Heidegger's Radicalism, the Destruction of the Philosophical Tradition, and the Call to Nazism

Martin Heidegger's joining of the National Socialist Party on 1 May 1933, the same day as other intellectual figures such as the jurist Carl Schmitt or the philosopher Erich Rothacker, does not reflect the intermittent enthusiasm of a man whose philosophical work stands independently. In reality, his writings from the 1920s reveal the increasing power of themes that would later be found at the heart of his most openly Nazi texts of the 1933–1935 period. Furthermore, the convergence of Heidegger's radicalism and that of Nazism does not constitute an isolated path but reflects the evolution of a whole group of German "philosophers." In Freiburg, Marburg, Bonn, and Berlin we see, besides Heidegger, the following figures corresponding and mutually inspiring one another: Oskar Becker, Ludwig Ferdinand Clauß, Erich Rothacker, and Alfred Baeumler. They will all adopt, in varying degrees of promptness and explicitness, the racial doctrine and anti-Semitism of the Nazis. In order to understand Heidegger's motivation during this period, we must bear in mind the real intellectual and existential relations these various figures maintained with one another and not reduce the Heidegger of the 1920s to a timeless dialogue with Aristotle or Immanuel Kant.

The evolution of the young Heidegger is not that of a scholar absorbed in pure philosophy. From 1910 to 1932, we see him moving from an antimodernist and nationalist Catholicism, nourished by the scholasticism of Carl Braig and his personal relationship with Konrad Gröber, to an affinity that lasted for several years (from 1919 to about 1923) with the antiliberal and decisionist theology of Friedrich Gogarten, and then to a radical conception of historicity (which became increasingly political) that he shared with Erich Rothacker, and which led him to vote for the Nazi Party from 1932 on.[1] The figures with whom he had been intellectually close during those three successive phases — the Catholic theologian Engelberg Krebs, the Protestant theologian Friedrich Gogarten, and the "philosopher" of history Erich Rothacker — manifested their adherence to National Socialism in 1933, as he himself did.

In the early 1920s, when Heidegger was working as Edmund Husserl's assistant in Freiburg until 1923, it was in the letters to Karl Löwith that Heidegger's radicalism was expressed most clearly. Löwith was, at the time, along with Oskar Becker, one of his two principal students. Heidegger wrote to Löwith in 1920: "Living in the present situation of a de facto revolution, I pursue what I feel is 'necessary' without worrying about knowing whether a 'culture' will emerge from it, or whether my research will precipitate the downfall." That radicalism of the pure decision on the part of an existent facing nothingness, which no rational motive can support nor any warning of its destructive effects forestall, inhabits the very foundation of Nazism. That is what Karl Löwith was able to see. "The 'spirit' of National Socialism had far less to do with the national or social element than with that resolute and dynamic radicalism that rejects all discussion and all agreement because it relies solely and exclusively on itself."[2]

This diagnosis is confirmed by the affinities between Carl Schmitt's political, Friedrich Gogarten's theological, and Heidegger's existential decisionism, affinities remarkably demonstrated by Löwith.[3]

The pure decision in preparation for an "authentic" existence, authorized only by itself, tends to deny all deliberation, all prudence, and eventually all real thought. It is, in this sense, the end of all philosophy. The particular fascination exerted by Heidegger over his students during the 1920s owes much to the fact that, unlike Gogarten, who, as a theologian, teaches decision by faith, or Schmitt, who transposes decisionism from theology to politics and law, the Heideggerian decision, which is pure resolve on the part of the existent facing death, remains suspended as it were in the void, only to bring about a program of destruction of the philosophical tradition, targeting most specifically the philosophy of human individuality and the Cartesian self. This is the plan announced in 1927 in *Being and Time* as a forthcoming second section. It was never published, but for many the effect of the announcement may have sufficed. As Löwith observed: "The main element in his effect on his disciples was not the anticipation of a new system, but to the contrary, the indeterminateness of the content and the character of pure call" in his teaching. "The inner nihilism, the 'National Socialism' of that pure resoluteness before nothingness, remained hidden at first."4 The Heideggerian radicalness of the pure decision and of authentic resoluteness certainly contributed to rendering his students and his German readership spiritually disarmed and open to the "call" of the "National Socialist" revolution.

In his teaching and writings prior to 1933, Heidegger's attitude was dictated in large part by the strategy of occultation and dissimulation. Of the group already mentioned — Clauß, Becker, Rothacker, and Baeumler — he was probably the best strategist, and for that very reason the most effective and influential over the long term. He alone was able to foster the belief that a work so permeated with Nazism could be a new beginning for thought. Ludwig Clauß began to show his true colors publicly by 1923; Heidegger, by contrast, reveals himself at first only privately, in a few letters. To attempt to understand the Heidegger of the 1920s thus requires several modes of approach. We must scrutinize the evolution of his writings, take his intellectual relations with the above-mentioned figures into account, not overlook the testimony of his former students, and examine the way his anti-Semitism is expressed in his academic politics.

But before undertaking that study, I must say a few words about another dimension of Heidegger, although this work does not claim to shed new light on that background, by nature difficult to grasp, and totally unrelated to philosophy. Behind his teaching, there is another visage of Heidegger, so to speak, characterized by his feel for clandestine action and his taste for secrecy. This other dimension of his played a non-negligible role in the aura in which he succeeded in surrounding himself from his first years of teaching, when he had published almost nothing. We know that Heidegger became involved very early — around 1909 — in the activities of the "Union of the Graal," or *Gralbund*, the spiritual head of which was Richard von Kralick, a Viennese close to the anti-Semite leader Karl Lueger.5 Subsequently, the taste for communities of which he would discreetly be the master does not seem to have left him, and in his correspondence with Karl Jaspers, for example, several allusions point in this direction. In his long letter of 22 January 1921, he evokes, not without condescendence, "a certain *circle*" who press themselves around Husserl and try to cling to Heidegger without realizing how much he himself "holds them tightly under [his] control." In the same letter, he speaks of the students in rather peculiar terms, the "best" being, in his words, most often "visionaries," "theosophists," and "adepts of George and the like."6 The circle he is alluding to is that of Stefan George — out of which was to emerge, for example, Heidegger's disciple Hans-Georg Gadamer — but also other circles, which are not further defined. He himself is constantly surrounded by a cohort of the faithful—which is the most visible aspect of his ascendancy. When he was called to Marburg in 1923, he spoke to Jaspers of "a *shock troop* of sixteen persons" who accompanied him.[7] (At the Davos meetings of 1929 between Heidegger and the philosopher Ernst Cassirer, Cassirer's wife, Toni, spoke of "Heidegger's elite troop who accompanied him.")[8] The oddest allusion is in a letter to Jaspers on 14 July 1923, in which after having lamented, as was his habit, the state of the German university, Heidegger asserts that "the more the overthrow is accomplished in an organized, concrete, and discrete manner, the more lasting and certain it will be." An action that is not individual but coordinated, all the more effective in that it acts discreetly and over a long period—such is Heidegger's recommendation. And "this requires," he declares, an "invisible *community*."[9] Heidegger says nothing further to Jaspers—although he then seems to want to draw him into what he calls their "community of combat"—but we find similar allusions in his *Contributions to Philosophy* of 1936–1938, which is an indication that these preoccupations must have played a decisive role in his political commitments of the 1930s. That activism, at once radical, concerted, and clandestine, which proceeds not from a spirit of research but from a power strategy, is not that of a philosopher per se. We can understand what made it possible for him to be able to tell Löwith that he was "not a philosopher."[10]

The Lectures of 1925 on the Present Struggle for a Vision of the Historical World

Very early on, from the late 1910s, Heidegger affirmed positions that would remain his at least until the beginning of the 1930s, if not to the very end, though his terminology would evolve considerably from the end of the 1930s. The critique of all forms of objectification in favor of lived experience, the rejection, by 1919, of universality as inauthentic, disdain for the ideal of humanity, the affirmation of self and of concern for oneself, as well as attentiveness to the historicity of existence: these salient points were affirmed by 1919–1923, while he was teaching at the University of Freiburg as Husserl's assistant. Heidegger relied at the time mainly on Wilhelm Dilthey, but also on Oswald Spengler, who had just published his *Decline of the West*. In 1920 Heidegger gave a lecture in Wiesbaden titled "Oswald Spengler and His Work *The Decline of the West*."[11] Heidegger drew closer to Jaspers at that time, with whom he said he shared a common struggle, a struggle that, for Heidegger, was directed against Neo-Kantianism but also, less overtly, against Husserl's phenomenology. Appointed to a chair as professor extraordinary (which in

Germany is a degree below that of ordinary professor) in 1923 in Marburg, thanks to Husserl's recommendation, Heidegger kept up an appearance of ties with Husserl until obtaining the latter's succession, in 1928, as ordinary professor at the University of Freiburg. Two months after his appointment, he broke off all relations with his former teacher.

Moreover, during those years of the 1920s, Heidegger's thought did not develop in an isolated manner. The sources of inspiration were multiple, as were the critical confrontations, though all that is partially hidden in *Being and Time*. Best known are his relations to Husserl's and to Dilthey's thought. I have pointed out his affinities with the theologian Gogarten, to which must be added a passing collaboration with Rudolf Bultmann. We should also keep in mind his relation to Erich Rothacker, who created the collection *Philosophy and the Sciences of Mind*, the first volume of which, appearing in 1923, was none other than *Correspondence Between Wilhelm Dilthey and Count Paul Yorck von Wartenburg*.[12] That correspondence, and particularly the figure of Count Yorck, fascinated Heidegger. It is mainly to him that he owes his conception of historicity and also his requirement of a soil (*Boden*) for philosophy. But we must take notice of the overtly anti-Semitic terms in which Yorck approaches the problem of the "absence of ground." When it is a question of how we are to understand absence of soil, Yorck refers to what he calls the Jewish race (*jüdische Stämme*). He writes to Dilthey: "I thank you for all the particular cases in which you keep teaching chairs away from the thin Jewish run-of-the-mill [*die dünne jüdische Routine*] who lack consciousness of the responsibility of thought, just as the whole race lacks a feeling for psychic and physical soil [*Boden*]."[13]

It is difficult not to be reminded of these words of Count Yorck when Heidegger, in paragraph 77 of *Being and Time*, in turn attacks what he elegantly calls "absence of soil" (*Bodenlosigkeit*) and alludes positively on that occasion to the letters of Count Yorck.

On 15 December 1923, a lengthy correspondence between Heidegger and Rothacker began, which continued at least until 1941. Rothacker invited Heidegger to write a review of the Dilthey-Yorck correspondence for a journal that had recently been created, *Deutsche Vierteljahrschrift für Literaturwissenschaft und Geistesgeschichte* [German Quarterly for Literary Scholarship and Intellectual History], of which Rothacker was co-editor. The review, completed in November 1924, was far too long to be published in the journal (it takes up seventy folios!) but in all likelihood constituted a matrix for the 1925 Kassel lectures and for *Being and Time:* paragraph 77 of that work contains the quotations and commentary relative to the thought of Count Yorck. Thus, not only does Heidegger's major work owe much to the correspondence published through Rothacker's initiative, but Rothacker was one of the very first to become cognizant of the thoughts that heralded *Being and Time*. In 1927, the same year *Being and Time* was published, Erich Rothacker published his own *Logic and Systematic of the Sciences of the Mind,* and then in 1934, his *Philosophy of History*—two works that reveal a certain community of thought with Heidegger and an understanding of his work that is worthy of taking into consideration for what it reveals to us about the racial background of Heidegger's preoccupations.

Another contemporary also serves as a connecting link between Heidegger and Rothacker: Alfred Baeumler, whom Heidegger wanted to make his successor when he left Marburg in 1928, and to whom he was particularly close in the early 1930s. Baeumler was, moreover, the chief editor of the *Manual of Philosophy,* in which the two monographs of Rothacker just cited appeared. Heidegger was certainly familiar with this manual, which he recommended to philosopher Elisabeth Blochmann. But before proceeding to a more detailed study of the intellectual relations between Heidegger and Rothacker, and what they have to tell us about Heidegger's underlying proclivities, we must approach the two major writings of his Marburg period: the 1925 lectures on *The Present Struggle for a Vision of the Historical World* [Der Gegenwärtige Kampf umeine historische Weltanschauung] and *Being and Time*.

For those familiar with German history and the editorials of the time, the association, in the title of the lecture, of the words *Kampf* and *Weltanschauung* related to the present and to historicity could not have been innocuous in 1925. One of the axes of the lectures is made up of a critique of René Descartes, and through him, of the philosophy of *self;* it is intimately associated with a challenging of Husserl's phenomenology and the Neo-Kantian theory of knowledge. Heidegger reproaches phenomenology with defining the person "as a lived manifold, the cohesion of which depends on the unity of the *self* as a manifold of acts," without asking itself about the "character of being" of that center (*Zentrum*).[14] In order to do so, one must have a soil, which, according to him, Husserl lacks. It does not appear that it is the idea of a center that is rejected. Earlier, in the third lecture, Heidegger alluded positively to Dilthey's essays on Novalis, Friedrich Hölderlin, and Johann Wolfgang von Goethe in *The Lived Experience of Poetry,* and following that, the efforts to understand concrete historical individuals on the basis of their "spiritual nucleus" and their center or "milieu" (*Mitte*) according to the expression in use in the circle or school of Stefan George (*George-Schule*).[15] This is a positive allusion to the historical monographs that appeared in the *Werke der Wissenschaft*—always stamped on the cover with a swastika, a symbol retained by George. What Heidegger rejected was therefore not the idea of "milieu" but consciousness and the *self* taken as center. For him, this milieu was founded not in human consciousness but in the surroundings (*Umwelt*) and the soil in which existence is rooted. The Descartes he stigmatizes is the one who characterized the person as *self,* without perceiving that this was not Descartes's thesis, but Heidegger seems to overlook everything in Descartes's philosophy about the unity of man or about *union,* such as it is set forth especially in his letters to Princess Elisabeth in 1643. What Heidegger retains, in order to reject it, is exclusively the *self* as point of departure, as it is subsequently taken up in the Kantian inquiry in the perspective of the theory of knowledge and of the subject-object relation.

Heidegger posits as primary what he calls the effectiveness of life, which leads him to affirm the primacy of the ambient world, of the *Umwelt.* This term is not forged by him. It is borrowed from the non-Darwinian biology of Jakob von Uexküll, and, before Heidegger, it is found not only in Husserl himself but also, and especially, as early as 1923, in an author coming from phenomenology, Ludwig Clauß. Clauß, in *The Nordic Soul,* explicitly applies Husserl's method to the description of racial identity (*Artung*), imprinting (*Prägung*), and the communal destiny (*Schicksalsgemeinschaft*) of the people. Clauß's work was published by Max Niemeyer, the press that would publish *Being and Time* four years later.[16] In 1925 Heidegger was certainly more moderate or less explicit than Clauß, but it is important to see what connotations, in that intellectual context, the substitution of surrounding world for consciousness, *Umwelt* for *Bewußtsein,* could have.

Moreover, it is assuredly Uexküll that Heidegger has in mind when he alludes to the fact that the knowledge of the correlation between life and its world has begun making its way into biology.[17] It is essential to understand that if Heidegger always fought against Darwinian biology and what in the 1930s he would call "liberal biology," he was a great champion of what he called in a letter to Elisabeth Blochmann "the new biology" — that of Uexküll. It is worth noting that Uexküll was to become the editor of the raciologist Houston S. Chamberlain. And as will be shown later in more detail, Heidegger received with great favor *The Philosophy of History* by Erich Rothacker, a study that evinces a virulent racism, entirely devoted to racial doctrine (*Rassenkunde*);[18] in two instances, when discussing the relation of the existent to its world, Rothacker associates Heidegger with Clauß, emphasizing the influence of Uexküll.[19]

Summarizing the spirit of the 1925 lectures, we can distinguish Heidegger's general orientation at that date: to work toward the elaboration of a soil, to seize the past at the point where, as he says, "we find the authentic roots of our existence," and the wherewithal to intensify the vital forces of our own present.

That quest for soil, for authentic enrootedness, and for a freeing of the life forces, is what energized Heidegger in his struggle for a vision of the historical world. History, it should be borne in mind, meant to Heidegger "the future that we ourselves are." As for this "we," it apparently refers to the Germans, since the horizon in which Heidegger presents his lectures is not humanity, or even Europe, but, in his words, "the existence of our Nation in its entirety." Already in 1925 he undertook to impugn conceptions foreign to his own way of seeing the historical community of the German nation: Cartesian philosophy, Neo-Kantianism, phenomenology in the form in which Husserl developed it, and which was characterized by its "loss of history" (*Geschichtslosigkeit*) and its status of being an enemy of history (*Geschichtsfeindlichkeit*).[20] Henceforth the adversaries are clearly identified.

Being and Time: *From the Individual Self to the Communal Destiny of the People*

Two years after delivering his 1925 lectures, Heidegger published the work that would make it possible for him to succeed Husserl at Freiburg and bring him increasing notoriety beyond the borders of Germany — particularly thanks to Sartrean existentialism in France, though the latter was of a quite different inspiration. *Being and Time* presents the paradox of an ontology without categories, a paradox heightened by the fact that at the same time that Heidegger rejects the Aristotelian category of substance, he nominalizes, in a very scholastic manner, the infinitive "to be" and speaks thereafter of *the to-be* (*das Sein*). Further, he replaces the Kantian transcendental analytic with an analysis of existence and proposes "existentials" — being-in-the-world, being-with, being-toward-death, and so on — in lieu of a table of categories. The contrast between the existential intent of the topic and the very scholastic ponderousness of the exposition has fascinated some and rebuffed others, but the apparent indetermination of the content has, as Löwith has shown, contributed considerably to its favorable reception. Yet there are, in this work, quite a number of signs that should have made philosophers wary, beginning with the elimination of the word "man," dropped for being too determinate, and to which Heidegger prefers the term, in appearance less determinate, "existence" (*Dasein*).[21] Thus the author maintains ambiguity. The reader may believe that he or she is dealing with a description of individual existence, while in fact something very different is involved, as sections 27 and 74 clearly reveal.

The book's overall line of argument is a double challenge, directed at once against any universal sort of thinking and any philosophy of individual existence. It is thus understandable that a major target of the book is the philosophy of Descartes. Heidegger rejects all attempts at an elucidation (*Aufklärung*) of existence that would depend on an understanding of the most foreign cultures (*fremdesten Kulturen*) and the search for a universal understanding of existence. According to him, such an effort leads to making existence foreign to itself, and to a loss of soil: *Entfremdung* and *Bodenlosenkeit* are the words that recur in this Heideggerian rejection of any universal. He also rejects all philosophy of the *I* and of human individuality. Heidegger develops an opposition between the *I*, which is reduced to nothing but a "formal indication," and the *self* (*Selbst*) of the existent, understood as being-in-common (*Mitdasein*).[22] In a formulation that summarizes all that has been accomplished in section 27, he affirms that "the sameness of the authentically existing *self* is ontologically separated by a chasm from the identity of the *I*."[23] This authenticity of the *self* has therefore nothing individual about it. It is accomplished only in the temporality and historicity of existence understood as fate (*Schicksal*). This fate is itself a "happening" (*Geschehen*) and a "destiny" (*Geschick*) that "is in no way made up of individual fates, no more than being in common can be conceived as the simultaneous presence of several subjects."[24] One cannot be more explicit than Heidegger is: authentic existence has nothing of an individual being about it. It can be accomplished only as a common destiny (*Geschick*) in "the historicizing of the community, of the people" (*das Geschehen der Gemeinschaft, des Volkes*).

On this page of section 74, which constitutes the culmination of the developments on the historicality of existence (and therefore of existence, and therefore of the entire work, since everything converges on the sections concerning historicality), the ideas that are at the very foundation of National Socialist doctrine are already present — namely, those of a community of destiny and of a community of the people: the *Gemeinschaft* understood as *Schicksalsgemeinschaft* and *Volksgemeinschaft*. Even the biological element is suggested by referencing the idea of "generation" (which is present in the same paragraph and taken from Dilthey, who uses it in a sense that is at once biological and social) and by appealing to the "elementary." In this context, the distinction between the authenticity of *Dasein* and the inauthenticity of the "they" takes on a clearly discriminatory sense.

The ideas of historicality (*Geschichtlichkeit*), of happening (*Geschehen*), and of generation are in fact already present at the beginning of section 6, on a page that deals with "the elementary historicality of existence" (*elementare Geschichtlichkeit des Daseins*) and thus also introduces the key reference to the elementary, which constitutes one of most cryptic pillars of *Being and Time*. It can be found especially in sections 41 and 42, in the context of the ontological "elementary totality" (*elementare Ganzheit*) of care, the "elementary traces" of which can be read in the fable of *cura,* care, related by Konrad Burdach in 1923 in the first issue of Rothacker's journal, to which Heidegger refers in a note.[25] This recourse to the elementary, associated with the idea of generation, was to have an ominous history among the "philosophers" of Nazism. I will give as an example the definition Alfred Baeumler proposes of race, identifying it with the "elementary lines of conduct" (*elementare Verhaltungsweisen*) that are also found in "the change of generations" (*im Wechsel der Generationen*).[26] Moreover, in Heidegger's recently published writings on Jünger, the "new relationship with the elementary" is explicitly linked to race.[27]

The real project of *Being and Time* is the will to destroy the idea of the *I* in order to make room for the "most radical individuation" (*radikalsten Individuation*), which is emphatically realized not in the individual but in the organic indivisibility of the *Gemeinschaft* of the people.[28] The "destruction" of Cartesian ontology, announced in the plan of the book as Division Two of Part Two, was never published and probably never written.[29] But the persuasive power of Heidegger's rhetoric seems to have been such that its mere announcement sufficed for many readers to take the non-realized project for a definitive accomplishment. Thus, Jürgen Habermas praised *Being and Time* as having taken "a decisive step along the path of argumentation that will make it possible to transcend the philosophy of consciousness" without noticing that in that entire work no philosophical and critical analysis of the Cartesian metaphysics of the *cogito sum* is accomplished; nor does he truly seem to discern the nature of the doctrine of *Gemeinschaft* toward which Heidegger was leading his readers at that date.[30] Though Habermas is lucid and severe with respect to the Heidegger of 1953, he is too indulgent of the one prior to 1929.

All that is to be found in *Being and Time* on the Cartesian *I think* are a few lines at the beginning of section 10, in which Heidegger asserts that "the approach of an *I* and a subject given at the outset fundamentally misses the phenomenal reality of existence."[31] Even sections 19–21, which constitute the only developed discussion of Descartes but focus on the *res extensa* and not the *ego cogito,* are presented by Heidegger as a provisional attempt, the "complete legitimization" of which will be obtainable only through the "phenomenological destruction of the *cogito sum.*"[32] In reality, this absence reveals that Heidegger has no real philosophical refutation with which to oppose the Cartesian *I think.* The anti-Cartesian diatribes of the 1933 courses will directly confirm this. The destruction of the individual and the human *I* in order to make room for the communal destiny of the people is in neither intent nor approach a purely philosophical undertaking but a "political project," embedded in the very foundations of National Socialism, with its *Volksgemeinschaft* doctrine.

Heidegger, Becker, and Clauß: Surrounding World, Community of the People, and Racial Doctrine

During his years as professor at Marburg, we have seen how Heidegger reveals the foundation of his doctrine only in small increments and with extreme prudence. All of *Being and Time* must be read in light of the sections on historicality and the propositions of section 74 on the communal destiny of the people, if we are truly to begin to understand where he is leading his readers. The fact that this way of proceeding is part of a long, thought-out strategy is clear from the following comment by Heidegger, related to Erich Rothacker by Ludwig Ferdinand Clauß after the war: "I'll say what I think when I'm a full professor."[33] The political radicalism of Heidegger's thought did not begin to become apparent until 1929, when he had moved into Freiburg as Husserl's successor. When in 1954 Heidegger was at the height of his fame and Clauß remained discredited, the latter regretted not having shown that same prudence in his youth.

Clauß was, along with Hans K. Günther, among the first and foremost theoreticians of the Nazi racial doctrine. But whereas Günther was originally a philologist, Clauß had received philosophical training, mainly from Husserl, and at the beginning he presented himself as the latter's disciple. It is therefore likely that Heidegger and Clauß became acquainted toward the last years of the 1910s or at the beginning of the 1920s, when Heidegger was Husserl's assistant at Freiburg. Heidegger's remark, therefore, was probably made in confidence directly to Clauß, or to their mutual friend Oskar Becker.

Becker, who was born in 1889 (and was therefore Heidegger's exact contemporary), was close to the raciologist Clauß. Their evolution from the common basis of Husserl's phenomenology is similar, and Becker took an interest in racial doctrine very early.[34] As a participant or at least a sympathizer of the Kapp Putsch, he began to collaborate before 1933 on the journal *Deutschland Erneuerung* by H. S. Chamberlain. Coming from a background of evangelical religion, he separated himself from it to take up an interest in Indo-Germanic religiosity and the thinking through of his relationship to the divine "in the sense of Goethe and Hölderlin."[35] Oskar Becker was equally close to Erich Rothacker and soon became his colleague at the University of Bonn, after having been Heidegger's assistant at Freiburg. After 1933 Becker contributed to the supposedly "philosophical" justification of Nazi racial doctrine to the point of collaborating, in 1933, in the journal *Rasse* and, like Heidegger, of progressively cutting off all relations with Karl Löwith because he was a Jew.

With these names, Rothacker, Becker, and Clauß, we are approaching interlocutors or figures close to Heidegger, both by their career paths, which were somewhat similar, and their political affinities. But while Rothacker and Becker, unlike Heidegger, did not completely reveal the Nazi substratum of their doctrine until the seizure of power of 1933 had been accomplished, Clauß had shown the racist thumbprint of his doctrine as early as 1923, with the publication of *The Nordic Soul*. That work is a major factor. It allows the reader to see how, before Heidegger, a phenomenologist formed by Husserl was able to claim he was using Husserl's method in proposing as early as 1923 a description of what is at the very basis of Nazism — namely, the communal destiny of a people united by blood. Because of this circumstance, a meticulous comparison of Clauß's *Nordic Soul* with Heidegger's *Being and Time* would be worth pursuing. Here I will limit myself to a few elements of their similarity.

In *The Nordic Soul*, Clauß claims from the opening pages to be following the "phenomenological method" and pays homage, in a note, as Heidegger will do in *Being and Time,* to the "fundamental works of Edmund Husserl" and particularly to the *Ideen* of 1913. But just as Heidegger removed his dedication of homage to Husserl in the fifth edition of *Being and Time,* which appeared in 1941, Clauß's homage to Husserl no longer appeared in the new, expanded edition of 1940, which henceforth bore the subtitle *An Introduction to the Doctrine of the Soul of the Race [Rassenseelenkunde].*[36]

In his undertaking, Clauß relies on ideas that will be equally pivotal in *Being and Time:* "surrounding world" (*Umwelt*), "destiny" (*Schicksal*), and "decision," which he hyphenates (*Ent-scheidung*), as if to illustrate the fact that decision is fundamentally the separation between what is homogeneous and what is foreign. As in *Being and Time,* the notion of the "call" (*Ruf*) is central, and on several occasions Clauß evokes "the decisive call of destiny."[37] Even more troubling, Clauß announces the Heideggerian *existentiale* of being in common or being-with (*Mit-sein*), using such neologisms as *Mit-erleben,* the "hearing" of which is in response to the call of destiny.[38] Here we also find the same requirement of a soil (*Boden*). The point is, Clauß writes, to "find a soil on which a new community of understanding may be founded."[39] The crowning moment of this research is, as in section 74 of *Being and Time,* the "communal destiny" or "destiny-community" (*Schicksalsgemeinschaft*) understood as the "people."[40] Let us note in conclusion the myth of a pure Greekness, evoked under auspices of the Nietzschean opposition of Apollo and Dionysus.[41]

It is true that Clauß, as emphasized in the passage quoted from his letter to Rothacker, reveals himself far more than does Heidegger during the 1920s. In

Being and Time, there is indeed the decisive reference to the community of the people who are united in a process of becoming and a common destiny, and the constant evocation of the soil and of enrootedness, but we have seen that the possibly racial background of *Being and Time* surfaces only in a euphemistic manner, as, for example, in the notion of "generation" or the references to the "elementary." Heidegger does not place blood and enrootedness "in the original German race" at the heart of his teaching until 1933 and thereafter. For Clauß, on the contrary, only his anti-Semitism remains discreet in 1923, and even that is a relative question, because at the end of the book, in a parenthesis that foreshadows the most dire prolongations, he advances the idea that *Judentum* "is not, as has often been believed, a pure character, a 'race,' but a *Volkstum* that is radically mixed [*artgemische*], quite the opposite of the German *Volkstum.*"[42] This is precisely the thesis that will be found in the Nazi racial doctrine, or *Rassenkunde,* in which Jews will be denied the designation of pure race. The goal of Clauß's work is to reaffirm the German people's community of destiny in order to restore its character as the pure race (*reine Artung*) and pure blood (*reines Blut*) of the Nordic soul. Clauß does not hesitate to refer the reader to Hans K. Günther's *Rassenkunde des deutschen Volkes,* published the preceding year, but he refers to it as a "biological" version of the question, while he insists on the fact that in his own view the word "blood" refers not only to the physical but to the soul "in its radical relation to its field of expression, the body" — that "German soul" that he means to describe by the phenomenological method.[43]

Incontestably, there are important points in common between Clauß's approach in 1923 and the doctrine set forth by Heidegger in *Being and Time,* and even more explicitly, of course, in the latter's courses of 1933–1934. As for *Being and Time,* as we have seen, the two authors share the same project of describing the existent in its surrounding world and its being in common, and in what is at the very basis of Nazi doctrine: namely, the "authentic" grasp of the existent in the community of destiny of the people, as the response to a call or to a decisive question, the precise tenor of which remains intentionally indeterminate in order to leave room for the pure decision. Nevertheless, important differences remain: Clauß speaks of soul (*Seele*), while Heidegger speaks of existence; Clauß speaks of homogeneity or racial identity (*Artgleichheit*) — a term taken up by Carl Schmitt and Ernst Forsthoff ten years later — while Heidegger speaks only of authenticity (*Eigentlichkeit*); Clauß speaks of blood and race, which Heidegger will never speak of openly until 1933.

If we compare Clauß's work with Heidegger's teaching in 1933–1934, the resemblance is even stronger, since both understand "blood" in a sense that is not simply physical and biological, the former author referring to the soul and the latter to the spirit, Clauß remaining close in this respect to Ludwig Klages, and Heidegger to Alfred Baeumler. Thus we see that as early as 1923 Clauß expresses a blood racism that he does not consider to be purely biological and that, far from presenting itself as a form of naturalism, claims to follow Husserl's phenomenological method. Now, this racism of Clauß's will be completely integrated with Nazi *Rassenkunde*. As Cornelia Essner makes clear: "It is the SS officers—Himmler first and foremost—who are the quickest, after 1933, to subscribe to Clauß's vision, for whom racial identity (*Artung*) has much less to do with consanguinity than with sensibility, with a 'way of taking life.'"[44] That point is paramount: it shows us that the taking up of a certain distance with respect to "biologism" is perfectly compatible with an unreserved allegiance to the most radical Nazi racism. What is true for Clauß also holds for Heidegger. Heidegger's critical remarks directed against "biologism" do not prevent him from speaking, in the unpublished seminar of 1933–1934, of the community of the people as a community of race; nor does it keep him, in 1940, in a passage contained in his course on Nietzsche that was not retained in the 1961 edition (the only edition translated into French) from using the word *Entartung* on several occasions, a term commonly used in the racist doctrine of Nazism to designate racial degeneration.[45]

It is therefore not without reason that Heidegger and Clauß have been closely associated by an author particularly well informed about the racial doctrine of this period, an author whose importance for the genesis of Heidegger's notion of historicality has already been pointed out. That author is Erich Rothacker.

Heidegger and Rothacker: "Philosophy of History" and "Racial Thought" in the Third Reich

We have forgotten that at the beginning of the 1950s the academic influence in Germany of Rothacker, a professor with Oskar Becker at the University of Bonn, the capital of the Federal Republic of Germany, was far greater than that of Heidegger, who had been forbidden to teach. Therefore it may seem surprising, for today's reader, to see these two authors placed side by side, now that one is known worldwide, while the other is scarcely mentioned outside Germany. Nevertheless, so many reciprocal relations link the two men that their comparison cannot fail to shed some light. Rothacker himself, in a lecture delivered shortly before his death, will go so far as to say that the notion of the world as developed by Heidegger in *Being and Time* was nothing but the reworking of what he himself had already said in 1926.[46]

We have seen that the gestation of *Being and Time* was closely linked to

Rothacker's publishing of the correspondence between Yorck and Dilthey, which fascinated Heidegger. To this we should add Konrad Burdach's study on Faust and care, which appeared the same year, 1923, in the first issue of the journal created by Rothacker — a study quoted by Heidegger in section 42 of *Being and Time* and that encouraged him in the idea of thematizing existence as care.[47] With the Nazi takeover, the ties between Heidegger and Rothacker were strengthened. The two men were together on more than one occasion — for example, during a program lasting several days at the beginning of May 1934 at the Nietzsche Archives of Weimar, at which Alfred Rosenberg was also present. Furthermore, Rothacker's National Socialist experience was very similar to Heidegger's.

Erich Rothacker, born in 1888, one year before Heidegger, joined the National Socialist Democratic Workers' Party (NSDAP) on 1 May 1933, just as Heidegger did, but he had already joined the League of National Socialist Professors (NSLB) in November 1932. He was rector of the University of Bonn from 1933 to 1935. In 1933 he developed a plan for National Socialist education and worked to that end for two weeks in April 1933 at Joseph Goebbels's private villa.[48] In August 1934, he sent Heidegger his monograph, *The Philosophy of History,* published in Volume IV of the *Manual of Philosophy,* edited by Alfred Baeumler. In that study, Rothacker shows that "the correlation of man and world" as "surrounding world" finds its meaning in the doctrine of race. The exposition of racial doctrine leads him to a defense of National Socialism and of Hitler, the virulence of which stands out in this *Manual.* It is, as I have indicated, in that study that Rothacker twice identifies Clauß closely with Heidegger, and the racial doctrine of *The Nordic Soul* with the existentialism of *Being and Time,* apropos of the "correlativity between world and man,"[49] according to which "the world in which a man lives is in a strict relation of exchange with his being."[50] This thesis leads Rothacker to speak of "struggles for life," for "we not only in each instance have our world: we affirm our world."[51] Thus what is at stake here is affirmation (*Behauptung*) in combat, a central motif shared by Rothacker, Baeumler, and Heidegger, which is one of the commonplaces of Nazi doctrine.

The last section of Rothacker's *Philosophy of History* is titled "The Existential Reduction: Race and Spirit of the People."[52] That reduction to race is explicated by Rothacker in terms that, even if his way of writing is very different, share the Heideggerian notion of historical existence. Rothacker writes: "The ultimate driving force behind historical life is existential: It is not thinkable without the urge of the emotions, whether those that flow forth spontaneously from the depths of being, or those reactive forces of anxiety and the pure and simple affirmation of life."[53]

Here we recognize the Heideggerian identity between the existential and the historical, the importance granted to moods, such as anxiety, and the positive value ascribed to the notion of assertion (*Behauptung*). In the same section, Rothacker develops his doctrine of race in the following terms:

> One must avoid at any cost that the good race [*gute Rasse*] should become the lap of idleness for the self-satisfied long heads, or that it should lead to underestimating the importance of training [*Zucht*] for the bearing [*Haltung*] and formation of men. Historically and personally, the good race is a task of very high responsibility, the carrying out of which can very well fall short. Our Teutonic ancestors, today largely transfigured, were not—due to the relatively higher percentage of Nordic blood by which they differed from that of today's average German—well protected from the dangers of drunkenness, gambling, and, above all, constant internal conflict. Thus, we are clearly not indebted to the Nordic race, which is purer in Scandinavia, for the decisive steps in the direction of German unity, but rather to "the Prussian spirit" and the spirit of the NSDAP, i.e., in both cases, to the lifestyles [*Lebensstilen*], the results of hard-won training, naturally engendered by the spirit of the Nordic tradition, but which were nevertheless formed from a racial material that is highly problematic, according to Günther's criteria.[54]

Rothacker could not have been more explicit, measured by the Nazi criteria of his day. "Long heads" is—as is made clear by Volker Böhnigk, who makes reference in this regard to Houston S. Chamberlain and Hans K. Günther—a rather common expression in Nazi racial doctrine to designate the Jews.[55] Moreover, Rothacker quotes the Nordic racial doctrine of Günther without contesting it, but he relativizes it by relying on the main argument of those among the National Socialists who wish to defend the notion of a "German race." To speak solely of the Nordic race is insufficient for a proper understanding of German unity, by the standards of the *völkisch* criteria of Nazism. It is the Prussian spirit and the spirit of the NSDAP, as well as the resultant discipline and training, that have produced the new unity of the German people and not just the "percentage of Nordic blood" based on Günther's criteria. Rothacker knows that in this he can draw on the authority of Hitler himself, who, in his speech at the end of August 1933, defined race as primarily "spirit."[56]

To this Nazi concept of "spirit" Rothacker adds that of "bearing" (*Haltung*). The "bearing" of the people is always enrooted, according to him, in a constant, which is none other than that of "racial origin" (*rassische Herkunft*).[57] But Rothacker doesn't stop there: he adds to his study a particularly enthusiastic and venomous appendix, titled "The Third Reich," which constitutes a sort of compendium of Nazism, under the auspices of Hitler, Jünger, and Rosenberg. It appears indispensable for our purposes to quote significant excerpts from this text, since we now know that Heidegger read and explicitly approved it.

> Meanwhile, the victory of the national revolution, with the establishment of the Third Reich, at the same time held up a new image of man. The accomplishment and realization of that image is the task, in terms of universal history, of the German people. — But what to the contemporary represents a call to action must impose itself to the philosopher of history as proof by example. The fundamental concepts must find the same confirmation in the most recent events as in those of the past: a new bearing [*Haltung*] vis-à-vis the world as the seed bearing a new future; new meanings opening up from the viewpoint of the new bearing; the adaptation to a new "world" and its correlate, a new ideal of life; that ideal, born into life as the expression of the taking up of a position toward life, and concerned with life. That new bearing, which did not appear "by itself," nor brought about as if by natural events, is not an "organic" process, or a utopian construction, but has issued forth from a determinate historical situation, has been won by dint of lofty combat and sacrifice, both internal and external — imposed in the face of resistance, hostile attitudes and dying worlds.[58]

We see how Rothacker's text is structured around the concept of "bearing" (*Haltung*), which corresponds to the "new image of man" held up by the Third Reich. The "ideal" Rothacker evokes corresponds to its new usage in *Mein Kampf,* in which it is defined solely in relation to struggle and sacrifice. Rothacker continues:

> While it is true that it is indeed in this gathering of all events into the center of a new lifestyle [*Lebensstil*] and life ideal that our fundamental conception of the philosophy of history is confirmed, it still remains for us to inquire into the most essential guiding thoughts — those thoughts that in the framework of this lifestyle struggle for their rank and participation and give life to our movement of renewal of the state and the people from the point of view of their contribution to the theoretical conception of historical life. There is first of all the new appreciation for the idea of the state, on which it is appropriate to insist most strongly in political terms, among a people so late in being unified as a nation, and nationally so little disciplined as is the German people, especially in the West. This is the guiding thought that imposes the obligation of a "political education" over long years, a forming and teaching of the young generation. These are totally indispensable, and must at all costs be strongly supported in opposition to the deep-seated liberal slackness; and they must be inspired with the greatest possible pathos, in the Hegelian as well as the classical sense, for the sake of stylistic formation and streamlining.[59]

Here we find Rothacker developing the same themes that were developed by Heidegger in his speeches and the unpublished seminar of 1933–1934: the new and heightened appreciation of the state implying the necessity of a political education directed against liberalism, the imposition of a new "bearing" and a new "style," terms that will be found particularly in Heidegger's speech of 25 November 1933, titled *The German Student as Worker.*[60] It must be borne in mind that in the language of the times the word *Stil* had become one of the key terms of the racial doctrine, not only in Clauß but also in Günther, whose work *Rasse und Stil* Rothacker quotes — from the second edition, which appeared in 1927.[61] Rothacker, for his part, becomes increasingly explicit as he develops his theme. He continues as follows.

> It is from this that Adolf Hitler, with the sure instinct of a great statesman, drew the conclusion, by the fact that in the book of his life he awards first place, in the scale of political values, to the idea of the community of the people [*Volksgemeinschaft*]. People in the twofold sense that was already germinating in Herder's concept of people: the people as the underlying bearer of an authentic national community, and of the spirit of national racial character [*Eigenart*].[62] National Socialist, then, if national means German, and socialism the cohesion of the people. To the extent that this social point of view is today for many reasons in the foreground of day-to-day domestic politics and its ideology, often even up to the limits of Jünger's apotheosis, which sees in the "worker" the sole stratum formative of the people of the state, it appears that a decidedly "national education" would therefore be indicated to furnish the third and indispensable guiding thought, alongside the "political education" and "social education" of an attentive cultural policy.[63]

Here we see Rothacker drawing authority from both Hitler's *Mein Kampf* and Jünger's *Der Arbeiter,* to bolster the notion of a "national education," the basis of which is, as the following lines specify, the "idea of the race," taken as what is common to the idea of the state and of the German people. "Next to the idea of the state, the idea of Germanness, the idea of a people, the common element essential to all of them is racial thought [*Rassengedanke*]."[64]

Here Rothacker uses a term, *Rassengedanke,* that Heidegger will make his own and legitimize in his course on Nietzsche in 1942. The continuation of Rothacker's text shows that he is particularly well informed on the contemporary controversy among Nazi authors about the definition of race.

> What immediately catches the eye is the tension between the race idea [*Rasseidee*] and the idea of the state: the framework of the latter might well be definitively blown apart by the regulation of action according to a community consciousness reaching beyond the consciousness of people, language, mores, and history. But the true importance of the other political consequences of the

idea of race is to be found particularly in its indestructibly aristocratic character. The fact that this trait stands in particularly felicitous agreement with the idea of a Führer hardly requires further argument; no more so than does the principle of honor [*Ehre*], admirably emphasized by A. Rosenberg, and which is closely tied to race consciousness. But profound tensions exist between, on the one hand, the two ideas united in the idea of race, that of descent from a pure race (Gobineau), and that of the "good race" in the sense of the highly qualified breeding race (H. Stuart Chamberlain), and on the other hand all the disguises of democracy and of the domination of the masses, as the inevitable favoritism of a racial heritage the average level of which can be lowered only as the numbers increase. According to the strictly biological criteria of the racial doctrine itself, on average the Nordic-Falish and the Eastern are as unequally distributed socially as are the results of social breeding for inherited gifts. In this sense, moving the concept of the racially noble from the purely somatic to the "heroic mind-set" and worldview so much more compatible with the Nordic hereditary share — a move that Hitler had strongly emphasized at Nuremberg[65] — removes a certain political embarrassment just as the Baltic pathos of the concepts of "character" and "personality" do in A. Rosenberg's *Myth of the Twentieth Century*. This also provides examples of how diverging ideas as such may find fruitful readjustment through practical application of new ideal images. That requires however, and above all, that the very quintessence of all the measures and all the ideas concerning "the national-political education" must be consciously put in the closest relation of complementariness with the idea of race. A racially satisfactory average level of population can be obtained only, given the existing racial mixture within the German racial stock, by encouraging in the most energetic way possible all eugenic methods that have recourse to the formation and training of human materials of youth, which is still malleable externally and internally, and this in the spirit of the best racial components of its hereditary mass. It is possible to encourage very manifestly the inherited percentage of Nordic and Falish blood by a conscious educative training in the Nordic-Falish spirit according to its phenotypical effects.[66]

As Cornelia Essner has clearly shown, the doctrinaire theoreticians of the Nazi *Rassenkunde* were at that time divided between Günther's Nordicist point of view, for whom the goal to be attained was the increase of "Nordic blood" in the German population, and the point of view of a Fritz Merkenschlager, for whom the notion of "German race" must prevail.[67] Now Hitler in a sense leapfrogged this debate in his speech at the end of August 1933, in which, far from placing himself on a strictly "biological" level, he uses, exactly as does Heidegger, the vocabulary of authenticity and essence, in making the "authentic" (*eigentlich*) belonging of the National Socialists to a specific race depend on "their essence" (*ihrem Wesen*).[68] It is to this speech that Rothacker refers, as well as to the racial notion of honor in Rosenberg, in order to develop an aristocratic conception of race, which plays on both levels distinguished by Rothacker in his doctrine: the genotype, or the hidden transmission of the racial type, which he intends to encourage by eugenic measures applied to the "human material" of malleable youth, and the phenotype, or visible manifestation of racial characteristics (in bearing, impression, style), that he intends to favor by an appropriate "national political education." The underlying intent of the text is continuous with the harshest abjection of Nazism: training and selection understood as the combining of a eugenics program and a National Socialist political education.

Since my goal here is not to study Rothacker's remarks in themselves, I have quoted only a small portion of his long disquisitions on what he calls the "existential reduction of race" and of his appended text titled "The Third Reich." The essential point is that Heidegger receives this text of Rothacker's very favorably. This capital point has never been stressed. Yet Heidegger writes to him about the philosophy seminar in Freiburg on 11 August 1934:

> Dear honorable Mr. Rothacker!
>
> I thank you emphatically for your invitation to a lecture. But it so happens that we have, beginning on 26 October, in the Black Forest, a camp [*Lager*] for the philological disciplines and those that are related to the natural sciences, the direction of which I have taken over. . . . I thank you very much for having sent me your *Philosophy of History*. As well as I can judge for the moment, you have made a fruitful approach to the construction of the whole thing. "Bearing" [*Haltung*] aims at an essential milieu of historical being, if it is not interpreted fallaciously in the "psychological" mode. It is a pity that your work remains too hidden in the framework of the manual. My speech broadcast on the radio, "Why do we stay in the Province?" will soon be republished *privatim;* you are already on the list to receive a copy. I was interested in hearing about the *New German Research.* I could soon have two works available for it. . . . Is there any possibility of placing these two works in the collection? Or is the whole thing not yet sufficiently advanced?
>
> Heil Hitler!
>
> Your Heidegger[69]

The beginning of the letter informs us of a fact hitherto unknown — namely, that far from being marginalized after his resignation from the rectorate, Heidegger continued to direct the Nazi work and study camps during the autumn of 1934, as he had so much appreciated doing in 1933. Moreover, with respect to Heidegger's relationship to Rothacker, the terms of his letter are most explicit. He praises the doctrine of *Haltung* developed by Rothacker, which, as we have seen, becomes meaningful only as a racial concept, and he goes so far as to relate it to an "essential milieu of historical being." The reservation expressed about the "psychological" interpretation is to be explained no doubt in part by the fact that Rothacker associates Heidegger with Klages, the doctrinaire theoretician of the soul, and this certainly repels Heidegger, given his hostility toward Klages, which he shares with Baeumler. In praising the "fruitful approach" (*fruchtbarer Ansatz*), is Heidegger perhaps indicating that he also approves Rothacker's appendix on "The Third Reich"? As we have seen, that text is intended solely to expound the racial doctrine of Hitlerism and Nazism, presenting it as the basis of a new "philosophy of history," intended to promote what Rothacker calls, in terms that are very close to those of Heidegger, "the enrootedness of existence in the affirmation [*Behauptung*] of the *völkisch* life on earth."[70] In sum, the reading of Rothacker not only does not dissuade him but motivates him to pursue an intellectual and editorial collaboration with him.

Heidegger's approval is doubtless largely due to the fact that Rothacker, like Hitler himself in his speech at the end of August 1933, and like Rosenberg in *The Myth of the Twentieth Century*, relates race not exclusively to "biological" considerations after the manner of Hans K. Günther, but to blood, spirit, and "training," just as does Heidegger himself. This is an extremely important point, because it must be understood once and for all that the fact of insisting on the importance of spirit and of expressing reservations with respect to "biologism" indicates not in the least a distancing from the Hitlerian conception of race, but on the contrary a perfect conformity with the "spirit" of Hitlerism.

Unfortunately, we do not have letters from Rothacker to Heidegger and do not know whether the latter kept them. It is possible that they were too compromising to be placed in the Heidegger archive at Marbach. If we did have the complete correspondence of Heidegger with such figures as Baeumler, Becker, and Rothacker, it is plausible that the perception that has been disseminated too long by his apologists would be transformed by them. In any case, there is at least one letter from Heidegger to Rothacker later than 1934. It confirms the particular esteem Heidegger had for him.

In 1941 the death of the Catholic thinker Erich Honecker, the holder of the "Concordat chair" at the University of Freiburg, left the position vacant, and the Nazis decided, in all likelihood with the agreement of Heidegger himself, to eliminate that Concordat chair and to change it to a chair in "psychology." Now, it was of Rothacker that Heidegger was thinking, and he wrote him on 4 November 1941 to try to convince him to leave Bonn for Freiburg. "Would you agree to come? That would make me very happy."[71] He was happy to see, in the person of Rothacker, someone coming who was a "psychologist" at the same time as a "philosopher." But we have seen the racial tenor of Rothacker's "philosophy of history." That is clearly not a problem for Heidegger in 1941. It may even be that this was a positive factor, if we consider what he himself would later say about the "idea of race" during that period. If intellectual and what were soon to be amicable relations between Heidegger and Rothacker are so important to our understanding of the underlying basis for Heidegger's doctrine during the 1920s (during which years the composition, for Rothacker's recently launched journal, of an account of the Dilthey-Yorck correspondence published by this same Rothacker was at the origin of *Being and Time*) and the 1930s (when the two men shared the same party line), it is not only because Heidegger's approval of his racist notion of "bearing" (*Haltung*) reveals to us that the author of *Being and Time* looks upon the racial doctrine of Nazism and Hitlerism with sympathy; it is also because we can then read his speeches and courses in a different way, revealing in his writings the presence of a vocabulary, that of "bearing," "style," "imprint," and so on, which comes directly from the racial language of a Rothacker or a Clauß. And the borrowings are not just in one direction, since we can discern the influence of Heidegger on Rothacker as the latter "ontologizes" his discourse, referring to existence and to being.

It is true that the comparison between Heidegger's writings and those of Clauß and Rothacker during the years 1923–1934 should be carried further, but the essential seems to me to be accomplished — namely, that henceforth it will scarcely be possible to study the notions of historicality and bearing in Heidegger without evoking the corresponding passages by Rothacker, or to analyze the notions of "surrounding world" and "being in common" in *Being and Time* without taking Clauß's work into account.

We shall now complete our approach at a more directly historical level, following, through testimonies and a series of letters and reports from Heidegger, the increasing forcefulness of his political positions, the progressive expression of his anti-Semitism, and the way he responds, in his university practice, to the "call" of Nazism, since the university is the very place in which he intends to act politically.

On the Political Orientation of Heidegger Before 1933

The closeness to the National Socialist movement begins very early. We know that his wife, Elfride, joined the ranks of the National Socialist youth movements as early as the beginning of the 1920s and was enthusiastic enough to want to win followers among her husband's students. Thus, in August

1922, during a house-warming celebration at the chalet nestled in the heights of Todtnauberg, she tried to rally Günther Anders, then a young student of Heidegger's, a Jew (unbeknownst to her), to National Socialism. Anders has also spoken of the prejudice of Heidegger himself, who was "not very far from *Blubo*" — that is, from *Blut und Boden,* the Nazi doctrine of blood and soil.[72] Indeed, Heidegger will explicitly endorse it on numerous occasions in his speeches and courses of the years 1933–1934. Heidegger's *völkisch* mentality during the 1920s is confirmed by another student, Max Müller. Müller, reminiscing about the professor's hiking and cross-country skiing with his students, relates that Heidegger would talk to them about the "relationship of the folk [*Volkstum*] with nature, but also with the Youth Movement [*Jugendbewegung*]. He felt an intimate closeness to the word *völkisch* and said he was tied 'to the blood and the soil.' "[73]

Moreover, Hans-Georg Gadamer himself, a disciple of Heidegger if there ever was one, places what he calls "the obvious sympathy" of Martin Heidegger "for the Nazi radicalism . . . far earlier than 1933."[74]

Equally important is the testimony of another student, Hermann Mörchen, who was among Heidegger's intimates. Mörchen, invited to his chalet in Todtnauberg on 25 December 1931, wrote in his diary what Heidegger had confided to him that evening. He said he was convinced that National Socialism was the only movement capable of opposing Marxism effectively: neither democratic idealism nor Brüning's honesty could be considered; halfway measures were henceforth worthless; a dictatorship was the only way. When it was a question of resisting threats to the spirit of the West, there was no shrinking back, not even from the Boxheimer method.[75] Heidegger was alluding to an affair that had marked the year 1931. Documents had been found on the person of a certain Dr. Best, who was later to become a high Nazi official, attesting to the existence of a National Socialist plot in Boxheimer Hof, in Hesse, with a list of political figures to be assassinated after the seizure of power. To accept the Boxheimer method, then, means to recommend the physical liquidation of political opponents when the National Socialist dictatorship took over in Germany. Such is the radical political "solution" recommended by Heidegger as early as 1931. He thus adhered to the Nazi violence that was already palpable in the streets and that would be given even freer reign after the Nazi takeover, with the arrest and imprisonment of all political opponents. With Mörchen's testimony, then, it is no longer a question simply of the mentality of Heidegger but of his actual political position before 1933.

Heidegger's rallying to the cause of Nazism before the 1933 seizure of power is confirmed by an unpublished letter of 16 December 1932 addressed to the Protestant theologian Rudolf Bultmann. Bultmann, having heard that

Martin Heidegger has joined the National Socialist Party, questions him about it. Heidegger responds by qualifying the rumor according to which he joined the Nazi Party as a "tale from the latrines," but he admits having voted for the National Socialist "movement." Doubtless in an attempt to win Bultmann over to his views, on 20 December he sent him a pamphlet written by a member of the Tatkreis, the ultranationalist and "socialist" group of the Protestant right, gathered around the journal *Action (Die Tat)*, which would rally massively to National Socialism after having prepared its arrival in the minds of its readers.[76]

The extremely clear declaration of Heidegger on his vote for the National Socialist movement in 1932 formally contradicts his son Hermann's declaration, according to which it was for "the little unknown party of the wine-growers of Württemberg" that he voted in 1932.[77] And yet Hermann Heidegger was familiar with the correspondence between his father and Rudolf Bultmann, since access to the manuscripts of the Heidegger archive was under his sole control, and he states precisely in the same text that the Heidegger-Bultmann correspondence is in preparation.[78] Therefore we have every right to wonder whether there is not, here, a desire to hide the historical truth.

Heidegger's correspondence with Elisabeth Blochmann displays the same tendencies, revealing a Heidegger essentially preoccupied with political questions in 1932, attacking, for example, the Catholic Party of the *Zentrum* for having "encouraged liberalism and a general leveling." Thus he reveals, in a letter of 30 March 1933, that his consent to the forces of the "process in progress" is based on analyses that have been established "for a long time."[79]

These testimonies and declarations by Heidegger himself confirm in advance what it says in the Nazi journal *Der Alemanne* of 3 May 1933: "We know that Martin Heidegger, with his lofty consciousness and responsibility, his care for the destiny and future of the German man, was at the very core of our magnificent movement. We also know that he never made any mystery about his German convictions and that for many years he has supported in the most effective way the party of Adolf Hitler in his struggle for being and power, that he has constantly proved ready for sacrifice for the holy cause of Germany, and that no National Socialist has ever knocked at his door in vain."[80]

This text is particularly important due to the fact that its author, a certain H. E. who signed only with his initials, associated characteristic terms of Heideggerian language such as "care" (*Sorge*) and "being" (*Sein*) with others that are just as central to Heideggerian terminology as to the language of Nazism, such as "destiny" (*Schicksal*), power (*Macht*), and "sacrifice" (*Opfer*). In short, the public rallying of Heidegger to Nazism in 1933 is not a transitory or circumstantial phenomenon. It constitutes the culmination of an inner fecundation and evolution that goes far back, as is evinced by his writings themselves.

The Politics of Heidegger's University Recruitment and His Anti-Semitism

It is not my purpose here to offer a synthesis of all the writings and testimonies that bear witness to Heidegger's anti-Semitism. That question will inevitably come up on many occasions during the various periods referenced in this work. I will limit myself to the consideration of four letters or reports from the period 1929–1934, certain of them being less well known than the famous report by Heidegger mentioning "the Jew Fraenkel," which rightly wounded Jaspers so deeply in 1934. These various reports by Heidegger, the tone and style of which approach those of the denunciatory letter, are part of a university politics; its orientation is set by a major but too little known fact — namely, whom the persons were that Heidegger chose and tried to get positions for when he left Marburg for Freiburg in 1928. Heidegger, although Jaspers recommended the Jewish philosopher Erich Frank to him, at first tried to get Alfred Baeumler, whose increasingly Nazi orientation was already apparent in 1928, named as his successor. Then, seeing that Baeumler was not retained, Heidegger succeeded in getting Oskar Becker on the top of the list. The latter was eventually dislodged by the social-democratic ministry in favor of Frank, and Heidegger took Becker on as his assistant at Freiburg.

I have already discussed Becker. I will therefore limit myself to recalling briefly who Baeumler was around the years 1920–1930. Born in 1887, Alfred Baeumler began to make himself known by his long introduction, in 1926, to an anthology by the mythologist Johan Jakob Bachofen. Baeumler's political positions became more clearly defined by 1927, the date at which he collaborated with Ernst Niekisch's national-revolutionary journal *Widerstand,* while allying himself actively with *völkisch* student organizations; he did not hide his support of Hitler, even though he did not join the Nazi movement until the very early 1930s.[81] Heidegger greatly appreciated his study on Bachofen[82] and wrote him in 1928 to have him send his vita when he was considering him as his possible successor.[83] This choice of Baeumler in 1928 thus confirms the direction of Heidegger's political leanings at that date. Heidegger developed personal ties at that time with Baeumler, who invited him to Dresden in 1932 to deliver his lecture on "The Essence of Truth" and to go on long forest hikes with him. We have seen, moreover, that Alfred Baeumler was the main editor of the *Manual of Philosophy,* which published the two monographs by Rothacker cited previously. In 1933 Baeumler was awarded a chair of political education at the University of Berlin, and he attended the first book-burnings in person. He soon became Rosenberg's main collaborator. We will have more than one occasion to point out the intellectual and political ties linking Baeumler and Heidegger up until the mid-1930s.

During the period of his teaching in Marburg, Heidegger does not publicly display an anti-Semitic position. True, he is still in need of the scientific support of Husserl, and several of his most brilliant students, such as Löwith, are Jewish, but for a complete assessment of the situation, three things must be borne in mind. The first is the terms in which he speaks, as early as 1923, not just of Husserl but also of his unfortunate rival, the Hegelian Richard Kroner, of whom he says that his right to teach should be revoked: "I have never until now met such a lamentable state of the human race—now he is trying to get people to take pity on him, like an old woman—the only kindness one could do him would be to withdraw his *Venia Legendi* [authorization to teach at a university]."[84] This disdain, unacceptable since we know how courageously Kroner stayed in Germany until 1938, is of virulence that it would be difficult to understand otherwise than proceeding in part at least from anti-Semitic resentment. The second is an expression of Heidegger reported by Ludwig Ferdinand Clauß that I have already quoted: "I'll say what I think when I am a full professor." In reality—and this is the third element, the most directly damning—although Heidegger does not show his hand immediately upon being promoted to full professor in 1927 since he still needs Husserl's backing in order to succeed him at Freiburg in 1929—after his appointment to the University of Freiburg his anti-Semitism will transpire in his research papers and correspondence before becoming crystal clear with his public adhesion to the NSDAP in 1933. There is, first of all, the letter addressed to Geheimrat Schwoerer, in which he lashes out against the "growing Jewification" (*wachsende Verjudung*) that is, in his view, taking over "German spiritual life," but there are also other more recently known letters and papers.

In 1928, during the processing of his appointment to Freiburg, Heidegger had had the opportunity to make the acquaintance of Viktor Schwoerer, a councilor [*Geheimrat*] to the government and the director of the Bureau of Universities of the Ministry of Public Education of Baden, a Swabian like himself, "extremely friendly and like one is with a fellow countryman," he points out to Jaspers.[85] The following year, the very same month in which the NSDAP reported its first favorable electoral returns before the stock market crash of 24 October (the Nazi Party got 7 percent of the votes in October 1929 in the state of Baden), Heidegger, in a letter to Viktor Schwoerer dated 2 October 1929, expressed directly in writing and for the first time (at least among the texts we know about today) the virulence of the anti-Semitic resentment that lived within him and from which he draws his main argument in favor of awarding a grant to Dr. Eduard Baumgarten: "What I could only hint at in my report, I can say more directly here. Nothing less is at stake than the ineluctable realization that we find ourselves facing the following alternative: Either we restore genuine forces and educators emanating from the native soil to our German spiritual life, or we abandon it definitively to the growing Jewification, in the broad and the narrow sense of the term. We will get back on track only if we are in a position to help fresh forces blossom forth, without strife and without sterile disputes."[86]

We will find again and again during the following years, and beneath Heidegger's pen, these *bodenständige Kräfte* and these *frische Kräfte*. As for the use of the word *Verjudung*, it is the most egregious example of anti-Semitism. It shadows precisely the discourse of Hitler, who, in the first part of *Mein Kampf,* speaks of the "Jewified universities" (*verjudeten Universitäten*).[87] Certain French apologists of Heidegger have, in order to tone down a bit its odium, "translated" Heidegger's term *Verjudung* as "Judaization." That is not defensible, for in German the word *Judaïsierung* exists. It is, for example, the word a Nazi "philosopher," Hans Heyse, a disciple of Heidegger later placed at the head of the Kant Gesellschaft by the regime, uses in 1935 in his work *Idea and Existence.* Heyse speaks of the "spiritual struggle against the Judaization of the Occidental world."[88] The use of the word "Judaization" seems to be the maximum of what a Nazi academic can use, even in 1935, even in a work published by a Nazi press like the Hanseatische Verlagsanstalt, which also published Carl Schmitt and Ernst Jünger.

In Heidegger's letter, *Verjudung* in the narrow sense clearly refers to the relatively high number of Jewish professors and students in the German universities and intellectual milieus at that time, and one thinks of the exasperation with which Heidegger depicts that state of affairs in a letter written in the winter of 1932–1933 to Hannah Arendt in which he responds to the rumor that had been spread about his "rabid anti-Semitism" (*enragierter Antisemitismus*).[89] As for the broad sense, "growing Jewification" designates everything Heidegger fought against to the very end: liberalism, democracy, the "time of the *I*" and subjectivism, and more specifically the intellectual and philosophical currents that he prioritized in his attacks, beginning with Neo-Kantianism (which developed in Germany from Hermann Cohen to Ernst Cassirer, Richard Kroner, and Richard Hönigswald) and younger academics whom Heidegger targeted in his reports. A case in point: during those same weeks, Heidegger is asked to give his opinion on the candidacy for full professorship of Siegfried Marck at the University of Breslau.[90] Marck, born the same year as Heidegger, was the son of a Jewish jurist and councilor of state from Breslau.

Notably, he had studied with Heinrich Rickert at Freiburg. An associate professor at the University of Breslau since 1924, he was, moreover, a member of the Social Democratic Party (SPD). Marck belonged to the Neo-Kantian school of Breslau, founded by the philosopher Richard Hönigswald, of Jewish origin. Hönigswald had been called to the University of Munich, and his successor was to be determined. Heidegger, in his first report on Siegfried Marck, dated 7 November 1929, began by giving a positive appreciation of his discussion of *Being and Time* in the last pages of his most recent work, *The Dialectic in Today's Philosophy*, which appeared the same year. His judgment of the work taken as a whole, however, was quite different: "As the preface explicitly states, the work's intent is precisely to constitute an 'introduction to the philosophy of the present.' Such undertakings, which are currently legion, are more literary and editorial by nature, but not indispensable and seriously scientific tasks. Thus it is that this book lacks, as does one of the same type [*gleichgeartet*] by Professor Heinemann from Frankfurt, all substance and all depth. I must go further into this book, because it definitely does not belong in the category of publications that can be taken into consideration as proof of qualification for a professorship."[91]

The other philosopher cited, Fritz Heinemann, is also an assistant of Jewish origin who comes from the Neo-Kantianism of the school of Cohen and Paul Natorp. In 1929 he published a book titled *New Paths of Philosophy: Spirit, Life, Existence in Today's Philosophy.*

What is very ambiguous in Heidegger's so negative assessment is the way he associates Marck and Heinemann in a common critique of their works as being devoid of all substance and all weight, which he does by the use of the adjective *gleichartig,* a term that will also be used by such authors as Ernst Forsthoff and Carl Schmitt to designate something pertaining to the same race. We are obviously all the more inclined to be of this opinion, given that this recommendation comes one month after the letter to Geheimrat Schwoerer on the "growing Jewification" of the German spiritual life. Moreover, the second report Heidegger produces on other publications of Marck in February 1930 is even more violent. In alluding to a review by Marck of the book by Karl Mannheim *Ideology and Utopia,* he reproves Marck for not having perceived the "absence of soil" (*Bodenlosigkeit*) of the work. And it should be pointed out that during the same time period Heidegger, in the text of his lecture "The Essence of Truth," linked "truth" in a *völkisch* way to the soil of the *Heimat.*[92]

Returning to Heidegger's recommendation, he concludes in the following terms: "This type of literature does not come into consideration for a serious discussion. M. will always know how to speak ably of what is modern from day to day, but he will never succeed in finding the center of gravity that will allow him to intervene with true questions in the tasks of philosophy. This type of philosophy professor is our downfall."[93]

The harshness of the final judgment and the use of the word *Art,* which in German means race as well as kind, give a heavy anti-Semitic connotation to these remarks, as will be confirmed by the report Heidegger wrote in 1933 against Richard Hönigswald, Siegfried Marck's teacher. Nevertheless, the 1930 report remains ambiguous and equivocal, because after having attacked Siegfried Marck in this way, he will praise two psychologists of Jewish origin, Kurt Lewin and Adhemar Gelb. When we consider the choice of terms (*gleichartig, Art*) and bear in mind Heidegger's contemporaneous judgment about the *wachsende Verjudung* and the report he will soon produce on Marck's former teacher, we are prompted to conclude that we are confronted with a strategy on Heidegger's part. While praising Lewin and Gelb, he preserves the ambiguity surrounding his formulations against Marck, since one cannot, given these circumstances, ascribe them unhesitatingly to his anti-Semitism.[94] Indeed, it seems there is no question that some calculation went into supporting Lewin and Gelb against Marck, since Heidegger knew very well that Marck was the favored candidate of the university as well as of the Ministry. He was in fact subsequently elected. That said, Heidegger seems to have truly appreciated Gelb's works. He gave them high praise in a letter to Elisabeth Blochmann, asserting that "it will be up to him to write the new psychology, the rise of which is based on the entirely changed problematic of the new biology."[95] This point is paramount, because it reveals the fact that Heidegger is not the adversary of all biology but specifically, as will be confirmed by other texts, of Darwinian biology, hence of Anglo-Saxon origin. To this he opposes the biology of form, which is of German origin, specifically that of Uexküll and Buytendijk. This means, for the case at hand, that Heidegger's anti-Semitism, undeniable in view of his letter to Schwoerer, targets in the present circumstance above all what he calls "Jewification" in the "broad sense": in his opposition to the extension of Neo-Kantianism, his bugbear, he tries to thwart the promotion of Hönigswald's followers and to promote instead the ascendancy of the supporters of Gestalt psychology.

In any event, the report Heidegger wrote on Richard Hönigswald in a letter to Dr. Einhauser, councilor to the Ministry of Culture of Bavaria, is unequivocal. The letter was sent on 25 June 1933, therefore after the National Socialist takeover, and Heidegger was able to be more explicit than he had been in his reports prior to 1933. The letter to Councilor Einhauser is worthy of being quoted in its entirety and commented on because it is one of the documents that best demonstrates how the abject thralldom of Heidegger to the Nazi doctrine of blood and soil unfolds within "philosophy," and how he conceives of the essence of man.

> Dear Mr. Einhauser,
>   I am happy to comply with your request and send you my judgment in what follows. Hönigswald comes from the school of Neo-Kantianism, which has defended a philosophy that goes hand in hand with liberalism. In it, the essence of man has been dissolved into a free-floating consciousness, and the latter, in the final analysis, diluted until it becomes a general logical world-wide reason. In taking this route, of ostensibly strictly scientific, philosophical foundations, our attention has been diverted away from man in his historical enrootedness and his tradition derived from the people and from blood and soil. This has been accompanied by a deliberate repression of all metaphysical questioning, and man's only worth was that of a servant to an indifferent, general world culture. It is from this basic position that Hönigswald's writings and obviously also all his teaching activities emanate. And we must add to this the fact that it is precisely Hönigswald who defends Neo-Kantianism with a particularly dangerous subtlety and an empty dialectic. The danger consists primarily in the fact that this bustle gives the impression of great objectivity and rigorous knowledge and has already fooled and misguided many young people. I still consider the appointment of this man to the University of Munich to be a scandal, the only explanation for which is the fact that the Catholic system prefers such individuals who are apparently indifferent to any vision of the world, because they are without danger to its own efforts, and because they are, in a well-known sense, "objective-liberal." . . . Heil Hitler!

> Your devoted Heidegger[96]

In that letter, we see a Heidegger denouncing Hönigswald's teaching to the University of Munich as a danger. The simplistic opposition, ponderously stressed by Heidegger, between a worldwide reason and culture and the enrootedness of man in the historical tradition of his people, sprung from the blood and the soil, is the product of the crudest *völkisch* and anti-Semitic mentality. What it means, in decoded language, is that for a Nazi like Heidegger, Hönigswald, as a Jew, belongs neither to the German people nor to the German blood.

Far from raising the level of the discussion, the "philosophical" considerations on the essence of man do nothing but make the whole letter more damning. Reading this report on Hönigswald, we can see more clearly what Heidegger's intent was, when, both in the conclusion of his Kassel lectures and in section 77 of *Being and Time,* he quoted the remark of Count Yorck according to which "modern man," that is, "man since the Renaissance[,] is ready to be buried."[97] In the report denouncing Hönigswald, logical and universal reason is presented as a threat to the essence of man, the latter being on the contrary associated with blood and soil. To identify the essence of man with the sacralization of a people and a race constitutes the most radically destructive challenge to an essence of man qua man. That is why, at whatever level the letter is understood, its reality is equally abhorrent. On the one hand, we see the confirmation of Heidegger's taste for denunciation, aimed on this occasion at a colleague whose position he is thinking about taking himself. Heidegger's report on Hönigswald is not without consequences, since the latter, despite his value and reputation as a philosopher, was dismissed from the University of Munich. When Heidegger hears that the Munich chair is vacant, he considers at a certain point having himself appointed to it, his motive being that in Munich he would be closer to Hitler. He writes in a letter of 19 September 1933 to Elisabeth Blochmann: "At the same time, Munich is prospecting; a full professorship is vacant. That would have the advantage of a larger theater of activity and would not be as remote as Freiburg is at the present time. The possibility of approaching Hitler. . . ."[98]

Furthermore, we can see the results of the sudden intrusion of Nazism into "philosophy" — to what a perverse conception of man Heidegger was led. But we are only at the threshold of the systematic undertaking that, beginning in 1933, will lead him to present a course in Hitlerian political education as a philosophy seminar. He will identify, in his teaching and his speeches, the fundamental question of philosophy with the self-affirmation of the people and of the German race, or with what he calls, in his course of the winter semester of 1933–1934, "the fundamental possibilities of the essence of the originally Germanic race."[99] It is time we ceased taking this ponderous racial fundamentalism for philosophical profundity.

2

Heidegger, the "Bringing into Line," and the New Student Law

Before approaching the reality of Heidegger's teaching through the lectures, courses, and seminars, recently published or even unpublished, it is important to realize that his influence was exerted not only through teaching but also through action, whether public and manifest, as in the case of his activities as rector, or much more discreetly and secretively, through the innuendos of certain letters and close ties made over an extended period of time with Nazi student organizations or government representatives in Berlin, Munich, and Karlsruhe. Indeed, it would take an entire volume to examine all Heidegger's activities and relations thoroughly, on the basis of the archival collections available in Germany and the still unpublished correspondence. That would be the task of a historian, not a philosopher, and therefore lies outside the purview of the present work. Nevertheless, it seemed to me indispensable to offer a general summary of Heidegger's activity in the framework of the "general bringing into line" (*allgemeine Gleichschaltung*) starting in 1933, from the moment of the seizure of power. Thus the reader will be sufficiently aware not to miss the fact that when Heidegger takes a position in his texts on such ideas as work, freedom, propaganda, or the annihilation of the enemy, these are not intellectual and theoretical views but prescriptions and directives intended to be translated into action. The official portrait of Rector Heidegger bears the inscription: "Professor Dr. Martin Heidegger was chosen rector of the University of Freiburg on 21 April 1933, as part of the 'general bringing into line,' " or *Gleichschaltung*.[1]

It was, then, quite officially that Heidegger's promotion to the rectorate was placed within the framework of the *Gleichschaltung*. It is not easy to find in English a precise equivalent of this term. The usual translation, "bringing into line," expresses the brutality of the operation, but the German word expresses at the same time the imposition of uniformity, homogeneity, and "synchronization." The Nazi *Gleichschaltung* was based on a global coordination for the entire Reich and constituted the maturation of a long process. Its underlying intention, as Carl Schmitt's interpretation has shown in a particularly clear and distinct way, was primarily racial.[2] The first step was to keep "non-Aryans" away from any public function, particularly the university system, in order to ensure the "racial homogeneity" (*Gleichartigkeit*) of the body politic. This was a prelude to the more complete discrimination that was carried out in 1935 with the Nuremberg Laws. Further, this process involved generalizing the introduction of the "Führer principle" inside the Reich's institutions, including the university.

The fact that Heidegger's rectorate was an integral part of this process is discernable at several levels. We must consider each of them individually in order to avoid watering down the reality, and the better to understand just how intense and decisive Heidegger's political activity was in the *Gleichschaltung* cause. Hugo Ott and Bernd Martin have already written useful studies on this topic, but many elements of Heidegger's activities require further investigation.

Heidegger's Approval of the New Anti-Semitic Legislation

When Heidegger assumed the functions of rector of the University of Freiburg, it was after having been elected, on 21 April 1933, by a teaching body that had just undergone the exclusion of all its Jewish teachers.[3] The universities of the Reich had indeed applied its sinister "law for the reconstitution of public functions" (*Gesetz zur Wiederherstellung des Berufsbeamtentums*) of 7 April 1933, also referred to as the GWB. The "bringing into line" of the university system began with that law, which automatically revoked "non-Aryan" teachers. In this national context, the Badenland, which included the universities of Heidelberg and Freiburg, was subject to an even more ferocious legislative measure, if that is possible, in the decree governing Badner Jews (*badischer Judenerlaß*), issued on 6 April 1933 by the commissioner of the Reich for the Badenland, Gauleiter Robert Wagner. Although the GWB granted exemption, in paragraph 3, to veterans who had fought at the front in World War I, the Badner decree of 6 April allowed no exceptions.

On 14 April 1933, Edmund Husserl, professor emeritus of the University of Freiburg, was stripped of his emeritus status and dismissed. Heidegger's assistant Werner Brock was also dismissed because he was half Jewish. Gerhard Husserl, the son of the philosopher and a World War I veteran who taught law in Kiel, suffered the same fate. The main reason why Wilhelm von Möllendorf, the preceding rector, had resigned after two weeks was because he did not recognize that ipso facto state of affairs. By taking over the rectorate less than ten days after Husserl's dismissal, Heidegger did, then, accept the situation. In fact, there is no known record of any protest on his part against the suspension of his former teacher or his assistant.[4]

Under these circumstances, the discussions as to whether Heidegger did or did not bar his teacher Husserl from access to the philosophy seminar and the university library do not go to the essential point, since it has been established that when Heidegger assumed his functions on 23 April, two days after having been elected, he thereby confirmed, in so doing, a situation in which Husserl was excluded from the university. Furthermore (and this is a point too often overlooked), during the following days and weeks, the terms in which Heidegger and his wife expressed themselves on this law show that they approved of it unreservedly. On 29 April, two days before Heidegger officially joined the NSDAP, Elfride Heidegger, in her name but also in the name of her husband, sent a solemn and compassionate letter to Malvine Husserl, in which she lists everything the Heideggers owe to the Husserl couple.[5] This lends the letter an air of farewell. Without saying a word about what has just befallen Edmund Husserl, Elfride Heidegger limits herself to speaking of the situation of their sons: "But to all this is added a deep gratitude for your sons' readiness to sacrifice, and it is indeed only in the spirit of that new law (hard, but reasonable from a German point of view) that we give our allegiance — without restrictions and with deep and sincere respect — to those who have given their allegiance to our German people in the hour of greatest need, in both word and deed."[6]

Thus we see Elfride Heidegger, in a letter written equally in the name of her spouse, qualifying the discriminatory law that dismisses "non-Aryan" civil servants as "hard" but "reasonable" from the "German point of view." A sinister assessment, which proves the deep anti-Semitism of the Heidegger couple and clearly means that, in their eyes, German Jewish citizens suspended by the law of the Hitlerian Reich can no longer claim that "German point of view" that supposedly justifies their exclusion. As for this qualifier "reasonable," it foreshadows in its very choice of the term the revisionist thesis of Ernst Nolte, who speaks of the "rational core" of Hitler's anti-Semitism. Moreover, Elfride Heidegger takes care to point out that by recognizing the "readiness to sacrifice" of the Husserl sons who fought on the front line during World War I, she stays within the law of the Reich, which in paragraph 3 exempts veterans wounded at the front. When Hugo Ott, in 1988, published his work on Heidegger, he did not yet have access to the full text of the letter, but only what Malvine Husserl in a private letter of 2 May 1933 said about it and the part of it that was translated by Frédéric de Towarnicki in *Les Temps Modernes,* in an article that was a defense of Heidegger solicited by Heidegger himself, in which Towarnicki did not say a word about this passage. In 1992, in a postscript — unpublished in French — to the second edition of his book, Hugo Ott was able to furnish the first complete version of the letter, as it had been copied by Towarnicki, in the winter of 1945, from the original text kept by Elfride Heidegger.[7] The historian from Freiburg says that "the text in parentheses is rather vigorously crossed out, doubtless by Elfride Heidegger herself, who, during the winter of 1945, no longer considered this passage expedient."[8] When he reprints the letter eight years later, in volume 16 of the supposedly "complete" works, Hermann Heidegger leaves out the text in parentheses, without any explanatory footnote. It is only in the appendix of the book, where in all likelihood few readers will go to see it, that the passage appears, crossed out with a horizontal line.[9] Hermann Heidegger says that Elfride Heidegger probably crossed the passage out not in 1945, but already in 1933. An expert assessment of the first draft of the letter and inks may perhaps make it possible to determine whether this passage was crossed out in 1933 or in 1945, but even if she didn't keep this passage in the letter she sent, we know today that Elfride Heidegger expressed in her own hand the Heidegger couple's approval of the new anti-Semitic legislation and that she did not want to affirm anything that was not "in the spirit" of that racist law.[10]

Moreover, we find explicit approval of that law written this time by Heidegger himself, in an official letter sent on 12 July 1933 to the ministerial counselor Eugen Fehrle, in which he intercedes in favor of two internationally famous Jewish professors, the philologist Eduard Fraenkel and the Hungarian chemist Georg von Hevesy, who subsequently received the Nobel Prize in 1943. Eduard Fraenkel was nonetheless dismissed, while Georg von Hevesy, whose status was different because he was not a citizen of the Reich, was granted a short reprieve. Now, that letter leaves no room for doubt about Heidegger's anti-Semitism. The arguments he makes are based solely on the negative consequences of suspending such well-known men of learning for the international reputation of the German university in "non-Jewish circles abroad." It is thus of no importance to him what "Jewish circles" abroad might think of these measures of exclusion. And we know today that in a secret report written on 16 December 1933 to discredit another professor,

Eduard Baumgarten, Heidegger included in his argument Baumgarten's frequentation of the "dismissed Jew Fraenkel."[11] These facts show that Heidegger was a realist: he knew how to play on several registers and was not politically naive, as he portrayed himself after the war in an effort to exculpate himself. Further — and this is the essential point — he does not fail to point out in his letter that he is acting "in full awareness of the necessity for the unconditional implementation of the law on reconstructing the Civil Service."[12]

Heidegger explicitly approves the new anti-Semitic legislation, and in the most insistent manner: nothing forced him to insist by adding the adjectives "full" and "unconditional."

Let us clarify that from a juridical point of view, the law of the Reich prevailed over the decree of Gauleiter Wagner, so that at the beginning of May, Brock and Husserl were provisionally reinstated. But that was only a temporary reprieve: Brock was definitively excluded from public service the same year and had to leave Germany (without the rector having lodged the slightest protest), while Husserl again lost his emeritus status and was also excluded from the university by the application of the Nuremberg Laws. As for Heidegger, far from distancing himself in the least from Gauleiter Wagner, on 9 May 1933, he sent him a warm telegram ending with a "*Sieg Heil* testifying to our solidarity in combat."[13] The telegram was published the same day in the Nazi newspaper of Freiburg, *Der Alemanne*.

Rector Heidegger and the Introduction of the Führer Principle at the University

Heidegger, having failed to protest against an exclusionary decree (in effect only in the Badenland) that had struck down both his former teacher and his assistant, going so far as to express his approval, in an official letter, of the anti-Semitic legislation promulgated by Hitler's Reich, now went on to become a crucial agent in the establishment of the Führer principle (*Führerprinzip*) at the universities of the Badenland, a principle that constituted one of the main facets of the *Gleichschaltung*. This capital fact proves to us that Heidegger was not only a consenting Nazi, as he had shown himself to be in the area of racial legislation, but also a very active Nazi, who successfully pursued a specific political goal.

Whether in the rectoral address, which begins and ends with considerations on the *Führung-Gefolgschaft* relation and explicitly rejects "academic freedom,"[14] or during the lecture tour from the end of June to the beginning of July 1933 at the universities of Freiburg, Heidelberg, and Kiel (the culmination being reached with the lecture at Heidelberg on 30 June 1933, at which Rector

Heidegger affirms that the university system must be reintegrated with the people and attached to the state),[15] Heidegger, in collaboration with Ernst Krieck, then the rector of Frankfurt, actively campaigned in favor of the academic constitution still in effect being repealed and replaced by a constitution that would apply the Hitlerian Führer principle. That new university constitution was in fact enacted for the Badenland on 21 August 1933. The Badenland then became the only one of all the *Länder* of the Reich to have a university constitution imposing the *Führerprinzip*. Neither Prussia, Bavaria, nor Saxony had one at that time. By the concerted efforts of Heidegger, Krieck, and of course Gauleiter Robert Wagner, the universities of the Badenland were then the avant-garde of the "movement" and constituted an example that would be followed by the entire Reich.[16]

Concretely, the new university constitution conceived in accordance with the *Führerprinzip* decreed that the deans of the faculties were no longer to be elected by the teaching body but directly appointed by the Rector-Führer. As for the rector himself, it was no longer the teachers who elected him; he was designated by the ministry. The university system thus lost all autonomy from political power. The new university constitution of the Badenland took effect on 1 October 1933. It was the Rector-Führer, then, who designated the new deans and, over the opposition of his colleagues, Heidegger appointed Erik Wolf as dean of the Faculty of Law, a man fanatically attached to the person of the rector and, as we will see by his writings, an enthusiastic propagandist for the racist and eugenic doctrine of Nazism. As Josef Sauer, the former rector of the University of Freiburg, writes in his diary shortly after the enactment of the new constitution: "This was the work of Heidegger. *The end of the universities!*"[17]

This epigrammatic remark by Joseph Sauer is replete with meaning. Given the date it was written, it cannot refer to the application by Heidegger of the new constitution, which did not really apply until 1 October 1933, the beginning of the new academic semester; it refers to the preparation of that constitution. What was Heidegger's role in that preparation? It would require more in-depth research into the archives to give a complete answer to that question. Nevertheless, a few points can be established.

First, let us recall the importance of the telegram already mentioned from Heidegger to Rector Wagner: it proves the solidarity of the rector of Freiburg with the decisions brought down from the ministry of Karlsruhe. The "community of combat" Heidegger speaks of in his telegram is intended to promote the realization of the *Gleichschaltung*.

Moreover, the introduction of the *Führerprinzip* at the university is not, to Heidegger, a local task limited to the confines of the Badenland: it involves the whole Reich. That national dimension of Heidegger's activity is proven by numerous facts and documents. It reveals the hierarchical level at which Heidegger is situated and the importance of his connections not only in Karlsruhe but also in Berlin. The first confirmation of this is a letter sent by Rector Heidegger on 3 July 1933 "to all the German universities." Being presumably far too compromising, the letter was not included by Hermann Heidegger in volume 16 of the so-called complete edition. It concerns the subordination of the chancellor of the university to the power of the rector. The second article of the university constitution for the Badenland concerning the rights of the rector stipulates that the Rector-Führer has the right to appoint a chancellor, for the entire duration of his mandate, chosen by him from within the teaching body of the university.[18] By means of that article, the rector no longer has any university authority above himself, since the chancellor of the university is henceforth dependent on him. Thus, the article in question makes the rector the true Führer of the university. Now Heidegger was almost two months ahead of the new constitution on this point. It was not until 27 June 1933 that he received, by a special decree of the ministry of Karlsruhe issued on his behalf, the right to appoint the chancellor himself. Not only did he exercise this decree immediately by appointing Julius Wilser, a professor of geology, as chancellor, but he also sent a circular to all the German universities, informing them of the situation.

> To all the German universities
> The Minister of the Cult, Education, and Justice has granted me the power, by the ordinance of 27 July 1933, and for the duration of my rectorate, to appoint a chancellor from the professorial body of the university to assist me. The determination of the purview of the tasks of the chancellor has been confided to me. Among the chancellor's tasks is that of signing "by power of attorney" for the rector; my responsibility in the conduct of the affairs of the university remains therefore entire.[19]

We see with what insistence Heidegger stresses the fact that the chancellor of the university is henceforth subordinate to him, so that the responsibility of the rector in the *Führung* (guidance) of university affairs remains entire. And Heidegger, by his letter, presents that situation as a model for the German university. Thus, the first partial introduction of the *Führerprinzip* at the university was accomplished by the end of June 1933, by this decree personally issued by the ministry in favor of Rector Heidegger. The constitution of 21 August, with its first article stipulating that "the rector is the Führer of the university," will merely ratify in this point a state of affairs already partially accomplished in Freiburg.

Another letter from Heidegger is equally revealing of the national dimension of his action: on 24 August 1933, he sent the entire teaching body of the University of Freiburg the text of the new constitution, accompanied by a letter in which he states explicitly: "With this, the first groundwork has been laid for the internal edification of the university in conformity with the new global task of scientific education."[20]

Now the new constitution begins with a general preamble clearly stating that it represents a first step in an undertaking that will involve the entire Reich. "The total renewal of the German universities can be achieved only if the reform of the universities is undertaken throughout the entire Reich in a unitary and global manner."[21]

The sentence is entirely Heideggerian in spirit. The question of whether he may not have been the direct inspirer, or even the redactor of it, is therefore not moot.

Heidegger's Appointments to Berlin and Munich and His Reputation for Political Extremism

The national scope of Heidegger's actions is confirmed by the fact that no sooner had the constitution been enacted for the Badenland than he was offered, in the early days of September 1933, a teaching chair at two universities, Berlin and Munich. It was the Minister of Education in person, Bernhard Rust, who appointed Heidegger to Berlin, spelling out his political motivation in a letter dated 7 September, addressed to the Berlin Faculty of Philosophy and cosigned by Secretary of State Wilhelm Stuckart. "The appointment of Heidegger is related to the implementation of the reform of the university and was required by considerations of politics of state."[22]

Things are thus entirely explicit, and Heidegger himself tells Elisabeth Blochmann, in a letter of 5 September 1933, that he "received a proposed appointment to Berlin yesterday — in connection with a political mission."[23]

Heidegger hesitated about the Berlin appointment for a long time. According to the terms of the new constitution, he was, on 1 October 1933, appointed (not elected) rector of the University of Freiburg by the Ministry of Karlsruhe. It was only at that point that he decided to remain in that city and to accept an appointment that consecrated the introduction of the Führer principle into the university and made him the first Rector-Führer of the new Germany. The following day, he wrote a draft of a communication intended for the professors of that university, in which his intentions are clearly expressed. "I will not go to Berlin; it is rather at our university that I will try to give an authentic and tangible reality to the possibilities offered by the new provisional constitutional regulations in the Badenland, in order thus to implement the uniform development of the future global constitution of the entire German university system. In conformity with the wishes of the government authorities of Berlin, I shall continue to remain in very close contact with the work being done there."[24]

The decision to remain at Freiburg, then, was not in the least, to Heidegger's way of thinking, a retreat in relation to the overall action he intended to carry out at the Reich level. The *völkisch* and peasant style of his radio broadcast "Why Do We Remain in the Province?"[25] published on 7 March 1934 in the Nazi Freiburg newspaper *Der Alemanne,* in which he spoke exclusively about his Todtnauberg lodge and the peasants of his *Heimat,* masks the reality of his political intentions and his activities at the Reich level. The application of the new constitution for the Badenland represented in his eyes a beginning and a model for the general "bringing into line," or *Gleichschaltung,* toward which he continued to work. The last sentence of the letter is perfectly explicit. Not only did Heidegger benefit from the support of the government authorities of Berlin, but he would continue to collaborate very closely with them.

On this topic, the correspondence with Elisabeth Blochmann gives us further particulars. Teaching in Berlin was only "an accessory thing." What was expected of him was that he should " 'lead' the Prussian body of instructors."[26] Heidegger was reserved, however. He feared the work might be limited to Prussia, while his intention was to work for the entire Reich. He preferred to expose his plan — for an "advanced school" — that, even after his refusal to go to Berlin, "*shows a brilliant outlook for the future.*"[27] Heidegger states specifically that his plan is "confidential" and says nothing further about it. But we can intuit what it was. Now that the *Gleichschaltung* was in the process of being realized and the Führer principle, in no small part thanks to Heidegger's efforts, had been introduced at the university, what was needed were "capable men."[28] Heidegger's concern, like that of the National Socialists in charge of education (Minister Rust, Secretary of State Wilhelm Stuckart, and so on), was to find and train men capable of being Führers of the institutions "brought in line." The fact that he conceived of "scientific camps," which he had up and running by October 1933 and in which those most "fit" by Nazi standards were chosen, belongs in this context. The same may be said of courses in political education, intended to produce, in his terms, a new "nobility" for the Third Reich, courses he taught in a seminar for advanced students during the winter of 1933–1934.[29] Moreover, Heidegger's plan was certainly contiguous with the projects of the advanced political schools, among which should be mentioned the one conceived no later than 1933 by Joachim Haupt, who was close to Heidegger and a counselor to Minister Rust: the Institutes of National Education (*Nationalpolitische Erziehungsanstalten*), also called "Napolas."

One year later, in August 1934, in response to the demand of Wilhelm Stuckart, Heidegger wrote a project for an Academy of Professors of the Reich—and in this instance the text has been preserved.

The conditions of the proposed appointment of Heidegger to Munich and the way in which he responded are also very instructive. That appointment involved the replacement of Professor Richard Hönigswald, against whom Heidegger had written such a vicious report. The decision in favor of Heidegger came not from the faculty but from the Bavarian Minister of Culture Hans Schemm and the Munich Deutsche Studentenschaft. The appointment raises a corner of the veil covering the network of connections Heidegger made with the National Socialist milieus of Munich, whether in the Bavarian government or the Nazi student associations. And indeed, Minister Schemm said he based his decision "on earlier conversations with Heidegger."[30] As for the Deutsche Studentenschaft, it had taken the initiative. In a letter dated 29 July 1933, when Hönigswald had not yet been dismissed, a certain Karl Gegenbach, in the name of the Deutsche Studentenschaft, had called for the replacement of Hönigswald by Heidegger, arguing that "the latter had made a name for himself both as a philosopher and as a champion of National Socialism."[31]

At that time, Munich was still the city where Hitler sojourned most frequently, and that seems to have been be a major consideration in Heidegger's view when he considered accepting the position. I have already mentioned the letter of 19 September 1933 to Elisabeth Blochmann in which he speaks of "the possibility, namely, of approaching Hitler" in Munich. His first response to Einhauser also refers to Hitler. "I am not yet bound, but what I know is that, to the detriment of any personal commitment, I must decide in favor of the task I will best serve the work of Adolf Hitler by accomplishing."[32]

To serve Hitler's work, to be able to approach him most easily if need be—that is what motivated Heidegger most at the time. But if he benefited from the support of the Nazi student organizations and the highest officials in Berlin and Munich, he did not find the same favor among university professors. At Munich, the commission that was formed to fill professor Hönigswald's vacancy believed Heidegger would be unsuitable at a university of Munich's standing. It concluded as follows. "The faculty would also be loath to suppress their suspicion that the effectiveness of his philosophy might prove to be less academic than inspirational, and especially that younger students, particularly, might allow themselves to be more readily intoxicated by the ecstatic language than instructed by the rather allusive deep content of that same philosophy."[33]

Furthermore, in the words of the minutes of the session of full professors of the Faculty of Philosophy of Munich, 26 September 1933, Heidegger "might be politically too extreme for the faculty," and "with such clap-trap, no philosophy could be offered the students."[34] This judgment should be pondered. We see that at that date the reputation of Heidegger in the German universities is so closely linked with the extremism of his political commitment that his colleagues at Munich consider him incapable of teaching philosophy.

The Action "Against the Un-German Spirit" and the New Student Laws

Heidegger's backers remained very much in the minority within the teaching body. He could count only on a small cohort of allies such as Baeumler, Krieck (who was to become his fiercest adversary in 1934), and Heyse. He also forms, with three other ultra-Nazi rectors,[35] a "shock troop" that worked actively for the "bringing into line" of the Association of University Professors. This point has already been studied, and I will not go over it here.[36] What I would like to explore in more depth now is the nature and significance of the relations between Heidegger and the associations of Nazi students. This is where we find one of the most somber facets of Heidegger's activities.

We have seen that the Nazi and Hitlerian *Gleichschaltung* was fixed on two main objectives, both of which were at once racial and political: to exclude political adversaries and Jews from the community of the people, defined as Germans of German extraction, and to introduce the *Führerprinzip* into all domains.[37] The realization of both these objectives took place in a methodical and concerted manner. I have already mentioned two important moments of that *Gleichschaltung*: the law of 7 April 1933 for the "reconstitution of the Civil Service" and the law of 21 August 1933, which introduced the *Führerprinzip* into the universities of the Badenland; and we have seen how Heidegger demonstrated his agreement with respect to the one and participated actively in the preparation, legitimation, and implementation of the other. Now we must go further and approach in this context the reality of the relations between Heidegger and the Nazi student associations. In the university, the *Gleichschaltung* was realized at the juridical level by the two laws already mentioned but also by the concerted efforts of the Nazi students. The latter organized the denunciation and boycott of teachers who were "non-Aryan" or politically suspect, forced the Jewish student associations to close down, and prepared other anti-Semitic actions.

On 29 March 1933 the *Völkischer Beobachter* published a proclamation by Oskar Stäbel, the Führer of the NSDStB, which, even before the application of the new anti-Semitic laws, organized the boycott of Jewish teachers in all the universities of the Reich, as expressed in the following terms:

In view of the almost total Jewification of the German universities, the federal guide of the German National Socialist Student Association, together with the president of the German student body, has demanded from the competent authorities of the Reich and of the *Länder,* as a first condition for the transformation of the German universities, the introduction of a *numerus clausus* for Jews, as well as the total separation of all Jewish professors and assistants in the German universities. Furthermore, in the context of the defensive measures on the part of the Reich, and in agreement with the central committee, the following measures are being taken:

Beginning on 1 April 1933 there will be installed, in front of all the classrooms and seminars of Jewish professors, student guards whose task it will be to warn German students against attending such courses and seminars, with the notification that as a Jew the professor in question is being legitimately boycotted by all respectable Germans. The respective university group leaders, together with the student SA and SS men, in cooperation with the local action committee, will oversee the execution of this measure.[38]

On 12 April 1933, an anti-Semitic placard written in red Gothic lettering on a white background was placed in the universities of the Reich. It was titled "Against the un-German Spirit" (*Wider den undeutschen Geist*). Shortly thereafter, on 10 May 1933, bonfires were lit throughout the Reich for the burning of works adjudged to represent, out of racial and political motivation, that un-German spirit. In Berlin, Goebbels and Baeumler made speeches before the flames. According to the city, these book-burnings were carried out with greater or lesser intensity throughout the months of May and June 1933.

Now there were two Nazi student associations whose rivalry became increasingly intense until the crisis of the month of August 1933. The first was called the Deutsche Studentenschaft, or DSt, and its leader was Gerhard Krüger; the second was the Nationalsozialistische Deutsche Studentenbund, or NSDStB, whose Führer was Oskar Stäbel. Officially, the former association was subordinate to the latter, but in reality the Deutsche Studentenschaft meant to keep its independence. It was the latter that would play the dominant role in carrying out the action "against the un-German spirit." Now the DSt, an association "radically anti-Semitic and anti-Marxist," had as its Führer a student in philosophy, "a friend and even a familiar of Heidegger," Gerhard Krüger, and as its "head of the central service of political sciences" Georg Plötner, with whom Heidegger also had particularly close ties.[39]

There is an entire correspondence between Georg Plötner and Rector Heidegger, which Hermann Heidegger was careful not to publish in volume 16 of the "complete" works. As soon as he assumed his duties, Heidegger wrote

Georg Plötner, on 24 April 1933, proposing that he organize daily workshops, bringing together the directors of the science section of the DSt.[40] Plötner sent Heidegger a series of letters. On 23 May 1934, he wrote to him on the subject of those workshop days that were in fact held in Berlin on 10 and 11 July 1933, with the participation of three "philosophers": Alfred Baeumler, Joachim Haupt, and Martin Heidegger. In another letter on the following day, Plötner broke the news to him of an article in the *Deutsche Zeitung* that had published an internal DSt document inviting the students to take part in espionage and the boycott of teachers who could not be immediately dismissed by the state. On 1 June, Plötner wrote to him again to inform him of contacts made, specifically with Joachim Haupt and Rudolf Stadelmann, a history professor at Freiburg, who was particularly close to Heidegger, and of whom I will have more to say later. Heidegger, for his part, sent another telegram to Georg Plötner on 3 June and a letter on 9 July 1933.

It is undeniable, then, that Heidegger cooperated actively with the Deutsche Studentenschaft throughout its action taken "against the un-German spirit." In these circumstances, contrary to what he claimed in 1945, we cannot give credence to a desire on his part to prevent the two main actions of the DSt: the posting of its proclamation "Against the un-German Spirit" and the bookburnings. Yet it was possible, while Paul von Hindenburg was still president, to take a critical position publicly. According to the testimony of Karl Löwith, three renowned men of the university protested in Germany during the action "against the un-German spirit": the Berlin rector Eduard Kohlrausch, the psychologist Wolfgang Koehler, and the philosopher and pedagogue Eduard Spranger.[41] Heidegger did not do so. On the contrary, he spitefully mocked Spranger in his letters to Elisabeth Blochmann.

Moreover, in his declarations after the war, Heidegger wavered. In his text of 1945 on *The Rectorate,* nearly all the affirmations of which have been refuted by the research of Hugo Ott, he affirmed that his first official act as rector was to prohibit the posting of the proclamation; in the interview with *Der Spiegel* he affirmed, on the contrary, that the prohibition was made by Rector von Möllendorf and that he himself only gave oral confirmation, after his election, of that prohibition to the representatives of the Nazi students. Heidegger thus took refuge behind an unverifiable assertion. Now, when we see in what terms the Studentenschaft of the University of Freiburg welcomed Heidegger's election in a declaration published by the newspaper *Der Alemanne* of 24 April 1933, reprinted on 2 May in the *Freiburger Studentenzeitung,* it seems implausible that the new rector had shown any opposition whatsoever to the Nazi students. Indeed, we read:

> The professors of the University of Freiburg have elected as their rector, instead and in place of Herr Professor Möllendorf, Professor Dr. Heidegger. That election took place in the context of the general bringing into line [*allgemeinen Gleichshaltung*]. This should make possible a collaboration of all the leading posts in a climate of confidence and closeness. We are convinced that the new rector will support and promote the work of the students, which organically integrates the new student law into the structure of the university. The students, on their part, in keeping with their duty, promise the rector, as Führer of the university, to follow him and collaborate.
>
> The departing rector has made his office available, in order to make possible a closer collaboration between leading posts. This sacrifice and its necessity are things that we can appreciate.[42]

A further proof that the declarations of Heidegger after the Nazi defeat are not trustworthy: on the book-burnings, he undeniably lied. The testimony of Ernesto Grassi and those of Freiburg residents gathered by Hugo Ott are categorical: the book-burnings did take place in Freiburg, as they did throughout the Reich.[43] A contemporary article speaks of "the great mass of books" that have "already burned on Exerzierplatz" in Freiburg.[44] And the Nazi students of the University of Freiburg launched the following call to action.

> The German Student Association has determined to wage a spiritual struggle, unto total annihilation, against the Judeo-Marxist dissolution of the German people. The symbol of this struggle will be the *public burning*, on 10 May 1933, of the Judeo-Marxist writings. Germans, gather yourselves for this combat! Demonstrate the collective willingness to fight publicly. . . . The fire of annihilation will then become the ardent flame of our enthusiastic struggle for the German spirit, German mores, and German customs.
>
> Students of the University of Freiburg.
> The Combat League for German Culture.[45]

It seems that this did not appear sufficient to the young Nazi population of Freiburg. Long after the destruction by fire of the mass of books taxed with "un-German spirit," the League of Combat for German Culture (*Kampfbund für deutsche Kultur*) announced again, on 20 June 1933, a "symbolic book-burning of literature of filth and trash" (*symbolischer Verbrennungsakt von Schmutz- und Schundliteratur*).[46] Originally planned for Saturday 17 June 1933 at Cathedral Square, the symbolic auto-da-fé was postponed till Wednesday, 21 June, for the festival of the solstice in the university stadium. In the end, the festival of the solstice and the book-burning were postponed till Saturday 24 June. In the university stadium that evening Rudolf Stadelmann and Martin Heidegger gave speeches before the flames.[47] Whether the rain, again present, did or did not prevent the material burning of the books, the flames before which Stadelmann, then Heidegger, gave their speeches certainly had, for the participants, the value of a symbolic auto-da-fé of "non-German" books. When Rector Heidegger exclaimed: "Flame, announce to us, light up for us, show us the path *from which there is no turning back*," he could not have been unaware of the symbolic meaning of the bonfire. Therefore, it cannot be denied that Heidegger participated in a book-burning symbolizing the destruction of the said "un-German" spirit.

But let us return to the circumstances surrounding the writing of the placard "Against the Un-German Spirit" and its distribution. The Deutsche Studentenschaft had finished writing it by 8 April 1933, and it was Alfred Baeumler, the "philosopher" then the closest to Heidegger, who put the finishing touches on the text before it was distributed throughout the Reich, beginning on April 12. Heidegger was not yet rector at the time, and if the displaying of the placard was forbidden in Freiburg, that could only have been due to Rector von Möllendorf, who was then in office, as Heidegger eventually confirmed in his 1966 interview. Further, as I have shown, it was not a letter prohibiting the placard distributed by the DSt that Heidegger sent the day after he took office as rector but, quite to the contrary, a proposal of increased collaboration with the DSt in the form of daily workshops in Berlin!

On the basis of an extremely troubling fact, not yet sufficiently taken into account thus far, we can go further. Ernst Forsthoff, one of Carl Schmitt's closest disciples, published in 1938 a second, enlarged edition of a work titled *German History Since 1918 in Documents*. Under this seemingly innocuous title, Forsthoff gathered, classified, and commented upon a set of documents, excerpts of laws and fragments of speeches that reconstruct in great detail the progress of the Nazi and Hitlerian undertaking until approximately 1936. Now Forsthoff published at the end — in such a way that they can be read side by side — the anti-Semitic placard of 1933 and a long excerpt from the speech of Rector Heidegger of May 1933 — an excerpt in which he praises the Nazi Deutsche Studentenschaft.

The presence in this book of an ample excerpt from Heidegger's rectoral address and the way in which Forsthoff inserts it are highly instructive. First, we see the fully official status given to Heidegger's address in 1938, published in a work approved by the printing commission of the NSDAP and presented as destined to take its place in the "National Socialist bibliography." It must also be stressed that the other speeches quoted in this book are exclusively speeches or texts by Hitler himself or by the highest Nazi dignitaries: Goebbels, Alfred Rosenberg, Richard Walther Darré, and Julius Streicher. Benito Mussolini is there as well. No other university figure besides Heidegger is present in the work. It is therefore proof of Heidegger's exceptional political importance — comparable, in Forsthoff's view, to that of the highest dignitaries of Nazism.

Moreover, it is important to specify in the most thorough manner the series of documents within which Heidegger's speech appears. In the section titled *Kulturpolitik,* we find, successively, on the topic of "university politics" (*Hochschulpolitik*): two speeches by Gerhard Krüger, the representative of the Deutsche Studentenschaft, the law of 22 April 1932 on the forming of student associations, Goebbels's speech given during the book-burning of "un-German writings" of 10 May 1933, the poster of the Deutsche Studentenschaft "Against the Un-German Spirit," an excerpt of the rectoral address by Martin Heidegger, and lastly an excerpt of the speech given by the Minister of Agriculture of the Third Reich, Walther Darré, in Heidelberg in 1936. Heidegger, then, occupies a good spot . . . moreover, we find the name Gerhard Krüger, who in 1932 had intervened in the name of the Deutsche Studentenschaft to demand the introduction of the *Führerprinzip* and the application of a *numerus clausus* against Jews at the university. We see, then, through these documents, that the *Gleichschaltung* was prepared by 1932 for the university, and its application, orchestrated throughout the Reich, was brought about by stages. Heidegger's speech plays the crucial role of academic and "spiritual" validation of the action of the Nazi Studentenschaft.

Now we must reproduce, despite its vileness, the text of the poster printed by Forsthoff, running directly across from Heidegger's speech. The placard of the Deutsche Studentenschaft is made up of the following twelve propositions:

> Against the Non-German Spirit:
> 1. Language and literature have their roots in the *Volk*. It is the German *Volk*'s responsibility to ensure that its language and literature are the pure and unadulterated expression of its *Volk* traditions.
> 2. At present there is a chasm between literature and German tradition. This situation is a disgrace.
> 3. Purity of language and literature is *your* responsibility. Your folkdom [*Volkstum*] has entrusted you with faithfully preserving your language.
> 4. Our most dangerous enemy is the Jew and those who are his slaves.
> 5. A Jew can only think Jewish. If he writes in German, he is lying. The German who writes in German but thinks un-German is a traitor, the student who speaks and writes un-German is, in addition, thoughtless and has abandoned his duties.
> 6. We wish to eradicate lies, we want to denounce treason, and we want for us students, institutions of discipline [*Zucht*] and political education, not mindlessness.

7. We want to regard the Jew as alien and we want to respect the traditions of the *Volk*. Therefore, *we demand* of the censor: Jewish writings are to be published in Hebrew. If they appear in German, they must be identified as translations. Strongest actions against the abuse of German script. German script is available only to Germans. The un-German spirit is to be eradicated from public libraries.
8. We *demand* of the German students the desire and capability for independent knowledge and decisions.
9. We *demand* of German students the desire and capability to maintain the purity of the German language.
10. We *demand* of German students the desire and capability to overcome Jewish intellectualism and the resulting liberal decay of the German spirit.
11. We demand the selection of students and professors in accordance with their reliability and commitment to the German spirit.
12. We demand that German universities be a stronghold of the German *Volk* tradition and a battleground reflecting the power of the German mind.

Die Deutsche Studentenschaft [*The Organization of German Students*][48]

The viciousness of the anti-Semitism of the text is unparalleled at that date in the writings of Nazi teachers. It is only after 1935 that we find similar proposals among certain Nazi academics. We see, for example, Carl Schmitt, in a colloquium he organized in 1936, *The Science of Law in its Struggle against the Jewish Spirit,* recommending the same measures as those stated in 1933 in theses 5 and 7 of the placard. The fact that Forsthoff published the theses of the Organization of German Students and an ample fragment of Heidegger's rectoral address side by side leads the reader to wonder whether there is a connection between the two texts, and if so, what it is. It is a fact that, in his address, Heidegger gives high praise to the Deutsche Studentenschaft, which he brings up three times. This is how he expresses himself in the first paragraph excerpted by Forsthoff: "The concept of freedom of the German students [*deutschen Studenten*] is now brought back to its truth. Out of that truth, the bond and the service of the Organization of German Students [Deutsche Studentenschaft] henceforth unfolds."[49]

And Forsthoff gives us only the second half of the paragraph. In the complete text, Heidegger stresses the Deutsche Studentenschaft even more clearly. He writes: "From the resolve of the Organization of German Students to support the German destiny in its most extreme distress comes the will of the essence of the university. That will is a true will to the extent that, thanks to the new student law, the Organization of German Students places itself beneath the law of its essence and thus is the first to delimit that essence."[50]

This declaration by Heidegger contains a concrete and precise reference that has not received the attention it merits from commentators. The laudatory reference to the "new student law," which allowed the Deutsche Studenten-schaft to delimit its essence, refers precisely to one of the most abhorrent juridical measures of the general *Gleichschaltung*—namely, the law "against the excessive number of enrollees in German schools and universities" of 25 April 1933.[51] Beneath the cloak of that administrative euphemism, the "new student law" in reality institutes a draconian *numerus clausus,* limiting the number of Jewish students thereafter to be admitted to the university to 1.5 percent. At the University of Freiburg, the new rector Heidegger had made provisions to activate this "new student law" on 1 May 1933, at the same time as the inauguration celebration of the rector and his official entry into the NSDAP. Readers of the Nazi newspaper of Freiburg, *Der Alemanne,* were informed: "The Academic Rectorate of the University of Freiburg announces the following: The solemn proclamation of the new student law, scheduled in the Prussian universities for the date of 1 May, will, in our university, in which the change of rector coincides with the beginning of the summer semester, be duly integrated with the *celebration of the transmission of the rectorate.*"[52]

Furthermore, only the Deutsche Studenstenschaft—totally under the control of the Nazis, and whose directors were required to be members of the NSDAP —were recognized in the new law as representing the students. Hence the Association of Jewish Students, "Neo-Friburgia," was forced to *dissolve.*[53] Thus we see that Martin Heidegger openly approved that anti-Semitic law, and his reference to the "new student law" indicates beyond a doubt the racist and anti-Semitic sense in which he understands the expression "to delimit one's essence."

It must be added that yet again the Badenland showed particular zeal. We learn on 12 June 1933: "The Ministry of the State of Baden has just taken a legal measure concerning students, which stipulates in paragraph 1 that, dur-ing registration, students must declare on their honor that their parents and grandparents are of German descent."[54]

If we now examine the content of the placard of the Deutsche Studenten-schaft, the radical anti-Semitism that is expressed in it has no entirely explicit equivalent in Heidegger, except in texts he took care not to make public, such as his letter of 1929 to Geheimrat Schwoerer. But the program of battle for "the German spiritual life" and against "the Jewification" defined in his letter announced precisely what the Deutsche Studenschaft brought to bear in its action "against the un-German spirit." Further, the insistent references in the twelve theses to language (*Sprache*) and to *Volkstum* coincide with the posi-tions of Heidegger himself. Thus he speaks, in his rectoral address, of "Occi-dental man," who, "on the basis of a folk [*Volkstum*]" and "a people-power of his language [*Sprache*]" rises up for the first time against being in its totality.[55] And in other texts of the same period we will have the occasion to revisit the importance of the reference to the *Volkstum* in Heidegger, which, in his speech of 6 May 1933 for student registration, he goes so far as to make the "root of the spirit."[56] It is therefore beyond doubt — and this is a capital point — that the racism of these twelve theses is not expressed in a "biological" way but, on the contrary, related exclusively to "the people," "the language," and "the spirit," exactly as in Heidegger. As for the so-called German writing — that is, Gothic letters — it should be recalled that Heidegger deliberately chose to have his speech published by a Breslau press that would print it in Gothic letters, whereas the collection in which his speech was supposed to be included continued, under the Third Reich, to appear in Latin letters.[57]

Further, we must point out that Ernst Forsthoff again published, in 1943, a third, enlarged edition of his work, henceforth titled: *German History from 1918 to 1938 in Documents*. It goes, therefore, up to the last year before World War II. In it, the rectoral address is also quoted following the twelve anti-Semitic theses, but a bit farther on Forsthoff adds a speech by Alfred Rosenberg, delivered on 16 February 1938 and titled "National Socialism and Education." Heidegger remains in good company. Needless to say, he and his apologists always kept silent, after 1945, about these two publications of edited excerpts from his address, *The Self-Affirmation of the German University* . . .

Many elements of Heidegger's real activity remain unknown. We know that he benefited from a sabbatical semester during the winter of 1932–1933 and therefore taught no courses between July 1932 and the beginning of May 1933. During that long period, as he was anxious to point out to Elisabeth Blochmann, he wrote no book but found himself caught up, as he says, for several weeks in "important university activities, among others."[58] It seems likely that he discreetly cultivated ties with the Deutsche Studentenschaft and its directors, Gerhard Krüger and Georg Plötner. Indeed, the most committed Nazi "philosophers" took part in the action "against the non-German spirit." Thus, we have seen that Alfred Baeumler put the finishing touches on the text of the placard and headed the procession of his students dressed in the SA uniform to go, after his class on 10 May 1933, to the book-burning in Berlin and deliver his speech there. And that notorious participation of Baeumler in the anti-Semitic action of the Nazi students did not in the least lead Heidegger to sever the close ties subsisting between the two men during the following months. As for Erich Rothacker, he was for a time the section head of the People's Education (*Leiter der Abteilung Volksbildung*) at the Ministry of Propaganda and "the liaison man between Goebbels and the student action against the non-German spirit."[59] As for Heidegger himself, his personal ties with Gerhard Krüger, his correspondence with Georg Plötner, and the initiative he took to help bring about the Berlin Workshop Days suffice to show that, far from having the slightest misgivings, he cooperated actively with the authors of the anti-Semitic campaign. It is even known that he sent his rectoral address to the main leaders of the Deutsche Studentenschaft: Gerhard Krüger, Georg Plötner, Andreas Feikert, and Hanskarl Leistritz, this last being the one who had proclaimed the "sentences of fire" during the book-burnings at Berlin.[60]

In short, given the ties of political affinity and personal friendship between Heidegger and Baeumler on the one hand, and the representatives of the Nazi Deutsche Studentenschaft on the other, we can affirm that he maintained the closest ties of solidarity with the main actors of the anti-Semitic campaign, and that his rectoral address, with its explicit and insistent stances in favor of the Deutsche Studentenschaft and its praise for the new student law, expresses not only the public and official academic backing of Rector Heidegger for the deeply anti-Semitic movement of the Nazi Deutsche Studentenschaft but the desire to appear as the one who gave it its "spiritual direction."

3

Work Camps, the Health of the People, and the Hard Race in the Lectures and Speeches of 1933–1934

The speeches, lectures, and proclamations of Martin Heidegger in 1933 and 1934 have now been republished — or, in the case of certain ones, published for the first time — in volume 16 of the work termed "complete." They make up a total of more than one hundred printed pages of ultra-Nazi prose. The reading of these texts reveals that neither the resignation from the rectorate at the end of April 1934 nor the bloody night of 30 June 1934 constituted a break in Heidegger's political career: proof that the resignation from the rectorate did not even remotely constitute an act of repudiation of Hitler's power. We must begin by turning to these texts in order to penetrate that dark period and make out the first contours of the doctrine Heidegger espoused at that time. Indeed it appears that in his acts as in his words, Heidegger is at the antipodes of the calm reflection and ability to make clear distinctions that one has the right to expect of a "thinker." We have seen him express his agreement with the new anti-Semitic legislation, collaborate with the authors of the action taken "against the un-German spirit," and campaign intensively for the Nazi transformation of the constitution of the university and the introduction of the Führer principle at the university. We discover, in his speeches and lectures, a Heidegger who does not hesitate to propose an enthusiastic apology for the new "scientific camps," exalt the hard race ready for combat, espouse the racial idea of "the health of the people," and outdo the Nazis in perverting

Official portrait of Rector Martin Heidegger in 1933.

the concepts of work, knowledge, and freedom. Emphasis must be placed on Heidegger's personal fascination with Hitler, which we will find expressed in all his courses, at least until 1936, to a pitch of intensity that has no equivalent among the other "philosophers" of Nazism, with the possible exception of Alfred Baeumler.

The Rectoral Address of 27 May 1933

The day after joining the NSDAP, Heidegger wrote an enthusiastic letter to his brother Fritz, enjoining him to support the movement "unreservedly." He writes: "You must consider the totality of the movement not from below, but on the basis of the Führer and his great objectives. . . . Henceforth we must think not of ourselves but only of the totality and destiny of the German people."[1]

Two days later, on 6 May 1933, the new rector delivered his first public speech on the occasion of student registration (during the early days of summer semester 1933). The beginning of the speech is almost identical to that of the course given the same week and titled *The Fundamental Question of Philosophy.* It begins thus: "The German people itself in its totality has found that it is under great leadership [*Führung*]. Under that *Führung,* the people comes to itself, creates for itself its state."[2] Just a little later in the rectoral address, Heidegger attacks academic freedom and redefines the concept of freedom in his own way: "Freedom does not mean being free with respect to . . . obligation, order, and law. Freedom means being free for . . . resoluteness with a view to spiritual and common commitment to the German destiny."[3] One of the major existentials of *Being and Time,* resoluteness (*Entschlossenheit*), is thus taken up again and oriented exclusively in the direction of the spiritual destiny of the German people, of what he designates in italics in his speech the community of combat and education (*Kampf- und Erziehungsgemeinschaft*). The "root" of this "spirit" is the "folk-dom," or *Volkstum,*[4] a Nazi word par excellence, and the goal of what Heidegger calls "politico-spiritual education" is the community of the people (*Volksgemeinschaft*). On the same day, in the name of their comradeship in combat (*Kampfgenossenschaft*), he sent a message of congratulations to Ernst Krieck for his election to the rectorate of the University of Frankfurt.[5] A few days later, on 20 May, he sent the following telegram to Adolf Hitler, concerning the accomplishment of the "necessary bringing into line" at the university. "I humbly request that the planned reception for the Steering Committee of the Association of German Universities be postponed until such time as the direction of the association of the universities is completed in the sense of the bringing into line that is particularly necessary here."[6]

What stands out most in Heidegger's conduct and writings during the first years of the Nazi Reich is the absence of all calm reflection, the frantic involvement in the political affirmation of Hitlerism: in sum, as I have said, quite the opposite of what one has the right to expect of a thinker.

One week after the telegram to Hitler, Heidegger delivered his address, *The Self-Affirmation of the German University*. The word "self-affirmation" (*Selbstbehauptung*) is pivotal for him. It is with this term that almost two years later he defined politics in the unpublished seminar of winter 1934–1935, dedicated to Hegel's doctrine of the state. It is not, therefore, a question of affirming the independence of the German university from National Socialist political power, let alone encouraging I know not what spirit of resistance. On the contrary, it is a question of affirming and upholding the political mission of the university as espousing the Nazi relation between *Führung* and *Gefolgschaft*. It is with these two terms that the rectoral address begins, and they define the political stakes contained therein. What is at stake is the introduction into the university of that same relationship between the Führer and his "following" that constitutes and structures the modality of political direction of National Socialism at all the levels of the state. In sum, it is a question, as I have shown, of realizing the bringing into line (*Gleichschaltung*) of the university by the introduction of the *Führerprinzip*. The rectoral address therefore has a specific political function: to announce and justify in advance what is to come, a process in which Heidegger will be one of the major actors — namely, the application of the Hitlerian mode of political functioning to the German university system.

Thus the interpretation some French apologists have tried to defend, according to which Heidegger's goal was to preserve the independence of the university, is substantiated neither by the historical facts nor by the texts. Worse yet, it does not tally with the words of Heidegger himself, such as they have been related by Jacques Lacant. The latter, a curator at the University of Freiburg after the German capitulation, relates his words as follows: "I saw Heidegger, I had him come. He entered into long considerations. He wanted to rejuvenate the university. He thought that with the Nazis he would have enough power. His idea was that the German university could not reform itself. . . . It would take an external power."[7]

We see that in 1945 Heidegger tried to justify himself in the eyes of Jacques Lacant by proposing the necessity of "rejuvenating the university," but he did not claim to have wanted to defend its independence. On the contrary, he admitted to having wanted to bolster his position by means of Nazi power to reform the university. And that is precisely what the introduction into the university of the *Führerprinzip* and the *Führung-Gefolgschaft* relationship represented to Heidegger, and it is explicitly central to his address, *The Self-Affirmation of the German University*. Moreover, the invocation in the speech of the figure of Prometheus shows clearly upon what force he relies: Prometheus is the Greek myth most frequently invoked and redirected by the Nazis for their own purposes ever since Hitler wrote, in *Mein Kampf*, that the Aryan "is the Prometheus of mankind."[8] What Heidegger develops around Prometheus is a discourse of power. He subordinates knowledge to the superpower (*Übermacht*) of destiny. These terms, "superpower" and "destiny," are not new beneath his pen: Heidegger already brought them together in section 74 of *Being and Time,* precisely in the passage in which he introduces the ideas of community and people. Similarly, this rectoral address is part of the continuity of what was foreshadowed as early as 1925 in the meetings held in Kassel on *The Present Struggle for a Vision of the Historical World*. We have seen that Heidegger intended to replace modes of thought such as that of Descartes, which take human consciousness or the *self* as their center, with the search for a soil (*Boden*) and a center or milieu (*Mitte*) that would make it possible to conceptualize existence no longer as a consciousness but as being-in-the-world and being-in-common. In this instance, under the reference to the "greatness" of the Greek beginning, Heidegger relates this middle to the "the inmost determining center of the entire *volklich*-state existence."[9] As for the world onto which existence opens by this center, it is, as Heidegger now makes clear, the "*spiritual world* of a people," understood not as "superstructure of a culture" but as "the deepest power of conservation of its earth and blood forces." The Heideggerian spirit is made of earth and blood. We are at the antipodes of the Cartesian *mens humana,* which is always related to thought. And this reference to earth (or soil) and blood, to *Blut und Boden* in short, is far from constituting a *hapax* beneath his pen, contrary to what those who, in the 1960s, felt free to assert, in their desire to diminish thereby the spiritual responsibility of Heidegger with respect to his public use of these superlatively Nazi terms. On the contrary, we find more than one occurrence of the association of these two terms in the letters, courses, and speeches of the time.[10]

Moreover, we must consider under what auspices, in May 1933, Heidegger's redefinition of the tasks of the German student is carried out. In that redefinition, the "service of knowledge" appears in third place after the "service of work" and the "service of defense." Heidegger places the service of work in the framework of the *Volksgemeinschaft,* that is, the community of people united by blood and race. That will be very explicitly repeated by Heidegger in the unpublished seminar of winter 1933–1934. Also, the overvaluation of work in the people has, with the Nazis, an unequivocal meaning, affirmed by Hitler in *Mein Kampf* when he presents the swastika as the symbol of "the mission of battle for the triumph of the Aryan man and simultaneously for the triumph of the idea of productive work, which was ever anti-Semitic and will ever remain anti-Semitic."[11] In short, Hitler made work into an idea that was itself anti-Semitic, so that it was no longer possible to redefine work according to the criteria of the "new German reality" without espousing that racist connotation.

Heidegger placed the service of defense beneath the sign of honor (*Ehre*), which since Rosenberg's *Myth of the Twentieth Century* was considered by the Nazis as the emblematic value expressing the relationship of the *Gefolg-schaft* to its *Führung*, as well as the community of combat united by blood and race. When, for example, Erik Wolf, Heidegger's most faithful lieutenant, brings up honor, it is to Rosenberg that he is referring. As for Rothacker, we have seen him explicitly relate honor to race in his *Philosophy of History*.

The service of knowledge, in conclusion, is exalted beneath the sign of the "spirit" and of its mission, but — as we have shown previously — it is a spirit related to blood and earth. Heidegger thus forms a triad without originality: people, state, spiritual mission, which echoes the triad set forth by Carl Schmitt at the same moment in *State, Movement, People*. Triads are in fact particularly in vogue in the Hitlerian movement since Hitler commented, in a page of *Mein Kampf* quoted above, on the three elements constitutive of the Nazi flag bearing the swastika.

What is proper to Heidegger, but does not make his discourse any more philosophical, is the pathos and bombast of his utterances, which come from what Theodor Adorno was right in calling "jargon." Much could be said about the poverty of the syntax, the purely assertive character of the utterances, and to borrow Adorno's terms, "the disintegration of the language into words in themselves"[12]: "a modest number of words that close in upon themselves and become signals."[13] The first of the words cited as examples by Adorno is that of "mission" (*Auftrag*), one of those terms Heidegger uses and abuses, and that he uses in his address to describe the service of knowledge. In short, it is not only because of its manifestly Hitlerian content and its immediate and real political stakes but also because of its pompous style that one may well be astonished at the blindness of those who, in France, were in ecstasies over "the admirable rectoral address."

The Apology for the Work Camps and the Selection

If the rectoral address is the best known of those given by Heidegger, it is far from being the only one. From May 1933 to the end of November 1934 —

that is, in the course of four academic semesters — Heidegger gave more than twenty lectures and speeches in which "philosophy" was radically put at the service of Nazism — in Freiburg, Heidelberg, Leipzig, Tübingen, and Constance. His period of intense activism goes far beyond the year of the rectorship, though the winter semester of 1933–1934 (from November to February) was a particularly virulent moment, as is confirmed by the unpublished seminar that will be discussed in Chapter 5 of the present work. More than half these texts were published in various newspapers, journals, and collective works, and a few of the speeches were broadcast on radio. While some of the texts are rather well known today — especially the tribute to the memory of Albert Schlageter, whom the Nazis worshipped, and the speech of November 1933 calling on students, professors, and the entire German population to vote for Hitler — the majority of them are accessible only in German. We will therefore turn to them, with special emphasis on the speeches and lectures not yet translated, or not available in any translation worthy of the name.[14] We will see to what degree Heidegger allowed himself be taken over by all the constituent parts of Nazism, including the apology for blood and race.

The speech of 14 June 1933 titled *The Service of Work and the University* is the first evidence of Heidegger's fascination with the Nazi institution of work camps (*Arbeitslager*), which he presents as a new manifestation of the *Volksgemeinschaft*. Schools no longer hold an exclusive place in education: alongside the schools there are henceforth the camps.[15] And in addition to these work camps for students, another sort of camp is formed, in which Heidegger himself participates actively: short-term camps where the teaching faculty of several universities gather, and members of the SS, among other activities, offer courses on racial doctrine. We have seen from Heidegger's letter to Rothacker that during the fall of 1934, thus well after his resignation from the rectorship, he was again to direct such camps. For the first camp he organized (from 4 to 10 October 1933) at Todtnauberg, near his *Hütte,* he ordered that the site should be "reached on foot" from Freiburg by the professors and students in close ranks. Furthermore, each of the participants was required to wear "the SA or SS uniform, possibly the steel helmet uniform with armband."[16] We might wonder what uniform Rector Heidegger wore at that time: doubtless the brown uniform and the party armband, for it is inconceivable that he participated in such marches in civilian attire. That seems more likely than the uniform of the SA, of which he does not seem to have been a member. On this question, Günther Anders observes, however, in an article that appeared in 1946, that he has in his possession a postcard, bought by him in Freiburg in 1933, in which Rector Heidegger can be seen parading at the head of the SA of the town.[17] And Jacques Lacant, who as a trustee of the university followed Heidegger's dossier quite closely in 1945–1946, affirmed that "several concordant testimonies say that he would come and give his classes in a brown shirt and salute the students with a *Heil Hitler!*"[18] These questions of uniform, the subject of spirited quarrels in the recent past,[19] should not be neglected, since the testimonies of Anders and Lacant, as well as the texts of Heidegger himself, prove the degree to which he personally identified with the Nazi militarization of university life. Heidegger's letters to his disciple historian Rudolf Stadelmann resonate with the pathos of the camp. Heidegger writes to him on 11 October 1933, when leaving the Heidelberg camp: "The camp was a dangerous atmosphere for each person. For those who left and for those who stayed, it was equally a trial."[20] The trial of the camps Heidegger praises in these terms is the selection: the progressive elimination of the participants who do not prove equal to the task. Heidegger himself proceeds to make the selection, and he boasts, in a letter of 16 October 1933 to Elisabeth Blochmann, of having eliminated twenty participants. "Eight days ago, I had the first camp [*Lager*] at Todtnauberg—I learned *a lot*. But right in the middle of the camp period, I had to dismiss 20 persons who didn't fit in there. Such a camp is a *great trial*—for each one—and dangerous."[21]

The above-mentioned speech devoted to *The Service of Work and the University* and the letters I quote show what feeds the Heideggerian pathos and how great a taste this "thinker" has for these places of selection—the Nazi camps. True, there are camps and there are camps, and the ones Heidegger directs are camps of indoctrination and of putting the participants to the test—very different from those that proliferated during the same years for the internment of political opponents. Still, given the context of those years, the importance Heidegger's remarks place on the justification of selection in the camps has a sinister quality. To this must be added his defense of the National Socialist conception of work, which is the overarching constant in several of his speeches.

The Heidelberg Lecture and the Exaltation of the Hard Race

On 30 June 1933, Heidegger was invited to Heidelberg to give the first lecture in the "Program of Political Education" established by the student federation.[22] It was an official event, and the entire professorial body of the University of Heidelberg, as well as the representatives of the town, were present in the *Aula* of the university to listen to the rector of Freiburg speak on "The University in the New Reich." Heidegger began by proclaiming that the German "revolution" had not yet reached the university, even if "the new life in the work camps" had opened the way. The university now had to be *inte-*

grated with the community of the people and allied with the state.[23] Thus it is a question not at all of defending the autonomy of the university but of "leading a rugged battle in the spirit of National Socialism, which must not be stifled beneath humanistic, Christian conceptions that would diminish its absoluteness."[24] To those who complain that the defense service takes time away from knowledge, Heidegger answers that *no danger* can come from *work* for *the state* but only from indifference and resistance.[25] Far from taking the side of spiritual resistance to the regime or the party, he specifically says that it is in such resistance that danger lies. Heidegger exalts a teaching and research rooted in the people and connected with the state.[26] It is a question of fighting like "a hard race" (*ein hartes Geschlecht*), based on "forces of the New Reich that Hitler, the Chancellor of the People, will bring about."[27]

The anti-Semitic connotation of the appeal to the "hard race" in that year of 1933 is quite clear, given the fact that Ernst Forsthoff concluded his work titled *The Total State* with a reference to "today's hard race" struggling against the Treaty of Versailles and "international Jewry" (*internationale Judentum*), for the purpose of preparing the "better future."[28] The appeals to the "hard race,"[29] the "German race to come,"[30] and "*our race*"[31] are a leitmotiv in Heidegger's speeches. The Heidelberg lecture, with its apology for a new student life in the work camps, the defense service, and the resolution to be a hard race in the "spirit" of National Socialism, closes the first university semester under the Third Reich in revealing what the rectoral address had been striving toward. It also inaugurated what was to dominate the following semester in German academic life — namely, the transformation of university teaching into a course in political education. As we will see, Heidegger was not behind the times.

Let us add that, on the impact of the lecture of 30 June 1933, we have the testimony of a listener, historian Gerd Tellenbach, who was then an assistant at the University of Heidelberg. Tellenbach related his experience in the following terms: "The man who was speaking there was a passionate National Socialist devoid of any wisdom, devoid of any sense of political responsibility, lacking all desire for measured distinctions. In 1933, people didn't stop at mere words. You have to know how many there were that summer who tried to adapt to National Socialism, in order to understand how daring this provocative question was: 'Is there revolution at universities, too? No!' Thousands of those on whom I had counted caved in under the influence of Heidegger."[32]

Heidegger, the Health of the People, and Nazi Medicine

During the summer of 1933, Heidegger attempted to extend his action in the direction of the faculties of law and medicine. His letter of 22 August

1933 to Carl Schmitt was a part of that action toward the jurists, which we will study in detail and which involves Erik Wolf. But Heidegger also intervened among the medical doctors. This can be observed particularly in the address he delivered in August 1933 to the Freiburg Institute of Pathological Anatomy. The "philosopher" came on that occasion to validate, for the benefit of the doctors who listened to him, the fact that in Nazism, what is healthy and what is sick is no longer determined on the basis of the human being properly so called, but according to whether or not he belongs to a certain people. Heidegger writes: "Now what is decisive and surprising is that the essence of health has not at all been determined in the same way in all ages and in every people."[33] The one and only criterion to determine the "essence of health" is the capacity to act for the state. Thus, Heidegger advances the idea that "for the Greeks, for example, 'healthy' means neither more nor less than being ready and strong to act in the service of the state. For one who no longer satisfied the conditions for such action, the physician was no longer authorized to come, even in the case of 'illness.' "[34]

All consideration for the human being having been thus swept aside, utility to the state authorized the severest eugenics. Like other doctrinarians of Nazism before him (one might think, for example, of the book by the raciologist Hans K. Günther, *Plato: The Guardian of Life*), Heidegger uses Plato's *Republic* to give an appearance of philosophical authority to his statement. But what is really at stake is the replacement of the human idea of health by the racial concept of the "health of the people," such as it underlies the racial doctrine of Nazi *Rassenkunde*. We are therefore far from Plato. Heidegger's statement is unambiguous. He continues in the following terms: "For what is healthy and what is sick, every people and age gives itself its own law, according to the inner greatness and extension of its existence. Now the German people are in the process of rediscovering their own essence and making themselves worthy of their great destiny. Adolf Hitler, our great Führer and chancellor, created, through the National Socialist revolution, a new state by which the people will assure itself anew of the duration and continuity of its history. . . . For every people, the first warranty of its authenticity and greatness is in its blood, its soil, and its physical growth. If it loses this good or even only allows it to become considerably weakened, all effort at state politics, all economic and technical ability, all spiritual action will remain in the end null and void."[35]

Heidegger adopts without restriction the Hitlerian perspective according to which politics and the economy ultimately depend on the "health of the people," understood in a strictly racial sense — that is, in terms of blood and soil. In this perspective, the "spirit" itself depends on the blood. That is confirmed in an even more explicit manner in the unpublished seminar of winter 1933–

1934, in which, at the end of the sixth session, Heidegger openly connects the "health of the people" (*Volksgesundheit*) with the unity of blood and race. Indeed, he declares that in "a word such as '*Volksgesundheit*,'" what is felt is nothing less than "the link with the unity of blood and stock, the unity of race."[36]

In his address to the medical doctors of Freiburg, Heidegger intends to legitimize, by that racial conception of the health of the people, the latter's expansion. The German people must be able to ensure its duration but also its "extension," and the listener is led to conclude that the "physical growth" of the German people authorizes it to extend its living space. The address does not, however, go so far as to develop a theory of the relationship between the people and its living space — a question that Heidegger will, however, develop in his unpublished seminar of winter 1933–1934 — and, at the end of the speech, he limits himself to preparing what will take place in autumn 1933 (namely, Germany's dropping out of the League of Nations), but, as we shall see, Heidegger goes further in his 1933–1934 seminar.

We have also recently learned that Heidegger was not content with bringing his "philosophical" warranty to the eugenics of German medicine. As rector, he himself worked actively to institute at the University of Freiburg an official and permanent teaching of racial doctrine (*Rassenkunde*) by the creation of a corresponding full professor's chair. On 13 April 1934, not many days before his resignation from the rectorship took effect, and therefore at a time when he was not obliged to any activism, Heidegger wrote to the ministry of Karlsruhe to demand the creation (and he reminds his reader that he has been demanding it "for months") of a "full professor chair in racial doctrine and hereditary biology" (*eines a.o. Lehrstuhles für Rassenkunde und Erbbiologie*).[37] After the preceding part-time lecturer in "racial hygiene," Alfred Nissle, was precluded in 1933, Heidegger began making personal inquiries for a replacement and had found the medical consultant Theodor Pakheiser of Karlsruhe, the district head of the Association of National Socialist Physicians, who, for reimbursement of the cost of his train tickets, had agreed to come to the University of Freiburg to teach "the National Socialist worldview and racial thought."[38] Following Heidegger's letter, Heinz Riedel, a member of the NSDAP, former director of the Office of Race of the SS of Freiburg and protégé of Eugen Fischer, was made full professor.[39] Thus Heidegger contributed in a very concrete way to the introduction of the teaching of the racial doctrine of Nazism at the University of Freiburg. We should bear in mind, in this connection, Heidegger's friendship with the doctor of eugenics and raciology Eugen Fischer, who was with him on 11 November 1933 at Leipzig for the National Socialist professors' "profession of faith in Adolf Hitler." Eugen Fischer, who directed the Institute of Berlin at which Josef Mengele, the doctor at Auschwitz, received his training, intervened on behalf of Heidegger in 1944 when he was drafted, along with the reservists of his (advanced) age group, into the *Volkssturm* defense service. That intervention seems to have been decisive, since Heidegger was almost immediately released from his obligations. It is rather pathetic to see him so eagerly seeking to avoid the draft—he who had taught his students the spirit of sacrifice for so many years and exhorted them to put "defense service" at the same level as "knowledge service." Heidegger continued to correspond in a friendly manner with Eugen Fischer after 1945 and to visit him.[40]

The Nazification of Work, Knowledge, and Freedom

The winter semester of 1933–1934 was Rector Heidegger's most active period, one in which "philosophy" was entirely corrupted by the role of political "education" at the service of National Socialism. A significant indication of that state of mind is the letter of 3 November 1933 that he sent to the ministry of the Badenland at Karlsruhe, demanding the transformation of the vacant associate professor chair in pedagogy and philosophy. "I demand that the general nature of that chair be imperatively transformed in the direction of the instruction of the entire field of political pedagogy."[41]

We are now at the eve of the referendum of 12 November 1933, which is on the approval of three issues at once: leaving the League of Nations, affirming the confidence of the German people in their chancellor Hitler, and voting in an uncontested list of Nazi candidates for election to the Reichstag. With three successive speeches, Heidegger intended to mobilize the students, the professors, and the entire German people in favor of Hitler. These speeches, republished beginning in 1960 in Switzerland and France, are not unknown. But it is important to stress the new tone they introduce compared with the lectures of May and June 1933. First of all, there is a hardening of vocabulary: it is no longer the word *volklich* but the term *völkisch* that Heidegger uses, a term that in the usage of the times had an even more strongly racist connotation. *Völkisch* is the conception of the people qua race. Today we have irrefutable proof that Heidegger does indeed understand the word in this sense. His course of summer semester 1934 attests to this in no uncertain terms.[42] Another important element to be considered is the group of key terms central to the Heideggerian doctrine: the words "essence," "beings," and "being" are called into the service of Nazism. Finally (and this is a first approximation of what will become Heidegger's "philosophy of law"—an expression used in 1934 by Erik Wolf about him, but in which the word "philosophy" can be understood only by antiphrasis), Heidegger on several occasions uses the word "law" (*Gesetz*) to proclaim that "the Führer and he alone *is* the present and future German reality and its law,"[43] and to speak of the "fundamental law of honor," by the strength of which "the German people preserves the nobleness and decision of its essence."[44] In bringing together in this way the words "honor," "law," "people," and "essence," Heidegger concurs, as does his disciple jurist Erik Wolf, with the positions of Rosenberg and Schmitt.

That these speeches of Heidegger's of November 1933 mark the unconditional and total allegiance of the rector of Freiburg to what he calls "the new German reality" is beyond doubt. But what of philosophy? We are witnessing, Heidegger proclaims, "the end of the philosophy" that had idolized a "thought deprived of soil and power."[45] What is left in place of that philosophy? A "return to the essence of being" that opens up the path of a "*völkisch* science" (*eine völkische Wissenschaft*) and the allegiance of the community of the people to the Führer. Heidegger's introduction of the basic elements of Nazism and Hitlerism into philosophy is indeed the end of philosophy, so much so that, as we shall soon see, the words "beings" and "being" will end up designating the people and the state.[46]

After the referendum of 12 November 1933, Heidegger devoted himself (in a series of speeches and lectures delivered and published from the end of November 1933 to the end of February 1934, while he was teaching his political education seminar) to inculcating his students with the National Socialist conception of work and knowledge that he had resolutely made his own. The first speech of this type, which was quite elaborate, was *The German Student as Worker*. It was given on Saturday, 25 November 1933, the day of new student registration at the beginning of the winter semester 1933–1934. Heidegger had planned and organized a ceremony combining the registration of new students with a commemoration of the Battle of Langemarck, which had become for the Nazis a symbol of the sacrifice of German youth in combat.[47] The rector's address was set for eleven o'clock in Prometheus Hall at the university. After his speech, everyone sang the *Horst-Wessel-Lied,* the official song of the Nazi Party. In the program of the ceremony conceived by the rector, the following order was planned for the procession of students and teachers who were to go to the monument erected in memory of the students fallen in combat: at the head of the procession the SA, followed by the SS, then the Steel Helmets and the university banners.[48] We should add that the speech was retransmitted by the radio station Südwestdeutsche Rundfunk and thus broadcast in the entire southwest of Germany — Frankfurt, Freiburg, Kassel, Trier, Köln, and Stuttgart — before being repeated in condensed form in the written press. This gives us an idea of the sizeable audience for his remarks.

In his speech, Heidegger wanted to show that the "new German reality" introduced a "total upheaval" of the state and of the relation between the university and the state, which could no longer be thought of in the manner of Wilhelm von Humboldt in 1810. In the liberal conception of the nineteenth century, the less the state got involved in university business, the better it was. Henceforth it would be totally different, and Heidegger drew all the conclusions for the life of the "new German student." Indeed, "the *being* of the German student also becomes different," and even his enrollment is changing in its meaning.[49] The new German reality requires of the student a new sacrifice, under the aegis of Langemarck. Heidegger will then marshal the rhetoric and pathos that is usual in his speeches of this period: the description of a state of affairs, followed by a demonstration that this will not suffice, that a higher "decision" is still needed. Thus, "the German student passes through the work service, he stands by the SA,"[50] and his studies are henceforth called "knowledge service." "That is something new." Yet that does not suffice. It is not yet the new reality of the German student, it is not, Heidegger says, *our* reality. What is occurring? The Germans are becoming a historical people. Being historical consists in knowledge. "This knowledge is realized *in* the people's becoming-a-state, this knowledge is the state."[51] Thus the identity between the state and the knowledge of the German people as a historical people has been posited. Henceforth state and knowledge, *Wissen* and *Staat,* will be indissociable.

Then comes a paragraph of decisive importance for an understanding of what Heidegger instilled in the collective student/professor body of the University of Freiburg. To the concepts of history and the state he adds that of nature, thus conjugating the three concepts that form the title of the unpublished seminar of the winter semester 1933–1934: *On the Essence and Concepts of Nature, History, and State.* What role does nature play in relation to the concepts of history and the state? As we shall see, in both the speech and the seminar, the reference to nature is not free of racial connotations.

The state is destined to activate the power of nature in the existence of the people. "The state *becomes* and it *is,*" Heidegger proposes, "to the extent that it brings the great powers of the human being into the existence of the people." Here is the paragraph in question.

> Thus, for example, *nature* becomes manifest as the space of a people, as countryside and homeland, as soil and ground. Nature, as the power and law of that hidden transmission of the inheritance [*Vererbung*] of essential instinctive predispositions and tendencies, is set free. Nature becomes a normative rule in the form of *health* [*Gesundheit*]. The more freely nature reigns, the more it is possible to put at her service, in the most excellent and controlled way, the formative power of authentic *technology*. By being tied to nature,

supported and overarched by her, at once fueled and limited by her, the *history* of the people is realized. In the struggle to trace out the *pathway* to its own essence and to assure its *duration,* the people grasps its identity in the growing constitution of the state. In the struggle to represent to itself its capacity for greatness and its destiny as essential truth, [the people] presents itself authoritatively in *art.* The latter attains to great style only by adopting the totality of the existence of the people in the imprinting [*Prägung*] of its essence.[52]

In this paragraph, to express the power of nature that is exercised in the transmission of the hidden essence of the people when the state implements it in technology and art, Heidegger uses the most characteristic terms of the racial doctrine developed by Clauß and Rothacker: the words "heredity" (*Vererbung*), "style" (*Stil*), and "imprinting" (*Prägung*). The term *Vererbung,* when it is used no longer solely apropos of an individual being but of a people, is one of the most characteristic ones of the racial doctrine of Nazism. The word *Stil,* borrowed from Nietzsche, is particularly used by Rothacker to designate racial characteristics. As for the word *Prägung,* we have seen that it is part of the very title of Ludwig Clauß's *Nordic Soul.* This racial background is confirmed by Heidegger's way of using the word "health" (*Gesundheit*) apropos of the nature of a people. We have already taken note of the background of racial eugenics against which he understands the "health of the people," both in his address to the Institute for Pathological Anatomy and in the unpublished seminar of winter 1933–1934, in which he links the "health of the people" to the unity of blood and stock (*Stamm*) — that is to say, to race (*Rasse*).

The hidden transmission of the people's heredity, insofar as it expresses the power of the law of nature and regulates the health of the people, is therefore the unity of the people based on blood and race. This hidden basis is manifested in technology, art, and the becoming-a-state — that is, the constitution of the state (*Staatsverfassung*) of the people, in which the word "constitution" no longer designates a body of juridical norms but the form and imprint taken on by the people within the state.

Condensed in the paragraph just quoted, we find the essence of Heidegger's doctrine. On the one hand, there is his (then) overvalued conception of technology as the manifestation of the natural power of a people, which obviously owes much to Jünger and reappears in his courses on Nietzsche. (Heidegger's critique of technology surfaces only with the defeat of the Nazi Reich). On the other hand, there is his idea of art and the state as manifestations of the truth of a people — an idea that constitutes the central theme of his lectures on the essence of truth, the origin of the work of art, and his courses of 1934–1935 on Friedrich Hölderlin. Indeed, it is "truth" that is in question here. Heidegger writes in the following two paragraphs:

> What is it, then, that takes place through the people's becoming-a-state? Those powers — nature, history, art, technology, the state itself — are imposed, and by that imposition, they are *confined* within their limits. And it is thus that *the very thing* that makes a people sure of itself, radiant and strong, becomes manifest. Now, the manifest character of these powers is precisely the essence of *truth*.
>
>   In imposing these powers, the developing state places the people back in its real *truth*.[53]

The manifestation of the powers constituting the people's becoming-a-state — nature, history, art, technology, the state itself — is for Heidegger the essence of truth. Thus art and truth, the two ideas that are the subject matter of his two best-known lectures, often delivered under Nazism, are indissociable from his doctrine of the people's becoming-a-state, earlier described in the vocabulary of the racial stylization common to Heidegger, Rothacker, and Clauß: heredity, style, imprinting, and bearing.[54] And philosophy's most essential concept, truth, is compromised here in this work of stylization of the racial essence of the people. Indeed, the passage from the hidden (*verborgen*) to its manifestation (*Offenbarkeit*) designates the moment at which the hidden transmission of the heredity of a people is manifested in the grand style of art, understood as being the imprinting of the essence of the entire existence of the people. Thus, the Heideggerian characterization of truth as unveiling (*aletheia*) really serves him in designating the passage of the hidden transmission of heredity (*Vererbung*) to the imprinting (*Prägung*) of the people manifested in its art and political constitution. When we take together the paragraphs of the speech on "the student as worker" and the unpublished seminar of the same period (one sentence of which I have quoted), the whole racial background of the Heideggerian conception of truth as unveiling becomes clear.

In very characteristic fashion, once he has dramatized, in the name of "truth," this passage from hidden heredity to the manifest imprint of the people — which is rather reminiscent of the distinction dear to Rothacker's racial doctrine between the genotype (which is transmitted in a hidden way) and the phenotype, or apparent character — Heidegger no longer has anything decisive to say, and his language begins to turn into jargon. Indeed, he proceeds in these terms. "It is from this truth that the authentic possibility of knowledge, the duty of knowledge, and the will to know arise. But knowledge means *to master in clarity the essence of things, and by the force of this power to be resolved to act.*"[55]

This definition of "knowledge," which involves essence, clarity, power, action, and resolve, is quite representative of that *Lingua Tertii Imperii,* or LTI, so minutely analyzed by Victor Klemperer.[56] In this case, "knowledge" fades away into something entirely different from knowledge in the usual sense of competency in a field of study or thought. To the student who is listening, all that remains is the pathos of action and resolve; in short, just the opposite of what constitutes knowledge for a philosopher.

From this moment on, Heidegger's speech becomes increasingly incisive and hard. The goal, in the popular, widespread tradition of the *Gauleiter* addressing the German youth, is to build up emotion and suspense until the moment of student enrollment, which becomes a veritable knighting ceremony initiating the students into the Nazi order. Heidegger begins by evoking the point at which "the *inviolate* people plunges down into the roots of its existence": "the German *youth. They* have no choice. They *must.*"[57] That obligation, a perversion of the Kantian imperative, is a constant in the Nazi pathos. As for "the decision," it has nothing whatsoever to do with individual choice. Heidegger is very clear on this point. The student is in the power of the command of the new German reality. "The student boldly addresses us and asks: 'What's your attitude toward the state?'"[58] "True, he is called 'primitive'; but fortunately so!"[59] And Heidegger goes on: "In this movement of aggression the will of the student has opened itself to the configurative powers of the state. In aggression, it [the will of the student] *follows* [*folgt*] the *Führung* of its firm will. In that *Gefolgschaft,* the individual no longer conceives of himself as an isolated individual — he has abandoned his own will to the powers."[60]

Here again we find that leitmotif of all the Nazism Heidegger adopted en bloc, the first elements of which, as we have seen, appeared already in *Being and Time:* the total renunciation of the existence of individual freedom for the sake of the community, structured by the exclusive relationship between the *Gefolgschaft* and its *Führung.* In this perspective, work is looked upon no longer as an individual effort but as a modality of being of the people, in the same way, Heidegger specifies, as care. It is, then, at the moment when the student has given up his or her own will that he or she becomes, in a sense, a "worker." The *Gefolgschaft* has become a *Kamaradschaft.*

It must be pointed out in this connection that in the Nazi language of the time, the word *Kamaradschaft* does not just mean "camaraderie" in the usual sense of the word, but the houses of communal life for students, instituted in 1933 and tightly controlled by the Nazi Deutsche Studentenschaft and the NSDAP organizations such as the SA. That Nazi meaning of *Kameradschaft* is, for example, totally explicit at the beginning of the text that the Nazi philologist Wolfgang Schadewald published on 27 July 1933 in the *Freiburger*

Studentenzeitung, titled "Der neue deutsche Student." Furthermore, it is no surprise that Schadewald refers specifically in that article to Heidegger's rectoral address, in explicating the three "figures" (*Gestalt*) of the *Gemeinschaft* corresponding to the three "services" enumerated by Heidegger: the "community of race [*Stamm*] and of the people" in the service of work, the "community of our destiny" in the defense service, and the "community of German spirit" in the knowledge service.

To return now to Heidegger, here are the terms in which he describes the new German student:

> It is the *Gefolgschaft* that creates the camaraderie and not the other way around. Such camaraderie educates these nameless, untitled Führers, who *act* more because they endure and sacrifice more.
>
> Camaraderie marks the individual with an imprint that carries it beyond itself and imprints on him the mark of a stamp that is distinctive to the young men of the troop. We know the resoluteness of their facial expressions, the stern clarity of their gaze, their decisive handshake, their uncompromising way of speaking. Both the isolated fanatic and the crowd without training or direction are demolished by the striking power of this breed of young men. This breed of student no longer "studies," that is, he does not remain *sitting* in some sheltered place, in order merely to "*aspire*" from there to some other place. This new race of those who wish to know is at every moment en route. Now this student will become a *worker.*[61]

Here we find, in its verbal form (*prägen*) or its noun form (*Gepräge*), that "imprinting" of the new German reality on the student as "worker." Heidegger plays to the point of satiety on the word *Schlag,* which can at once mean "brand," "blow," and "stamp;" and, like the word *Art,* it can mean "race." With the "new German reality," must one not recognize that "the *essence of work and of the worker has changed?*"[62] Work no longer designates one activity of the individual among others, but, like care, a new modality of being (*Seinsart*) of existence.

This linking by Heidegger of work and care deserves special attention. With "the essence of work," henceforth understood as determinative of the existence of *man in a fundamental manner,*[63] "our existence begins to move toward another modality of being, the nature of which I specified years ago as *care.*"[64] This clarification on the part of Heidegger is of major importance for the interpretation of the relation between *Being and Time* and the "new German reality," which did not triumph until 1933 but prepared its takeover throughout the 1920s. According to him, care therefore designated not an "existential" belonging to human existence as such but rather a new modality of being that did not begin to emerge until 1933, with the change in the essence of work, in conformity with the imprinting of a new "race" of "workers." For Heidegger, this is also a way of showing that he anticipated Jünger and that the Jüngerian figure of the worker, which was not set forth until 1932 in *Der Arbeiter*, would merely rework a determination already attained by Heidegger in 1927 and called "care."

In any case, Heidegger makes clear the precise Nazi meaning that will henceforth attach to the concept of work. He writes: "Work places and sets the people in the field of action of all the essential powers of being. The structure of the *völkisch* existence that is in the process of being formed [*sich gestaltend*] *in* work and *as* work is the *state*. The National Socialist State is the Work State."[65]

One could not be more explicit! Let us point out also that here the state represents the essential powers of being. Heidegger announces in this formulation what he will say in February 1934 in his unpublished seminar, in which the state is directly identified with being, and the people with individual being. Henceforth the concept of work is a *völkisch* one. We are not far from *Mein Kampf*, in which Hitler affirmed that creative work is and will always be anti-Semitic. Knowledge also becomes a *völkisch* concept to which the new student is forced to bow. Heidegger writes: "The new student, however, is integrated into the new order of state existence and its *völkisch* knowledge, and this in such a way that he must himself, for his part, contribute to the configuration of that new order."[66]

But as Heidegger advances toward the conclusion of his speech, the mythification of the student as worker intensifies. "The new student *is a worker*. But where do we find that student? Perhaps there are only in each university a *half-dozen*, perhaps *even less,* and in all less than the *seven* with which the Führer once began *his* work."[67] We can see, with the mention of this number seven, to what degree Heidegger is part of the Hitlerian cult of the Führer. The latter relates, in *Mein Kampf,* that when he asked in March 1920 to join the German Labor Party or German Party of Workers (*Deutsche Arbeiter Partei*) of Anton Drexler — from which the NSDAP would soon emerge — he received "a temporary card with the number seven."[68] That was, Hitler wrote, "the most crucial decision of my life."[69] To evoke the number seven was thus to put oneself back into the "heroic" times of the foundation of Nazism by Hitler and have the students participate in that legend.

In reality, that number seven was just a "conscious lie" on Hitler's part, "intended to create the legend," a lie that "has contributed considerably to the birth of the cult of Hitler since that publication of the first volume of *Mein Kampf*."[70] Hitler was not the seventh but the fifty-fifth member of the DAP, and his card bore the number 555. The number seven was therefore chosen by Hitler to suggest "mystic relations" among the initiators of the movement. We can see by this choice that Hitler's idea of the "worker" had nothing socialist about it, and that it came rather — as was equally the case with the "form [*Gestalt*] of the worker," dear to Jünger — from a mythified and mystical "aristocracy," from a cult of the Führer and his close "guard."

In Heidegger's speech, it is suggested that the new mythical student, understood as "worker," should soon take over, teaching in turn and joining the "work front of the new teaching body." Meanwhile, the meaning of the enrollment of students has been turned upside down by this. Henceforth, Heidegger concludes, "the examination for the new student is held no longer *at the end* of the time of studies, but at the beginning."[71] What does this mean, if not that one must begin by making sure that the enrolled student is a *Volksgenosse? Volksgenosse* is a word as untranslatable as the term *völkisch*. In the Nazi language of the time it designated exclusively the racial companion; never would a "Jew" be called the *Volksgenosse* of an "Aryan." It also meant that the new student was ready to let himself be dominated by the "new state forces" of the National Socialist state.

Rector Heidegger, after having invoked his native Black Forest (the homeland of Schlageter, mythicized by the Nazis), calls on the philosophy student Fischer to come forward for his enrollment. He speaks in the following terms. "I charge you to respect the will and work of our Führer Adolf Hitler. I bind you to the law of existence of the new German student. I require of you discipline and seriousness, and hardness toward yourself. I require of you willingness for sacrifice and exemplarity of bearing [*Haltung*] toward all the German comrades of the people [*Volksgenossen*]. Heil Hitler!"[72]

Five days later, on 30 November 1933, Heidegger gave a lecture in Tübingen titled *The University in the National Socialist State*. A long account of the lecture appeared the following day in the *Tübinger Chronik*. Heidegger is presented as "one of the strongest pioneers of National Socialism among German scholars."[73] The purpose is more or less the same as in the preceding speech: The New University must be "a part of the National Socialist state."[74] Once more Heidegger affirmed the complete opposite of what certain apologists would have the public believe by claiming that he wanted to save the autonomy of the university against Nazi power. In this speech, Heidegger adopts the extremism that prompted Karl Löwith to say that he was more radical than Messrs. Rosenberg and Krieck. Indeed, he proposes that the revolution at the university has not yet begun and concludes with the necessity of being a "hard race."

It is at this time — in a letter of 13 December 1933 to the deans of the University of Freiburg inviting the teachers to subscribe to the funded publication of a *Denkschrift* commemorating the "demonstration for German science" of 11 November 1933 in Leipzig (the day during which Heidegger could be seen beside the eugenicist and raciologist Eugen Fischer, sitting before a row of SA banners bearing the swastika) — that Heidegger adopts the anti-Semitic terminology of Nazism by using the term "non-Aryan" (*Nichtarier*). Thus he writes: "It is unnecessary to point out that non-Aryans should not appear on the subscriber list page."[75]

The exclusion of "non-Aryans" is presented as something that goes without saying and is therefore unnecessary to spell out. The work Heidegger invites the "Aryan" professors to subscribe to is none other than the *Profession of Faith of Professors of German Universities and Institutions of Higher Learning in Adolf Hitler and the National Socialist State,* published in Dresden by the League of National Socialist Professors (NSLB) in five languages — German, English, Italian, French, and Spanish — in order to be distributed throughout Europe. This book, then, contains one of the first French translations of a text by Heidegger, and it seems to have been distributed throughout Europe. Beneath the pen of a translator who is clearly not French, Heidegger's *Bekenntnis* (profession of faith) speaks of "the blossoming of an entire adolescence purified down to its deepest roots," of "the spineless idolatry of a thought without basis or force, which we hope to see disappear from philosophy," and of "not hiding from the terror of the raging madmen and turmoil of darkness" and praises "the National Socialist revolution" as bringing "a transformation in our existence as complete as it is radical."[76] Furthermore — and this is an important fact to be brought out — the two main non-Jewish disciples of Heidegger, Hans-Georg Gadamer and Gerhard Krüger, are among the few philosophers whose names are found at the end of the work, in the list of teachers having adhered to the "profession of faith" in Hitler. These two names, Gadamer and Krüger, are the ones Heidegger recommended to Stadelmann in 1945,[77] when the issue was to arrange for the replacement in Tübingen for the chair in philosophy left vacant by Theodor Haering, barred from university activity, as was Heidegger himself soon thereafter, because of his Nazi activism.

To return to early 1934, Heidegger begins by giving a speech on 22 January for the opening of a course intended for the "emergency workers" (*Notstandsarbeiter*) of the city of Freiburg. This speech, as well as the one devoted the following day to a call to "work service," manifests most explicitly the National Socialist transformation of the concepts of work, knowledge, and freedom that Heidegger espoused, thus following "the Führer of our new state."[78] What we have been calling until now knowledge, science, and work has taken on, he says, another meaning.[79] For what purpose? To "become hard for a fully valid existence as a *Volksgenosse* in the community of the German people,"[80] which includes in particular the understanding of "what the rehabilitation of the future body of the people means" and the significance of "the fact that 18 million Germans belong to the people, but, since they live outside the borders of the Reich, do not belong to the Reich."[81] Here, Heidegger anticipated the major measures that the new Reich would soon take: the law for the defense of German blood, or Nuremberg Law, the reunification of Austria and Germany (*Anschluss*) and the expansion of the Reich, which would soon include the Sudetenland and the Danzig Corridor. Similarly, we must understand "worker" and "work" as "National Socialism understands these words"[82] — that is, precisely, to conceive of the state of work as the NSDAP does. Here, the legend of a Heidegger opposing the Nazi Party breaks down. Indeed, here is what he proposes. "There is but *one sole* German 'condition of life.' It is the *condition of work,* rooted in the foundation carrying the people and freely ordered in the historical will of the state, whose imprint [*Prägung*] is molded in advance in the movement of the *National Socialist Party* of the German *workers.*"[83]

Heidegger manifests his total allegiance to the Nazi movement represented by the party. It is no longer possible to say, henceforth, that his goal was to free the university from the ascendancy of the party, as he tried to make people believe after 1945. What he says of the German "condition of life" molded in advance by the NSDAP is very close to what Rothacker affirms during the same period in his *Philosophy of History* on the "lifestyle" the Germans owed to the "spirit" of the NSDAP.[84] Furthermore, Heidegger brings together in this paragraph Carl Schmitt's triad of people, state, and movement. Thus the freedom alluded to is not freedom, since the imprint of the condition of work is molded in advance by the NSDAP. If work makes one free, that freedom is nothing more, here, than servitude and total submission to the party. The perversion of the ideas of work and freedom could not be more radical.

In his speech at Constance, delivered at the end of May 1934 (therefore after his resignation from the rectorate), Heidegger confirms the very special way in which he understands freedom. "Freedom means *to be bound by the most intimate law* and the orders of our essence."[85] In the context of the lecture, Heidegger clearly shows what is at stake. That law of "our" essence is to be understood in a *völkisch* and racial sense. What is involved is "the health of the impetus of *völkisch* life," and we know, by the definition he gives of it in his seminar of the same period, the explicitly racial meaning that the idea of "health of the people" has in Heidegger, as in all the National Socialists. Henceforth freedom no longer designates the autonomous will of the citizen but the bond of blood uniting the German *Volksgenossen* to one another and to a common allegiance to the Führer.

The Justification for the War, the "Spiritual Combat," and the Cult of the Dead

The speech at the end of the month of May 1934, delivered before his former fellow students of the Lyceum of Constance, was dedicated to the cult of the Great War and the announcement of the war to come. Heidegger evokes the two million German dead in the Great War, their endless gravestones forming, he says, "a mysterious crown around the borders of the Reich and German Austria."[86] His purpose goes far beyond ordinary patriotism in the context of the times. In two instances he embraces the Nazi way of integrating the community of war-dead comrades, in keeping with a cult of the dead intended to prepare for the coming war, into what he calls "our race" (*unser Geschlecht*).[87] At this point Heidegger invokes, as in several of his courses from the years 1933–1934, Heraclitus's aphorism 53 on strife, father of all things, which is also mentioned in his letter to Carl Schmitt.

We will return to the use he makes of that aphorism.[88] The Constance lecture reveals above all that, contrary to what Heidegger tried to maintain later, and particularly in 1945 in order to make up for his past misdeeds,[89] the *polemos*, the war of which is questioned in the aphorism of Heraclitus, is indeed evoked by him in direct relation to real wars, since the paragraph in which he cites the aphorism begins with the evocation of the Great War, thought of not only as a past event but as being imposed presently "on us"[90] — this "us" referring to the German people and the German race. As for that war, declares Heidegger, we must "win it *spiritually*, which means that the *struggle* becomes *the most intimate law* of our existence."[91] He asserts: "For the essential man, the struggle is the *great trial* of every being, in which it is decided whether we are ourselves slaves or masters. . . . Our race — we in our camaraderie full of mystery with the dead comrades — is the bridge toward the historical/spiritual conquest of the Great War."[92]

We must take seriously this Heideggerian theme of spiritual struggle, conceived of as taking over where the military war leaves off. In certain respects we are always in that situation. Indeed, the most recurrent theme in Heidegger's speeches, lectures, and, as we shall see, his courses, is struggle (*Kampf*), which for him is at once actual war (*Krieg*) and spiritual struggle. When military struggle coincides with the overwhelming victory of the armies of the German Reich, Heidegger elevates military victories to the rank of a metaphysical trial by ordeal, in which the essence of the peoples and their historical destiny is played out. This will be the case, as we shall see, in the courses of June 1940, at the moment when the armies of the Reich rush into France.[93] When on the contrary Heidegger must face defeat, he maintains that war decides nothing. That is what he proposes in 1934, in connection with the German defeat of 1918. "The war has in its immediate end not yet brought any decision,"[94] and that is what he will maintain again, after 1945, in *What Is Called Thinking?*[95]

I will not dwell on the rather comical nature of that sanctification of effectiveness, which varies according to the occasion: ready to express itself on the most concrete plane when the historical event is favorable, ready on the contrary to move to another plane, called "spiritual" (but we have seen how Heidegger himself defines spirit) when the winds of history shift. What it is important to stress at this point is that Heidegger never drew any lessons from the fact that in 1945 it was a question not, as in 1918, of the outcome of a war between nations but of the military defeat of the Hitlerian and Nazi domination of Europe, which was revealed to be the enterprise of destroying the Jewish people, of massacring Slavic populations and of enslaving prior to progressively annihilating all non-*völkisch* peoples — including in France. On this point, which is in reality at the center of his doctrine, there would be no turning, no *Kehre*. After 1945 Heidegger continued, as he had done after 1918, to transpose a struggle that had been lost in the military theater of action onto the plane of the "spirit" or the "word."

The ease with which he succeeded in executing that transposition, the absence — almost total for an extended period — of resistance to this new circumstance, particularly in France, leads one to raise a number of questions about the lack of reflection that followed the Nazi capitulation of 1945. In any case, the way Heidegger evolved during the 1920s and 1930s after the German defeat of 1918 is full of helpful information for us in trying to understand how he and his most committed followers — beginning with Ernst Nolte — would behave after 1945. That is why an in-depth study of the years 1933–1935 not only makes it possible to appreciate how deeply compromised he was but turns out to be indispensable for an understanding of the strategy he adopted later on.

The Secret Germany, "Veneration," and Hitler's Triad of Poet, Thinker, and Political Action

The resignation from the rectorship of 23 April 1934, which was connected, as Hugo Ott has demonstrated, to Heidegger's radicalism and that of his disciple Erik Wolf, marks by no means the end of Heidegger's public activities in the service of Hitler's *Führung* but, on the contrary, its "deepening." Heidegger henceforth has time to produce lectures and texts that are much more elaborated, such as the lectures of 15 and 16 August 1934 on "The

German University," the text on "The Instituting of a School of Professors" in the new Reich, sent on 29 August of the same year to Dr. Stuckart, and the lecture of 30 November 1934 on "The Present State and Future Task of German Philosophy."

We now know that the attempt at self-justification of 1945 is nothing but a string of falsehoods. Heidegger claims that from 1934 on he no longer had a hand in the affairs of the university.[96] In fact, at the request of Secretary of State Wilhelm Stuckart, a high dignitary of the party close to Hitler and Himmler and the first president of the German Association for Racial Hygiene, he agreed to participate in the constitution of a new school of professors of the Reich. There was even question of his taking over its direction personally.

Now, Heidegger wrote in 1945 that after 30 June 1934, "anyone who accepted a position in the direction of the university could know unequivocally with whom he was dealing."[97] In submitting his project for the institution of that new Academy of Professors to the ministry, he indeed did know with whom he was continuing to deal.[98]

The lectures of August 1934 on "The German University" show no weakening of his commitment. Heidegger begins by asserting: "Our present-day Germany is swept by a great upheaval that is taking hold of the entire historical existence of our people. We see the beginning of this upheaval in the National Socialist revolution."[99]

Then Heidegger gives a historical summary of the foundation of the German university and its development in the nineteenth century in which its vocation and role are overrated. In his view, if we consider not the external image but the "intimate essence" of the German university, its history is that of the German spirit, which coincides with the destiny of the German people.[100] If we add to that the fact that Heidegger considers the philosophy faculty to be "the milieu that bears and determines the new university,"[101] we can see more clearly why he considers himself to be the repository of the "spiritual" *Führung* and destiny of the German people. It is a question not only of personal pride but, on the collective level, of a nameless disaster, because the "mission" (*Sendung*) that Heidegger intends to define for the German people is identified with "work" and "honor" as Nazism conceives of them. In the outline he provides, it is the three ideas of work, honor, and mission (*Arbeit, Ehre, Sendung*) that allow the people, through the state, to elevate itself to "knowledge" and "science."[102] Doubtless what Heidegger condenses here is the teaching that he dispensed in 1933–1934 in a seminar on "The People and Science," apropos of which he cannot refrain from reminding us in 1945 that it was very popular (*stark besucht*).[103] Heidegger espouses the ideas of Nazism theorized by Hitler and Jünger (on work) and Rosenberg (on honor). He takes up in particular the speech on "the worker of the fist" and the "worker of the head,"[104] a long-standing commonplace in Hitler's speeches.[105]

Nevertheless, Heidegger adds to work and honor the idea of "veneration," *Ehrfurcht,* derived from honor (*Ehre*), and defines it in terms of his own existentials, such as "the care [*Sorge*] of nobility and the resoluteness of the essence" of the people. This "care of the historical determination of the people" remains, he says, a secret (*Geheimnis*), which remains hidden (*verborgen*) and watched over by the people.[106] These determinations appear at the same time that he is relating being to what is hidden and veiled, and truth to what is unveiled (*Unverborgenheit*), in his course on Plato's cave allegory. Heidegger takes up the theme of "hidden Germany" (*geheimes Deutschland*)[107] from the circle of Stefan George and Norbert von Hellingrath's lectures on Hölderlin, but he does so in order to make them into the very origin of "truth" and the most intimate determination of the essence of the German people.

What Heidegger intends to found is neither a philosophy nor a way of thinking but rather the secret cult and veneration of the German people for its hidden essence. There is in this no taking up of a distance with respect to National Socialism. Indeed, Heidegger is nourished from the occult depths of Nazism. For the essence in question is "the essence of the National Socialist revolution," conceived as "the transformation [*Verwandlung*] of the German reality."[108] When he evokes "the secret Germany" that continued to live at the beginning of the nineteenth century, despite "the political powerlessness" (*politische Ohnmacht*) of the German nation in the face of the victories of Napoleon, Heidegger recalls the creation of the word *Volkstum,* which is itself linked to the word *Volksgeist,* conceived in its "natural and historical essence." He writes: "The natural and historical essence of the spirit of the people [Volksgeist], not the rules of mere understanding and not the calculations of a free-floating universal reason, determined the essence of man. It was then also, and not by accident, that the word *Volkstum* arose. This new knowledge and will applied necessarily also to the state. . . . The state was intuited in advance as a living order and a law, in and by which the people itself won its unity and the assurance of its duration."[109]

This text of Heidegger's, the beginning of which is very close to the report against Hönigswald already quoted, is reminiscent of the developments published a little earlier by Rothacker in his *Philosophy of History* on the "reduction of existence to the *Volkstum* and the race." Heidegger does not have to go any further: The reference to the *Volkstum* and to honor — and all the National Socialists know, since Rosenberg, that it is identified with the myth of the blood — suffice to give us an idea of the tenor of the "veneration" Heidegger speaks to us about.

In reconstituting in his own way the history of the German university, and in placing himself beneath the sign of the secret Germany, Heidegger takes up a position on the plane of long duration: he is no longer at that time (August 1934) in immediate involvement but dreams of the perennial Hitlerian state. Just as he would say in his introduction to the following winter's seminar, titled *Hegel, on the State,*[110] so here the realization of a "new higher school of the spirit"[111] cannot, in his view, be accomplished immediately, but "perhaps in 50 years."[112] There follows a defense of "greatness" including praise of the Führer. Thus we see where the Heideggerian veneration is leading us: veneration for what is said to be "great": today the cult of the Führer, tomorrow the cult of the very person who celebrates the cult. Indeed, "he who truly wishes to see what is great must himself have greatness."[113] Thus the pathos of "greatness" and the chain of veneration can be extended to become nonnegligible factors in the favorable reception and eventual cult of the "master" from Meßkirch. One thinks, for example, of the words chosen by Elfride Heidegger in speaking to Frédéric de Towarnicki of her husband: *Er ist zu groß* (He is [just] too great).

As for the new university of the spirit projected by Heidegger — which in his view constituted the task of the German university both present and future — its role was clearly defined. *"The education of the people, by the state, for the people* — such is the meaning of the National Socialist movement; such is the essence of the new state education. An education *of such a kind,* leading to the highest level of knowledge, is the task of the new university."[114]

Once again, the fact that Heidegger has no intention of affirming the autonomy of the university vis-à-vis the "movement" — that is, the party — and vis-à-vis the state is corroborated. On the contrary, this new education is conceived of as a political education. The unpublished seminar of winter 1933–1934 will confirm this.

I will not go over in great detail the last, long lecture of the year 1934, delivered on 30 November, on "The Present State and Future Task of German Philosophy," since its themes are close to the courses of the same year, and they will be studied in the next chapter. I will only bring out two major elements of its conclusion. The first is an astonishing sentence in which the state is identified with historical being, and the people with individual being. Heidegger writes: "A state *is* only while it *becomes, becomes the historical being* of individual being, which is called the people."[115]

On reading this sentence when the volume appeared in 2000, I was profoundly struck at seeing the ontological difference between being and individual being — which is always presented as the heart of Heidegger's "doctrine" and always kept carefully at a distance from any relationship to politics by his apologists—placed here by Heidegger in a relationship parallel to that of the state to the people. Since then, I have found in the unpublished seminars of winter 1933–1934 the developed confirmation of what is expressed here in only one instance. This sheds an entirely new light on the intimate relationship (not to say identification) between ontology and politics in Heidegger.

The other major point is that Heidegger concludes his lecture with a quotation from Hölderlin that evokes the fatherland (*das Vaterland*) and presents the poet as "the most German of Germans" (*das Deutscheste der Deutschen*).[116] Veneration for the essence of the secret Germany passes through the cult of Hölderlin, elevated since Hellingrath to the rank of poet and prophet of the *geheimes Deutschland*.

Finally, Heidegger introduces the triad that is found in the course given the same semester on "Germania" and "The Rhine": *Poetry, Thought, and the Political Action of the Creator of the State* (*Dichten, Denken, politische Tat*).[117] In thus placing within a continuous series the poet, the thinker, and political action, Heidegger Nazifies the traditional vision of Germany as the people of poets and thinkers. In so doing he is textually following Hitler, who, we must remember, concluded *Mein Kampf* with the evocation of poets (*Dichter*) and thinkers (*Denker*) as leading to action (*Tat*).[118] Heidegger's triad is thus the exact repetition of Hitler's.

4

The Courses of 1933–1935: From the Question of Man to the Affirmation of the People and the German Race

The recent publication of the courses from the years 1933–1934 radically enhances our ability to perceive the true nature of Heidegger's work.[1] What we discover is that his Nazi commitment was not limited to a few occasional speeches but deeply permeated the teaching he dispensed to his students. Beneath the philosophical-sounding titles of his courses (an impression reinforced at present by the division into paragraphs introduced by editors), it is really the very tenor of Nazism that erupts at the heart of his doctrine. The first course, from the summer semester of 1933, is titled *The Fundamental Question of Philosophy*, the second, from the winter semester of 1933–1934, *The Essence of Truth*, and the third, from the summer semester of 1934, *Logic*. But the "fundamental question" that motivates Heidegger in the first course is none other than the one the German people asks itself, in the supposed grandeur of its historical instant and metaphysical destiny. The following course is about showing that man is essentially political and that Hitler's worldview brings with it a radical mutation of the essence of man. In the course on logic, again it is mainly a question of the German people seen in its historical essence and its relation to the state. In short, as in the lectures and seminars of the same period, the ideas pertain primarily to the people and the state but also include the racial conception of the German people, which Heidegger specifically embraces, championing, in opposition to a "biologism"

Heidegger among Nazi rectors come to lend their support to Hitler at the Leipzig Conference of 11 November 1933.

that he characterizes as "liberal," an alliance of blood and spirit that is also found in Baeumler and even Rosenberg.

Furthermore, we can identify as a leitmotif running through these three courses the very distinctive way in which Heidegger develops the question "What is man?" — borrowed from Kant, but radically transformed. Here we witness not a true challenge to this question, but its perversion, by means of an explicit and deliberate shift of the interrogation from man to the self-affirmation of the German people and race—with Heidegger ringing the changes on the words *Rasse, Stamm,* and *Geschlecht,* which all belong to the current vocabulary of Nazi anti-Semitism.

This review may seem harsh, but it is certainly less so than the violence of these courses. In any event it appears indispensable that we familiarize our-selves with the content of courses that are unfortunately crucial to our under-standing of "the path" traced out by Heidegger, especially since they will probably not be translated into French for a long time.[2] The attention given to their content will show us that the Heideggerian shifting of the question "What is man?" to the question "Who is man?" — the passage from the *quid* to the *quis* or from the *Was* to the *Wer*—constitutes not a liberation of thought with respect to the metaphysics of essence for the purpose of obtaining an existential and more authentic understanding of man but rather the passage from the *I* to the *we,* and from the individual to the people.

The ipseity advocated by Heidegger, from section 74 of *Being and Time* to the recently published courses of the years 1933–1934, is the ipseity of the people, and, as it happens, of the German people. The "great transformation of the existence of man" to which he summons the German people,[3] and which he also calls the "total transformation" (*Gesamtwandel*), is in reality quite simply "reeducation in the direction of the National Socialist world-view" of which, he says "our Führer speaks to us continually at present."[4] To pass over this in silence would be tantamount to refusing to take into account the most explicit intention of Heidegger himself.

The Völkisch *Transformation of the Question of Man in the Spring Semester Course of 1933*

Heidegger's reservations with respect to the reduction of philosophy to anthropology are well known. They are expressed in 1927 in section 10 of the work on *Kant and the Problem of Metaphysics,* and in a particularly detailed way that same year, at the beginning of the course on German idealism.[5] The still unpublished lecture of 24 January 1929 should also be mentioned because it expresses very well, in its title, "Philosophical Anthropology and Meta-physics of Existence," the distinction on which Heidegger's words focus.[6]

In his debate with Kant, Heidegger wants to show that the question "What is man?" taken from Kant's *Logic* should be construed not as an inquiry that places the essence of man at the foundation of metaphysics but as the sign of the finitude of existence and the necessity of proceeding from the question of man to the question of being, and to what Heidegger calls from 1929 on the "struggle for being."[7] During the years 1933–1934 (and even during a longer period that could extend up to the composition of the *Beiträge zur Philoso-phie*), the struggle, the *Kampf* for being, far from consisting in a binary philo-sophical struggle opposing man and being, in reality includes a third term that will reveal itself, in certain of Heidegger's courses, as much more central than the two others. This third term is the *Volk,* the people, and even quite ex-plicitly *das deutsche Volk,* the German people. In short, Heidegger takes up the struggle for the meaning of being in the name of what he will designate, in the *Beiträge zur Philosophie,* as the "*völkisch* principle." In the courses from the 1930s, it is not a philosophical thought of being that we find but an explicit and resolute endorsement of the National Socialist struggle for the grandeur and primacy of *das deutsche Volk,* the German people.

When only a few official political pronouncements, such as the openly *völ-kisch* speeches of November 3, 10, and 11 were available, one could still, perhaps, though not without considerable self-delusion, try to maintain that these proclamations, identifying the German reality with the Führer and with him alone, represented a political commitment distinct from the philosophical work — although it would have been necessary, in doing so, to explain what philosophical principle justified Heidegger's having been able to identify, in these texts, the "return to the essence of being" with the unconditional alle-giance of the German people to Hitler's *Führung.* Today, however, we discover that he was not satisfied with expressing before his students his radical alle-giance to the Hitlerian movement but wanted to drag philosophy as a whole into that commitment, in such a way that for anyone following him in his "decision" (his *Entscheidung*), no indignation, no revolt of the spirit, was subsequently possible.

Let us first consider the course of summer semester 1933. Given in May–June 1933, when Heidegger assumes almost simultaneously the functions of rector of the University of Freiburg and membership in the NSDAP, the course begins by evoking "the grandeur of the historical moment" in which "the German people in its entirety comes to itself" — that is, finds its *Führung.*[8] Such is its "spiritual-*volklich* mission." For Heidegger, the fundamental question of philosophy is simply the question that the German people ask themselves, and that finds its first formulation in the question "Who are we?" (*Wer sind wir?*). This course tends to confirm what we could already anticipate in reading section 74 of *Being and Time* — namely, that the question of being and the political question of the destiny of the German people are but one and the same. And indeed, what is at issue here? It is about "taking stock of the present political situation of the German people,"[9] in affirming that if "philosophy is the questioning and incessant struggle for the essence of the being of the individual being," then "this questioning is in itself historical, i.e., it is what a people — in the name of the harshness and clarity of its destiny — requires, quarrels over, and venerates."[10]

This is not rhetoric devoid of concrete focus. At the end of the course, Heidegger will attack those of his contemporaries who, he says, "in our present existence as a state" believe it is enough for them to carry the insignia of the NSDAP (*Parteiabzeichen*) and that "everything be called National Socialist" (*alles jetzt nationalsozialistisch hießt*), while hoping everything will return to the way it was before. They have not understood that if "the new German state is not yet here, we desire and we shall create it."[11] Such is, for Heidegger, who intentionally assimilates all of philosophy to Nazi politics, what he calls the "metaphysics of the German people identified with its "destiny." "We are a people who must *first conquer* its metaphysics and *will* conquer it, which means that we are a people who still has *a destiny*."[12]

The author is careful not to clarify what he means by the "metaphysics" of the German people. In reality, with this course of spring 1933, a new usage of the word "metaphysics" begins — a singularly distorted usage that will continue to be used until the beginning of the 1940s and that, as the courses on Nietzsche show, has more to do with power than thought. Although he titled his course *The Fundamental Question of Philosophy*, we can see that for Heidegger it is neither a question about man nor a question about being per se, but the question that the German people is summoned to ask itself through the National Socialist "revolution," as dramatized by Heidegger. From the outset, philosophy is considered from the angle of a *we* that is none other than the German people. From the outset, philosophy's function is to address, in a privileged, or even an exclusive way, the German people alone. All others but this originally German man are excluded from the *we*. The political/spiritual and, following his expression, "spiritual/*volklich*" inquiry that the German people addresses to itself about its history and destiny is at the same time a question about its being, and even about being tout court, since henceforth being is always *our* being. Thus Heidegger goes so far as to write: "*That* question, through which our people rides out its historical destiny, enduring it through danger, holding it high in the greatness of its mission — that question *is its philosophizing, its philosophy.*"[13]

But Heidegger doesn't stop here. His intent is not only to define the philosophizing of the German people, a highly problematic notion, since it is not widely assumed that peoples are in the business of philosophizing, and even less so one particular people rather than another: he unflinchingly identifies philosophy as such with that question! Thus he writes: "Philosophy is the question about the law and structure of our being."[14] Such is, then, for him, philosophy's fundamental question: the one that bears on the being of the German people, the one, he says, that people, qua *our* people, puts to itself.

We can therefore infer from these texts that the question of being has become, in Heidegger's teaching, beginning in 1933, explicitly a *völkisch* question: it concerns exclusively the being of the German people and arises only with respect to this people.

That national and *völkisch* inveiglement of philosophy has something unbearable about it. And the most serious problem is not that Heidegger personally belonged to the Nazi Party, to the Hitlerian movement and doctrine: it is that he purposely tried to take the whole of philosophy down with him and to compromise it radically in that unconditional allegiance to Nazism and Hitlerism, or to what he calls, as one did at the time, the *völkische Bewegung.*

The essence of the 1933–1934 courses can be reduced to the same truly obsessional leitmotif: the identification of all contemporary philosophy with the questioning and the decision (*Entscheidung*) of the German people about its history, its destiny, and its being. Henceforth, this conception of *Entscheidung* — so laden with connotation since it has been thematized by such Nazi theoreticians of constitutional law as Carl Schmitt, but also by such "National Bolsheviks" as Ernst Niekisch, or yet again by Oswald Spengler, during that same year, 1933, in his *Jahre der Entscheidung,* in which he depicts what he calls the world struggle of the white race — will be present, as either a noun or a verb, on almost every page of Heidegger's courses. Let us be clear: that *Entscheidung* has absolutely nothing to do with a reflective choice calling for individual free will but, as Heidegger says, a resolve and a struggle to confront the "hardness and darkness of our German destiny and of the German calling."[15]

The Teaching of Descartes in German Universities, Reduced by Heidegger to a "Spiritual Degeneration"

It is within the framework of this course, between two developments devoted to the destiny of the German people in the new National Socialist state still "in the process of becoming," that Heidegger proceeds to a rather brief presentation of modern metaphysics from Descartes to Hegel. A ten-page section is devoted to Descartes. It consists in a virulent denunciation of the philosopher, challenging what he calls the latter's inauguration and meta-physics of *self*. If the "destruction" of the ontology of the *cogito sum* that was announced in *Being and Time* is undertaken in this course, we must recognize that there is nothing philosophical about it. These pages merit our attention because in them we can see with particular clarity the identity of the adversary Heidegger intends to destroy, Descartes — and through him all philosophy committed to defending human individuality and the human spirit understood as intellect and reason. The paragraph begins with a long diatribe in which the teaching of Descartes in German universities is presented as an unequivocal sign of a "spiritual dissolution" and "lack of thought," for which the instruc-tors are responsible by their laissez-faire attitude: "Descartes . . . with his generalized doubt and at the same time his 'accent' placed on the *I* is the most popular and usual object of the supposedly philosophical examinations and written evaluations in the German universities. This practice, which has been common for decades, is but *one* sign, but an unequivocal one, of the lack of thought and the irresponsibility that have thus been propagated. This spiritual dissolution of the students and examining authorities would not have taken place if the instructors had not themselves perpetrated and permitted it."[16]

This clearly indicates that the teaching of Descartes must disappear from the German universities. It is, moreover, what Heidegger himself put in practice after 1930. Between 1919 and 1930, besides the 1923–1924 course I have mentioned, he devoted four seminars to Descartes. The first, taught at Freiburg during the summer semester of 1919, is titled *Introduction to Phenomenology in Its Relation to Descartes;*[17] the second, which was held during the winter semester of 1920–1921, is titled *Phenomenological Exercises for Beginners in Relation to Descartes's* Meditations;[18] the third, with a similar title, was held in Marburg during the summer semester of 1924; the fourth and last took place at Freiburg in 1929–1930: *On Certainty and Truth According to Descartes and Leibniz.*[19] After 1930, Heidegger will never again devote a course or seminar explicitly to Descartes or to an author who is not either German or Greek.[20] Furthermore, beginning in May 1933, he adopts, by his anti-Cartesian diatribe, the position that will be that of the most radical Nazis throughout the 1930s, culminating in 1938 in Franz Böhm's *Anti-Cartesianismus.*

In the 1933 course, the entire tenth paragraph deals with Descartes and is titled: "The Metaphysics of the Modern Period and Its Apparent New Begin-ning with Descartes." After the diatribe already quoted, Heidegger begins by abruptly asserting his thesis: "I affirm that 1. The radicalism of the Cartesian doubt and the rigor of the new foundations of philosophy and of knowledge in general are an illusion and consequently the source of disastrous delusions that are now difficult to eradicate. 2. This so-called new beginning of the philosophy of the modern period with Descartes not only does not exist but is in truth the beginning of a further fundamental decline of philosophy. Descartes does not bring philosophy back to itself, to its foundation and soil, but thrusts it even further away from the questioning of its basic question."[21]

In support of this condemnation, Heidegger develops a lengthy rejection. First, he reproaches Descartes for presupposing that the philosophical method of questioning and reasoning is the "mathematical" one. That assertion will recur like a leitmotif, without Heidegger's ever specifying exactly what he means by it. There is obviously no study of the Cartesian distinction between the analytic way and the synthetic or geometric one, nor any consideration of the fact that for Descartes it is not the geometrical method or the order of deduction that is the most suitable in metaphysics, but the analytic way, or the order of discovery, the analysis showing "the true way by which a thing has been methodically discovered."[22]

Second, and in perfect continuity with *Being and Time,* Heidegger does not forgive Descartes for setting out from the *I* or *me* of man and not from his *self.* In other words, the return to the *I* is only an illusion of radicalness: there is no consideration of whether the *self* of man may not be something more original than the *I.* In short, Heidegger criticizes Descartes for having determined the essence of the *I* as consciousness (*Bewußtsein*), thus missing "the historicity of man and his essential bond with his being-in-common."

Behind this philosophically unclear distinction between the *I* and the *self* of man, which takes on a certain meaning — but a particularly problematic one — only to the extent that the *self* is identified with the community, the *Gemeinschaft,* Heidegger criticizes Descartes for having conceived of man on the basis of his individual conscience and not on that of the existence of the historical community of the people. Heidegger goes so far as to speak of the "historically and spiritually deprived nature of the Cartesian *I*"! How can it be maintained that the *mens humana* — that is, the human mind — is "deprived of spirit"? In reality, Heidegger uses the word "spirit" in a sense that no longer has anything philosophical about it.

To those who pretend that one must "spiritualize the National Socialist revolution," Heidegger responds that first one must know what spirit is: that it should be understood neither as "an endless agitation of analysis and decomposition by the understanding" nor as "the unbridled activity of a form of reason that claims to be universal." Indeed, "spirit has for a long time been breath, wind, storm [*Sturm*], commitment, and resolve. Today we have no need to spiritualize the great movement of our people. Spirit is already there."[23]

This text of Heidegger's is very important. The identification of spirit with storm or attack (two possible ways to translate the word *Sturm*) is a clear indication that the Heideggerian usage of the word "spirit" no longer has anything to do with philosophy or metaphysics. It is common knowledge that the term *Sturm* was used by the Nazis to designate their assault divisions "storm troops" (*Sturmabteilung*), or SA. Heidegger himself had already used the word in a philosophically indefensible translation of Plato, on which he had concluded his rectoral address.[24]

Let us note in passing that the interpretation of Jacques Derrida, who wanted to see in the Heideggerian "spirit" a remnant of metaphysics,[25] is contradicted here by Heidegger himself. Far from continuing the movement of modern metaphysics, Heidegger radically opposes all modes of universalistic thought, as well as all recognition of the individual value of human spirit, and therefore of the whole of modern philosophy as developed on the basis of Descartes. That same interpretation maintained that Heidegger wanted to spiritualize National Socialism.[26] Now, Heidegger says precisely the opposite: the spirit is already there, for "us" who can seize "German history" in its historical instant and "the greatness of the beginning of our spiritual/*volklich* existence."[27] This *volklich* "spirit" is part and parcel of the commitment of the German people to the Nazi "revolution." There is therefore no reason to want to "spiritualize" the National Socialist "revolution."

Finally, Heidegger reproaches Descartes for having identified the subject with the *I*, for having conceived of the *ego cogito* as a *subjectum*.[28] This point is at the beginning of the subsequent developments that can be found, much more amply, seven years later, in 1940, in the course on Nietzsche, *European Nihilism*, in which Descartes's first philosophy is reduced to a metaphysics of "subjectivity." But that terminology, to which Heidegger's influence has too quickly accustomed us, is not without its problems. Indeed, never in the *Meditations* does Descartes use the word *subjectum* to refer to the *mens humana* or the *res cogitans*.[29] It is in fact Thomas Hobbes who introduced the term *subjectum* in his objections to the *Meditations*, apropos of what thinks,[30] and Descartes expressed the greatest of reservations on that usage, esteeming it too "concrete" a term to designate unequivocally the *res cogitans*.[31] One cannot, then, speak, apropos of Descartes, of a "metaphysics of the subject" without doing violence to his most explicit terminological choices. The presentation of the first paragraphs of the summer semester course of 1933 allows us to conclude that Heidegger, in attacking Descartes, is not engaging in serious philosophical reflection but only manifesting a radical hostility on principle, which stems from the fact that Descartes, in basing his argumentation on the *I* and on consciousness, can only be an obstacle in the way of asking the "basic question" of "philosophy," according to Heidegger, which bears on the German people in its historical destiny and "decision" in the "movement" that leads it to create the new German National Socialist state.

Heidegger's Racism and His Critique of Biology in the Winter Semester Course of 1933–1934

While the preceding course was relatively brief (given in May and June 1933, it was probably shortened due to the duties required of Heidegger upon entering his new function as rector), the winter semester course of 1933–1934, titled *The Essence of Truth,* is much more developed, being the reworking, though radically transformed, of an earlier course on the cave allegory. In this course Heidegger will identify, in paragraph 29, the question of the essence of truth with that of the "history of the essence" of man (*Wesensgeschichte des Menschen*).[32] This presupposes, according to him, the transformation of the question of man: one no longer asks, as did Kant and after him the entire philosophical anthropology that claims him as their ancestor, "What is man?" (*Was ist der Mensch?*) but "Who is man?" (*Wer ist der Mensch?*)[33]

How is this transformation to be interpreted? It does not demarcate the abandonment of the vocabulary of essence. Heidegger continues to speak of the essence (*Wesen*) of man. That essence, however, no longer resides in a possible definition of man but in the "decision" about oneself, by the knowledge that "man is a *self*," and that in that "decision" it is of his being that it is questioned. In the same page in which Heidegger thus poses the question "*Who* is man?" he again takes up the existentials of *Being and Time* to identify that being of man with care, but to add that on that foundation of being as care, man is not only a historical essence but also a *political* one (*ein politisches Wesen*). This political essence of man is not in the least reducible to a repetition of the classical definition of man by Aristotle. It resides in the struggle for "*the great transformation of the existence of man*,"[34] a struggle in which the adversary is identified in the writings of Heidegger of the 1930s, now as the *Asiatic* (and we cannot overlook the very precise use the National Socialists made of this term at the time), now as "liberalism," a liberalism that can, according to him, go so far as to pervert the National Socialist revolution itself. Indeed, Heidegger says that he fears a "liberal National Socialism"![35] This point is key. It is similar, but in a still more radical way, to the exaggerated language that is found, for example, in Jünger, in a text from 1930 titled *On*

Nationalism and the Jewish Question, in which he criticizes Mussolini's fascist state as still being nothing more, according to him, than a condensed form of liberalism![36] In this same text, Jünger does not hesitate to advocate seeing the figure of the Jew separate from the authentic German figure (*Gestalt*), just as one can see an oil slick stand out distinctly on still, clear water.[37]

It remains to be shown, however, precisely what constitutes this "liberalism" whose aftermath Heidegger still finds in the Nazi movement. Let us be clear, first, that there is in these courses no critique of Nazism as such, nor of Hitlerism; quite to the contrary, their author underlines and justifies the radicalness of the Führer's words. In fact, he teaches his philosophy students: "When the Führer speaks continually of reeducation in the direction of the National Socialist worldview, that does not mean — inculcate some slogans — but rather — bring about a *total transformation, a worldwide blueprint,* on the foundation of which he educates the entire people. National Socialism is not just any teaching but the fundamental transformation of the German and, as we believe, also the European world."[38]

In reading this justification of the National Socialist *Weltanschauung,* one cannot help but remember how Heidegger answered Cassirer in 1929. He affirmed that "philosophy does not have as its task to supply a worldview, but rather a worldview is the condition for the act of philosophizing."[39] In short, in that doctrine, philosophical thought is neither primary nor foundational: it *derives,* on the contrary, from a pre-given *Weltanschauung.*

In addition, in at least two instances in the winter course of 1933–1934, the critique of liberalism coincides with the critique of biology. It is vital that this point be clarified, for today, the Heideggerian critique of biology serves as a last bastion for those who, like Hartmut Tietjen, the editor of the course himself, deny Heidegger could ever have been a Nazi, since he critiqued biology. Unfortunately, this revisionist-oriented argument is untenable for at least two reasons. First, Heidegger does not decline to speak of race. He uses the terms *Rasse* and *Geschlecht* very explicitly in this same course. Far from rejecting them, he simply proposes that race should be thought of on the basis of existence (hence on that of his own analyses of existence), and no longer on the basis of what he disdainfully refers to as "liberal biology" (*liberalistische Biologie*).[40] This means, then, that Heidegger considers his own doctrine the only one equal to the task of founding the doctrine of race. In *Contributions to Philosophy* from 1936 to 1937, he will again speak, and in a similar fashion, simply reversing the noun-adjective relation, of a "biological liberalism" (*biologischer Liberalismus*).[41] Second, when Heidegger critiques biology, exactly what is he referring to with this term? Definitely not to the racial discrimination that is at the foundation of Nazism, but rather quite explicitly to a science that is not of German origin, since it is based on the Darwinian doctrine of life and therefore on what Heidegger calls "the liberal understanding of man and human society,"[42] in vigor in nineteenth-century British positivism.[43]

It is not, then, Nazism per se with its racial doctrine that is targeted by the Heideggerian critique of biologism; quite to the contrary. He is not saying anything different than does Ludwig Clauß in his quite limited critique of Hans K. Günther.[44] Moreover, it must be remembered that in *Being and Time* it is apropos of Georg Simmel that the biological approach to human life and death was challenged. In the winter semester course of 1933–1934, Heidegger, in the anti-Semitic context of those years, affirms unhesitatingly that that "liberal biology" comes from the same universe as the psychoanalysis of Freud and company, and Marxism[45] . . . and he goes on to make fun of a biological doctrine that does not allow for a true conception of German nobility, and which would on the contrary lead one to consider, he says, Prussian nobility (*Preußischer Adel*) no differently from the way one thinks of apples growing on a tree. Reading these pages, it is apparent that it is not discrimination against Jews that disturbs him: his concern is rather to preserve the superiority of Prussian nobility.

The occasional reservations expressed during these years by Heidegger with respect to the word *Rasse* are in reality the same as those formulated with respect to the word *Kultur*.[46] Heidegger uses the word *Rasse* sparingly, just as he avoids using what he calls Roman words, *römische Wörter*. But he frequently uses, and with no restrictions, the equivalent Germanic term *Geschlecht,* in contexts in which this word can only mean race,[47] and he is not reluctant to speak of *Stamm, Sippe,* and so on. As for the expression *Blut und Boden,* used on many occasions in the proclamations, speeches,[48] and even courses of the years 1933 and 1934, Heidegger's attitude is unequivocal: he always affirms, in this same course, the force and necessity of the terms "blood" and "soil" (*Blut und Boden sind zwar mächtig und notwendig*), while at the same time adding to them the terms "knowledge and spirit" (*Wissen und Geist*), knowledge being necessary, he writes, to orient the flow of blood (*das Strömen des Blutes*).[49]

Thus we see here — and this is paramount — that there is neither incompatibility nor opposition in Heidegger between the vocabulary of the blood and that of spirit, but a conjunction, not to say fusion, of the two. Moreover, we must bear in mind that the vocabulary of *Geist,* the words *geistig, Geistesleben,* and so on, belong to the pro-Hitler literature of the period just as much as the vocabulary of blood and race. In short, in this course of winter 1933–1934, to ask "Who is man?" is to ask "Who are we?" It is to decide in favor of what Heidegger calls "the fundamental possibilities of the essence of the originally Germanic root."[50] Faced with that "decision" that is presented as "radical," biologism, not being originally Germanic but of "liberal" origin, must henceforth give way to what he calls the "new German reality."

Given the semantic context of their Heideggerian usage, we see that the word "liberalism" and the adjective "liberal" refer, exactly as in the Nazi attacks of the era, both to Anglo-Saxon culture and to Jewish thought — whether it be politically, to the various forms of democracy, or "philosophically," in Heidegger, to the thought of the individual and of the *I*, in what he calls the *Ich-Zeit*.

The Völkisch *Identification of the People and the Race in the 1934 Summer Semester Course*

We now come to the examination of the third course of the years 1933–1934, that of the summer of 1934, titled *Logic as the Question of the Essence of Language*. Special attention must be given to its content. This is the text in which the central axis of Heidegger's doctrine — namely, his idea of the people — appears the most clearly. And this course, which was billed as an instruction on logic, was in fact explicitly addressed to the Germans and centered on the constant reference to the people.[51]

The course begins with a series of moves, some of which we have already seen. The question of logic leads to that of the essence of language, which leads in turn to raising the question "What is man?" The Heideggerian response to the question of man is not in the *I*, which is explicitly repudiated, but in the *we*.[52] This *we* is *the* people.[53] To the question "Who are we ourselves?" (*Wer sind wir selbst?*) Heidegger answers, "we are *the* people" (*Wir sind das Volk*); not primarily *a* people, but *the* people; we, qua existents, are this very people. "Our being-ourselves is the people."[54]

Then there begins in paragraph 14 a long investigation of the idea of the people, which will be envisaged in turn as body, soul, and spirit, without any of these three determinations being rejected.

But first of all Heidegger introduces and embraces, for his own part, a series of statements in which it is a question of the people.[55] And here once again, the untenable takes place: at the end of a string of apparently harmless sentences about song, dance, and popular festivals, about census-taking and measures to be taken to reestablish the health of the people (but we have already seen how, in those years, Heidegger envisaged the health of the people), the author unreservedly and uncritically brings up the action of the "*völkisch*" movement," which, he says, "desires to restore the people to its racial purity."[56] This adjective, *völkisch*, which Heidegger made his own in his three proclamations in favor of Hitler in November 1933, thus reappears in the course of summer semester 1934, *after* his resignation from the rectorate, and indisputably in the openly racist and Nazi sense that it has at that time.

Henceforth it will be impossible to deny that the racist use of the word *Volk* is accepted by Heidegger without the slightest reservation and from among the different acceptable senses, which, he argues, are connected by "a hidden unity" (*eine verborgene Einheit*).[57] Besides, Heidegger doesn't have to remind his listeners of his *völkisch* commitment: all his Freiburg students are obviously aware of his appeals favoring Hitler and his *völkisch* movement, launched and published six months earlier at the time of the November 1933 plebiscite. And if their memories needed refreshing, Heidegger's reminder in the following paragraph spelled it out for them. He again quotes a series of sentences illustrating the uses of the word "people" (*Volk*) among which are: "On 12 November 1933, the *Volk* was consulted."[58] And a bit further down on the same page: "By the plebiscite of 12 November 1933, the entire *Volk* was consulted."[59]

Such insistence in referring to that decisive date in the consolidation of Hitler's absolute power shows conclusively that Heidegger, after his resignation from the rectorate, never reconsiders either his unqualified commitment to the Führer and the *völkisch* movement or his grave responsibility in the adherence of the German people to the dictatorship of Hitler during that plebiscite.

Now, how can that "hidden unity" of the Volk be fathomed? Not by thinking of it as an "aggregate of men taken one by one."[60] Heidegger points to "another path": we are *here*, "integrated with the order and will of a state, we are *here*, integrated with what is happening today, in belonging to this *people*, we are this people itself."[61]

Thus Heidegger's words leave room for no possible retreat with respect to the historical actuality of the state and the German people in that year of 1934. The entire movement of the course is directed toward inducing its listeners to identify themselves resolutely with this "we" of the German people, who have obtained their harmony and unity from the order and will of the Hitlerian state. In short, what we find here is the "decision," the *Entscheidung* that will be a pivotal term in the course. Belonging to the people as a group is on the order of a "decision."[62]

Does this mean that it is a free decision of voluntary association expressed by isolated individuals? Far from it. As Heidegger clearly pointed out earlier, the unity of the *Volk* is the same thing as the order and will of the state. No latitude is given to the individual consciousness, the value and existence of which are totally denied.

Thus, "to exist," *Da-sein,* is to be *the* people, and this people, "we," are it, first, he says, as body. The determination of the people as body (*Volk als Körper*) is not at all rejected by Heidegger, but on the contrary assumed as self-evident.[63] He begins by repeating two "examples" already quoted: the one about census-taking and the one about the *völkisch* understanding of the word "people." In the census-taking of the people, only those who live within the borders of the state are counted: the Germans living outside the country (*die Auslandsdeutschen*) — the Sudeten Germans, for example, one might appositely add — are therefore not counted in the population census. In this sense, they are not part of the people. But, he adds: "On the other hand, among those included in the count there may be those who, considered in a *völkisch* way, are radically foreign, are not part of the people."[64]

Obviously, none of Heidegger's listeners can be unaware that those who were previously counted as Germans but henceforth, according to the *völkisch* construal of people, are no longer a part of the German people are the Jews.

The rest of the text shows specifically that it is not the point of view of the census that is, for Heidegger, the most authentic reality of the people, but the *völkisch* understanding of it. The census of the population is merely the calculation of the number of inhabitants.[65] The *völkisch* understanding of the people sees it quite otherwise, Heidegger reminds us, by identifying people with race. One could not be more explicit about the meaning of the word *völkisch* than Heidegger is: "We often use the word 'people' in the sense of 'race' as well (for example, in the expression '*völkisch* movement')."[66]

We must be particularly attentive to this use of "we," which removes all distancing. Heidegger does not say "one" (*man*), but indeed "we" (*wir*). Furthermore, he shows that he is perfectly aware of the fact that to use the word *völkisch* is to back the identification of people with race. He takes the same care to define the idea of race in these terms: "What we call 'race' [*Rasse*] has a relationship with what binds the members of a people to one another — according to their origin — by body and by blood."[67]

Thus the idea of race is in no way rejected, even if the word *Volk* is more essential to Heidegger's purposes than the word *Rasse,* doubtless because only the former is a *völkisch* word with a German root. And the use of the word *völkisch,* explicitly taken by Heidegger in the racist sense he recognizes in it, shows that he accepts a relationship of strong correlation, or even perhaps of identity, between the terms *Volk* and *Rasse.*

The reason we bring up these courses from the years 1933–1934 is not solely to show their radically pro-Hitlerian and *völkisch* tenor; it is also to ask whether there is the least bit of philosophy to be found in this "teaching." In the summer semester course of 1934, we see, still in the context of the question of man, two main ideas: besides that of the people, there is that of historicality. Thus Heidegger is revisiting a major "existential" from his 1927 work. But let us see in what terms.

After having covered more rapidly the people as soul and spirit, Heidegger affirms that "concepts such as 'people' and 'state' cannot be definitive, so to speak, but must be grasped as historical, as falling within the domain of a historical being."[68] We should, then, no longer ask "What is a people?" but "What is *this* people we ourselves are?"[69] This question falls within the domain of the resolute decision. It is an *Entscheidungsfrage*.

Heidegger allows no critical distance for thought, since the legitimacy of the individual consciousness is destroyed and the question is reformulated in such a way that it can only lead to resolute adherence to the German political reality of 1934. Thus, we can no longer speak of philosophical reflection here, which always assumes the legitimacy of critical thought, but of a true indoctrination of students.

To this must be added the examples he gives to back up his idea of historicality. After having identified man with the people and maintained that the people can be grasped only as history, he does not hesitate to affirm that there are, nevertheless, "men and groups of men who have no history."[70] Who are they? Well! he says, "negroes, the Kaffirs for example."[71] Let us note that here Heidegger does not speak, as in the Kassel lectures, of peoples without a history[72]: he no longer even uses the word "people," but only "groups of men." Inversely, he adds, history can come in by the medium of a nonhuman entity, such as the plane, for example, that carried the Führer from Munich to Venice to meet Mussolini. (The allusion is to Hitler's trip to Venice of 14 and 15 June 1934, in the course of which he tried to convince Mussolini to accept an early annexation of Austria by the German Reich.) Heidegger comments on this trip as follows: "When the plane takes the Führer from Munich to Venice, of course, history happens."[73]

In short, the Führer's plane, a technical artifact, can contribute to making history happen (to the point, Heidegger adds, that it can be placed as such in a museum), but not the Negroes and the Kaffirs . . .

There will be many other passages to be singled out in these various courses, as, for example, the elaborations on the "voice of the blood" (*Stimme des Blutes*),[74] or those on the "struggle against humanism."[75] We will have occasion to return, apropos of the relations between Heidegger and Carl Schmitt, to the long developments Heidegger devotes to war and struggle in his winter semester 1933–1934 course.[76] What we may conclude at this point, on the basis of these three courses, is that despite the constant references to philosophy and its "fundamental question," they contain no philosophical clarification of man. What we find, on the contrary, is the destruction of individual consciousness and an almost obsessive concern to replace the philosophical question of man with the politico-historical "decision" of a self-affirmation of the German people that is in reality nothing but a declaration of allegiance to Hitler's *Führung*.

Heidegger and Hölderlin: Being as Fatherland, the Hitlerian Triad, and the Swastika

The year 1934 is not a turning point in Heidegger's Nazi commitment, but a "deepening" and a projection toward the future. After his year of intense activity of the rectorate, followed by his contribution in the summer of 1934 to the setting up of an Academy of Professors of the Reich, Heidegger is no longer involved in immediate action but in the entrenchment and prolongation of the new Hitlerian state. In this endeavor he embraces the process of consolidation of the Nazi movement itself. In this respect, the course Heidegger dedicates for the first time to Hölderlin during the winter semester of 1934–1935 is perhaps the most radically Nazi one of all. The choice of Hölderlin is neither original nor the result of chance. Since the publication of Hölderlin by Norbert von Hellingrath and his two posthumous lectures,[77] Hölderlin tends to take Goethe's place as the poet of the Germans. Hellingrath saw in the Germans "the people of Hölderlin" and linked that vision to the theme of "secret Germany" (*geheimes Deutschland*)[78] — an expression I have found in Heidegger's lecture of 30 November 1934, in which Hölderlin is introduced at the end. The veneration of Hölderlin and secret Germany is cultivated with intensity by Stefan George and his circle. One thinks in particular of Max Kommerell, who came from this circle, was a friend and correspondent of Heidegger, and was the author, in 1928, of *The Poet as Führer*, or of Kurt Hildebrandt, who published *Hölderlin: Philosophy and Poetry* in 1939,[79] and who reappears in 1943 with Heidegger in the same Nazi collective work celebrating the centenary of Hölderlin's death and published by Serlot Editions, the spearhead of Paris collaborators.

But Heidegger wants to go further than Hellingrath, and if he does homage to him as a soldier fallen at Verdun in the dedication of his 1936 Rome lecture, "Hölderlin and the Essence of Poetry,"[80] he does not omit to criticize his interpretations in his course. This is because he furthers as much as he can the Nazi preempting of the poet and no longer follows Hellingrath when the latter, faithful to Hölderlin, accepts the juxtaposition of the gods of antiquity with Christ. Heidegger, on the contrary, tries to dim down Hölderlin's Christianity, just as he brushes aside his reference to Rousseau.[81]

Starting with the preliminary remark in the introduction to the course,

Heidegger declares that Hölderlin's work opens up "the beginning of a different history" for the Germans, which "begins with the struggle over the decision about the coming or the flight of the gods."[82] The theme of the "other beginning" that is found constantly in the courses, and even more in the posthumous works of the following years, is therefore already present as the introductory motif of this course in 1934–1935. This proves, despite what his publishers and apologists would have had people believe after the war, that the Heideggerian "other beginning" was definitely not introduced by him as an alternative to historical National Socialism but, on the contrary, to designate the movement that took hold of the German people in National Socialism.

Indeed, what are the dominant lines of Heidegger's interpretation of the two hymns titled "Germania" and "The Rhine"? The poet is invoked only as he who founds the existence of the people. It is the poets who, in their *saying,* "announce the future being of a people in its history."[83] But history, Heidegger adds, "is always the unique history in each case of this particular people, in this case the people of this poet" — namely, the poet Hölderlin — and therefore "the history of Germania."[84] It is the same question that recurs in all Heidegger's courses of these years of 1933–1935: the question of "us," of the people that "we" are. This "we" — the author specifies here, are "the Germans."[85] To the question "Who are we?" the Germans can answer only if they know what their time is — namely, that of the "people between peoples."[86] Thus there emerges the theme of the German people as the people of the middle, which will be central to the *Introduction to Metaphysics* of summer semester 1935. That postulated middle position of the German people is tied to a radical ontological privilege. Indeed, all the courses on "Germania" are directed toward the goal of identifying the German fatherland with being (*Seyn*) — henceforth written with a *y.* Heidegger goes so far as to maintain, in underlining it, that "the 'fatherland' is being itself"![87] In the course on "The Rhine," he similarly declares that by the poem, "enveloped in the word, unveiled being is placed in the truth of the people."[88] That identification of being with the fatherland, which is the continuation of the identification of being with the state in the unpublished seminar of winter 1933–1934, confirms that Heidegger's "ontology" is in essence a "politics."

In the last passage quoted, Heidegger intends to show that only the poem reveals to the people the power of its "destiny." Thus we see the Heideggerian conception of being and truth as one with his conception of the "destiny" of the German people. Further, we must consider in what terms Heidegger qualifies the word "destiny." He writes: "We must learn to use this essential German word as the naming of an essential being in its German bearing in an essential way, and that also means — seldom."[89]

In reality, Heidegger's writing hardly practices this recommended discretion in the use of a word as "essential" and as "German" as the word "destiny" (*Schicksal*). In certain pages of *Being and Time,* as in the courses of the 1930s, Heidegger cannot avoid the immoderate use of a word—a true *Schlagwort* or slogan of the LTI—that brings together everything he has to say about being, time, history, and politics.

In these pages of the course on Hölderlin there is thus a confirmation of the interpretation I have incrementally drawn from the lectures of 1925, and then from *Being and Time.* Heidegger declares frankly that "this being that is ours" —that is, the being of the German people—"is not the being of an isolated subject, but the historical being in common as being in a world."[90] And, "the fact that this being of man is in each case mine does not mean that this being is 'subjectivized,' reduced to the isolated individual, and determined on that basis."[91] In short, the existent, or *Dasein,* is never an individual, even in the experience of being-mine, and there is no other destiny than the one for the historical community of the people. Heidegger's clarifications confirm how profound the continuity is between his writings of the 1920s and his Nazi teaching of the 1930s.

In the course on Hölderlin, however, Heidegger goes further. The poet's *saga,* explicitly conceived of as "political," allows him to embed his teaching more than ever in the opaqueness of the occult underpinnings of Hitlerism and Nazism. Hölderlin is identified with "that hidden and latent thing": to be the "poet of poets qua poet of the German"; as such he has not yet, Heidegger says, "become the power in the history of our people,"[92] and "to contribute to it is 'politics' in the most authentic and highest sense."[93] It is up to the "thinker" — that is, to Heidegger himself, as he understands his role—to bring it about that Hölderlin's word becomes the active power in the history of the German people, and that he inspires the political action of the founder of the state. Heidegger takes up the Hitlerian triad of poetry, thought, and political action, just as it appears (in a moment of dramatic crescendo) in *Mein Kampf,* and as we have seen it evoked in the lecture of 30 November 1934, which was contemporaneous with this course. But while Hitler condensed this triad in the person of one sole inspirer, Dietrich Eckart, Heidegger distinguishes the three persons and forges the myth of a *völkisch* trinity of sorts: the poet of Germany is none other than Hölderlin; the creator of the state is quite obviously "the true and unique Führer"—that is, Hitler. As for the thinker, he is not named. Much later, in 1944, at which time he was be careful not to put himself forward as the spiritual inspirer of the Führer, Heidegger turned to Nietzsche to occupy this spot alongside Hölderlin. But here, it is quite clear that it is his own teaching that Heidegger has in mind as the work of the "thinker," in that he alone can bridge the gap between the poet and the statesman. In place of the name of Dietrich Eckart, an anti-Semitic "poet," a "thinker" of an obscure *völkisch* religiosity, but also a man of action, and a member, along with Rosenberg, of the Thule Society (*Thule Gesellschaft*), the matrix of the NSDAP, Heidegger substitutes three names: Hölderlin; implicitly Heidegger himself, the "thinker" and author of the course; and Hitler, the sole Führer.

But, in contradistinction from Hellingrath, for Heidegger it is a question of severing all ties between the new *völkisch* political mythology and Christianity. Thus he proposes that Hölderlin's return to his fatherland is not a return to Christianity.[94] In this connection, Heidegger lashes out against those who speak from the pulpit "of Christ as the Führer," which can be nothing, he says, but blasphemy.[95] This text has been interpreted by one apologist as challenging Hitler. To interpret it in that way is to be singularly inattentive to the text of the course, and little informed about the history of Germany. There were indeed such attacks at the time by Hermann Goering, aimed at the Catholic clergy, against those who spoke of Christ as of a celestial Führer. That was not to defend Christianity. For Goering, it was against the Führer that there was "blasphemy."[96] These attacks were contemporaneous with Heidegger's course, and they announced the circular decreed by Goering on 17 July 1935 ordering the ecclesiastics "to pronounce themselves in a positive manner for the National Socialist state."[97] We are, indeed, entering the period in which — after the euphoria of the Concordat in the most blinded German Catholic milieus, which allowed Hitler to neutralize the Catholic center (*Zentrum*) — the Nazi power began to tighten the vise sharply and to organize trials and deportations of priests who refused to yield.

In Heidegger's course, his attack against the assimilation of Christ to a Führer allows him to clarify how he conceives of the Führer: "The true and only Führer makes a sign in his being toward the domain of the demigods. Being the Führer is a destiny, and consequently finite being."[98]

The mythologizing of the Führer is openly assumed, since he becomes the one who makes signs toward the demigods. And the distinctive trait of the Führer is at once his unique character and his finitude. Like the *Gestalt*, which is evoked by Rosenberg in *The Myth of the Twentieth Century*[99] and by Jünger in *The Worker,* and which is characterized by its limits, it is finitude (which was at the center of Heideggerian doctrine since his book on Kant) that determines Heidegger's vision of the Führer here. For him, as for Jünger and Rosenberg, there is no creative power unless it finds its configuration in a destiny and figure that is delimited and finite. So it is that at the end of his course on Hölderlin, Heidegger affirms that the being of the demigods is delimitation and finitude.[100] That is the only thing that allows us to understand how the

Heideggerian "care" can, as he maintains,[101] be linked with "work" as it is conceived of by Jünger and the National Socialists. In Rosenberg, "that limitation [of the figure] is conditioned by race."[102] But what is true of Rosenberg is just as true — though expressed in a less trivial manner — of Jünger, who brings the worker back to "the law of race," and of Heidegger, who determines "work" on the basis of "*völkisch* existence." The "finiteness" of destiny and the community of the people or of *völkisch* existence is, in Heidegger, what opposes all thought of the universal, roots existence in the determination of a people and a race, and finds its highest configuration in the figure of a Führer.

But one must be particularly attentive to Heidegger's dexterity and malice as it is manifested in his "clarification" of Christ and the Führer. First let us consider his relation to Catholicism. Today we know his true feelings, especially by the letter he wrote to try to outlaw the Catholic student association Ripuaria, despite the Concordat.[103] But in his course on Hölderlin's hymns, instead of attacking the Catholics directly, he sends them back to their own dogma, reminding them that the idea of the Son being consubstantial with the Father, such as it has been defined in the Church since the Nicene Council, forbids the likening of Christ to the demigods and therefore to the Führer. He adopted a similar tactic in January 1939 against Max Müller. After having questioned his political reliability with respect to National Socialism in a report, he responds to Max Müller, who asks that he withdraw his attack because he is endangering his very existence: "As a Catholic, you must know that one must tell the truth."[104]

Furthermore, the way he evokes the Führer is no less clever. In the context of the times, to speak of the "true and unique Führer" can refer only to Hitler. Besides, at the beginning of the year 1935, Heidegger's allegiance to Hitler was still intact. The conversation with Karl Löwith in Rome the following year and the praise of the Führer in the 1936 course on Shelling are sufficient proof of that. But Heidegger probably no longer nourished his illusions (which he had during the period of the rectorate, when he was considering accepting a chair in Munich) of being able to approach Hitler personally and perhaps play a role comparable to that of Gentile toward the Duce. Yet far from giving up, using Hölderlin for support in this course and Hegel in the concurrent unpublished seminar, Heidegger presented himself as the only one equal to the task of "thinking" the future evolution of the people and the German state and thus of prolonging the movement, by projecting their future beyond the person of Hitler himself. In short, he claimed to be the one and only thinker of National Socialism and Hitlerism, and, in so doing, he also presented himself as he who, in a sense, went beyond them, so that he succeeded in both prolonging the movement in spirit and in giving the appearance of being distinct from it. It is this constant duplicity that was his strength and allowed him to last and to extend his influence well beyond 1945. Thus, in the course of the summer semester of 1935, he hailed "the internal truth and greatness" of the National Socialist movement, and in the summer semester of 1936 it was this time to the Führer and the Duce, to Hitler and Mussolini, that he explicitly paid homage, while at the same time affirming that they had not been able to think Nietzsche's metaphysics in all its "profundity."

But to evoke the finitude of the Führer in contrasting him with Christ also implies the opposition between the Christian cross and another cross, the extremities of which end in perpendicular lines: the swastika, adopted very early by Stefan George and designated by him as the "*völkisch* sign,"[105] which consequently became the distinctive sign of "secret Germany" before being taken up by Hitler. The most obscure and unsettling passage of the course on Hölderlin proposes a cryptic exegesis of a cross that in many ways resembles the swastika. This cross requires an axis, around which all the poetry gyrates: this will be the beginning of stanza X of the poem "The Rhine" by Hölderlin (in which the writing of the number doubtless already has symbolic value), quite precisely the first four verses, which bear on the knowledge and love we owe the demigods.[106] That thought of the demigods is, Heidegger declares, as he takes up the same representation, "the axis around which the entire poem turns."[107] Also, the "thought" that is played out there is the thought of a "superman," since "the superman and the demigods are the same thing."[108] Here, two opposite directions cross, for "to think the demigods means: beginning from the original middle, to think toward the earth and to think toward the gods."[109]

The cross of which Heidegger "makes a rough sketch" will be based on four words that he picks out in stanza IV of "The Rhine": birth (*Geburt*) — ray of light (*Lichtstrahl*) — distress (*Not*) — discipline (*Zucht*). Birth expresses "the pure origin" (*reinen Ursprung*) and the "ray of light is the zigzag of a flash of light."[110] While the words are indeed taken from Hölderlin's poem, in the context of a revealed secret that invites an esoteric reading, the cross is not there, and it is Heidegger who draws it, going so far as to propose a schema that is quite precisely that of the *Kruckenkreuz*:[111] the square cross, or "cross potent," which can be considered as either the origin or the combination of two antagonistic *Hakenkreuze*, or swastikas, one clockwise and the other counterclockwise. Heidegger draws the schema shown in Figure 1.[112]

So it is, for example, that Guido von List, one of the very first disseminators of the swastika in Germany along with Alfred Schuler and Lanz von Liebenfels, considers the *Kruckenkreuz* the most essential, in that it is the conjunction of both swastikas.[113] Here, we offer the explanatory schema proposed by

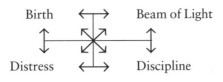

Figure 1.

Wilfried Daim on this topic, in his reference work on Lanz von Liebenfels (Figure 2).[114]

The chosen schema, as well as the words picked out and their commentary, lead one to think that Heidegger has taken on the role of the esoteric interpreter of the gestation and occult meaning of the swastika. The words *Geburt* and *Zucht* are key words in Hitlerism and the racial doctrine of Nazism. When Heidegger's former disciple and assistant Oskar Becker proposes, at the Congrès Descartes of Paris in 1937 (before re-exposing his theses in 1938 in the journal *Rasse*), a "metaphysics" of race, conceived in a relation both imitative of and oppositional to Heidegger's doctrine, it is on the word *Geburt* that he bolsters his argument.[115] As for the word *Zucht*, we find it exalted once more by Oskar Becker in 1942, the very year in which Heidegger, in a course on Nietzsche, links two terms immediately derived from *Not* and *Zucht*, not hesitating to maintain that "racial selection is metaphysically necessary."[116]

In the pages of Heidegger's course dedicated to the esoteric exegesis of that *Kruckenkreuz,*[117] we are far from any real philosophy, and we can understand even Max Kommerell's reproaching Heidegger, in a letter of 1942, for translating the esoteric poetry of Hölderlin "not into a public language, but into a new esoteric."[118] That murderous configuration does not lend itself to lightheartedness. The cross potent that, from the "purity" of origin passes through "distress" and necessity of discipline (*Zucht*) and selection to lead to the beam of light, tends toward the esoteric and murderous justification for racial selection (*rassische Züchtung*), which Heidegger will call "metaphysically" necessary in 1942, the same year that the "Final Solution" will be chosen. It is more than a little disturbing to see Heidegger subsequently succeed in reviving something of that configuration after the war, in the falsely pacified representation of the cross in the square of the *Geviert*, in which the same demarcation between the earth and the gods is decided.

It must be added that the racial meaning of the course on Hölderlin is explicit. The historical continuity between the Greeks and the Germans, a theme borrowed particularly from Hellingrath and George, but also from Rosenberg, is exacerbated by Heidegger in a radical sense. Using Hölderlin as his springboard, Heidegger evokes "the German race" (*das deutsche Ge-*

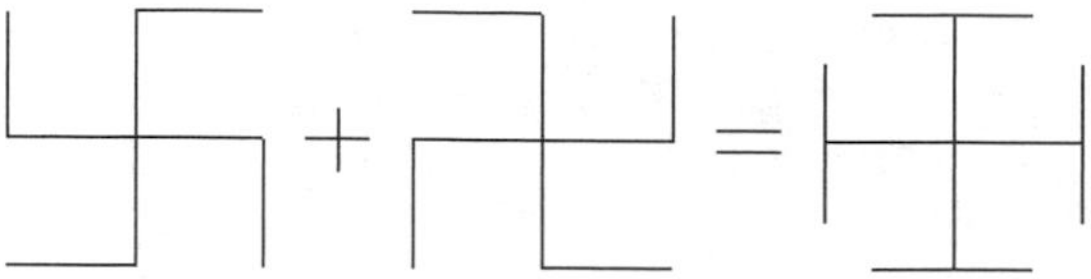

Figure 2.

schlect), supposedly originating in the East, somewhere in the neighborhood of a mythic Caucasia. Matching the "German race," Heidegger conceives of the Greeks as "a people of related race" (*ein stammverwandtes Volk*).[119] Now we can understand why, in his rectoral address, he was able to speak of the Greeks as a *volklich* people. If, in this *völkisch* mythologizing of history, the originator of German philosophy is, for Heidegger as well as Rosenberg, Meister Eckhart, Heidegger sees the original German power in Heraclitus! He writes: "The name Heraclitus is not the title of a philosophy of the Greeks long run dry, no more than it is the formula for universal humanity as such. In truth it is the name of an original power of Occidental-Germanic historical existence, and it is such in its first confrontation with the Asiatic."[120]

This Germanizing of Heraclitus has no historical basis. It can spring only from a mind won over to the racial mythology of Nazism in which, in Rosenberg for example, the Hellenic people and the Germanic people are related as Aryan peoples. Thus Oskar Becker, in a passage from his article in the journal *Rasse* titled "Nordic Metaphysics" as related by Karl Löwith, presents Heraclitus as "the ancient Nordic thinker of the first Greek era."[121] Becker and Heidegger are also of one mind in bringing up the struggle against the "Asiatic" idea of destiny, and in countering it with the Germanic or Nordic one.[122] In Heidegger, the confrontation with the "Asiatic" is a recurrent theme, found, for example, in his text of 1937, "Paths of Expression." The Greek moment was but a first confrontation, and it is clear that for him, as for all National Socialists, the German "new reality" calls for a new confrontation and a new struggle. Need it be spelled out that, in the language of the times, the "Asiatic" designates primarily the Jewish people, as well as does "Bolshevism"? These are the terms in which Heidegger speaks of the struggle against the Asiatic in his lecture of 30 November 1934, contemporaneous with his course on Hölderlin: "But the true historical freedom of the peoples of Europe is the precondition for the Occident's return *to itself* in a historical-spiritual way and ensuring its destiny in the great decision of the Earth against the *Asiatic*."[123]

Earlier, Heidegger, repeating almost word for word the terms of Hitler's speeches, was careful to point out that the "true historical freedom" was not "the illusory organized community of a 'Society of Nations' but was to be accomplished only 'within the state,' understood neither as a 'work of art' "[124] nor as a limiting of freedom, but on the contrary as the deployment of "all the essential powers of the people, according to the law of their hierarchic order,"[125] which distinctly foreshadows the future domination of Hitler's Reich over all Europe. The conclusion of the course on Hölderlin goes in the same direction, ending on "the mission and heralding of the eagle,[126] the symbol of the German Reich, which, in Nazism in general, including in the insignia of the party,[127] is represented holding a swastika in its claws.

In this course of Heidegger's, the new *völkisch* mythology he exposes is rooted in the Aryan mythology of Nazism. That the "German race" related to the "original Greek race" came from the East to establish itself in the North and in the German country is precisely what Nazi racial doctrine teaches. Heidegger's astuteness is to partially metaphorize that doctrine and give it the power of myth through his exegesis of the poet's hymns. What is decisive in this regard is the development on the change in direction of the river's flow, which comes in just before the passage on the German race and the original Greek race. "There, the vector of the direction taken by the river manifests something decisive. The direction, initially pointing east, turns suddenly . . . north toward the German country."[128]

Like Ludwig Clauß in his Nordic doctrine, Heidegger begins to speak here of the soul, a "royal soul" that, through Asia, "thinks the totality of being." It alone is capable, in its "kingly dignity," of "ensuring the accomplishment of its essence." While the expression "royal soul" appears in Hölderlin's poem, all the commentary of the "totality of being" and the "accomplishment of the essence" of the soul, which precedes the passage on the German race, is Heidegger's. What is soul doing here next to race? It is worth remembering, in this connection, how Rosenberg conceives of the soul. At the beginning of the *Myth of the Twentieth Century,* he declares, following the doctrine of Clauß in this, that "the soul signifies the race seen from within."[129] Thus we are better able to understand the importance of the *Innigkeit,* the "intimacy" of the secret, on which Heidegger insists particularly at the end of his course. Similarly, his insistence on "birth" (*Geburt*) certainly conjures up, for the listener of that era, the theme, constantly reiterated by Rosenberg, of the "rebirth" (*Wiedergeburt*) of the German people. Rosenberg speaks, after a development on mythic Greece and Homer's "world of the gods," of the "great river of German-Nordic rebirth."[130]

A certain knowledge of the writings of Ludwig Clauß, Oskar Becker, and even Alfred Rosenberg is not, then, without value in achieving a heightened awareness of what is really at stake in Heidegger, beneath the ideas of soul and essence. Doubtless it would be important to go further, proceeding to in-depth comparisons of the canonic texts of these different doctrinarians of Nazism. For it is not in Kant or Hegel that we will find the key to understanding what is at stake in Heidegger's commentaries on Hölderlin, but rather in comparison with the other mythologists of Nazism. And it is because this work is generally not done by philosophers that the latter are so defenseless and sometimes so seduced when they discover Heidegger's texts. Without completely carrying out this critical work — for first the main patterns of the writings of Heidegger themselves must be brought out in their relation to Nazism, which is the purpose of the present work — we at least want to show the need for it. For without that realization and the vigilance that it arouses, there is a great risk that the reading of Heidegger might, in the reader's eyes, win acceptance for ideas and themes that would not be so easily accepted were they found beneath the pen of Clauß or Rosenberg, as the racial character of their doctrines is better known.

In any case, the text of the course contains ample indications for the attentive reader to perceive that the Heideggerian use of the words "being" and "essence" no longer has anything philosophical about it, and to recognize that Heidegger does nothing more here than publicize — more adroitly than others perhaps, but without any great originality of substance — the basic elements of the *völkisch* mythology that was disseminated during the first decades of the twentieth century under the name "secret Germany" before being taken up and assimilated into Nazism. Particularly labored, but dangerously effective on the minds of his subjugated students, is the final commentary on the intimacy of the secret and its "unveiling" in poetry.[131] For in the breaking of the river's flow and the "intimacy" of this secret, it is not peace that is announced but battle,[132] in "the crisscrossing of adverse tendencies,"[133] symbolized by the cross potent and the swastika.

5

Heidegger's Hitlerism in the Seminar
On the Essence and Concepts of Nature,
History, and State

We now approach the main text: the one in which we see the total identification of Heidegger's teaching with the principle of Hitlerism itself—namely, veneration of the Führer and justification for the relationship of radical domination, instituted by Nazism, between the Führer and his *Volk* in the Hitlerian state, or *Führerstaat*. In the winter of 1933–1934, and therefore during the time he held the political and administrative academic power of Rector-Führer, Heidegger taught, concurrently with his course *The Essence of Truth,* a seminar for advanced students that was originally to be on Johann Fichte's science of logic but was ultimately titled *On the Essence and Concepts of Nature, History, and State.*[1] This seminar is generally passed over in silence, and it appears that its publication is not included in the projected edition of the so-called complete works. It must be noted, in this connection, that although the courses of the years 1923–1944 have been ordered chronologically, there is to be no complete publication of the seminars in chronological order. All that has been announced is a selective and partial publication, with no justification for the choices made or indication of seminars left out. Thus the *Gesamtausgabe* does not live up to its name.

Yet Heidegger seems to have given particular importance to this seminar, so much so that he brings it up in 1945, at the beginning of the attempt to justify his rectorship.[2] He speaks of a "very popular seminar" on "the people and science," which was the completion of his course of the same semester on Plato's cave allegory, titled *The Essence of Truth,* itself the repetition of a course given two years earlier.[3] Like almost every sentence of his justificatory text of 1945, this information contains a series of dissimulations, if not falsifications. Not only does he refrain from saying anything about the overtly political content of his seminar, but he modifies the title radically, specifically eliminating any reference to its main concept, the state. Furthermore, Heidegger presents his course *The Essence of Truth* as the simple repetition of an earlier course, whereas we can appreciate today, by comparing them, the radical transformation in 1933–1934 of the course given in 1931–1932.[4]

Recently it has become possible to form some idea of the partial content of this seminar on the basis of a summary in English of the last three sessions[5] and the German publication of part of a report on the seventh session.[6] Moreover, thanks to the cooperation of several researchers, I have had access to more ample transcriptions of the manuscript kept in Marbach, which has made it possible for me to carry out a more complete study of the last five sessions, devoted to the state in its relation to the people and the Führer. Heidegger's seminar was presented explicitly at the time as a course in Hitlerian "political education." Now, this seminar is vital in reestablishing the historical truth, in spite of the revisionism of the authorized parties and principal figures responsible for the so-called complete edition, who attempt to deny all substantive relation between Heidegger's teaching and Nazism. The analyses I propose, and the quotations I publish to back up my demonstrations, are therefore intended to serve the right to historical truth that the public can legitimately claim, seventy years after the holding of this seminar.

It is a seminar for advanced students. A summary, assigned at each class meeting to a different student, is entered into a seminar book, which is subsequently reviewed and sometimes annotated by Heidegger. The seminar consisted of nine two-hour classes, the first of which was held on 3 November 1933, the last on 23 February 1934. The fifth session, which took place on 12 January 1934, was a transitional one. After the usual recapitulation of the preceding session, which dealt with the relations between time and space according to the interpretations of Kant and Newton, Heidegger undertook a rather lengthy development on time in its relation to history. The point was to understand the time of history as *"our past."* From then on, "we understood time not as a framework, but as the fundamental and authentic constitution of man."[7] Time appears as the being of man himself, understood as historical existence, which leads Heidegger to turn his questioning directly to "the nature of the state."

This summary is laden with meaning. By means of the detour of history, it is to the state that time is related. The terms used in connection with time — "being" and the "fundamental constitution" of man — will reappear later in the seminar, but this time to qualify the state. Under the cover of "philosophy," in reality it is something quite different that Heidegger introduces into his teaching. The entire remainder of the seminar will have no other object than the state — not just any state but precisely, according to the term used in the last session, the *Führerstaat,* that is, the Führer's state, the Hitlerian state.

State, People, and Race

The end of that fifth session and the sixth are concerned with the three ideas on which Heidegger founds what he calls, in the seventh session, his course on "political education": the idea of the state, the political, and the people. Lodged at the heart of these three ideas there is, explicitly assumed by Heidegger, the Nazi conception of the people as "unity of blood and stock" and as "race" (*Rasse*).

On the subject of the state, after having asked whether there can be a history without there being a state, Heidegger maintains that to ask questions relative to the state is to ask questions relative "to ourselves."[8] It is not about inquiring into the goal of the state or about its origin. The state is not a domain of history but must be grasped primitively (*primitiv*) in its essence as "a modality of being in which there is man."[9] The state is therefore related to being itself. This ontologizing of the state leads Heidegger to ask what beings correspond to this being. To which he responds: "The people?"[10] That reply is still in the interrogative form, for it remains to be seen how we are to understand "people." "During the French Revolution," he says, "they also answered: 'The people.'"[11] There is no need to be more explicit; in the political context of the era, any allusion to the French Revolution acts as an absolute bugaboo. One must therefore seek a concept of people that owes nothing to any usage connected with the French Revolution; one must direct one's inquiry toward the people in its essence, in view of a response that is only possible, according to Heidegger, "on the basis of a decision for a state." Indeed, "the determination of the people depends on how it is in its state."[12]

This circularity in the reciprocal reference from people to state and from state to people simply expresses the Nazi conception of the state. The state does not constitute the expression, representation, or delegation of the will and sovereignty of the people: it desires nothing short of being the people itself, taken in its "essence" — that is, in reality, in its racial unity, as Heidegger himself makes explicit. He continues in the following terms: "We had first formally established that the people are those beings that are in the manner of the state—that are or can be the state. Then, formally, we pursued the questioning: What is the imprint [*Prägung*] and form [*Gestalt*] that the people gives itself in the state, and that the state gives the people? . . . Is it order? Formulated in this way, it is too general, for I can put anything in order—stones, books, etc. What hits the mark, on the other hand, is the idea of an order in the sense of domination [*Herrschaft*], rank, leadership [*Führung*], and submission [*Gefolgschaft*]."[13]

Heidegger's terminology here is identical to that of his speech of the same period, "The German Student as Worker": imprint (*Prägung*) is a term we have shown to be equally central to the racial doctrine of Clauß and Rothacker; form or figure (*Gestalt*) and domination (*Herrschaft*) obviously bring back the subtitle of Jünger's *Worker*—namely, *Form and Domination* (*Gestalt und Herrschaft*). As for what is intended by "state," it is the *Führerprinzip* of Hitlerism—namely, the relation *Führung-Gefolgschaft,* introduced here and placed at the center of the later development of the seventh session on politics and the state. It is a matter not only of characterizing the state as an organism, or even as order, if the term is taken in too general a sense, but of providing an introduction to the precise relationship between the Führer and his "following," which, in Hitlerism, concretely structures the relations of power. One can, then, speak of an order within which the distinctions of rank and the relationships of domination are distributed. The question then becomes: "Who should lead?"[14]

After the recapitulation of the preceding session, the sixth session proceeds to an explication of the political. Heidegger reminds his listeners that the term is derived from the Greek *polis,* which designates the community of the city-state, from which "all state being" comes. Then he reinterprets Aristotle's saying about man as a *zôon politikon.* This means not that man is, according to a possible Latin translation, a social animal, but that "to be man means: to bear within oneself the possibility and necessity of fashioning and accomplishing both one's own being within a community, and that of the community."[15] What fascinates Heidegger is the relationship between man and the *Gemeinschaft,* his ability to fashion (*gestalten*) a community and to create a *polis,* a state. Thus it is not the state that is the condition of politics. The state is possible only if it is based on the political being of man. Heidegger means to designate by this not the individual will of man but the power of the community that encompasses all. That totalizing—not to say totalitarian—conception of the political community is the foundation of his entire doctrine. He therefore rejects all vision of politics as a limited domain, alongside one's private life, economics, technology, and so on. For him, that conception leads to a degradation of the political, which he assimilates to the politician who knows how to play "low parliamentary tricks" (*parlamentarischen Kniffen*). It makes one wish that the criticisms of Heidegger would focus on the term *Schlag,* the murderous blow of totalitarianism; when he uses the term it is, by contrast, to justify that violence and legitimize it by inscribing it within being itself.

To return to the seminar, Heidegger does not limit himself to impugning parliamentary democracy: he includes the entire modern period in a movement of decline that he sees as beginning with the Renaissance, when the individual was taken as an end in itself.

> This development began with the Renaissance, when the individual as a person was held up as the goal of all being, the great man, according to the two ideals, the *homo universalis* and the specialist. It was the new will to develop the personality that has brought about that total transformation, according to which henceforth all things are here merely for the great individual. Everything, and therefore politics as well, is then included in a sphere in which man has the possibility and will to live as he pleases. So it is that politics, art, and science fall back into areas that are dependent on the desire for individual development, and this becomes all the more pronounced, the more these areas become, through powerful achievements, both wider and more specialized. But in subsequent times all the cultural domains were allowed to grow apart to the point of stretching beyond any synoptic overview, until our time, when the perils of such goings-on have become apparent with an elementary clarity in the downfall of our state.
>
> This is why we have recognized as the urgent task of our era the confrontation of this danger, by attempting to restore to *politics* its rightful rank, to teach us to see it once again as the fundamental character of the philosophizing man in history, and as that being in which the *state* develops, so that it can truly be called the mode of being of a people.[16]

In that negative recapitulation of the modern era (which reminds us of the quotation of Count Yorck on the man of the Renaissance, who is "ready to be buried," taken up by Heidegger in *Being and Time*), we are back to the unchanging basis of Heidegger's position — namely, the rejection of all consideration of the individual value of man, such as it is expressed both in the humanist conception of the universal man and in the valuing and blossoming of the individual and the specialization of personal style in modern societies. For him, a culture that seeks the blossoming of individuals, instead of obeying the exclusive cult of the unity of the community, leads to excessive specialization and the downfall of the state. Heidegger thus joins with the National Socialists in rejecting the liberalism of the nineteenth century and the Weimar Republic. The autonomization of the spheres of activity is looked upon as leading to the constitution of "indirect powers" (political parties, unions, associations) that set individual freedom in opposition to the state and are perceived as a menace to its unity and authority.[17] In reaction to that "dissolution," politics is viewed by Heidegger no longer as one human activity among others but as "the fundamental character of philosophizing man in history."

In reality, politics thus identified with the "being in which the state develops" is based on something completely different from human thought and free will, so that its tie with philosophy is really problematic. Indeed, the rest of the passage shows that for Heidegger (who is merely taking up the National Socialist position on this), the "mode of being of the people," with which politics is identified, expresses in fact nothing but the unity of blood and race. The people is considered by Heidegger to be "the beings of the state, its substance, the basis that sustains it."[18] Announcing the procedure repeated here from the course of summer semester 1934, Heidegger goes through several expressions that use the word "people." This time the concern is to characterize the people in relation to the state, and for that purpose Heidegger gives special emphasis to three expressions. First there is the counting of the population (*Volkszählung*), which, he points out, "includes the state members of *one* state." In this expression, "what is emphasized as constituting the demarcation and definition of the people is the characteristic of belonging to the state." What constitutes that belonging remains to be defined. Until now, says Heidegger, we were going around in a circle. On the one hand, the people was conceived of as the substantial basis that carried and sustained the state, while on the other, it was determined according to its belonging to *one* state. At the end of the sixth session, Heidegger reveals his pivotal point: the unity of blood and race, without which, in his view, it is impossible to conceptualize the unity of the people. This time he relies on the notion already encountered in his speeches of 1933: the "health of the people" (*Volksgesundheit*). We read in the conclusion of that sixth session: "But closely related to this is a word like 'health of the people,' in which additionally all that is felt is the tie with the unity of blood and a common stock [*der Blut- und Stammeseinheit*], with race [*Rasse*]."[19]

The intent, this time, is totally explicit. The unity of the people is first and foremost a unity of blood and "stock," as related to race. Such is the *völkisch* concept of the people that Heidegger explicitly makes his own. That this *völkisch* idea is for him, as well as for all the authors of the time who use it, a racial concept is henceforth beyond question, whatever debate there may be about the best way to translate the term *völkisch*. And we have seen, in his address to the Institute of Pathological Anatomy of Freiburg, the sinister consequences of the racist conception of the "health of the people," which Heidegger embraced to the point of justifying the harshest eugenics.[20] With the conclusion of the sixth session, we touch upon the most intimately Nazi foundation of Heidegger's teaching (which is normally hidden beneath terminology that seems more philosophical, such as "essence" or "mode of being") — namely, what we have no choice but to call the racial basis of his conception of the people. Heidegger continues in these terms. "But the broadest use we make of [the term] people is when, for example, we speak of 'people in arms'; for we understand by that not only those who have received their draft papers, and something different still from the simple sum of citizens of the state, something that represents an even stronger bond than that of a common stock and race — namely the nation, and that means a significant mode of being arrived at under a common destiny and formed within *one* state."[21]

If the mode of being of the nation in the unity of *one* state constitutes an even stronger bond than that of blood and race alone, it is clear that to Heidegger this mode of being continues to encompass the supposed unity of blood and race, and to be based on it. Therefore, after having read this seminar, it is no longer possible to affirm that Heidegger was not a racist.

Furthermore, the way Heidegger, setting out from the people understood as a race, draws conclusions about the state and the nation must have reminded his listeners of that period of one of the most sadly famous developments from *Mein Kampf* — Chapter 11 of the first part, titled "Volk und Rasse," in which Hitler draws conclusions about the German nation and the state. The author of *Mein Kampf* contrasts the state as a mechanism with the organic, *völkisch* state, a distinction that will become, after him, a commonplace of Nazism and will be taken up both in *The Total State* by Ernst Forsthoff and in the works of Nazi jurist and disciple of Heidegger Erik Wolf; or in Heidegger himself, in his unpublished seminar on Hegel and the state. Indeed, Heidegger speaks of "creating the granite foundation upon which someday a state will rest that represents not a mechanism alien to our people . . . but a *völkisch* organism: A Germanic state of the German nation."[22]

It is indeed one and the same conception of the nation that is expressed in Heidegger's seminar and in *Mein Kampf.*

The Political Education of the Nobility of the Third Reich

Beginning with the seventh session, which was held on 2 February 1934, the "philosophy" seminar of winter 1933–1934 turns out to be quite explicitly a course on "political education" (*politische Erziehung*), according to the expression then made official by the Nazis and that Heidegger unhesitatingly makes his own at the beginning of the session. In what does this "political education" consist? He intends to give a "philosophical" legitimacy to the Hitlerian conception of the state and to the domination of the Führer. In this "political education" à la Heidegger, this introduction of the advanced students into the very foundations of Nazism and Hitlerism (that is, the triad of people, state, and Führer), there is at the same time an attempt to introduce Nazism into philosophy and to radically pervert the latter. The lesson begins as follows: "Politics, as the fundamental possibility and modality of being distinctive to man is . . . the basis on which the state is. The being of the state rests anchored in the political being of the men who, as a people, bear that state, and have decisively committed themselves to it. This political, that is, historically fateful decision requires the clarification of the original bond between the essence of the people and the state. For every man an understanding and a knowledge of the essence of the state and the people are necessary. This knowledge, the concepts and cognition, belong to political education — that is, to the introduction [*Hineinführung*] into our own political being."[23]

Heidegger begins by recalling a definition of the political already formulated in the preceding class session. Politics considered as a possibility and a modality distinctive to man seems traditional and echoes Aristotle's well-known definition. Doubtless, hermeneuticians could be found to assert that Heidegger's conception of the political comes from Aristotle. In reality, and as the following will show, the emphasis placed several times in these initial sentences on being, and later on essence, transforms the perspective radically. The pathos of the fundamental and the essential in politics is not neutral. It is a process of indoctrination exploited by the Nazis. Enlisted in the service of a fundamentally destructive cause, it constitutes a fearsome and "essentially" totalitarian arm, in that nothing and no one eludes it. Indeed, the originary political distinction between public and private space, between individual liberties and collective ones is rejected out of hand, since the basis, the essence, the very being of man are enlisted here in such a way that no listener can escape. Heidegger also uses the rhetoric of "decision," of *Entscheidung*, but that word is used in a sense that excludes all deliberation, all reflective use of free will. It is there only to indicate the identification of an entire people with the "historical destiny" of the present event.

The main point is that the "political being of man" for Heidegger as well as for all National Socialists has no consistency except as a people, never as an individual. The only reality of the political thus conceived is the bond uniting people and state, which is itself indissociable from the bond that attaches the people and the state to the Führer. There is no place for a contract, or even a pact — at the very most a plebiscite ratifying a situation already established, if we think of 12 November 1933. Heidegger proceeds to a radical ontologization of the state. He speaks of the "original relation of essence between the people and the state." It is the knowledge of these concepts that necessitates "political education," defined as their "introduction [*Hineinführung*] into our political being proper." Heidegger plays on the words, as usual, and will show that this *Hineinführung* reveals to us the necessity of a Führer. He continues as follows: "That does not mean, however, that just anybody who gets this knowledge can act politically and be authorized to do so as a statesman or *Führer*. For the origin of all political action and *Führung* is not in knowledge, but in being. Every *Führer is a Führer, must* be a *Führer*, in accordance with the stamp of his being, and simultaneously, in the living unfolding of his proper essence, he understands, thinks, and puts into action what the people and the state are."[24]

Thus, political education cannot make us into supreme leaders. Being a supreme leader, a Führer, comes not from a knowledge that we could acquire but from the very being of the one who guides us. Again, that ontologizing of the status of Führer places the latter beyond all calling into question. As in his speeches of November 1933, Heidegger underlines the verbs (the *Führer* is . . . , he must be . . .) in order to win acceptance for the tautological affirmation of a *Führer* who is a *Führer* by his very being. Heidegger's purpose is very close to that of Hitler's minister Walter Darré, who, in *The New Nobility of Blood and Soil,* speaks of distinguishing those who, in the totality of the *Volkstum,* are born Führer (*geborene Führer*).[25]

But what, in the seminar, do the following obscure formulations cover: "the stamp of his being" or "the living unfolding of his proper essence," if not the sacralization, at once ontological and political, of the Führer? Let us recall that one year later, in his first course on Hölderlin, Heidegger affirms that the "true and unique Führer" beckons toward the domain or empire (*Bereich*) of the demigods. That the Führer alone can, by his own being, understand and activate the being of the people, and the state presupposes between him and the people, to repeat the expression used in the ultimate conclusion of this seminar, a "living bond" (*lebendige Verbundenheit*), which can have obtained its substance only from a supposed "unity of blood and race" between the Führer and the German people, as Heidegger had expressed it to define the people in the conclusion of the sixth class meeting. That is what Carl Schmitt maintained the preceding year, in the fourth part of *State, Movement, People.* The Nazi jurist spoke of homogeneity or racial identity between the Führer and his people, using the term *Artgleichheit,* which was immediately picked up, as we shall see, by Hitler's closest disciple during his rectorship, jurist and "philosopher" of the right Erik Wolf.

Heidegger himself does not need to use such a term. As I will show later, he only partially adopts Schmitt's vocabulary. The ontologizing that typifies his language is sufficient for him, once it has been affirmed that the unity of the people and the nation bears a racial dimension. He can now speak of the "relation of essence" that is supposed to unite the people and the state, and of the identity of will that binds into one same destiny *Führung* and *Gefolgschaft*, the guidance of the supreme leader and the allegiance of his loyal followers. The racial connotation, which is undeniable in the context of the era, of the expressions used by Heidegger during the seventh session — "*völkisch* destiny," "breeding" (*Zucht*) — suffice to confirm to the listeners that he is firmly established on the very foundations of the National Socialist conception of the state and its Führer.

A political education is, however, necessary, for Heidegger intends to inculcate in his public of advanced students the spirit of "service" and "sacrifice" that was supposed to unite the Führer and his supporters or faithful followers. He does nothing but repeat, all through the session, and particularly at the end, the core of Hitler's political doctrine both in the second part of *Mein Kampf*, which appeared in 1927, and in his *Führung und Gefolgschaft*, published in 1933. The basic idea of that political doctrine was to impose a relation of dominance for one and of radical subordination for the others — as between Hitler and the totality of the German people, but also as between the head and his following, and as here, in the university, between the Rector-Führer and his troop of professors and students. The relation cannot be equal, and political education is only for the *Gefolgschaft*. Heidegger spells it out as follows.

> A *Führer* does not need to be educated politically, but a troop of guardians [*Hüterschar*] within the people, who contribute to bearing the responsibility of the state, must be. For every state and all knowledge of the state grows within a political tradition. Where this nourishing, securing soil is lacking, the best ideas of state cannot take root and grow forth and develop out of the sustaining bosom of the people. Otto the Great founded his empire [*Reich*] on the spiritual princes, requiring of them political and military allegiance and knowledge. And Frederick the Great educated the Prussian nobility to be guardians [*Hüter*] of his state. Bismarck neglected this enrootedness of his idea of the state in the solid and powerful soil of the political nobility, and when his protective arm loosed its grip, the second empire collapsed unsupported. Today we must not neglect the foundation of a political tradition and the education of a political nobility.[26]

We can see how concrete political education becomes here. There are two things at stake: the handing down of a political tradition and the formation of a political nobility for the Third Reich that would become the "guardian" of a new empire. "Guardian" (*Hüter*) is a word found during this period in a racial or political context: thus in 1928 the Nazi raciologist Hans K. Günther published an apology for racial eugenics titled *Plato as the Guardian of Life* (*Platon als Hüter des Lebens*), and Carl Schmitt, in 1929, published *The Guardian of the Constitution* (*Der Hüter der Verfassung*), with an enlarged edition in 1931, in which he describes for the first time the "turning toward the total state" (*Wendung zum totalen Staat*).[27] In Heidegger's seminar, the formation of that political tradition as guardian of the Third Reich is based on the evocation of the two previous ones, the better to bring out the present task of the new Reich. The idea is, by means of the handing down of that "political tradition" and the formation of a "political nobility" (addressed to an audience of advanced students, a few of whom belong to the SA or even the SS and come to class in their uniforms), to recall the people to their *völkisch* destiny — "*völkisch*" being a term whose racial meaning was explicitly set forth by Heidegger in his course of summer semester 1934. Heidegger continues thus: "Each one must now . . . try to attain knowledge of the people and the state and his or her own responsibility. The state rests on our vigilance, our willingness, and our lives. Our way of being stamps the being of our state. Every people thus takes a position toward the state and no people is without a yearning for the state. The people that turns down the state, that is stateless, has just not yet found the gathering of its essence; it still lacks self-control and strength for the obligation to its *völkisch* destiny."[28]

Heidegger and Stadelmann: The Nazi Preempting of German History

The fact of German history's being henceforth integrated into the political education of Nazism is well illustrated not only by the content of the unpublished seminar but also by the close and privileged relationship between Heidegger and historian Rudolf Stadelmann. In the *Gefolgschaft* of Rector Heidegger, his two main lieutenants, who remained faithful to him to the end, were jurist Erik Wolf and Stadelmann, who, after a thesis on Nicolas of Cusa and Giordano Bruno, had become Otto von Bismarck's editor and historian. In 1933 Stadelmann was a young instructor of history at the University of Freiburg and a member of the SA. Heidegger chose him as director of the press (*Presseleiter*) of the university. For the midsummer festival of the student body (*Sonnenwendfeuer der Studentenschaft*), instituted by Heidegger on the evening of Saturday, 24 June 1933, in the university stadium, he was the one Heidegger invited to address the students in honor of the memory of Bismarck before he himself, in the dark, before a burst of flames, delivered the eulogy of the "German Revolution." Reviewed in the Freiburg student newspaper, Stadelmann's address gives us an idea of the pathos of the ceremony.

> The privat-docent Dr. Stadelmann then stepped forward and delivered a speech. On that day, he said, youth everywhere were facing the flames to celebrate the solstice. He spoke of the meaning of the solstice, of the prewar years, when the German youth, on the heights of the Meißner,[29] would celebrate the change; he spoke of the days that have marked the destiny of the German people, and of the days of the year 1933 when a new generation stood ready to demonstrate its faithful German will. And [he declared] that it was particularly fitting, at such an hour, to commemorate those builders of the people who had carried out great things for it. One of those builders was our former chancellor Bismarck, to whom this homage was especially dedicated. The spirit of Bismarck was that of chivalry, self-moderation, and that spirit should be the one to show the way to the new Germany. The youth, who were then facing the flaming bonfire, were to aspire to form a united people; they should take to heart the words of Bismarck: "I would have no friends, if I had no enemies." The absolute spirit of chivalry is reserved for the strong. The fundamental trait of the Germanic character lies in satisfying its own requirement. Our combat should be joined for God, liberty, the fatherland, the youth, and the people![30]

We see how, in this speech, Bismarck, the man of the Second Reich, was presented to the student youth as a precursor of the Third Reich. It is significant that Stadelmann quoted a sentence of Bismarck's that could have been written by Carl Schmitt: "I would have no friends, if I had no enemies."[31] The unity of the German youth and people is thus structured, in Nazism, according to the opposition friends/enemies. As we will see, this dichotomy is primarily, in Schmitt, a discrimination of a racial nature. Under the guise of "the spirit of chivalry" there is something far more sordid going on, for this invocation of a "new Germany," these appeals to the "united people," and these speeches to the young people of the university before the bonfires are indissociable from the book-burnings organized at precisely the same period by the Deutsche Studentenschaft (with which Stadelmann, like Heidegger, cultivated close relations) and at Freiburg by the League of Combat for German Culture (*Kampfbund für deutsche Kultur*). And I have shown that the flames before which Stadelmann, then Heidegger, perorated had the value of a symbolic burning of "non-German" books, regardless of whether the rain did or did not allow the material burning of books to take place.[32]

In October 1933, when Rector Heidegger organized his first camp at Todtnauberg, where the Nazi members met, hand picked from the universities of Freiburg, Heidelberg, and Kiel, it was to Stadelmann that he entrusted the task of being the Führer of the group from Freiburg. One of the most explicit objectives of these camps, clearly stressed both in the announcement prospectus written by Heidegger and in the Stadelmann bequest of Koblenz,[33] and in the correspondence of that time between Heidegger and Stadelmann, was to put to the test and to reinforce the bond between *Führung* and *Gefolgschaft.* So it is that, in a tragicomic episode, Heidegger "sacrificed" his faithful Stadelmann by ordering him to leave the camp on the day before he was supposed to give his speech. He later takes him to task, in a letter of October 11, for having stayed in the camp until the early hours of the following morning.[34] Stadelmann responded with a pathetic letter, assuring him of his "obedience" and affirming that he understood very well that "the goal of the revolution in the university is the SA student."[35]

Shortly thereafter, it was again to Stadelmann that Rector Heidegger turned, this time to open a public lecture series, required for all students, on "The Tasks of Spiritual Life in the National Socialist State." The titles of several lectures organized by Heidegger show the intended goal: to introduce at the University of Freiburg a requirement to teach the political and racial doctrine of Nazism. We find, for example, for the winter semester of 1933–1934, the following titles, at times difficult to translate, the terms being so charged with connotations in the language of the Nazis: "The Present-Day Economic Life Considered in a Historical and Political Manner (Liberalism, Fascism, Socialism)," "Racial Hygiene and Its Significance for Demographics Policy," "From Work Camp to Work Service," "The Teaching of the Fatherland [*Heimat*] of National *Deutschtum.*" And for the summer semester of 1934: "Social Hygiene and Demographics Policy," "The Teaching of the German *Heimat* (*Rasse, Volkstum, Heimat*)."[36]

On 9 November 1933, the tenth anniversary of the march of 9 November 1923 in front of the Feldherrnhalle of Munich[37] and three days before the plebiscite in favor of Hitler, Stadelmann gave a lecture in the presence of the rector and the assembled professors and student body. It was titled: "The Historical Self-Consciousness of the Nation."[38] The presentation in broad strokes that is given of German history, from Luther to Bismarck, is very close to Heidegger's historical evocations in his seminars. Moreover, this lecture by Stadelmann helps us understand why and in what direction Heidegger would, in his seminar on political education, use a term, "self-consciousness" (*Selbstbewußtsein*), that had been banished from his vocabulary since *Being and Time.* Stadelmann speaks of a "self-consciousness" that is in reality "devoid of reflection on self" (*ohne Selbstreflexion*).[39] What is really involved is the "experience of self" (*Selbsterfahrung*) of the nation as historical consciousness of self. This latter presupposes, as in *Being and Time,* the "passage from the *I* to the self" (*der Schritt vom Ich zum Selbst*).[40] In short, the use by Stadelmann of the expression "self-consciousness" is characteristic of the hijacking of philosophical concepts in the language of the Third Reich. What we have here is a consciousness with neither *I* nor reflection, entirely identified with the "historical existence" of the nation and its destiny[41] and even, as we shall see, with the politics of the Führer.

Without summarizing the entire Stadelmann speech, I will approach certain points that sufficiently demonstrate the spirit of it. He begins by speaking of the change that has taken place in the German universities between the summer semester of 1933 and the winter semester of 1933–1934. Though a more emphatic and naive version, willing to pile on the ultranationalist and Nazi commonplaces, his pathos is close to Heidegger's speeches. In that vein he exclaims: "Why continue to have schools, when men grow up in the camps and the assault sections? Why give time to reflection, when the distress of a people calls for deeds?"[42] "We must harden ourselves against the temptation of breaking the discipline [*Zucht*] of the spirit to shorten the path that leads to action."[43] Stadelmann then distinguishes among three forms of "*völkisch* self-consciousness." First, the naive or instinctive self-consciousness, that consciousness that can respond to the "call," and apropos of which he brings up the imminent plebiscite of 12 November, presenting the "yes" as going without saying—a foregone conclusion. "The foreign policy of the *Reichsführer,* to which the German people will adhere [*sich bekennen*] next Sunday, is the expression of that self-consciousness, at once brave and obligatory, that on the basis of self-respect commands respect from others."[44]

What motivates that self-consciousness is the "political greatness of one's country" and "love," in Hitler's words, which Stadelmann repeats abundantly, quoting in particular this phrase from the author of *Mein Kampf:* "I can fight only for something I love."[45] We notice that in introducing this theme Stadelmann anticipates the theme of eros, of the amorous desire of the people for their Führer and the state, which Heidegger will himself develop in his seminar. As for the Hitler quote, Stadelmann comments on it, placing race alongside history in the "consciousness" of the nation. "History, in this, is quite simply a moment alongside other moments, alongside countryside, lifestyle, industry, and race [*Rasse*], moments upon which the pride of a nation can be built."[46]

Then comes the "mythic consciousness," a second form of "*völkisch* self-consciousness." Indeed, he asserts, "it is not in history but in myth that the genius of the nation is recognized."[47] What Stadelmann has in mind is a mythologized remembrance of the grandeur of the German past: the "courage of consciousness" (*Gewissensmut*) of Luther, the "figure of the Iron Chancellor," that is, Bismarck, "the Prussia of Frederick as a symbol of the German state." In matters of myth, we have here the same commonplaces of German history as those that will reappear in Heidegger's seminars. When Stadelmann becomes more original in his references, his motivation is no less questionable, for then we see the historian of the Renaissance put his knowledge at the service of Nazi nationalism. Thus, he enlists "the Alsatian Beatus Rhenanus"[48] in the cause, without saying that this humanistic philologist was the friend and editor of Erasmus and that it was at the University of Paris, in the Collège du Cardinal Lemoine alongside Jacques Lefèvre d'Étaples and Charles de Bovelles, and not in the German universities that he chose to pursue his training. In his developments on mythic consciousness, moreover, we see Stadelmann referring to Hegel as the brilliant thinker of the German race (*germanische Rasse*), following which he does not hesitate to present Ernst Krieck, the most virulent of Nazi "philosophers," as the continuator of Dilthey. He writes: "In a magnificent passage of his 'Philosophy of Universal History,' Hegel defined the fundamental tonality of the Germanic race as '*Gemütlichkeit*,' pointing out in a brilliant philosophical interpretation that *Gemütlichkeit* is the 'sentiment of natural totality.' Wilhelm Dilthey, and more recently, in his wake, Ernst Krieck, isolated the fundamental trait of the German spirit as being objectivity: devotion to the endlessness of life and a feeling for the manifestation of strength for its own sake."[49]

At that date, Krieck is still Heidegger's ally. Thus, shortly before this, he had sent his representative, Johann Stein, and his *Gefolgschaft* from the University of Heidelberg to the Todtnauberg camp. On the theme of mythic consciousness, Krieck and Heidegger will continue, to some extent, to concur, for Krieck makes myth the motor of history, and Heidegger himself will say, in his course of summer semester 1935, that "the knowledge of primordial history is . . . mythology."[50]

The third sense of "self-consciousness" of the nation is historical self-consciousness properly so called, and this time Stadelmann's development leads him to come to the defense of Hitler. "We have, in the self-presentation of Hitler, a very living testimony to that synthetic power of historical memory."[51]

I will spare the reader the final development, in which Stadelmann magnifies "the spirit of the National Socialist revolution"[52] and asserts that the "breakthrough toward truth" is the present and exclusive "mission" of the German people. I quote only this excerpt from it. "The breakthrough toward the truth is the mission of the German: it is for its sake that he goes forward. At the highest point of German history, Hegel expressed it thus: 'Every time it is the people who have seized the highest concept of the spirit that comes at its moment and dominates them.' "[53]

Stadelmann concludes on the same page with a quotation from Nietzsche, who, along with Hegel, Dilthey, and Hitler's *Mein Kampf,* is one of the four major references of his lecture.

Need I underline the fact that Stadelmann's lecture hardly rises above the level of an ultranationalist and pro-Hitlerian propaganda speech? The quotations from Hegel and Nietzsche cannot conceal the philosophical bankruptcy of the speech. This does not prevent Stadelmann's text from meeting Heidegger's full approval, and an approval that is not transitory. It is worth noting that Stadelmann, far from distancing himself from his initial political positions and soon to be promoted to full professor at the University of Tübingen, included this text of his 1933 lecture in a work published in 1942 titled *Vom Erbe der Neuzeit.* Heidegger did not forget about this lecture: in his correspondence with Stadelmann in 1945, we find a letter from Heidegger dated 20 July 1945 that begins with a transparent allusion to the theme of Stadelmann's 1933 lecture. He writes: "An hour before your letter came I was pondering over historical self-consciousness . . . and thinking vividly of you in the process."[54]

We will have occasion to return to these letters exchanged in 1945, which confirm the permanence of Heidegger's exaltation of the German "essence." What was important to show at this point was that the two men shared the same conception of German history as finding its meaning in the advent of the Hitlerian Reich.

The People, the State, and the Führer According to Heidegger and Carl Schmitt

When Heidegger brings up the notion of politics, he spontaneously tends to mention two conceptions, Carl Schmitt's and Bismarck's. We might wonder why he chooses these two authors, but Stadelmann's speech just quoted puts us on the right track, since it contains a proposition of Bismarck's that is very Schmittian. We have seen that Heidegger intends by the "political education" of his seminar to contribute to the gathering into its essence of the people in its "*völkisch* destiny." He then goes back to the still largely indeterminate conception that he formulated of the political, and it is in that context that he introduces Schmitt's conception of the political.

> This is why we should try with a very special willingness to further clarify the essence of the people and the state. To this conception one could contrast other concepts of the political, for example the concept of the friend-enemy relation, which goes back to Carl Schmitt. This concept of the political as a friend-enemy relation is based on the viewpoint that combat, i.e. the real possibility of war, is the precondition for political conduct, and that the

possibility, then, of decisive combat, which can also be led without military means, sharpens the existing oppositions, whether moral, confessional, or economic, down to the radical unit of friend and enemy. In the unit and totality of this friend-enemy opposition resides all political existence. Decisive for this viewpoint, however, is that the political unit does not have to be identical to the state and people.[55]

Heidegger will not express himself more explicitly on Schmitt in this seminar. As we will show, it is a year later, in the seminar titled *Hegel, on the State,* that he returns in a more precise and elaborated manner to his relation to Schmitt.[56] But we can already retain the fact that Heidegger does not conceive of the essence of politics without referring to Carl Schmitt, even if it is to differ from him in part. The precise point that we would like to stress now is the way Heidegger conceives of the relation among the people, the state, and the Führer. It appears that the purpose of the reference to Bismarck is to introduce that issue, which is central to the seventh session.

It must be added that the way Heidegger sustains his line of argument on the First and Second Reich shadows the attitude of Hitler himself. Hitler often echoes Bismarck's definition of politics as "the art of the possible." That reference is to be found, for example, in his speech of 13 July 1928, which appeared in the *Völkischer Beobachter* of 18 July of the same year.[57] Similarly, Heidegger also retains Bismarck's conception of politics as "the art of the possible," to interpret the possible not as the result of a choice but as "the sole possible" that must "by essence and necessity spring from a historical situation"; a "possible" that is not based on deliberation but imposed by destiny. This destiny is identified with the "creative project of the great man of state," who sets himself a goal "from which he will never deviate." Thus it is a matter of a radical decisionism, without rational justification, in which the state depends entirely on the personality and the decisions of its director, its Führer. Heidegger expresses himself in the following terms.

> A different grasp of the political is expressed in these words of Bismarck: "Politics is the art of the possible." What is meant by possibility, here, is not just any one, that might be thought up by chance, but the one possible, the only possible. Politics for Bismarck is the capacity to see and achieve what must spring forth of essential necessity from a historical situation, and at the same time the *teknç,* the skill to accomplish what has been recognized. Therewith politics becomes the creative project of the great statesman, whose gaze embraces the overall events of history, not just the present; he who sets in his idea of the state a goal, which he keeps steadily in focus despite all contingent changes of the situation. This view of politics and the state is closely tied to the person of the brilliant statesman, upon whose eye for the essential, upon

whose strength and bearing, the being of the state depends. Where his power and life end, there begins the powerlessness of the state.[58]

Immediately afterward, however, Heidegger affirms that "a state that is to have consistency and durability and that is to mature, must be grounded in the being of the people." There is in this an obvious logical contradiction: How can a state be at the same time entirely dependent on its leader and based on the people? From a rational point of view, the state cannot be at once a dictatorship and a democracy. Even in the plebiscite, democracy is abolished the moment it brings a new tyrant to power. But this contradiction is precisely what the National Socialist state embodies,[59] so that any rational idea of the state is thereby destroyed. Or rather, Hitlerism intends to overcome the opposition, but in an occult and irrational manner, by affirming the substantial unity of the "being" of the leader and the "being" of his people, which is dependent on no deliberation and rests on a racial presupposition. That is the conception Heidegger makes his own—that of the people understood as "a unity of blood and stock," as a race. It is the very principle of Nazism, developed at length in 1933 by Carl Schmitt in the last part of *State, Movement, People,* that deals with the indissociable relation between the "principle of the Führer," or *Führerprinzip,* and "racial identity" (*Artgleichheit*). Although Heidegger does not use this last term, preferring to speak, even more explicitly, of the "unity of stock" and "race" (*Stammenseinheit und Rasse*), they both use expressions that are so close that one might wonder whether Heidegger is not repeating some of Schmitt's vocabulary here. When Heidegger speaks of the "living bond" (*lebendige Verbundenheit*) that unites the "will of the Führer" and his *Gefolgschaft* to produce the community, one thinks immediately of what Schmitt calls the "living bond" (*lebendige Verbundenheit*) between the Führer and his *Gefolgschaft.*[60]

There is, however, a difference between Schmitt and Heidegger that may help us to understand the distance, relative though it is, that Heidegger will take from Schmitt's conception of the political. Schmitt insists more on the role of the "movement," that is, the party, and the "council of the Führer" (*Führerrat*), along the same lines as the council instituted by Goering in Prussia at the suggestion of Carl Schmitt in person, and to which he belonged until 1945. As for Heidegger, he mobilizes, as I will show, what is at the heart of his doctrine, namely the ontological difference between being and beings, to put it at the service of the Hitlerian conception of the relation between the Führer's state and the people.

Both these positions are equally ridiculous. The Council of State instituted by Goering turned out to have no effective political power and was scarcely more than an alibi, intended to give the appearance of the maintenance of a legal system in Prussia. Similarly, Heidegger's ontological difference, in this function, if it serves to give an appearance of philosophical legitimacy and profundity to the relation of the people to the state, has no other content than the presupposition of a vital and sound bond, of a racial nature, between the Führer and his people. Carl Schmitt attempts to create the illusion of an order of law, while the new state is the ipso facto destruction of the autonomy of law. Heidegger would like to create the illusion that a form of thought subsists at the foundation of the *Führerstaat,* whereas the latter marks the annihilation of all truly free choice and all rational will — in short, of all philosophy and even all thought, for no thought can be formed without freedom and reason.

The Relation Between the State and the People Identified with the Relation Between Being and Beings

It is in the middle of the seventh class session of his seminar that Heidegger identifies the relation between beings and being with the one that unites the people and the state. He "ontologizes" the relation between state and people and presents it as the exact equivalent of the relation between being and beings. Let us note that he speaks not merely of an "ontological difference" but of a "relation." The *Staat-Volk* relation is identified with the *Sein-Seiendes* relation, as Heidegger affirms that "the people, that is, beings, bear a very precise relation to their being, that is, to the state."[61]

This sentence radically modifies the way Heidegger's entire work can be viewed. We discover that he does not hesitate to identify the political difference between the people and the state with the ontological difference, which is always presented as the centerpiece of his work, between being and beings. Furthermore, it is not a matter of a passing identification, since it is found notably in his Constance lecture of 30 November 1934, titled *The Current Situation and Future Task of German Philosophy.* There, Heidegger affirms that "a state *is* only when it *becomes — when it becomes the historical being* of beings, which are called a *people.*"[62] The "philosophical" and the political can, therefore, under no circumstances be separated for Heidegger. The terms of one are immediately translated into those of the other. What this seminar reveals is that the foundations of his "doctrine" are political through and through. Because of this, the ontological difference between being and entities is always liable to carry within it, in a veiled fashion, a political dimension indiscernible at first glance. We must therefore be vigilant, faced with the perversity of this seemingly philosophical artifice that consists in speaking to us about being, while what is in fact taking place is the communication, to listeners, of the

Hitlerian conception of the *Führerstaat*. Beneath the words "being," "beings," "truth of being," and so on, Heidegger succeeds in circulating the very principles of Nazism. I will give several examples of that in this work.

How to Anchor the Will of the Führer in the Being and Soul of the People

Although I do not want to write a detailed commentary on this lesson, which would come down to sanctioning the academic appearance Heidegger gives his words all the better to transmit a radically Hitlerian content, it is worth paying attention to the way he proceeds and the meditations he entertains — in short, to his strategy. Thus, why the long detour through intermediary of the ontological difference based on the purely academic example of the piece of chalk? What is he trying to elicit from his students? The question, familiar to his readers and listeners, about the use of the verb "to be" in expressions as varied as "the chalk is white" or "the chalk is present-at-hand" (*vorhanden*), does not just allow one to conclude that, since the use of the verb "to be" is not definable in a univocal way, being is not "visible" and escapes representation. Heidegger dramatizes his words. We are faced with an understanding that becomes obfuscated when we question it. Here, questioning introduces something occult. Since we cannot ask, "What is being?" and it eludes our questions, is it not because "the entire world, ourselves, are nothingness?" The interrogation opens upon the chasm of the nothing; it causes distress and dread . . . Heidegger plays heavy-handedly the same note as in the 1929 lecture, "What Is Metaphysics?" But this pathos of anguish and danger tends now toward a resolution that is expressed in a new way. He declares: "Man, in whose essence it is to question, must expose himself to the danger of the nothing, of nihilism, in order to seize the sense of his being on the basis of the overcoming of nihilism."[63]

Without further explanation, Heidegger objectifies this "danger" with a term, "nihilism," which, like "liberalism," has become one of the National Socialists' favorite words to designate everything they are fighting against. It is thus far less a matter of leaving a question open than of touching the "nothing," of arousing in the student a movement of anguish or dread, in order to induce him to react, to seek something solid, to cling to what Heidegger calls, in his speeches of this period, the "new German reality."

Let us note already at this point that if the state is to the people what being is to beings, this state, in a certain sense, "is" nothing. What Heidegger will say further about the constitution no longer representing any "legal order" confirms this for us. In truth, there is in him neither political philosophy nor a rational doctrine of the state. His procedure expresses the paradox of Nazism: during the first years of its domination in Germany, there is talk of nothing but the state in the speeches, courses, and works of the period, while at the very time the juridical foundation of the state of law, in practice as well as in the texts, is destroyed in order to make room for the undivided domination of the *Führerprinzip*. It is this situation that Heidegger describes in his seminar, in order to legitimate it. The state, in this, is no longer conceived of as a legal institution but as an invisible and occult foundation, "anchored [*verankert*] in the political being of men," when "the existence and superiority of the *Führer* are sunken [*eingesunken*] in being, in the soul of the people." It is not a political thinking that is expressed here but the justification of the occult possession of the being and soul of each individual person by the will of the Führer. Heidegger understood the principle of Hitlerism perfectly and made it his own.

We must be aware of the modality of Hitler's domination, as Ian Kershaw has so remarkably depicted it.[64] Hitler's power is not only that of a dictatorship in which the decisions of the Führer are immediately executable and never questioned. Everyone is also trained to "work toward the Führer," according to the expression used on 21 February 1934 (the same month in which Heidegger held the last three sessions of his seminar) by a Nazi functionary, Werner Willikens, state secretary in the Prussian Ministry of Agriculture. Now Heidegger's whole detour through "the question toward being," as preparatory to the inquiry concerning the state, carries out precisely this intent by penetrating the heart, the spirit, and finally the very being of his hearers. The idea is to let the Führer's will enter into you to the point of your becoming one with him, in "one sole destiny" and "the realization of one idea."[65]

A familiarity with this seminar enables us to understand that it is not only a "doctrine" that Heidegger wants to transmit. He proceeds to something much more insidious and radical, not hesitating to penetrate the inner life of his students by appealing to the forces of their "consciousness," and especially of their eros.

The evocation of "consciousness" (*Bewußtsein*) has something unusual about it if we reflect that the entirety of *Being and Time* was directed against that notion. But the use Rudolf Stadelmann makes of the term during this period has made us grow wary of the way this word "consciousness" can be diverted. Now that is the case here. Heidegger relates consciousness far less to acquired knowledge than to a certain mode of being that expresses our relation to the surrounding world. It is a question here not of self-consciousness but of "consciousness" understood as "knowing and care about the height and depth, the greatness and the powerlessness of one's being in the totality of the world," without which man "no longer is, as man."[66] Height and greatness: in the indetermination of the expression, we recognize the hierarchy of the orders, and that is precisely what it is about. It is a matter not of recalling the human being to himself but of relating the "consciousness" that man has relative to his "being-man" to the people's care about its state. It is therefore always about the people and the state, and not about the individual discernment of the human being. Despite the use of the word "consciousness," Heidegger's remarks should come under the heading of collective affect rather than thought.

What follows shows this clearly. It is a matter of presenting the people's will and love (*eros*) for the state as being as imperative as the will of each man to live and to "be there" or to exist. Thus he affirms that "the people love the state; that is their type and modality of being as people. The people are governed by *eros* toward the state."[67]

Far from expressing rational deliberation, this "will" of the people has the imperious character of an "urge" (*Drang*) and affect. Heidegger derives from this a very odd notion of the "constitution" (*Verfassung*) and of law. "The form, the constitution [*Verfassung*] of the state is an essential expression of the meaning the people want to give their being. The constitution is not a rational contract, a juridical order, political logic, or anything arbitrary and absolute. The constitution and law are the realization of our decision with respect to the state; they are the factual testimonies of what we hold to be our historical and *völkisch* task, and of what we try to live."[68]

Heidegger is playing on the word *Verfassung* here, the first meaning of which is not that of "governmental constitution" but of "state" in the sense of fashioning, *fassen*, which is apparently derived from the old German *fazzon*. This allows him to set aside the "liberal" conception of the constitution as a "rational contract" and the normative conception, which identifies it with "juridical order" and a logical construction. Like Carl Schmitt before him, whose influence is recognizable here, it is the "decisionist" conception of law and the constitution that is the only one retained by him. In the rest of the paragraph, Heidegger comes back to the importance of that "decision" that concerns each one of us. "Thus also, then, knowledge of the constitution and of law is not something that is only the concern of the so-called 'politicians' and jurists, but is, as thought and consciousness of the state, an integral part of the existence of every single man who takes it upon himself to fight for the responsibility of his people. In this historical instant, the clear formation and transformation of the thought of the state are part of our task. Now, every man and every woman must learn to know, be it only darkly and confusedly, that his or her individual life decides the destiny of the people and the state, and carries or rejects it."[69]

Heidegger's words are intentionally ambiguous. The affirmation that the "thought" and "consciousness" of the state do not concern exclusively the "politicians" and jurists but are "an integral part of the existence of every single man" may seem like an appeal to the individual consciousness of each person, whereas in reality it is nothing of the kind. The "decision" sweeps up all the members of the *völkisch* community, not by individual deliberation, which is explicitly rejected along with the idea of a "rational contract," but in the sense that the existence of all is concerned. We are back to the concept of the total state. It has nothing to do with a deliberation of individual consciousnesses but with the idea that each one should be prepared, according to the terms used later, for obedience, combat, faithfulness, and sacrifice. It matters little, then, that this "clear" thought of the state is learned by each in a manner that is "dark and confused." As we will see further along in the seminar, what counts is being prepared at every moment for the sacrifice of one's existence. Heidegger takes up the doctrine of sacrifice (*Opfer*) given by Hitler in *Mein Kampf*.

This passage should help us to overcome what has seemed to many to be an aporia in *Being and Time*. It has often been asked how Heidegger was able to pass from a description of existence that seems to leave room for singularity (notably in solitude in the face of death) to the affirmation according to which that existence accomplishes its destiny only in being in common, that is, within a people, a community. In reality, as he clarifies, as all existence is destiny, destinies are not individual: they are always-already guided.[70] There is thus no place, in the doctrine of *Being and Time*, for individual freedom. This is what was not perceived with sufficient clarity by Sartre, whose existentialism has, for this reason, the merit of maintaining the radical freedom of individual consciousness, though within the limits of its "being set within a situation."

Getting back to the 1933–1934 seminar — the guiding intention of this course in "political education" is diametrically opposed to all philosophy, since the individual thought of the human being, far from being activated, is in reality annihilated. Indeed, the intended goal is that all should become one with the will of the Führer.

We can now take up the last paragraph of the seventh session, without doubt the most important, though left aside by Theodore Kisiel. It is here that we discover just how far Heidegger wanted to lead his students. He begins by insisting on the notion of "order": "the order of the state" or "true order" (*wahre Ordnung*). The presence of this idea immediately following a development on "decision" denotes the influence of Carl Schmitt on Heidegger, who appears to have been inspired both by the former's "decisionist" conception of law and by his notion of "concrete order." This tends to confirm the interpretation according to which "decisionism" and the idea of "concrete order" in Schmitt, or of "true order" in Heidegger, are not opposed to one another but proceed from the pursuit of the same goal.[71]

Before investigating this point further, it may be useful to consider the following coincidence. The eighth session of the seminar, which was held on 16 February 1934, took place one week before the Berlin lecture of 21 February 1934 in which Schmitt set forth his conception of the "concrete order." In that lecture he rejects, as Heidegger had just done, the expression "juridical order" (*Rechts-ordnung*) as still pertaining to the "normativism" against which he is struggling. Schmitt writes the word with a hyphen to stress the fact that it is a compound word, in which the link between the two concepts is not self-evident, and he rejects the expression in these terms: "A term like 'National Socialist' [*Nationalsozialist*] is necessary in that form because it puts an end to the violent separation and play of oppositions between the two words. . . . But there exist equally compound words whose terms bear a relation of exteriority. . . . Today the compound word and concept 'juridical order' is no longer among the compound words from whom we may draw felicitous profit, because it can be used to veil the difference that exists between thought oriented according to the rules, and thought oriented according to order."[72]

For Schmitt, the "juridical order" is an expression in which order is still in reference to the rules of laws, according to the normativistic representation of law he opposes, while "concrete order" emanates directly from the Führer. It is the doctrine of *Nomos basileus*: we shall see in the next chapter to what a great degree it is common to Heidegger and Schmitt. Order, then, is no longer thought of according to the rules regulating it and according to law. On the contrary, we may say that it is order that dictates what the law is, if we take order equally in the sense of command. Here, French is more suggestive than German, in that the word *ordre* can designate both an order that is given (*Befehl*) and a constituted order (*Ordnung*). In any case, the temporal propinquity between the two rejections of the "juridical order" by Heidegger and by Schmitt confirms the similarity and interpenetration of the two approaches. How, then, are "decisionism" and the doctrine of "concrete order" (Schmitt) or "true order" (Heidegger) reconcilable? The answer lies for Schmitt in the fourth part of *State, Movement, People,* and for Heidegger in his seminar *On the Essence and Concepts of Nature, History, and State.* Carl Schmitt relies on the concept of "substance of the people" (*Volkssubstanz*), the racial content of which is explicit. "National Socialism," he writes, "protects and takes care of each true substance of the people where it encounters it, in the landscape, in race or state. It has created law applicable to hereditary agrarian goods; it has saved the peasantry; it has purified the German civil service from elements foreign to the race and thereby established it in its standing. It has the courage to treat the unequal unequally and to impose the necessary differentiations."[73]

The racist concept of "substance of the people" was commented on by Schmitt in reference to the racial laws that had just gone into effect: the laws governing the peasantry dear to Walter Darré (we will see that they were praised by Erik Wolf), which limited the transfer and possession of cultivable land exclusively to "Aryans," and the law of 7 April 1933 on the "reconstruction of the Civil Service," which, as we have seen, dismissed Jewish civil servants. As Schmitt said, "without the principle of racial identity, the National Socialist state could not exist, and its juridical life would be unthinkable."[74] That "racial identity" (*Artgleichheit*) not only served to "define" what for Schmitt constituted the "substance of the people": it also made it possible to give its full racial meaning to the "living bond" that united the Führer and his *Gefolgschaft*. This he stressed emphatically. "This concept of *Führung* comes down to us entirely from the concrete and substantial thought of the National Socialist movement. . . . It is not a descendant of the baroque allegories and representations, or of a Cartesian *general idea*. It is a concept of immediate contemporaneity and of real *presence*. For this reason it includes, as a positive requirement, an *unconditional racial identity between the Führer and the Gefolgschaft*."[75]

We note the rejection of Descartes, which we will find at the end of Heidegger's seminar, and the willingness to use expressions borrowed from Catholic theology, such as "real *presence*," which should be compared with similar uses but this time is inspired by Lutheranism, found in the seminar. Against this background, we see that it is henceforth the "substantiality" of the people such as they are "revealed" in the National Socialist movement that constitutes the concrete basis of the decision.[76] Here we find in Schmitt the "juridical" equivalent of the "*völkisch* basis" dear to eugenicist and Nazi physician Eugen Fischer in his Leipzig speech of 11 November 1933, printed in five languages along with Heidegger's profession of faith.

Now, Heidegger relies on the same doctrine. We have seen that he considers, in his seminar of winter 1933–1934, the people as "the beings of the state, its substance, the basis that sustains it."[77] When we recall how much he insists, in *Being and Time*, on the inadequacy of any determination of the thinking *I* as "substance"[78] (a determination that, philosophically, has a meaning, since that Cartesian denomination rests on the experience of self-conscious thought), it is rather laughable to see him use the word "substance" unreservedly in order to join the theoreticians of National Socialism in identifying the "people" with "substance" and with the "basis" that sustains the state.

It is true that in *Being and Time* not all use of the word *substance* is forsworn. On four occasions, its author affirms that "the substance of man is existence."[79] And as we have seen, that existence is never the existence of an individual *I*, but, as affirmed in section 74, that of the community of a people united by a "destiny." The concept of "substance" is thus, in Heidegger, an "existential" one. That is equally the case for Schmitt, as I will show in the following chapter apropos of the 1933 edition of the *Concept of the Political*. But — and this is the essential point — the fact that the "substance" of the people is to be taken in an "existential" sense in no way safeguards us from the racial determination of the "people" and their "substance." Indeed, just as "order" and "decision" are united in Heidegger as well as in Schmitt in the same conception of the "living bond" between the Führer and his *Gefolgschaft,* similarly "substance" and "existence" both refer to the unity of the "people," explicitly conceived of by Heidegger as "the unity of blood and stock," linked to "race."

And indeed the seminar of winter 1933–1934 follows, in its last sessions, a movement similar to that of the fourth part of *State, Movement, People,* entitled "Principle of the Führer and racial identity as fundamental concepts of National Socialist law."[80] Just as Schmitt must begin by positing the existence of the "substance of the people" (*Volkssubstanz*) and marking the racial meaning of this concept by referring to the racial laws that constituted the first "bringing into line" of April 1933, so must Heidegger designate the "people" as "substance" (*Substanz*) and "supporting foundation" (*tragende Grund*) of the state and determine the people as "race" (*Rasse*) in order to subsequently give body to his concept of state and the "living bond" uniting the Führer to his "people."

The consequences of this demonstration on the understanding of Heidegger's "existentials" are radical, because they mean that Heidegger's conception of existence is at root a racial one. What we saw in our second chapter, on the connection he establishes in his speeches between the notion of "care" and the Nazi concept of "work," already tended decisively in that direction. Similar to that of Oskar Becker or Carl Schmitt, Heidegger's proven racism is not to be confused with a biological naturalism he rejects for having the too "liberal" character of a "science" that likes to think of itself as positive. This doesn't mean that his racism is less than that of a Hans K. Günther or a Eugen Fischer, but on the contrary that it is even more radical, in that it no longer lends itself to any scientific (or supposed scientific) discussion, nor therefore to any possible rational refutation. It merges into the pure self-affirmation (*Selbstbehaupt-*

ung) of the *völkisch* existence of the German people, the only one of all the peoples to still have a "history," a "destiny," the sole "metaphysical" people, capable of giving meaning to the "great transformation of the existence of man," initiated, according to him, by Hitler's *Weltanschauung*.[81] It is clear that this position of Heidegger's is far more than political nationalism: this "existential" exclusiveness of the German people, presented as the only people capable, under the direction of Hitler, of taking charge of the transformation of the existence of man, proceeds from the adoption of a position that is deeply racist and discriminatory through and through. If the expression is less crude, the extremism of the intent rivals that of the theses of *Mein Kampf*.

A passage from his course *The Essence of Truth*, which dates from precisely the same period as his seminar, confirms my reading. Heidegger writes: "The corporeal must be transposed *into the existence* of man. . . . Race and lineage also are to be understood in this way, and not described on the basis of an outdated liberal biology."[82]

We see in an explicit and definitive way that Heidegger does not in the least reject the idea of race but refuses to understand that idea on the basis of a science qualified as "liberal" and thus opposed in principle to the *völkisch* foundations of National Socialism. Furthermore, in qualifying that biology as "outdated," he is targeting the biology inherited from the nineteenth century. Heidegger speaks on the same page of delivering the Germans from an error that "has lasted a century." Thus, he means to found the understanding of race in "existence." In short, it is his own doctrine of "truth" that he presents henceforth as alone being equal to the task of providing a foundation for the Hitlerian doctrine of "race" and of grasping the "total transformation" (*Gesamtwandel*)[83] of the existence of man initiated by the Führer's *Weltanschauung*.

I can now quote in its entirety the unpublished conclusion of the seventh session of the winter 1933–1934 seminar, one of the texts that best reveals the intensity of Heidegger's Hitlerism. We read the following.

> The bond with the order of the state is also a part of this knowledge. Order is the way of being of man and thereby also of the people. The order of the state expresses itself in the delimited field of duties of specific men and groups of men. This order is not just organic, as one might suppose, and did suppose, based on Menenius Agrippa's fable; rather it is something that is spiritual/ human, i.e., at the same time voluntary. It is grounded in the domination-servitude relation of men to one another. Like the medieval order of life, so also today the order of the state is sustained by the free, pure will to loyalty and leadership, that is, to combat and faithfulness. For when we ask: "What is domination? In what is it grounded?" then in a true, essential answer, we hear nothing of might, servitude, oppression, force. We hear rather that domina-

tion, authority, and service, subordination, are grounded in a common task. Only where leader and led together bind each other in *one* destiny, and fight for the realization of *one* idea, does true order grow. Then spiritual superiority and freedom respond in the form of deep dedication of all powers to the people, to the state, in the form of the most rigid training, as commitment, resistance, solitude, and love. Then the existence and the superiority of the *Führer* sink down into being, into the soul of the people and thus bind it authentically and passionately to the task. And when the people feel this dedication, they will let themselves be led into struggle, and they will want and love the struggle. They will develop and persist in their strength, be true and sacrifice themselves. With each new moment the Führer and the people will be bound more closely, in order to realize the essence of their state, that is their Being; growing together, they will oppose the two threatening forces, death and the devil, that is, impermanence and the falling away from one's own essence, with their meaningful, historical Being and Will.[84]

We can see clearly in this text that the insistence on the "spiritual" rather than on the "organic" indicates no distancing from Nazism. Quite to the contrary, to want to introduce the existence and superiority of the Führer into man's very being and into the soul of the people, is in effect to carry out a form of possession, since the principle of "decision" is not free individual choice but submission and training. Thus we see how Heidegger identifies totally with the principle of Hitlerism. The order of the state is assimilated to the *Führung-Gefolgschaft* relation, and "true order" consists in being *one* with the Führer.

As for the struggle of the Führer and his people against death and the devil, Heidegger's listeners could scarcely be unaware that in the chapter on "people and race" of *Mein Kampf* the Jew is identified with the devil. "No one need be surprised if among our people the personification of the devil as the symbol of all evil assumes the living shape of the Jew."[85]

In orchestrating the pathos of the devil in reference to the Führer, Heidegger awakens and cultivates the darkest side of Hitlerism in his students.

The tactic is analogous to the one Carl Schmitt used a few years later, at the end of his 1936 speech titled "The German Science of Law in Its Struggle Against the Jewish Spirit." When he affirmed that "in defending myself against the Jew, I struggle for the work of the Lord,"[86] he was repeating the conclusion of Chapter 3 of *Mein Kampf*.[87] Hitler used the same tactic in the chapter already quoted on "People and Race." There indeed we find a very political reference to Christ, who "took to the whip to drive from the temple of the Lord this adversary of all humanity," whom the Jew represented for Hitler.[88] We may conclude, then, that Heidegger, like Carl Schmitt after him, was striking, as Hitler did (and in referencing him), a religious chord to work in a particularly odious anti-Semitic allusion.

Heidegger and the Völkisch *State*

At the beginning of the next session, Heidegger's summary (with which he begins every session) returns to his critique of Bismarck and the shortcomings of the Second Reich. He does not stop at a simple reminder, but goes much further.

> I had something further to add on the internal causes of Bismarck's political failure. We have learned that, besides a Führer, a people also needs a tradition, passed on by a political nobility. If, after Bismarck's death, the Second Reich knew a hopeless decadence, the reason should be seen not only in the fact that Bismarck had not succeeded in creating that political nobility. He had not succeeded, either, in considering the emergence of a proletariat an occurrence justified in itself, nor in integrating it into the state and going forward to meet it in an understanding way. But the main reason is doubtless the fact that the *völkisch* character of the Second Reich was limited to what we call patriotism and fatherland. In themselves, these elements of the 1870–1871 unification should not be evaluated negatively, but they are totally insufficient for a truly *völkisch* state. Nor did they any longer have the least roots in the people.[89]

This time Heidegger proposes new reasons for the failure of the Second Reich. Not only did it lack a true Führer, not only was Bismarck unable to create that tradition-protecting "political nobility" that the Third Reich would create in the form of SA and SS officers: there were two other reasons that explained his failure. First, according to Heidegger, he did not succeed in integrating the proletariat into the state the way the Third Reich did. Must I evoke the reality of the Nazi "socialism" to which Heidegger refers here in a positive light? It begins by dissolving all unions and arresting, on 1 May 1933 (the day Heidegger officially joined the party) all the leaders of the workers. The Nazis created the Workers' Front, entirely controlled by the NSDAP, in its place. They also introduced the *Führung-Gefolgschaft* relation between the boss and the workers in all businesses. Such was the "understanding" integration of the proletariat with the state of the Führer.

But this still is not the most important point for Heidegger. The Second Reich's main shortcoming is to have kept to traditional patriotism, without being capable of founding a true *völkisch* state. Thus Heidegger embraces unreservedly the central term in *Mein Kampf*, that of the *völkischer Staat*. We know how Hitler, in his long developments on the *völkisch* state, characterizes it by the fact that it *"must place race at the center of all life."*[90] And he rebukes the former Reich for having neglected "the racial foundation of our *Volkstum,"*[91] whereas it is "the qualities of its essence which root in its blood"[92] that alone give a people the right, according to Hitler, to a life on earth. In embracing the notion of the *völkisch* state and the very particular conception of enrootedness in the people that is inseparable from it, Heidegger unquestionably adheres to the racist foundation of Hitlerism.

Heidegger and the Extension of the Living Space of the German People

In his seminar, Heidegger distinguished two ways of approaching the question of the state in its relation to the people. I have addressed the first: it proceeds by "setting out from above, from the general, from being and beings," considering the relation between the state and the people on the pattern of the relation between being and beings. And we have seen that it leads eventually to advocating the unity of the people with their Führer. The second, which I will now analyze as set forth in the eighth session, proceeds on the contrary "from below, from the people and the state, from ourselves." While reminding us that "it is impossible to consider the people without the state, in other words, beings without their being," Heidegger proposes a separation that is methodological and entirely provisional, in which the people and the state will be envisaged no longer together, but severally. It is the question of the people that will be taken up first, and, reminding us that "the process of nature and the events of history unfold in space and time," he invites his listeners to reflect on the determination of the people in space. The passage begins as follows: "When we inquire about the people in space, we must begin by eliminating two erroneous representations. When we hear those two terms, we first think of a contemporary slogan: 'a people without space.' If we understand by that living space, there is no doubt that it goes too far. One could perhaps say: a people without sufficient living space, necessary for its positive development. We should never forget that space is always necessarily a corollary of the people in their concrete being, and that literally there is no 'people without space.' "[93]

We get a sense of the initial climate of ideas from which Heidegger sets out, as he begins by mentioning the title of the then famous work by Hans Grimm, *People Without Space,*[94] the 1,200 pages of which constitute "a vehement diatribe against England" and the "skillful preparation for a politics of territorial conquests."[95] But Heidegger outdoes Grimm. His ontologizing of ideas leads him to say that every people as such has a living space. Here he is doing no more than espousing the thesis of the "correlation of man and world," to use Rothacker's terminology, or of the essential relation between *Dasein* and its surrounding world, to speak like Heidegger himself. *Lebensraum* is therefore just another formulation of *Umwelt*. Taken literally, the expression "people without space" is therefore meaningless. We must add: "without living space that is sufficient, necessary for its positive development." It is a clever way of justifying out of hand the living space of the German people.

After having thus ontologized the living space of the people by using a vocabulary inspired by *Being and Time*,[96] Heidegger approaches the difference between nomads and natives (*bodenständige Menschen*) in the following terms. "History teaches us that the nomads did not become what they are because of the bleakness of the desert and the steppes, but that they have even left numerous wastelands behind them that had been fertile and cultivated land when they arrived, and that men rooted in the soil have been able to create for themselves a native land, even in the wilderness."[97]

For him, the difference between natives and nomads apparently derives not from the necessary adaptation to the environment, of which all men are capable, but from a specificity of their own being. This comes down to suggesting that certain human beings and certain peoples are creators by essence, and others sterile. Thus Heidegger prepares, in the minds of his students, the discriminatory conclusions, which we will see later, on the "Semitic nomads," incapable of having access to the nature of the "German space."

But if an "authentic" people is characterized by enrootedness in a soil, how can the expansion of a people be justified? Here Heidegger declares that it is inaccurate to think that the ideal of a people consists solely in its autochthonous character, in its *Bodenständigkeit,* like the peasants who develop a sense of having sprung from the soil (*Bodenverwachsenheit*) and of belonging to it. "Circulation" (*Verkehr*) is equally necessary. Thus, the concrete way in which human beings operate in and shape space includes both enrootedness in the soil and "circulation": *Bodenständigkeit und Verkehr.*

Heidegger can now return to the question of the state, on the basis of what has just been affirmed about the people and their space. He uses all the resources of his vocabulary to introduce the notion of empire (*Reich*), affirming that the space of the state is in a certain sense the space of the autochthonous people understood as the actual development of its "circulation" in business and trade, the extension (*Be-reich*) of its power and the empire (*Reich*) of its regime and law. Hence the conclusion that we can speak of a state only when the will to extension, to "circulation," is added to enrootedness in the soil or the autochthonous characteristic (*Bodenständigkeit*).

Heidegger now comes down to distinguishing one's homeland (*Heimat*) from one's fatherland (*Vaterland*), which allows him to raise, in a very concrete way, the problem of those Germans who live outside the borders of the Reich. They have a German *Heimat* but do not belong to the German state, the Reich, and, Heidegger adds, they are thus deprived of their proper modality of being. We can see how he leads the listener to draw the conclusion that it is necessary to eliminate the existential gap between *völkisch* being and the official state being of Germans. Concretely, this means giving credibility to one of the two goals of Hitler's anti-Semitism: namely, the promulgation of the idea that the German people's living-space, which Schmitt later called their *Großraum*, extends far beyond the then current space of the Reich. Heidegger's teaching also tends to legitimate in advance the politics of annexation of Austria, the Sudetenland, and the territories of the east where German colonists resided—in short, the politics Hitler himself was preparing to put into action.

At the end of the eighth session, Heidegger justifies in advance, and in a truly criminal way, the discrimination that, in the eastern territories in which German colonists resided, would be put into practice between the German people, the Slavic peoples, and those he now calls the nomadic Semites—that is, mainly, the Jews, in reference to whom he no longer even speaks of a people. The "Semitic nomad" is therefore essentially deprived of all space of its own. This is indeed what Rector Heidegger taught his students, many of whom were to become combatants at the beginning of the following decade on the eastern front. "The nature of our German space would surely be apparent to a Slavic people in a different manner than to us; to a Semitic nomad, it may never be apparent."[98]

Thus the eradication of the Jews, essentially incapable of having any knowledge of the "German space" that is "specifically the *Völkisch*,"[99] is legitimated in advance by Heidegger.

Heidegger's Justification of Hitler's Domination

At the end of the eighth, and in the ninth and last session, Heidegger comes back to what makes up the major obsession of his seminar, namely the relation to the Führer. He is bent on specifying the conditions for a veritable political direction or *Führerschaft* and expresses himself as follows: "Führer is involved with the will of the people; the latter is not the sum of individual wills, but a whole constituted by an originary character of its own. The question of the awareness of the will of the community is a problem that is posed in all democracies, but one that of course can become fruitful only when the will of the Führer and the will of the people are identified in their essence. Today, the task consists in structuring, in accordance with this reality of the people and the Führer, the fundamental relation of our common being, in the course of which, both being one reality, they are not to be sundered. Only then, when that fundamental schema has essentially been successfully brought about through a sudden impulse, is a true *Führerschaft* possible."[100]

Let us make no mistake: Heidegger intends to advocate a notion of the "will of the people" that owes nothing to the general will according to Rousseau, whose notion of the social contract is explicitly rejected during the same session, along with all the "attempts at a deduction of the state in the seventeenth and eighteenth centuries." What is involved here is the identification of the will of the people with the will of the Führer, reducing all being to the latter. If, as Heidegger says in the same session, "the people are beings, the being of which is the state," that state in reality has no other being than the Führer's — that is to say Hitler's — total domination. And in the last session, Heidegger will justify that domination. He asserts the following. "A part of domination is power; the latter creates a hierarchy that allows the dominator to impose his will, if his power is real: in other words, it allows him to show the dominated ones the means and the ends."[101]

The question thus becomes: How can the Führer impose his will? Heidegger then coldly considers two possible "modalities of the imposition of will": "persuasion by words" and "coercion by action," it being understood, he says, that "in our time, the Führer persuades by words."[102] Heidegger goes so far as to give a radical apology for Hitler's inimitable and thumping (*trommelnd*) style, in which he does not shrink from comparing him to Thucydides![103]

But words are not enough: the superiority of the Führer is to be seen, according to Heidegger, in his adroitness in combining words and action. Indeed, "the active will persuades most effectively through action. The great implementer, he who acts, is at the same time the powerful, the dominant one, whose existence and will become decisive by persuasion, that is, by the knowledge and acknowledgment of the highest will of the Führer."[104]

What, then, is the goal of political education? Heidegger emphasizes it clearly: "Current political education = the fashioning of a new fundamental bearing of a volitional sort."[105]

The terminology is close to Rothacker's regarding the creation of a new "bearing" (*Haltung*). Thus we grasp more clearly what Heidegger has in mind when he speaks, in the course of winter 1933–1934 (contemporaneous with this seminar), of a "transformation of our entire existence," presented as "necessary,"[106] or again "the *great transformation of the existence of man*,"[107] and in reference to Hitler's words and to National Socialism, of "the fundamental transformation of the German world."[108] That radical transformation of man is not at all philosophical: it amounts to nothing less than a mutation of man's existence initiated by Hitler himself.

In the same spirit, Heidegger declares that "the will of the Führer begins by shaping the others into a *Gefolgschaft* from which the community springs forth. It is from this living attachment that their sacrifice and submission result, and not from compliance and institutional constraint."[109]

We can gauge on the basis of these words the radicalness with which Heidegger defends and advocates the principle of Hitlerism.

It is necessary, for a more precise understanding of the reality of the Third Reich and the way Heidegger participates in it, to distinguish between Nazism and Hitlerism. These two forces certainly made use of each other and joined in the same enterprise of destruction, but they are not identical. Nazism is dedicated to the promotion of a "pure" race in the community of the people and tends toward radical discrimination, followed by the physical elimination of all that opposes it or simply differs from it. Hitlerism seeks primarily to impose domination and total possession of each and all by the will and spirit of the Führer. The domination and destruction of individual consciousnesses targets first and foremost minds, and spreads through speech and writing.

Now, we see that Heidegger identified perfectly with and embraced this principle, to the point of thinking of himself as a — if not the — "spiritual" Führer of the movement. The seminar of the following year on Hegel and the state will confirm this for us. It is therefore impossible to reduce Heidegger's action to one or the other of the "variants" of National Socialism: what he received from Nazism and Hitlerism, and the direction that he himself wanted to impart to them, concerns the *integrality* of the phenomenon. On this point, therefore, I do not follow Victor Farías when he affirms in the preface of his book that "Heidegger chose the faction headed by Ernst Röhm and his Storm Troops [*Sturmabteilung*, or SA] and tried to base this variant of National Socialism on his own philosophy."[110] Indeed, although, as his correspondence with Rudolf Stadelmann shows, Heidegger initially approves of the increasing role of the SA at the university, he enters into conflict with their student representatives at the end of his rectorship. Further, the courses given after 30 June 1934, his renewed support of Hitler during the summer of 1934, his project written during the same period of an Advanced School of Professors of the Reich, as well as his participation in the activities of the Academy for German Law prove that Hitlerian and Nazi commitment was not shaken by the night of 30 June 1934. And we have no knowledge of relations established between Röhm and Heidegger, while we know that Heidegger was close to Goebbels's circle and, above all, totally fascinated with the physical person of Hitler, as evidenced, in addition to the Hitlerian seminar, by his declaration of

1933 to Karl Jaspers about "Hitler's admirable hands," or that of 1936 to Karl Löwith on his complete faith in the Führer, not to mention a considerable number of declarations taught or published during these same years. Finally, I have shown that there is no one "philosophy" of Heidegger, constituted in a coherent and distinct way, independent from his radical involvement in Nazism. This is sufficiently proven by the unfinished state of *Being and Time,* the way it already relates the destiny of authentic existence to the community of the people, and his affirmation at Davos about there being a *Weltanschauung* at the foundation of every philosophy.

I do not make these points to add to the criticisms that have been unjustly heaped on Farías. His book is definitely not based on that briefly articulated thesis, and the documents he has assembled in the third part of the work counterbalance the partiality of that view. My purpose is solely to demonstrate that the line followed by Heidegger cannot be identified with any particular "variant" of National Socialism. There is, then, no basis for speaking of a "Freiburg" National Socialism, or of a "private" one, as has sometimes been done by authors seeking to mitigate the importance of his participation. Too many texts, beginning with his rectoral address, reveal to us that he identified himself not only with Nazism but also with Hitlerism, and that he nourished the ambition of taking charge of the intellectual and "spiritual" direction of the entirety of the movement in combating its "liberal" deviations.

Heidegger and Hitler's Speeches

Having reached this point in our analysis, we must ask a question that will be submitted to the wisdom of future investigators. The high esteem in which Heidegger holds Hitler's speeches and style, his total defense of the principle of Hitlerism's domination as the basis of politics and the state, leads to a deeper questioning of the nature of the relation between Heidegger and Hitler. Is Heidegger simply one who comes to the support and defense of Hitler's work—which already represents an appallingly base act—or is his participation in the dictatorship of Hitlerism still more active? Anyone who, in his or her research, has had to carry out a close reading of Heidegger's speeches, lectures, and courses of the years 1933–1934, as well as certain of Hitler's speeches of the same period, cannot but be quite struck by the similarity of style and doctrine between many passages in the two men's speeches. That could be explained by Heidegger's mind having been steeped in the Hitlerian style.

But Heidegger did not just welcome and seek sustenance in Hitlerism: he also contributed actively in its supremacy, as we have seen in the ardor with which he dedicated himself to the introduction of the Führer principle at the university. How far did his pro-Hitler activity go? In this regard, we should be attentive to the fact, far too often overlooked, that many of the speeches delivered by Hitler were not written by him. To one who has had occasion to leaf through the *Völkischer Beobachter* of the years 1933–1934, it appears materially impossible that the Führer could have written entirely by himself all the countless run-on speeches he gave almost daily. Now, there is no exhaustive study on those who, in Hitler's close or distant entourage, had occasion to write notes, memoranda, and speech outlines addressed to his attention. In this connection, the telegram Heidegger sent to Chancellor Hitler on the attitude to take concerning the university union (*Hochschulverband*) looks like a public gesture of willingness to advise the Führer, the scope of which remains to be assessed. That would be a task far beyond the limits set for this work, but one that would be valuable to undertake one day. Indeed, when Heidegger declares at the beginning of his rectoral speech that "Führers are themselves also led," this is not idle talk. Today, now that we are able to compare Heidegger's speeches, courses, and certain still unpublished seminars, it indeed appears that he himself wanted to set the spiritual direction expressing Hitlerism's will to total domination over minds.

Without pretending to do more than take a few steps along the way of that task that remains to be undertaken, I would simply like to propose a hint in that direction. An important passage from the memorandum, or *Denkschrift*, of Hitler dated 15 December 1932, entitled "On the Internal Foundations for the Disposition to Produce a Stepped-Up Strike Power of the Movement,"[111] is, in conception, terminology, and style, particularly close to Heidegger's proposals found in his speeches and seminars of 1933–1934. Now, this memo has remained unpublished, and when in January 1943 Goebbels esteemed that it contained "such classical arguments" that it could be reused without amendment, Hitler had totally forgotten the document,[112] which would tend to indicate that he was not the author. Here is the passage in question.

"The *basis* of the political organization is loyalty. In it is revealed as the most noble expression of emotion the recognition of the necessity for *obedience* as the *premise* for the construction of every human community. Loyalty in obedience can *never* be replaced by formal technical measures and institutions, of whatever sort. The aim of the political organization is the enabling of the widest possible dissemination of the knowledge seen as necessary for the maintenance of the life of the nation, as well as the will that serves it. The final aim is thereby the mobilization of the nation for this idea. The *victory* of the National Socialist *idea* is the *goal* of our struggle, the organization of our party a means to attaining this goal."[113]

Ian Kershaw, in commenting on this text, remarks that "such ethereal language emphasizes how remote Hitler's conception of the party was from any notion of a bureaucratic organization." Now, it must be noted that this conception of the political, which reduces everything to the *Führung-Gefolgschaft* relation and the bond of faithfulness connecting the community to the will of the Führer, both united in the same "idea," is exactly what Heidegger constantly defends, in both his speeches and his seminar of winter semester 1933–1934. And Heidegger's conversation with Karl Löwith in 1936 still tends in the same direction. Indeed, he affirmed that "the only thing that seemed of concern to him was an excess of organization at the expense of living forces."[114]

I should, moreover, direct the reader's attention to the fact that if we do not know precisely what Heidegger's activities were from July 1932 to April 1933, during which time he benefited from a leave from teaching, his correspondence with Elisabeth Blochmann and what we know of his letters to Bultmann in December 1932 prove to us that his preoccupations were mainly political and linked to the rise to power of the NSDAP, for which he had voted. In any case, the way of italicizing key terms, the value placed on the one sole *idea*[115] and the pathos of loyalty (*Treue*)[116] are found particularly in the Hitlerian seminar dealt with in this chapter. The affinities between the *Denkschrift* attributed to Hitler and the orientation and words of Heidegger are thus substantive enough for the hypothesis I have formulated to merit examination.

Heidegger and the Führerstaat

We have seen Heidegger embrace the main component parts of Nazism and Hitlerism: the definition of the people as a community of blood and race, the *Führung-Gefolgschaft*, the justification of the *völkisch* state, and the legitimation of the extension of the living space of the German people; we have seen him express his fascination for the speeches of the "drummer" — as Hitler called himself — and for the persuasive power of his propaganda; finally, we have seen him deliver an apology for the principle of Hitlerism and even contribute to its creation, specifically on the subject of the community of the people's consisting in a living bond uniting it with its Führer. In all the developments of this seminar on the state, there is nothing philosophical, then, and nothing more than the expression of an active and complicit fascination on Martin Heidegger's part for everything Hitler represents.

What is more, in the conclusions of the last session, he pushes his absolutizing of the Hitlerian state to the very end, not hesitating to affirm the following. "The state . . . is the most real reality, which must give a new meaning to the totality of being, an original meaning. It is in the state that the highest realization of what the human being is takes place."[117]

Now the state, which is supposed to give a new meaning to the "totality of being" and allow "the highest realization" of the human being, is, as Heidegger now says explicitly, the Hitlerian state, the *Führerstaat*. Here he places, as did Hitler himself, the Third Reich in the continuity of the preceding ones, and thus of the Prussian state, and he does not hesitate to claim the political legacy of Lutheranism, obviously gone astray in that confusion. That is Heidegger's conclusion, with which I will also end this chapter, for the radical Hitlerism of the author of *Being and Time* has now been sufficiently demonstrated.

"The *Führerstaat* — such as we possess it — means the accomplishment of the historical development, the realization of the people in the *Führer*. The Prussian state, such as it was perfected by the formative thrust of Prussian nobility, is the preliminary form of today's state. This relation bears witness to the elective affinity that exists between Prussianism and the Führer. It is from that grand tradition that the words, imbued with the Lutheran spirit, of the great Prince Elector spring forth, and we hold to them as we profess their meaning: *I will administer the domain in such a way as not to forget that it is the people's good, not my own.*"[118]

6

Heidegger, Carl Schmitt, and Alfred Baeumler: The Struggle Against the Enemy and His Extermination

Heidegger's two unpublished seminars—the Hitlerian seminar we have just studied and the one titled *Hegel, on the State,* which we will approach soon—shed new light on the relations between Martin Heidegger and Carl Schmitt. There we discover that when he treats politics, Heidegger is led to bring up Schmitt's conception of the political in an explicit manner, and he does so not to identify himself with it but in order to differ, without, however, refuting Schmitt's conception. Yet it would be wrong to place the relation between the two men on a strictly intellectual level. In reality, their relation does not consist in a dialogue between two thinkers but unfolds within the framework of the most brutal world of action of Nazi politics and the Hitlerian undertaking, at the moment of the "bringing into line," or *Gleichschaltung,* which both of them support and even assist in carrying out, in several decisive ways. I have shown the active role played by Heidegger; I will say a few words about the activity of Carl Schmitt, as well as Baeumler, in justifying the struggle against "the enemy" and the call for his extermination.

Carl Schmitt and the Gleichschaltung *as a Means Toward the Racial "Homogeneity" of the People*

I have already mentioned the publication by Ernst Forsthoff of a substantial passage from Heidegger's rectoral address, published alongside the twelve anti-Semitic theses "Against the Un-German Spirit."[1] It must be added that Forsthoff is an insufficiently recognized link between Heidegger and Carl Schmitt. Born in 1902, he is, with Ernst Rudolf Huber and Theodor Maunz, one of the main ultra-Nazi and virulent anti-Semitic disciples of Carl Schmitt. Well before the 1933 power takeover, he collaborated under various pennames on several anti-Semitic magazines. In 1930 Carl Schmitt helped in having him defend his habilitation thesis. After an unsuccessful attempt at Bonn, it was at the University of Freiburg that Forsthoff defended it, on 12 May 1930, under the direction of jurist Fritz Freiherr von Marschall. A junior lecturer in the Faculty of Law of Freiburg until spring 1933, Forstoff was then appointed at Frankfurt to the chair of jurist Hermann Heller, who had been an opponent of Carl Schmitt in the legal case of the "Prussian coup," or *Preußenschlag,* of 1932 and dismissed in April 1933 as a Jew by the law of "Restoration of the Professional Civil Service." Forsthoff, a Protestant, was close to Erik Wolf and remained so until after 1945, as attested to by an exchange of letters between the two men after the defeat of the Reich. The correspondence has been preserved in the Wolf Archives of the University of Freiburg.[2] In view of these various connections, it is likely that Forsthoff and Heidegger met at Freiburg during the years 1930–1933. Furthermore, Forsthoff was the author, in 1933, of *The Total State (Der Totale Staat),* a work of considerable impact, notably quoted by Erik Wolf the same year as a reference. And when Heidegger himself in his unpublished seminar of 1934–1934 speaks of "the total state," it is not only to Carl Schmitt's but equally to Forsthoff's work that he is certainly alluding. But let us get to Schmitt himself.

The commentary Carl Schmitt published on the current *Gleichschaltung* on 12 May 1933 in the *Westdeutscher Beobachter,* titled "The Good Right of the German Revolution," explicitly shows the anti-Semitic and racist goal of that "bringing into line." As is his custom, he plays on the word *gleich,* which means both "equal" and "identical" and is found in the term *Gleichartigkeit.* The term is ambiguous, and Schmitt will play at length, and despicably so, on that ambiguity before 1933. Indeed, it can be associated with the word *Gleichheit,* which means "equality" — but also "similarity" — and can thus coincide with the democratic concept of political and social equality. But Schmitt uses the term *Homogeneität* as a synonym of *Gleichartigkeit,* and by the end of the 1920s, it becomes clear that what he calls, specifically in his *Theory of the*

Constitution of 1928, "the substantial homogeneity of the people" (*die substantielle Gleichartigkeit des Volkes*) is a reference not in the least to social equality but to something entirely different—something of a racial order. Now what amounts to a verbal shell game is that during that period Schmitt retains the term "democracy" to oppose it to "liberalism," but the way he understands the *demos*, the people, is already pre-Nazi, and he does not conceal the fact that "political democracy" such as he understands it is perfectly compatible with dictatorship. In the long notice to the second (1926) edition of his work *The Historical-Spiritual Situation of Present-Day Parliamentarianism*, Schmitt reveals himself a bit more. He affirms that "what necessarily belongs first to a democracy is homogeneity, and second—if need be—the expulsion or extermination [*Vernichtung*] of heterogeneity."[3] That "if need be" (*nötigenfalls*) is particularly nefarious, for all of Schmitt's work in Nazism will consist in justifying the "extermination of the heterogeneous."

And yet—to return to his commentary on the "bringing into line"—in May 1933 Schmitt can allow himself to be much more outspoken. He writes: "German law and the German state no longer rest on the empty and formal 'equality of all before the law' or the deceptive phrase 'equality of all that has a human face,' but on the real homogeneous and substantial nature of the entire German people, unified in itself and homogeneous. *Gleichartigkeit* is something more, and something more profound than *Gleichschaltung*, which is but a means and an instrument for *Gleichartigkeit*. . . . The decisions concerning magistrates, doctors, and lawyers purify public life from non-Aryan elements foreign to the race."[4]

It is therefore evident not only that the *Gleichschaltung* is a political "bringing into line" but that its goal is racial "reconstruction" or "homogeneity," by the exclusion of "non-Aryan elements of a foreign race" from "public life." That is the goal of the "Law for the Restoration of the Professional Civil Service" of 7 April 1933, but that law is only a beginning. Nazism will go much further with the racial laws of Nuremberg of 15 September 1935 (of which Schmitt will become an enthusiastic commentator in a document titled "The Constitution of Freedom"), then with the *Kristallnacht* of 1938 and the "Final Solution" decided on in 1942. This series of events was openly announced prior to 1933, since we have seen Carl Schmitt as early as 1926 cold-bloodedly envisage, as did Hitler in *Mein Kampf*, "the extermination" of so-called heterogeneous elements.

What it is of the utmost importance to be clear about is that the "bringing into line" accomplished by Nazism was brought about simultaneously by deeds and by words, both spoken and written. In this respect, the jurists appear at the center of the plan, at least until 1936, for soon the time will come when the police and the army will definitively take over from the "law." But the succession of laws that impose the ever more radical racial exclusion of "non-Aryans" from the German community merely translates into acts what already existed in the texts. Behind the jurists there are the "philosophers," and the evolution we witness in the works of Schmitt, from his *Theory of the Constitution* of 1928 to his writings of the year 1933, is comparable to that of Heidegger, from *Being and Time* in 1927 to the courses, speeches, and lectures of 1933–1935, via the courses of winter 1929–1930 on the *Fundamental Concepts of Metaphysics,* in which the political orientation of Heidegger begins to transpire clearly, especially in paragraph 38. There he evokes in the same sentence "the political imbroglio" (*die politische Wirrnis*) and "uprootedness of philosophy" (*die Bodenlosigkeit der Philosophie*), followed by the necessity of leading *Dasein* back to "the enrooted unity of an essential action" (*wurzelhaften Einheit eines wesentlichen Handelns*) and of "being strong at the foundation of our essence" (*in Grunde unseres Wesens stark zu sein*).[5]

It is therefore indispensable that we dig deeper into the nature of the relationship between Heidegger and Schmitt, because that will enlighten us on the actual responsibility of Heidegger and on the way in which the "philosophers" of Nazism and its "jurists" (the terms must be put in quotation marks) mutually encourage and inspire each other. I will begin by recalling what we know currently of the Schmitt-Heidegger relationship in 1933 before proceeding to the manner in which the relationship is manifested in their writings of the period.

Heidegger's Letter to Carl Schmitt of 22 August 1933, the Desire for a "Decisive Collaboration" Between the Two Men, and the Nazification of the Faculty of Law at Freiburg

The year 1933 was not only that of a common commitment to Nazism on the part of Heidegger and Carl Schmitt, who both joined the NSDAP on the same day; it was also that of an intellectual and political collaboration between the two men, confirmed by the fact that their writings of the period bear the mark of a deep and undeniable reciprocal influence. This is why Karl Vossler and Karl Jaspers were right in associating them in a common political destiny.[6] Still, it seems difficult to speak of an "exchange of letters" between Heidegger and Schmitt,[7] since, as I will show, we possess at the present time only one letter from Heidegger to Schmitt, with no known response from the latter. Nevertheless, the revelation by that letter of the fact that the two men agreed in 1933 on the same conception of the *polemos* allows us to bring to light how deeply racism runs in their doctrine.

On 22 August 1933, soon after the proclamation of the law on the introduction of the Führer principle at the universities of the Badenland, Heidegger wrote to Carl Schmitt as follows.

> Most honored Mr. Schmitt,
>
> I thank you for having sent me your text, which I already know in the second edition and which contains an approach of the greatest importance. I would be most appreciative if I could speak with you about this *viva voce* some day. On the topic of your quotation of Heraclitus, I especially appreciated the fact that you did not forget the *basileus,* which alone gives the whole saying its full content, when it is fully interpreted. For years I have had such an interpretation ready, concerning the concept of truth — *edeixe* and *epoiçse* [reveals and makes], which appear in fragment 53. But I now find myself also in the middle of the *polemos,* and the literary projects must give way. I would only like to say to you today that I am counting very much on your decisive collaboration, when it comes to the entire rebuilding, from the inside, of the Faculty of Law, in its educational and scientific orientation. Here the situation is unfortunately quite hopeless. The gathering of spiritual forces, which should lead up to what is coming, becomes increasingly urgent. I conclude today with my friendliest salutations.
>
> Heil Hitler!
>
> Your Heidegger[8]

Heidegger's letter is in response to his having been sent the third edition of *The Concept of the Political,* published by Carl Schmitt in 1933 with many revisions. It is possible that Schmitt's mailing was itself preceded by that of Heidegger's rectoral address, because the first edition of the address is found in the *Nachlaß Schmitt* of Düsseldorf. We learn from Heidegger that he already knew the second edition, dated 1932, and that he particularly appreciated the important modifications introduced by Schmitt at the beginning of the third, published by the Hanseatische Verlagsanstalt. The preceding year that Nazi workshop in Hamburg published Jünger's *The Worker,* and then, in 1933, Forsthoff's *The Total State* and Schmitt's *State, Movement, People.*

The reference to Heraclitus seems all the more enigmatic in that Schmitt does not quote the fragment in his third edition of *The Concept of the Political* but is content with alluding to it in a note added in 1933, apropos of Baeumler's interpretation of Nietzsche and Heraclitus. It is possible that Heidegger was referring to the handwritten dedication of the book, in which Schmitt may have quoted the fragment in question. It seems less likely that Heidegger was answering an accompanying letter, despite that suggestion by the American editors of the journal *Telos,* because Schmitt was in the habit of keeping a copy of his letters. There is no trace of a letter from Schmitt to Heidegger in the

Nachlaß Schmitt. If indeed there was a letter, that would mean that Schmitt intentionally hid or destroyed it to conceal the reality of their relations.

An analysis of the sources leads one to believe that all that exists (or at least all that has been kept in the recorded public archives) is one letter from Heidegger to Carl Schmitt. Indeed, the existence of a prior letter dated 22 April 1933 is supported by no known text. The first mention of such a letter appears in a study by Joseph Bendersky, *Carl Schmitt: Theorist for the Reich,* in 1983. Bendersky simply notes that Heidegger wrote to Schmitt in 1933, inviting him to "collaborate," and he gives the date of 22 April. In 1987 Victor Farías wrote that "it was Heidegger who invited Carl Schmitt to join the National Socialist movement, in a letter dated April 22, 1933, located in Schmitt's personal archives."[9] But since Farías gives the reference not to the *Nachlaß Schmitt* but only to the page from Bendersky already referred to, we may conclude that he overinterpreted the invitation to collaborate laconically alluded to in the latter.[10] In short, it is probable that Bendersky saw the actual handwritten letter of 22 August 1933, or a copy of it, and misread the month. In that case, the invitation to collaborate was not an invitation to join the Nazi Party but the wish for a "decisive collaboration [*entscheidende Mitarbeit*] on the restructuring of the Faculty of Law," which we find mentioned in the letter of 22 August.[11] Whatever the case may actually be, after the efforts of Bendersky and Farías, the letter of 22 "April" and Heidegger's supposed invitation to join the NSDAP have been brought up more than once by commentators on Schmitt in France, without anyone having taken it upon themselves to verify whether the letter really existed.

Carl Schmitt was doubly attentive to the suggestions in the only letter currently known from Heidegger, that of 22 August 1933. First, it induced him to use it in his own writings. In his two lectures at the beginning of 1934, *The Three Types of Juridical Thought,* he proposes a rather long exegesis of the notion of *nomos basileus* and refers to a saying from Heraclitus[12] (fragment 22, it is true, not 53). Schmitt, however, relates the *nomos basileus* or "*nomos king*" not to Heraclitus but to Pindar.[13] After having mentioned that the expression had been interpreted in a normative way, taking it in the sense of law as king, he maintains that *nomos* means not "law" but "right," and not only means the norm but decision, and even above all the order. This allows him to arrive at "the concrete order of the king or *Führer.*" We have, then, in Schmitt's terms, "a true coordination. Just as *the nomos is king,* so *the king is nomos.*"[14] And Schmitt goes on to make hay of a note that Hölderlin placed beneath his translation of Pindar and that was published in the edition of his works by Norbert von Hellingrath. In Hölderlin's note, which Carl Schmitt quotes, the *nomos* includes inherited statutes that safeguard "*the living conditions* in which *a people found and finds itself in the presence of itself.*"[15] As we can see, Heidegger was not the only one to make use of Hölderlin.

As a jurist and academician, moreover, Schmitt fulfilled Heidegger's expectations. He underlined, in those same 1934 lectures, the necessity of reinforcing the rector of the university's power. From the fact that in the *Gleichschaltung* the rights of the senate were conferred on the rector, Schmitt asserts that "it would be an error to exclude from this transfer of powers those involving the exercise of disciplinary law and tribunals of honor, under the pretext that those would constitute [conflict of] jurisdiction [with courts of law]."[16] Therefore he wants to add disciplinary and judicial powers to those of Rector-Führer, which would allow him to exercise an absolute dictatorship at the university. According to Schmitt, not to confer this judicial power on the rector would be tantamount to giving in to the arguments of a "normativism separating the powers and destroying the concept of *Führung.*"

In addition, Schmitt will participate in the Nazification of Freiburg's Faculty of Law. We have seen that the date of the letter addressed to Schmitt is not insignificant: Heidegger sent it shortly after the proclamation by the minister of the Badenland of the new constitution of the universities. That constitution introduced the *Führerprinzip,* according to which the new rector was no longer to be elected by the full professors but directly appointed by the minister and empowered with appointing the deans of the various faculties himself. The new constitution, by eliminating the principle of election and therefore of academic freedom, instituted de facto the "bringing into line" of the university, which Heidegger expressed his ardent hope for as early as 20 May 1933, in a telegram to Hitler.[17] We have seen that Heidegger hurried to spread the news of this change in the university constitution to all professors and assistants on 24 August 1933,[18] but as he wrote shortly afterward to Elisabeth Blochmann, although the rector and deans found themselves endowed with considerable powers, the men to carry out this alignment were lacking.[19] That was true at the time especially of the Faculty of Law—whence no doubt the call to Carl Schmitt, which made up the second part of the letter. In this also, Heidegger's call did not fall on deaf ears.

The problem he encountered in his desire for a "bringing into line" of the Faculty of Law was that the latter, which was actually called "Faculty of Law and Political Sciences," grouped together, besides the jurists, the economists, among whom he was to encounter his main adversaries in the persons of Walter Eucken and Adolf Lampe. He therefore turned to a young Nazi jurist, Erik Wolf, at once a fanatic follower of his and, as we shall see from his writings, ideologically very close to Forsthoff and Schmitt. Though Wolf was not yet a member of the NSDAP, he did belong during the summer of 1933 to the *NS-Juristenbund,* which in fact constituted adhesion to the "movement." That partially Schmittian orientation of the Faculty of Law, marked by the presence at its head of Dean Erik Wolf, would later be reinforced by the appointment of Nazi jurists. Of the two professors of Roman law, one had been and the other was soon to be dismissed for racial reasons, so that there were vacancies for two new tenured professors to be appointed. The first, Theodor Maunz, was one of the closest disciples of Carl Schmitt, who, moreover, would recommend him warmly to the University of Freiburg and vouch for the National Socialist orientation of the new *Dozent.*[20] The second, Horst Müller, was a declared anti-Semite who would participate, as well as Maunz, in the Days of 1936 against the Jewish spirit, organized by Schmitt in the presence of Julius Streicher. Thus we may say that Heidegger's wishes were, in 1935, on the way to being fulfilled, and that the following year, in 1936, with the active participation of the two new professors in the Anti-Semitic Days organized by Schmitt, the Nazification of the Faculty of Law had been brought about in a Schmittian spirit — that is, by the application, in the "science" of law, of the principle of racial identity, or *Artgleichheit.*

That organization was perfectly orchestrated, and, on 1 May 1937, the three young Nazi jurists of the Faculty of Law at Freiburg, Wolf, Maunz, and Müller, joined the NSDAP together, thus reenacting what had been carried out four years earlier by Heidegger, Schmitt, Rothacker, and Freyer. We see then how far Heidegger's letter to Schmitt was from being just a polite response on receiving a book: it was a concrete call for the realization of a joint plan for the Nazification of the university, and of law in particular.

Schmitt's Identification of the Enemy with the Racial Foreigner in the 1933 Edition of The Concept of the Political *Praised by Heidegger*

I will now go into more detail on the way in which Heidegger recognizes himself in Schmitt's writings and how that is reflected in his own writings. I will not try to establish which one inspired the other first, because it seems rather to have been the case that there was between them an interaction. In Nazism, in which individuality is abolished, the various figures communicate subterraneanly with one another and make up one body, like members irrigated by the same "blood" — or rather the same poison. In order to bring to light the reciprocal influence between Heidegger and Schmitt, I will turn successively to the third edition of *The Concept of the Political* sent by Schmitt in 1933, the reference to Baeumler that was added to it, and the conception of the enemy developed by Heidegger himself in his course of winter 1933–1934.

What was the beginning or the approach (*Ansatz*) that, in the 1933 edition, takes on such great importance for Heidegger? We will note that in his letter to Schmitt he uses the same word (*Ansatz*) that he used a year later in his letter to Rothacker. In the 1933 edition, the entire first chapter, as well as the first paragraph of the second chapter, are eliminated; thus Schmitt begins his exposition directly with the discrimination between friend and enemy, which is no longer stated as "specifically" but as "properly [*eigentlich*] *political*."[21] He takes up on his own behalf the most central term of the existential analytic of *Being and Time,* thus confirming the correctness of those who identify Heidegger's distinction between proper and improper (or authentic and inauthentic) existence with Schmitt's distinction between friend and enemy. It is important to emphasize, in this connection, that *Being and Time* and the first edition of *The Concept of the Political* appeared the same year, 1927. To speak of "properly *political*" discernment is indeed to indicate that it is those who are capable of discerning the enemy who possess the "proper" conception of political existence, whereas the "liberal" conception of politics, which tends toward the peaceful resolution of conflicts through discussion, is "improper."

Furthermore, two important additions must be pointed out, because they are what quite probably attracted Heidegger's interest. As we will see, there is an almost exact echo of Schmitt's considerations in the course Heidegger gave during the winter semester of 1933–1934, *The Essence of Truth.*

First, following the passage in which the author of *The Concept of the Political* points out that the political enemy is the other, the stranger, he adds in 1933 a series of considerations that show, for those familiar with the racial vocabulary of the period as it was constituted from Clauß to Schmitt and Forsthoff, that the words "friend" and "enemy" are to him racial terms. The friend is identified as "of the same race" (*gleichgeartet*) and the enemy as "of another race" (*andersgeartet*). Thus Schmitt makes it clear that "the possibility of specifically political relations is given by the circumstance that not only are there friends — of the same race and allied — but also enemies."[22] The following sentence is almost identical to the one in the preceding edition, with one nuance of difference that is not without significance. The adjective "existential," already used in 1932 to emphasize the fact that the enemy is constitutively something other and foreign, is, in 1933, put in italics and repeated. "The enemy is, in a particularly intense sense, *existentially* an other and a stranger, with whom, in an extreme case, *existential* conflicts are possible."[23]

Thus, in the 1933 edition, the racial vocabulary of "homogeneity" (*Gleichartigkeit*) and the existential vocabulary of the proper, of authenticity (*Eigentlichkeit*), and of existence, common to both Heidegger and Schmitt, come together and merge explicitly for the purpose of justifying the radicalness of the "political" conflict. If the enemy is "existentially" such, that is, by his very "essence" and race (*Art*), a stranger, then the friend/enemy conflict is existential in the sense that it is the existence of the other that is at stake, without there being any mediation possible, whether by norms or a third party. The annihilation of the enemy becomes not only justified but "existentially" necessary.

The danger of this doctrine cannot be overemphasized. On the one hand it rejects the legitimacy of an international law and the possibility of a legal resolution of political conflicts, and on the other it reduces politics to a racial struggle. It opens the path to a war of annihilation; already in 1933 it foresees and legitimates the path on which the Hitlerian Reich will set out.

In the 1933 edition Schmitt adds a long development that deserves to be quoted, because it may be the one that so interested Heidegger.

> A foreigner could decide neither the question whether the "extreme case" is given, nor the broader one of what "extreme means" are vital in order to defend one's own existence and preserve one's own being — *in suo esse perseverare*. He who is a foreigner and of another race [*Andersgeartete*] might well claim to be strictly "critical," "neutral," and "purely scientific" and under the cover of similar disguises he might smuggle in his foreign judgment. His "objectivity" is but a political *disguise* or else a total *isolation* that misses all that is essential. In the political decision, the only possibility of fair recognition and understanding, and therefore also the competence to give one's advice and to judge, can rest only on an existential *having-a-stake-in* and *taking-part-in*: the authentic *participatio*. That is why only the participants *themselves*, among one another, can discern the extreme case of conflict; and more specifically, each one of them can only decide *himself* the question of knowing whether, in the case of the conflict presenting itself concretely, the other-being of the foreigner means the negation of one's own type of existence [*eigene Art Existenz*] and must for that reason be kept at a distance or combated, in order to save one's own type of life, in keeping with one's own being.[24]

In this long addition, the word *being* is central. Indeed, Schmitt introduces a third distinction, posited as the equivalent of the first two: there is no longer just the *Freund/Feind* and the *gleichgeartet/andersgeartet* distinction, but also the one between the own-being and other-being — *das eigene Sein* and *das Anderssein*. In short, the words *Art* and *Sein,* "type" or "race" and "being," are used as synonyms. Schmitt procures for the Nazi struggle between the races an existential and "ontological" support taken from Heidegger's "doctrine" itself. Thus he gives us a racial reading of the Heideggerian "ontology" that we may consider to have been approved by Heidegger, since the latter expressed, in his letter to Schmitt, what a high opinion he had of the 1933 version of *The Concept of the Political.*

This is a very important point, revealing to us as it does the racial connotations of Heidegger's expressions, constantly reiterated, involving being, such as "the rank of being" or even "the truth of being." We will find the confirmation of this in many of Heidegger's texts, especially in the recently published ones on Ernst Jünger.[25] We can say that Heidegger is, in comparison to authors like Clauß, Becker, Rothacker, Wolf, or Schmitt, the one who has taken the greatest care to hide, beneath apparently indeterminate terms such as "being" or "existence" (*Dasein*), the racial content of Nazism, revealing the true meaning of his "doctrine" only at particularly chosen moments.

To return to Carl Schmitt, the racial meaning of the *gleichgeartet/andersgeartet* distinction is undeniable: we have only to read his work that came out the same year by the same publisher to be persuaded. In *State, Movement, People,* Schmitt inverts, so to speak, the word *Gleichartigkeit* and speaks thereafter of *Artgleichheit,* a term whose racial meaning is already manifest in Clauß's *The Nordic Soul* (1923), and one that, in Schmitt, denotes the racial identity uniting the Führer with his people in the "community of the people" (*Volksgemeinschaft*). If, in 1933, the anti-Semitic goal of Carl Schmitt was not as brutally thematized as it would be in 1936, for example, during the congress he organized against "the Jewish spirit," it must be said that we are at a time when, by calculation and strategy, Hitler himself muted his anti-Semitic utterances. In German academic life, explicit, brutal anti-Semitism was not prevalent at the time, except among a few extreme agitators like Krieck — whose career was purely political and who was taken seriously only out of fear of power, when, during the years of 1935–1937, he was able to avail himself of powerful supporters in the SD — or in a more controlled but no less abhorrent way, among the younger authors like Forsthoff, who did not hesitate to go even further than their master. In Ernst Forsthoff, the anti-Semitic meaning of the term *Artgleichheit* is explicitly asserted. In *The Total State* he writes: "The consciousness of racial identity and *völkisch* solidarity is realized above all in the ability to recognize racial difference and to distinguish the friend from the enemy. In truth it all depends on recognizing racial difference even when it is not immediately visible through an affiliation with a foreign nation, such as in the case of the Jew, who through an active sharing in cultural and economic life has sought to create — and successfully so — the illusion of racial homogeneity and of belonging to the people."[26]

For this disciple, things are totally explicit: Schmitt's discrimination between friend and enemy is a racial one, and it is directed first and foremost against the "Jew," who, despite all his efforts to assimilate and become integrated in the cultural and economic life of a people, is exposed by racist awareness, which recognizes in him his radical difference. As for Schmitt, he is more adumbrative and wily: in the page quoted, the anti-Semitism transpires in an allusive and indirect way, through Spinoza's Latin quotation: *in suo esse perseverare.*

Carl Schmitt's Note on Baeumler and Jünger and Baeumler's Reference to Heraclitus

As we have seen, Heidegger's letter seems to refer both to the beginning of the new 1933 edition of *The Concept of the Political* and to a long additional note in which Schmitt speaks of the relationship among combat, politics, and war; and he refers specifically to Heraclitus. That note is important, since it is most probably what motivated Schmitt's quotation of aphorism 53, either in a handwritten dedication or an accompanying letter. Now, this is how Schmitt brings Heraclitus in at the beginning of the note.

> A. Baeumler interprets Nietzsche's and Heraclitus's concept of combat in a totally agonistic mode. Question: Where do the enemies in Walhalla come from? H. Schaefer, in *Form of the State and Politics* (1932), refers to the "agonistic underlying character" of Greek life; even in bloody confrontations between Greeks and Greeks, combat was only "agon," the opponent only an "antagonist," a player on the other team, an opponent, not an enemy, and consequently the conclusion of the contest was not a peace treaty (*eirçnç*). That did not end until the Peloponnesian War, as the political unity of Greece was shattered. In every in-depth examination of war, the great metaphysical opposition of *agonistic* versus *political* thought emerges. Regarding the most recent times, I would like to mention here the great polemic between Ernst Jünger and Paul Adams . . . , which hopefully will soon be available in print. There Ernst Jünger represented the agonistic ("Man was not made for peace") while Paul Adams saw the meaning of war in the bringing about of domination, order, and peace.[27]

This note is quite representative of Schmitt's way of expressing himself, which jumps from allusion to allusion without offering a well-constructed and clear line of argument. For the well-informed reader, the appearance of erudition cannot mask the deficiency of thought, and if his knowledge of Latin allows him to make use of concise and striking formulations, I do not see on what basis certain interpreters have managed to speak about him as a great political thinker. Though I will not be able to analyze the content of the note completely here, I will retain several things. First of all, the reference to Baeumler, which I will examine for its own sake; then the reference to Jünger, which is equally important; finally, and more generally, the fact that the question of the enemy (*Feind*) — understood as *hostis* and not as *inimicus* — is explicitly envisaged by Schmitt in relation to war. This means that the political enemy in question is not a private adversary, distinguished by a feeling of personal antipathy, but a public enemy, whom one combats to defend one's existence. This enemy corresponds to the Latin *hostis* or the Greek *polemios*, and Schmitt, on the same page, explicitly translates *polemos* as war (*Krieg*). We shall see the importance of this point as it relates to Heidegger.

The way Schmitt refers to Baeumler and Jünger is, then, partially critical. In his view, they perceived only the "agonistic" character of combat, valued in its own right, so to speak, by its character of being a violent struggle between two antagonists: they did not recognize what was, in Schmitt's view, the true meaning of the struggle of a people for its existence. But there is intentional misdirection in this note, as is constantly the case with Schmitt. In speaking of the opposition of Paul Adams to Jünger, Schmitt seems to want to favor a political conception of war, which alone would make it possible to arrive at a conclusive peace treaty, while the agonistic struggle, which has no goal beyond itself, would be endless. But another note on the same page, in which he bases his opinion on his reading of Plato to define his way of understanding *polemos*, reveals what he really has in mind. An internecine struggle, a struggle between Greeks, could not be a true battle between enemies. "Only a war between Hellenes and barbarians [who are, according to Schmitt, 'enemies by nature'] is a true war." There is, then, no true war except between opposing peoples, "enemies by nature," that is, those not of the same race. Far from leading to peace, the "true war" in his view is a war "for one's existence," and it leads necessarily to the annihilation of the enemy. By 1926 he makes reference to *Vernichtung,* and in his correspondence with Jünger he enjoys quoting Léon Bloy's "War is meaningless unless it is exterminatory."[28] The spirit in which Schmitt quotes Baeumler and Jünger is comparable to the spirit in which Heidegger uses Schmitt in his seminars. These references show the Nazi context in which their "reflections" on politics evolve, as well as each one's concern to show that he is the only one to define the political in all its radicalness. But the reference to Baeumler is in itself very important, because it refers to a text that was a source common to Schmitt and Heidegger. The work by Baeumler to which Schmitt alludes is none other than *Nietzsche, the Philosopher and the Politician,* published in 1931 and of considerable influence. The author, who had just reedited *The Will to Power* with a postscript that Heidegger praised, had undertaken, with this book on Nietzsche, to "treat [him] as a thinker of European standing and placed alongside Descartes, Leibnitz, and Kant." Well before Heidegger, he took Nietzsche's "metaphysics" seriously, highlighted his "perspectivism," and centered his interpretation on the "will to power." One chapter is dedicated to what he calls "the world of Heraclitus," and that is where the page mentioned by Schmitt can be found. Here is what Baeumler wrote.

> The assumed preconditions of justice are inequality and struggle. This justice does not rule over the world; it does not rule over the tumult of conflicting parties; it knows neither culpability nor responsibility, nor judicial procedure nor sentencing. It is immanent to struggle. That is why it is not possible in a peaceful world. Justice can exist only where forces are given free reign to measure themselves against one another. Under an absolute authority, in an order of things that recognizes a divine master, in the domain of the *Pax Romana,* there is no longer any justice, because there is no longer any struggle there. The world is petrified in a conventional form. Nietzsche, to the contrary, asserts: Justice is regenerated at every moment out of struggle, which is the father of all things. It is conflict that makes the master, master and the slave, slave. Thus speaks Heraclitus of Ephesus. But this is also an originally Germanic conception: in struggle is revealed who is noble and who is not; it is by his innate courage that the master becomes master, and it is by his cowardliness that the slave becomes slave. And it is precisely in this way that eternal justice is expressed; it structures and separates, it creates the order of the world, it is at the origin of every distinction of rank. This is how, out of Nietzsche's nodal German/Greek metaphysics, his great doctrine arose: that there is not one morality, but a master morality and a slave morality.[29]

We find on this page from Baeumler several oft-repeated themes of Heidegger's, in particular the central reference to fragment 53 of Heraclitus, reinterpreted in keeping with Nietzsche's *Genealogy of Morals.* We see first of all how Baeumler borrows Nietzsche's notion of a "justice" immanent to strife, to which Heidegger will give the status of one of the five key words of Nietzsche's "metaphysics." This "justice" is precisely the opposite of what is normally understood by this word, since it does not serve equality but, on the contrary, consecrates the radical inequality between master and slave and founds the "distinction of rank" with which Baeumler is intoxicated. The critique of Romanism, that of the world without struggle envisaged by Christianity and democracy, the exaltation of Heraclitus, whose fragment is identified with the "originally Germanic conception" — these points are found not only in Heidegger's courses on Nietzsche but also, for many of them, in the winter course of 1933–1934.

It should be added that while for Baeumler the meaning of struggle is derived from what he calls "German/Greek metaphysics," what is "political" about his interpretation is that he identifies the enemy clearly. In the developments that follow the page quoted, he insists on what he calls Nietzsche's "warlike nature" (*Kriegernatur*).[30] The author of *Also sprach Zarathustra* was, in his view, "a warrior down to his very instincts."[31] Baeumler then posits the opposition between "peoples like the Germans and the Greeks," warrior peoples who know only "the force of their destiny," and those they are confronted with — namely, "the world of priests" and "the world of the upholders of the Enlightenment." What Baeumler is describing thus goes far beyond the agonistic conflict to which Schmitt would reduce it. What we have here is truly a war between peoples, between those who by nature possess a sense of war and those who don't. The Nazism of this conception is manifest, in which the master holds his rank with an innate courage, and in which certain peoples are said to be warriors (the Greek and Germanic peoples) "by nature," whereas others cannot be: the peoples of priests and supporters of the Enlightenment, in which the Latin peoples, the Jews, and the French are lumped together in his mind. So the attempts of certain apologists to have us believe that Baeumler, by his "heroic realism," is only a Fascist, or even a simple representative of the "conservative revolution," and not a Nazi, are ridiculous in the face of these texts and the reality of the facts. Alfred Baeumler is one of the very rare German academics to belong to the NSDAP before 1933. He is, in 1932–1933, the Nazi figure closest to Heidegger and will be able to play the role the "movement" expects of him when he is appointed, immediately after the Nazi power takeover, to a chair of "political education" created for him at the University of Berlin.[32] As we have seen, it is Baeumler who puts the finishing touches on the anti-Semitic theses of the Deutsche Studentenschaft and delivers a speech on 10 May 1933 after Goebbels, before the flames fed by "non-German" books.

The "Truth" Related to the Heimat

In 1933–1936, Heidegger — far more even than Baeumler, but doubtless influenced by him and, as I will show, by Schmitt's conception of the enemy — makes the interpretation of Heraclitus's fragment 53 the centerpiece of his doctrine. We have seen how in his letter to Schmitt he tied his reading of that aphorism to his interpretation of the concept of *truth* and said that he had had that interpretation "ready for years." This would appear to indicate that his theses on *polemos* or struggle (*Kampf*) and war (*Krieg*), taught in his winter course of 1933–1934, had been elaborated over a long period of time and therefore that the Nazi foundations he openly claimed in 1933 had for years been at the basis of his work.

In this connection there is a text, still unpublished, that requires our scrutiny: the first version of his lecture "On the Essence of Truth," given in July 1930 during the *Heimattag* of the Badenland, held on 11 July 1930 to celebrate the recent withdrawal of French troops from the Rhineland. Heidegger was joined for the occasion by Nazi figures as well known as Eugen Fischer and Ernst Krieck. We should be able to determine whether the premises of the interpretation of the concept of "truth" in relation to *polemos* are already present. From what has been reported to us about the first version of that lecture, we do indeed know that Heidegger was already referring to Nietzsche and the pre-Socratics, and that he linked "authenticity" (*Wahrhaftigkeit*) to enrootedness in the native soil (*Bodenständigkeit*). It is these two concepts that the review of the convention published by the *Karlsruher Zeitung* chose to retain.[33] Charles Bambach states specifically that it contains "*völkisch* themes," but these do not appear explicitly in the edited version of the text.[34] In the version of this lecture read after the war, to which special prestige was attached because Heidegger had led the public to believe it had almost been banned in 1943 (without divulging the fact that the lecture in fact had appeared with the support of Mussolini and Goebbels),[35] the underlying basis of his "doctrine" is intentionally disguised and veiled — but it is very perceptible to the reader already informed (by the courses of 1933–1934) of how Heidegger understands "the historical existence" of man. In the original text, on the contrary, "truth" is related in a very explicit way to the soil of the *Heimat*.[36] These details are crucial because they reveal that Heidegger's conception of "truth" as "uncovering" (*aletheia*) is in reality conceived as the manifestation of a depth that is enrooted in the earth and native soil: it is the *völkisch* conception that bears Nazi principles within itself. Heidegger's work does not contribute a new notion of truth capable of enlightening all thought, but on the contrary it promotes the downfall of truth grasped in its universality, in favor of a discriminatory doctrine that abuses the word "truth" by relating it to "the historical existence" of man, who is essentially rooted in the soil of his *Heimat*.

The Extermination of the Enemy in the Winter Course of 1933–1934

To return now to Heidegger's interpretation of Heraclitus, which he says he has held ready for years — he delivers it to his students in his winter semester course of 1933–1934, titled *The Essence of Truth*. In the introduction to the course there is an entire paragraph under the heading "The maxim of Heraclitus. Strife as the essence of the entity." What it is about, Heidegger announces, is "listening to the voice of the great beginning," not to become Greeks but to perceive "the original laws of our race as Germanic men,"[37] or what he calls on the same page "the fundamental possibilities of the essence of the original Germanic race."[38] The racial character of these theses on the Greek beginning in its relation to the "Germanic race" is therefore totally accepted. Thus he sees in Heraclitus, in his course of the following year on Hölderlin's "The Rhine," "the name of an original power of Occidental-Germanic historical existence"![39] Heidegger's "doctrine" is therefore to be related to the version of the racial doctrine of Nazism that considers the Greeks as the Aryan people who were precursors of the Germans.

Then there begins a strange exegesis of the fragment from Heraclitus, as follows.

> With grandeur and simplicity, at the beginning of the fragment, there appears the word *polemos, war [Krieg]*.[40] What is so designated is not the external event or the advance of the "military" but rather that which is decisive: to stand up against the enemy. I have translated this as "struggle" to seize the essential; but it is also important to reflect on the following: it is not a question of *agon*, vying/competition, in which two friendly [*freundliche*] adversaries measure forces against one another, but of *polemos*, war [*Krieg*]; which means that there is something serious in struggle; the adversary is not a partner, but an enemy. Struggle as a holding out in the face of the enemy; more precisely, as endurance in confrontation.[41]

Polemos is not a simple competition (*agon*) between friendly (*freundlich*) adversaries but indeed a struggle, a war, which means that "the adversary is not a partner, but an enemy." Heidegger repeats precisely the same assertions made by Carl Schmitt in *The Concept of the Political*. Schmitt is therefore his starting point, and we will have to remember this point when we see that after being so much in debt to him, he declares that Schmitt's concept of the political is merely derivative, his own idea of the political being the more originary.[42]

The only element of the development that differs somewhat in tone from Schmitt's is the insistence on "holding one's own," or the fact of standing up (*Stehen*) against the enemy. Heidegger will use all the linguistic variations surrounding this word *Stehen* to make of struggle the "rising up in being," "the original surging up from being," and the manifestation of "truth." It is in this that Heidegger is undoubtedly more dangerous than Schmitt, because his "ontologizing" of violence and struggle, which he inscribes at the very heart "of being," gives that murderous doctrine a deceptive appearance of existential "nobility" that has seduced and fooled a considerable number of readers. But recently published texts prompt us to be more vigilant.

We also see two occasions on which Heidegger translates the Greek *polemos* as "war." Even if it is not his intention to reduce that term to the advancing of "the military," even if he undertakes to "ontologize" the concept of war, it is clear that actual warfare is included in this concept. Other texts, such as the speech of Constance of the end of May 1934, or the previously mentioned lectures of August 1934,[43] definitively confirm this. Heidegger introduces his interpretation of Heraclitus's fragment 53 by evoking the Great War,[44] and he makes of the "world war" the "great trial for *each* people," and the question put to all peoples: whether they want "to renew their youth or get old."[45]

Returning now to the courses of 1933–1934, the three ways of translating *polemos* used by Heidegger — "war" (*Krieg*), "struggle" (*Kampf*), and "confrontation" (*Auseinandersetzung*) — are therefore indissociable, any one of them being replaceable by another; and although Heidegger can play on one or another of these terms depending on the tone he wishes to impart to his texts, his denials in 1945, in which he attempts to foster the belief that the term *polemos* in his work has nothing to do with war,[46] appear laughable today in light of the reading of these texts.

Here a development by Heidegger that, in perfect harmony with the words of a Schmitt or a Forsthoff, explains that it is a matter of finding and flushing out the enemy at the innermost root of the existence of a people, and of unmasking him, the better to exterminate him.

> The enemy is one who poses an essential threat to the existence of the people and its members. The enemy is not necessarily the outside enemy, and the outside enemy is not necessarily the most dangerous. It may even appear that there is no enemy at all. The root requirement is then to find the enemy, to bring him to light or even to create him, in order that there may be that standing up to the enemy, and that existence not become apathetic. The enemy may have grafted himself onto the innermost root of the existence of a people, and oppose the latter's ownmost essence, acting contrary to it. All the keener and harsher and more difficult is then the struggle, for only a very small part of the struggle consists in mutual blows; it is often much harder and more exhausting to seek out the enemy as such, and to lead him to reveal himself, to avoid nurturing illusions about him, to remain ready to attack, to cultivate and increase constant preparedness and to initiate the attack on a long-term basis, with the goal of total extermination.[47]

That is one of the most indefensible pages of Heidegger because the struggle he describes against the enemy lying in wait at the very root of the people describes precisely, in his own characteristic language, the reality of the racial fight of Nazism and Hitlerism against the Jews assimilated to the German people, which will lead, in the course of those years of 1933–1935, from the first anti-Semitic measures I have described as being a part of the *Gleichschaltung* to the anti-Jewish laws of Nuremberg and the *Endlösung,* or "Final Solution."

Moreover, it is not just a question of recognizing the enemy, or even, in some sense, of "creating" him by identifying him, but of exterminating him. Heidegger, like Schmitt and Hitler, does not hesitate to use the word *Vernichtung*. If, in this course, Heidegger's racial vocabulary is not entirely the same as that of Schmitt or Fortsthoff, since the former speaks *Stamm* (but also, in other passages, of *Stammesart*) while the two latter speak of *Artgleichheit*, they all strive toward the same goal: to recognize and flush out the enemy, who is adjudged a threat from within to the innermost essence of the Germanic people and race, and to provoke an existential struggle that will lead to his extermination.

What is particularly perverse in Heidegger's doctrine is that if struggle is understood as a "decision," that decision can express only "the essence of being." Just as in Baeumler, when he affirms that a people is warlike by nature, Heidegger maintains that one is a master or a slave, according to what is harbored within one's "being." So there are, exactly as in Hitler, peoples who by their essence are destined to dominate, and others fated to be subjugated. Of the long and miry expositions in Heidegger's course that tend in this direction, I give the following passage as an example.

> The essence of being is struggle; all being passes through decision, victory, and defeat. One is not simply either a god or a man, but with being in every case there falls a combative decision that places struggle in being; one is not a serf because that exists among other things, but because that being harbors within itself a defeat, a lack, an insufficiency, a cowardliness, and perhaps even a wanting to be inferior and weak. Hence it becomes clear: struggle is that which places within and maintains within being; it is what decides on the essence of being, and it does so in such a way as to *invest* every entity with a *decisional character*: the constant acuity of the either/or; either them or me; either hold out, or succumb. This combative decisional character of every being brings into the entity a *fundamental mood*, which is at once victorious rejoicing and will, the awesomeness of the untrammeled rush (resistance), elevation, and ferocity in one—which we are not equal to expressing in a word, but for which the Greeks had a word, recurrent in the great poetry of the tragedians: *to deinon* [that which inspires terror].[48]

Heidegger's strategy gives him greater effectiveness in the long run compared with Baeumler. What is that strategy? It is, to use an expression Baeumler applies to Nietzsche (and which Heidegger applies to Jünger), to have succeeded in converting "heroic realism" into maxims about "being" and its "truth," and in giving his words a captivating tone that has engulfed many a reader. I, for one, think that there is nothing more twisted than the enjoyment Heidegger claims to derive from the experience of war and struggle. It is true that Jünger and Hitler preceded him down that path. Jünger, in his work

Struggle as Inner Experience (1922), writes the following. "It is struggle that makes men and times what they are. Never yet has a race like ours stepped into the arena of the earth to decide in battle who will hold sway in their time. . . . War, the father of all things, is ours as well; he has hammered, welded, and hardened us into what we are. And ever, so long as the swinging ring of life turns within us, will this war be the axis round about which it whirs. War has reared us for struggle, and fighters we shall remain, as long as we exist."[49]

When Jünger writes these lines, he cannot be unaware of the fact that the *Freikorps* had adopted the swastika as its emblem in 1918. He himself will soon praise the swastika, and we may legitimately wonder whether that whirring ring of life he celebrates in combat may not correspond to that emblem.

To return to Heidegger, we now know the nature of the doctrine on war he transmitted to his philosophy students at the University of Freiburg, during those years when the teaching body and soon the student body itself were being "purged" of their non-Aryan members. It is important that we realize that that doctrine of the enemy and *polemos,* however "ontologized" it may be by Heidegger, is in no form or fashion a simple theoretical view or intellectual game but indeed a radically murderous doctrine, the translation of which into the real world cannot but lead to the war of extermination and the concentration camps.

As for the enemy, Heidegger often designates him as "the Asiatic." In the language of the National Socialism of the times that he openly embraces here, the term unequivocally designates first and foremost the Jews, then the Bolsheviks, and more generally it can ultimately refer to all the potential enemies of Germany, to the extent that they are considered to be in the clutches of what Heidegger, in his letter to Geheimrat Schwoerer, called "Jewification . . . in the broad sense." Now, the term already comes up in Heidegger in the 1933–1934 course, in which he speaks of the powers that are let loose "like something frantic, unbridled, spellbinding and wild, furious, Asiatic."[50] And as in Ludwig Clauß's *The Nordic Soul,* he assimilates "the opposing forces in warfare" to "what Nietzsche calls the Apollonian and the Dionysian."[51]

Frequently thereafter we find Heidegger identifying the enemy with the Asiatic. This is the case in the lecture of 30 November 1934, in which he speaks of "the great decision of the earth against the *Asiatic*";[52] in the course on Hölderlin's "Germania" in which we saw that he makes Heraclitus "the name of an original power of the historical Occidental-Germanic Dasein . . . in its first confrontation with the Asiatic";[53] in the lecture delivered in Rome on 8 April 1936 and titled "Europe and German Philosophy," in which, already in the beginning lines, he advances the idea that the salvation of Europe depends on "the preservation of the European peoples against the Asiatic";[54] and in the 1937 text titled *Wege zur Aussprache*. The war between the Hellenes and the Barbarians appears, then, exactly as in Carl Schmitt's *The Concept of the Political,* as the model and the matrix of the wars, present and future, between the historical *Dasein* of the Germanic people and its existential adversary, in which it will be decided in each instance who will be master and who slave. Thus we understand why this struggle can become externalized into a world war but begin with an internal conflict—obviously of a racial nature—the very one to which the Nazis commit themselves in Germany beginning in 1933. Hence the conclusion is inevitable. Hitler announces on 30 January 1939, in his most frightful speech, that the world war will mean "the extermination of the Jewish race in Europe." He calls it "his prophecy," which he will carry out with the "Final Solution," decided upon in January 1942. Now, this is quite simply the ultimate translation into action of what Heidegger theorizes in 1933, at which time he already spoke, as we have seen, of a "total annihilation."

Therefore we must take seriously what authors such as Heidegger or Schmitt spell out in their writings or express in their lectures and classes. When they use the word "extermination" (*Vernichtung*), it is no mere idle fancy. Coming from much-heeded sources, these statements catch on and prepare the future, pending their translation into deeds, and history has shown how rapidly these fatal statements are implemented in Hitlerism.

It is impossible to overemphasize this point after having seen the author of a work like *The Politics of Friendship* (which has unfortunately contributed greatly to the planetary dissemination of the ideas of Schmitt and Heidegger), allowing himself to be caught up in all the snares devised by these two Nazis. Taking the case of Heidegger alone, Jacques Derrida affirms that "Heidegger never names the enemy,"[55] although the texts in which he designates "the Asiatic" as the enemy—that is, in the language of the period, mainly the Jews—are legion. The author also declares in several instances that the Heideggerian *polemos* is "certainly not" a "human war,"[56] and he goes so far as to magnify "the originary . . . *Kampf.*"[57] It is true that he fleetingly perceives that Heidegger could furnish a "justification" to "those who have nothing but *Kampf* on their lips," but he suggests that that justification is "the most worthy and the most thoughtful."[58] Now even if Derrida could not have had access to all the texts now published in the so-called complete edition, the courses already published, such as those of 1934–1935 on Hölderlin's hymns, should have alerted him to the danger of the doctrine and its true objectives, since their racial content is clear and the designation of the adversary as "the Asiatic" is explicit.[59] To call upon his listeners to hunt down the enemy at the root level of the people and to exterminate him entirely — surely this tends in the direction of the destruction of all human dignity and all thought. It is indeed nothing short of a call for the physical, moral, and spiritual destruction of the enemy, who is identified by Heidegger and Schmitt with what is foreign to the racial "essence" of the people.

7

Law and Race: Erik Wolf Between Heidegger, Schmitt, and Rosenberg

In order to assess the activity and the "doctrine" of Heidegger during the period of his rectorship, but also during the years that followed, it is indispensable that we direct our attention to the figures he surrounded himself with, and the ones he himself appointed to important academic responsibilities. After having invited the collaboration of Carl Schmitt to restructure the Faculty of Law "from within," he appointed Erik Wolf, a young jurist who was already entirely devoted to him personally, as well as to his "doctrine," dean of that faculty. From then on and to the end Wolf remained the closest of Heidegger's close friends. He participated in the seminar on Hegel and the state during winter semester 1934–1935, the analysis of which will be the topic of our next chapter.

The increasingly spirited resistance encountered by Erik Wolf's activism at the university was the most decisive element in Heidegger's resignation of the rectorship on 27 April 1934. Later on, Wolf accepted responsibilities in the Confessing Church, which might give the impression that his Nazi commitment had diminished. In 1945 Heidegger capitalized on his ties with Wolf to give his resignation the appearance of the expression of some reservations with respect to the National Socialist powers. Since then, many apologists have repeated and embroidered on the same argument.

But Erik Wolf's complicity in National Socialism was radical. He had been a member of the League of National Socialist Jurists since the summer of 1933, and in his lectures and articles published from 1933 to 1935 he embraced the Nazi racial doctrine and eugenics, and adopted the idea of the total state of Carl Schmitt and Ernst Forsthoff, becoming its apologist. Hugo Ott recalled that Erik Wolf was "completely aligned, and even beyond" in 1933,[1] but it remains to be determined, on the basis of the texts, what his commitment to National Socialism was in terms of "doctrine." In order to accomplish this we have a certain number of texts at our disposal: the lectures, articles, and works published by Erik Wolf from 1933 to 1944, the rough draft of a justificatory letter intended for Karl Barth (written after the Nazi defeat, it was not sent, and was published after his death by Alexander Hollerbach), and finally a second justificatory text written with the French authorities in mind and never published, which I discovered in the Colmar Archives of the Ministry of Foreign Affairs. I will also base my arguments on the unpublished letters of Wolf to his editor, which I was able to consult in the Klostermann Archive recently deposited at Marbach.

The Racist and Organic Conception of the Total State and the People Developed by Erik Wolf Under Heidegger's Rectorship

Born in 1903, Swiss and German by nationality, Erik Wolf comes from the school of Neo-Kantianism. He met Heidegger in 1928, the same year he befriended Gerhard Husserl, a jurist like himself, a colleague at the University of Kiel and son of the founder of phenomenology. From the following year on, Erik Wolf was Heidegger's disciple, and he frequented the circle of Stefan George with intensity. That "conversion" to Heidegger contributed decisively to the destruction of the ethical boundaries that might have kept him from becoming an unconditional supporter of Hitlerism. In 1933 he broke off all ties with Gerhard Husserl and showed no solidarity or compassion during the anti-Semitic persecutions of his former friend. He acceded to the university senate in May of that year, at the moment Heidegger became rector. He became involved in a violent conflict with the economist Walter Eucken, who criticizes him for being a Heidegger fanatic. We have already seen that during the summer of 1933 he joined the *NS-Juristenbund*. On October 1, using the powers invested in him by the *Führerprinzip*, Heidegger appointed Erik Wolf dean of the Faculty of Law, replacing Eduard Kern. Again, Wolf's fanatic activism met with the opposition of his colleagues, but its effect was to draw Wolf's student disciples into the paramilitary organizations of Nazism. In the end, the opposition from his colleagues and within the Karlsruhe ministry — which eventually became alarmed by the ensuing problems — constituted the main cause of Heidegger's resignation from the rectorate. Erik Wolf no more distanced himself from Nazism on that account than did his teacher Heidegger. The titles of the courses he taught during the summer semester of 1934 bear witness to this: "The Idea of Law for National Socialism" or "The Battle Against Criminality in the National Socialist State."[2]

Among the texts he published during the years 1933–1935, there are two that must attract our attention. The first is titled *The True Law in the National Socialist State*. It is the text of a lecture given at the University of Freiburg on 7 December 1933. This is one in the series of lectures all students were required to attend on "the tasks of spiritual life in the National Socialist state," instituted by the Rector-Führer, who attended it personally in an official capacity. The text appeared in 1934, constituting the thirteenth issue in the series of "Freiburg University Addresses" — the eleventh being none other than Heidegger's rectoral address (there were only four addresses in that series under Heidegger's rectorship). Thus we see how many things connect the text of that lecture by Wolf to Heidegger himself: Wolf was then a young Nazi jurist, a member of the NSLB, appointed two months earlier by Rector Heidegger, who had him speak in a series of official, mandatory lectures that he attended personally as rector, thus lending it his authority. To this factual data must be added factors that are even more decisive, because they are more internal to the text itself and therefore to the "doctrine" of the young dean. It suffices to read the first paragraph to appreciate how much the terminology and style are tributary to Heidegger's work. "Law belongs to the original essence of man himself, since we recognize man's essence by the fact, among others, that it possesses a world of law. This being-in-the-world-of-law is inescapable, and the question of true law undeniably follows from it. It is not something that is derived from the broodings of modern times, and it does not consist in anything that can be written down on paper. It is something that lives in the blood."[3]

Erik Wolf takes on the role of disciple, partly by referring to the "original essence of man himself" (*ursprünglichen Wesen des Menschen selbst*), and partly by borrowing the notion of "being in the world" from *Being and Time*, to form a new existential: "Being-in-the-world-of-law" (*in-der-Welt-des-Rechts-sein*). In very Heideggerian fashion, the term *Mensch* disappears in the following paragraphs, yielding to the word *Dasein*. Further, the reference to blood is precisely in the tone of Heidegger's speeches and courses of that period. It is not the simple mention of what is called the "right of blood": as the rest of the passage proves, it is an explicitly racial idea.

Erik Wolf, after a first critical part in which he dismisses both the natural law of the eighteenth century and the positive law of the nineteenth,[4] relates the essential component of our existence or *Dasein* to the "destiny of the community of the German people."[5] "Our true law," he says. "can only be . . . the law of National Socialism in the Third Reich."[6] What does this mean? In order to define the law of National Socialism today, the fact of referring back to the old program of the NSDAP, or to the "war book" of Hitler (*Hitlers Kampfbuch*), is not sufficient. Not that the reference to Hitler is unnecessary in Erik Wolf's view; on the contrary, as he points out, it is a question of defining not an administrative law of the state but a "law of the people," for as the Führer so well expressed it, the state is but a means for him to an end that is "the complete realization of the *Volksgemeinschaft*."[7] In the National Socialist perspective that he accepted as his own, the reference to the people could not suffice without it being immediately made clear to what ideas the notion of the people was to be connected. Therefore Erik Wolf becomes more explicit. "There are, first of all, two realities of natural historical life: the people and the race. From these come two requirements regarding each individual life: the common interest and the sense of sacrifice. And two values aspire to realize these requirements: the unity of the nation and the social community. The totality of the life in which that happens is called the state, the total state. Within it, the constitution of the new law must be realized."[8]

Thus, the people is understood in its relation to the race, from which emanate the "values" that are to be realized in the total state. The fundamentally racial dimension of the community of the people and of the "sense of sacrifice" in National Socialism is therefore very explicitly affirmed by Erik Wolf.

Need I again emphasize that these words and this racial conception of law were apparently approved and encouraged by Rector Heidegger? Indeed, he not only got Erik Wolf appointed dean of the Faculty of Law two months earlier, but he refused to accept the resignation tendered to him by the latter in a pathetic letter, the very evening of his lecture, and retained him in his position, in the name of the Führer principle, without taking his arguments into consideration. Following that refused resignation, Heidegger sent a letter on 20 December 1933 to all the deans and teaching faculty of the university, in which we read that in the National Socialist state, "the individual, wherever he may be, counts for nothing. The destiny of our people in their state counts for everything."[9]

From the point of view of doctrine, Erik Wolf's clarification reveals a well-informed National Socialism. He introduces the idea of a "total state," forged in Germany by Carl Schmitt before being taken over in 1933 by his disciple Ernst Forsthoff (whose name, as we shall see, Erik Wolf specifically invokes), not in reference to the Italian, fascist *stato totalitario,* which is not what this is about, but on the basis of the racial conception of the life of the people, which is specific to Nazism. The state is total in that it brings together the totality of the German life of the race and the people. In short, as in Forsthoff, the Wolfian concept of the *totaler Staat* is explicitly racist.

As for the people, the term is not at all limited to designating the citizens of a state grouped within the same borders. Here Erik Wolf proposes a clarification identical to Heidegger's in his 1934 summer semester course. "But the people in the National Socialist sense does not correspond to the population within the borders of the *Reich,* either; it also contains, in a larger sense, all those who are of the German race in other territories. For the National Socialist, the organism of the people is not the accumulation of a mass of single individuals, but a unity structured within by groups according to occupation. The corporative structure rests on the natural order of the people, which are marriage and family, community and race, and finally the state."[10]

The spirit of the people thus understood becomes directly the source of law. The *Volksrecht* is nourished by the *Volksgeist.* But we must take note of where the "spirit of the people" is to be found, according to Wolf: in the SA and SS movement, and the *Hitlerjugend.* He writes: "And above all we must not forget this: the law of the people, emanating from their spirit, is also growing at present. Where there is an authentic life of the people at the present time — that is where the beginning of the new law is to be found. In the unwritten law of the camaraderie of the SA and SS, in the new forms of life of the Hitler Youth, in many a truly grown professional organization, in the NSBO [National Socialist Factory Cell Organization] and the Work Front, living law is practiced, which bears within itself the strength necessary for generalized validity."[11]

What we must always bear in mind in reading these pages of Erik Wolf is that we are dealing with the words of a jurist — words that not only pertain to the order of discourse but are intended to be translated into social practices, decrees, and laws. If, for the Nazis, the *Volksrecht* is at the origin of an unwritten law, it is destined to be translated into laws such as the Nuremberg Law on the "safeguarding of German blood."

It is indispensable at this point to quote the passage in which Erik Wolf sums up his understanding of race (*Rasse*). His positions take up those of Heidegger himself very precisely and condense in a particularly explicit manner the entirety of the positions expressed by the latter in his courses, speeches, and proclamations of the years 1933–1934, as well as his Hitlerian seminar of winter 1933–1934. There we find the same racist attachment to the German stock, the same partial distancing from biology alone (on which the "modern anthropology" relies too exclusively, in unfavorable contrast with the "being-authentic" of the Germans), the same care taken to conceive of the racial community as being equally a linguistic one, and the same legitimizing of the most radical eugenics. We read:

The new life of the people understands itself and its history on the basis of a new lived experience of *race*. And the very heart of that experience resides less in reflection on the biological origin of the evolution of peoples than in the living experience of the racist being-authentic of the Germans, whose cultural development has taken place, over the course of a thousand-year development, without any significant influence from those of alien race. Of alien race means not belonging to one of the four German races that are intermingled with one another: the Nordic, the Phalian, the Dinaric, and the Alpine, which derive from the Indo-Germanic or Aryan root race. In opposition to the theory of imperialistic nationalism, which only admits the concept "people" as determined on the basis of economic and cultural communities of a human mass governable by the state, for National Socialism the foundation of the community of the people is the racial and linguistic community; it is to the latter community that National Socialism grants priority, and not at all on the basis of merely biological considerations. It is not based solely on that outcome of modern anthropology according to which, to use an expression of Eugen Fischer, "the destiny of peoples and states is the most strongly and decisively influenced by the racial characteristics of their members." Rather it has succeeded (and this had previously been accomplished only fragmentarily) in turning the fact of belonging to a specific race into the spiritual and political experience of large portions of the people. This involves a communal experience with very diversified traits; the foundations of it are not only, or even essentially, natural. The experience of the race carries intrinsically within itself spiritual elements, such as tradition, family, nobility, bearing [*Haltung*], and convictions.[12]

This text is essential to the purpose of my work, specifically because it furnishes the proof that one can perfectly well express reservations about a solely biological comprehension of racial doctrine and bring up the "spiritual" and political dimensions of the people understood as race, while at the same time adopting, in the most radical manner, the racial doctrine of Nazism. Thus it is not because Heidegger, like his disciple Erik Wolf, criticizes "biologism" and wants to connect blood to "spirit" that he is not deeply racist all the same in his *völkisch* conception of the Germanic people and nation.

Erik Wolf now draws the "legal" consequences of his development.

Consequently, this new experience also has an effect on legal thought. The insight becomes increasingly widespread that a people's law cannot make abstraction of the racial origin of the people. In this process, the issue of the participation of the various Aryan races in the construction of our community of the people should not be put in the foreground. That could easily lead to a rivalry that would imperil unity. All the German races must take part in the legal construction of the National Socialist state. The legal meaning of racial thought cannot reside in a legal preference for the Nordic types of race to the detriment of the others. It rests on the measures that will be taken to preserve the composition of the German race such as it is today, among which are protection from the foreigner, by excluding those who are of a foreign race from the acquisition of land and real estate,[13] in making their civil integration more difficult, in restricting their immediate influence on education, jurisdiction, conduct of affairs of state, and publications. In order to keep the degradation of the race from progressing at the heart of the German people, it is appropriate to impose prescriptions such as social eugenics, forced sterilization of professional criminals and those afflicted with grave hereditary diseases, and finally the curbing of emigration.[14]

Such then is the racist and eugenic doctrine of the man Heidegger himself and his apologists presented after the war as a non-Nazi jurist. Such misrepresentation requires that I pause to stress several important points.

1. The terminology used shows clearly that the words *Rasse* and *Stamm* are used interchangeably, which is an important point for our reading of Heidegger, who, avoiding as much as possible *Fremdwörter* and other *römische Wörter,* uses the word *Stamm* far more frequently than *Rasse.* This does not mean, then, that Heidegger is less racist than Wolf, but on the contrary that he is, if that is possible, still more racist, since his *völkisch* racism is expressed in the form of an unparalleled vigilance in his choice of words and in the language itself.

2. As I have emphasized, Erik Wolf's speech proves that it is perfectly possible for a "jurist" like himself, or for a "philosopher" like Heidegger, to take up a distinct distance from an exclusively biological interpretation of the German people and race (such as that of a Nazi "doctor" like Eugen Fischer), without being any less of a racist than those who explain race exclusively by biology. For a Nazi to criticize the exclusively biological approach therefore does not in any sense mean that he is not a racist. This is perspicuous in Erik Wolf's unreserved adhesion to the Nazi identification of the "German race" with the allegedly "Aryan" races, and to the fate reserved for those of foreign races — that is, above all, the Jews.

3. Among the Nazis themselves, we have seen that there are certain divergences in the definition of the Aryan race. Those who, like Alfred Rosenberg or Hans Günther, praise mainly the so-called Nordic race, clash with the breakaway group of Nazi theoreticians, generally from southern Germany, who express their reservations about that preference. Among this group there are those, like Fritz Merkenschlager (in whom Ernst Jünger was particularly interested), who rely on the concept of "German race" and those, like Erik Wolf or Erich Rothacker, who accept Günther's classification into four — then

five — German races but try to temper "Nordicism" by insisting on the participation of the different races, and in a jurist like Wolf, by insisting on the eugenic and racist measures to be taken.

We can, then, retain the fact that Wolf shows himself to be an expert on the *Rassenkunde* of the times and the debates then going on between the defenders of the "Nordic race" and the proponents of the "German race";[15] and that he is inclined to side more with the second tendency, which though as racist as the first will ultimately not prevail, despite its being the one that tends more toward the *völkisch* identification between "race" and "people."

4. We notice in Wolf, as in Heidegger, the concern to define racial affiliation not only in biological terms but also and especially in "spiritual" ones. There is nothing original about this. It can be found in most of the Nazi writings and speeches of the era, especially in the first Nazi years, when the word *Geist* is even more frequently used than *Rasse*. The directly Hitlerian origin of that Nazi appropriation of spirit is seen in the use of the word *Geist* in *Mein Kampf* and in the famous speech of August 1933, in which Hitler defines race by spirit, a speech Rothacker specifically uses to bolster his position.

5. The reference to Eugen Fischer is worthy of particular emphasis; the bonds of friendship that existed between him and Martin Heidegger, which continued until after the war, are known today. Here, Wolf's reference to Eugen Fischer is laden with significance. It is generally known that he was one of the very first and major theoreticians of eugenics, racial hygiene, and genocide of supposedly "inferior" peoples, even before the Nazi takeover. It was at the institute he directed in Berlin that Doctor Josef Mengele, among others, would receive his formation. In 1933, Eugen Fischer, who was to be promptly appointed rector of the University of Berlin by the Nazis, presents himself not only as a theoretician of Nazi medicine but also, in a speech that was immediately printed by two different publishers, as a political theoretician of the *völkisch* state. His speech is titled *The Völkisch Concept of the State, Considered from a Biological Standpoint*. As the title indicates, the reference to biology is of major importance to this doctor. But he claims to take into account both the "corporeal" and the "spiritual," and refers, for example, at the same time to "corporeal and spiritual differences," which, in his view, differentiate "Aryans" from "Jews."[16]

We may consider that there are degrees of horror and that a certain distance still separates, on the one hand, Wolf's speech at Freiburg, which emphasizes the "spiritual" at least as much as the "biological," avoids pronouncing the word "Jewish" but nonetheless contrasts persons of "Aryan race" with those of "foreign race," and, on the other hand, the brutality of Fischer's Berlin speech, which explicitly attacks the "Jew" and insists much more strongly on the biological foundation of Nazi racism. But it must be stressed that Wolf's mention of Fischer takes the form not of a categorical rejection, but of the "not only . . . but rather. . . ." Thus his intention is not to refute Eugen Fischer but to nuance and complete his words. Furthermore, and especially, the measures recommended by Wolf match those recommended by Fischer. Wolf enumerates, against those who are of a "foreign race," a long series of measures to be taken that affect all facets of their existence. The mention of these racist measures is immediately followed by the legitimating of social eugenics, forced sterilization of criminals and those afflicted by hereditary diseases. It is the same alliance between racism and eugenics as in Fischer.

If the abjection is more manifest in the doctor of medicine who concretely applies the measures decreed by the jurist, and if the jurist is more explicit than the academic "philosopher," since it falls to him to translate into specific laws what the "philosopher" expresses only in general terms, the same chain of responsibilities links the "philosopher," the jurist, and the doctor. The responsibility of the "philosopher" is not the least, for it is he who provides the theoretical justification of discriminatory concepts — such as the distinction between authentic and inauthentic existence — which are then transposed to the level of laws, and of decrees affecting their application, and finally acted upon in medical and law enforcement practices, which destroy human beings in their flesh, their souls, their minds, and their lives. Therefore we must be particularly vigilant about what happens in philosophy.

After having explained at length the meaning and relationship to law of expressions such as the sense of sacrifice (*Opfersinn*), Erik Wolf returns to his definition of the "total National Socialist state." As a Nazi specialist in criminal law, he wants to criminalize resistance to the total state. "In the total National Socialist state, crime appears first and foremost in the form of disobedience and rebellion, and in [striking the] the criminal, it is the enemy of the state that is stricken."[17]

If in the total state the crime par excellence consists in opposing the state, the political opponent becomes the foremost criminal. This is how Wolf justifies the nature of a regime in which the political prisoner is treated far more brutally than the criminal under common law. It is well known that in the Nazi concentration camps the "political" prisoners were at the mercy of the "common criminals," who had for all practical purposes power of life and death over them. The criminal is no longer defined by Wolf as one who infringes on the rights of another person, but as the enemy (*Feind*) of the state. Therefore we can speak, given the context of the times, of a Schmittian element in Wolf's speech, given that in *The True Law* he continues his presentation of the total state in referring to Ernst Forsthoff, who was himself a disciple of Schmitt and the author of *The Total State*. Erik Wolf writes:

> The ambition of the National Socialist state grasps the earthly existence of man in an all-encompassing manner. It finds its limits neither in historical traditions nor in certain fundamental rights, or rights of man. As Ernst Forsthoff has lucidly demonstrated, we must not understand this conception of the total state in a mechanistic way, as if it were necessary henceforth to organize and schematize, with the help of the apparatus of the state authorities, all the other domains of existence. The total state is not a mechanical unit, but an organic one; it does not schematize, it structures. Through that being-structured, it tends toward an order of aristocratic domination, culminating in the personal Führer, and is built on a series of hierarchies and functions.[18]

The total state is therefore built on the rejection of all appeal to fundamental rights or rights of man that could be used to oppose it. This presentation of the *totaler Staat* has nothing original about it, but we had to quote it because the conception of the state, no longer mechanical but organic, borrowed in this case from Forsthoff (but which we also found at the end of the chapter on "Volk und Rasse" in *Mein Kampf*), was taken up again by Heidegger himself in the unpublished seminar that he organized in 1934–1935, with the participation of this same Erik Wolf.

In the total state, what remains of man? No personal life subsists, no recognition of the intrinsic value of the individual existence of the human being. Erik Wolf could not be more explicit. Taking up an expression of Forsthoff, he underscores the "total assumption of sworn responsibility of each individual in the nation" and uses the Hegelian notion of *Aufhebung* to affirm "that assumption of sworn responsibility annuls the private character of individual existence."[19] Heidegger will echo that affirmation when he sweeps aside all the personal arguments of the young jurist and refuses his resignation, countering, as we have seen, with the argument that henceforth "the individual counts for nothing."

In the part of the text immediately following, Wolf develops a theme particularly dear to him, and one that, revolting in itself, brings him dangerously close to the group who called themselves *Deutsch-Christen,* or pro-Hitler reformed, the very same that would be a source of such concern for Jean Cavaillès.[20] The Nazi jurist wanted to establish "the essential and necessary link between National Socialism and Christianity."[21] This is an orientation that distinguishes him from Heidegger, but it is probable that for reasons that may be simply strategic, or may run deeper, the latter was not displeased to rely on a Protestant National Socialist in the struggle — which came first in his view — against the dominant Catholicism at Freiburg. Indeed he was particularly repressive and hard with respect to his Catholic disciple Max Müller, whose political trustworthiness and conception of the state he questioned in a report from the end of the 1930s, which dashed any possibility of an academic career under the Third Reich for Müller and put his life at risk, and this at a time when the latter had published, in September 1933, the most outspoken apology for the *Führerstaat,* but also associating — in an unacceptable manner, no doubt, to Heidegger — religious goals with *völkisch*-state ones.[22]

Erik Wolf: Disciple of Rosenberg and Schmitt

Neither his own resignation from the deanship of the Freiburg Faculty of Law in March 1934, nor that of his "guide" Heidegger, nor the Night of the Long Knives dampened Erik Wolf's enthusiasm for Hitler. Nearly a year after his lecture of 7 December 1933, he returned to the podium, this time before the Freiburg section of the League (*Bund*) of German National Socialist Jurists, on 20 November 1934. The pompous title of his lecture, "The Ideal of Law in the National Socialist State," cannot disguise the fact that it is an even more abominable text than the preceding one. This time, Erik Wolf does not hesitate to put his remarks beneath the banner of both Alfred Rosenberg and Carl Schmitt. He also trades on the authority of the pro-Nazi rector who succeeded Heidegger at Freiburg, he too a jurist: Eduard Kern. The text of the lecture appears in 1935 in the journal *Archiv für Rechts- und Sozialphilosophie.* If it is necessary to stop and take a look at the main points of that text, it is because it gives us the state of Wolf's "doctrine" at the precise moment when Heidegger — in an exceedingly rare occurrence — called upon Wolf to intervene at length in the seminar he devoted that winter of 1934–1935 to Hegel's doctrine of the state. Thus we know exactly on what "philosophy of law" Heidegger based his seminar, in deciding to invite Erik Wolf. Essentially, the lecture of November 1934 (from which all reference to Christianity and the authority of God disappeared this time) reproduced Schmitt's only slightly modified triad, *Staat, Bewegung, Volk* (state, movement, people),[23] while unifying the totality of the legal order under the notion of honor (*Ehre*), which was explicitly taken from Rosenberg's *Myth of the Twentieth Century.* Its goal was therefore to show the unity of the two doctrines, Schmitt's triad expressing, according to Wolf, the same reality as Rosenberg's concept of honor. This text bears close scrutiny by those who think they can make a clear distinction between a "theoretician" (Schmitt) and an "ideologue" (Rosenberg). Here is the context in which the reference to Rosenberg comes up, at the beginning of the article: "It is part . . . of the characteristics of the authenticity of the National Socialist revolution that the movement has renewed a source of law previously dried up: the community of the people, and discovered a new source: the principle of the *Führer*. . . . It is no longer the traditional ideal of the formal equality of subjects of abstract law, but of the idea of the status-graduated honor of the *völkisch* legal participant. It is thus that honor — by which a Führer of the movement [Rosenberg] said German juridical life has always been inspired — becomes the fundamental value that encompasses the totality of our juridical order, the juridical ideal of National Socialism."[24]

Erik Wolf will show at length how this "honor," a conception distorted and perverted by Hitlerism, as pivotal to Rosenberg as to Schmitt, and one that, in the total state, took the place of legal equality proper to rights-based states, henceforth assumes the value of the "honor of the people" (*Volksehre*) and is embodied in the Führer himself.[25] He writes: "In the battle against the pernicious tumors of the age of liberalism, it is important, no doubt, on the one hand, to eradicate without mercy asocial egotism and anything odd or unfamiliar to the people [*Volksfremdheit*], but also, on the other hand, to cultivate the moral, spiritual, and legal freedom of the community of legal participants [*Rechtsgenossen*], for this is where the life-giving roots of the authentic principles reside — the principle of the Führer and the principle of heroism — as well as in the field of the *völkisch* renewal of law."[26]

Whereas the lecture of December 1933 emphasized the racist conception of the people in the total National Socialist state, that of November 1934 insists on this new "source of law," the Führer principle. The properly Hitlerian spirit of the new law as understood by Wolf is, then, particularly emphasized. What ensures the unity and the bond between the Führer and the German people is "racial identity" (*Artgleichheit*), a term taken up again in the fourth part of the work by Carl Schmitt, *State, Movement, People*. Wolf adopts Schmitt's triad, the only difference being that, closer here to the *völkisch* conception defended by Heidegger in his 1933–1934 course, it is the people Wolf puts in the foreground and not the state. His tripartite division is thus the people, the state, and the movement, to which corresponds element for element the tripartite division of blood, status or rank (*Stand*), and tradition. In the very passages in which he refers explicitly to Schmitt's work, we see that he formulates the Nazi doctrine in a slightly different way, more *völkisch* than the manner of the *Kronjurist*. We note, moreover, that he insists on points that will be treated in the seminar on Hegel and the state that he will teach with Heidegger. The following passage — in which we find certain formulations from his 1933 lecture — thus deserves special attention: "The ambition of the National Socialist state grasps the earthly existence of the human being in an all-encompassing manner. . . . One must not conceive of this new state in a mechanistic way, as if it were henceforth a matter of organizing, with the help of an apparatus of domination, all the other domains of life: the Church, art, science. . . . Western sociological thought sees nothing in it but an apparatus, but the German sense at its highest level of development has perceived in it the reality of the idea of morality. The state must never be envisaged independently of the people, for it is political unity itself, visible now as the people, now as the state, now as the political movement."[27]

We recognize in that last sentence the thesis of the work by Carl Schmitt, *State, Movement, People,* cited in a footnote in the 1934 edition. The critique of the conception of the state as a mechanism and an "apparatus" (*Apparat*) turns up again in the same terms in Heidegger's seminar of the same period, as well as does the critique of sociological thought applied to the state. Furthermore, the long circumlocution on "the German sense at its highest level of development" that "perceived in it the reality of the idea of morality" is a transparent allusion to Hegel's conception of the state that concludes his *Elements of the Philosophy of Right.* Finally, it is important to note that this implicit reference to Hegel comes just before the more explicit one to Schmitt. In this lecture, as in the seminar on Hegel and the state, the Schmittian doctrine of the state is perceived by Wolf, as by Heidegger, in relation to the Hegelian philosophy of the state as the concrete realization of the idea of morality. There is something odious in the idea that one can still speak of "morality" here, and at the right moment we will have to take a closer look at why Wolf, like Heidegger, places Hegel and Schmitt in relation to one another.

We must, moreover, keep in mind the fact that we are dealing with a text that is not only a "theoretical" one but also a study, written by a specialist in penal law, and published in the *Archives for the Philosophy of Law and Society.* Wolf will, in the following text, take it upon himself to clarify the precise "content" of this new law, founded no longer on the legal equality of citizens but on "honor," making the tripartite schema of blood, status or rank, and history, correspond to the modified version of Schmitt's triad of people, state, and movement.

> The essential characteristics of the people founded on honor are at the same time the essential characteristics of its law. These characteristics are blood, status [*Stand*], and tradition. With them, we come to the content of the new legal ideal of honor. This ideal is made up of *völkisch* values, status [*ständisch*] values, and historical values. The moment has come to speak of them in more detail.
>
>   1. The conception of identity by blood, race [*Blut- oder Artgleichheit*], or folkdom [*Volkstum*] designates that unity of many branches, grown on the

natural soil of the racial heritage of German stock in its deepest essence; the one described by the terms spirit of the people or soul of the people. This is the reason why a conception of law that sees the root of law in the spirit of the people, and its goal in the service rendered to the *Volkstum,* must necessarily require that certain functions particularly important to the building of the community of the people be restricted to the community of the authentic race (which is not the same thing as the legal "citizens of the state"!) — since the *völkisch* predispositions necessary for this are lacking in foreigners or citizens of foreign race.[28]

He unceremoniously draws a practical consequence from this that is much harsher even than in the 1933 lecture: whereas there only public responsibilities, membership in the civil service, and the acquisition of land were forbidden to non-Aryans, this time those who are declared of foreign race fall completely outside the law. Erik Wolf could not be clearer on this point. "Those who are racially of foreign stock and foreigners belong to the category of other-racial guests of the people, having no claim to any legal status."[29]

Henceforth, there are no more rights outside the *völkisch* community: no more "*jus gentium*," or even any recognition of "mixed subjects" who would still belong partly to the legal order regulating the German community. "A *völkisch* legal order cannot recognize so-called 'mixed subjects' in the sense of the former international law."[30]

The drift toward a murderous policy becomes more distinct. Non-Aryans no longer have any legal protection. The Nuremburg Laws are already present in this text in spirit. Not belonging to the *völkisch* blood community, "non-Aryans" are no longer part of the state. They are thus potentially, in the Schmittian sense, "enemies" of the state and can be criminalized, since we have seen the way Wolf, the "specialist in criminal law," recognizes resistance to the state as a crime.

Such then is the "doctrine" of the man Heidegger counts more than ever among his intimates and chooses to call upon in the seminar on the state he is in the process of organizing at that time.

Jean-Michel Palmier's Justification of Erik Wolf and Heidegger

Once we have become familiar with the actual "doctrine" professed by Erik Wolf in 1933–1935, it is only with great perplexity that we can read what Jean-Michel Palmier wrote about him in 1968, in *Les Écrits politiques de Heidegger* — a work marred by serious errors that would require rectification point by point. The constant desire for justification shown by this work is all the more unacceptable for being virtually devoid of in-depth research. Moreover, the author seriously adjusted his position when he became better informed of the actual facts.[31] But in 1968, Jean-Michel Palmier was still writing the following: "Professor Erich [*sic*] Wolf, whose entire work is worthy of translation, taught law, and was well known for his attacks on the Hitlerian jurists, especially Carl Schmitt. He even directed a seminar with Heidegger against Carl Schmitt. One of his essential works, *Vom Wesen des Rechtes in deutscher Dictung,* devoted in part to Heidegger, contains a series of courses taught at Freiburg on "The Essence of Law in German Poetry" (Klostermann, 1946). A simple reading reveals the greatness of the work and the man who was, with Heidegger, one of the rare professors to have publicly fought against Nazism by his teaching."[32]

In reality, if we want to find opponents of Nazism at the University of Freiburg, it is not to Erik Wolf that we must turn but, on the contrary, to those who, like Walter Eucken and Adolf Lampe, refused to commit themselves to National Socialism and who by this fact opposed the excesses of Erik Wolf in 1933. Furthermore, we have seen that far from opposing Schmitt and Nazism, Wolf, at the end of the year 1934, took up the theses and concepts of *State, Movement, People,* developing them in the most explicit and radical way. He was not content simply to be Schmitt's disciple: he used the authority of other Nazi jurists such as Eduard Kern, who was appointed rector of the University of Freiburg after Heidegger. At the conclusion of his lecture given on 29 May 1934 and published as the fifteenth issue of the series *Freiburger Universitätsreden,* Eduard Kern thanked Hitler for having worked for the foundation of a Reich destined to last a thousand years.[33] As for Eduard Kern's rectoral address, titled *Führertum in der Rechtspflege,* it was published as the eighteenth issue of the same series and constitutes, as indicated by the title, an illustration of the application of the *Führerprinzip* to the domain of law. Kern explicitly drew his authority from one of the Nazi jurists who was the most virulent in his repression of political opponents, Ronald Freisler. Now we must bear in mind that Erik Wolf never broke with Eduard Kern. In 1941 we find in a list of the twenty-nine individuals who were to receive his work *Der Rechtsgedanke Adalbert Stifters* (Adalbert Stifter's Thought on Law) Eduard Kern in sixteenth place and Forsthoff, the Schmittian theoretician of the total state, in twenty-fourth position.[34] Still after the war, in the list of fifty-eight addressees of the new edition of these *Dichterstudien* alluded to by Jean-Michel Palmier, we find Eduard Kern in third place, Ernst Jünger fifth, Erich Rothacker tenth, and Martin Heidegger fourteenth.[35] Karl Jaspers ranks only fortieth. . . . Therefore we may have legitimate doubts about the reality of attacks by Wolf on the Nazi jurists and wonder, given these facts, whether it is possible to speak of a break with Nazism on the part of Erik Wolf, even after 1945.

Let me note in passing a point that goes beyond the purpose of this work and would require a separate historical investigation. We learn through a series of letters from Vittorio Klostermann to Erik Wolf[36] and another letter from the Office of Military Government for Hesse to Klostermann[37] that Klostermann had encountered difficulties in publishing Wolf's work on Adalbert Stifter in Frankfurt and had to request a justificatory document from the author. It seems that the *Dichterstudien,* reprinted in one volume in 1946, could not have been distributed before 1948, since we have seen that Wolf did not draw up his list of recipients until February of that year. The publisher informs Wolf specifically in a letter of 2 December 1946 that in the American occupied zone, in order to be authorized to publish, an author had to furnish proof that he or she had not adhered to National Socialism or its goals by spoken or written word.[38] The very existence of the lectures published from 1933 to 1935, if it had been brought to the attention of the American authorities, would have inevitably brought about the refusal to republish his studies published under the Nazis at the beginning of the 1940s. Unfortunately, we do not have his answers, and we do not know who gave him enough cover for the authorization to be given for him in the end. What is certain is that Wolf, protected by his belated activity in the Confessing Church, carefully concealed the radical nature of his Nazi involvement, so much so that no trace of it transpires in either the proceedings of the colloquium dedicated to him in 1967,[39] or the necrology in the *Frankfurter Allgemeine Zeitung* of 1977, in which Wolf is presented exclusively as the person who oriented his students at Freiburg toward the human, democratic, and ethical foundations of law![40] No allusion is made to the racist and eugenic theses he taught with such enthusiasm.

To return to Jean-Michel Palmier's remarks, I must draw the reader's attention to a team-taught seminar by Heidegger and Wolf, which can be none other than the seminar on Hegel and the state, the subject of the next chapter of this book. We will see that the reservations expressed by Heidegger (but not by Wolf himself) about Carl Schmitt cannot by any stretch of the imagination be considered as attacks and, especially, that they in no way express an anti-Nazi point of view. Research would have to be undertaken to determine who it was that "informed" or rather misinformed Jean-Michel Palmier in this way about an unpublished seminar that was inaccessible at the time, since the manuscript courses of Heidegger had not yet been gathered and deposited in a public archive collection. It cannot reasonably be assumed to have been anyone but Heidegger himself, or someone in the small circle of his intimates, such as François Fédier, for example, whom the author thanks at the end of his book.[41]

In the second part of his projected justificatory letter to Karl Barth, Erik Wolf avails himself of this unexpected support from France, citing what he presents as "a brochure for the rehabilitation of Martin Heidegger."[42] But he is careful not to claim for himself the theme — which could not bear scrutiny in his own writings — of an opposition on his part to Carl Schmitt and the Nazi jurists.

Whatever the case may be, and quite to the contrary of what Palmier has asserted, we know today that Wolf and Heidegger were among the rare academic professors at Freiburg to have publicly taught, in a radical way and at a time when they held in their hands the university power initiated by the *Führerprinzip,* what we must call the application of Hitlerism and Nazism to law and philosophy.

This book does not treat the way in which Heidegger's work has been received. I have made an exception in bringing up Jean-Michel Palmier's work because he shows how far afield authors who reason on entirely distorted historical givens — without taking the precaution of seriously backing up their allegations — may be led. Palmier makes much of the relationship between a glorified Erik Wolf (unaware of, or ignoring, what he wrote in the 1930s) and Rector Heidegger in order to try to clear the latter's name. Palmier, the impeccable Germanist, has taken the time to go to Wilflingen to meet Ernst Jünger, but not to read Wolf's published writings.[43] And yet he does not hesitate to amplify his apology to the maximum. In a particularly spirited controversy against the work devoted to Heidegger by Alexander Schwan,[44] which is quite moderate and infinitely better informed than his own book, Jean-Michel Palmier writes as follows:

> A greater attentiveness to the historical reality of Heidegger's rectorship would have refuted such an interpretation [of Alexander Schwan]. Heidegger was not satisfied with making a few "critical remarks" about "ideology." He opposed the very foundation of National Socialism by attacking totalitarianism specifically in the person of the great Nazi jurist Carl Schmitt. Let us recall here the community of ideas that united *Heidegger to the anti-Nazi dean that he had himself appointed, and whom he refused to dismiss:* Professor Erich [sic] Wolf. Erich Wolf was probably one of the greatest adversaries of National Socialist law and totalitarianism, of which Carl Schmitt was the official representative. One of the most important works of Erich Wolf, published in 1946, *Vom Wesen des Rechts in deutscher Dichtung* (Of the Essence of Law in German Poetry), is, moreover, in large part dedicated to Heidegger. *One must after all admit that it would be rather paradoxical that the fiercest enemy of totalitarianism would dedicate a work devoted to the defense of the essence of law to a man whose entire philosophy is the justification of totalitarianism.*[45]

To speak of a "greater attentiveness to the historical reality of Heidegger's rectorship" is but an empty phrase. In Palmier's book there is no firsthand research on the reality of Heidegger's rectorship, nothing but the repetition of the mantra elaborated by the small circle of his apologists, based on information from the master himself.[46] Thus Heidegger's nomination, in his view, "was absolutely not of a political nature."[47] Nothing is said about Heidegger's active role in the *Gleichschaltung;* his membership in the NSDAP was "without a doubt the expression of a simple administrative formality."[48] Furthermore, Palmier quotes the sentence from the rectoral address in which Heidegger praises the "new student law,"[49] without for a moment inquiring into the content of this "new law." The *völkisch* and racist reality of the new student law that I have shown above[50] is far more accurately perceived in a recently published study by Reinhard Brandt, who appropriately reminds us of the racist content of the law of 22 April 1933.[51]

Returning now to Jean-Michel Palmier, his entire reasoning rests on the premise that Erik Wolf is "the fiercest enemy of totalitarianism." Now in reality his writings show that this premise is false and its opposite true. In many articles, Wolf becomes the enthusiastic propagandist of the total state and its eugenic and racist law, and he explicitly draws his inspiration from Ernst Forsthoff (to whom he is personally close), the theoretician of the total state and a disciple of Schmitt, if not from Schmitt himself. Although it is accurate to speak of "the community of ideas" uniting Heidegger and Wolf, it is clear, on the basis of the texts, that it is by their common apology for the Hitlerian *Führerstaat* that they are united.

It remains for us to examine in what sense it can be said that Erik Wolf's study, published in 1941 and dedicated to Martin Heidegger, is "devoted to the defense of the essence of law." Nineteen forty-one is the year in which the armies of the Nazi Reich dominate Europe, their only adversary being an England that is exposed to massive bombardments by the Luftwaffe. Now, here is the quotation from Adalbert Stifter that Wolf chooses as an epigraph for his study, just before the dedication to Heidegger. "Law and custom are the loftiest things in the world, and since in my opinion the German people is first in spirit and soul, it has always wanted to stand at the forefront of law and custom."[52]

The choice of that quotation shows the indissociable link Wolf is determined to establish between his peculiar "defense" of "law" and his conception of the German people as the foremost of all peoples, expressed in the historical context of the year 1941. Is it any surprise that Wolf will take care not to retain that quotation in the new 1946 edition?

Moreover, one would have hoped that Wolf would take the Stifter quotation in the sense of a cautionary reminder of the requirements of ethics and law, but the conception he presents of law in his study remains deeply essentialist and discriminatory and tends to prove that he had not burned his bridges with National Socialism. In his studies *On the Essence of Right in German Poetry,* Wolf depicts a Stifter who seeks his inspiration in "thoughts of Herder in his *volkstümlich* conception of the state." The author opposes those who, like Josef Domandl, present Stifter as "a declared liberal."[53] Wolf argues that justice "is realized in each human existence [*Dasein*], but not in each in the same way [*nicht in jedem auf gleiche Art*]."[54] Everything depends on the "bearing" (*Haltung*) and discipline (*Zucht*) of men and of peoples,[55] or on the rank (*Stand*) understood as "the form of the community" (*die Form der Gemeinschaft*). What Wolf appreciates in Stifter is that he "sees as a poet not the abstract man or historical humanity, but the living human figure" (*die lebendige menschliche Gestalt*). In short, in justice "the bearing, the direction, and the substance of a man who fulfills himself with seriousness, who wants to come to himself, is manifested." This is the lesson to be drawn: "Only the essential man is truly right. He is in the right, remains in the right, and sets things right. Nothing inessential can be right."[56]

We see the direction in which Erik Wolf is evolving. He takes refuge in an evocation of "the essential man," which leaves little open to direct criticism, but lets a specific message through: there is nothing universally right for man as such. Rightness belongs to the essential man and to him alone. It is thus the discrimination between the essential and the inessential that founds "rightness." But is this what it means to defend the essence of rightness? Is it not, quite to the contrary, after having denied the universal character of the right, the positing of a discrimination more originary than rightness itself, that of the essential and the inessential, which is reminiscent of the Heideggerian distinction between the authentic and the inauthentic, or, even more explicitly, that of Oskar Becker between essence (*Wesen*) and "non-essence," which allows the latter to found his racial ontology? As for what makes up that "essential," we may fear the worst, on seeing the terminology taken up by Erik Wolf: *Haltung, Zucht, Stand, Gestalt*. . . . These are terms we have encountered elsewhere many times among the "intellectuals" of Nazism, from Rothacker to Heidegger himself.

The study on Hölderlin, which originally appeared in 1940, is still more explicit than the one on Adalbert Stifter. We see Erik Wolf reducing law to the "originary orders of family, race and people, the city as a true life-community, the fatherland"[57] and praising Hölderlin for having shown that "the voice of the people" is "a tempestuous movement" (*stürmisch bewegte Stimme*). Moreover, justice is not only "something original": it is also "something fated." "The manifestations of justice in nature, the hero, the people, are the very manifestations of destiny."[58] Wolf also wants to show what he believes

Hölderlin got from Heraclitus: "his idea of the right of destiny, his affirmation of war, his heroic requirement of the commitment of all the forces of the people in the battle for the fatherland."[59] (Wolf published these lines the year of the invasion of France by the Nazi armies.) He contrasts the "right of the hero" and the "order of destiny"[60] with the "degenerate state" (*entarteter Staat*), and Hölderlin's "German humanism" with a humanism that is "alien to life." In Wolf's view, the state according to Hölderlin is "common, community, corporation, *polis,* but not Leviathan, society, or a simple administrative apparatus."[61] As will see in the next chapter, what we have here, in condensed form, is the same critique of the state qua apparatus of the liberal society — as opposed to the community, corporation, or *polis* of the National Socialist state — that we saw in Heidegger and Wolf's seminar on Hegel and the state.

That eulogy of the corporate and communal state is followed by Erik Wolf's apology for war, conceived of not as "a simple struggle on the level of ideas" but as "a true struggle with bloodshed" to "lead a just life in keeping with the eternal order of nature." In sum, a "renewal of the people" (*Volkserneuerung*) understood as "a struggle for self-affirmation" (*Kampf um die Selbstbehauptung*).[62] These pages, as well as the concluding apology for "German rightness" as opposed to the "*Aufklärung* of the West,"[63] go beyond simple nationalism: these are the specific language and ideas of Nazism, and in the very year of the victory of the Third Reich.

On the Necessity for New Research on Erik Wolf's True Evolution

The subject of this book is not Erik Wolf. Nevertheless, it is indispensable that sufficient information be brought to bear to prompt a totally new assessment of the validity of his almost hagiographic image as a "resistant." Heidegger made use of that legend to clear his own name by association, and several apologists have taken their cue from the master. We must therefore introduce a certain number of unpublished documents — or published ones that have never been studied — bearing irrefutable proof of the radicalness and constancy of Erik Wolf's pro-Nazi commitment.

I have already touched upon the lists of individuals to whom Wolf's publications were sent in the 1940s, both before and after the defeat of the Reich. They prove that he was far from having broken all ties with certain of the most radical Nazi legal scholars. In addition to this — as attested to by a series of letters kept in the Wolf archives of the University of Freiburg (especially one of two typed pages, dated 8 November 1945, in which Ernst Forsthoff requests his help in justifying himself before the American authorities who have jurisdiction over him, since he is in Heidelberg) — his relationship with Ernst Forsthoff was sufficiently close for the latter to turn to him for protection in 1945.[64]

Another important document is the (unpublished) five-page typed justification, signed by the hand of Erik Wolf and addressed by him on 2 November 1945 to the French military government at Baden-Baden, which I found in the archives of the Ministry of Foreign Affairs kept at Colmar. In it he is more explicit than in his first draft of a letter to Karl Barth, published by Alexander Hollerbach. He cannot hide facts that the French authorities are then in a position of being able to verify by consulting the Karlsruhe Archives. Thus, he admits to having become a member of the League of National Socialist Jurists during the summer of 1933 and to having paid a monthly contribution to the Nazi Party from then on, and then to having joined the NSDAP on 1 May 1937. To justify his 1933 commitment, Wolf advances two main arguments: he was carried away by the decisive influence of Martin Heidegger, and, moreover, being more "to the left" than the latter, he was motivated by his desire for social reform. He makes the following assertions. "It was not as a concession to the 'circumstances' . . . but to show my social good will that I entered the *NS-Juristenbund* in the summer of 1933, and paid a monthly contribution for what was called the 'ring of sacrifice,' with the assumption that the money would be directed toward social goals."[65]

That strong influence of Heidegger, according to his account, dated back to 1929 and was compounded by the influence of the Stefan George circle. "Since 1929, I found myself under the profound influence of the existential philosophy of Martin Heidegger, which I came to through Neo-Kantianism, the phenomenology of Husserl, and the reading of Kierkegaard. The poetry and the research of the Stefan George circle had also influenced me strongly in 1924–1927, and especially my personal interaction with [Friedrich] Gundolf, who introduced me to Plato's idea of the philosopher-king and expected the salvation of Germany's future to come from a 'great man.' "[66]

But in the Nazi commitment of 1933, it was Heidegger's influence that was decisive. "I tried to rectify the error to which I had succumbed in 1933 under the suggestive influence of a very significant thinker [Heidegger]. That error consisted in the fact of having believed in the possibility that the ideal of social justice could be realized even under National Socialist domination."[67]

That Wolf is being truthful in insisting on Heidegger's strong influence on him is confirmed by the episode (which he does not mention here) of the refusal of his resignation on the evening of his December 1933 lecture. And Wolf's testimony in his letter of 1945 confirms that Wolf's National Socialist commitment in 1933 comes directly from Heidegger's influence.

Moreover, Wolf's progressive involvement in the Confessing Church is undeniable, but it appears, upon reading the texts he published, that his effort was directed far more toward reconciling than opposing the religious and the Nazi orientation of his existence. This is perfectly explicit, for example, in the article he writes in 1934 in Walter Künneth's evangelical journal *Wort und Tat,* titled "The Tasks of the Christian Evangelical Youth Movement in the Third Reich." In it, Erik Wolf exalts "our Christian, *bündisch, völkisch* life"[68] and continues with the following words.

> Now it is a question of truly persisting in our Christian being, our *bündisch* being, our German being, of which we have become aware through the three great experiences of the Gospel, the Youth Movement, and National Socialism. That is why what is important is not to divide these experiences according to their respective specificities and differences but to consider them according to their indissoluble unity in our very lives. We know that it is as Protestant youth that we live within the congregation and that we remain faithful to our Church; we know that it is as *bündisch* youth that we lead the life of the *Bund* and respond to our *Bund*; we know that it is as German youth that we preserve our *Volkstum* and stand behind our Führer Adolf Hitler. Now these are not realities that stand next to one another, but one inside the other, and the specificity of our lives does not consist, as some think, in being a good Christian and a bad comrade of the people, a good element of the Bund and a bad member of the congregation, a good comrade of the people and a negligent Christian, but on the contrary in forming a living unity of the triple unfolding of our essence, from which new forces accrue to the Church, the people, the state, and the *Bund*.[69]

A conception that unites so closely an existence that calls itself Christian and a commitment to Hitler is not much different than the "German Christians," those Hitlerian Protestants who in 1933 formed a church officially subordinate to the Führer, though Wolf did not belong to so extreme a group as that. By the theses he upholds, Wolf is close to Walter Künneth, the author of *The Present-Day Völkisch Religion,* who is determined to promote what he calls "the völkisch dogma of the unity of race, people and religion"[70] without falling into all the excesses of those who reject the Old Testament in its entirety as "Jewish," thus resuscitating the "Marcion vision of the world."[71]

It was in a collective work, co-directed by Walter Künneth and titled *The Nation before God: On the Message of the Church in the Third Reich,* that Wolf published another, more elaborated "evangelical" text. The work edited by Künneth features racial and eugenic studies such as "The Race as Biological Greatness," "The Race as Principle of the Vision of the World," and "Possibilities and Limits of the Eugenic." Wolf's study went through two different versions, that of the 1933–1934 editions and the much reworked fifth edition, published in 1937. A comparison between the two editions and an in-depth study of the 1937 version, which is longer and includes the "achievements" of Nazi law during the year 1935, furnish proof that Wolf is far from renouncing Nazism in 1937.[72]

In the first version, we find chief among Wolf's main references Forsthoff's *The Total State*, Carl Schmitt's *Political Theology*, with its critique of the political secularization of theological concepts, and Heidegger's *Being and Time*, with its existentials such as the call of conscience, on which he relies in evoking what he dubs "ownmost authority-being" (*eigensten Autorität-Sein*).[73]

In 1937 the Heideggerian point of departure of his work is still affirmed — namely, what Wolf calls "the-being-in-the-world-of-law" (*das-in-der-Welt-des-Rechts-Sein*).[74] In contrast, the omnipresent discourse on race of the first version is dropped. But is this the sign of a critical retreat? It is true that Erik Wolf's fundamental racism and anti-Semitism are more immediately visible in the first version, which is devoted entirely to illustrating the "ethnic unity of the people in race and language" as "creation," it being understood that "the Christian order of the people rests on the existence of the people as *ethnos,* not as *demos,*" and is opposed to what is called the "old Jewish order" (*alt-jüdisch*).[75] That unity is the effect of "the National Socialist total state of the people" (*nationalsozialistischer totaler Volksstaat*) that preserves the "racial inheritance" (*rassisches Erbgut*).[76] In short, his entire purpose is to make explicit and illustrate what he does not hesitate to call "the necessary relation of essence between National Socialism and Christendom."[77]

The fact that these developments on race are not retained in the second version may be explained by the fact that Erik Wolf's racism was publicly attacked in 1935 in the Freiburg newspaper *Der Alemanne* for being insufficiently "nordicist."[78]

A similar fate befell Rothacker. At that date, the question of the orthodoxy of the racial doctrine had become a burning issue in Nazi circles. That is probably the main reason why from 1937 on Wolf took cover behind a more nebulous and therefore less easily attackable form of discourse, directly inspired by Heideggerian language. Indeed, we read: "We feel and recognize in law a part of our being, a quality of existence that is proper to the determined structure of our existence. That structure of being is the structure of the community in which we are, and which first makes us conscious of law as a moment of our specific existence."[79]

We see that law is reduced by Wolf to the structure of our being, given that it is the structure of the community. From this he asserts that "the true law of present-day Germany"[80] relates back to "the politico-cultural totality of the community of the German people."[81] Setting out from the presupposed identity between being and community, between *Sein* and *Gemeinschaft*, he rejoins, in the end, the Nazi concept par excellence of the *Volksgemeinschaft*.

The doctrine of law exposed by Wolf in 1937 is not, therefore, less Nazi than the one formulated in 1933, but it corresponds in its language to an evolution similar to that of other "philosophers" of Nazism like Erich Rothacker or Carl Schmitt. Wolf eclectically combines Hegelian elements (by the mediation of Karl Larenz, no doubt, that neo-Hegelian Nazi jurist from Kiel whom he often cites with approval), as well as Heideggerian and Schmittian ones. Once law has been related to *"the political existence of a community of the people,"*[82] the relationship of the *Volksgemeinschaft* to law must be made explicit. Wolf then borrows from Schmitt the critique of law understood as a positive "norm" and sets it in opposition to law understood as "the order of a concrete community"[83] and "as a state of historical/spiritual things that can truly be grasped and felt only on the soil of an existential affiliation with the community."[84] Behind these verbose definitions, Wolf pursues a precise objective. He wants to have a concept of the community that will be applicable on the one hand to the Nazi concept of the community of the people, and on the other to the community of the Confessing Church: on the one hand to the "political content of the state," and on the other to "the spiritual content of the Church."[85] On this point, there is unquestionably an evolution from 1933–1934 to 1937 in that it is no longer a question of affirming the unity of state and church but of coordinating them without fusing them. The polemic with the "German Christians" thus becomes explicit, since that group tends to eliminate any distinction between the German *Volkstum* (folkdom) and the Church. But the opposition as Wolf conceives of it between "German Christians" and the Confessing Church does not at all correspond to the opposition between a Nazi conception of the Protestant Church and an anti-Nazi conception of it. In reality—and this point is essential—Wolf's arguments remain explicitly Nazi. What we have here, then, is a polemic that remains to a very large extent internal to Nazism itself. What Wolf blames the "German Christians" for is having remained prisoners to that "same error" (*gleicher Irrtum*) as those who, "after the First World War, identified the church's 'people' with the liberal-democratic concept of people."[86] In short, it is (in Wolf's view) the Confessing Church and not the "German Christians" who best understood and were able to apply the new concept of the organic community to the Protestant Church. Wolf therefore does not hesitate to rely on Nazi law, specifically the "law for the security of the German Evangelical Church of 24 September 1935"[87] and "point 24 of the Party Program of the NSDAP," which provides for the "freedom of all the religious confessions in the state," but on the condition that they do not run counter to the "German race" (*germanische Rasse*).

Thus Wolf explicitly adopts the racial limits within which Nazism circumscribes "freedom of religion" as his own. There is in this an obvious hypocrisy. You leave the responsibility of defining what is declared good for the "German race" — for example, the rejection of all the Jews from the "community of the people" — in the hands of the state, and yet you are determined to safeguard "religious freedom" in this radically racist political context! That is indeed what Erik Wolf's position amounts to: "the people is not the congregation, but the Church gathers its congregation within the people,"[88] it being understood that this people is the German *Volkstum* as defined by the Nazis. On this score he does not hesitate to speak in 1937 (thus well after the Nuremberg Laws) of "the fundamental reorganization of the political self-awareness of the German people in National Socialism."[89] In short, the congregation of the Confessing Church as Wolf conceives of it remains explicitly inscribed within the community of the people as conceived of by Nazism. Indeed he maintains that "the Church also stands within the world of law of the community of the people, within which it gathers its congregation."[90]

It is understandable, then, that Wolf was able to accept joining the NSDAP that same year of 1937. This reaffirmation and more narrowly focused commitment within the Nazi movement is the conscious and concerted repetition of what had taken place on 1 May 1933. This time, it is the Nazi jurists of the Faculty of Law of Freiburg, Theodor Maunz, Hörst Müller, and Erik Wolf, who join the party together on 1 May 1937. Need we recall that Maunz and Müller had participated the preceding year in the violently anti-Semitic convention organized by Carl Schmitt "against the Jewish spirit"? The "reorganization of the Faculty of Law" of Freiburg, wished for by Rector Heidegger four years earlier in his letter to Carl Schmitt, was now accomplished, and Erik Wolf had not shrunk from the task.

It is sufficient, moreover, to consult the texts related to law that Wolf continued to publish after 1934 to be convinced that he did more than give the regime his token support. This is visible, for example, in the works that he chose to review in 1937, and the way he did so: the book by Hans K. E. L. Keller, which in 1935 defended the idea that there was "an originally German and at the same time supra-national thought of 'the empire,' distinct from the Christian-Roman one of the *Imperium,* and in opposition to the French concept of empire" that was about to be accomplished in "the law of the twentieth-century peoples such as it is announced in the community of the people of Adolf Hitler."[91] The "egalitarian universalism" of the French empire is set in opposition to "the dynamic-vital idea of the German Reich." Wolf expresses only a few reservations about the way the author treats the "religious foundations of the thought of the empire," but he judges in conclusion that "considered from the political point of view, Keller's book sheds new light on the present-day European political situation."[92]

Even more revealing, if that is possible, is the review he gave the work that came out the following year: *The Present-Day Natural Law* by Hans-Helmut Dietze.[93] That author is one of the main Nazi theoreticians of *völkisch* law. Wolf unreservedly approves Dietze's distinction between two possibilities of realization of the idea of natural law, the "organic-*völkisch*" and the "abstract-individualistic," as a thesis "true in itself." In order to be able to "think" that distinction, however, it is not enough to rely, for example, on Ferdinand Tönnies's distinction between "community" (*Gemeinschaft*) and "society" (*Gesellschaft*). In order to go beyond that still abstract opposition and speak adequately of the "form of the present-day German community," one must, in his view, rely on "the new idea of a law of existence [*Daseinsrecht*] that derives not from idea but from form, not from the theory but from the *praxis* of political existence." Upon which Wolf commences to poke fun at the "vitalism à la Bergson," in a way that in the context of the times inevitably carries a hint of anti-Semitism. The way he intends to base the *völkisch* law of Nazism on the "law of *Dasein*" corresponds to the way Heidegger himself—in his 1933–1934 classes—relates race to the political-historical existence of the people. This review confirms the fact that Wolf definitely does not seek to avoid political topics that force him to take up a position, and that he remains tributary to the way Heidegger himself meant to "found" Nazism.

A more developed piece from 1939 reveals to us that far from distancing himself, Erik Wolf has the ambition of appearing as a "philosopher of law" of record for National Socialism. The article in question is titled "The Conflict of Method in the Doctrine of Penal Law and Its Overcoming," published in April 1939 in the Nazi law review *Deutsche Rechtswissenschaft* of the Academy for German Law, founded and directed by Hans Frank.[94] The review was published by the Nazi press in Hamburg, Hanseatische Verlagsanstalt. The author exposes the conflict between the Kiel school of jurists and that of Marburg, each group having a tendency to present itself as "the sole founder of the true spirit of the science of National Socialist law."[95] What are at stake, according to Wolf, are "the determinate values and protective thoughts such as: the race, the people, the fatherland, honor, faithfulness, the defense force . . . , in which the spirit of renewal of the National Socialist penal law is expressed."[96]

Without hiding a certain proximity to the Neo-Hegelianism of the "philosopher of law" of Kiel, Karl Larenz (it should be recalled in passing that the latter takes his inspiration largely from the "political realism" of Krieck, Baeumler,

Schmitt, and Freyer),[97] Erik Wolf maintains it is beyond question that these two schools have a fundamentally National Socialist orientation. He proposes a surmounting of the controversy, basing his view on Hegel and even more on the very words of Heidegger, and affirms that "the historicity (finitude) of being" also obtains in law, and that "its truth" is not an immanent logical rightness in the rationalist sense but "the temporal openness to historical existence."[98]

These few texts confirm that Wolf does not have an original "doctrine" and scarcely does more in the way of "philosophy of law" than transpose what he has retained of Heidegger to the field of law, on each occasion in view of proposing what he considers to be the most "truthful" legitimation of Nazi law. The way he keeps repeating the word "law" (*Recht*) corresponds to Heidegger's incantatory use of the word "being." In both men, the strategy is the same: to seize hold of a central term of philosophy or law to use as cover to smuggle through a "doctrine" that in its discriminatory and racist foundations is neither philosophical nor legal, but Nazi.

At the beginning of the 1940s, Wolf's writings on law in German poetry or in the first Greek thinkers reveal to us how far his mimicry of Heidegger's approach can go. Furthermore, we have seen that an attentive reading of his studies on the German poets attests, though in a more muffled way, to the presence of the same essentialism of people and race (*Stamm*) as in his writings of the 1930s, and to the same *völkisch* enrootedness of law in the community and the *Volkstum*. What gave Erik Wolf the aura of a "resister" after the war is that he was one of those Germans who, when Hitler's defeat became probable, then certain, began to reflect seriously about the "after Hitler," and that he approached the *Freiburger Kreis,* or Freiburg Circle (though not being strictly speaking a part of it), composed of Protestant academics such as the historian Gerhard Ritter and the economist Constantin von Dietze, who redacted a secret memorandum in 1942 titled "The Order of the Political Community. An Attempted Introspective Evaluation of the Christian Conscience in the Political Distress of Our Times."[99] When Gerhard Ritter was arrested (he was to be released only thanks to the advance of the Russian army), Wolf was interrogated for a few hours by the Gestapo in Berlin during the winter of 1944, but without being seriously harassed. In the context of the times, the members of the Freiburg Circle undoubtedly constituted a small resistance group to Hitler; but the memorandum includes a last section written by Constantin von Dietze titled "The Jewish Question," which seems awkward to say the least. In 1942, at a time when the "Final Solution" was being decided on and put into practice and the horrifying fate of the Jews under Nazism could no longer not be known, the memorandum accepts the legitimacy of the return of Jews to Germany and countries from which they had been banished but affirms that this will not solve the "Jewish question"! Far from defending the reintegration of German Jews into the German people, the memo presents the constitution of an "international status of Jews" according to which they would have "in all the states in which they reside, the position of foreigners."[100]

In any event, Wolf's contacts with the Freiburg Circle were but one aspect of his activity. He continued at the same time to take part in the Wehrmacht's war effort by agreeing to publish his studies on the great German legal thinkers in the form of booklets for the army, and in February 1944 he went to Paris to teach courses at the École supérieure de la Wehrmacht . . . [101]

One last point is worthy of mention: the way the Faculty of Law of Freiburg reformed after 1945. Theodor Maunz and Horst Müller, the two Nazi legal scholars who had been called to Freiburg in 1935 and had joined the NSDAP at the same time as Erik Wolf on 1 May 1937,[102] were both reinstated at the university, one after the other. Maunz, who had participated in Carl Schmitt's anti-Semitic convention with a lecture on "The Jews in Administrative Law," benefited, as "a Catholic," from the protection of the Archbishop Konrad Gröber (who also intervened on Heidegger's behalf), which allowed him to be granted emeritus status on 13 October 1945.[103] He complained at the time that his reinstatement was being delayed by the fact that, in his words, "three Jews are already back on the faculty."[104] The following year the university senate proposed the reinstatement of Maunz, who then worked toward the reinstatement of other Nazi legal scholars of Freiburg. With that goal in mind, he presented the anti-Semitism of Horst Müller — the author of a particularly virulent contribution, "The Jews in the Science of Law," during Schmitt's convention — as a "youthful slip-up" (*jugendliche Entgleisung*). Müller himself and Erik Wolf succeeded in obtaining his reinstatement in 1951,[105] over the protests of the prorector Friedrich Oehlkers, who rose against the "present-day re-Nazification" of the university that the reinstatement of a man like Horst Müller represented.[106] Thus we see that Erik Wolf did not hesitate to collaborate with Maunz in that enterprise of "re-Nazification" of the Faculty of Law.

After Horst Müller, Ernst Rudolf Huber — a professor at the University of the Reich at Strasbourg in 1941 and revoked in 1945, a disciple of Schmitt, and one of the most compromised Nazi law scholars[107] — was able to begin a second career thanks to the active complacency of the Faculty of Law at Freiburg, which agreed to receive him.[108]

It is important to note in this regard, for it is a fact too little known, that Ernst Rudolf Huber belonged to "the most intimate circle" (*engsten Kreis*) gravitating around Martin Heidegger.[109] From 1933 to 1937, he was a professor at Kiel, the most "Nazified" university in the entire Third Reich. I have discovered, moreover, that Heidegger was authorized by the ministry to go to Strasbourg on vacation in the middle of World War II, in October 1943, and it is possible that he met with Huber, who had been a professor at the University of Strasbourg since 1941. Now 1943 is the year that Huber published (again with the Hanseatische Verlagsanstalt, the Nazi press in Hamburg) a collective work on National Socialist law titled *Idea and Order of Empire,* in which, as we shall see, a long article by Theodor Maunz appeared.[110] These specifics open the door for researchers who may undertake to dig deeper into the many ties that existed between Heidegger and several ultra-Nazi legal scholars.

To return to Theodor Maunz, his subsequent evolution gives pause for thought, because it proves that time did not remedy the fundamental Nazism of Schmittian legal scholars. Soon called to the University of Munich and a member of the CSU (Christian-Social Union), Maunz became the Minister of Culture of Bavaria. But the rediscovery of the fact that in a work edited by Huber in 1943 he had published a 100-page study titled "Form and Law of the Police" forced his resignation.[111] In particular, his article contains a development on the relations between the police, the SS, and the Wehrmacht.[112] Subsequently, it was not until after 1993, the year of his death, that it came to light that for decades he had kept up secret relations with the neo-Nazi party Deutsche Volksunion and had even written an article for that party's press.[113]

As for Wolf himself, whose career remains to be studied in more depth, we have seen that after 1945 he did not in the least break his ties with other Nazi jurists such as Forsthoff, Maunz, or Kern. In addition, he bequeathed the entirety of his writings and bound offprints, including the various deeply Nazi articles and book reviews I have quoted piecemeal, to the library of the Institut für Staatswissenschaft und Rechtsphilosophie of Freiburg. All this clearly demonstrates that he did not repudiate that aspect of his work. Moreover, in his less openly marked works, his conception of being as *nomos* appears as a synthesis of the positions of Heidegger and Schmitt.[114] But we have to be aware of the connotations of the words used by the author of *Greek Thinkers on Law* when we read a sentence like the following. "Justice as fate of being for all entities also means the unity and self-affirmation [*Selbstbehauptung*] of the essential being in all entities."[115]

That sentence was inspired by the course on Parmenides taught by Heidegger during the winter semester of 1942–1943, and which Wolf attended. The vocabulary is characteristic: the author reduces justice to being, just as Heidegger identified the *völkisch* state with being in his Hitlerian seminar of 1933–1934. Furthermore, the word *Selbstbehauptung,* used, as is well known, in the title of Heidegger's rectoral address, is the same one with which the master thought to define politics in the unpublished seminar of 1934–1935, and which they taught in common.[116] Once again, terms that appear philosophical, such as "being," or juridical, such as "justice" and "law," mask in reality a very different content. Thus Erik Wolf's deep convictions (like Heidegger's), after having been expressed in a radical way in the early years, seem remarkably consistent, though later they are formulated in an increasingly nebulous and cryptic fashion.[117] It appears that he did not break with Nazism; like his master, he continued to feed on it in an occult way, like a fire smoldering beneath the ashes.

Heidegger and the Longevity of the Nazi State in the Unpublished Seminar on Hegel and the State

It has been said that Hegel died in 1933; on the contrary, it was only then that he began to live.

— *Heidegger,* Hegel, On the State

Heidegger's writings of the years 1933–1934 that we have considered thus far, whether in the form of speeches, lectures, or courses, exalt the "grandeur" of the historical moment represented by the Führer's takeover of power and the "transformation in the essence of man" brought about by that event. The Hitlerian seminar of the winter of 1933–1934 revealed a Heidegger attached to the consolidation of the institution of the Third Reich by the formation of a "political nobility" that, in his view, Bismarck lacked, a nobility destined to serve the furtherance of the domination of the *Führerstaat* body and soul, by arousing the eros believed to unite the German people to Hitler. The text we are about to examine, the second of the unpublished seminars to which the present work is dedicated, will enable us to progress further in our grasp of Heidegger's National Socialist commitment. It dates from the winter of 1934–1935 and bears the double title *Hegel, On the State.* There we find a Heidegger concerned with ensuring the very long-term durability of the Nazi state.

Already in the introduction of the seminar he does not hesitate to assert: "The [present] state should to continue to exist beyond fifty or one hundred years."[1] This statement, made at the end of 1934, shows that Heidegger projects the political reality of the Nazi state into the most distant future — even beyond the year 2034! We will see him enjoining his students to contemplate the perdurance of that state even beyond the person and lifespan of the Führer. This has nothing to do with any critical distance taken with respect to Hitler. The positive interpretation he gives to the finiteness of the "one and only Führer" in his course on Hölderlin of the same period, the praise for Hitler and Mussolini in his course given the following year on Schelling, and Karl Löwith's relevant statement in Rome in 1936 — all testify to his undiminished Hitlerism despite the assassination of Ernst Röhm and Schleicher on 30 June 1934, and the Nuremberg racial laws of September 1935. We must see in this long-term projection Heidegger's way of presenting himself as the one best suited to ensuring the "spiritual" direction and survival of the Nazi state over the long haul.

This ambition shows that the aim of his teaching is not philosophical, but political. It is not a question of contributing to the progress of human thought, but of reinforcing the unconditional dominance of the Nazi state. Now at the time we are discussing, there was no longer any possible doubt: the Nazi state's violence was radically destructive to the human being and his fundamental freedoms, as shown by the racial laws instituted from 1933 to 1935, the daily acts of violence of the SA, the increasing grip of the SD and the Gestapo at all levels of administrative and academic activity, the opening of the first concentration camps, and the murders of the Night of the Long Knives. The fact that Heidegger considered himself to be the "thinker," instituting in "spirit" the Nazi state that had been created by Hitler in concrete form and making its perpetuation possible, is confirmed as the seminar progresses. He even goes on to compare his "doctrine" of the state and its future realization to Aristotle's thought on movement, which, twenty-five centuries later, made possible the flourishing of mechanics and ultimately the automobile! Similarly, the ternary relation that unites poet, thinker, and creator of the state in the course on Hölderlin of the same period is further illustrated and reinforced by the way Heidegger conceives of the relation of his writings to the Führer's actions: that is, to the longevity of the "present-day state" instituted by Hitler.

The will to project himself into the most distant future is what is most troubling about Heidegger. On the one hand, what he intends to make everlasting is quite simply the Nazism that came to power in 1933. On the other hand, his strategy of postwar "reconquest," which has turned out to be such a tremendous success, tends to camouflage the Hitlerian and Nazi aquifer sustaining him from below. In this connection, the fact that this seminar is still not accessible but only announced as forthcoming in an indefinite future, in volume 80 of the *Gesamtausgabe,* which is supposed to contain all the seminars devoted to Hegel and Schelling (but this seems materially unrealizable), shows that Heidegger's intention is still operative today, since the plan is to publish, in the guise of a work of philosophy on Hegel, a teaching whose avowed purpose is to give permanence to the Nazi domination.

In proposing a critical examination of this seminar, backed up by significant quotations intended to exercise our "right to history," my intention is to draw the reader's attention to the danger of the increasing ascendance of Heidegger's works over many minds. In order to protect the future, to free the horizon of philosophy, the time has come to confront this and to reveal the true nature of these works.

Heidegger and the "Commission for the Philosophy of Law" Created in May 1934

Martin Heidegger's political projections over the long term did not lead him to neglect the present: witness his involvement beginning May 1934 in the Academy for German Law created by the Führer of Nazi jurists, Hans Frank. In order to understand the context surrounding this seminar, we must begin by evoking the institutional commitment behind Heidegger's positions taken up with respect to the "philosophy of law" and to a jurist such as Carl Schmitt, whose conception of the political he will discuss.

Although Heidegger's relation to the "philosophy of law" is one of the issues involved, the seminar is far less philosophical than institutional and political. In 1934–1935, the introduction of the Führer principle was no longer an issue. That process had already been accomplished, and if Heidegger resigned the rectorship, it was not only because of obstacles encountered. It was also in order to devote himself to other tasks that would enable him to act in a less local, and less exposed, way. Scarcely had he left the rectorship when he took on a role in the creation of a new institution: the "Commission for the Philosophy of Law of the Academy for German Law" (*Ausschuß für Rechtsphilosphie der Akademie für Deutsches Recht*).

Hans Frank, the creator of the Academy for German Law, was one of the very first National Socialists. In 1919 he had belonged (with Dietrich Eckart, Adolf Hitler, Alfred Rosenberg, Rudolf Hess, and Karl Haushofer) to the Thule Gesellschaft, a secret society that was the matrix of the Hitlerian movement. In 1933 he became a minister of state for Bavaria and a commissioner of justice of the Reich. The Academy for German Law was founded in 1933 as a public law association seated in Munich. By the law of 11 July 1934, it received the status of Institution of the Reich. In 1933, Hans Frank, in his address to the Congress of Jurists in Leipzig, specified the constitutive relation between law and the concept of race (*Rassebegriff*) in the following terms. "Race is the creative substance of a people and the sole essential condition of its duration. The task of law is to protect the race in every sense. . . . It is only by means of the concept of race that the healthy part of the peoples of the world will be freed from insanity and decadence."[2]

The Commission for the Philosophy of Law was officially founded at the beginning of May 1934, at the time of a demonstration that was held from 3 to 5 May at the Nietzsche Archives in Weimar. The members of that commission were chosen by Hans Frank. Among those sitting on the commission were "philosophers" such as Martin Heidegger, Erich Rothacker, and Hans Freyer; a legal scholar who held second rank after Hans Frank in the Academy for German Law, namely Carl Schmitt; and finally, dignitaries of the party like Alfred Rosenberg and the agitator Julius Streicher, editor-in-chief of the anti-Semitic newspaper *Der Stürmer*.

In his inaugural lecture, Hans Frank asks that "the commission be constituted like a National Socialist combat commission." It is a question of linking together concepts such as "race, state, Führer, blood." Indeed, he declares, "the breakthrough of philosophy of law means therefore: to bid a solemn farewell to the conception of a slave philosophy in the service of non-German dogmas. The law of life and not formal law must be our goal. . . . It must be a law of masters and not a law of slaves. National Socialism's concept of the state will be reconstructed by us based on the unity and purity of the German man, formulated and put into practice in the law and the *Führerprinzip*."[3]

We see how Frank connects the racial basis of Nazi law to a distinction crudely borrowed from Nietzsche's *Genealogy of Morals* — to which he refers explicitly — and transposed into law: the distinction between a law of the masters and a law of the slaves. We also see that one of the main tasks of the Commission for the Philosophy of Law must be to work on the conception of the Hitlerian state, in its relation to Nazi law and the *Führerprinzip*. It is in this sort of task that Heidegger explicitly participated in his two unpublished seminars.

But the political aspect of the commission's work remained subordinate to its racial goal. Hans Frank did not conceal this fact at the press conference he held on his way out of the demonstration, on 5 May 1934, in front of two hundred journalists, forty of which represented foreign presses. Indeed, he pointed out that "the basis of our legislation is the safeguard of the value of our people's racial substance."[4]

Such is the commission in whose work Heidegger participated for several years. We do not know at the present time the content of the work sessions he took part in or what proclamations he may have made in them. It may be considered regrettable that in 1945 no serious examination of the past afforded clarification on that point. The commission of the University of Freiburg charged to rule on his case was too exclusively focused on his rectorship and was restricted to calling on the testimony of a few colleagues, without undertaking the least investigation that availed itself of the archive collection. It is true that most of the records of the proceedings of the Academy for German Law, kept at Munich, were destroyed at the end of the war. At least we know, through the testimony of Karl Löwith, that in 1936 Heidegger continued to be widely known as belonging to the institution and that he accepted to sit on a commission with a man like Julius Streicher. In an embarrassed response to Löwith, reluctantly uttered after an interval of silence, Heidegger conceded that Streicher's *Stürmer* was "nothing but pornography," but he tried to run interference for the Führer by affirming that he "didn't understand why Hitler didn't get rid of that fellow."[5] Clearly, at that time, Heidegger's Hitlerism was still intact. Löwith confirms this by revealing that his former teacher did not "leave any doubt as to his faith in Hitler."[6]

Now it must be borne in mind that the Academy for German Law participated actively, under the tutelage of Hans Frank and Carl Schmitt, in the elaboration of the racist and anti-Semitic Nuremberg Laws of September 1935. Furthermore, it has been established that at least from 1934 to 1935 Heidegger was present and active in that institution. That is why his participation in the Commission for the Philosophy of Law, which continued after the proclamation of the racist laws of Nuremburg, appears, given the evolution of the Hitlerian regime, morally even more serious and more compromising than his rectorship. In any event, it is in the context of that intellectual collaboration with the work of the Nazi jurists that Heidegger taught a seminar with Erik Wolf on Hegel's philosophy of law and the state.

Presentation of the Seminar on Hegel and the State

It appears that there remain, for the seminar titled *Hegel, On the State,* neither the seminar book in which the minutes of each session were written by a different student and reread by the teacher, nor any text written by Heidegger, but only course notes, very complete, taken down by two students, Wilhelm Hallwachs and Siegfried Bröse, and kept at the DLA of Marbach. At present the reader has access only to a brief but useful synthetic presentation by Jeffrey Barash, the first to have referred to the content of this seminar.[7] To this must be added three short quotations concerning Carl Schmitt, published by Theodore Kisiel and Marion Heinz, excerpted from a *reportatio* (course notes) by Siegfried Bröse,[8] and finally a more recent development by Francesco Fistetti, who relies solely on Barash's presentation and not on a direct study of the *reportationes*.[9]

In contrast to the Hitlerian seminar of the preceding winter, which does not appear among the projected publications of the *Gesamtausgabe,* and the existence of which is never mentioned by the heirs (probably because the intensity of Heidegger's Hitlerism is so blatant in it that it cannot be masked by philosophical-looking section headings), the seminar *Hegel, On the State* is supposed to be published in volume 80 of the *Gesamtausgabe.* Since the latter is not a critical edition, it is impossible to predict whether its future editors will follow the Hallwachs or the Bröse text, or some mixture of the two — in which case, in the absence of justificatory notes, the reader will have no way of verifying criteria or pertinence. In any case, although the transcriptions of all the notes of Wilhelm Hallwachs are available to me, it is not my business to publish this seminar in its entirety. But it is necessary to inform the public at this time of the reality of what was taught in this seminar — and also to explore its significance seriously and in depth, as well as the presence of Erik Wolf alongside Heidegger — specifically because the existence of this text, as well as the participation of Erik Wolf, have been used by certain apologists, as we have seen from the example of Jean-Michel Palmier, to lend credibility to the notion that Heidegger distanced himself from the National Socialist state after 1934. Now, once we have we familiarized ourselves with the content of the seminar, it is precisely the opposite that is seen to be the case, which leads us to conclude that these apologists had read neither the seminar nor the Nazi writings of Erik Wolf, or else that they knowingly dissimulated what they knew. My task is thus to reestablish the historical truth, which can be done only by furnishing a minimum number of supportive quotations and excerpts. In Wilhelm Hallwachs's *reportatio,* consisting of ninety folios front and back, it seems that eight sessions can be distinguished, held between the beginning of November 1934 and 23 January 1935. (Only the last five sessions carry precise dates.) The entire seminar cannot, of course, be summarized here, but I can propose a preliminary approach that will make it possible to bring out several important points: the introduction to the seminar, which announces the political goal sought by Heidegger; the fiasco of the first three sessions, in which he gets bogged down in general considerations and provokes the protests of his students; the intolerable identification of Hegel with the Nazism that came to power in 1933; the very odd way in which Heidegger uses Hegelian concepts, especially in the fourth session; his remarks and those of Erik Wolf on the "philosophy of law" and the "constitution" in the fifth and sixth sessions; and finally the development of the eighth session, in which Heidegger portrays the total *völkisch* state, relates the state to the *polis*, and then develops a distinction between his conception of the political and that of Carl Schmitt.

The Introduction of the Seminar: How to Make the Nazi State Last Beyond Fifty or One Hundred Years

The seminar is presented as an academic work, intended for beginning philosophy students. In fact (and this is very often the case with Heidegger's courses), it often tends to take the form of commentary, or even of a simple paraphrase of the paragraphs of Hegel's *Elements of the Philosophy of Right* that have to do with the state. Furthermore, the recalling of the great Hegelian concepts of "spirit" and "freedom" gives the impression that the seminar unfolds in the philosophical realm. But that is mere appearance. In reality, what is at issue is not philosophical, but out and out political. The way Heidegger spoke of Hegel's doctrine of the state as early as spring 1933 already shows the spirit in which he conceived of it. He writes: "When Hegel was leaving Heidelberg, he declared in a farewell text that it was not with philosophical but political intentions that he was going to Berlin: the philosophy of the state was completed. He hoped that political efficacy would come from it; he had no taste for mere teaching. His philosophy achieved a most noteworthy influence on the state's cast of mind."[10]

Heidegger, basing his opinion on the letter Hegel wrote to the senate of the University of Heidelberg (which he was leaving for the University of Berlin), interpreted the acceptance of that chair as the expression of the latter's will — not philosophical, but political — to inspire the actual constitution of the state. Far from being solely a work of theoretical reflection on the basis of political law, Hegel's doctrine on the state would, in Heidegger's view, take on its full meaning only to the degree that it was translated into the most concrete political reality. This is not the place to discuss in depth and in its own right the much debated issue of the relation between Hegel's philosophy of the state and its historical context. What we should retain is how Heidegger himself understands the question. This tells us a lot about his way of viewing work realized in his seminar. We can even go further. Heidegger seems to identify with Hegel's position. Immediately following the paragraph that I just quoted from the 1933 course, he writes that "Hegel manifests the specific nature and racial character [*Stammesart*] of the Swabian." In a fully *völkisch* manner, Heidegger gives the highest importance to these Swabian roots of the author of *Elements of the Philosophy of Right;* they were also his own, as he liked to recall a propos of *Geheimrat* Schwoerer, "a Swabian like me," as he used to say, and with whom he referred in 1929 to what he did not hesitate to call "the increasing Jewification" of "German spiritual life." That "Swabian" and *völkisch* approach to Hegel is found similarly in one of his exegetes, Theodor Haering, a professor at the University of Tübingen who lapsed into Nazism in 1933. In his lecture "Der werdende Hegel," given in 1931 at the Hegel Convention at Berlin on the occasion the anniversary of Hegel's death, Theodor Haering stressed the Swabian roots of Hegel, born in Stuttgart like himself, and intended to form a concept, based on Hegel, "of the separate, concrete unity-of-the-people, the German one."[11]

Returning to Heidegger, it is likely that he saw in Hegel's trajectory from Heidelberg to Berlin the equivalent of the career that could have been his, when he was called on two occasions to the University of Berlin—only to decide in the end to remain at Freiburg. In any case, the Hegelian doctrine of the state certainly represents for him, in 1934–1935, the shining example of a way of thinking destined to inspire the "creators of state," according to the triad laid out in the course on Hölderlin of the same period.

We may go even further. The Hegelian determination to influence the constitution of the state of his time allowed Heidegger to take up that political intention himself and to present himself as the one who "thinks," over the long term, "the current state"—that is, the National Socialist state instituted in 1933 and reinforced by a succession of edicts in such a way that it would continue to exist beyond the following century. That is in fact what he announces from the outset in his seminar. "The goal of the exercise is *philosophical reflection on the state,* which is to be conducted by following Hegel's lead. People might consider reflection on the state untimely today, since it is said today that the present state was born not of books, but of struggle. Such an affirmation rests on the view that the spiritual is found only in books. It is forgotten thereby that the state will continue to exist beyond fifty or one hundred years. But then it must have something *from which* it exists. It can last only through the spirit. But men must be educated."[12]

We see that the objective affirmed by this seminar is the same as that of the one of 1933–1934: the perpetuity of the state as instituted by the Third Reich. To attain this goal, Martin Heidegger uses the "philosophy of right" as a simple means. He uses it to attain ends absolutely extrinsic to it, since what is at stake for him is the long-term preservation of the total and *völkisch* state of Nazism. In the end, it is philosophy altogether that is reduced to the role of means toward an end, not only because Heidegger maintains that the whole of Western philosophy is subsumed in Hegel, but also because the explicitly stated goal is not to elaborate a theoretical conception of the state but to contribute to the longevity of the Nazi state. As I have stated, the goal is therefore not philosophical but political. It is a question of providing for the "spiritual" education of men expected to make that state last. And we have seen how, in his course, Heidegger conceives of "the spirit": neither as a form of reason nor of understanding, but as "wind," "storm," "drive," "commitment,"[13] as what moves and transports a people and not as what brings enlightenment to human thought.

Thus we may say that in this seminar Heidegger pursues the "political education" begun in the speeches and courses of the years 1933–1934, and in the unpublished seminar of the preceding year. And there is no reason to be surprised that he reverts at the end of this new seminar to the definition of the political and the discussion of Schmitt initiated a year earlier. That he thinks more than ever of the survival of the state instituted in 1933 shows clearly that he has not in the least renounced his engagement in Nazism. There is, however, a change of perspective, which it is essential to see clearly because it commits the entire future.

In the spring of 1933, Heidegger had the presumption to believe he could advise Hitler directly. We saw this from the telegram Heidegger sent him on 5 May 1933, in which he goes so far as to suggest what line of action Hitler should take. I have, moreover, asked the question as to whether Heidegger — whose close political contacts with high-ranking political figures in Berlin and Munich have been verified — may not have participated in the elaboration of certain memoranda and even the countless speeches of the Führer. In November 1933, at the time of the plebiscite, Heidegger put all his energies into the service of the immediate consolidation of the Führer's power. Furthermore, we have seen that he considered accepting the chair at Munich in order to be closer to Hitler.

As late as August 1934, and therefore a few weeks after the murders of the Night of the Long Knives, Heidegger signed a public declaration of allegiance to Hitler (in the presence notably of Carl Schmitt and Eugen Fischer) at the moment when the latter, upon Hindenburg's death, acceded to the function of head of state. The declaration in favor of Hitler, which constituted, after that of November 1933, a second profession of faith by Martin Heidegger toward the Führer, was entirely in the style of the speeches he gave when he was still rector. Indeed, we read: "The impact of the matter both abroad and at home requires the renewed expression of the unity and resolve of the German people and its will to freedom and honor through a declaration of faith in Adolf Hitler."[14]

Nevertheless, in the autumn of 1934 he seems to have understood that it was not easy to influence Hitler directly, and that it was a completely different scenario than in Italy, where a theoretician like Gentile could collaborate directly with the *Duce*. But far from throwing in the towel, Heidegger continued to consider himself the true "spiritual" Führer of the movement. He presented himself, then, in his seminar as the one who was the best able to prolong in spirit the long-term survival of the National Socialist state. That ambition was later confirmed. Indeed, Heidegger affirmed in an important passage: "In sixty years, our state will surely no longer be led by the Führer; therefore what it becomes *then* will depend on *us*."[15]

This is an astounding statement, because it reveals hidden intentions on Heidegger's part. That "we" is intended partially to motivate his students, but what it expresses even more is the way Heidegger understands his own political/"spiritual" role: to guide, over the long haul, the National Socialist movement, to ensure its survival even beyond the temporal duration of the existence of Hitler.

This declaration must be taken seriously. Other indices confirm that this is the way Heidegger perceived himself. Furthermore, and most important, it is the role his work has played since 1945, notably when he chose to republish his (1935) *Introduction to Metaphysics* in 1953, retaining his praise of the "internal truth and greatness" of the National Socialist movement. His work will continue to play its intended role in the future if we do not resist it — if we do not succeed in freeing ourselves from it and definitively ending the spread of this "movement" in philosophy.

As we read the seminar on Hegel and the state today, Heidegger reveals himself as a man who wanted to ensure the survival of Hitlerism and its dictatorial and destructive domination over minds beyond the historical person of the Führer. And he resolved to take on this role of true spiritual Führer extremely early, with a prescience that allowed him to survive the defeat of 1945, to perpetuate his action, and to extend his influence on minds after Hitler, his exact contemporary, had failed on the battlefield. And he did this despite the fact that his writings, which until 1945 had taken up the cause of the Third Reich itself (as I will show in the next chapter), were *completed* by that date — the defeat of the Reich marking the end of a work whose main raison d'être was to legitimate the domination of the Third Reich and, as we will see, its principle of racial selection.

In that undertaking, the most difficult thing to grasp fully, and the thing that has in fact ensured the current planetary success of Heidegger's writings, is the way he has succeeded in using philosophy, or rather its verbal appearance, to win acceptance for and disseminate a work rooted in the foundations of Nazism. In this respect, the seminar titled *Hegel, On the State* is one of the best examples of his strategy: to make use of a major philosopher in such a way as to lend his own words the greatest possible philosophical authority; to deal in fact far less with that philosopher's thought itself than with the concept of the state — and those considerations on the state will give way, at the end of the seminar, to the properly Heideggerian conception of the state; to enter into discussion with his only rival within Nazism as far as the conception of the political is concerned, namely Carl Schmitt, and to affirm his own conception as being the more fundamental, in such a way as to retain for himself the "spiritual" *Führung* of the movement.

It remains for us to examine in more detail how he goes about implementing his aim. To return to the introduction of the seminar, he continues in the following terms.

> Why have we chosen precisely Hegel for this work, while other philosophers, for example Plato, Kant, and Fichte, have equally meditated on the state? It is because, first, Hegel's philosophy is not just any philosophy; we should rather see in it the fulfillment of Occidental philosophy altogether, a fulfillment in a great beginning, with a view to the *Aufhebung* of classical and Christian thought into *one* great system. Hegel had a clear awareness of that; he had the conviction that with him philosophy had arrived at its end point. And it is true. What comes after Hegel is no longer philosophy. Not even Kierkegaard or Nietzsche. Those two are not philosophers but men without category, who will be understood only in later eras. Until Hegel there is philosophy — which he, as we have said, concludes.[16]

Heidegger goes a step beyond the Hegelian thought of the fulfillment of philosophy. He makes it into a factual term. In short, he reinterprets fulfill-ment (*Vollendung*) as end (*Ende*), which is the most reductive reading possible of Hegel's work. Let us note also that this former disciple of Husserl goes so far as to assert as self-evident that there is no philosopher after Hegel. The contri-butions of philosophers of the caliber of Husserl, Henri Bergson, or Ernst Cassirer are thus brushed aside. Heidegger specifically states here what he had already implied in his course of spring 1933: that "the completion of Western metaphysics" took place with Hegel, in relation to which Kierkegaard and Nietzsche were a manner of "departure" (*Ausgang*).[17]

The arbitrary nature of these affirmations is seen by the fact that shortly afterward it was to Nietzsche and no longer to Hegel that he applied the same paradigm, this time making Nietzsche's thought the completion of Western "metaphysics." We will examine, in its place, the precise meaning of this move from Hegel to Nietzsche. At this point we may note that there is in this mode of presentation a considerable amount of pathos. The idea is to give the stu-dents the feeling that their teacher has a command of the entire history of thought by taking as his interlocutor, from a supposedly more profound perspective, the very one who, before him, led all Western philosophy to its culmination. That implies, if it is consistent, that Heidegger himself cannot pretend to do philosophy, since he comes after the culmination of philosophy. Nor does the way he projects himself into the future constitute the invention of a new mode of thought that would surpass philosophy. In reality, his objective remains political: to ensure the longevity of the *Führerstaat* instituted in the year 1933.

To complete our picture of the introduction to the seminar, here is the essential part of the third paragraph.

> That is why to reflect on Hegel's philosophizing on the state is the equivalent of reflecting on the fundamental beginning and direction of Occidental thought on the state. The second reason is that Hegel's doctrine of the state, turned toward the future (toward the era that *followed* it) was decisive in both a direct and an indirect way, and it was so in a sense that was both positive and negative. Thus Karl Marx goes back to it in a negative sense. Further, one does not learn to understand the liberalism of the nineteenth century until one has understood Hegelian thought on the state. This is, then, how this exercise is to be understood. It is intended as a study for beginners. That means that nothing will be presupposed, in a negative sense — in that the mastery of the philosophical work tools will not immediately be required. This does not mean we will not appropriate certain of these tools in the course of the exercise. Nor will any *certain* knowledge of the object be presupposed. Such knowledge you may confidently leave at home. But all the more will a true *will* for an authentic knowledge be presupposed. Therein lies the will to know the *essence* of what we are treating: the requirement of *conceptual clarity,* and the requirement of the *original foundation* of this knowledge. These are the three fundamental presuppositions.[18]

Heidegger expresses the two reasons for his interest in Hegel. First, once it has been posited that we have in Hegel the gathering together of the entire Western tradition, to invoke his name makes it possible to give the illusion that we are going back to the beginning of Western thought on the state. What matter, then, that all we are given is a set of superficial notions on political philosophy?[19] Second, it is Hegel who, under this dispensation, makes it possible for us to understand what took place after him, beginning with the "negative" — namely, the work of Marx and the "liberalism" of the nineteenth century. There is much talk of Marx and of "liberalism" in the seminar.

The details furnished as the text progresses are important if we are to understand the result sought by Heidegger. When he affirms that the "the mastery of the philosophical work tools will not immediately be required," that must be understood in several senses. In the first sense, it expresses the fact that he is addressing himself to "beginners" (*Anfänger*). Heidegger almost always gives two seminars: one for beginning students, the other for advanced students who have been carefully "selected" by the professor. The one titled *On the Essence and Concepts of Nature, History, and State* is a part of the series of seminars for advanced students who have already had at least four or five semesters of study. The seminar can therefore entail an elaborate protocol redacted by a different student for each session. *Hegel, On the State,* however, is one of those seminars for beginning students who — since philosophy is not systematically taught in German high schools — most often have no philosophical basis or culture. Thus the level of conceptual elaboration and argumentation is not very high.

But Heidegger's introductory remark may also be taken in a different sense: what is required is not of an intellectual order. What he wants is the "the authentic," the "original," the "fundamental." All that I have read of Heidegger has taught me to be suspicious of this vocabulary or, in Adorno's words, this jargon, but novices in philosophy can be taken in by it.

What is the functional role of this pathos? There is, in Heidegger, a taste for the domination of beings and minds that can attain — as we have seen in his relations with Rudolf Stadelmann and Erik Wolf — levels beyond the ordinary. There is also evidence that the goal envisaged is not philosophical but political. Heidegger says Hegel has no taste for teaching for its own sake, but this is especially true of Heidegger himself. What he is after is "political activity," less in the sense of competing for official functions — though in the National Socialist state to be Rector-Führer is precisely that — than in the sense that what he likes is to act on minds and direct the will of others. He manifests no respect for individual freedom. All his teaching is oriented by that will to dominate minds, which explains his total disdain for discussion and that deeply dictatorial temperament noted by Karl Jaspers[20] and previously stressed by Robert Musil, who saw in Heidegger the paragon of the "intellectual dictator."[21]

Furthermore, this seminar is political not only in its subject matter but in the way it is conducted. This is amply confirmed by the rejection of Marx, sociology, and liberalism, as well as the reference to 1933, the "present state," and the Führer.

Heidegger and Richard Kroner

In order to get a better grasp of the context in which Heidegger appropriated Hegel, so to speak, by Nazifying him, a few words must be said about Richard Kroner and his Hegelian critique of Heidegger's ontology. Kroner had formulated, at the beginning of the 1930s, remarkably pertinent criticisms of

Heidegger based on the philosophy of Hegel. Richard Kroner was a former student of Heinrich Rickert and the director of the philosophical journal *Logos,* as well as the author of *From Kant to Hegel,* a work that had attracted considerable attention. Kroner was an unsuccessful competitor of Heidegger at Marburg in 1923 before being elected by the University of Kiel. He had founded the International Hegel Society (*Internationaler Hegel-Bund*) at The Hague in 1930. That society was responsible for organizing three international colloquia devoted to commemorating the centennial of Hegel's death: at The Hague (1930), in Berlin (1931), and in Rome (1933). There is a very high degree of diversity in the Proceedings of the Colloquia, in which we see, for example, a universalist Hegel defended by Richard Kroner alongside the Hegel of Swabian roots and already *völkisch* in spirit, as depicted by Theodor Haering. And at the Berlin congress, Giovanni Gentile, the theoretician of fascism, came to speak in Italian about the state in Hegel.

Richard Kroner's introductions to the Proceedings of the three colloquia are worthy of being republished. In his view, the key issue of the times lies in the tension between the philosophy of infinite spirit, inherited from Hegel, and Heidegger's ontology of finitude. In each new writing Kroner's critique deepens, as he shows that the very possibility of thought requires dimensions other than that of finitude. He raises the question of how man could know his finitude, if he did not have the consciousness of infinity within him. As he sees it, it follows that it is consciousness of infinity, and not finitude, that is the condition of thought.[22]

Hitler's seizure of power in 1933 put an end to these international colloquia. As for the journal *Logos,* it was soon brought into line. Its original title, *Logos, Internationale Zeitschrift für Philosophie der Kultur,* became, in 1935, *Zeitschrift für deutsche Kulturphilosophie. Neue Folge des Logos.* The Jewish philosophers who sponsored it, Ernst Cassirer and Edmund Husserl, were driven out of the journal and replaced by university professors who had rallied to Nazism: Hans Freyer, Theodor Haering, Nicolai Hartmann, Heinz Heimsoeth, Erwin Guido Kolbenheyer, Hans Naumann, Erich Rothacker, Max Wundt. . . . The director himself, Richard Kroner, was replaced by two National Socialist Neo-Hegelians: Hermann Glockner and Karl Larenz. In the editorial, with its heavily *völkisch* content, we read the following.

> On the basis of the new relation to the community and to the eternal forces of the Folksdom [*Volkstum*] that our era has just won through struggle, we will also develop a new understanding of culture and history, as well as of law, the state, and economics. The so-called sciences of mind, stronger than before, will aspire to free themselves from the isolation of the disciplines and will seek

a center in the philosophical penetration of all the forms of the life of the community. This new bearing [*Haltung*] of the sciences of mind determines the new orientation of the journal.

Our will is expressed in the new title. An "International Journal for the Philosophy of Culture" has become a "Journal for the Philosophy of German Culture." But we do not want to isolate ourselves thereby from intellectual exchange with other peoples. With the same resolution with which we refuse the pale phantom of a philosophy of international culture, we salute every philosophical contact with the spirit of other nations on the one fruitful and life-giving soil of *völkisch* particularity.[23]

Such is the atmosphere that weighed on philosophy in Germany at that time, and that is what became of the journal that had been directed by Richard Kroner before 1933. The *völkisch* manifesto of the realigned journal *Logos* constitutes an illustration at once representative and sinister of what the present work means to indicate by its title — namely, the introduction of Nazism into philosophy, and into all the domains of culture. We see, then, that there was at that time, among the National Socialists, a very conscious will to penetrate all the domains of intellectual and spiritual life.

Heidegger himself did not participate in the redaction of the journal. He always kept at a distance from editorial committees of journals, whether before or after 1933. But he did respond, in his own way, to Richard Kroner's criticisms. In 1928 Kroner had published an essay titled *Die Selbstverwirklichung des Geistes, Prolegomena zur Kulturphilosophie*. Heidegger's rectoral address, titled *Die Selbstbehauptung der deutschen Universität*, reads like a response to Kroner. To the "self-realization of the spirit" in culture according to Kroner, there corresponds "the self-affirmation" of "German existence" according to Heidegger, in which the latter reduces "spirit" to the elementary forces of "earth" and "blood." Heidegger subsequently sent a copy of his *völkisch* speech to Richard Kroner, who had been forbidden to publish.

The Inconsistency of Heidegger's Teaching and His Response to the Protests of His Students

Returning to the seminar — it is conducted in an odd manner, and seems to reflect the difficulty, for Heidegger, in penetrating the text of Hegel's *Philosophy of Right*. Despite his title and subject, he does not begin by laying out Hegel's doctrine of the state. The first three sessions are essentially nothing but long preliminaries, alternating, in an improvised and rather disorganized way, elementary and very scholastic considerations on the Hegelian method, summary remarks on the history of metaphysics that by their generality do not go beyond the level of a textbook introduction, and a few allusions to what he calls "our" present state (that is, the Hitlerian state) intended to recall the political goal of that instruction.

Heidegger very quickly gives his students their first assignment: the reading of Hegel's text on "the constitution of Germany."[24] In his view, this text on the constitution is more or less incomprehensible. Hence there are two ways of mastering it: (1) by attempting to get clear about Hegel's way of philosophizing and (2) by conducting an independent reflection on the state.[25] It is in reality the second path that Heidegger undertakes, as the last session of the seminar will show. He uses Hegel to lead us to his own doctrine of the state.

After some mention of Plato's dialectic, Heidegger returns to Hegel and comments on his method, alluding to texts of the Jena period, in which we find considerations on nature, work, and the tool. Heidegger dwells on the working of metal and iron, and on the hammer as an example of the tool, thus returning to a theme exploited at length in *Being and Time*.[26] The tool has "essentially the character of the passive and at the same time the character of activity."[27] When we hold the hammer, the tool is passive; but when we strike, it is active. It can therefore be said that the hammer is at once itself and its opposite: that contradiction is in its essence. Thus we may affirm with Hegel that "the essence of the thing is contradiction."[28]

But the example that has been chosen scarcely seems probing, for it is not in the same relation that the hammer is said to be passive and active, so that one does not see clearly where the contradiction lies. The hammer is passive in relation to the person holding it but can be said to be active only in relation to what is hit and to the result that is produced. In truth, the nature of the examples chosen and the way Heidegger explains them does not indicate a clear comprehension of the Hegelian dialectic. What is clear, in any case, is the manner — at the very least sophist — in which he conceives of the contradiction.

After the hammer, Heidegger chooses the *I*: "When I say 'I am you,' or 'you are me,' where is the dialectic in this case?" In the fact that that *I* am neither *everyone* nor *no one*. Then comes the example of the donkey. "Donkey" being a word whose sound is in me when I pronounce it, to say "It is a donkey" implies that we admit in so doing (at least so it is in Heidegger's view) that "it is therefore *I* who am the donkey" (*Also bin* ich *der Esel*).[29] How does this elementary sophism illustrate the contradiction in the Hegelian dialectic? That remains a mystery to me. But if Heidegger is addressing himself to "apprentices," it is difficult, when we think of all those studies that present Heidegger to us today as a "great thinker," not to be astonished at the heavy-handedness of the examples and argumentation. Even in the exposition of principles, an authentic philosopher can be subtle: we have only to think, for example, of Descartes or Leibniz.

In reality, the entire beginning of the seminar is particularly labored. There is no building up of thought but a succession of remarks that show especially the great difficulty Heidegger has in penetrating Hegel's text philosophically. As so often in his courses, moments of simple paraphrase alternate with short digressions that suddenly reveal an aspect of his words by their polemic character but do not truly bring about the advance of thought. I shall give two examples of this. After having introduced, through a series of paraphrases, Hegelian negativity and Hegel's doctrine of being, which is, and is not, nothingness, Heidegger remarks abruptly: "The true nihilists are those who do not see that we could not conceive of being if it were not nothingness."[30]

For the well informed, that remark is of interest, because we see in it a possible rejoinder to the attacks formulated only a few months earlier by Ernst Krieck in his journal *Volk im Werden*—attacks in which Krieck criticized Heidegger for speaking of nothingness, thereby displaying a "metaphysical nihilism." But for the students, who were probably unaware of the polemic point involved, the remark could scarcely have contributed to the furtherance of reflection.

The other example immediately follows. After a traditional development on the difference between finite understanding and "infinite" reason, on the occasion of which Heidegger finds nothing more apposite than to return to the example of the tool, he quotes the famous proposition of Hegel according to which "all the real is rational, and all that is rational is real," and immediately adds: "The Treaty of Versailles is real, and yet it is not rational."[31]

This time the example seems more in keeping with the flow of logic. Indeed, the point is to show that "real" does not mean simply "existent," but "the *realization* of the *essence* of the thing." Still, the choice of example remains problematic. It goes considerably beyond the argumentation, which remains quite summary. The example of the Treaty of Versailles assumes that the thesis of there being no rationality to the Treaty of Versailles is self-evident, and that it expresses nothing but the dictate of the victors.

If I have taken the time to go into some detail on Heidegger's way of proceeding in the first session of this seminar, it is mainly because it seems that several of his students complained about his teaching. At the beginning of the following session Heidegger answers them. His response, not without adroitness, or perhaps I should say cunning, begins with a rather amusing anecdote but continues in a much more troubling way, if we fully grasp what is being said. I have already quoted one sentence from this response, but now we must consider it as a whole.

Now we would like to round out and clarify what was said in the preceding session, but first there is yet one more preliminary question to take care of. Several listeners have approached me with the comment that the theme of our work was too remote from them, and that the proposed discussions could not be "*used*" for anything. I recently visited a local family. The servant girl who introduced me let the following words slip out: "Heidegger! Is he the one the students don't learn anything from?" The servant had worked a short time previously in the home of a chemistry professor. That was the best definition of my teaching. You learn practically nothing here! The question as to whether one may need philosophy is not to be decided at the outset. Perhaps you will know after four years, when you have finished your studies, or only when you are forty years old, but then it will be too late. To produce an automobile or a bicycle, one certainly has no need of philosophy, but rather of mechanics, that is, of physics, such as it was founded by Galileo. We would have had neither Galileo, however, nor Newton, if there had been no Aristotle. But Aristotle does not philosophize in foreseeing that there might be a need for his philosophy in order to build automobiles. At present it is a question not of automobiles but of the state. The state is not lying over against the wall in such a way that we could take it and look at it closely. We don't even know what the state is; we only know that something like the state is in the process of becoming. In sixty years, our state will surely no longer be led by the Führer; therefore what it becomes *then* will depend on *us*. That is why we must philosophize.[32]

It requires a certain degree of vigilance to perceive the specious, not to say monstrous, nature of Heidegger's argument. Let us not make too much of the fact that he equates rather too quickly the flimsiness of his first session with the cause of "philosophy" itself. Heidegger tends to make this sort of assimilation. Let us give more weight to the following fact. Heidegger seems to be making a plea for the practice of philosophy, the usefulness of which, as is well known, appears not immediately, but retrospectively, when we take stock of how far the practical application of its concepts can go. Thus, today we can follow the thread that leads from Aristotle's physics to modern mechanics and from there to the construction of automobiles. The problem is that the reality Heidegger is speaking to us about is of an entirely different nature, and radically incompatible with any form of philosophizing. It is the development of the state that he wished to make philosophy serve, and not just any state. At issue is the total and *völkisch* state instituted in 1933 by the Führer and led by him since the month of August 1934, following the death of Hindenburg. It is the future of that state—which Heidegger hopes to see last over a hundred years, and therefore far beyond the person of the Führer himself—that must now be "thought," and such is the task in the service of which he means to enlist philosophy! To put all philosophy at the service of the future of the *Führer-*

staat—that is what Heidegger proposes. Further, he himself seems to be expressing the mad ambition of being to the future of the Nazi state what Aristotle was to the foundation of physics—unless it is Hegel and his doctrine that he casts in that role, assigning to himself a position analogous to that of Galileo or Newton.

We can now discern the significance Heidegger gives his work: he puts it entirely at the service of the future of the National Socialist state. And we will see that this will remain the case until the beginning of the 1940s. That is why Heidegger's work may legitimately be considered *finished* in 1945. With the defeat of the Third Reich in 1945, the raison d'être and underlying motivation of his work will cease to exist. Nevertheless he will attempt to project his work into the future, to further the spread of the principles of Nazism to the minds of future generations.

The Identification of Hegel with the State Inaugurated in 1933

We have just seen Heidegger trying to escape the criticism of his listeners by radicalizing the stakes of his message. This procedure is so constant, and the effect produced so effective with so many readers of his texts, that it seems absolutely necessary to focus on Heidegger's strategies. It is the same ploy he used again after 1945, when trying to make his writings acceptable despite their Nazi roots. He painted such a desolate picture of modernity and the globalization of "technology" that National Socialism lost all specificity and was thus exonerated (along with Heidegger) from all its responsibility for the devastation it inflicted on all humanity.

In his seminar, Heidegger's main strategy consists in playing successively on two frames of reference. He does not hide that duality, since we have seen how he distinguishes "two paths" in the first session: one that inquires into the philosophy of Hegel taken as a whole, and another that deals, independently of Hegel, with the state. And now we can see that, in its brevity, the title of the seminar itself expresses this. It is made up of two parts, separated by a comma: on the one hand "*Hegel*" and on the other "*On the State*." Hence the title makes it impossible to tell with any certainty whether it is about studying Hegel's thought on the state or about dealing with the state itself, taking Hegel as the point of departure. At the end of the second session, for example, Heidegger treats in turn, and in a distinctly different way, Hegel, then the present state, emphasizing the dramatic vigor of each inquiry.

On one hand he presents Hegel as he who recapitulates all. "In that thought on the state," he writes, "Hegel has *gathered together* the Occidental tradition." "Even at the risk that there may not remain of the Hegelian doctrine of the state one stone standing," he goes on to say, "we must therefore confront him, precisely because the philosophy of Hegel is thus far the *only* philosophy of the state."[33] All the contemporary doctrines of the state proceed therefore from Hegel, even the one that in Heidegger's view is the worst—namely, Marxism. Marx, he declares, draws "his spiritual power, his conceptual firmness and depth from the philosophy of Hegel."[34] This is why Heidegger could write in a prior passage that "the dialectic is in itself a frightful thing in thought. With Hegel, you can do anything."[35]

On the other hand, Heidegger returns without transition to his questioning of "the present state," expressing himself as follows.

> Now we wish to speak of the state from the other point of view, from the point of view of *ourselves,* in improvising. *Where* is the state today? "The state" is *a priori* an equivocal term. Is it *our* state? What is going on right now? Or do we mean "the state as such"? Any state, in the sense that any state has a historical character? Are we speaking of the different states and forms of state? *The* state, what does that mean in a general sense? We see that the question of the state is in itself unclear, already confused. If we ask about *our* state, *where* is it? . . . *Today* no one yet knows who the state *is.* A state is *in the process of becoming,* that is, we *believe* in it, we believe that it will be; it is a state of this people, so that each one in his own way *really* knows what the state is. . . . But what does *being* (the state *is*) mean here? We are totally lacking in ideas, all is confused.[36]

It is striking to see in this passage how Heidegger uses the same rhetoric of aporetic questioning as in so many of the texts he has authored in which the question of being is raised. Like being, the state is used in several senses, and we cannot seize it in a determined concept. Thus it would seem radically to elude all thinking. What might, at first reading, give the sense of deep thought reveals itself as technique when it is found indifferently applied to both being and the state. And we understand better now why Heidegger had been able, in his Hitlerian seminar of the preceding winter, to bring together—and even to identify with one another—the relation of being to the entity, on the one hand, and that of the state to the people on the other.

In reality, underlying Heidegger's questioning there is not, as in Bergson, for example, any spiritual intuition or inspiring thought, but on the contrary a void and a radical abandonment of thought, which acts on the listener or reader like a power of seduction and fascination all the greater in that no one can intellectually and mentally get a firm grip on it. Here we are very far from, and even at the antipodes of, all philosophy. The real danger of this technique is that it acts as a manipulative power. When Heidegger says about the Hegelian dialectic that "with it, you can do anything," he is simply describing his own style, which is not, as in Aristotle's inquiries or Descartes's meditations, meant to bring philosophical clarity to the mind but to endow it with the most occult and least verifiable basis: *eros* for the Führer in the Hitlerian seminar, or, as we shall now see, a Nazified Hegelianism in this seminar.

Heidegger makes a parallel between the Hegelian system's affirmation of fullness and totality, and the impossibility of giving a determined content to the current state, in such a way that as nature abhors a vacuum, he ends up identifying the National Socialist state with the Hegelian spirit. The culminating point of the seminar is doubtless the moment when Heidegger, with no preliminary justification, abruptly makes the following assertion. "It has been said that in 1933 Hegel was dead; on the contrary, it was only then that he began to live."[37]

This loathsome assertion — it is the shock I felt when coming upon it that led to the writing of this book — cannot be justified, whatever one's judgment may be of Hegel's philosophy and his doctrine of the state. The brutality of the statement confirms, in that winter of 1934–1935, the radical nature of Heidegger's Nazi commitment. What he appreciates in Hegel's doctrine is not a bygone moment in past conceptions of the state but the possibility of finding within it the very image of the state such as it was being realized since Hitler's seizure of power in 1933. What is indefensible in the utterance is both the fact that in it Heidegger reaffirms his allegiance to the power of Hitler before his students in the beginning of 1935, and that he associates and merges philosophy and Nazism by identifying Hegel with the year 1933. In a seminar in which Heidegger affirms that "in that Hegelian thought of the state, the Occidental tradition was *gathered*," to say that it was in 1933 that Hegel began to live, is to make of Hitlerism the very culmination of the "Occidental tradition."

Heidegger's affirmation further represents, within the economy of the seminar, the precise moment at which he makes what he had called the two ways coincide: the questioning on the subject of Hegel and the interrogation on the present state. Not only does he misrepresent the philosophy of the author of the *Phenomenology of Spirit* in this way, he abusively procures the philosophical authority of Hegel for the Nazi power grab. There can be no question of attributing the epithet "great thinker" to an author who, by perversion or blindness, thought he could elevate the advent of Nazism to the dignity of a "philosophy of history." It is true that there are, in the Hegelian doctrine of the state, a certain number of elements that open onto particularly dangerous slopes, such as the conception of the state as a totality, or the fact of relating the state to the spirit of the people (*Volksgeist*). Moreover, we know what inspiration the Italian theorists of fascism would subsequently draw from the

Hegelian state. Although I do not intend to make an inordinately strong case for Hegel's doctrine of the state, I do consider the identification of the historical sense of that doctrine with the seizure of power by National Socialism to be an unacceptable perversion of his thought. From the conception of the state as an organic whole to Nazism's total state, and from the *Volksgeist* to the Hitlerian *Volkstum*, there is more than just a distance. The passage from one to the other can be accomplished only at the cost of a totalitarian and *völkisch* appropriation of Hegel's philosophy of law. Such an appropriation largely sweeps aside the dialectical tension between the particular and the universal, which constitutes the dynamic of Hegel's body of thought devoted to the state.

We see then that Heidegger, in his assertion, does not hesitate to Nazify Hegel entirely. We must not forget this fact when we approach the question of the relationship between Heidegger and Nietzsche, with whom, contrary to what he attempted to make people believe after the war, he proceeded in a similar fashion.

Heidegger and Erik Wolf: From the Lack of Distinction Between the Concepts of Law and the Constitution to Their Ontologization

After the extreme generalizations of the third session on the Hegelian system and the history of modern metaphysics, it is in the fourth session that we begin to understand what Heidegger is trying to do. He wants to assert that the question of law and the state cannot be determined by jurists. The definition of the state comes not from law but from "spirit," the "substantive will," and "freedom," and law is not taken "in the sense of the law of the jurists, but has a metaphysical meaning."[38]

Such an assertion sounds like an encouraging prelude to a true "philosophy of law." In reality, that is not what he has in mind. Philosophical thought tends toward conceptual distinctions. Heidegger, on the contrary, will proceed to an identification of all the Hegelian concepts gravitating about his "doctrine" of the state in such a way as to show that each of them says nothing but being. He thus tends toward a climate of intellectual non-differentiation and tautological assertion in which all clear distinction of thought is neutralized.

Let us begin by examining what he says about "knowledge" (*Wissen*): "knowledge *belongs* to willing";[39] "Simple knowledge that wills nothing is only *familiarity with* [*Kenntnis*] and is not knowledge in the sense of being, and of being as it stands within the thing."[40] "Knowledge," in the sense the author gives the term, refers neither to familiarity with nor to mental discernment, but to being. It is therefore not a philosophical concept but a discriminatory one: the only one who "knows" is the one who is a certain way by his or her "being." Indeed, Heidegger continues in the following terms. "We say for example . . . 'I know I am determined'; in *this* way, knowledge is not taken in the sense of familiarity with something, but as 'I *know* [myself] to be *resolved,* I *am* that.' "[41]

In this we find Heidegger's constant position, from *Being and Time* to the courses of 1933–1934. "Decision," "resolution," and henceforth "knowledge" do not express the human being's use of his or her free will and faculty of discernment but merely manifest his or her "being." Only one who is of such and such a "being" can "decide," "be resolved," or "know." Heidegger proceeds in like manner with each concept. "Knowledge is will and will *is* freedom." He goes so far as to assert that freedom belongs to the will just as depth and surface belong to a painting. In short, "freedom" no longer has anything to do with the free will of the human being. Heidegger is not afraid to spell it out, assuring us that "we cannot grasp what Hegel means by freedom when we take it as the determination of one *sole* me. . . . Freedom only really is, where there is a community [*Gemeinschaft*] of I's, of subjects."[42]

What maintains a dialectical meaning in Hegel, nourished by the tension between the individual and the universal, disappears here, since all reference to the universal has disappeared, and all that remains is the tautological identification of "knowing," "willing," and "being free" (*Frei-sein*). Heidegger then borrows Hegel's concept of "recognition," but in order to relate everything to the people and the state. "The accomplished reality of recognition is the *state*. In the state, the people attains to itself, on condition that the state is the state of the people."[43]

This tautological circularity leaves no place for the expression of human individuality. We find at the end of the above quotation the same affirmation of the reciprocal relationship between the people and the state as in the seminar of the preceding winter, in which Heidegger maintained that the people is to the state as the entity is to its being.

It remains for us to see what "philosophy of law" it is possible to elaborate on the basis of such premises. The next session, which took place on 5 December 1934, has a particular status, because that is the one in which Erik Wolf intervenes at length. He responds to the twofold desire expressed by Heidegger: the elucidation of what law means in the *science of law*, and "how the reality of law and the state reveal themselves to us *metaphysically*."[44]

Erik Wolf's intervention is hardly deep. Long considerations on justice and law tend to show that law is not just a "normative decision" and that one must go back to the idea of *gerechtes Recht*. This pleonastic expression in German is difficult to translate, as is also the related expression used in a lecture the preceding year: *richtiges Recht*. Indeed, we cannot speak of "right right": one might eventually speak of a "just right" or of a "legitimate right," but in the perspective of our authors, this does not refer at all to a notion of intrinsic right that would be introduced to shed light on the formation of law: it is a way of reducing law to the "people," or, as Wolf or Heidegger would say from their *völkisch* perspective, to "us," to "our [collective] self," to what Heidegger in his writings on Jünger called "the German essence." And it is of course on this "ontological" assertion of law that Erik Wolf concludes, with a question. "When we question ourselves, do we stand facing law as facing a part of ourselves, with the question *about ourselves?*"[45]

The borrowing from Heidegger is unequivocal. After having asked whether the law is merely a norm, he relates right to the "knowledge" of a "being-right" (*Rechtsein*) and law not to a proposition, but to the "specific way of a being" (*bestimmte Weise eines Seins*).[46] That specificity is no more legal than it is, in the philosophical sense of the word, "metaphysical." It is profoundly discriminatory, as was shown, in the preceding chapter, by the study of Erik Wolf's writings of the same period, in which Wolf relies on the Heideggerian "existential" of "being-in-the-world-of-law," to conclude that those whose "being" is foreign to the German race have no rights. In the seminar, Erik Wolf appears as the disciple who brings to his master his backing as a jurist and prepares the way for him. Heidegger can now condense Wolf's words by declaring, not without a surfeit of heaviness and neologisms, that "the law is tied to the self's knowing-itself [*Sich-selbst-wissen*]. But the self's knowing-itself is not a simple knowledge and a being-instructed of situations; the self's self-knowing is the foundation of being. A very precise form: the power of being is that in which *state-being* is realized."[47]

This tautological fundamentalism, in which "knowledge" and "power" on the one hand, "being" and "state" on the other, are all merged into one, marks the end of any true philosophy of law.

At the beginning of the sixth class meeting, when Erik Wolf begins by reminding his listeners how he had distinguished three conceptions of law, Heidegger responds dryly: such distinctions or decisions on law are from a time when "we had no state. When a state is truly *present,* such decisions are impossible."[48] This means that henceforth what is necessary, in the state that was set up in 1933, is what he calls "the historical reality of the people and the state."[49] Thus he will be able, in the seventh session, to use Hegel to identify "the substantial unity of the state" with "the absolute power on earth"[50] and with "the spirit of the people."

In wielding the terms "power" and "spirit," borrowed from Hegel, Heidegger can give a gullible listener or reader the impression that he is "philosophiz-ing." In reality, he conflates spirit and power and relates "the spirit" not to a human being but to "the spirit of the people" (an expression whose radicalized meaning appears explicitly in these years in the usage of such Nazis as Roth-acker, Stadelmann, Larenz, and many others) and to the self-affirmation of the people in the state as an absolute power. There remains no distinction what-soever among concepts. Freedom, will, knowledge, and spirit refer at once and equally to the undivided domination of the *völkisch*, organic, and total state. It is no doubt possible here to impute a large historical responsibility to the author of the *Principles of the Philosophy of Right,* given the theses he exposes in his doctrine of the state. It is nonetheless Heidegger who, by suppressing the properly Hegelian question of the conciliation of the individual and the uni-versal and retaining solely the identification of the state with absolute power and the spirit of the people, asserts, as we have seen, that Hegel's philosophy came to life in the state instituted in 1933!

The introduction into the discussion of the "philosophy of right" allows Heidegger to get a step ahead of the jurists (Carl Schmitt in particular). In order to accomplish this he uses the authority of Erik Wolf. His words are not surprising, and his adversaries are the adversaries of Nazism. Hegel makes it possible for him to refute Rousseau, Marx, liberalism, and sociology. By af-firming that this theory of law is the *only* philosophy of the state, he cuts short all discussion and prepares his own conception of the political in relation to the foundation of the *polis,* in which a people, a race, an ethnic group take on specific shape and form.

We can therefore conclude that there is nothing philosophical in Heidegger's remarks. Instead of distinguishing ideas as all philosophers do, he proceeds to a reduction of all concepts to the pure affirmation of "being" and of *self* in which "knowing" = "willing" = "freedom" = "law" = "state" = "absolute power" = "spirit of the people" = self-affirmation of the people and the race.[51] As for the word "metaphysical," which Heidegger takes care not to define even though he sketches out a brief history of the first uses of the term, it henceforth means nothing but the identification of the spirit with power, and of being with the state.

Great vigilance is therefore indispensable if we are to understand what is going on in Heidegger's courses and seminars. The fact of using words from the language and tradition of philosophy does not necessarily mean one is in fact doing philosophy. If we do not try to accomplish greater distinctness of conception, more clarity and discernment in thought — if we tend on the con-trary toward a murky indistinctness between all the concepts, it is because in reality there is neither true cognitive labor going on, nor philosophy. Specifically, despite Erik Wolf's assertion, there is no philosophy of law in Heidegger, and that is noticeable particularly in his tautological definition of the "constitution" as the way in which the state itself *constitutes* itself.[52]

Thus we can appreciate the distance between Heidegger and Hegel. In the latter, even if the theses he formulates on the relations among the legislative, governmental, and sovereign powers are highly debatable in that they lead, in paragraph 273 of his *Principles of the Philosophy of Right,* to the exclusive esteem of constitutional monarchy, he nevertheless presents an argument built on the separation of powers that it is then possible to argue about and challenge. Heidegger by contrast reduces the "constitution" to the "self-knowledge" of "authentic being." That ontologizing of the word "constitution" suppresses all possibility of legal reflection on the actual formation of constitutional law and of reflective political argument on the relationship of the different powers to one another. Furthermore, it rests on a discriminatory concept, because there can only be, "properly" speaking, one constitution for the being affirmed as "authentic."

The Total and Völkisch *State of 1933 and Its Relation to Hegel According to Carl Schmitt and Heidegger*

We have seen the delicacy of the question of the relations between Hegel's doctrine of the state and the Heideggerian one. Just as delicate is the more general question of the possible influence of the Hegelian doctrine of the state on fascism and National Socialism. When we read, for example, the writings at once neo-Hegelian and *völkisch* of a Karl Larenz who in the 1930s taught "philosophy of law" at the University of Kiel, and also when we revisit certain moments of the text of Hegel himself (for example, paragraph 358 of *Principles of the Philosophy of Right,* with its considerations on the people of Israel and the Nordic principle of the Germanic peoples), it is difficult not to ask oneself a lot of questions, although the resolution of them would require specific research not part of the present work. That said, we can propose the following few conclusions.

On the one hand, it appears that while Heidegger bases his considerations on several propositions from *Philosophy of Right,* especially the conception of the state as an "organism," the differences between his ontological fundamentalism and dialectic thought remain very great. As we have seen, he abandons the properly Hegelian question of the reconciliation between the individual and the universal, retaining only the identification of the state with absolute power and the spirit of the people.

On the other hand, it is historically unquestionable that the Hegelian doctrine of the state was, along with Fichte's *Discourse to the German Nation* and the first dissertation of Nietzsche's *Genealogy of Morals,* one of the texts of nineteenth-century German philosophy most frequently quoted by the National Socialists. That their use of them was dubious and even abusive — of that we are convinced, particularly in the case of Hegel, whose Marxist legacy went in quite a different direction, but that does not account for all the problems raised by these various texts.

It is true that the expression *total state* does not come from Hegel directly. When Ernst Forsthoff chose it in 1933 as a title for one of his works, he took it from Carl Schmitt. The genesis of the expression also owes much to Ernst Jünger's "total mobilization." But as Forsthoff pointed out after the war, the expression "was the result of an analysis applied to the situation at the time, with the means of reflection that go back essentially to Hegel."[53] It is indeed the case that there is in the latter's work a conception of the totality of the state that influenced Italian fascist doctrine and is at the origin of the Nazi formulation as well.

Nevertheless, the Hegelian influence has its limits. "The total state" described by Forsthoff is historically identified with Hitler's *Führerstaat,* and not with the Prussian state the author of *Principles of the Philosophy of Right* had in mind in 1820. Hence Heidegger's identification of Hegel with the year 1933 remains historically and philosophically unacceptable.

To return to the seminar — at the end of the sixth session Heidegger develops at length the conception of the state as an organism, which he borrows from Hegel, and as a figure (*Gestalt*), which is reminiscent of Jünger. Thus he speaks of "the inner self-formation of the state as an *organism.*"[54] That organism is not understood in a biological way, but as a unity (*Einheit*), a self (*Selbst*), and a *totality* (*das Ganze*).[55] Heidegger then asks the following question. "How is the constitution of the state thought? (Biologically? Racially, *völkisch* — or as spirit of the constitution?)"[56]

As we can see, the equivalency between the German words *rassisch* and *völkisch* is stated by Heidegger as taken for granted. This fact refutes once again the efforts of apologists to have us believe that he invented a use of the word *völkisch* that distinguished it from its racist meaning. Moreover, Heidegger's question, as recorded by Hallwachs, may seem ambiguous because it is not immediately apparent where the alternative is demarcated. Do we have on one side the solely "biological" conception of the state, and on the other a conception that is simultaneously racist, *völkisch,* and spiritual? Or is the racist and *völkisch* conception related to the biological one and set apart from the spiritual one? The rest of the seminar, in which Heidegger speaks of the "total state" and the "*völkisch* state," without impugning these expressions, is an indication to me that the former reading is the right one.

Furthermore, it is possible to distinguish in Heidegger the biological sphere and the considerations on "race": his critique of "biologism" did not begin with the courses on Nietzsche but is present much earlier, as early as section 10 of *Being and Time,* and is energetically expressed in the *völkisch* and racist courses of 1933–1934.[57] It is unquestionable that there is a form of racism in Heidegger, so stated. We have seen the confirmation of this in the conception of the people he embraces at the end of the sixth session of his Hitlerian seminar, a conception that is not of a biological nature but conjoins "spirit" and blood. We are therefore never, in Heidegger, in the realm of the purely spiritual but in a corrupted, perverted conception of the "spirit" related to soil and blood, and of the "spirit of the people" conceived of in a *völkisch* way.

In the text of the response at the beginning of the second session, Heidegger affirms that for Hegel, "*organism* is conceived neither in a biological way, nor in a general metaphysical way, as a system; this way of operating together not only functions, but it knows itself in the *government, it is* present to *itself.*"[58]

So we see what Heidegger retains. The state, as an organism, is thought of not in a universal manner, but in relation to itself. What the nature of this "self" is remains to be seen. It is well and good that he says, at the beginning of the seventh session, that the state, as an organism, is spirit.[59] But what does this term, borrowed from Hegel, mean to him? It is not in the least a question, with the word "spirit," of the understanding or of a universal reason. Heidegger, on the contrary, considers at length paragraphs 257 and 259 of *Principles of the Philosophy of Right* and retains the idea that the substantial unity of the state must be put in relation to the *Volksgeist,* the spirit of the people. "While the state itself is in the process of becoming, it becomes necessary in that act to affirm itself [*Sich-selbst-behaupten*] = a distinguishing-oneself from another. . . . The state is what gives the impulsion in the becoming of the peoples, inasmuch as the state is nothing other than the spirit of the people."[60]

It should be clearly understood that if Heidegger borrows Hegelian terms and propositions, he does so only partially, and his intention is in reality quite different. Indeed, here he introduces in verbal form the concept of the affirmation of self (*Selbstbehauptung*) of the state, which becomes itself in its confrontation with another state, and we shall see that this concept, taken from the title of his rectoral speech of May 1933 and equally important in Alfred Baeumler's works, is used at the end of the seminar to define the political.

In short, Heidegger retains from Hegel the notion of the state as an absolute power, and at the end of the seventh session, he thinks he can use the Hegelian conception of spirit and freedom to claim that liberalism rests on a misconception about freedom,[61] the essence of which is not to be determined on the basis of individuals, but on that of spirit itself, that is, in reality, through the intermediary of the *Volksgeist*, on the basis of the people in their relation to the state. Thus we find, subjacent, the same struggle against liberalism and the same affirmation of the relation of essence between the people and their state as in the Hitlerian seminar of the preceding winter.

It is not until the last session that, ceasing to hide behind Hegel, Heidegger shows himself more directly and says what is on his mind. After a few rapid allusions to paragraphs 258–271 of *Principles of the Philosophy of Right*, on the subject of which he declares that the Hegelian conception of community (*Gemeinschaft*) is not sociological but historical/metaphysical, he attacks, in wording intended to draw attention, and which I have already quoted: "But now what is the *present* conception of the state? It has been said that Hegel died in 1933; on the contrary, it is only then that he began to live."[62] And he continues: "We are indeed speaking of the *total* state. It is not a particular *domain* (among others), not an apparatus intended to protect society (from the state *itself*), a domain with which only certain persons are to be involved. But politically, what is 'the total state'? How are things arranged in it, such as the university, for example? In the past, the relation of the university to the state had been such that the state only supported it, and it followed its own path. How do things stand with it today?"[63]

It must be pointed out that according to Siegfried Bröse's *reportatio* Heidegger speaks not only of the "totaler Staat," but also of the "völkischer Staat,"[64] and he never rejects these designations. He wants only to relate the total state and the *völkisch* state to "an essential determination of a metaphysical nature."

With these affirmations and these questions on the total and *völkisch* state, the more essential developments of the seminar begin: Heidegger gives, in a more explicit manner than in the Hitlerian seminar, his definition of the political and specifies at the same time how it differs from that of Carl Schmitt. The first thing to be pointed out, for it is paramount for the understanding of what follows, is that Heidegger begins by citing an affirmation of Carl Schmitt in order to invert it. It occurs in one of the most radically racist and Nazi works of Schmitt—namely, *State, Movement, People*, published in 1933 by one of the principal National Socialist presses, the Hanseatische Verlagsanstalt, in the series titled "The Present-Day German State" (*Der deutsche Staat der Gegenwart*) directed by Schmitt himself. Schmitt writes, at the end of the third part of *State, Movement, People*: "On this day . . . , it may be said, 'Hegel died.' "[65]

That affirmation by Schmitt has been quoted and commented on by numerous interpreters,[66] who generally draw the conclusion that the National Socialists distanced themselves from Hegel. That conclusion is hasty. First, as we have seen, this utterance of Schmitt's, far from expressing unanimity among the Nazis, is openly contradicted by Heidegger. Second, the continuation of Schmitt's text corrects and nuances his affirmation considerably. He adds the following, which is generally omitted from the quotations. "That does not mean, however, that the great work of the German philosopher of the state has become meaningless and that the idea of a political *Führung* maintaining itself above the egotism of the interests of society has been abandoned. What is timelessly great and German in the powerful intellectual edifice of Hegel remains still active within the new configuration."[67]

Thus we see that on the underlying issues, and despite his weakness for the striking phrase, Schmitt maintains the idea of a strong continuity between Hegel and the *Führerstaat* instituted in 1933, overriding the historical mutation of forms of the German state. As he points out: "Only the forms of the Hegelian civil-servant state that corresponded to the domestic situation of the nineteenth century are abolished and replaced by other configurations, suited to our present-day reality."[68]

Need I add that Schmitt's grandiloquent recommendations are far from qualifying as a true philosophy of state? Indeed, the text that follows shows the vileness — the word is not too strong — of the way Schmitt conceives of "what is timelessly great and German." When he proposes, on the same page, that "the German civil service is freed from a hybrid situation that has become suspect and untenable,"[69] it is, in the context of the year 1933, a transparent allusion to the law of April 1933 on "the Restoration of the Civil Service," which ordered the dismissal of non-Aryan civil servants. To put an end to the "hybrid" situation of the German public civil service, to restore "the political unity of the German people," is quite obviously, in Schmitt's mind, to ensure what he calls in the fourth part of his book the homogeneity or racial identity (*Artgleichheit*) of the German people.

The subsequent portion of his text is unambiguous. Schmitt writes at the beginning of the fourth part: "National Socialism . . . protects and cares for every true substance of the people wherever it finds it, in region, race [*Stamm*] or rank [*Stand*]. It has . . . cleansed the German civil service of elements foreign to the race [*fremdgearteten*] and restored it as a professional rank. It has the courage to treat the unequal unequally and to proceed to the necessary differentiations."[70]

In Schmitt's view, then, this "courage" of Nazism consists in imposing racial selection on the civil service of the German state and in creating new corporate law according to the different "ranks" — for example, he proposes, "in specific organizations of the Party such as the SA and the SS."[71] What this means concretely, as he made so bold as to write above, is that "one cannot incriminate the Party or the SA for any civil responsibility."[72] Stated unequivocally, a private citizen can no longer take legal action to require reparations for acts of violence on the part of the SA.

When Heidegger opposes Schmitt's statement on Hegel, we should not conclude that he is in fundamental opposition to him but that behind this role playing, this desire to impress his listeners with an equally grandiloquent phrase, he in fact subscribes to Schmitt's thesis of a deep continuity between Hegel and the state as instituted in 1933, once the elements inherited from the "liberalism" of the nineteenth century have been eliminated—an elimination that, as we have seen, rests essentially on racist discrimination. Schmitt maintains that "the ternary organization" of the twentieth-century state—which in his view finds its fulfillment in the total Hitlerian state, bringing state, movement, and people under one sole *Führung*—corresponds "to the great German tradition, founded by Hegel, of the idea of the state."[73] What has given the illusion of a discontinuity between Hegel and the Hitlerian state is, Schmitt says, "only that in the second half of the twentieth century it [that German tradition that goes back to Hegel] has been repressed in the consciousness of the German people, under the influence of theorists and liberal writers and racial foreigners."[74] In this sense, the "law on the Restoration of the Civil Service" reestablished the continuity.

We see that Heidegger's formula is in no sense a criticism, even veiled, of Schmitt's Nazism, but on the contrary a form of radicalization, since it goes even further than Schmitt's actual thesis, that of a deep continuity between Hegelian thought and the totality of the state, with its corporate dimension, and the ternary organization of the Hitlerian state.

Nevertheless, Heidegger's words remain nebulous. He does not construct a clear line of argument but advances a series of discontinuous remarks. One of the most interesting is the reference to the total, *völkisch* state, which comes just after the phrase on Hegel and the year 1933. The association of ideas denoted by that allusion appears to be a confirmation of what Forsthoff said after the war, when he related the genesis of the formulation *totaler Staat* to "ways of thinking that go back essentially to Hegel."

Heidegger expresses no reservations about the formulation "total state" and the expression "*völkisch* state." In using the "we" (*wir*), he includes himself, and certainly Erik Wolf, among those who "readily" speak that way. It should be recalled that in his publications of 1933–1935, Wolf repeats the expression in referring explicitly to Forsthoff to designate the state taken not as a mechanism but as an organism,[75] which leads us back to what Heidegger himself, in his seminar, vindicates at length in the Hegelian state. And it is not irrelevant to recall that Wolf, Heidegger's disciple, emphasizes during these same years the profoundly racist meaning of "the total National Socialist people's state" (*nationalsozialistischer totaler Volksstaat*), intended to safeguard the "racial inheritance" (*rassisches Erbgut*)[76] of the German people.

If Heidegger embraces the expression "total state" inherited from Schmitt and Forsthoff and adopted not only by Erik Wolf but by Hitler himself in the fall of 1933, and if he also invokes the idea of the *völkisch* state that comes from *Mein Kampf*, the difficulty comes, according to him, when it is a question of defining the *totaler Staat* "politically." What, for example, is the relationship between the university and the total state? We have seen the answer he gives on 30 June 1933. Far from continuing to affirm its autonomy and to exercise its academic freedom, "the university must *return to the community of the people* and *attach itself to the state*."[77] Such is the true meaning of the self-affirmation (*Selbstbehauptung*) of the German university according to him. It is not a declaration of independence, but a proclamation of his will to incorporate the German university into the community of the people and to tie it *politically* to the state of the Führer. Not only does Heidegger not struggle against the politicization of the German university — as he will attempt to make us believe after the Nazi defeat — but he wants to affirm its "political" vocation.

But we must give self-affirmation (*Selbstbehauptung*) its "true" meaning. That is what Heidegger will take pains to do in this seminar. He therefore dismisses the theoretical considerations on the university in its relation to the state and concentrates instead on the relationship between the state and the political, continuing in the following terms.

> It is not with such questions and such considerations that we will make progress, but only by means of an *essential* meditation, of a *metaphysical nature*.
>
> The meaning of the confrontation with Hegel's philosophy of the state and first and foremost of our meditation consists in learning *what* a metaphysical and deep reflection on the state looks like. What is at issue is the *form* of the idea of the state. It is certain that our new struggle for the state is *freed* from *sociological* questioning, even though it may fall back into it again and again.
>
> These paragraphs, in particular paragraphs 262 and those following, are the ones in which *Marx* intervenes with his critique; that is where he puts Hegel on his head.
>
> That connection between the universal and the individual, anchored as what occurs in the effective reality of the state, is *in its place* here. But that is still only a completely *general* determination.
>
> In these paragraphs (namely in the last, paragraph 267), Hegel speaks for the first time of "the political": "the necessity of ideality . . . , etc.", "*the political state*." What does *political* mean here? Is there a state that is *not* political? In contrast, there is in Hegel the *external* state, or the *necessity-state,* or the *understanding-state.* That *external* state is the entire system of bourgeois society, the regulation of its needs, and the gradation of its states,

all that intricacy regulating the needs of the individual and of the different groups. Hegel speaks, thirdly, of the *spiritual* state; that is the entire becoming of the history of the world, of the process of the state that attains to itself *in* the advent and the decline of the particular states, in this cosmos that encompasses all. Thus Hegel also forms the concept of state in a larger sense, which *does not correspond to the political.* The political state is the *more* state, the truly *national* state.[78]

Heidegger's considerations here are not very clear. He resumes the opposition he had set up earlier in the seminar between the "sociological" and the "metaphysical" conception of the state, but without specifying what meaning is to be attached to the word "metaphysical," unless it is a matter of relating something to its "essence" (*Wesen*). What is certain is that the opposition does not reflect any retreat from the National Socialist view of the state. The so-called sociological conception is the one that reduces the state to its role of regulating the relations among individuals within a society, or *Gesellschaft,* and guaranteeing individual freedoms and the rights of man (explicitly repudiated by Erik Wolf);[79] it is therefore the so-called liberal conception of the state constantly fought against by the National Socialists. Moreover, Heidegger invokes what he calls "our new struggle for the state," which is proof that he thinks of himself as entirely committed to the ongoing struggle for the establishment of the *Führerstaat.*

The continuation of the text appears relatively less discontinuous, and it is very important because of all his writings known at the present time it represents his most explicit definition of what he calls "the essence of the political."

> What does the political mean? Put in relation to the *polis,* the *political* is the particular property of the *politeia;* it goes together with the *polis,* occurs within a *polis.*
>
> One can, however, also understand it thus: the political is what *constitutes* precisely the *essence* of the state (of the *polis*). It can therefore be understood first as an attribute, second as a grounding essence.
>
> Depending on which of these two ways of understanding the political we adopt, the proposition according to which we say that "the essence of the state must be determined on the basis of the political" will be correct or not. The proposition is *correct* when it is applied to a non-state, and trivial (tautological) when the state is already an actual state.
>
> In order to determine the essence of the political, one must first of all return to the essence of the *state.*[80]

After having traced, on the basis of Greek etymology, the political back to the city (*polis*), Heidegger distinguishes two ways of understanding the political in its relation to the *polis,* depending on whether the determinant element is taken to be the *polis* or the "political." Where is he going with this? We see that he quotes a proposition that is close to one of the best-known theses of Carl Schmitt. According to the terms Heidegger uses, as reported by Hall-wachs, "the essence of the state must be determined by setting out from the political." To establish precisely to which text of Schmitt's Heidegger is allud-ing requires some attentiveness. Although one thinks initially of the first sen-tence in the 1932 edition of *The Concept of the Political,* "The concept of the state presupposes the concept of the political,"[81] Heidegger's terminology is closer to a passage from the second part of *State, Movement, People,* in which Schmitt declares with emphasis that *"today, the state can no longer determine the political; it is the political that must determine the state."*[82] We can there-fore consider that the proposition reproduced and discussed here is a partial quotation, with the addition of the word "essence," of a sentence from *State, Movement, People,* which demonstrates the special attention Heidegger de-votes to that work.

He opposes that proposition with a dual critique. First, it would be correct if we relate the state to the political in the way Schmitt does this, but false if on the contrary we relate — according to the etymology and to the position that will be that of Heidegger — the political to the *polis* and therefore to the state. Second, Schmitt's proposition would be tautological and therefore trivial when the state is already an actual state — meaning apparently that the exis-tence of the state itself determines de facto the meaning of the political. This argument also has in its favor the fact that when Nazism's total state is in place, Schmitt eliminates (from the 1933 edition of *The Concept of the Politi-cal,* which he sends Heidegger) the whole opening development in which he subordinated the state to the political and begins directly with his definition of the political.

Let us recall how much the 1933 edition has been modified. It has ten chapters instead of eight, and the whole first chapter, as well as the first para-graph of the second chapter of the 1932 edition, has disappeared. The book no longer begins with the relation between the concept of the state and that of the political, which it presupposes, but with the distinction between friend and enemy. And the equivalency posited between the foreigner (*der Fremde*) and he who is of another race (*der Andersgeartete*), the idea of a difference in the very being of the enemy when Schmitt speaks of "the being-other of the for-eigner" (*das Anderssein des Fremden*) — all this suggests that the friend/enemy discrimination is of an ethnic and racial order.[83]

Returning now to Heidegger's seminar, the question of the definition of the political should, according to him, leave room for the question of the meaning of the *polis.* He continues along these lines.

What does *polis* mean? *Status* means *state, status rei publicae* = state of the public thing (in modern usage, first appeared in the Italian *stato*). *This state has absolutely nothing to do with the polis.*

Nor is *polis* the community of the *politeia.* We already learn what *polis* is from Homer, *Odyssey,* book 6, verse 9ff. "Around the *polis,* he drew (ran) a wall and built houses, the temples of the gods and divided up the land."

Polis is therefore the authentic *center* of the empire of existence. This center is properly the temple and the *marketplace,* in which the assembly of the *politeia* takes place. The *polis* is the authentic and determinative center of the historical existence of a people, a race, a clan; that around which life revolves; the center to which everything is related, the protection of which, as self-affirmation, matters. The essential of existence is self-affirmation. Enclosing wall, house, earth, gods. It is from this starting point that the essence of the political is to be grasped.[84]

The Heideggerian explication of the meaning of the *polis* takes us through the rejection of the Latin term, from which the modern word "state" (or *Staat*) is derived — namely, the word *status,* which reappears in the Italian *stato.* That rejection not only sets aside the Latin term, as is usual in Heidegger, in favor of the Greek, in the name of a fundamentalism that borders on the sacralization, not to say mythologization, of Greek words: it is directly aimed at Schmitt, who at the beginning of the 1932 edition of *The Concept of the Political* made the state in the strict sense of the term and in its historical appearance "status par excellence."[85] And Heidegger probably also intended to reject the reference to the Italian state as well, the better to establish the idea of the state such as he wished to impose it, on basis of the Greek conception of the *polis.*

The Temple, the Lecture on the Work of Art, and the Nuremberg Congress of 1935

Heidegger does not seek the meaning of the Greek *polis* in the writings of the philosophers. He does not refer us to Plato's *Republic* or Aristotle's *Politics,* but quotes two verses from Homer. Later, in his course of summer semester 1935 titled *Introduction to Metaphysics,* he will claim that history, at its origin, was mythology. Here his thought is to posit an existential foundation that would be more originary than the community and human assembly of the *politeia,* a "middle" (*Mitte*) that would be determinative of "the historical existence" of a people, race, or clan. Let us note that he does not offer a commentary on the verses that follows the precise order of the words. Where Homer first evokes the enclosing wall and the houses, Heidegger identifies this milieu first with the *temple.* In thus associating the *polis* with a sacred center, he shows that his conception of the political is not philosophical but (as we might say, in the absence of a better expression, and to take up one of his own terms) mythological.

Now this high esteem of the temple on Heidegger's part is further elevated the same year in a lecture on "The Origin of the Work of Art." This lecture was delivered for the first time on 13 November 1935 in Freiburg, a second time on 17 January 1936 in Zurich, and a third time (in three parts) in Frankfurt on 17 and 24 November and 4 December 1936. The text published in 1949 in *Holzwege* reproduces the three Frankfurt lectures, probably retouched after the war. Two earlier versions have also been published, one in 1987 (by Emmanuel Martineau), the other in 1989.[86] In the best-known version, that of *Holzwege,* Heidegger alludes to the Greek temple and thus seems to refer to the past.[87] But in the original version, published in 1989 by Hermann Heidegger (the year of the centennial of the birth of Heidegger and Hitler), there is no explicit reference to a real Greek temple.[88] The reference to Greek architecture is, to be sure, always in the background, but the temple is only spoken of as an architectural work, in that it "opens the There, in which a people comes to itself, i.e. comes into the dispensatory might of its god."[89]

Now in November 1935, the fact of referring to the temple as an "enrooted and outspreading middle, in which and on the basis of which a people founds its historical sojourn,"[90] and of doing so in a lecture in which the German people are explicitly at issue,[91] necessarily brings to the mind of the listeners of the time the congress that had taken place two months previously at Nuremberg. That year, the congress of the NSDAP and the Führer's speech had been held on the grounds of the *Zeppelinfeld,* bordered by a 394-yard grandstand, complete with colonnades and basins intended to recreate the atmosphere of a Greek temple. That *Zepplintribüne* was inspired by a classical structure: the Pergamon Altar.

It is widely known that Hitler chose Nuremberg as a symbolic site in the middle of Germany for the party's annual congress, which met for a week, generally in September. And with architect and future Minister for Armaments Albert Speer, he had conceived the site for the congress of the National Socialist Party, the only part of which was ever entirely completed was the *Zeppelintribüne.* The backdrop, "grandiose" on every occasion, was intended to display the solidarity of the people and the Führer. Now 1935 was the year in which under the name "Freedom Congress," the anti-Semitic laws, or "Nuremberg Laws," were proclaimed. That year, 150 air-raid defense projectors raised columns of light to the skies, delimiting the space in which the crowd gathered to listen to Hitler and extending the temple of marble by a temple of light. The *Zeppelinfeld* was "but a sea of swastikas, lit up at night by torches."[92] To speak two months later, in his lecture, of the "temple" in which the people "comes to itself" (which is not a Greek but a Nazi conception) and of the "clearing" (*Lichtung*), such was the way chosen by Heidegger to celebrate the congress of Nuremberg of September 1935. That is why the lecture "The Origin of the Work of Art" is, in its true historical and political meaning, a text that is not far from being as odious as the one published by Carl Schmitt in the *Deutsche Juristen Zeitung* on 1 October 1935 to celebrate the Nuremberg Laws, titled: "The Constitution of Freedom."

That obvious fact has never been perceived, because until now too little attention has been given to the (always precise) correlations between Heidegger's texts and the corresponding historical and political situation, which he comments on or celebrates in his own way. And when we consider the inordinate influence of that piece in contemporary reflection on art, we are better able to appreciate all the potential risk Martin Heidegger's work exposes us to, and what it conveys.

When, in his seminar, Heidegger puts the accent on the temple conceived of as the "authentic *center* of the empire of existence," "in which the assembly of the *politeia* finds its place," when he reduces the state to the *polis* and the *polis* to the "temple" defined as the "authentic and determinative milieu of the historical existence of a people, race, or clan," he reveals to us that his conception of the temple and the work of art is deeply political. His Rome lecture of 8 April 1936, "Europe and Its German Philosophy," confirms this: in it, he speaks of the work of art as being between political action and the organization of the order of the people.[93]

It is quite likely that in his seminar at the beginning of 1935 he was already aware of the Nuremberg site, which was often discussed in the party paper that Heidegger received daily. What he describes a few months later under the name "work of art" is therefore the political foundation of the people united within the temple walls and in the mythology, or *Sage,* of the "poem." And when he adds that the *polis,* as "temple," is "that around which life revolves; the center to which everything is related, the protection of which, as self-affirmation, matters," this theme of self-affirmation and of "protection" of the people, the race, and the clan has a sinister ring, in that year of 1935 in which the main law among the racial laws of Nuremberg is called the "law for the protection of German blood and honor."

The Concept of the Political According to Martin Heidegger and Carl Schmitt

What Heidegger intends to advance at the end of his seminar is the concept of "self-affirmation" (*Selbstbehauptung*). It is remarkable to see him adopting the well-known term from the title of his rectoral address, *The Self-Affirmation of the German University,* to define the essence of the political. Retrospectively, this proves that the conception of the university exposed in his address was fundamentally political. As for the concept of *Selbstbehauptung,* it is not of Heidegger's own making but comes from Spengler's definition of politics, which Heidegger quotes with praise in his courses on Nietzsche.[94] The concept is also found at the center of the propositions of another "philosopher" of Nazism, Alfred Baeumler, both in his *Nietzsche, the Philosopher and the Politician* of 1931 and in his *Alfred Rosenberg and the Myth of the Twentieth Century* of 1943, in which the word "self-affirmation," chosen by Heidegger to define the political, is used by Baeumler to express his understanding of world history. We read the following. "The Führer's struggle against Versailles was the struggle against the Jewish/democratic myth. It was Rosenberg's task to lead this struggle to its conclusion at the level of the fundamental. The Führer's comrade-in-arms accomplished the task by proving that world history cannot be understood as an imaginary 'development' of an imaginary goal, but as the self-affirmation and the struggle of being-shaping myths against one another."[95]

To return to Heidegger, what he writes is perfectly trivial. It comes down to maintaining that the affirmation of existence is primary and that it is on that basis that the struggle for life ensues. In the continuation of the seminar, he brings up Schmitt's concept of the political directly, not to reject it outright but to say that it is secondary and derived, and that the discrimination between friend and enemy comes into play only after "self-affirmation." Heidegger's concern, then, is with affirming the primacy of his own positions, in having them appear to be the most fundamental. Still, he does not succeed in thinking up an idea of the political that would be radically distinct from Schmitt's. In both cases, it is the competitive struggle for being that is placed at the heart of the political. Heidegger continues as follows: "Recently the *friend/enemy relation* has appeared as the essence of the political. It *presupposes the affirmation of self,* and is therefore an essential *consequence* of the political. There is only friend and enemy where there is self-affirmation. The affirmation of self taken in this sense requires a specific conception of the historical being of a people and of the state itself. Because the state is that self-affirmation of the historical being of a people *and* because the state can be called *polis,* the political consequently appears as the friend/enemy relation. But that relation *is* not *the* political."[96]

I also give the version of the same passage in Siegfried Bröse's *reportatio.* While the meaning is the same, Carl Schmitt's name is explicitly cited in his version: "Recently there has appeared, as the essence of the political, the friend/enemy relation. *Cf.* on this point the friend/enemy relation according to Carl Schmitt as being the political. The latter presupposes the affirmation of self; but the friend/enemy relation does not reach the political, but the self-affirmation, which is of a historical nature. To the extent that the state is that self-affirmation of the historical being of a people, the *polis* is revealed in its becoming through the friend/enemy relation; the latter is not the political."[97]

Thus, while Schmitt's concept of the political rests on the discrimination between friend and enemy (*die Unterscheidung von Freund und Feind*), Heidegger's conception identifies the political with historical "self-affirmation" (*Selbstbehauptung*) and claims to state the original determination of the political, of which Schmitt's discrimination would be but the derivative expression. But we have seen, in Heidegger's winter 1933–1934 course and in his Hitlerian seminar on the concept of the state, how close he is to Schmitt: the same dramatization of the existential strife that can go as far as to the other's annihilation, the same *völkisch* conceptions of the "people" qua "substance" and of the "living bond" between the Führer and his "partisans," the same doctrine of law and the constitution conceived of not as a "juridical order" related to a rational contract and norms, but at once as existential "decision" and as "true order" (Heidegger) or "concrete order" (Schmitt). It is true that these assertions on strife, the people and the Führer, and in opposition to the democratic and "liberal" conception of law, run along the same beaten track of Hitlerism and Nazism.

We now understand how Heidegger differs from Schmitt, and this seminar sheds retrospective light on what he said about him in the Hitlerian seminar of the preceding winter. There is no criticism of Schmitt's Nazism here, and Jean-Michel Palmier's affirmations according to which it was as a Nazi jurist that Schmitt was taken to task in the seminar held by Heidegger and Erik Wolf are seen to be unfounded. Schmitt's concept of the political is not impugned but simply presented as not fundamental, and derived from "self-affirmation." Heidegger wants to show that his conception of the political subsumes Schmitt's discrimination between friend and enemy, and accounts for it. We have, in studying the 1933 edition of *The Concept of the Political*, shown that the discrimination in question is mainly a racial one. So what we see is not a true rejection of Schmitt but, far more trivially, a struggle for supremacy within Nazism itself.[98]

Heidegger is committed to what he calls "our new struggle for the state." He thinks of himself as the thinker capable of getting at the "authentic" foundation that would justify that political enterprise. In order to do so, he goes back to a mythological vision of the *polis* and the temple, which leads him to posit as first principle the self-affirmation of a people and a race. Thus he presents himself as the "spiritual guide" of the German people, in keeping with a strategy that is also at work in the course on Hölderlin's hymns "Germania" and "The Rhine," contemporaneous with the seminar on Hegel and the state, and in which poets and thinkers appear as those who inspire the creators of the state. In short, he continues to think of himself as the "spiritual" Führer of Nazism, as he who would still dare, well after World War II, when Nazism's politics of extermination was known to all, to affirm that as far as the possibility of coming to a "satisfactory relationship" (*zureichendes Verhältnis*) between man and "the essence of technology," "National Socialism indeed went in the direction" (*der Nationalsozialismus ist zwar in die Richtung gegangen*).[99] Martin Heidegger therefore continues to consider the direction taken by Nazism to be "satisfactory." Far from challenging it, he clearly intends to revive it after 1945.

9

From the Justification of Racial Selection to the Ontological Negationism of the Bremen Lectures

"It is only where unconditioned subjectivity becomes the truth of the entity in its totality that the principle *of the institution of a racial selection, that is, not the simple formation of race developing on its own, but the* thought *of race that is aware of itself, is possible, that is, metaphysically necessary."*

— *Heidegger, 1941–1942*

Martin Heidegger's complicity in National Socialism emerges from a radicalization that began much earlier than 1933. It is equally true that his commitment did not end in 1934, or afterward. It continued until the end, and was never disavowed by him. But beginning in 1936, his deep involvement with National Socialism entered a new phase. It was mainly characterized by his official participation in the work of the Nietzsche Archives of Weimar, which Hitler publicly honored as a Nazi shrine, and by his courses on Nietzsche, which constitute the most significant part of his teaching from 1936 to 1940. As late as autumn 1944, in his last course, *Denken und Dichten*, partially taught before the Nazi defeat, he brought together the two figures most celebrated by the "intellectuals" of Nazism: Hölderlin and Nietzsche. This new period, more complex due to the internal discord of the various inimical currents and personages (a case in point was Krieck versus Heidegger), is no less revelatory of the fact that Heidegger's work continued to find its inspiration in the evolution of the National Socialist movement. Thus it was that at the beginning of the 1940s one of his most obsessive themes was none other than the cold-blooded legitimation of racial selection, which he presented as "in its *principle* metaphysically necessary"!

For the years 1935–1944 alone, the published courses in the *Gesamtausgabe* fill sixteen volumes,[1] to which must be added the personal notes of the *Nachlaß*, six volumes of which have been published,[2] and the seminars, only one of which has appeared to date.[3] The sheer bulk of courses and of notes published in the *Gesamtausgabe* thus constitutes a true material obstacle to be overcome for anyone undertaking to produce a critical synthesis of Heidegger's work. Therefore it is not physically possible to furnish textual demonstrations in this chapter as complete as those for the years 1933–1935, studied in the preceding chapters.

We can, nevertheless, open up several essential perspectives. The study of the volumes mentioned has progressively revealed to me that the Heideggerian themes popularized in his writings published *after* 1945 — the "turn" (*die Kehre*), "the other beginning" (*der andere Anfang*), as a way of creating an opposition between "the event" and "the truth of being" on one hand and the "history of metaphysics" on the other, as well as the identification of metaphysics with "nihilism" — all these are but so many decoys intended for a dual purpose: to propagate the belief in an exculpatory reversal in his relationship with National Socialism and to shift the responsibility for the Third Reich's enterprise of annihilation from those who served as Nazism's guides to the whole philosophical tradition.

We must not allow ourselves to be taken in by these decoys, because in reality the only important change in Heidegger's discourse took place during the years 1942–1949, and the motivation was strategic. It is only faintly visible during the period in which the defeat of Nazism began to come into view; then it becomes more distinct as he had to face the failure of the Third Reich, an event that spelled the total failure of his work, which had accompanied the movement of that regime. As he said in 1945 to the sister of the archbishop Konrad Gröber, to whom he had come to ask for protection: "It is all over with me" — *Mit mir ist es jetzt zu Ende*.[4]

The courses of the years 1933–1944 show us today that his work was in profound harmony with the victorious progress of the National Socialist movement both in the intellectual sphere and in the theater of war. That is why it lost its raison d'être and *ended* with the defeat of the Nazis in 1945.

But Heidegger, like the majority of the most extremist Nazis, did not accept that total defeat, at once general and personal, as is clearly visible in the letters he wrote in 1945 to one of his faithful followers, Rudolf Stadelmann.[5] Subsequently, Heidegger went on to develop a variety of maneuvers and strategies to win acceptance for his work and to disseminate it in the postwar period.

In order to succeed in his undertaking he did not hesitate, as Hugo Ott has proven in the case of his "justification" of his rectorship, to hide the reality of his past actions behind the most untenable denials and, as I shall demonstrate, to engage in numerous rewrites and falsifications of his own texts. He claimed, in the case of his praise of National Socialism in the *Introduction to Metaphysics,* merely to have restored parenthetical material already written but not delivered orally, and in the case of his Nietzsche classes, only to have made a few purely formal modifications, whereas in fact we now know that he tried to hide the true nature of his message to make it acceptable. These facts are extremely serious, because they involve not only the hiding of the truth but also a deliberate attempt to transmit the themes and basic principles of Nazism after World War II.

Given these circumstances, if we want to attain a sufficiently complete and objective overview of Heidegger's work on the basis of the texts and documents now available, we must take into consideration both the texts as written between 1933 and 1944 and the way they were edited after 1945, sometimes twice, and in very different ways. We must distinguish, in this regard, the period that preceded the publication of the *Gesamtausgabe* and the one that begins in 1975 with the publication of the first volume of the so-called complete edition. That is the only way we can tell the difference between the strategies brought into play and the author's true intentions. Only then will we be sufficiently well informed to understand the importance of exercising great caution today, in the face of the publication project of the *Gesamtausgabe,* also referred to as the "definitive version." As has been rightfully emphasized,[6] the fact that Heidegger refused the establishment of a critical edition poses a problem. When we cannot compare the volumes of the *Gesamtausgabe* with earlier editions or the author's manuscripts themselves, his later rewrites are no longer discernable. And when comparison is possible, it requires lengthy and painstaking research that few commentators have the patience to carry out successfully, especially in France, where many studies continue to be based solely on the *Nietzsche* of 1961, without ever referring to the courses actually given on Nietzsche, even though their publication in the *Gesamtausgabe* began in 1985 and has been completed since 2003.

I will add a final observation, probably the most important one, since it bears the key to the understanding of the period after 1945. Heidegger envisaged two goals successively. At first his goal was to make his most Nazi courses of the 1930s acceptable, and to that end he added a parenthesis intended to attenuate his praise of the National Socialist movement of 1935, removed the apologetic statement on Mussolini and Hitler from his 1936 course on Schelling, and modified the conclusion, in which he exalted the motorization of the Wehrmacht in his course taught during the time of the invasion of France. At the same time, he wanted to show that he hadn't repudiated anything fundamentally, but he could only do so in an extremely prudent and gradual manner.

Thus the *Letter on Humanism* of 1947 speaks only by allusion, and as Heidegger himself will say later, "in veiled terms,"[7] as in the case of the reference to the young Germans who, because they "knew about Hölderlin," "thought and lived something entirely different faced with death."[8] In 1949, before the chosen public of the "Bremen Club," he ventured — in a lecture titled "The Frame" (*Das Ge-stell*), on the subject of the death camps and gas chambers — to assert a radical revisionism, which he took care not to include in his publication of the 1962 lectures. And as we shall see, he went much further in another lecture, written at the same time but not published until 1994, in the *Gesamtausgabe*.[9]

It took the interview that appeared after his death in *Der Spiegel* in 1976 and the texts now available in the *Gesamtausgabe* for readers to begin to see clearly that he had renounced none of his deep-seated Nazism. That is why the "complete edition" is so destructive. By its very content, it disseminates within philosophy the explicit and remorseless legitimation of the guiding principles of the Nazi movement.

But when Heidegger conceived the plan for the *Gesamtausgabe,* he did not pursue his "disclosure" to the end. For example, he omitted from that publication the seminar from the winter of 1933–1934, doubtless because his Hitlerian *eros* was so patent there that it was impossible to dissimulate it behind philosophical-sounding titles. That is why the presentation and study of that seminar are one of the major subjects of the present work. And there are undoubtedly a good many other writings and letters kept in reserve. Yet today we have a sufficient number of texts to bring out the whole truth about Heidegger's work, so that we need no longer remain prisoner to its enticements. It is that in-depth investigation pushed to the darkest regions of Heidegger's doctrine that I present in this chapter.

The Introduction of Nazism into "Metaphysics"

Before taking up the first of the courses published after 1945, the *Introduction to Metaphysics*, which appeared in 1953 (exactly twenty years after Hitler's takeover), we must provide some historical information of a general nature on the year 1935, during which the course was taught. That year, a decree by the ministry of the Reich added more stringency to a directive that had been formulated two years earlier: it definitely forbade professors from doing politics in their courses. As Karl Löwith relates, not without humor: "No less deplorable was the general pandering to the political 'worldview.' The new program of courses was chock full of courses that had added 'the State': 'Physics and the State,' 'Art and the State,' 'Philosophy and Politics,' 'Plato and National Socialism,' etc. That resulted, the following semester, in a note from the minister of education forbidding teachers to deal with political subjects that were not within their specialty. Two years later, the situation had become so much worse that the minister, in light of the miserable exam results, decreed that he would no longer tolerate any professor doing politics. The results of the learning that was 'close to the people' led to a depoliticization, for political reasons, and the total state became paradoxically the advocate of neutrality in things intellectual!"[10]

What Löwith reports is crucial. We now know that if Heidegger, after his seminar on Hegel and the state, offers no further courses on explicitly political subjects, it is not from a personal choice to distance himself from the regime but in order to conform to the general evolution of the Reich and the refusal to let teachers treat political subjects. There is a relative depoliticization of the university system beginning in 1935, affecting professors teaching in the classical disciplines. Thus it may be that Heidegger's struggle against specialization at the university does not reflect a rejection of "politicized science," as he would have us believe after the defeat, but on the contrary his aversion to the depoliticization of the university. We now know that the word "self-affirmation" (*Selbstbehauptung*), by which he chose to designate the mission of the German university, is the very term he uses to define the "essence" of the political. How then is it possible for him to claim that he always opposed the politicizing of the university?

Henceforth the taking up of political positions in Heidegger's courses becomes rarer — but does not disappear. It even becomes more incisive and abrupt, as if he meant to compensate for the diminishing of the political in his university courses by more striking formulations. We may, for example, consider (as he leads us to believe in the letter to *Die Zeit* of September 1953), that the 1935 course on the *Introduction to Metaphysics* is entirely conceived in order to lead the listener toward the final eulogy[11] of what he does not hesitate to call "the inner truth and greatness of this movement" (*der inneren Wahrheit und Größe dieser Bewegung*) — that is, National Socialism.[12]

That "introduction" (*Einführung*) to metaphysics is really the introduction into philosophy of the principle of the "spiritual" direction (*Führung*) of the

National Socialist movement, whose "internal truth and greatness" he exalts. The violent tone that characterizes many of the pages of this course is due to the tenor of the "message" but also to the fact that Heidegger was then involved in a savage polemic with another "philosopher" of Nazism—namely, Ernst Krieck. In that year of 1935, the political strife within Nazism became harsher. Krieck and several of those close to him were, at the time, active in the SD (*Sicherheitsdienst*), the security service branch of the SS, and it was not solely a question of a struggle of ideas, as is demonstrated by the fate of Joachim Haupt, who was close to Heidegger.

Haupt, a long-standing member of the NSDAP, was a specialist in education. He founded the "Institutes of National Political Education" (*Nationalpolitische Erziehungsanstalten*) or "Napolas." Like Heidegger, he praised the new racist student law[13] and distinguished himself by participating in the Deutsche Studentenschaft Days with Alfred Baeumler and Martin Heidegger, which were apparently organized as a result of the personal initiative of the rector of Freiburg. Now Krieck, who from that time on opposed Baeumler, did not take part in them, and it may be that his absence was an indication of his future break with Heidegger. Haupt himself tried, in a work published in 1935 by the Armanen Verlag under a pseudonym and titled *Sinnwandel der formalen Bildung,* to develop themes close to those of Heidegger, and in all likelihood inspired by him. In Haupt's view, the similarity between the German and the Greek peoples was their "fight for true being [*wahres Sein*]." Like Heidegger in his Hitlerian seminar, he relates the people to the "blood community" and places *völkisch* existence beneath the sign of *eros*. He is equally insistent about the importance, in this respect, of language and race, in a chapter titled *Rassen und Sprache.*[14] In October 1935, Reinhard Hoehn,[15] who was close to Krieck and, like him, a member of the SD, had Haupt arrested under pretext of homosexuality, on the strength of his private correspondence, which was intercepted and monitored. Haupt did two months of prison time and was barred from the NSDAP in 1937 at the conclusion of his trial.

With respect to these struggles, the first example given in the 1935 course to elucidate the question of the being of the state reveals the climate of the times and the concrete meaning of *Führerstaat*. "A state—is. In what does its being consist? In that the state police arrest a suspect . . ."[16]

The two other examples formulated by Heidegger are those of typewriters in action at the chancellery of the Reich and the Führer's conversation with the British minister of foreign affairs. State police, typewriters, Hitler's foreign policy—this is indeed a good summary of the Hitlerian state so vaunted and advocated by Heidegger in his Hitlerian seminar of 1933–1934 and envisaged by him in connection with its prospects of longevity during his 1934–1935 seminar on Hegel and the state.

In the first part of the course, Heidegger reduces the main question of "metaphysics" to the "question of being." That question is understood in a sense that has absolutely nothing to do with true philosophy, which is concerned with all human beings and cannot therefore be confiscated for the benefit of one people or one "race." It is no longer a question, he says, of constructing ontology: on the contrary, the time has come to give up that term.[17] Henceforth it is the historical being of man, of "our" ownmost future that is the issue. Heidegger continues as follows. "We are concerned with reconnecting man's historical being-there — and this always means at the same time our ownmost future being-there in the totality of the history intended for us — to the power of being that was originally to be opened out. . . . That is why we have related the question of being to the destiny of Europe, where the destiny of the earth is being decided — while our own historic being-there proves to be the center for Europe itself."[18]

The two sentences just quoted, evoking historical existence, related in reality in an extremely banal manner to the temporality of the future, to which is added a note of pathos with a Nazi intonation on destiny, authenticity, and the power of being, constitute a good condensed sample of the *Lingua Tertii Imperii*, or LTI, in its Heideggerian version. But the bombast of the passage does not succeed in hiding the brutal and very concrete reality of what is at stake, infinitely far removed from any philosophy, any metaphysics. . . . What is in fact the status of this "we"? It designates exclusively the people who are in the middle of Europe and decide on the destiny of the earth. Heidegger conflates the historical existence of man and the "we" of the sole Germanic people, united under the Hitlerian *Führung*, a people who are preparing themselves at that date, with a massive rearmament, to invade, subject, and annihilate — mentally, spiritually, and even physically — the other peoples of Europe. We know how quickly the "destiny" of Czechoslovakia, Poland, France — and England if it had not managed to hold on — was successively played out shortly after 1935, once the fate of Republican Spain was sealed with the help of the Luftwaffe.

The apparently dominant project of *Being and Time*, which is to be a fundamental ontology, yields to the reality of what is at stake behind the verbal window-dressing. Beneath the indeterminacy of the discussion of being and nothingness, the most precise and radical determinacy springs up when it is a question of the German people as "the metaphysical" people (*das metaphysische Volk*) positioned at the center of Europe and the only one capable of saving the West from destruction.[19] A major point to be noted is that the theme of "the other beginning" is already present, and it is essentially a Nazi theme. It is a beginning that is a "more original recommencement," in which it is a question, according to Heidegger, "of *repeating* the beginning of our historical/spiritual existence and of transforming it into the other beginning,"[20] thanks to which *Dasein* will find its soil (*Bodenständigkeit*) and re-root.[21] The interrogation about being is related to the destiny of Europe in which the destiny of the earth will be decided, a Europe in which the historical existence of the German people is conceived of as the *middle,* caught in the vise between Russia and America, which are, as he vehemently says several times, the same thing.[22]

It is essential to understand that the theme of "the other beginning" does not appear solely in the unpublished pieces such as *Contributions to Philosophy,* and that it therefore does not constitute an alternative to the teaching given in the courses, whether it be the *Introduction to Metaphysics* or the courses on Nietzsche; nor is it the esoteric version of an exoteric teaching, as has sometimes been affirmed. In reality, it is in his courses that Heidegger first introduces "the other beginning," identified with the moment when the German people comes into the "might of being" for the purpose of deciding on the historical becoming of Europe and even of the entire world. Hitler does not think differently. The "other beginning" is not at all "other" than Nazism and Hitlerism with which it is, moreover, identified; it is only other in relation to the "first beginning" posited as originary, which is supposed to have taken place in Greece. Furthermore, the 1935 course is one of the texts of Heidegger in which the Nazi exaltation of the German people takes its most violent turn. Through the rejection of Russia and America, what Heidegger is formulating is the sort of blanket rejection that levels all differentiation. Western democracy and Marxism are equally targeted. In the middle of a paragraph against Marxism there is a passage, the exegesis of which, presented by certain commentators, has succeeded in propagating the belief that it indicated some degree of distance taken from National Socialism — but this is mainly due to the translation. The expression in question is: "the organizational directing of a people's vital resources and race."[23] The target of that criticism of Heidegger is the idea of "organizational directing" (*organisatorische Lenkung*): he has no problem with considering the people as a race. The word *Organisation* — not of German root, but one of those "Roman words" Heidegger rejects in the name of his *völkisch* conception of language — had been used by him in a pejorative way ever since his 1929 work, *Kant and the Problem of Metaphysics.* At the end of that book, in a manner that may have seemed enigmatic at the time, but the discriminatory significance of which is manifestly clear to us today, he sets up an opposition between the "fools of the organization"

(*Narren der Organisation*) and the "friends of the essential" (*Freunde des Wesentlichen*).[24] Behind the word "Organisation" Heidegger targets the political regimes opposed to the community, or *Gemeinschaft,* whether in the context of Soviet Bolshevism or of Western liberalism; he attacks the latter in particular, because in his view it risks contaminating the way the NSDAP is directed and leading to what he calls, in one of his courses, "liberal National Socialism,"[25] the sort of National Socialism in which bureaucratic organization would outstrip the dictatorial violence of the *Führerprinzip*!

In this connection it must be remembered that this celebration of the "friends of the essential" is contemporaneous with the moment when Heidegger, opposing Cassirer, as did all the National Socialists of his generation, affirmed not without violence that "it is . . . the vision of the world [*Weltanschauung*] that is the condition of the act of philosophizing."[26] That should lead future commentators to greater vigilance, and to reread the *Kantbuch* in keeping the declarations of its author in mind. In any case, we now know how Heidegger, by his teaching during the years 1933–1935, intended to develop the "question of man" that he had borrowed from Kant. In all likelihood he already identified in his mind the existence or *Dasein* of man with the "historical/metaphysical" destiny of the German people alone.

Several major questions can no longer be dodged. What meaning can the words "metaphysics" and "metaphysical" still have, when Heidegger uses them in this way, to characterize the existence of the German people alone, united beneath Hitler's yoke? And how can such a usage be taken seriously from a philosophical point of view? There is in him a patent usurpation of the terms of philosophical language pressed into the service of a "worldview" that is nothing but the destruction of all philosophy.

Heidegger's perverse use of the word "metaphysical" reaches such a level that in June 1940 he will speak of the "motorization of the Wehrmacht" as "a metaphysical act"! That is why it is essential today to realize fully that what Heidegger means when he uses the word "metaphysics" bears no relation to true metaphysics or first philosophy, the science of principles and causes, such as we see it at work in philosophers as different as Aristotle or Descartes.

The Rewriting of the Courses on Nietzsche and the Appreciation of Baeumler

From 1936 to 1940, Heidegger devoted almost all his courses to Nietzsche. That instruction is closely tied to his official involvement in the publishing projects of the Nietzsche Archives of Weimar, which may be said to be his most visible contribution to the progressive extension of National Socialism into philosophy itself. Far from being a reasoned discussion of differences in point of view between himself and National Socialism, and an "intellectual resistance," as he would claim when attempting to clear his name in 1945 before the Freiburg commission, the courses on Nietzsche are a constant, resolute effort to legitimate Nazism, particularly during its first military victories in the spring of 1940.

The Nietzsche Archives of Weimar, an institution founded by Elisabeth Förster-Nietzsche, became an official shrine for the new regime after 1933. One week after his enthronement, Hitler went there to be photographed beside the bust of Nietzsche, and he directly supported the institution that thus became an ideological pillar of the National Socialist state.

At the beginning of May 1934, right after his resignation from the rectorship, Heidegger participated, with Alfred Rosenberg, Hans Frank, Carl Schmitt, and Erich Rothacker, in the Days of the Commission for the Philosophy of Law of the Academy for German Law, organized in the buildings of the Nietzsche Archives. The theme of the Days was "the realization of German Law."[27] The fact of organizing that event in the Nietzsche Archives of Weimar shows the will of the Nazi leaders to make Weimar a sacred city for "philosophy," paralleling Bayreuth's corresponding role for music.[28] Heidegger's official involvement with the work of the Nietzsche Archives began in 1935; he sat on the research commission that met on 22 and 23 February 1936 in Weimar. Another Nazi "philosopher," Hans Heyse, was named at the same time he was.[29] For eight years, from 1935 to 1942, and very actively until 1938, Heidegger was a member of the "scientific commission for the complete historical and critical edition [*Gesamtausgabe*] of the works and letters of Nietzsche." As Karl Löwith wrote: "while in reality he covered over evil in this way with his good name."[30]

Heidegger took charge of the preparation of the new edition of *The Will to Power* planned by the Nietzsche Archives. It was at his suggestion that *My Life,* the autobiography of Nietzsche as a young man, was published the same year and sent to those most likely to support the institution financially: Hitler, Mussolini, Frank, Rosenberg, and Baeumler.[31] Heidegger had reproductions of the unpublished writings available to him for his work; they were particularly useful to him for his summer semester course of 1937, *The Fundamental Position of Nietzsche. The Eternal Return of the Same.* Additionally, he spent long periods at the Nietzsche Archives for his research. On 11 July 1936 he wrote to Henry Corbin: "I got back only last evening from Weimar, where I roved around in the *Nietzsche-Archiv.* I am a member of a scientific commission for the new historical and critical edition."[32]

When a conflict broke out in 1938 between the Nietzsche Archives and the

"Rosenberg Office [*Amt*]," which claimed oversight of the publication, it was Hans Heinrich Lammers in person, the head of Hitler's chancellery, who intervened and attempted to find a compromise. As for Heidegger, he felt in a strong enough position to resist the authority of the *Rosenberg Amt,* stressing the importance of the works of Nietzsche "for the German people and the future of the Occident." But he was careful to point out that in his view "an ideological [*weltanschaulich*] review of new German works appearing today is politically necessary and is not being contested here."[33]

Heidegger admits, then, in 1938, the "political need" for Nazi censorship of publications.

Let is now consider the Nietzsche courses. Heidegger republished them all in 1961, along with five texts composed between 1940 and 1946, under the titles *Nietzsche I* and *Nietzsche II.* In order to make his teaching of Nietzsche acceptable sixteen years after the Nazi defeat, he made very numerous and significant intentional omissions, modifications, and additions. He said nothing about this to his readers,[34] with the result that a whole generation of philosophers had access to only a mutilated text that did not allow them to form an accurate opinion of the propositions that were in fact taught by Heidegger from 1936 to 1940. This is particularly true for France, which for over thirty years (since 1971) has had nothing at its disposal but the French translation of the 1961 edition. Those who read German, however, now have access to the text of the courses published in the *Gesamtausgabe,* making it possible for them to assess the extent and significance of the modifications introduced by Heidegger in 1961. Without being able to be exhaustive — for that would require an entire volume — I will examine several of these alterations or intentional omissions, referring in all cases to the text of the courses as reedited since 1986.

The first fundamental point to be made is that far from opposing the Nazi interpretations of Nietzsche current at the time, Heidegger referred his students to them as positive references. The two best-known Nazi interpreters of Nietzsche were Alfred Baeumler and Kurt Hildebrandt.[35] Now what was the first reference Heidegger gave his students? What he calls Baeumler's "judicious afterword" to his 1930 edition of *The Will to Power.*[36] It is therefore important to see what is contained in that afterword of Baeumler's, given such high priority in being recommended to students.

Baeumler, exactly like Heidegger six years later, presented *The Will to Power* as Nietzsche's "key philosophical work" and insisted on the systematic coherence of his thought, which he compared to that of Heraclitus.[37] In Nietzsche, it is "the legislator of a specific epoch of Occidental history" who speaks to us as "the dictator of the future."[38] It is a question of "bringing to expres-

sion the countermovement that opposes European nihilism,"[39] and in conformity with "the essence of life," of replacing "the rotted foundations of Christian culture" by "new foundations, in truth older."[40] Indeed, "he who wishes
to educate must go back to the basis of life. He must begin with life and the
engendering of life." He must, as Nietzsche did with the title of book 4 of *The
Will to Power,* go back to the "Greek concept of education" understood as
"training and selection" (*Zucht und Züchtung*).[41] In short, he must transfer
the "Greco-Germanic concept of education" to its "reality, which gives pause
for thought."[42] Nietzsche pits "life against consciousness, instinct against
knowledge," the will being understood as "drive, affect, organizing force,
creative, formative power, and life becoming 'power' in forms." But we must
have a correct understanding of these major concepts, such as "will to power,"
"superman," "master in morality," and "slave in morality." They are not to be
understood in "an idealized sense." Already the young Nietzsche had succeeded in understanding how to "protest against the concept of humanity"
and pit "culture against civilization." The proper role of Nietzsche is to have
managed to show that "instincts and affects express in every race [*Rasse*] and
in every status [*Stand*] something of their conditions of existence. To require
that these affects give way before 'virtue' amounts to demanding that these
races or states be annihilated."[43] It is therefore "not the moral concept of
virtue but the historical concept of greatness that stands at the center of the
Nietzschean ethics." Hence "the critique of philosophy, which Nietzsche takes
up exclusively — except for the Greeks — with the Germans."[44] Whence also
his social doctrine: "democracy represents the fact of not being able to believe
in great men." And Baeumler proceeds to quote that other affirmation of
Nietzsche's as well: "my philosophy is built on the hierarchical order, not on a
morality of the individual." This he sums up in his own way, when speaking of
the Nietzschean "superman." "He shows the image of the master of the earth,
the heroic man, who knows he is a destiny. He haughtily dismisses the liberal
verbiage about nobleness of spirit: there is no authentic spirit without authentic life. It is first and foremost blood [*das Geblüt*] that ennobles the spirit."[45]

Education understood as training and selection, liberalism and democracy
replaced by the hierarchical order based on race and rank, spirit connected
with blood nobility — these are the things Baeumler professes openly in this
short text that Heidegger recommends to his students as being judicious. It is
the quintessence of the political and racial teaching of Nazism that Heidegger
approves unreservedly in his course of winter 1936–1937. This is not just the
indication of an isolated case of convergence. We frequently find in Heidegger's teaching, whether in 1933–1935, or in the texts on Nietzsche from the
1936–1941 period, propositions similar to those stated here by Baeumler.

This approval of Baeumler's afterword is a decisive element if we want to understand Heidegger's *Nietzsche*. With it we have the proof that Heidegger approves an interpretation of the will to power that essentially consists in relating it to race and blood. This observation does not corroborate the usual interpretations of Heidegger's *Nietzsche:* they, based on the fact that Heidegger seems to distance himself from what he calls "biologism" (but we shall see that even on this point there are nuances that must be taken into account), conclude quite mistakenly that he rejects the racial interpretation of Nietzsche's will to power and that he opposes the National Socialist interpretation of Nietzsche as being based on "biologism," that same "biologism" that is held to underlie Heidegger's supposed critique of Baeumler. But what the texts show is that Heidegger does not reject the racial interpretation of Nietzsche's will to power and of his superman, but on the contrary legitimizes them. As a matter of fact we see that in the projected (but never taught) course of 1941, he relates the superman to "the racial selection of man,"[46] without expressing the slightest reservation about the racist reading of Nietzsche.

Moreover, the texts do show that Heidegger questions the "biological" interpretation of Nietzsche, but the truth is that he does so in a way that is always ambiguous and that cannot be understood without consulting the ample excurses of 1939, edited out of the 1961 version of *Nietzsche*.[47] It must be concluded that for Heidegger racism and biologism are not identical, and that there is a racism that is not exclusively "biological." In sum, Heidegger's questioning of biologism does not make him any less a racist.

Further, is it the usual Nazi interpretation of Nietzsche that he is challenging when he questions biologism? Not at all. In 1937, the principal representatives of that Nazi reading are Baeumler and Hildebrandt. We have seen how Heidegger refers his students very approvingly to their works. It is true that there is, in the first course on Nietzsche, a critical passage concerning Baeumler, which we will analyze carefully. But that passage ends with yet another encomium of the latter, expressed as follows. "Apart from this, Baeumler is among the extremely few to have opposed the psycho-biological interpretation of Nietzsche by Klages."[48]

Contrary to what has until now been affirmed by commentators, Baeumler's interpretation of Nietzsche was therefore considered by Heidegger not to be "biological" but, quite to the contrary, to oppose that reading.[49] This proves that the fact of invoking race and blood is not at all what Heidegger is rejecting as "biologism." Moreover, we see that the Heideggerian critique of "biologism," which here is associated with "psychologism," is directed not at Baeumler but at Ludwig Klages, an author who in 1936–1937 lost the quasi-official position he had held during his lectures in Berlin in 1934. Klages lived in

Switzerland thereafter, and in 1936–1937 was not considered in Germany as a major representative of National Socialist "philosophy." In reality, as is proven specifically by the course of winter semester 1933–1934,[50] the fact of associating blood and spirit in order to have them serve a racist and explicitly Nazi conception of the superiority of the German people is common to both Heidegger and Baeumler. Moreover, it seems that this same position is to be found in Hitler and Rosenberg. It should be noted that in a recent work on *The Political Religion of National Socialism,* devoted mainly to the writings of Hitler and Rosenberg, the author maintains that there is no social Darwinian biologism in Hitler and Rosenberg, and that "the entire basis of National Socialist racism . . . remains hidden" if one applies a "biological characterization of the ideologeme race."[51]

In any event, what Heidegger criticizes Baeumler for does not involve his interpretation of Nietzsche in terms of blood and race. His criticism bears exclusively on the importance to be given to Nietzsche's idea of the eternal return of the same. On this point, taking his cue from Karl Löwith but without naming him, Heidegger refuses to get involved in the controversy between Baeumler and Jaspers, and he is dismissive of both of them at a time when the latter is about to be forced to retire and forbidden to teach, as a professor whose wife is a "non-Aryan." This is a good indication that the criticism is not aimed at Baeumler as a National Socialist "philosopher."

In reality, the interpretations of Baeumler and Heidegger are very close at that date. Both place the will to power at the center of Nietzsche's thought, both see that thought as culminating in the idea of the superman, both attack "nihilism," and both target what Nazism, too, is struggling against: the values of Christianity, democracy, and individual freedom that is then designated by the word "liberalism." And finally, both oppose the narrowly "biological" interpretation of Nietzsche. The only important point opposing them is the following: Baeumler claims that the eternal return of the same contradicts the will to power interpreted as irreversible becoming. Heidegger maintains to the contrary that these two doctrines are concordant, but that this can be understood only by relating them to their "metaphysical" foundations; he considers Baeumler's conception, in his 1931 work, *Nietzsche, the Philosopher and the Politician,* too political to succeed in doing so.

In his winter 1936–1937 course, Heidegger limits himself to a nuanced remark, suggesting that it is less the compatibility between the doctrine of the eternal return and the political conception of Baeumler that is the issue than the insufficiency of his analysis of this subject. He writes: "The Nietzschean doctrine of the eternal return is not suitable to Baeumler's politics, or at least he thinks it isn't suitable."[52]

In the *Nietzsche* of 1961, Heidegger rewrites the sentence in order to make it look like a radical criticism of Baeumler's Nazism, which in reality is completely absent from the course taught in 1936–1937. The revised version reads: "Nietzsche's doctrine of the eternal return of the same militates against Baeumler's conception of politics."[53]

In German, the homophony between *Wiederkehr* and *widerstreitet* accentuates the strength of the criticism, and all seems to be conceived in such a way as to suggest to the reader that Heidegger opposed Baeumler directly and thereby performed, through his reading of Nietzsche, a spiritual act of "resistance" (*Widerstand*), as he claimed in 1945. Furthermore, that radical modification of the sentence is not the only way Heidegger manipulated this passage. He attenuated the praise that followed by taking out the "very" (*sehr*): Baeumler is no longer "one of the very rare" but only "one of the rare" to rise in opposition to the psychobiological interpretation of Nietzsche. And he attenuates considerably the criticism of Jaspers that comes after that. We find in 1936–1937 a long paragraph that expresses a virulent attack on Jaspers: Heidegger blames him specifically for "not taking philosophical knowledge in its innermost foundation." Philosophy becomes "a moralizing psychology of the existence of man."[54]

In 1936–1937, the reader is confronted with the contrast between two critical attitudes: the one expressed toward Baeumler concludes with an insistent encomium, while the other ends radically by uniting Jaspers and Klages in shared opprobrium, both men having been wrong to limit themselves to "psychological" considerations. In 1961 the situation is reversed: the entire critical paragraph on Jaspers, in which he is presented as a psychologist and not a philosopher, is removed, and the criticism of him, thus shortened, seems quite moderate in comparison with that of Baeumler, which on the contrary has been stiffened. These changes are a first illustration of Heidegger's manipulations after the war, which are intended to make his courses acceptable to that postwar public. If then, there really is a "turning," a *Kehre*, in Heidegger, it is on the order of a falsification, not a turning of thought.

If the transformations of the 1961 text had reflected an authentic and profound evolution of Heidegger after twenty-five years, they would certainly have been a positive point. Unfortunately, the fact that Heidegger claims in the 1961 preface to have made only purely formal corrections and the existence of the *Gesamtausgabe*, in which the courses on Nietzsche are republished, this time in their unchanged form, prove that the 1961 modifications were in essence motivated solely by tactical considerations connected with the intellectual and political context of the immediate postwar period. Martin Heidegger's only concern was to avoid his work's being rejected by the readers of our democracies, which would facilitate what Carl Schmitt spitefully referred to as his "comeback" after his forced retreat in the wake of the Nazi defeat.

Once his worldwide fame was ensured, in the mid-1970s, Heidegger could allow his courses to be republished just as he had taught them. He has given us his doctrine to read today in a form in which he deems it still to be operative and actively preparing a future for itself, in which it will once again be able to take part in the movement of history.

Praise for Spengler, "Biologism," and the Foundations of Politics

One of the scandals of the 1961 edition of Heidegger's *Nietzsche* is that it omits, without saying so, most of the long passages in which he reiterates points from the preceding lesson in order to make them more concrete. Despite their name, these "repetitions" (*Wiederholungen*) do not simply repeat what has already been exposited. It is in these passages that Heidegger reveals the sources from which he drew his "doctrine," revealing the close ties that bind his teaching on Nietzsche with the current politics of Nazism. Thus, in the 1939 courses on *The Will to Power as Knowledge,* the chapter on "Nietzsche's Biologism" contains a vital, twenty-six-page development that was not included in the first volume of the *Nietzsche* of 1961[55] and was not published until 1989, in volume 47 of the *Gesamtausgabe.*

Although it has been twenty years since their publication, these pages have not been mentioned in any article in France, where the *Nietzsche* of 1961 generally continues to be the only one referenced. Yet it is in this long suppressed section that we can see in what spirit Heidegger discusses biologism. It is above all the use of words ending in *-ism* that he ridicules — such words as "biologism," "idealism," and "liberalism." To him, these neologisms fall into the category of public, contemporary communication in which everything is of equal value and gets run together, the ancient and the modern; in which, for example, as he says, "we see photo-essays on the Acropolis and a village of Negroes [*Negerkral*] displayed alongside one another."[56]

The use of the word *Negerkral* is the mark of a deeply anchored racism. The German term *kral,* seldom used, comes from *Kraal,* a Dutch word for "village," which turns up in the English *corral,* and in South Africa it designates an enclosure for livestock. We are not far here from Sloterdijk's "human zoo." . . . *Negerkral,* then, means "village of Negroes," or worse: an "enclosure for Negroes." Obviously, for Heidegger's deep racism, the fact of juxtaposing the Acropolis and an African village constitutes a scandal in itself and requires no commentary. The racist connotation of this passage reminds us of what he had already said about the "Negroes" and the Kaffirs in his course of 1934.[57]

We then find a long, critical development on the evolution of *Die Tat,* a publication connected with the movement of "Young Conservatives" (*Jungkonservative*) that Heidegger, as well as his disciples Hans-Georg Gadamer and Erik Wolf, had been close to. The directors of the journal had helped prepare — before celebrating it unreservedly — the power takeover of 1933.[58] Heidegger evokes, not without pathos, the "German youth," until recently gathered around that journal, militating before the war in the "free academic corps" (*akademische Freischaren*) of the universities of Jena, Göttingen, and Marburg, before falling in battle at Langemarck. It is deplorable, he then adds, that in that year of 1939, "in the present distress of our people," the journal *Die Tat* adopted a new subtitle, "The Twentieth Century," and that "from an uprising of the most German of men" it was "transformed into a fairly sophisticated American magazine."[59]

Immediately afterward, Heidegger makes fun, as he does more than once in his courses, of the "Confessional Front," a gathering of Protestants who are the least subservient to Nazism. These attacks did not alienate Erik Wolf from him, which confirms that he had other attachments to Heidegger. But what is the most revealing of Heidegger's true thoughts is the long passage on biologism involving Oswald Spengler and Ludwig Klages.[60] Heidegger has merely a few words of contempt for Klages, since the only thing he respects him for is being the founder of graphology. What he says about Spengler, on the contrary, is quite detailed and entirely positive. After having risen in protest against considering Spengler, on the strength of his title *The Decline of the West,* as a "pessimistic preacher with a weak and hopeless mood of doom and gloom,"[61] whereas he is "quite the opposite," Heidegger embarks on an insistent panegyric in the following terms. "As a result of a biological interpretation of the 'Will to Power,' he became one of the foremost and essential political educators in the decade between 1920 and 1930, during which time he undertook to write history for the statesman and to trace the historical development of statecraft."[62]

As we can see, Spengler's "biologism" is not ill viewed. Furthermore, Heidegger appreciates the "political educator" in him. For us, who know of Heidegger's will to play the role of "political educator" himself, it is important to see that in 1939 he has not changed his mind about that ambition he had flaunted earlier, in his Hitlerian seminar, at a date when it was still possible for him to openly transform his teaching into a course of Hitlerian and Nazi propaganda.

In 1939, Heidegger reverts to that earlier ambition, covering his tracks this time with the authority of Spengler. Here are the quotations from the book *Der Staat* that he gathers for his students in this spring of 1939. "In the preface to his work titled *The State* (1924), in which he summarizes the fundamental philosophical thoughts of the *Decline of the West* (1917), we find the statements: 'where we find ourselves: in the transition from parliamentarianism to Caesarism. We are living through a great era. . . . The destiny of Germany depends on the influence attained by men who have understood the situation and risen to the occasion' (Preface, iv). 'The successes of the English have always been introduced by failures, and secured only by doggedness in the final struggle.' "[63]

After having chosen these excerpts from the preface of the book, Heidegger quotes several sentences taken from the first few pages of the third part, "Philosophy of Politics": "There are no politically gifted peoples. There are only peoples who are solidly placed in the hands of a directing minority and who feel that they are well off. The English as a people is as deprived of judgment, as narrow and impractical in things political as any other nation, but they possess a *tradition of confidence* despite their taste for public debate. . . . Confidence means spontaneous renunciation of criticism. . . . *Political ability in a mass of people is nothing but confidence in leadership* [*Führung*]. But it needs to be acquired, to mature slowly, to be preserved by successes and to have become tradition."[64]

The suspension points mark reflections on the English omitted by Heidegger in order to get at what interests him: the assertion of *Führung*, which sums up for him, as for Hitler, the essential of politics.

The continuation of his course is particularly important for us because it reveals the sources from which Heidegger drew his conception of the political as "self-affirmation" (*Selbstbehauptung*). He continues as follows.

> The grasp of the underlying and essential elements of politics from which Spengler's political position and historical reflection emerge appears in the following sentences, which often bring Nietzsche literally to mind: "Politics is the modality in which the influx of human existence affirms itself [*sich behauptet*], grows, and triumphs over other vital currents. *All of life is political,* in each one of its instinctive traits, down to its innermost marrow. What is often termed these days vital energy (vitality), that "id" that is within us, that will go forward and upward at any cost, our blind, cosmic, longing drive for recognition and power, which remains bound plantlike to the earth and racially to "our native land," existence directed and *made* to act—this is what seeks, and must seek everywhere among superior men in the form of political life, the great decision: to be a destiny, or to suffer a destiny. For one can only *grow* or *die out*. There is no third possibility."[65]

The comparison of that page by Spengler quoted by Heidegger with the end of the unpublished seminar on Hegel and the state shows us that Heidegger's definition of the political as "self-affirmation" (*Selbstbehauptung*) is directly inspired by Spengler's definition of politics as the "modality in which the influx of human existence affirms itself [*sich behauptet*], grows, and triumphs over other vital currents."[66] Thus the source from which Heidegger was able to borrow his conception of politics as early as his 1920 lecture on Spengler is revealed to us. Politics (or, in the seminar on Hegel and the state, *the political*) is simply the self-affirmation of existence. It is true that Heidegger transposes into an existential and ontological vocabulary what Spengler expresses in a more vitalistic vocabulary, but the substance is the same, and we have seen that Heidegger does not hesitate to speak on occasion of the "flow of blood" (*das Strömen des Blutes*).[67]

Now, what is that "existence" (*Dasein*) that affirms itself in politics, according to Spengler? The preceding sentence tells us. "We call the currents of human existence history the moment we envisage them as movement: race [*Geschlecht*], order [*Stand*], people, nation . . ."[68]

Thus, existence is "political" in that it affirms itself, and "history" in that it is movement. It is as race, then, that it is initially apprehended. It is from this doctrine that Heidegger draws sustenance.

The extremely deleterious nature of these pages must be emphasized; they constitute the source that will be tapped by the major "doctrinaires" of Nazism, such as Alfred Baeumler, Alfred Rosenberg, Walter Darré, and Martin Heidegger. Nearly every one of Spengler's words shows up in Nazi doctrine. Such is the case, for example, with his praise of "nobility" (*Adel*) as an expression of the "strong race," and with "discipline" or "training" (*Zucht*) as the method of political education. Spengler writes: "That is why nobility as the expression of a strong race is of a properly political order, and discipline, not learning, is the properly political method of education."[69]

The Heideggerian definition of the political as "self-affirmation" is therefore devoid of originality. It comes from the same racist source as the developments of Spengler. The demonstration has thus been definitively made that Heidegger is not at all combating that "biologism." What he continually critiques is Darwinism, because it is Anglo-Saxon and therefore "liberal." But he is careful to point out later in his course on Nietzsche that "Nietzsche's biologism is not Darwinism." Indeed, he adds, Darwin understands life in a "*sociological/metaphysical*" manner, while Nietzsche interprets it in an "*ontological*/metaphysical" way — the word "ontological," he specifies, not to be taken in the scholastic sense.[70] Therefore we can affirm that the Heideggerian "doctrine" constitutes in its premises the appropriation, and the existential and "ontological" transposition, of the struggle for life and total domination such as it is to be found in the interpretations of Nietzsche by Spengler and Jünger, who remain his two main sources throughout the 1930s.

It is true that Heidegger will constantly try to defend his originality, notably in forging his own terminology, but on the substance, the racist inspiration remains common to all three authors. It may even be argued that the racial element, being expressed in an "ontological" way, becomes more radical in Heidegger. What is the most important for him, however it may be expressed, is the defense of what he calls in his summer semester course of 1934 "the creative possibilities and self-affirmations [*Selbstbehauptungen*] of the strength of the German people."[71] For that, one must draw on what he calls "the fundamental possibilities of the essence of the originally Germanic race" (*die Grundmöglich-keiten des urgermanischen Stammeswesens*).[72] And what has made the great success of his work is that Heidegger was able to give the underlying racism of that doctrine a more "philosophical" appearance than had either Spengler or Jünger, even though that doctrine, by its discriminatory nature, constitutes the radical perversion and destruction in an act of philosophy.

Heidegger and Oskar Becker: Being, Essence, and Race

On the racist factor of Heidegger's "ontology," the controversy raised in 1937–1938 by Oskar Becker, one of his disciples, sheds important light. Becker, along with Karl Löwith, is one of the main students of Heidegger in the early 1920s. During these same years, disciples and master maintain an abundant correspondence, which has remained unpublished, on the theses of *Being and Time*. Beginning in these years, Becker proves to be very close to the raciologist Ludwig Clauß. In 1928 Heidegger has enough esteem for Becker to propose him as his successor at Marburg. But as Becker was degraded by the ministry in favor of Frank, Heidegger took him on as head assistant at Freiburg, before himself being elected as professor at Bonn, where he became the colleague of Erich Rothacker.

In 1937 Becker was a member of the delegation selected by the regime to represent Germany at the Descartes Congress. His intervention was published the same year, in volume 8 of the *Travaux du IXe congrès international de philosophie. Congrès Descartes*. It was titled "Transzendenz und Paratranszendenz." The summary reads as follows: "Plato's well-known expression *epekeina tes ousias* and Aristotle's considerations on the theme of first philosophy bring about the recognition, in the idea of transcendence, of a double meaning that is not clarified. The systematic pursuit of this problem leads to a separation of the traditional idea of transcendence into a 'transcendence' properly so called (in an eminent sense) and a new form, hitherto given insufficient attention, 'paratranscendence.' It corresponds to the 'natural': organic growth, maternal powers, blood and earth. The research concerning it founds a new metaphysical discipline of the same kind as ontology: 'parontology.' "[73]

The reader will have understood that what is involved here is the founding of the National Socialist racial doctrine of *Blut und Boden* on a pseudo-metaphysics elaborated on the basis of the fundamental ontology of Heidegger and in keeping with it. What is bewildering about this undertaking is first the appearance of philosophical technicality that it assumes, with a scholarly pseudo-discussion between Plato and Aristotle, studded with Greek quotations, and second the fact that the organizers of the congress published this text. We can see by this example how the routine functioning of the institution and the absence of any serious and deep grasp of what is being said under the guise of a philosophical statement allows the most devastating doctrine to be disseminated in thought. It is a warning to be heeded today.

Are we, today, more diligent than in 1937? Have we, to use a traditional phrase, learned the lessons of history? The reality of what is currently being published leaves room for doubt. Here is an example. In 2003 an article by the Schmittian Reinhard Mehring was published in which the author, without hiding the *völkisch* and racist character of the conceptions of Larenz, but passing over in silence the racism of Wolf, who is presented as a "personalist," delivers a strong panegyric for the "philosophy of law" of Erik Wolf and Karl Larenz and contrasts it with "the democratic ethos of relativism," which, in his opinion, can only incline its followers to "resignation."[74] In short, it is Wolf and Larenz who must, in his view, be emulated, and not Gustav Radbruch, who was under Nazism an authentic, albeit discreet, opponent. Thus, in a publication devoted to *Leftist Jurists in the Weimar Republic,* it was possible for an article to promote the Nazi conception of law without anyone, apparently, being alarmed. It is true that the author takes shelter to some extent behind the usurped reputation of Erik Wolf, which confirms how necessary it was to bring the true doctrine of that disciple of Heidegger out into the daylight.

To return now to Oskar Becker, the thing that must be underlined is that his project takes its lead from Heidegger. By going one better, so to speak, he intends to constitute a new "ontology" that would give a better account of race than that elaborated by his master. Becker begins by capitalizing on the concept of "birth" (*Geburt*) — a major theme in Nazism and, as we have already seen, in Heidegger's first course on Hölderlin. *Geburt* for Becker is an "originally pagan" concept, rooted in the "original myth" (*Ursprungsmythos*). He presents "birth" as the "metaphysical counterpoint" (*metaphysisches Gegenspiel*) of the Heideggerian "*existentiale*" of "thrownness" (*Geworfenheit*). In short, he sees in the author of *Being and Time* one who has succeeded in describing the thrownness of *Dasein* in inauthentic existence, characterized by the absence of soil and the fact of not belonging to the *Gemeinschaft,* while he himself undertakes to found belongingness to the race in a new "ontology."

It is pathetic to see this disciple try to exist in relation to his master by inventing even more barbaric neologisms such as "paratranscendence" and "parontology," and sink into the most nauseating mire of Nazism in attempting to do a better job than Heidegger in implanting its racial doctrine into philosophy. Becker shows his hand at the end of his study. Speaking of the "phenomenon of birth," he affirms: "It is here that the fundamental experiences, such as belonging to a specific *Volkstum*, a specific race and a native landscape, have their place. What become visible in these fundamental experiences are the ancient maternal powers of blood and earth, mythically connected from time immemorial."[75]

And Becker blithely proceeds to recycle all the metaphorized racial vocabulary of National Socialism that had been worked out by Clauß, Rothacker, and Jünger. As we have seen, this vocabulary was used over and over by Heidegger himself, particularly in his course of 1933: "the strength that stamps" (*prägende Kraft*), the "type" (*Typ*), the "blow" (*Schlag*), and the fundamental figure (*Grundgestalt*). Becker then asks whether we do indeed find reflected here the human *Dasein* described by Heidegger in his existential analytic. Doubtless we do, he suggests, but on the condition that we make a terminological shift. Invoking the "philosophical nature of the German language," which speaks of the child as a "little essence" (*kleines Wesen*), we should no longer say *Dasein*, but *Da-wesen*, no longer speak of *Sein*, but of *wesendes Wesen*. Becker pursues his divagations, constantly defining himself in relation to Heidegger, with the idea of completing the "ontological difference" between being and the entity by "the parontological identity" (*parontologische Gleichung*) of essence with essence. In reality, far from differentiating himself from his master, he merely confirms a tendency that is detectable in Heidegger's texts themselves, in which the reference to "essence" (*Wesen*) becomes increasingly insistent during the 1930s. Thus we shall see Heidegger, in his writings on Jünger, speak of "the not yet purified essence of the Germans."[76]

In 1938, in the journal *Rasse*, Becker publishes an even more explicit article, which he entitles "Nordic Metaphysics."[77] That monthly was published at the time in Leipzig by Teubner, the publisher of Aristotle. That second "study" of Becker's, having already been mentioned by Karl Löwith and Hans Sluga, is a bit better known than the first.[78] It is just as instructive by its way of "ontologizing" a racist substratum. The disciple takes up in a more direct manner what the master had accomplished more secretively. But there is a difference between the two authors in that Heidegger is, like Erik Wolf and according to his own expressions, a partisan of an "essence of the Germans" and of an "essence of the originally Germanic race," whereas Becker, like Ludwig Clauß, bases his work on the "Nordic race." Thus the article starts out with affirmations to the effect that "not all peoples have a metaphysics" and "metaphysics is a Nordic possibility," while Heidegger affirms, a bit differently, that the Germans are "the metaphysical people."

In that article, Becker no longer discusses exclusively the existentialism of Heidegger, but also the form given it by another of his disciples, Hans Heyse, in *Idee und Existenz*. The context of the journal *Rasse* allows him to be more explicit, and he goes so far in his conclusions, in which he bolsters his views with the raciologists Houston Stewart Chamberlain and Ludwig Clauß, as to express the relation between the essence of man and race in these terms: "The essence of man pertains to the safekeeping [*Geborgenheit*] of his race."[79]

Becker's terminology accurately foreshadows Heidegger's later developments and especially his *Bremen Lectures* of 1949, in which we find words from the same root as *Geborgenheit*, as when Heidegger speaks of "sheltering" (*bergen*) and of the "saving" (*Bergung*) of man in the truth and "the essence" of being.[80]

In a general way, the evolution of Heidegger's terminology under Nazism takes the same direction as Becker's vocabulary: it is more and more constantly a question of "essence." In the 1930s, the word *Existenz* has long been absent from Heideggerian language. The "essence of being" (*Wesen des Seins*), in contrast, is henceforth at the heart of his discourse.

⋅ Let us also point out that Becker wanted to continue a friendly controversy about race that had begun in the mid-1920s on the subject of art. He cast doubt on the ability of the existential analysis of *Being and Time* to account for art. But as Hans Sluga successfully demonstrates,[81] Heidegger had already entirely reconsidered the question of art a long time before 1938 and founded it on the people's belonging to the "earth," comparing, in his 1935 lecture, *The Origin of the Work of Art*, the foundation of the city (*polis*) to the foundation of the work of art, especially in connection with the example of the temple. Becker's criticisms in 1937–1938 are therefore out of date in relation to the actual evolution of Heidegger's writing at the time.

Actually, not only is Heidegger no slacker in comparison with Becker when it comes to orphic utterances on "the essence of the original Germanic race," but he will go further than him in the area of anti-Semitic ostracism. Indeed, when in 1942 Oskar Becker publishes, in the series of "war lectures" of the University of Bonn, a lecture titled *The Thoughts of Frederic Nietzsche on Hierarchy, Training, and Selection*,[82] he includes in his short bibliography the book published by Karl Löwith in 1935: *Nietzsche, Philosophy of the Eternal Return of the Same.*[83] Heidegger, on the contrary, though he profited greatly from Karl Löwith's highlighting of the Nietzschean eternal return, never refers to his book, and not once does he pronounce Löwith's name in his courses on Nietzsche.

Heidegger was clearly not upset by Oskar Becker's racial discussion of his ontology, since after World War II the two men remained friends. In a letter of 20 March 1966 addressed to Eugen Fink, Heidegger spoke to him of "our highly esteemed friend Oskar Becker, recently deceased."[84] In 1963 the latter, shortly before his death, had produced a new edition (with Neske, the same press as Heidegger's) of his considerations on *Dasein* and *Dawesen*, stripped of anything that, in his writings of 1937–1938, showed the racial meaning of his idea of "essence."[85] And as recently as 1984, his study titled "Para-Existenz. Menschliches Dasein und Dawesen" was published by a student of Heidegger's, Otto Pöggeler, in a collective work on his master.[86] So even though the racial content of Becker's doctrine is deliberately obfuscated after 1945, Heidegger and Pöggeler continue to welcome Becker's writings without ever showing the least reservations about what remains fundamentally a racial discussion of Heidegger's work.

The Interpretation of Descartes and of "Metaphysics" at the Time of the Invasion of France

Let us return to the courses on Nietzsche and the position that emerges from them at the beginning of the 1940s. It is particularly important to see how Heidegger considers Descartes at this time, since it may seem, at a first reading, that he has changed markedly in his assessment of the author of the *Meditations* since his condemnation without appeal of 1933. In reality, the apparent about-face reflects the upheaval of the power relation between Nazi Germany and France. We are in spring 1940: the armies of the Nazi Reich are rushing into France. That is the moment Heidegger chooses to speak at length of Descartes. The original course was far more developed than the text published in 1961 in *Nietzsche II*, in which over twenty pages of a summary involving Descartes — specifically in his relation to Pascal's critique — are omitted. Nevertheless, this can hardly be considered a philosophical elucidation of the work of Descartes: on the contrary, it contains the earlier "interpretations," already present in his course of winter 1923–1924,[87] and in a rigid form, as can be seen by the formulations Heidegger attributes to Descartes but that, in reality, are not his. The expressions used — *cogito me cogitare, ego cogito,* as well as *fundamentum absolutum inconcussum veritas*[88] and *subjec-*

tum[89] — are not in the *Meditations*. In them, Descartes never speaks of *fundamentum* in the singular, he never qualifies the human *I* as "absolute," and as we have seen, in the *Meditations* he does not use, in speaking of the *res cogitans,* the term *subjectum.*

Furthermore, in 1940 and 1941 we find the same reductive presuppositions as in 1923–1924, proving that Heidegger's conception of the author of the *Meditations* did not change fundamentally in two decades. He continues to interpret Descartes's *philosophia prima* in a completely scholastic manner, as a philosophy that remains "within the sphere of the question concerning the *ens qua ens.*"[90] Also, and although he sometimes says he doesn't want to use the word *secularization,* he continues to interpret the metaphysical position of Descartes as the translation and philosophical equivalent of a theological position. The Cartesian freedom and its determination of truth as certainty are understood as a "certainty similar" to "the certainty of salvation" in faith.[91] This parallel allows Heidegger to associate Descartes with Luther, identifying them as the two reference points at the onset of modernity.[92] But besides the fact it is not established by any solid argument, the idea of a relationship between philosophical certainty and religious faith is not acceptable from a Cartesian point of view. It presupposes a conflation of belief and rational certainty that Descartes always rejected. For the author of the *Regulae,* belief is the adherence of the will to something dark,[93] while rational certainty is born of the evidence of a fully clear and distinct perception. There is therefore no common measure between the two.

In thus diminishing the distance between the certainty of faith and rational certainty in human knowledge, Heidegger tends to absolutize human certainty, contrary to the spirit of the *Meditations.* That allows him to present Cartesian metaphysics as the anticipation of the absolute "domination of the subject in the modern period," which in his view found its highest expression in Hegel's "absolute knowledge" before being fulfilled in the Nietzschean "will to power."[94] Here, the deformation of the Cartesian project is at its highest point. Descartes's first philosophy is a philosophy of clear perception and truth. It is not a doctrine of the self-affirmation of power. The Cartesian spirit is neither an "absolute spirit" à la Hegel nor a self-production à la Fichte or Gentile, but a *mens humana* that does not at all pretend to identify itself with the *ens infinitum.*

All the originality of the metaphysics of the *Meditations* resides in the subtly preserved equilibrium between human clarity (*evidence*) and divine truthfulness (*véracité*). Descartes thus avoids two pitfalls: that of a pure self-affirmation of the mind that would posit itself as an absolute foundation, and that of a submission of the human "subject" to an unintelligible foundation of which it can have no thought. If we cannot understand the infinite, we nevertheless do have a clear and distinct thought of it: an *idea* and not a belief. Now, Heidegger's reading destroys that equilibrium of thought, making no mention of the metaphysical quest for divine truthfulness, and absolutizing the certainty of the existence of our minds. That clarity is, according to Descartes, only the point of departure and the principle of philosophy, not its ultimate end and apotheosis. Thus the *I* of the *Meditations* is without any true relation to what Hegel was to call "absolute knowledge."

In order to impute to Descartes the responsibility of the relation of domination of modern man over all that is, Heidegger, like all who will take their cue from him to attack Descartes in the future, quotes without comment the famous passage from part six of the *Discourse on the Method,* in which the author speaks of "making us like masters and owners of nature," a formula that resonates like an attenuated echo of Francis Bacon's project. If it is isolated from its context, if it is considered without attention to the nuance of the "like," and if it is associated in a totally anachronistic way to Nietzsche's "will to power" and the ravages of today's overexploitation of nature, Descartes's phrase seems excessive. But we must see clearly what it means. The continuation of the text explicates the meaning of the passage in question (but Heidegger does not quote it): the goal is not primarily all the "comforts" that are on earth but "the conservation of health," in order to make men "wiser." That presupposes knowledge of the "causes" of our illnesses and of "all the remedies which nature has provided us."[95] That way of considering health as the precondition for wisdom does not convey any will to exploit nature unrestrainedly, but on the contrary a deep attention to life, with a view to preserving man's unity.

After these critical analyses, which were necessary in order to show how far away Heidegger kept from an attentive and precise reading of Descartes, we must now approach the way his contribution is, in the spring 1940 course, ostensibly reevaluated but in reality manipulated to the point of being negated. Indeed, if Heidegger continues to point out from time to time the scholastic and medieval sources of Descartes's metaphysics, he insists henceforth far more on his role in the beginnings of the modern period. Descartes appears as the man who, making the *I* into the *subjectum* par excellence, established within the certainty of the world qua representation, inaugurates the "metaphysics of subjectivity." On that view, he thus announces the "domination of the subject in the modern period," which Nietzsche's will to power would then bring to completion.

This conception of the modern "history of metaphysics" as the history of subjectivity, in which we would rattle off the names Descartes, Hegel, and Nietzsche like beads strung on an invariable line of fate, has been reiterated countless times by many commentators since the publication of the *Nietzsche* in 1961. But it does not seem that anyone has seriously asked how Heidegger could pass in this way from the Cartesian *mens* to the Nietzschean *Macht*. The fact is, nothing permits us to translate the human mind such as it becomes conscious of itself in the *Meditations* into terms of power. Furthermore, if we factor in the texts that were left out of the 1961 *Nietzsche,* we discover that Heidegger conceives of modern subjectivity in a sense radically opposed to the philosophy of Descartes. It is no longer to the mind and the human *I* that he ties subjectivity. The attachment to the *I* is, he writes, nothing but "degeneration" (*Entartung*) of the being-oneself. Heidegger does not hesitate, in this passage, to use the term *Entartung* several times, a word that belongs to the racial vocabulary most charged with Nazi connotations. Thus it is not at all the human being in his or her individual value but, on the contrary, the people and the nation as a community, and therefore the *Volksgemeinschaft,* that Heidegger understands by the word "subjectivity." This is confirmed by his writing the following.

> When a man sacrifices himself, he can do so only to the extent that he is entirely himself — on the basis of selfhood and the abandonment of one's individuality. . . .
>
> Subjectivity can never be determined on the basis of I-hood or be founded on it. Though it is difficult for us to get the false undertone of the "individualist" out of our ears when we hear the words "subject" and "subjective," the following must be inculcated: The more, and the more universally, man qua historical humanity (people, nation) rests on himself, the more man becomes "subjective" in the metaphysical sense. The accent placed on the community [*Gemeinschaft*] in opposition to the egotism of the individual is not, metaphysically conceived, the overcoming of subjectivism but indeed its fulfillment, for man — not the separate individual, but man in his *essence* — is now getting on track: all that is, all that has been implemented and created, undergone and overcome, must rest on him and be comprised beneath his domination.[96]

This passage shows us how, from the National Socialist theme of the *Opfer,* the sacrifice that seals the bond of the individual to the community, and under the cover of the usual attack by National Socialists on the supposed "egotism" of the individual, Heidegger identifies in 1940 the culminating achievement of modern subjectivity with the domination of the Nazi *Volksgemeinschaft,* and the latter with the emergence of man understood "in his *essence*"! Thus it is clear that what Heidegger understands by "metaphysics of subjectivity" has basically nothing to do with Descartes or with metaphysics as such, which entails the discernment of thought and not the affirmation of self and the domination of a national and racial community.

The very unusual way in which Heidegger uses the word "metaphysical" is also manifested in the "metaphysical" way he chooses to interpret the invasion of France by the armies of the Reich. One is indeed struck by Heidegger's identification of what he calls "metaphysics" with the brutality of the military events — and that at the time when, in hundreds of unpublished pages assembled after the fact, selectively, into volumes (*Beiträge zur Philosophie, Besinnung*, etc.) and published after his death, he puts himself forward as a thinker of the "event" (*Ereignis*) and of what he calls "the other beginning" — which does not keep him from reaffirming, in these same pages, his adherence to what he calls "the new German will."[97]

In this key passage of the 1940 course, which follows long disquisitions on Cartesian "subjectivity," he comments on the defeat of France in these terms. "These days we are ourselves witnesses to a mysterious law of history, according to which a day comes when a people no longer measures up to the metaphysics that has sprung from its own history; and this, at the very moment when that metaphysics has transformed itself into the unconditional."[98]

This means, baldly stated, that for Heidegger, the invasion of France by the German army is not just a military but a "metaphysical" event, revealing to the Germans — referred to in these pages by the expression *wir selbst* — that France as a people no longer measures up to the metaphysics instituted by Descartes. In the context of the invasion of France by the German armies and the signing of the armistice on 22 June 1940 between Hitler and the representatives of Philippe Pétain, Descartes appears no longer as a hereditary enemy to be brought down but as a bygone moment that it seems henceforth possible to include in a "history of being" ending with the domination of the European continent by Nazi Germany and its satellites or allies of the moment.

Contrary to the assertion of one commentator, wanting to make this course pass for a critique of National Socialism while in fact it is the explicit legitimation of its domination, the people called into question are quite clearly the French, not the Germans.[99] This is clearly shown in the continuation of the text, which this time does refer to the Germans. What is necessary "for modern technology and its metaphysical truth" is a "new humanity, surpassing the man of today" (*ein neues Menschentum . . . das über den bisherigen Menschen hinausgeht*), a new human type dedicated to the "unconditional domination of the earth." That this "new humanity" is none other than the community of the German people under Nazism is confirmed by the fact that it is in the recapitulation (*Wiederholung*) of these pages that we find the passage quoted earlier on the "subjectivity that finds its culminating achievement in the people, the nation, and the community" (*Gemeinschaft*).

Unfortunately, the rewrites of the 1961 *Nietzsche* have fooled many readers, especially in France. It was believed that in 1940 Heidegger was criticizing the Nazi domination of Europe, whereas the opposite was the case. Numerous passages from the course in the form in which it was actually taught in 1940 bear this out. Besides the text quoted on the community, we should mention, among others, the modifications in the conclusion of the course. In 1961 Heidegger added a paragraph on the "history of being" and dropped the three pages of the real conclusion of the 1940 course. Now in that original conclusion he maintained that the "motorization of the Wehrmacht" — which had just secured the military victories of the Nazi Reich during the French campaign — was not a phenomenon having to do with "technicism," but "a metaphysical act"![100]

Victor Klemperer has demonstrated that the word "historicity" had become a key word in the language of the Third Reich, or the LTI.[101] It may be argued that the word "metaphysical," with its use by Heidegger, was also about to become a word in the LTI.

The Legitimization of Racial Selection as "Metaphysically Necessary"

In his attempt to forcibly enlist Descartes in a "history of metaphysics" identified with the globalization of the relations of power and domination, Heidegger maintained, without ever demonstrating or even explaining it, that the essence of subjectivity would "necessarily" develop from the *animal rationale* (an expression he mistakenly presents as being taken up by Descartes)[102] to the *brutalitas* of the *bestialitas* demanded, according to him, by Nietzsche in his evocation of the "blond beast."[103] This was not a criticism but a legitimization of Nazism, noted by Heidegger as participating in "the history of being" and in the fulfillment of "metaphysics" — Nazism being in his view, in 1940, the only historical movement equal to the task of realizing the globalization of the dominance of man over all entities.

Such was Heidegger's accomplishment. Beginning with the first courses on Nietzsche, in an important passage of the course of 1936–1937 (excised from the 1961 *Nietzsche* but restored in the 1985 edition of the course), he launches a violent attack against democracy, which is presented as the "historical death" of Europe in that it rests only on "values" and not, like "great politics," on "form-giving forces" (*gestaltgebende Kräfte*).[104] In 1941–1942, in his course redacted but ultimately never taught on *Nietzsche's Metaphysics*, he does not hesitate to present the "breeding [*Züchtung*] of men" and the "*principle* of the institution of a selection of race [*Rassenzüchtung*]" as "metaphysically necessary" (*metaphysisch notwendig*)![105]

Moreover, Heidegger speaks in this regard of "racial *thought*" (*Rassengedanke*), underlining the word "thought." He thus elevates racial doctrine to the dignity of "thought," with the intention of endowing it with a legitimacy that is not only historical but "philosophical" as well. In that perspective of cold-blooded legitimation of the very foundations of Nazism, in which the "racial breeding of man" (*rassische Züchtung des Menschen*) is presented as a "metaphysical" necessity (which constitutes, however we may construe the phrase, an unacceptable perversion in the use of the word), Heidegger leads us to the destitution of the human being, the exact opposite of the Cartesian philosophy of the perfection of man. Consequently, in Heidegger's modus operandi, Descartes's contribution is disfigured beyond recognition: he no longer even represents the figure of an adversary and therefore a spiritual alternative or possible resistance. In the univocal and dictatorial determinacy of what Heidegger abusively calls "the history of metaphysics," which in reality leads in 1940 to the legitimation of the domination (which he believes soon to become global) of the Nazi *Volksgemeinschaft* under Hitler's Führung, the manipulation, or rather negation, of Descartes's contribution approaches its apogee. We are very far removed from any philosophical approach to Descartes, and we will be even more so, if that is possible, after the war when, with the defeat of Nazi Germany, Heidegger revises once more his discourse in keeping with "the event," henceforth asserting that "the war has decided nothing"[106] — even though the war in question was one that saved Europe from Nazi domination.

Thus Heidegger intimates — and this will be amply developed by his epigones — that it is metaphysics itself and Cartesian "subjectivity" in particular that are truly responsible for unleashing the planetary fury of technology; the gas chambers and death camps (*Gaskammern und Vernichtungslager*) being presented in the *Bremen Lectures* of 1949 solely as one particularity among others of the apparatus (*Ge-stell*) of modern technology. That is a particularly serious form of negationism, which openly denies the specificity of the Shoah — the "Final Solution" — and tends to exonerate National Socialism from its radical responsibility in the annihilation of the Jewish people and the destruction of the human being to which the industry of Nazism was committed.

The "Völkisch *Principle*" and Heidegger's Anti-Semitism in the Beiträge Zur Philosophie

It is not possible in discussing Heidegger's work in the second half of the 1930s to omit an in-depth examination of *Contributions to Philosophy (Beiträge zur Philosophie)*, usually referred to as the *Beiträge*. At the same time, we must be particularly conscious of the fact that it is a late and posthumous work, and not one that was entirely composed in the second half of the 1930s in the form in which we can read it today. The *Beiträge* appeared in 1989 in the so-called complete edition, for the centennial of Heidegger's birth, and they were presented by Heidegger's beneficiaries (*les ayants droit*) as the second great book of the "master" after *Being and Time*. Moreover, the implication was that this book would prove, even better than the courses on Nietzsche, how strongly Heidegger opposed Nazism.[107] Two authoritative studies by Nicolas Tertulian have dashed that attempted defense, however.[108] I assume, then, that these articles are known, and I will restrict my efforts to completing them on several major points.

The *Beiträge* are one of the volumes of the so-called complete edition for which the absence of a critical edition is the most shocking. Unable to consult the original manuscripts, we have no other recourse than to take into account several remarks formulated by a defender of Heidegger whose interpretations are quite unfounded but who, having a literary background and being in personal possession of the manuscript, has offered some information on its composition. We learn that Heidegger "numbered in pencil the folios to be copied by his brother Fritz, thus excluding from the copy a great number of them," which "have not, moreover, been included in the complete edition."[109] The author of this remark does not notice that by his own admission, the expression "complete" edition is therefore inappropriate. Nor does he indicate what editorial fate awaits these numerous folios excluded from the copying process. What we have read since 1989, then, under the title *Beiträge* is a work composed by Heidegger not during the years 1936–1938, but only after May 1939 — and very probably carefully revised after 1945 — on the basis of a selection of his notes written on loose leaves independently of one another.

Furthermore, we cannot be certain about the actual dating of the folios. Silvio Vietta has shown that Heidegger's dating is sometimes substantially wrong, as in the case of the study titled "Transcending Metaphysics," presented in the first (1951) edition of *Essays and Lectures* as a text from 1939–1940, whereas in fact it contains a reference to an event that did not take place until 1942.[110] As for the *Beiträge*, it is possible that the entirety was partially antedated. Thus it is not certain that the overall theme of the "passage from metaphysics to the historical thought of being" characterizes Heidegger's position during the years 1936–1937.

In any case, if most of the selected folios were in fact written in 1936–1938, we may conjecture two things. It is likely that the project of writing a work made up of fragments assembled by sections was inspired by the example of Nietzsche's *The Will to Power,* a new edition of which Heidegger was working on during the years 1936–1938. Furthermore, during those same years, he still adhered entirely to Hitlerism, since according to a postwar testimony published in a work by Vietta, Heidegger didn't develop any reservations about Nazism prior to 1938.[111] It is therefore unquestionable that the Heideggerian ideas of "new beginning," "event" (*Ereignis*), and "mutation of the essence of man" were conceived at a time when he was fully committed to Nazism.

The work takes its place within the continuity of the Heideggerian theme of historicity and decision. The words "historicity" (*Geschichtlichkeit*) and "decision" (*Entscheidung*) are still the main ones.[112] The difference from the classes of 1933–1934 is that Heidegger is not enveloped in the pathos of the present but rather, since the courses and seminars of 1934–1935, projects himself passionately into the future. This corresponds precisely to the new phase into which the Third Reich is entering: the time of the seizure of power (*Machtergreifung*) is over. Now the time of consolidation is coming, a time to ensure the longevity of the *Führerstaat* by prolonging the state of legal exception created by Hitler and the Nazi jurists, and to prepare the military conquest of a new living space for the German *Volkstum.*

The awaited event (*Ereignis*), which is the subtitle, is "an essential transformation [*Wesenswandel*] of man from rational animal to *Da-sein*."[113] Now, far from constituting a new motif in his writings, this mutation in the essence of man is already a central theme in the courses and seminars of the years 1933–1934, and it is an explicitly Hitlerian one. Let us recall here how, in the course of winter 1933–1934, Heidegger insistently spoke of "the great transformation [*Wandlung*] of the existence [*Dasein*] of man,"[114] identified, as we have seen, with the German people, and then went on to specify that the "fundamental transformation of the German world"[115] took place within the "total transformation" (*Gesamtwandel*) initiated by the Führer himself and his "vision of the National Socialist world." This is not just about the formation of an "ideology" but about a domination and total possession of the human being by the Führer. This is one of the reasons why I have not adopted the traditional presentation of the problem of Heidegger's Nazism in terms of the relationship between philosophy and an ideology—the other reason being that the results of my research have led me to question the very existence of a "philosophy" of Heidegger.

In a still more explicit manner than the courses I have mentioned, the Hitlerian seminar of 1933–1934 showed, in an unpublished passage I have quoted more fully in Chapter 5,[116] how "the will of the *Führer* begins by transforming the others into a *Gefolgschaft,* out of which the community [*Gemeinschaft*] then arises."[117] The *Ereignis* of the *Beiträge* thus always constitutes the same obsessive motif, that of a transformation of the essence of man, the clearly Hitlerian basis of which is none other than the *"völkisch* principle" of discrimination and racial selection. Now as for this *"völkisch* principle" — Heidegger continues to embrace it in the *Beiträge.* He declares, in a passage we may well take to be the most important of all these "Contributions to Philosophy," that "the meditation of what pertains to the people [*das Volkhafte*] is an essential point of passage. It is as important for us not to overlook it as it is for us to know that a supreme rank of being must be achieved if a '*völkisch* principle' as determinative for historical *Da-sein* is to be mastered and brought into play."[118]

Thus the *völkisch* principle, which is by definition a racial one — as Heidegger himself affirms in his summer semester course of 1934 — continues to be conceived of as decisive for "historical existence." And he openly inscribes the Nazi mystique of "rank" into being itself, henceforth writing that word (as a kind of fundamentalist archaism) with a *y, Seyn* — which is by this fact transformed into a *völkisch* term. Along these same lines, the theme of passing from "metaphysics" to the "historical thought of being," on which Heidegger would rely after 1945 to give the appearance of having surpassed all and of breaking new ground, is but a verbal surface phenomenon and a false appearance, given that the racist principle of Hitlerism continues to be at the center of his preoccupations, in both the 1933 courses and the *Beiträge.*

In light of this it should be no surprise that certain essential passages in the *Beiträge* contain explicit references to the rectoral address,[119] as well as to the course of summer semester 1934, in which Heidegger offers the most explicit demonstration of the *völkisch* equivalency: people = race.[120] Hence it is quite clear that the *Beiträge* in no sense constitute a departure from the underlying Hitlerian and *völkisch* content of the courses and seminars of 1933–1935. This fact is of major importance, since the idea of the event (*Ereignis*) developed in the *Beiträge* is presented today by some of his apologists, specifically on the strength of a note added by Heidegger to his *Letter on Humanism,*[121] as constituting the "thought" of the "last Heidegger."

Now we must consider in more detail certain elements of the book. We must not be fooled by the *Beiträge* into mistaking Heidegger's disparagement of the ambient mentality for a critique of Nazism. In truth there is no such critique, as must now be demonstrated. Heidegger asserts that in being content with speaking of "politics" and of the "racial," one accomplishes nothing more than a new version of Scholasticism.[122] This assertion, surprising at first—and in any case abhorrent in that it contemplates the possibility of racial considerations being integrated into a philosophy—is explained further on. In this ambient mentality, the transcendence of the God of Christianity has been rejected and replaced by the people itself (sufficiently indeterminate in its essence) as the goal and end of history. This anti-Christian "worldview," according to Heidegger, only appears to be non-Christian, for it agrees essentially with the mode of thought called "liberalism." Indeed, this transcendence of the people is an "idea," a "value," or a "meaning," something for which one does not lay down one's life, something that is realized merely through a "culture." This produces a mixture of *völkisch* ideas, political culture, and Christianity that makes up the present-day "worldview" but does not rise to the level of the decision.[123]

In this critique, which comes up frequently in the *Beiträge,* it is not the principle of racism or the idea of the *völkisch* as such that is rejected, but the lack of radicalness of a "worldview" (which demotes the *völkisch* to a simply "cultural" level, therefore not going beyond the "liberal" mode of thought) that Nazism vigorously opposes. Here we find the same obsessive fear as was expressed in the course of winter 1933–1934—the fear of Nazism's drifting off course in a "liberal" direction! Heidegger's targets, then, are the same as those of Hitlerism: Christianity and liberalism. It is simply that the various "worldviews" that dominate the scene and appear to be tearing each other to shreds are not, from Heidegger's perspective, up to the level of "struggle" that is to be taken up. Once more, it is not racism per se, it is not the idea of the *völkisch* itself that Heidegger rejects, but just the fact of reducing the *völkisch* —in the way Heyse does, for example—to "ideas." It is not the conception of the people per se that is challenged, but its insufficient determination in the various "worldviews" confronting one another. And when he mockingly casts aspersions on "political-*völkisch*" anthropology, it is an obvious allusion to the work by the same name by his main adversary at the time, Ernst Krieck, and not in the least a rejection of the "*völkisch* principle" as such.

What Heidegger had against "total" worldviews is that they did not, in his opinion, succeed in thinking through to the hidden depths whence they emerged—namely, the "essence of the people."[124] The content of these worldviews mattered little. His lack of differentiation went so far as to prompt him to say that "total political belief" and "total Christian belief" were "of the same essence" and that "propaganda" went hand in hand with "apologetics" in their common lack of creative struggle. Far from expressing any criticism of Nazism and Hitlerism in their specificity, Heidegger immersed the targets of his obsessive fear in an undifferentiating murkiness: on the one hand Christianity, on the other the ideology of those who wanted to represent National Socialist "philosophy," and against whom he thereafter struggled with varying degrees of intensity — men like Krieck, Heyse, and so on.

But the *völkisch* basis of Nazism is never challenged. It must be clearly understood that the reference to the "essence" of the German people (*Volk*) is never rejected. On the contrary, for Heidegger the issue is to "think" even more profoundly that reference to the people and that "essence." In this respect, paragraph 15, titled "Philosophy as 'Philosophy of the People'" is key to the understanding of the significance of the *Beiträge*. The author considers it self-evident that philosophy is always that of a people: is it not that of the "Greek people"? And "the grandiose end of Occidental philosophy, of 'German idealism' and of 'Nietzsche' — is it not the philosophy 'of' the German people?"[125] Yet this assertion according to which philosophy is the philosophy of a people still says nothing as long as we do not know "what we ourselves are" (*was wir selbst sind*). Here again we find, in a form at once more insistent and more coded, the same thought as in the Nazi courses of the years 1933–1934. What has changed is that to the ongoing rejection of "liberalism" there has been added, due to the influence of his reading of Nietzsche, a destruction of the "Platonism" that supposedly continues to make its way into the world-views. It is not a question, then, of the people qua idea or value but of the meditation of the people's essence. In place of "*völkisch* ideas," which are considered too "metaphysical," Heidegger proposes, as we have seen, what he calls a "*völkisch* principle," which he considers determinative of historical existence if it is based on an "ultimate rank of being."

It is not the Nazi reference to the people that is rejected. On the contrary! Heidegger's target of rebuttal is scarcely different from that of the Nazi "Nietzscheism" of the period. What he wants to root out are the remaining elements of "Platonism" he believes to be still circulating. And the "*völkisch* principle" is quite simply the "law" that the people has given itself in the "struggle," when it "decides itself for itself," for its existence or historical *Da-sein*. Further on, in paragraph 19, titled "Philosophy" and subtitled "Toward the question: Who are we?" we find the same pathos as in the summer semester course of 1934, to which a note in the *Beiträge* refers us. We must study this paragraph carefully. It is a clear indication that Heidegger's Hitlerian, Nazi, and radically anti-Semitic orientation is still just as present during the period of the *Beiträge* as it was in 1933–1934. We read the following.

> Here, the asking of the question who we are is in fact *more dangerous* than any other opposition found at the same level of certainty about man (the final form of Marxism, which has essentially nothing to do with either Judaism or even

with Russia; if somewhere a non-developed spiritualism is still slumbering, it is in the Russian people; Bolshevism is originally Western; it is a European possibility: the emergence of the masses, industry, technology, the extinction of Christianity; but inasmuch as the dominance of reason as an equalizing of everyone is but the consequence of Christianity and as the latter is fundamentally of Jewish origin [*cf.* Nietzsche's thought on the slave revolt with respect to morality], Bolshevism is in fact Jewish; but then Christianity is also fundamentally Bolshevist! And what are the decisions that become necessary on that basis?). But the danger of the question "Who are we?" is at the same time — if danger can necessitate what is highest — the sole path by which to succeed in coming to ourselves and thus in initiating the original salvation, that is, the justification of the Occident on the basis of its history. The danger of this question is in itself so essential for us that it loses the appearance of opposition to the new German will.[126]

In the middle of this obscure, and even sibylline pathos — in which it is not said, for example, what this "most high" is that must be imposed — precise ideas do nevertheless transpire. They go in the opposite direction from what several apologists have thought they could draw from this text. It has been said that this passage proves that Heidegger was not a Nazi because he, unlike Hitler, was able to distinguish Marxism from Judaism. But this takes into account only the beginning of the long sentence constituting the essential part of the text, without considering what comes after it: the part that affirms at the end, as do all the Nazis of the period, that Bolshevism is a "Jewish" phenomenon. Heidegger's position joins the same anti-Semitism as Hitler's. It is simply that, in passing, he has included Christianity itself in his "demonstration," or rather rejection, as being beyond all possible discussion fundamentally "Jewish."[127]

That single sentence from the *Beiträge* summarizes the nauseating confusion that typifies all the unpublished manuscripts or *Nachlaß* of the years 1936–1944, from the *Beiträge* to the *Koinon* and other texts. And in them we find the hateful clichés of Hitlerism and Nazism of the period in their harshest form: the "domination of reason" that brings with it the equalization of all the individuals in the democracies of the West and the radical rejection of Christianity as an originally "Jewish" phenomenon, chiefly responsible for that much despised egalitarianism, even though the historical receding of Christianity as a religion is noted. This is Heidegger's obvious goal, and the obsession manifested in his writing since 1933, when he declares his will to ban *Ripuaria,* the Association of Catholic Students of Freiburg, as well as the Association of Jewish Students:[128] not to spare Christianity, to show that a term should be added to the Nazi equation Bolshevism = "Jewish" — namely, Christianity = Judaism = Bolshevism. As for the decision that this entails, it suffices to refer to Hitler's politics as they are asserted in the years 1936–1937, far removed from the 1933 Concordat: the progressive dissolution of the religious youth movements in favor of the Hitler Youths alone, persecution and deportation of priests and pastors, the internment of Pastor Martin Niemöller at Dachau . . .

Heidegger's intent is in fact totally transparent. It is only at the beginning that he appears to contradict the "new German will" by questioning the directly "Jewish" origin of Marxism. In reality, his conclusion moves in the same direction as Nazism, after having assimilated along the way the entirety of Christianity, the Western democracies with their egalitarianism and human reason itself, as phenomena equally "Jewish" at root. It would therefore be difficult to show oneself more radically anti-Semitic than Heidegger is on this page, in which he reduces everything he and the Nazis are struggling against to a supposedly "Jewish" root phenomenon.

The considerations with which the *Beiträge* are filled show a uniform strategy: to ridicule a few commonplaces of the current ideology, not in order to oppose Nazism, but on the contrary to bring the reader back to its fundamental tenets. For the considerations on the people are always central to his discourse. The word *völkisch,* as we have seen, is not rejected: when Heidegger attacks "*völkisch* ideas," it is not the *völkisch* he is objecting to but the residual "Platonism" he sees lingering about the word "idea," after the fashion of Hans Heyse's *Idee und Existenz.* Similarly, his rejection of *völkisch-politisch* anthropology[129] targets the political anthropology of Ernst Krieck and not the *völkisch* as such. Not only does Heidegger maintain that all philosophy is the philosophy of a people, but he asserts that "the essence of the people is its "voice"[130] and goes on to say that "the *voice* of the people speaks rarely, and only through a small number."[131]

Now we cannot forget that this theme of the voice has sinister precedents in his courses: in 1934, Heidegger spoke, as we have seen, of what he unhesitatingly called "the voice of the blood."[132] The fact that the organic conception of the people's essence as related to generation and race always underlies the doctrine of the *Beiträge* is confirmed in a number of passages, as, for example, in paragraph 251, titled "The essence of the people and of *Da-sein.*" This paragraph is part of the most disturbing passages of this book, which are dedicated to the "last god"; it concludes with "the future ones" (*Die Zukünftigen*).[133] There we read the following: "The essence of the people is grounded in the historicity of the belongingness-to-*oneself, setting out* from the belongingness to the god. Out of the event in which this belongingness-to is historically grounded there first arises the rationale according to which 'to live' and 'living body,' breeding and generation [*Geschlecht*], race [*Stamm*] — the earth, to sum it up in a fundamental word — belong to history."[134]

I will not stress the redundant vocabulary and style of the passage (and what follows it), because the truth is that this trait characterizes the entire book, so much so that independently of the danger of the themes treated and the "principles" it brings up, all this rehashing would be enough make a reader with common sense doubt that the book could "contribute" to philosophy in any way at all. As for the content, the nebulous and beyond blurred mythology of the *Beiträge* does not prompt one to wish that humanity should ever experience the advent of the "last god," especially since the title of the section itself that includes these developments, *Die Zu-künftigen,* is reminiscent of *Die Kommenden,* the title of the journal of the *Bund* of the Artamanen (from which Himmler emerged), to which Ernst Jünger notably contributed numerous articles.[135]

It remains for us to wonder about the identity of that small number of men (*die Wenigen*) of the future, the only ones empowered to articulate the "voice of the people." Under the title "The Decision," paragraph 45 — a number that, if it was chosen after the defeat of the Third Reich, may not be accidental — lists the members of a sort of secret society and *völkisch* conspiracy or, to use Nicolas Tertulian's ironic expression, a "Heideggerian charter of the future,"[136] that cannot help but be disturbing. Need I remind the reader that these pages were written by Heidegger at a time when, according to his own statements, he was entirely devoted to Hitler and that they were published in the *Gesamtausgabe* in 1989 to celebrate the centennial of the birth of the "master," which was also the centennial of the birth of Hitler?

Heidegger distinguishes three circles: the solitary (or those who are unique), the few, and the many (*die Einzelnen, die Wenigen, die Vielen*). Apropos of those who are "unique" and thus respond to the "uniqueness of being itself" (*die Einzigkeit des Seyns selbst*), we find the Hitlerian triad already taken up by Heidegger in his course on Hölderlin in 1934–1935: poetry-thought-action (*Dichtung-Denken-Tat*), to which this time a fourth term is added, equally central to *Mein Kampf:* sacrifice (*Opfer*). Then there are the few who ally themselves within the *Bund,* and then the many. What binds them to one another? Heidegger tells us that the agreement between the three circles remains hidden (*verborgen*). That is how what is to be called *a people* is prepared and gathered, and becomes historical. And, he adds, "In its origin and determination this people is unique, corresponding to the uniqueness of being itself, the truth of which this people must found but once, in one sole place, in a single moment."[137]

So we find in Heidegger's *Nachlaß* the same *völkisch* and Nazi teaching as in his courses: one sole people, obviously the German people, can and must "found the truth." And the whole point here is, as Heidegger specifies in the following paragraph, to maintain the law and the mission of the West—the sole guarantor of which, as is clear to him, is "the German essence."

We are still dealing with one and the same idea of the historical foundation of the German people in "being" itself. The fact that Heidegger no longer speaks of the foundation of the people in a state (*Staat*) but in one sole "place" (*Stätte*), and that he no longer explicitly refers to the *Führung* of Hitler but to the submission (*Fügung*) to being, does not change the permanence of the Hitlerian and Nazi content that is at work. It is still the same idée fixe, which goes far beyond a simple sense of nationalism, according to which the German people and they alone are the guardians of the historical destiny and law of the entire West, and even of the "earth." In all this we may say that Heidegger's only "contribution" to philosophy consists in having devoted all his energies to introducing into it, in a variety of ways, the very principles of Nazism, hiding behind terms such as "truth" and "being," which in his writings are only apparently "philosophical"; their hidden (*verborgen*) meaning is always essentially the same and has nothing to do with philosophy as such.

If we had the least doubt about what is really going on in the *Beiträge,* a passage from his recently published writings, *On Ernst Jünger,* would dispel it. In a series of paragraphs grouped under the heading "The Question of Truth" (*Die Wahrheitsfrage*) and subtitled "Truth and figure" (*Wahrheit und Gestalt*), we can now read the following. *"The attribution of rank is the total representation of total mobilization* (for the passive, active, and dictatorial types) (the many, the few, the unique)."[138]

This time, Heidegger shows his hand. The conjuration of the three circles exposed in the *Beiträge* isn't a triad of ideas but the concerted and clandestine activation of a power directed toward the historical advent of a dictatorship. The idea is to inveigle the three types of men: those who, being passive, allow themselves to be pulled in by the strength of numbers and their submission to the dictatorial *Führung* as it imposes its law on the *Gefolgschaft;* those who, being active, require resolution and "decision" and organize themselves into a *Bund;*[139] and finally those, who may be only one, who have the vocation to rule and are by their "being" itself destined to be the Führer.

Heidegger continues, in the *Beiträge,* to hold to his interpretation of Jünger's "total mobilization," which he conflates with the Hitlerian and dictatorial relation between *Führung* and *Gefolgschaft.* It is true that what Heidegger describes in the *Beiträge* forms an invisible and apparently idle community, a silent conjuration. But its purpose is to prepare and wait for the unique time and place at which the "people," assembled according to and by means of that invisible community, will be able to found their "truth," whose law they will enforce over the whole Western world, or even the entire earth.

This is the message Heidegger transmits to his most attentive and well-informed readers of the *Gesamtausgabe,* such as it is to be found today in the philosophy section of libraries. It is nothing but a conjuration of Nazi mentality, the advent of which his writings usher in. We also see in them a confirmation of the fact that the distinction proposed in the postwar period between "the fulfillment of metaphysics" and "the other beginning" is no more than a decoy and a ploy. Indeed, that "other beginning" is conceived by Heidegger in connection with Jünger's "total mobilization" (which he relates to the "fulfillment of metaphysics"), since the "conjuration" of the *Beiträge* is found precisely, with its three "types," in his writings on Jünger and total mobilization. Heidegger's attempts, after the collapse of the Third Reich, to make a distinction between the advent of that "other beginning" and what was accomplished from 1933 to the defeat in 1945 is nothing but a survival strategy. The trick is to distance himself just enough from an entirely failed project, not to disavow it (since he will still, in his posthumously published interview, give full credit to the direction taken by National Socialism) but to prolong it at whatever cost and prepare its return, in new forms, foreshadowed by the dissemination of his work, which he intended for that purpose.

The "Double Game" of "Judeo-Christianity" Denounced in Besinnung

The *Nachlaß* of the *Beiträge* is just the first volume of an oddly broken-up series. Besides the volumes already published (GA 65–69), three volumes of "reflections" (*Überlegungen*) have been announced as volumes 94–96, and in the notes to the *Beiträge* and *Besinnung* there are several references to them. Limiting myself to what is currently available, I will say a word about *Besinnung* (GA 66) before dwelling at greater length on *Koinon* (published in GA 69).

In *Besinnung,* which is presented as the continuation of the *Beiträge* and which assembles the writings of 1938–1939, Heidegger's constant reiteration becomes even more obsessive and insistent. He concentrates especially on and around a term that already appeared in the *Beiträge* and that he never tires of repeating: *Machenschaft,* a difficult word to translate, a possible approximation for which might be "machination." This term allows him to designate indistinctly all the modern forms that the "will to power" is supposed to assume, including "racial selection," which thus becomes legitimized as a "necessary" form of will to power at the service of "total mobilization." Heidegger even goes so far as to identify *Machenschaft* with *poiesis.*[140]

Paul Celan, as is revealed in a preparatory note to his writing of *Der Meridian* (which may also contain some reference to the "Goll Affair"), was able to see the outrageousness of these Heideggerian puns surrounding power. "[Das Machen] Die Mache — Machenschaft. . . . Certain among you should know what and who is at work here. It is a *literary* game of the infamous, that is — a form particularly monstrous because rhymed [in words], of the nameless."[141]

In *Besinnung* and *Koinon,* Heidegger's words are not contained in paragraph form: he gets carried away and launches into long speeches on *Machenschaft* and race in which no thought breathes, developments devoid of all restraint that bear witness to the activity of a maniacal spirit, fiercely determined to unleash the fury that is devouring it. In a more ponderous and abstract language, certain of these texts resemble, by their obsessive repetition, a German counterpart of the pamphlets written by Louis-Ferdinand Céline during the same period.

We find, specifically in *Besinnung,* the anti-Semitism already expressed in the *Beiträge.* By way of proof, consider this passage, in which Heidegger writes as follows. "*Judeo-Christian* domination plays . . . in conformity with its nature [*Art*] a double game, standing both on the side of the 'dictatorship of the proletariat' and on that of liberal-democratic cultural solicitude; this double game continues to veil, for a time, the already existing rootlessness and lack of strength for the essential decisions."[142]

The querulousness with which the author challenges "*Judeo-Christian* domination" while writing in post-Kristallnacht Nazi Germany is abhorrent on many levels. First there is the will to use the context of the times the better to disqualify Christianity by treating it as a "Jewish" phenomenon. Then there is the amalgamation of the two forms of "*Judeo-Christian* domination": the Bolshevism of the East and the democracies of the West. Finally, there is, in the accusation of duplicity, the characteristic repetition of the case Nazi anti-Semitism brings against Judaism, accused of pulling the strings and being the hidden force behind a worldwide plot. And one cannot help but think of Heidegger's words to Jaspers in 1933, warning him of what he had no compunctions about calling "a dangerous international collusion of the Jews."[143] To say that the disguise will continue to work "for a certain length of time" is particularly sinister in 1938–1939, at a time when the German Jews, having been deprived of all rights, are beginning to be interned en masse in concentration camps.

Another passage from *Besinnung* merits being singled out: the one in which Heidegger comments critically on a sentence from one of Hitler's speeches. The sentence is one of totalitarian Nazi propaganda. Hitler asserts that all behavior, all "bearing" (*Haltung*) can ultimately be justified by the service (*Nutzen*) it performs for the overall group (*Gesamtheit*).[144] Heidegger questions not the assertion itself contained in the sentence but the terms Hitler uses: *Gesamtheit, Nutzen, Haltung.* It is possible that this page of Heidegger's translates a certain disenchantment with Hitler in 1939, or at least with language that does not seem to him to rise to the level of the "hidden relation of the essence of man to being." Nonetheless, it is difficult to read Heidegger's commentary without feeling a profound malaise. For what sense is there in writing in 1939 that the Führer's language (which—and particularly the word *Haltung*—has long been used by Heidegger himself) expresses the abandonment of all essential questioning on the hidden relationship between the essence of man and being?[145] Though one can in principle only be in favor of any challenge to Hitler's words, the tenor of Heidegger's criticism remains no less appalling. It reveals to us that after having long believed and said that Hitler's words expressed the truth and hidden law of German being and announced the complete transformation of the essence of man, Heidegger did not discover "the indigence of thought" of certain utterances of the Führer until 1939— even though *Mein Kampf* appeared in 1925–1927. If we are to believe this, then it wasn't until that late date that he found his way to the position that he was later to express in *Der Spiegel,* where he states that despite the indigence of thought of its leaders, National Socialism went in the direction he calls "satisfactory," doubtless because the Heideggerian *Führung* continued to the end to remain active somewhere.

Furthermore, and this is even more serious, the very mediocre sentence on which Heidegger chooses to concentrate is part of one of Hitler's most murderous speeches, the one most laden with consequences—in which, before the Reichstag on 30 January 1939, he "prophesies" what he does not hesitate to call the "annihilation of the Jewish race in Europe" should another world war break out. One would have hoped Heidegger would dwell on Hitler's "prophesy," to express concern about it, and not on the comparatively rather harmless sentence on which he does comment. This is a confirmation, if one was needed, that he has no reservations on the substance of what he refers to at the time as Nazism's "racial thought" (*Rassengedanke*). Quite to the contrary, he will devote his energies in the texts written during the years of 1939–1942 to legitimating racial selection. This we have seen in his writings on Nietzsche, and we will see it confirmed by the text titled *Koinon* and his writings on Jünger.

"Racial Thought" Related to the Experience of Being in Koinon

In the texts grouped under the title *Koinon,* we find several long passages that establish in a monstrous way—Celan's adjective was not too strong— that what Heidegger unhesitatingly calls "racial *thought*" (*Rassen*gedanke), emphasizing the word "thought,"[146] corresponds for him in a necessary way to the fulfillment of "metaphysics." The most important development in *Koinon* on race begins as follows. "Racial *thought,* this means that the fact of taking race into account springs from the experience of being as subjectivity, and is not something 'political.' Racial breeding (*Rasse-züchtung*) is a means of self-affirmation (*Selbstbehauptung*) for dominance. This thought opposes the explanation of being as 'life' — that is, as 'dynamics.'"[147]

Here, as in the course on Nietzsche of winter 1941–1942, written but not taught, Heidegger elevates the doctrine of race and the human "breeding" (*Zucht*) implied by it to the dignity of a "*thinking*" and claims it has arisen from an "experience of being," understood as subjectivity! This he purports to be a "thinking" that belongs to the ontological and not the "political" in the current sense of the term, the one, for example, referred to by Krieck when speaking of a "political-*völkisch* anthropology." But for us, now well advised on the importance Heidegger gives to the term *Selbstbehauptung*, the second paragraph of the text confirms that this "racial breeding" to which all "racial thought" leads does indeed belong to the "political" in the sense defined by Heidegger himself in his seminar on Hegel and the state, and which consists in the self-affirmation of a people or race and the power and dominance it necessarily implies. It is thus still one and the same racial basis of Nazism that Heidegger continues to harbor and to express throughout the *Koinon* more explicitly than ever, in order to legitimate it. He continues:

> Cultivation of race is a power-related action. That is why it can be activated at one moment and put aside the next. Its use and promulgation depend in each case on the situation of dominance and power. It is nowise an "ideal" in itself, for it [cultivation of race] should then lead to the renunciation of claims of power, and the estimation of the value of all biological dispositions. This is why all doctrines of race already contain, strictly speaking, the idea of a racial *preeminence* [*Rasse*vorrang]. The preeminence is founded variously, but always on things that the "race" has achieved — achievements that are assessed by the criterion of "culture" and the like. But what if culture, considered from the limited viewpoint of racial thought, is nothing but the product of race? (The circle of subjectivity.) Here there appears in the foreground the self-forgetful circle of all subjectivity that contains a metaphysical determination not of the *I*, but of the human essence in its entirety in its relation to the entity and to itself.
>
> The metaphysical foundation of racial thought is not biologism, but the subjectivity (to be thought metaphysically) of all being of entities (the consequence of the overcoming of the essence of metaphysics, and especially of the metaphysics of the modern era).
>
> (Thought of all the refutations of biologism too crude: therefore useless.)[148]

Despite its extreme nebulousness, this text from *Koinon* is doubtless one of those in which the well-informed reader can better understand what is going on. First of all, there is in the background of this page a certain interpretation of Nietzsche and of Jünger's reading of him in *The Worker*. Very recently published texts of Heidegger on Jünger, which I will soon examine, will confirm this. What Heidegger calls "racial thought," "the breeding of race," "attention to race," or yet again "racial preeminence" — in short, all that is quintessentially racist — is not reduced to simple biological presuppositions but to "an experience of being" conceived of "metaphysically" as subjectivity and power. What Heidegger holds against biologism is its not being sufficiently "deep," but he does say there is no reason to reject it, because all refutation would be just as crude. Thus it is quite clear that the reservations expressed at times by Heidegger with respect to what he calls biologism are intended not to challenge racism but to relate it to an "experience of being" considered by him as being more essential, and as founding it.

What is monstrous about Heidegger's thesis is that it makes racism the ultimate expression of "metaphysics." In affirming that the doctrine of racial preeminence — which constitutes as such the very principle of Hitlerism and Nazism, is in itself neither the reason nor the goal but, for those capable of penetrating more deeply than the "circle of subjectivity," simply the highest expression of being understood as power — Heidegger lends the strongest support to racism one could possibly find. He procures for racism a legitimacy beyond its wildest dreams, deeper and even more difficult to uproot than that of Nazi "doctors" like Eugen Fischer, with their perverse use of Mendel's tables, or that of Nazi "jurists" like Hans Frank or Carl Schmitt, with their appeal to the principle of the "defense of German blood," which had legitimated the Nuremberg Laws. This time, it is no longer law or medicine but philosophy itself that is taken over, derailed and destroyed by that monstrous utilization of the term "metaphysics."

Metaphysics, since Aristotle and Descartes, has been understood in philosophy as the science of principles and first causes, which rests on the thought of the human being considered as such and in his or her integrality. To claim to discover or posit a "metaphysical" concept of being understood as "power" and "subjectivity" at the basis of a doctrine that asserts the preeminence of a race — with racial breeding, racial selection, and soon the resultant extermination — is not only a derailing of the terms of philosophy but the negation of humanity and of man as such. The "work" of the Nazi "philosopher" is even more criminal than that of the jurist and the doctor because he supports and justifies in depth what the latter will put into practice.

The fact that Heidegger believed himself personally entrusted with this mission — that he meant to transmit his Nazism to doctors and jurists — is evidenced by the speech he delivered in 1933 to the Institute of Pathological Anatomy of Freiburg, as well as by the influence he had on jurist Erik Wolf. The fact that the "philosopher's" action is less apparent than that of the magistrate or the medical practitioner does not make his influence any less dangerous. One could even assert the opposite, as is regrettably confirmed by Martin Heidegger's present worldwide public, as well as his personal, direct influence on the most revisionist historians, such as in the cases of Ernst Nolte and Christian Tilitzki.[149]

But Heidegger does not merely destroy metaphysics. He annihilates at the same time the very possibility of a moral attitude, which constitutes the heart and soul of all philosophy. Indeed, he does not hesitate to identify the defense of morality with the protection of what he calls "the *völkisch* substance," deriving both from the same aspiration for power! In one of those sentences in which he takes pleasure in accumulating the derivatives of the word "power" (*Macht*), he declares: "Precisely the most honest fight for the rescue of freedom and morality serves only to maintain and increase of the possession of power [*Machtbesitz*], the powerfulness [*Mächtigkeit*] of which cannot tolerate any challenge, precisely because the forward-moving urge of power [*Macht*] qua being of entities has already mastered morality and its defense as an essential means of power [*Machtmittel*]."[150]

Here we are very close to the most perverse passages of Carl Schmitt arguing against an appeal for respect of humanity in politics. Morality no longer has for Heidegger any consistency of its own; it no longer appears as anything but a means in the service of the same goal as the racial doctrine! By this nebulous and truly criminal lack of differentiation, for any possibility of moral resistance to Nazi racism is hereby eliminated, morality is subordinated to racism itself, which has preeminence and alone defines "the highest goals," so that he who does not submit to the radical objectives of Nazism "would succumb" in his view "to an absurd reduction." He adds: "And one would succumb to an absurd reduction of all the real tensions brought into play if one did not recognize as the highest goals the protection of the folkdoms [*Volkstümer*] and the preservation of their 'eternal' racial composition."[151]

Having arrived at this point, Heidegger's speech gets carried away as is constantly the case in *Koinon*. He continues:

> It is only in this manner that the entry into the struggle for the possession of world power takes on its significance and acuity, for this objective also is a means that is placed along the way through the forward-directed thrust of power.[152] These types of goal-setting and the modalities of their promulgation

and inculcation are indispensable in the struggles for world power; for the defense of the "spiritual" goods of humanity, and the preservation of "corporal" "substance" of the nationalities [*Menschentümer*] must be retained as tasks and set anew, wherever the entity is dominated through and through by the fundamental structure of "metaphysics," according to which spiritual "ideals" must be realized, and according to which that realization requires the undivided psychophysical life-force. But this same structure [*Gefüge*] of metaphysics is the historical foundation of the fact that, beyond the explanation of being as reality and effectuality, it is ultimately the essence of being as power that imposes itself in the foreground. These goal-settings are metaphysically necessary; they are not imagined and put forward as unmotivated *desiderata* and "interests."[153]

It is necessary to quote these crazed, perverse texts in order that the reader should also wonder whether their author has not lost his "mind" in the human and philosophical sense of the term. There seems to be nothing more in him, according to his own definition of *Geist,* than "storm" (*Sturm*) and no longer any understanding or reason. It is with such texts that we can see to what extremes the will to introduce Nazism into philosophy may lead. When he teaches, Heidegger knows how to give his words a smooth, professorial tone that — at least superficially — makes them more acceptable, but when he expresses the conceptions that possess him directly on paper, they give the reader a very different impression.

Further, the time at which *Koinon* was written contributed to increasing the confusion of the text. As the author says at the outset, we are at the beginning of World War II — that is, in that complex and turbulent period when the Nazi-Soviet Pact signed by Ribbentrop and Molotov in the name of Hitler and Stalin had just come into effect. "Bolshevist" communism, the total enemy of the Nazis from the start, was now their main ally. This inevitably precarious pact would allow, as we know, the dismemberment and partitioning of Poland and the mobilization of all the forces of the Third Reich to turn the attack toward the West — that is, first and foremost, France and England. That was the moment Heidegger chose to summon up his vision of "communism." But it is perhaps problematic to speak of choice, since his writings and courses constantly bear traces of the historical and military events in which they are inscribed, and which they comment on, from the supposedly "destinal" perspective of the "history of being." Heidegger's thesis is that communism should not be conceived of in a "political," "sociological," or even merely "metaphysical" way, but "like a certain destiny of the entity as such, grasped in its totality, which marks the accomplishment of the historical age, and in so doing, the end of all metaphysics"![154] And he blithely proceeds with a "definition" of communism worthy of being retained as an extreme example of what the agglutination of the German language and the obsessive use of the term *Machenschaft* are capable of producing. Indeed, we find a string of six occurrences of the words "power" (*Macht*) or "to make" (*machen*) in a single short sentence, which makes it literally untranslatable. Here is what Heidegger writes. "*Der 'Kommunismus' ist die Durchmachtung des Seienden als solchen mit der Ermächtigung der Macht zu Machenschaft als dem unbedingten Sich-einrichten der Macht auf die vorgerichtete Machsamkeit alles Seienden.*"[155]

Despite the "destinal" claim of these words, their historical/political — not to say military — concerns are perfectly clear. It is odd to see him attribute the paternity of Jünger's idea of "total mobilization" to Lenin,[156] an assertion found in his writings of the same period on Ernst Jünger.[157] Moreover, his passages centering on the idea of "total war" should be noted.[158] What he expresses above all is the fact that for him, as for the leaders of the Nazi Reich, the enemy to be annihilated was at that time not primarily the Soviet Union, which had provisionally become an ally, but England. How could that tactical about-face be made acceptable, given that years of propaganda had brainwashed everyone into believing that the adversary of the German people was Bolshevism? The solution was crude but simple. All that was needed was to assert that the English state was "the same thing [*dasselbe*] as the Union of Soviet Socialist Republics," the only difference being that the English state had succeeded in giving itself "the appearance of morality" (*der Schein der Moralität*). That was precisely wherein its greater danger lay. And Heidegger would go on to assert that "the Christian and bourgeois form of English 'Bolshevism' is the most dangerous. Without the annihilation [*Vernichtung*] of the latter, the modern period continues to maintain itself."[159]

We see that Heidegger's "destinal" considerations lead him to very concrete prescriptions indeed, the same as those of Hitler at the same date: annihilate England. The "overcoming of metaphysics" does not make him forget the military objectives of Nazism.

On Ernst Jünger, *or the Worldwide Dictatorial Domination of the German Race and Essence*

The entire set of Heidegger's notes and developments on Ernst Jünger, recently published,[160] henceforth constitutes a document of prime importance for those interested in understanding the history of the development of Nazism in thought. We had long been aware that Heidegger found inspiration for his own writings in those of Jünger, especially in *Total Mobilization* and *The Worker,* but his postwar article of homage to Jünger, "On the Line," mainly showed the distance he intended to take from him on the question of nihilism, technology, and metaphysics. The vast majority of texts available today show, in a noticeably different way, how much Heidegger owes to Jünger's work, with respect to such important concepts as "metaphysics," "power," "form," "organic totality," "work," the "type," and "the elementary," not to mention *race*. In contrast, there is very little said about nihilism in his texts on Jünger before the defeat of the Nazis. I will offer only a few sample probes into a subject that would require a far more complete study, but they will suffice to bring in new and decisive elements in connection with Heidegger's conception of worldwide and total domination of the German race, which he, like Jünger, openly desired.

Let us note at the outset that Peter Trawny, the editor of the volume of the *Gesamtausgabe* titled *On Ernst Jünger,* specifies that it contains the text of the "Talk on Ernst Jünger" (*Aussprache über Ernst Jünger*)[161] delivered in January 1940 before a small circle of colleagues at the University of Freiburg.[162] This is the seminar Heidegger made so much of, claiming in 1945 that it had been banned. Yet the editor doesn't say a word about this alleged ban. Might it be, once again, one of those fabrications with which Heidegger studded his plea to try to exculpate himself? Whatever the case may be, as we shall see, there does not appear to be anything in that text that would have worried the Nazi authorities.

Given the date, coupled with what we have learned of Heidegger's own preoccupations in his course on Nietzsche that same year and also in *Koinon,* it will come as no surprise that war is a central theme. He lays special emphasis on the fact that, already in Jünger's first writings, the "battle for materiel" (*Materialschlacht*) appears as a manifestation of the will to power (that is probably how the "motorization of the Wehrmacht" becomes a "metaphysical act" for Heidegger after the defeat of France, and that "work" comes to take on an "animal character" in war).[163] It is not all, then, the question of "nihilism" that chiefly interests Heidegger in Jünger—as the role-playing of the *Festschriften* and the false leads of the postwar period will induce many to believe—but rather the world war and its potential: the planetary domination of a new type or new race issuing from what Heidegger calls at the end "the essential power of the Germans" (*Wesenskraft der Deutschen*)[164] and what Jünger himself, at the end of *The Worker,* designates as "the maternal soil of the people, bearer of a new race" (*der Mutterboden des Volkes als der Träger einer neuen Rasse.*)[165]

Is Jünger's conception of the "worker," which is qualified as "metaphysical" because it merges with the manifestation of "power," in keeping with Nietzsche's thought? To resolve the issue, Heidegger quotes two aphorisms successively, which had been edited in such a way as to follow one another in *The Will to Power*. He begins with the second. "The workers must one day live as the bourgeois do today; but *above* them, distinguishing themselves by their frugality as the *highest caste:* poorer and simpler, then, but in possession of power."[166]

To Heidegger, "this statement of Nietzsche's sounds like a mockery in relation to what Jünger thinks in *The Worker*,"[167] but, he points out, that is just an aphorism of youth, quite poorly edited, since it is the preceding aphorism that, in *The Will to Power*, reedited in 1930 by Alfred Baeumler, corresponds to the mature Nietzsche. That aphorism is titled *On the future of the workers*, and begins thus: "The workers should learn to feel like *soldiers*."

This time Nietzsche's words seem to Heidegger to agree with what Jünger thinks, and with what he himself approves. The present-day "worker" has no longer anything of the bourgeois. He is a *soldier*, and his "work" is called *war*. Heidegger writes: "The worker is thought of in a soldierly-warlike way, and assessed according to *race* [*Art*]—i.e., as type [in German, *Schlag:* stamp]."[168]

He then goes on to capitalize on the fact that Nietzsche spoke of the *future* of the workers, in order to bring out what, in his own view—in that month of January 1940—is at stake in the world war between the Western democracies and the Nazi Reich. "The powers of the West had carried to the highest degree of clarity and acuity their will, expressed until then to maintain in their possession the world power as understood in the national democracies. With us, it was only in the premonitions of a few important warriors that premonition began to turn into the certainty that a change in the way of possessing world power was being prepared. The Western powers fight to save the past: we struggle for the formation of a future."[169]

Reading these lines, we must give Heidegger this much: he knows how to use the rhetoric of a military leader. What might be more surprising in itself—though it can no longer astonish us after having seen so many texts that say the same thing—is that he presents this martial discourse as leading toward "a new truth of being" (*eine neue Wahrheit des Seyns*). I must quote a substantial part of a long passage that ends his "Talk on Jünger," because it contains the most explicit indication of what he really has in mind when he speaks of the "overcoming of metaphysics" and the "truth of being."

> The question of who the eighty million [Germans] *are* is not to be resolved on the basis of what their ancestors created but according to what they themselves are able to know and want as a mission for the future, on which basis only then can it be assessed whether they are worthy to invoke their ancestors. In the next zone of decision, the struggle concerns world power alone, and not so much in the sense of the mere possession of power, as in the capacity for maintaining,

within power, power as essence of reality, and that always means: to increase it. The decision consists above all in knowing whether the democratic "empires" (England, America) remain capable of power or whether the imperial dictatorship of absolute arms for arms sake becomes capable of power.[170]

Here we can see definitively what is behind Heidegger's drive and intoxication. It is not in the least as a philosopher and metaphysician that he argues, but as a Nazi bent on announcing and upgrading the unconditional and dictatorial domination of the Nazi Reich over the planet to the status of reflective thought, at the very moment when that regime is concentrating all its efforts on the rearmament and motorization of its forces — all this instead of the democratic Anglo-Saxon "empires." Behind the name "metaphysics" nothing is to be found but the Nazi exaltation of power and the dictatorial domination of Hitler's Germany, which Heidegger embraces and — though here he was able to deceive thinkers like Derrida — we now see the laughable inadequacy of his late denials, intended to delude us into thinking his conception of strife had nothing to do with war, that the *Kampf* of which he speaks bears no relation to a *Krieg*.

At the same time, as the continuation of the text will show, Heidegger has the personal ambition of being the one who will lead Hitler's Germany to the fulfillment of its "truth." Such is no doubt his wildest and most dangerous ambition, for he managed to give the illusion of being capable of going beyond Nazism, while in fact he did nothing but ensure its fulfillment by completing and justifying it through his own contributions. He has attempted to make Hitlerism respectable, so to speak, but in using his ability to captivate and possess minds to do so. What he has spread over the entire planet is quite simply Nazism, with all its power of radical destruction of the human being.

Heidegger continues in the following terms.

> But this decision is only a preliminary one; its discharge may require a century or more. For supposing the possession of power in the sense of the imperial dictatorship of absolute armament for armament's sake harbors at the same time within itself the essential possibility of the total devastation of the world, the question arises as to whether the highest possession of power with a view to supreme power becomes capable of going beyond power itself as essence of reality, and, if not of founding a new truth of being, at least of preparing it in its foundations. It is only if the place of such a decision is reached that the age of the modern era may be considered transcended. That the strength of the essence, hidden and not yet purified, of the Germans should extend this far, such is *our* belief. But because the elementary decisions concerning the essence of being can neither be made, nor blindly grow, but are a gift or a privation of Being itself, therefore we must not want to skip over the zones of decision.[171]

Visibly the strategy of Heidegger is always the same. He presents himself as the one who is able to see further, even beyond the next century, but there is definitely never a question for him of opposing what in the *Beiträge* he called "the new German will." At this point we are in 1940: the world war will continue and the armed power of the Hitlerian Reich will be pitted against the democracies of the West. It is not only, Heidegger asserts, a matter of contrasting "German socialism" (*deutscher Sozialismus*) with the "plutocracies of the West."[172] The old ideological justifications, clumsily excerpted from the works of Werner Sombart, for example, no longer suffice for him. The power of the German Reich must win out because it alone, he says, fights for the configuration of a future. Nor is it enough to draw on the idea of the living space necessary for eighty million Germans. Heidegger invokes something far more fundamental, in his view — namely, what he calls "*our* belief" (unser *Glaube*) — and which therefore has nothing of a philosophy or reflective thought about it: the belief in a hidden link between "the essential power of the Germans" and "the truth of being"!

Thus we have the confirmation of what had already proved to be the case in the study of the Hitlerian seminar and the *Beiträge* — namely, that the Heideggerian being is a *völkisch* being, the manifestation or withdrawal of which is in his view indissociable with what he calls the "purification" of the German essence. Thus it will come as no surprise that there should be much about *race* in his writings on Jünger.

Need we go so far as to think Heidegger's declaration on what he calls "*our* belief" discreetly affiliates him with those who at the time were called *Deutschgläubigen*, those for whom the *völkisch* belief in the essence of the German race had supplanted all authentic religious faith, and among whom numbered, as it seems, his former student Oskar Becker[173] and his former classmate and student of Husserl, the raciologist Ludwig Clauß? Or is this just a "political" profession of faith? I leave the question open, and make two comments on the issue. On the one hand, we find in the early 1940s, particularly in the letters Heidegger sent to the parents of students fallen on the front, very strange declarations on the relation of the people to their dead, which are in keeping with the *völkisch* "religiosity" of Nazism and its cult of the dead. And in the Bremen lecture titled "The Danger," he will go further than anyone else in that direction.[174] On the other hand, and in a more general way, I must express serious reservations about the idea, which is very widespread since the works of Eric Voegelin and those more directly related to the National Socialism of Claus-Ekkehard Bärsch, which would attach Nazism and Hitlerism to what has been dubbed "political religion." Without being able to develop all the elements of a discussion here, it is not certain that the term "religion" can, in whatever sense it is taken, be suitable to Nazism except superficially, even though Dietrich Eckart, Hitler, Rosenberg, Schmitt, and even Heidegger (as we saw in his Hitlerian seminar) occasionally take that tack. I think that it was Nazism that penetrated religion, as it did politics, art, history, law, and philosophy — in each case submerging them and destroying them completely. Therefore it is not a specifically religious phenomenon.

Getting back to Heidegger's writings on Jünger, we must take note of the ample developments they contain on race and what Heidegger calls "the new rank of the future 'race' " (*der neue Rang der künftigen "Rasse"*).[175] Far from expressing the least reservation about Jünger's speech on race, Heidegger does not hesitate to elaborate in a direction that confirms the racial content of other texts already examined, particularly in his courses on Nietzsche or in *Koinon*. He relates "racial thought" (*Rassengedanke*) to the "soil of subjectivity"[176] and assures us that "man is no less subject, but on the contrary more essentially so, when he conceives of himself as a nation, a people, a race, a somehow self-dependent humanity."[177]

In the enumeration contained in that sentence, race is presented as a perfectly legitimate way to conceive of man. But in what follows in that statement Heidegger takes the same line of thought to even more hateful lengths. He continues: "But there is a world of difference between belonging to a race [*Rassehaben*] and establishing a race particularly and intentionally, as a 'principle,' the result and goal of being-human; especially when racial selection is specifically conducted *not only as one* condition for being-human, but when that being-race and domination qua that race are held up as the highest goal."[178]

This way of considering racial selection as the principle, result, and goal of being-man, in short this exultation of "race-being," constitutes one of the most substantially Nazi texts he has written. It is true that he then waxes ironic, as in other passages already quoted from *Koinon*, over any appearance of morality that might be attributed to this goal. Indeed, he adds that "the oft-claimed primacy of the general interest over the particular is but a semblance."[179] But though he makes fun of presenting a racist goal such as this as defending the primacy of the common good over individual interest, he nonetheless continues to consider the most radical racism as the metaphysical truth of the modern era.

That is why it is paramount that the reader has a clear understanding of my critique. Heidegger proceeds not to a moral condemnation but to a historical and ontological legitimation of racial selection. In the Nietzschean tradition, he places himself "beyond good and evil" and to that end presents all moral judgments, including that of the common weal, as the disguise of a position of power. He maintains that all Western philosophy necessarily leads to what the

Nazis are in the process of putting into practice beginning in the summer of 1941 — namely, a war of extermination against all those whom the National Socialists consider not to be a part of the new "humanity" that is asserting itself. Hence there is indeed, on Heidegger's part, a monstrous historical and ontological legitimation of the Nazi genocide that is being readied.

Now what fascinates Heidegger in Jünger is the will to take "the culture of the race as principle,"[180] with the goal of creating through the "type" or the "stamp" of the "worker" a new race that ensures planetary domination for itself. He stresses that in this way the elementary is related to race, and he takes a particular interest in the ideas of the "figure" (*Gestalt*) and the "organic construction" (*organische Konstruktion*), noting that "an organic construction is, for example, the SS."[181]

For Heidegger, to speak of "organic construction" according to Jünger is therefore to refer to the Hitlerian *Schutzstaffel* of which Himmler is the *Reichsführer* and which constitutes, for the Nazis, the true nobility of the Reich. It is doubtless also the SS that Heidegger was thinking of in his Hitlerian seminar when, before his students in their SS and SA uniforms, he spoke of the necessity of a "new nobility" for the Third Reich.[182]

To return to the relation between these two authors, its importance cannot be understood unless we know exactly who Ernst Jünger was. It is not possible in this book to treat that question in its own right, though it is a fundamental research project that remains of some urgency, particularly in a country like France, where the apology of Jünger has reached absurd heights — as opposed to Germany, where his true nature is better known. After World War II, it went without saying that Jünger had been a Nazi. The Germanicist Emond Vermeil, for example, spoke of him as a "talented Nazi,"[183] and Karl Löwith in 1946 published this sentence in *Les Temps modernes,* aptly summarizing Jünger's status. "He [Heidegger] was a 'National Socialist' and has remained one, as has Ernst Jünger — on the fringe, and in isolation, but that isolation is not without its effectiveness."[184]

Jünger's "isolation," like Heidegger's, is similar to the isolation of those "unique ones" who are at the center of the invisible community described by Heidegger in both the *Beiträge* and his writings *On Ernst Jünger.* But the concerted efforts of a certain number of apologists have produced the result that over time the substantial ties between Jünger and the National Socialists before and after 1933 have been lost sight of. A strategy that has proven to be particularly effective is that of his former secretary Armin Mohler, who, in order to clear the name in part of the author of *The Worker* and to exonerate the "intellectual elite" by distinguishing it from Nazism, ably used the idea of a "conservative revolution."[185] Yet Jünger corresponded personally with Hitler, published Goebbels in one of his journals, greeted the rise to power of the National Socialists very explicitly and warmly in his writings during the 1920s, and signed publicly in favor of Hitler on 7 November 1933.[186] We know, moreover, from Schmitt's diary that during a conversation between the two men on 29 January 1933 Jünger had expressed his entire satisfaction in seeing Hitler come to power.[187] Furthermore, Jünger, like Heidegger in his conversation published by *Der Spiegel,* calmly asserted long after the end of World War II that "in the beginning, obviously, they [the National Socialists] had a whole series of right ideas."[188] Among the "intellectuals" of Nazism such as Erich Rothacker or the jurist Otto Koellreutter, Jünger appears, in the years 1933–1934, as *the* theoretician of "work" such as conceived and put into practice by Hitler and the NSDAP.

It is true that Jünger's Nazism appeared very early. From this point of view he had a great lead on Heidegger and Schmitt. Jünger had already heard Hitler at the Kröne Circus. Later he recalled the moment in the following terms. "Then I was seized by a special feeling, which was like a purification. . . . An unknown person spoke and said what had to be said, and everyone felt he was right. . . . What I had just experienced was not a speech; it was an event having the power of the elementary."[189]

In that same year of 1923, in the NSDAP newspaper *Völkischer Beobachter,* Jünger published an article titled "Revolution and Idea" in which he says the following. "The true revolution has not yet taken place, but progresses irresistibly. . . . Its idea is the *völkisch* idea, honed and given a cutting edge hitherto unknown. Its banner is the swastika; its form of expression is the concentration of the will into a single point — dictatorship! . . . It is not money that drives it, but the blood that unifies the nation by its mysterious currents. . . . The blood must guarantee the freedom of the whole by the sacrifice of the individual. . . . It must eliminate all the elements that are harmful to us."[190]

From these texts we can see how unacceptable, in the case of characters like Jünger, the use of the distinction between "conservative revolution" and National Socialism is for apologetic reasons. The fact that much later Jünger took a certain distance with respect to Hitler, whom he looked upon "from on high," so to speak, although he had for a long time been fascinated by him, does not obliterate the crushing responsibility that remains his in the public legitimation of Nazism before the Nazi power takeover. As a former hero of the Great War, a writer, the director of a number of journals, and a political leader, Jünger had a considerable public and considerable charisma, which directly served Hitler and inspired Heidegger and Schmitt. He could express himself openly at a time when the German university professor would not have been able to do so without risking dismissal, as occurred, for example, in the case of Ernst Krieck in the very early 1930s.

The radicalness of Jünger's underlying positions are also to be seen by the fact that on 27 August 1926 he published an article, "Der Jungdeutsche," in *Der Jugendbewegung der Tat,* in which he developed a long defense of the *Bund* of the Artamanen. The Artamanen, apparently founded in April 1924 by Bruno Tanzmann, constituted, beneath the guise of promoting farm work and public funding for youth movements, the most deeply racist *Bund* there was, characterized by a subterranean, secret racism that expressed itself only in forms that were acceptable, and whose true meanings remained hidden. It was from the Artamanen that Heinrich Himmler and Walter Darré emerged, as well as the commanding officer at Auschwitz, Rudolf Hoess. Now Jünger saw in the Artamanen "a new aristocracy" and approvingly cited their slogan: "Work ennobles" (*Arbeit adelt*).[191] The conception of "work" that was formed in this *Bund* was, however, a racist one, and their idea of "aristocracy" foreshadowed the role of the SS in the Third Reich. The fact that Jünger says he is close to the Artamanen and that he commends them speaks volumes about the true significance of the conceptions of "work" and the "new race" he developed in *The Worker*.

Now we have seen that Heidegger takes up, in his writings on Jünger, the latter's conception (which he develops in paragraph 45 of the *Beiträge*) of the three secret circles: between the dictatorship of the "unique ones" and the "many," there is the "small number" of those who are united in a *Bund*. We do not know precisely to which movements Heidegger may have felt close after his membership as a young man in the *Gralbund,* but we may wonder whether he might have been thinking, among other groups, of the *Bund Artam* praised by Jünger. That would explain his stated desire in his Hitlerian seminar to contribute to the formation, with Walter Darré, of a "new nobility" for the Third Reich. On these questions, new research — which I leave to others to carry out, since they have no relation to philosophy — would be necessary.

In order to better understand the true nature of the interest Heidegger has for him, one last point must be established touching the reality of Jünger's racism. On 27 June 1934, Ernst Jünger sent Carl Schmitt a copy of the letter he had just sent to the "Service for the Preservation of Professional Ethics" (*Abteilung zur Wahrung der Berufsmoral*) of the NSDAP. He had been asked to justify his relations with the biologist and racial theorist Fritz Merkenschlager. We are at the moment at which a fierce polemics was being waged between the conceptions of the "German race" defended by Merkenschlager, a member of the NSDAP and SA from the beginning, and Hans K. Günther, a partisan of the "Nordic race," which was favored by the SS. Now, we learn from Jünger's response that he knew Merkenschlager "by his publications on the racial question" and considered them "important," which is the reason why he corresponded with their author and visited him at the Institute of Biology of the Reich.[192] Jünger himself thought the activity of the "worker" should be recognized as "a form in which the law of the race finds expression."[193] It would be useful to be able someday to read—if it has not been destroyed—the correspondence between Merkenschlager and Jünger. In any case we know enough of it by his letter sent to Schmitt to conclude that the conception of race set forth in *The Worker* must be taken seriously and not as a simple metaphor. It is based on one of the two versions of Nazism's racial doctrine.

To return to Heidegger, it is extremely troubling to discover, in reading *Koinon* (1939–1940), as well as pieces on Jünger and courses on Nietzsche composed in 1941–1942, that it is during these initial years of World War II that he begins to bring up on a regular basis and to legitimate "racial *thought*" and racial selection. It is precisely at that moment that the Nazis are preparing the means to bring about the fulfillment of the "prophesy" stated by Hitler in his speech of 30 January 1939—namely, "the annihilation of the Jewish race in Europe," decided on during the Wannsee Conference of 1942. At that conference, the most virulent participant is none other than Wilhelm Stuckart, who was, as we have seen, in close contact with the former rector of Freiburg and the promoter of an "Academy of Professors of the Reich."[194] Given the extreme gravity of the context, I think an in-depth study of Heidegger's writings during the wartime years (1939–1945) comparable to the one I have attempted to carry out in this work for the years 1933–1935 would be indispensable. We can simply say today that there is every indication that it was not just a question, in what Heidegger calls the "decisions that announce themselves," of defeating the democracies of the West but also, as he himself writes, of making progress in the "purification" of the German essence, and in doing so by racial selection with its concomitant destruction.

Let us go even further in our questioning. We must ask ourselves whether there is not, in his writings on Jünger, something akin to a "prophesy" on Heidegger's part that, on a different plane, would accompany Hitler's, and its realization as well. The texts in which Heidegger announces a "new truth of being," speaks of "the hidden and not yet purified [*ungeläutert*] essence of the Germans," and praises to the skies "the race-being" (*Rassensein*) held up as an "ultimate end" all belong to the same period and the same point of view. Hence the attentive reader is led to wonder whether the heralded "truth of being" and "race-being" held up as the ultimate end and "essence of the Germans" that remains "to be purified" does not represent, in Heidegger's mind, one sole idea.

This would be the prolongation, equally horrifying, of what he had already said in the *Beiträge* about the "*völkisch* principle" that he related to the conquest of the "ultimate rank of being," just as his remarks on "the not yet purified essence of the Germans" may seem like the repetition, a decade later, of what he said in 1929 about the "Jewifying" (*Verjudung*) of German spiritual life.

On that hypothesis, unfortunately prompted by too many texts not to be seriously entertained, the Heideggerian distinction between "the fulfillment of metaphysics" and the "truth of being" would begin to reveal its hidden (*verborgen*) meaning. "Metaphysics" in Heidegger is manifestly just a name dislodged from philosophy to improve the image of and win acceptance for something entirely different: the "motorization of the Wehrmacht," taken by him as a "metaphysical act"; "racial selection," qualified by him as "metaphysically necessary"; the defeat of France by the armies of the Nazi Reich, commented on by him as the "day when a people no longer measures up to the metaphysics that has sprung from its own history." In short, all of this points in the direction of the realization of the planetary domination of Hitler's Nazi Germany. As for the "truth of being" that would be unveiled following such a realization, we can begin to get some sense of what it may involve by reading his texts on "race-being" (*Rassesein*) and "the essence of the Germans," who are not yet "purified": *the "truth of being" appears henceforth as indissociable from the future "purification" of the German essence and race.*

When Heidegger insists on the fact that "metaphysics" must be positively fulfilled and transcended, we can now understand, given what he actually calls "metaphysical" in the preceding examples, what is really going on. Power and domination are for him but means intended to facilitate what he calls "the purification of the German essence" and the unveiling of the "truth of being." The indetermination of that "truth" that, as "unveiling," suggests something hidden, not to say occult, is what lends Heidegger's voice its strength, being elusive enough to appear unscathed by criticism and mysterious enough for everyone to read into it whatever they were looking for: for the Thomist theologians, God; for mystic souls, the ineffable . . . But if we read attentively the writings of Heidegger accessible to us today, it is something entirely different that is progressively unveiled — which I have analyzed as the introduction of the very foundations of Nazism and Hitlerism into philosophy. The Heideggerian "transcending" of "metaphysics" is thus not at all a transcending of Nazism with its racist foundations, but on the contrary the announcement of a "truth" of "being" that remains that of Nazism itself — namely, the belief in the necessary "purification" of the German essence. As such, it is less a "political religion" than a racial mythology in an ingratiating and cryptic form that continues to motivate Heidegger to the end.

Today we must be aware of the nature of that enterprise, recognize it for what it is, and have the patience to analyze its monstrous character, in order to free ourselves of it definitively. To lead astray, lay waste, and radically destroy philosophy — such was indeed Heidegger's intent. He himself did not conceal after the war, specifically in the *Letter on Humanism* sent to Jean Beaufret, that the "thought that is to come" and that he advocated would "no longer be philosophy."[195] It is not even certain that what Heidegger said he was preparing merits the name of "thought." For my part, I am convinced, after the research that has gone into this book, that Heidegger's work never belonged to philosophy in the deeper sense of the term. It is not enough to have written on Aristotle, Descartes, or Hegel to be a philosopher, if the basic tenets of one's thought constitute the very negation of the moral obligation to respect the human being as such, independently of his or her belonging to any particular community, people, or "race."

Heidegger's Anti-Semitism in 1944

By an effort comparable to the one carried out in this book for philosophy, there should be, the better to resist Heidegger, a parallel attempt to assess his devastating influence on poetry. I would like, along these lines, to draw the reader's attention to a text that reveals Heidegger's intentions in choosing the figure he designates as "the" poet of Germany. This will make it possible to show the ongoing nature of his anti-Semitism in 1944. In the course titled *Poetry and Thought*, which he wrote for the winter semester of 1944–1945, and of which he taught only two sessions before being enlisted to serve in the *Volkssturm,* Heidegger quotes the following saying from Nietzsche and adds his own comment immediately afterward. " 'Germany has produced only one poet, besides Goethe: that is Heinrich Heine — and he is a Jew into the bargain . . .' This saying casts a strange light on the poet Goethe. Goethe — Heine, 'the' poet of Germany. What happened to Hölderlin . . . ?"[196]

This is all he says about it. The mere fact of Nietzsche's association of Goethe with a "Jewish" poet, Heine, sufficed for him to disqualify Goethe, whose name will not come up again. Hölderlin alone will be singled out as "the" poet of the Germans.

We are now at the end of the year 1944, a time when the enterprise of the extermination of European Jewry by the Nazis is certainly a known reality, and in particular by Heidegger. But he continues to develop the Germanic myth of the poet and thinker, and to draw on the argument of his own anti-Semitism and that of his listeners to choose "the" poet of the Germans. During these times of imminent defeat, he no longer adds, after the poet and the thinker, the third term — namely, the political activity of the creators of the state — as he did a decade earlier in his course on Hölderlin's "The Rhine," following Hitler's example at the end of *Mein Kampf*. Still, Heidegger persists in retaining the only two names magnified by the Nazis — Hölderlin for poetry and Nietzsche for thought, both abusively interpreted. And the first long fragment Heidegger quotes from Nietzsche in *Denken und Dichten* concerns the "strong races of Europe."[197]

Moreover, we know that since Norbert von Hellingrath and Stefan George, the German extreme right had replaced Goethe with Hölderlin. Carl Schmitt emphasizes this still after the war in his *Glossarium*. "The tragic aspect of J[ewish] assimilation since 1900: They could not, on the whole, keep up and take the great step from Goethe to Hölderlin, but remained in the old culture, with which they criticized the new one, out of an unconscious and provoking feeling of superiority. They did not understand the passage from the concept to the *Gestalt* and what that meant in the German spirit. Or else they understood too well, like Gundolf."[198]

Schmitt does not hide what is at stake from a *völkisch* point of view in the substitution of Hölderlin for Goethe, particularly in the Stefan George circle, to which Gundolf, though Jewish, was connected — a circle that had already adopted the swastika as its symbol in 1918. The idea was to break with the culture of assimilation by no longer relying on the universality of the concept but rather on the racial particularity of the *Gestalt*.

This whole anti-Semitic factor resurfaces in Heidegger's course of 1944. In order to reject Goethe and the universalism of the culture he represents, Heidegger, not without malice, uses Nietzsche's association of the names Goethe and Heine and the fact that Nietzsche emphasizes the Jewishness of Heine (whose name was radically proscribed by the Nazis) to disqualify Goethe himself. The "strange light" cast on Goethe, according to Heidegger, means of course that if Nietzsche himself was able to associate a "Jew" with Goethe's name, it is because the latter is somehow "sullied" and cannot qualify as "the" poet of the Germans.

After the defeat of Nazism, Heidegger persists, in the *Letter on Humanism*, in affirming that Hölderlin's thought is "essentially more primordial and thus more significant for the future than the mere cosmopolitanism of Goethe."[199] This clearly demonstrates that Heidegger did not change after 1945, even though he may henceforth mask the anti-Semitic basis of his rejection of "cosmopolitanism."

From the Revisionism of the Response to Marcuse to the Ontological Negationism of the Bremen Lectures

Much as been said about Heidegger's "silence" with respect to the annihilation of European Jewry by the Nazis. In reality, he did not keep silent, and what he expressed is far worse than silence. On 28 August 1947, Herbert Marcuse wrote to him from Washington: "A philosopher can be mistaken in politics, in which case he will openly acknowledge his mistake. But he cannot make a mistake about a régime that killed millions of Jews simply because they were Jews, who made terror a normal state of affairs and transformed everything that ever truly pertained to the concepts of spirit, freedom, and truth into its bloody opposite."[200]

He expects, then, from his former teacher a declaration not only admitting his past "mistake" — since his adherence to Nazism constitutes much more than a political "mistake" — but publicly declaring that he has changed his views. Without such a declaration, philosophy and Nazism being incompatible, one could only refuse to see Heidegger as a philosopher. The revisionism of Heidegger's response is mind-boggling. Sent on 20 January 1948, his response consists of six carefully numbered points. After having said "how difficult it is to argue with people who have not been in Germany since 1933," but without saying a word about the reasons why Marcuse had been forced to flee Germany in 1933, (1) he begins by justifying his public adherence in 1933 in wording that clearly shows he believes himself still perfectly justified (he expected from National Socialism "a spiritual renewal of the totality of life") and asks Marcuse whether he has "read *in its entirety*" his rectoral address! (2) He then claims to have acknowledged since 1934 what he calls his "political mistake." Yet Marcuse had clearly pointed out that the word "mistake" cannot possibly be appropriate when the issue is one of adherence to an enterprise such as Nazism, the exterminatory objectives of which were clearly displayed by Hitler from the start. (3) Then Heidegger takes cover behind a statement by Jaspers: "to have survived, that is our offense." But he fails to make any distinction between the tragic situation of Jaspers, who was forced to retire in 1937, whose wife's very life was continually threatened because she was Jewish, and his own situation as a recognized Nazi, still authorized in 1943, for example, to take a holiday in Strasbourg in the middle of the world war! (4) Heidegger then declares that his teaching from 1933 to 1945 protected his students from the Nazi ideology. We have seen, on the contrary, the devastating effects, emphasized by Gerd Tellenbach, of his influence on the German student body, his disastrous influence on disciples like Erik Wolf, and the true content of his presently accessible courses and seminars. The disdainful bad faith of point 5 reaches a pinnacle: Had he made a declaration after 1945, it would have identified him with the Nazis who had publicly changed their views. The reality is that all of those condemned at Nuremberg, with the exception of Hans Frank, persisted in affirming their positions.

Then comes the sixth point. Heidegger is content with repeating the sentence of his correspondent about the millions of Jews annihilated by the Nazis and simply adding that in the place of "Jews," one could have written "East Germans" (*statt "Juden" "Ostdeutsche" zu stehen hat*), the difference being that everything that was done by one of the Allies (the Soviet Union) after 1945 was done with the knowledge of everyone worldwide, whereas what the Nazis had done remained hidden from the German people.

But where was Heidegger when, during Kristallnacht in Freiburg, the Nazi bands burned the old synagogue *that stood at the heart of the university* and arrested many of the city's Jews? Where was he on 22 October 1940, when the Germans grabbed and deported all the German Jews of Baden who had not already been arrested? How could he not have known how the Nazi forces had acted in the east, he with two sons on the eastern front? How could he not have known anything, he who proclaimed throughout the 1930s the necessity of the "fight against the Asiatic," a term the National Socialists used specifically to designate Jews? Further, although the Russian troops — three million of whom had starved to death in the Nazi camps — often showed unusual brutality, there was no genocide of the German population of the east.

The "revisionism" of the response is patent. As Hugo Ott writes: "Heidegger anticipated the quarrel among historians of the year 1986."[201]

Is it possible to proceed with a reasoned discussion after such assertions? As Marcuse said in his response to Heidegger on the substitution of "Germans of the East" for "Jews": "With that sentence, do you not stand outside the dimension in which any conversation between men is still possible — outside the *Logos*?"[202]

And in fact, as we shall see, after 1945 Heidegger abandons all that sets philosophy on a human foundation.

It is in the four *Bremen Lectures* of 1949, titled respectively "The Thing" (*Das Ding*), "The Frame" (*Das Ge-stell*), "The Danger" (*Die Gefahr*), and "The Turning" (*Die Kehre*), that Heidegger's negation of the specificity of the Nazi genocide finds its extreme expression. Two passages require special attention. Heidegger took care not to publish them during his lifetime. The first text is from the lecture titled "The Frame," delivered before the public of the "Bremen Club" on 2 December 1949 but omitted by Heidegger in the first edition he offered of the text in 1962.[203] It was not revealed until 1983, in a study published by Wolfgang Schirmacher.[204] The text finally appeared in 1994 in the *Gesamtausgabe*. In the same breath, Heidegger launches into unbearable comparisons. "Agriculture today is a motorized industry of alimentation, the same thing in essence as the fabrication of corpses in the gas chambers and the death camps, the same as blockading and the reducing of countries to famine, the same thing as the fabrication of hydrogen bombs."[205]

By uttering such a sentence, Heidegger excludes himself from philosophy and shows that he has lost all humanity. After having exalted, in his courses, the motorization of the Wehrmacht as a "metaphysical" act—and we know that the first gassings took place in trucks—he now uses the planetary nature of modern technology to deny the irreducible specificity of the Nazi genocide and to associate it with one of the most banal manifestations of the technological transformation of existence—namely, the transformation of agriculture into a mechanized food industry. The deranged nature of that assertion is reinforced by the fact that he assimilates the programmed murder of millions of human beings to an industry intended to manufacture corpses, as if the SS had had the intention of producing corpses mechanically as one might produce sugar, by annihilating millions of men, women, and children, completely cut off by them from the human species. So it is that the dehumanization by Nazism of the victims of the death camps is perpetuated in Heidegger's statement.

Heidegger knew perfectly well what he was doing in articulating that statement. That is why he decided to forgo publishing it during his lifetime, leaving it to the *Gesamtausgabe* to share it with the public, which is what would have occurred had Wolfgang Schirmacher not decided to take action.

There is a second text on the death camps in the *Bremen Lectures*. It is less well known, but even more filled with the dark shadows that invaded Heidegger's mind, and it testifies to what we have chosen to call his *ontological negationism*. In truth it pertains to what Paul Celan has called "the unnamable." But the expression *ontological negationism* expresses clearly the fact that Heidegger attacks not only the historical reality of the facts by substantially reducing the number of victims of the camps and by refusing to grant any specificity to the Nazi genocide, but also the very *being* of the victims of the camps.

The text is found in the lecture titled "The Danger." It has been available only since 1994, with the publication of the four *Bremen Lectures* in the *Gesamtausgabe*. In this case, no listener was able to take the initiative. If we are to believe the testimony of Heinrich Wiegand Petzet, the document not only remained unpublished until that date, but was not delivered at all in 1949.[206] If this testimony were to be confirmed, it would mean that by refraining from delivering that fourth lecture, Heidegger showed he was aware that he was going much further than in the first passage quoted, from the lecture titled "The Frame." In any case, this text is now part of the *Gesamtausgabe*. Here is what he writes.

Hundreds of thousands die *en masse*. Do they die? They perish. They are put down. Do they die? They become supply pieces for stock in the fabrication of corpses. Do they die? They are liquidated unnoticed in death camps. And also, without such — millions in China sunken in poverty perish from hunger. But to die means to carry out death in its essence. To be able to die means to be able to carry out this resolution. We can only do this if our essence likes the essence of death. But in the middle of innumerable deaths the essence of death remains unrecognizable. Death is neither empty nothingness, nor just the passage from one state to another. *Death pertains to the* Dasein *of the man who appears out of the essence of being.* Thus it shelters the essence of being. Death is the loftiest shelter of the truth of being, the shelter that shelters within itself the hidden character of the essence of being and draws together the saving of its essence.

This is why man can die if and only if being itself appropriates the essence of man into the essence of being on the basis of the truth of its essence. *Death is the shelter of being in the poem of the world.* To be able toward death in its essence means to be able to die. Only those who can die are mortals in the apposite sense of the word.[207]

This text surpasses anything the National Socialists could assert. The death camps are not just the culmination of a process of segregation and destruction. The "Final Solution" becomes the point of departure for something even more unspeakable: the direct and total eradication of the very possibility of human life. The monstrousness of what Heidegger says places him outside all philosophy. The words "truth of being," "poem of the world," and "loftiest shelter" cannot conceal the atrocity of the intended meaning. The "Do they die?" (*Sterben sie?*) thrice repeated elicits from the reader an indefensible response: *According to Heidegger, no one died in a death camp, because none of those who were exterminated there bore within their essence the possibility of death.*

We must bring our minds to focus on the absolute insanity of these words. We are no longer just in revisionism but in total negationism, and even in something beyond words — something that is properly unspeakable. Heidegger does not say that the conditions of the murder of millions of human beings were such that they were not able to die in a manner that was human and worthy, and to which every human being is entitled. After having denied, in a revolting way, the extent of the Shoah by speaking of "hundreds of thousands," whereas several millions of human beings were exterminated by the Nazis, he gives us to understand that no one died in the death camps because none of those who were liquidated were *able* to die there.

It is intentional that at the beginning of his text he never uses the word "man" in connection with the victims of the death camps. Heidegger claims the only ones who "can" die are those to whom "being" has given the "power": those who are in the "shelter" of the "essence" of being. Those who disappeared in the death camps could not be "saved" in this way by "being." They were not "mortal," therefore not human.

It is impossible to go further in the negation of the human being than Heidegger does. The genocide of the Jews — the Shoah — and the murder of all who also disappeared in the Nazi concentration and death camps — German political opponents, French and Polish resisters, Gypsies, Russian and Polish war prisoners — never happened for Heidegger. The entire populations who were gassed, the children burned alive at Auschwitz, none of that involved human beings. Not only did the massacred populations not die, but they could not even live. The madness of that condemnation is without bounds. It leads to the elimination of all human life and even of the possibility of its reappearance.

Heidegger's words outdo, in their abjection, National Socialist racism and the physical, moral, and spiritual annihilation it sought to attain. After having associated in his writings on Jünger the "truth of being" with the "purification of the German essence," he now maintains that those who "by essence" are outside "the essence of being" do not have the "possibility" of "wanting" death. They do not have being, they *are* not. What Heidegger is saying, then, is not just tied to the conditions of programmed extermination in the camps; he goes still further and attacks the very "being" of those who were exterminated. It is not just a question of destroying them completely, but of showing that they were nothing. To the Nazi extermination, which afflicted human beings unbearably in their flesh, is added a radical ontological negationism, which cuts off human life at its root.[208]

The fact that Heidegger mixes "poetry" in with the atrocity of that negationism casts a black light on what Paul Celan, whose parents had died in deportation, may have endured during his long visit to Todtnauberg.[209] There has been talk of the illness of the poet, but it is rather of Heidegger's madness as it transpires in the *Bremen Lectures* that we must be aware. Now that we know how far he went mentally in the direction of the destruction of humanity, his remark on Celan, "He is incurable," echoes like a condemnation without appeal.

It seems that Paul Celan expected from his visit at Todtnauberg not reconciliation, but "redemption," so to speak. For this reason, he had to lead Heidegger to the quagmires of the Black Forest, where the Nazis had set up their camps. He had to tread with Heidegger

Die halb-
beschrittenen Knüppel-
pfade im Hochmoor.[210]

He had to show in this way that the earth of the Black Forest does not consist solely of the granite celebrated by Heidegger in his homage to Schlageter.

Hermann Heidegger claimed his father didn't know Celan was Jewish. But Martin Heidegger's remark, "I know everything he wrote,"[211] proves the opposite. Heidegger knew perfectly well what he was doing.

The poet left the following sentence in the album presented to the hosts of the *Hütte* on 25 July 1967: "In the cabin book, gazing at the star in the well, with the hope in the heart of a word to come."[212] Here is how his host answers, on 30 January 1968: "My own wish? That at the hour that will be the right one you hear the language in which the poetry that is to come will address you."[213]

The star of the *Hütte* is not a star of redemption. Jean Bollack has rightly emphasized the offhandedness and "impertinence" of Heidegger's response. But what Heidegger says about the victims of the camps in the *Bremen Lectures* and his remark about Heinrich Heine, a "Jewish" poet, whose name being juxtaposed to that of Goethe sufficed to cast a "strange light" on the latter, requires that we go further in our understanding of what he intends. He suggests to Celan that he has not yet heard the call of the "word" and therefore has not attained to poetry. It is the negation of his poetic being and the destruction of everything he lives for. Heidegger's response casts Celan into the quagmire of death.

Returning now to the *Bremen Lectures,* the monstrous meaning of the assertions just quoted is confirmed by the fact that it was not until 1945, with the total defeat of the Third Reich, that Heidegger said he feared "the annihilation of man," as he expressed it in *Feldweg Gespräche,* conversations between two German war prisoners.[214] While the Nazi politics of extermination brought to bear from 1942 to 1945 stirred no burst of revolt in him, it was only when "the essence of the Germans" seemed to him to be threatened in its "being" once Nazism was defeated that he expressed his radical fear. From this fact we can assess the total impasse of that doctrine, in which there remains no possibility of forming a clear notion of the human being as such.

In 1933 Heidegger had answered the question "What is man?" with the assertion "We are the people," and the only people still to have a "history." After the defeat of Nazism, he identified "the essence of man" more radically with the destiny of native-born Germans. In 1945, his belief in the future of the "German essence" remained intact. As he writes in a rather obscure sentence to Rudolf Stadelmann, "We Germans cannot . . . sink because we have not even risen yet and must first pass through the night."[215]

For Heidegger, the passage through the night began in 1945 with the defeat of Nazism. We must therefore be lucid about what he expects from this "journey to the end of the night" and the hoped-for coming of the "last god." There are gods whose advent cannot be wished for.

The Danger of Heidegger's Works and
His Negationist Posterity

The gravity of the peril presented by the dissemination of Heidegger's works today may be seen in its continuation among his closest followers, who, one after another, have drifted toward an increasingly radical revisionism, when they have not sunk into negationism. It is true that there are, among those who approve of the content of Heidegger's works, all possible varieties, from those who share his National Socialist convictions to those who in themselves have nothing Nazi about them, but who, remaining on the surface of the work, do not attempt to explore it in depth, and yet take the personal risk of assimilating it and the moral responsibility of contributing to its legitimation. Now the more we realize the radicalness and permanence of Heidegger's Nazism, the more we are confronted with an essential moral, intellectual, and spiritual choice. Once we have understood that his work constitutes the continuation of Hitlerism and Nazism in thought, either we decide to resist it with the same determination that was necessary in the recent past to resist Nazism, or we allow ourselves to be pervaded, possessed, and dominated by it. On a question this vital, there can be no possible arrangement or half measure.

Now the acceptance of Heidegger's work as a source of thought is particularly dangerous. It is not possible to approve morally anything connected with Nazism without risking the progressive destruction of one's humanity. In addition to the risk of personal ruin there is the following danger. Those who allow themselves to be possessed by the cult of Heidegger to the point of seeing in him a "great thinker" risk, as they discover the intensity of his Nazism, drawing the conclusion that there must be something "great" in Nazism. Thus we soon end up with the type of question an Anglo-Saxon commentator recently formulated as follows. "His deserved rank as a great thinker in the philosophic tradition, however, must be considered alongside the terrifying possibility that he was right about National Socialism."[216] The same author continues in a no less odious vein: "As shocking as that suggestion is to our moral sensibility, our intellectual integrity obliges us to wonder whether National Socialism represents *the* genuine answer to the question of how we ought to live."[217]

It seems to me that the intention of that author is not to present an apology for National Socialism but to impress the reader with the dramatic effect of his words. The questions he formulates are no less revolting for that fact. They assume that we contemplate the unacceptable rehabilitation of Nazism, and they presuppose the opinion, the shallowness of which my book has tried to expose, according to which Heidegger would merit being raised to the level of "great thinker." Indeed, not only did he explicitly attempt to destroy the integrality of the Western philosophical tradition by describing ethics as obsolete and metaphysics as nihilistic, but his blindness and complicity with respect to the most monstrous enterprise humanity has ever known prove that he was nowise a true "thinker."

There remains the problem of those authors who work dispassionately for the rehabilitation of Nazism and Hitlerism by stages. Here we encounter the present reality of revisionism and negationism. Several strategies are at work, and often in the same author. At one moment they may try to minimize the issue of anti-Semitism to the point of making it a secondary question: for this, the revisionists need the "work" of negationists such as Robert Faurisson, who go so far as to deny the existence of the gas chambers and more generally of the Shoah — the *Endlösung*. At another moment they claim that Nazism, and even Hitler's anti-Semitism, contains a "rational nucleus" and a "grain of truth," as does Ernst Nolte. Nolte maintains that Nazism is merely a defense mechanism of German existence threatened by Bolshevism, as if the Soviet Union, with which Hitler had colluded to crush the Western democracies, in any way justified Hitler's politics of extermination and genocide of entire populations.

Let us recall that this revisionist historian was a student and close friend of Heidegger's. He relates an anecdote that reveals the closeness of his ties with the Heidegger family and symbolically foreshadows the support he will give his former teacher. In 1945, the Allies were advancing toward Heidegger's native town of Meßkirch, where he had taken refuge with his wife and Nolte himself. Fearing arrest, he hopped onto his bicycle and fled eastward. The revisionist historian rushes to the rescue. "I caught up with him on my own bicycle to give him a knapsack full of clean clothes and food his wife had given me for him."[218]

Almost half a century later, when the radicalness of Heidegger's involvement with Nazism began to be better known thanks to the works of Hugo Ott and Victor Farías, Hermann Heidegger, Heidegger's son and director of the so-called complete edition, announced in the course of a televised interview the imminent publication of an authorized biography. That was the monograph on Heidegger that Nolte published in 1992 as *Heidegger, Politik und Geschichte im Leben und Denken.*

Now, in that book, Ernst Nolte approves and justifies Heidegger's Nazi involvement. He was within his "historical right,"[219] Nolte argues, like all those who had opted for Hitler in 1933. Nolte explains the meaning he gives that expression, in a "summing-up" published in 1998 with the very Heideggerian-sounding title *Historical Existence.* Presenting himself not just as a "historian" but as a "thinker of history"[220] and of "historical existence," he speaks like the author of *Being and Time* of "existentials" such as "religion, the state, the nobility, war."[221] According to him, the "singularity of the National Socialist 'Final Solution'" is the "dogma" of the left "since 1968." (By "left" Nolte means more or less everything that is not on the extreme right.) Thus it is insinuated that the "Final Solution" is not a historical truth but an ideological bias, if not, according to his expression, a "quasi religion" (*Religionsersatz*). Furthermore, National Socialism should not be considered solely "in a moral, but also in a historical way." In reality, Nolte separates history from morality and coins the expression "historical right," by means of which he would justify the inexcusable. Considered in its "historical right," Nazism should no longer be considered "absolute evil" and "total wrong" but "as the phenomenon by which historical existence became aware of itself as threatened" and led a "last political battle"![222]

So it is that Nolte presents Nazism as a form of self-defense, as if the extermination of peoples undertaken by Hitler could be justified in such a way! And deliberately identifying, exactly as Heidegger does, "historical existence" exclusively with the destiny of the German people united under the *Führung* of Hitler, he elevates Nazism to the rank of an "existential"! Moreover, it is not the destruction of European Jewry that he emphasizes but the character of "self-destruction" (*Selbstzerstörung*) of Nazism. Beneath his pen, Nazism became a legitimate historical phenomenon, the only regrettable thing about which is that it turned out badly for its instigators. In short, it is the 1945 defeat, the collapse of Nazi Germany, and not the Shoah, that he regrets.

Nolte's revisionism, foreshadowed in Heidegger's response to Marcuse, undertakes to rehabilitate Nazism in its supposed "historical right" and then comes to the aid of Heidegger to justify his involvement. The snare is set, ready to tighten its grip around those who have allowed themselves to be taken in.

A parallel case, that of another Heidegger disciple who played a crucial role in his master's dissemination in France, and whose teaching (and that of his followers) has wreaked ongoing havoc in the higher levels of our school system, has completed the journey leading from revisionism to negationism. I refer to Jean Beaufret, a man in whom suspect areas remain that the adulation of his admiring followers has not succeeded in dissipating entirely. Beaufret's fascination with a certain vision of Germany merits study. He went to Berlin in 1932–1933 for at least seven months, when he wrote a still unpublished memoir, "The State in Fichte." Did he make contact in the course of his research with members of the Fichte Society (*Fichte Gesellschaft*)? That is a question worthy of being looked into, because of all the German philosophical societies, the Fichte Society is the one that became the most radically and completely National Socialist.

Furthermore, after World War II, Jean Beaufret held aggressively revisionist positions on the beginning of Nazism. During the winter of 1963–1964, a controversy developed on the opinion page of the newspaper *France-Observateur,* following a quote by Étiemble from the Germanist Robert Minder on Heidegger's Nazism. It was a letter from Dominique Janicaud that touched off the controversy,[223] to which Jean Beaufret made three contributions. In a letter published on 31 December 1963, he asks the following question: "The whole question, i.e., the one that has never been asked, is in my opinion whether or not the appearance of Hitler as chancellor in 1933, facing a properly German situation, the tragic nature of which was studiously ignored by the rest of Europe, did not contain sufficient ambiguity for a man who was not 'more than man,' as Descartes put it, to give credence for a time to one who promised to 'correct in four years the mistakes committed for fourteen years' (Hitler's speech of 3/1/33), to the point of accepting at that date, though conditionally, to become a member of the NSDAP of that period."

This text reveals unquestionably that in 1963 Jean Beaufret was already well involved in the twists and turns of revisionism. We see him using the name of Descartes in an unacceptable way, citing an expression from *Discourse on the Method* that concerns the salvation of the soul and cannot therefore by any stretch be applied to the political question of the relationship with Nazism. And Beaufret does not hesitate to reinforce his argument with a speech by Hitler, as if the statement he quoted could expunge in the minds of his listeners the reality of a deeply discriminatory and racist doctrine, a doctrine that had been proclaimed even before *Mein Kampf.* Furthermore, the contorted way the question is put contains in fact the response: according to Beaufret, the "properly German situation" of 1933 "contained sufficient ambiguity" for Heidegger to rally to Hitler's cause and adhere to the NSDAP.[224] Now if one can always say of a historical situation that it is ambiguous, the "response" of Hitler and the NSDAP was not. The "bringing into line," the introduction of the "Führer principle," the racist laws that were immediately enacted and enforced, the book-burnings, the opening of the first concentration camps, the exactions of the SA — all of these actions unambiguously revealed the discriminatory brutality of the new political power. In this regard, Alfred Grosser's statement, published in the *France-Observateur* on 9 January 1964, unequivocally sets the record straight: "My disagreement with M. Beaufret is total. I plead in favor of indulgence for those who have unwittingly yielded without knowing exactly what they were yielding to, for the young whose enthusiasm was misplaced. But a great philosopher who preaches against freedom of mind, who invites his students' unconditional obedience to a man and an ideology whose effects on the life of the mind were perfectly obvious at the time (the purging of the universities, arrests and imprisonment, the burning of 'bad books,' etc.): no, really, indulgence does not appear to me fitting in the case of Martin Heidegger!"

But can we continue to use the term "great philosopher"? The texts that have come to light since then, and particularly those revealed in the present book, lead today, on this point, to a negative response.

Jean Beaufret, in the long article published on 6 February 1964 on the subject of what he calls "the substance of the issue," claims that the facts mentioned by Alfred Grosser "are precisely the reasons for Heidegger's resignation." We know they were nothing of the kind, not only because the destructive radicalism of the Nazi enterprise was manifest even before his commitment to Hitler and the NSDAP on 1 May 1933, but because today it has been definitively proven that Heidegger actively participated in the general "bringing into line" by the introduction of the "Führer principle" into the university and the promotion of racist and anti-Semitic legislation that, after having imposed the dismissal of "non-Aryan" professors, put in place, under the expression "new student law," a *numerus clausus* considerably restricting the access of Jewish students to the university.

I will not give further details on Jean Beaufret's statements. I will simply point out that he embraces the oft-stated sophism that if a "poet" like Gottfried Benn and a "great philosopher" like Heidegger were able to "opt" for Hitler, surely there must have been reasons for it. Once again, we see how any attempt to justify Heidegger's Hitlerism sooner or later comes down to justifying Hitler himself.

Today we know just how far Jean Beaufret traveled down that slippery slope. He embraced the most radical historical denial of the Holocaust, adopting the theses of Robert Faurisson — that is, the negation of the existence of the gas chambers and of the extermination of the Jews by the Nazis. On 22 November 1978, in a letter to Faurisson, who had been his student and whose address he had through his "old friend" Maurice Bardèche,[225] Beaufret commends Faurisson's "courage" and expresses his "esteem" for him. And he tells him this. "I have for my part taken more or less the same path as you, and have made myself suspect for having entertained the same doubts."

Robert Faurisson published the letter, along with another from his former teacher Beaufret, in the *Annales d'histoire révisionniste*.[226] The following year he dedicated one of his articles "to the memory of Martin Heidegger and Jean Beaufret, who preceded me in revisionism."[227]

Revisionism among the Heideggerians did not end with Jean Beaufret. François Fédier, Beaufret's leading disciple and the current French representative of

Heidegger's successors, attempts to exculpate Heidegger in an open letter to Hugo Ott by formulating a singular argument.[228] According to Fédier, Heidegger didn't know, in 1978, who Robert Faurisson was.[229] But by that date Faurisson had already made his negationist theses known to the public. And it is a fact that Jean Beaufret expressed the "same doubts" as Faurisson about the reality of the gas chambers and the extermination of the Jews by Hitler. François Fédier's argument cannot change that reality. Furthermore, it should be observed that nowhere in his article does Fédier himself reject Faurisson's negationist theses.

As a matter of fact, François Fédier embraced Nolte's revisionism to the point of participating, in 1993, in an apologetic volume in favor of the latter. In his contribution he maintains: "Nihilism, which remains the foremost historical achievement of Nazism, is not criminal in itself. Nor is it *neutral,* but as a historical phenomenon, the conveyer — on equal terms — of positive possibilities just as much as negative ones."[230]

These affirmations come down to saying that there are as many "positive possibilities" as "negative possibilities" at the foundation of Nazism. If the author does not go as far as does Nolte in explicit historical revisionism, he goes still further in the partial rehabilitation of the very foundations of Nazism. And the intertwining of Nolte's revisionism with the direct posterity of Heidegger goes so far that in the presentation of lectures given by Nolte in Italy, his Italian editor Massimo Amato uses the passage I have quoted from Fédier's text to bolster the theses of the revisionist historian.[231]

A new step has recently been taken with the revisionist "general survey" by Christian Tilitzki, which appeared in 2002 from the Akademie Verlag and is titled *Die deutsche Universitätsphilosophie in der Weimarer Republik und im Dritten Reich.* The author presents himself as a disciple of Ernst Nolte, who undertook "the historicizing of the new writing of the history of philosophy."[232]

In reality, he reiterates the revisionist theses of Nolte, only stiffening them. The "German position" from 1918 to 1945 is presented as "politically legitimate" in an international situation described in Noltean terms as that of a "civil war."[233] The "National Socialist vision of the world" is presented as containing a "rational kernel," which consists in "the opposition between particularity and universality."[234] Quite obviously it is not a question of just any "particularity," but of the "particularity of '*völkisch* existence' as opposed to all the universalisms."[235] Now, the "*völkisch* particularity" means nothing short of the discriminatory assertion of the supremacy of a "race," and therefore no historical situation could possibly legitimate it in any way. So we must face the reality: behind the subterfuge of borrowed words and specious arguments, Christian Tilitzki's book undertakes to rehabilitate Nazism, and it is extremely serious that such a work has been published by a press that has also published the works of Aristotle and Leibniz.

To make his undertaking of a "revision" of Nazism less unacceptable, Tilitzki says that "racism is but *one* element of particularism."[236] In reality, the extensive nature of the developments the author devotes to race proves that it is not just one element among others.[237] Nazism's racial obsession invades even "philosophy," as can be seen, for example, by the fact that in the *Philosophical Dictionary* of a Nazi author like Heinrich Schmidt, the article "Race" grows from 12 pages (in 1930) to 148 pages (in 1934).[238] Now, in Tilitzki's work, Martin Heidegger is not put on the same level as the other university professors quoted. He is less an object of analysis than an exemplary figure and a major source of inspiration for the author's revisionist agenda. This fact confirms the existence of substantial ties between Heidegger's work and revisionism. Thus it is Heidegger's "profession of faith in Adolf Hitler" of 11 November 1933 that is taken as an example of the legitimate attitude of self-affirmation of German existence and of "true being" (*wahres Sein*).[239] Tilitzki lashes out at Victor Farías — qualified as a "simplifier" and rejected for his "utopian cosmopolitanism" — and at Hugo Ott, George Steiner, Bernd Martin, and Alexander Schwan. Only the "alternative interpretations" of Ernst Nolte and Hartmut Tietjen, the former private secretary of Martin Heidegger and one of the principal artisans of the *Gesamtausgabe,* find grace in his eyes.

Not only does Tilitzki say that Heidegger's allegiance to Hitler was legitimate, but in his book he studies the academic careers of such Nazi "philosophers" as Alfred Baeumler, Erich Rothacker, Arnold Gehlen, Ernst Krieck, and Hans Heyse, as if academic life had continued normally in Germany after the dismissal and emigration of the Jewish philosophers, and as if those "figures" of Nazism were authentic "philosophers." With Tilitzki, negationism no longer perverts just history, but the view one may have of philosophy itself.

Against that radical perversion of thought, it must be reaffirmed that no philosophy can be based on the negation of the existence of man as such. From behind the proclamation of a so-called particularity (a term the Nazis scarcely used and to which the author resorts to try the make his words acceptable), it is the murderous assertion of the domination of a "race" that emerges. Tilitzki's book confirms that beneath the appearances of historical "objectivity," it is the legitimation of Nazism that is being carried out, and with increasing insistency.

We also see, through many "figures" whose careers are presented by the author, the degree to which Nazism systematically took over all the fields of academic "philosophy," progressively destroying all possibility of thought. In short, this book confirms the peril Nazism represents for the life of thought, and the need for resolute opposition to any attempt to legitimate that movement.

The gravity of the aberrations I have had to point out reveal the danger of Heidegger's work. There is a manifold of causal reciprocities between his direct influence on negationism and Holocaust denial, and the support that the revisionism of authors such as Nolte, Beaufret, Fédier, or Tilitzki brings to the Heideggerian cause. Particularly striking are the resemblances between the loss of all ethical reference in the Noltean idea of "historical right" and the way Heidegger himself violently disqualifies any reference to morality, especially in *Koinon*. It is certain that once the moral attitude has been destroyed, and therefore philosophy as well, which cannot be constituted except on that condition, then there is no longer any strict separation between what is humanly acceptable and what is not. Then one can, by making use of such indeterminate expressions as "truth of being" or "historical right," promote progressively — or brutally, should the movement of history gather momentum — the most discriminatory and murderous deeds.

Finally, it must be admitted that it is Heidegger's responsibility that is the greatest, for in introducing Hitlerism and Nazism into philosophy, he used every means to ravage and destroy it from the ground up. The basis of Nazism thus legitimized was able to expand into fields as diverse as law, medicine, and history. Now the harmful effects of that enterprise did not end with the Nazi defeat of 1945. They have been perpetuated by the texts, especially today, by the publication of the *Gesamtausgabe*. Furthermore, as we have seen, Heidegger's negationism assaults not only the historical truth but the very possibility of human life at the most elementary level. A careful study of his work has shown us that Nazism, going beyond its negation of a people and a "race," aims at the destruction of the human being as such. It is therefore of the utmost importance at the present time that we realize the danger of the dissemination of Heidegger's works.

Conclusion

An in-depth assessment of the human loss and inner destruction to which National Socialism has led so many minds is no easy task. For my part, I would never have conducted this research if I had not been guided, as I became aware of the gravity of the disaster, by the growing conviction of the vital necessity of seeing philosophy free itself from the work of Heidegger. His writings continue to spread the radically racist and human life–destroying conceptions that make up the foundation of Hitlerism and Nazism.

In the work of Martin Heidegger, the very principles of philosophy are abolished. No place is left for morality, which is openly and radically annihilated. Respect for individual human life, the refusal of destruction, the inner scruple of conscience that, turning inward upon itself and measuring the responsibility for one's thoughts, words, and deeds, not to mention generosity and the giving of oneself — all those qualities essential to man, and that it is philosophy's vocation to cultivate and reinforce, are eradicated to make room for the exaltation of the "hard race."

Further, what we now know of Heidegger's way of acting — his many letters of denunciation and his secret relations, his active role in the introduction of the "Führer principle" into the university, the close ties he made among those responsible for the book-burnings of Jewish authors, his efforts to falsify his own writings after 1945, and then, having secured a worldwide audience, the reintegration into his complete works of the most Hitlerian and racist courses and texts — forbid our viewing him as a philosopher.

We must also consider his continual attacks — often as violent as those of Baeumler or Krieck — on understanding and reason, without which there is neither human equilibrium nor rectitude of thought. If, in his sacralization of Greek words, Heidegger retains the term *logic,* he brings about the downfall of its meaning. This is sufficiently demonstrated by the course of this name taught in the spring of 1934, which exalts the voice of the blood and identifies the people with race, and also by his wild assertion that "in logic, too, one can introduce the figure of the Führer."[1] It is therefore not surprising that in the tens of thousands of pages left by Heidegger, there is almost no mention of Socrates. To the dialectic that, since Plato, has made possible the vitality of the philosophical dialogue and founded the intellectual requirement of questioning on the level of concepts, he substituted the dictatorial use of the word and exalted combat unto the annihilation of the enemy.

As for metaphysics, the vocation of which is to enlighten the mind in its search for principles and the critical examination of its faculties, Heidegger smuggled in under this name, at the end of the 1920s, a pathos of angst that has nothing to do with thought's requirement of truth. In 1930 he went so far as to deny the universality of the concept of truth and to destroy it by using it to designate the enrootedness of the historical existence of the German people in the soil of the native land or *Heimat.* Moreover, if in his book on Kant he took up the key question "What is man?" it was in order to give it, in his courses of 1933 and 1934, a racist and murderous response. Indeed, we have seen him commend the "fundamental transformation of the German world," accomplished in his opinion by Hitler's "worldview." And during World War II he used the word "metaphysical" in a radically perverted manner to glorify the motorization of the Wehrmacht, racial selection, and the invasion of France.

How can we consider an author who uses the loftiest words of philosophy to exalt the military power of Nazism and justify the most homicidal discrimination a philosopher? The example of Heidegger shows us that it does not suffice to use philosophical terms or to comment on philosophers to be one. When Heidegger uses the term "freedom" to mean the possession of the human being by the Führer, or when he defines the word "spirit" as the equivalent of the word "storm" (*Sturm*) to enthuse the students of the SA (*Sturmabteilung*) present in the classroom, it is not as a philosopher that he is expressing himself but as a being who has agreed to put all his faculties at the service of the supremacy of Nazism.

Heidegger's Nazism is already present in his works prior to 1933. If, in *Being and Time,* he becomes discreet because his goal is to obtain Husserl's former position, we already find in it the assertion that human existence cannot accomplish its "authentic destiny" except within "a people, a community." In the context of the times, that thesis refers clearly to the ideas of "community of destiny" and "community of the people," which are the distinctive terms of the National Socialists of the day.

What is particularly serious is that these texts — as fundamentally destructive of the human being and of philosophy as those that exalt the "voice of the blood" and the "forces of earth and blood," those that legitimate "racial selection" and "racial thought" and deny the specificity of the Hitlerian genocide and even the human essence of its victims — have been included in the *Gesamtausgabe* without the least disclaimer on the part of either their author or the editors. Thus it is definitively established at present that Heidegger's Nazism was absolutely not a "mistake" from which he subsequently recovered. The author of the rectoral address identified himself willingly with that enterprise and affirmed the "inner truth," the "greatness," and the — in his view — "satisfactory" direction taken by the Nazi movement. With the work of Heidegger, it is the principles of Hitlerism and Nazism that have been introduced into the philosophy libraries of the planet.

In this connection, it is deeply shocking to see Hermann Heidegger, the responsible party for the entire project and its principal executor, publish the most frightening and offensive lectures and speeches, such as those of April 1933, in which the entire eugenics policy of Nazism is justified in volume 16, under the title *Speeches and Other Signs of a Life Path*. Indeed, how is it possible to propose to young philosophers as a "life path" texts in which respect for human life is openly destroyed? Furthermore, I cannot accept the denial of the editor, who, in the presentation of the volume, dares to say that Martin Heidegger had no fascist leanings. And we are led to wonder whether Hermann Heidegger, who was, according to his own testimony, much more of a National Socialist than his parents during the 1930s, and whom we know to be close to the revisionist historian Ernst Nolte, may not share the political views expressed by Martin Heidegger in his rectoral speech. After all, Hermann Heidegger did not hesitate to discuss Heidegger's work recently in the *Junge Freiheit*, a periodical of Germany's extreme right.[2] In the course of that interview he states specifically that the rectoral address — which, as we have seen, praises the "new student law," the "forces of earth and blood," and the *Führerprinzip* — parts of which were published on two occasions by Forsthoff (with the official stamp of approval of the NSDAP) next to speeches by Goebbels and Rosenberg — "was not a National Socialist speech"! It would be difficult to go further in the direction of the denial of historical truth.

That is why it is necessary today to wonder whether it is acceptable for the manuscripts of authors like Heidegger or Baeumler, sixty years after the Liberation, to continue to be inaccessible and controlled by close relatives whose intentions are openly revisionist and apologetic. These archives should be open to all scholars in the name of historical truth.

In order to preserve the future of philosophical thought, it is equally indispensable for us to inquire into the true nature of Heidegger's *Gesamtausgabe*, a collection of texts containing principles that are racist, eugenic, and radically deleterious to the existence of human reason. Such a work cannot continue to be placed in the philosophy section of libraries; its place is rather in the historical archives of Nazism and Hitlerism. That is why we must hope that that work, translated and commented on worldwide, will be the object of far deeper research, which will facilitate a clearer view of its meaning, an awareness of its dangers, resistance to the destructive principles it harbors, and opposition to their being spread both in philosophy itself and in philosophical instruction.

These questions call for a fundamental debate. They also require further research, focusing specifically on Heidegger's writings and activities during the war (1939–1945) and his strategy for legitimating his past writings during the decades following the war and preceding his death (1946–1976). Studies must be conducted on how the myth and the cult of the person of Heidegger were developed. They will reveal that his power of fascination was largely tributary to the considerable sway Nazism and Hitlerism exerted over minds, whether directly or insidiously. It is deeply troubling to observe that two of the main defenders of Heidegger, Jean Beaufret and François Fédier, who played a major role in the spread of his doctrine in France, went so far, in the case of the first, as to embrace Robert Faurisson's negationism, and in the second to write in favor of Ernst Nolte.

Outside the circle of apologists grouped in their unconditional allegiance to the "master," the influence of Heidegger in France underwent three great waves. They must be brought up in order to focus on the reasons behind the lack of serious research and absence of vigilance that may have led their representatives to participate, with varying degrees of explicitness and directness, in the dissemination and legitimation of that work.

The first wave, associated with the translation of the lecture titled "What Is Metaphysics?" and excerpts from *Being and Time* published together by Henry Corbin in 1938, was mainly that of Jean-Paul Sartre's existentialism. The author of *Being and Nothingness* did much to popularize the Heideggerian "being-with," or *Mitsein*, but in a very watered-down version. Despite Heidegger's insistence on the necessity for "struggle" in order to free the "power of destiny," Sartre does not seem to have perceived the whole political dimension of "community" or *Gemeinschaft*. To him, the "empirical image" that seemed be the best suited to convey the Heideggerian "we" was not the "struggle" but the *"team"* [*"équipe"*]. It is true that Sartre did not have at his disposal, in 1943, texts and documents now in print.

The second wave, quite different and even in opposition to the first in its presuppositions, followed the publication of the letter to Jean Beaufret in 1947 known as the *Letter on Humanism*. This was the "anti-humanism" of the generation of Louis Althusser and Michel Foucault, who, in their last years, acknowledged the ascendance exerted on them by Heidegger. It was a time when his influence led many to challenge all philosophy of man and consciousness. It was fashionable to brush aside Sartre's "humanism" with disdain. The fact that Heidegger had begun by writing to Sartre and commending him, even inviting him to Todtnauberg, was generally not known. It was not until after having understood that Sartre was not going to lend him his support that, in an about-face whose motives were strategic rather than philosophical, Heidegger set about attacking him publicly.

The third wave, inspired mainly by the collection of lectures published in 1968 in *Questions I* and by the publication of the translation of his *Nietzsche* in 1971 (the reading of which also left its mark on Foucault), was the result of a more insistent reading of Heidegger. His representatives imposed the theme of the "end of metaphysics" and of its being "gone beyond," without any deep inquiry into the real meaning of "metaphysics" in his writings, especially in the courses of the years 1939–1942. This is the provenance of "deconstruction," which, translating Heidegger's *Abbau* and *Destruktion*, departed France in conquest of the "humanities departments" of American universities, at first with the critical support of Paul de Man.[3] That endeavor made it possible for Heidegger to expand to the United States and subsequently to the entire world, to the point of making him appear to be the chief representative of what has been called "continental philosophy." The Heideggerian hermeneutics also penetrated large domains of academic life in France, even in the area of Cartesian studies, where it spread the view—which could be read in 1981 on the flap copy of the books in the collection "Épiméthée"—that Heidegger represented the "end" of metaphysics and the "only path" for thought, whereas we know today that his doctrine is a journey without return, in which philosophy's contribution is discredited and destroyed.

I, having chosen a very different path, have long concentrated my research on humanist thought, in order to show the remarkable contribution to modern philosophy of thinkers as different as Charles de Bovelles, Michel de Montaigne, and René Descartes, whose efforts have resulted in a better understanding of the evolution of the human being and the achievement of his own perfection, without confining him within a preconceived doctrine or system. Moreover, I have been led to inquire into the nature of the premises from which a work such as that of Heidegger's proceeds. It does not fall within the tradition of philosophy that stands at the service of human evolution, but has on the contrary aimed at destroying its essential contribution. After having intervened in the public debate on Heidegger's opposition to the humanist thought of the Renaissance and having developed, in several conferences and seminars, a general critique of Heidegger's texts devoted to Descartes, I wanted to get a clear view of the origin of the problem itself by investigating the foundations on which Heidegger's positions were based.

As I discovered new texts, my research brought me to the realization that Heidegger was intimately nourished on National Socialism and that he served it whole-heartedly, to the point of trying to introduce the racist basis of Hitlerism into philosophy. Thus, Heidegger spoke in his courses, with reference to National Socialism, of a "great transformation in the existence [*Dasein*] of man" and intended to raise racial selection to the dignity of a way of thinking! Refusal to consider such a work as philosophical and resistance to the spread, through teaching, of writings that have let the most destructive principles infiltrate the mind: these are the measures necessary if we do not wish to see the eventual return, in other forms, of an endeavor that nearly led to the spiritual, moral, and physical annihilation of humanity.

We must acknowledge that an author who has espoused the foundations of Nazism cannot be considered a philosopher. The vocation of philosophy is to serve the evolution of man. It is totally incompatible with a doctrine that, claiming to promote a particular people, language, and "race" by dominating to the point of annihilation everything that is different from them, destroys the very being of man, both in his individual existence and in his universality. Further, it is historically established that Heidegger did not simply give in to the temptation of a partial and temporary compromise agreement with the regime in place, but that he put all his energies at the service of Hitler's rule and derived from that undertaking a taste for dictatorial authority that has lived on in his followers.

How was such a work able to procure for itself a planetary public? The objective of this entire work is to call for a general consciousness-raising. The moment has come to resist the ill-advised opinion that Heidegger was a "great philosopher" of the past century. An author who, in both his writings and his deeds, has destroyed all morality, impugned the faculties of understanding and reason, destroyed metaphysics by confusing it with "nihilism," and related the "truth of being" to a racist principle cannot appropriately be called a "philosopher."

In our societies we recognize the vileness of deeds and the monstrousness of those politically responsible for them, but we do not see with sufficient clarity the danger of writings. While the atrocity of the genocide ordered by Hitler is very widely condemned, we are not ready to assess the danger that the introduction of Hitlerism and Nazism poses for thought. Yet it is *through the texts* that the homicidal movements continue to act upon minds, destroying all critical sense and insidiously rehabilitating the most devastating worldviews. It is the role of philosophy to prevent these risks and preserve men whole from them. Philosophy has the capability to sound the depths of works and gauge what they bring to human evolution, opposing all that would destroy man's very being.

The crises we go through should prompt us to the greatest vigilance. Let us remember the premonitory way in which Henri Bergson already in 1914 had foreseen the dangers of a "culture" adrift, which had accepted the idea of a "chosen people, a race of masters next to the others who are a race of slaves." We must therefore study with more critical lucidity the real content and meaning of certain works intended to captivate minds. We must be mindful that behind its masks of legal "erudition" and political "vision" the works of a Carl Schmitt signal the demise of justice and the radical perversion of the idea of a European space; that behind the pretense of a false historical "impartiality" those of an Ernst Nolte constitute the negation of historical truth; and that beneath the cover of philosophical "greatness" those of Martin Heidegger aim at the destruction of philosophy and the eradication of human meaning. We must be aware of this if we wish to put an end to the progressive spread of underlying Nazi principles these texts intend.

The *völkisch* and fundamentally racist principles Heidegger's *Gesamtausgabe* transmits strive toward the goal of the eradication of all the intellectual and human progress to which philosophy has contributed. They are therefore as destructive and dangerous to current thought as the Nazi movement was to the physical existence of the exterminated peoples. Indeed, what can be the result of granting a future to a doctrine whose author desired to become the "spiritual Führer" of Nazism, other than to pave the way to the same perdition? In that respect, we now know that Martin Heidegger, in his unpublished seminar on Hegel and the state, meant to make the Nazi domination last beyond the next hundred years. If his writings continue to proliferate without our being able to stop this intrusion of Nazism into human education, how can we not expect them to lead to yet another translation into facts and acts, from which this time humanity might not be able to recover? Today more than ever, it is philosophy's task to work to protect humanity and alert men's minds; failing this, Hitlerism and Nazism will continue to germinate through Heidegger's writings at the risk of spawning new attempts at the complete destruction of thought and the extermination of humankind.

Appendixes

Appendix A
The Political Trustworthiness of the *Parteigenosse* Heidegger According to the Secret Reports of the SD

      Hoping to pass for an adversary of the regime plagued by persecution, Heidegger claimed, in 1945, that his teaching during the time of his courses on Nietzsche had been under surveillance by the security service of the Reichsführer of the SS, or the SD. The "Heidegger file," probably seized by the French authorities in 1945 from the Karlsruhe ministry for Baden, and today kept at the Ministry of Foreign Affairs, makes it possible for us to give an update on that question, and more generally to establish how Heidegger was seen by the Nazi regime.[1]

It is true that there was at least one SD report on Heidegger. There is nothing surprising about that in a Nazi state in which this was current, if not general, practice, especially if, as in Heidegger's case, you had adversaries like Ernst Krieck in the party or even in the SD. The important thing is the overall impression given by the documents collected about him. It is extremely unpleasant to deal with such documents, which bring us into contact with the dregs of the functioning of a totalitarian police state, but it is necessary if we are to know the historical truth, given that Heidegger personally brought up the SD surveillance. I will not present a complete inventory of the file on Heidegger, which contains twenty-eight items, ordered from the most recent to the oldest. Many are just administrative forms. I will limit myself to quoting elements of significance for our purpose. But I should point out that, viewing the file from the oldest to the most recent items, two parts may be distinguished. Items 28 through 12 contain exchanges of letters and Nazi expert opinions from April 1938 to October 1943, while items eleven to one concern Heidegger's "de-Nazification" by the French authorities. I will not discuss that second part of the file, which would require a separate study, which has already been begun by Silke Seemann. Item 27 is a typed letter dated 12 April 1938 in which the regional service head (*Gaustellenleiter*) requests that the district National Socialist Party leaders (*Kreisleitung der NSDAP*) of the Freiburg Personnel Office furnish expert opinions and inquiries by the twenty-sixth of that same month on Dr. Martin Heidegger. Item 26 is a "questionnaire for political evaluation"; it is a printed document marked "Strictly Confidential" (*Streng vertraulich!*). It is dated 11 May 1938. Section 2, titled "Political antecedents," reads:

> *Has he ever given concrete proof of his opposition to the NSDAP?* No.
>   *Has he ever been a Freemason?* No.
>   *Did he speak out in favor of the NSDAP before its coming to power?* Yes.

In section 3, titled "Position with Respect to the National Socialist State and the National Collectivity," we read the following responses.

> *Does he have a subscription to the party press?* Yes.
>   *Do his children belong to a National Socialist Youth Organization?* Yes. . . .
>   *Is he a generous donor?* Yes, sometimes that could be better [*ja, dürfte manchmal besser sein*].
>   *Does he approve of the National Socialist state?* Yes.
>   *Has he ever made negative remarks about it?* No.
>   *Is he capable of exerting a positive effect on the people pedagogically?* Yes, on a theoretical level [*ja, in der Theorie*].
>   *Does he buy from Jews?* No.
>   *Does he have political/confessional ties?* No.

In section 4, titled "Willingness to Cooperate," we find the following clarifications. Beyond the fact, which is well known, that he had been a member of the NSDAP since 1 May 1933 (membership number 3-125-894), Heidegger was also a member of two other organizations since 1933–1934: the RLB/Dozenten, which grouped the teachers attached to the "National Air Raid Protection League" (Reichsluftschutzbund), and the NSV (Nationalsozialistische Volkswohlfahrt).

Section 5, titled "Psychological Evaluation," reads: "Character somewhat withdrawn, not very close to the people, lives only for his scholarship, does not always have a firm footing in reality."[2] And to the question *Reactionary, argumentative, critical?* the response is: No.

In section 6, titled "Overall Judgment," the fact that he is a "virulent adversary of Catholicism" (*erbitterter Gegner des Katholizismus*) is emphasized. And to the question, *Is he politically reliable or unreliable?* the answer is "reliable."

In short, we see that Heidegger's political reliability is evaluated in a positive way, and at all levels. He has a subscription to the NSDAP press — that is, he presumably receives daily deliveries of the *Völkischer Beobachter* and probably also of *Der Alemanne* at his domicile from 1933 to 1945. Now you have to have examined one day in your life a copy of the *Völkischer Beobachter* to understand what it might mean to receive and read such a newspaper daily in one's home. Heidegger does not buy "from Jews" and has sometimes been a "generous donor." Not only has he never criticized the Nazi state, but he spoke up in favor of Nazism *before* it took power. He is a member not only of the party but also of two other affiliated organizations. Only the character study expresses some reservations, but it is stressed, as an obviously positive point for the NSDAP, that he is a virulent adversary of Catholicism.

We also find, in item 23, a one-page typed anonymous report on Heidegger, which was probably sent less than a month after the questionnaire as a supplement to it. Indeed, we find as item 22 a mailing receipt dated 3 June 1938, by the Security Service or SD (Sicherheitsdienst des Reichsführers SS). Thus we have in this document a clear idea of the SD's judgment of Heidegger in 1938. The report briefly summarizes the stages of his career. The resignation from the rectorship is mentioned, as well as the reason for it. "He left his post in 1934, given the fact that he did not possess the tactical capacities required for that post."[3]

We see that Heidegger's resignation was absolutely not perceived as the expression of a political distance taken up toward the regime.

The author of the report notes that Heidegger cuts himself off from the outer world before associating again with his colleagues beginning in the years 1936–1937. The appreciation of his "philosophy" and his character are not unmitigated, and it is probable that they show the effects of the campaign mounted against him beginning in 1934 by such men as Walter Gross, Erich Jaensch, and Ernst Krieck. Nevertheless, the report ends on a positive note, insisting on his hostile attitude toward Catholicism. "Setting out from Kierkegaard's conflicts with the Church and from Husserlian phenomenology, in an independent development, he placed himself in increasing opposition to the Church and to Christianity in general. . . . In sum, it may be said that within the framework of the University of Freiburg, Heidegger represents a positive force, due to his sharp and clear attitude toward Catholic power groups and other Christian groups."[4]

Just as in the questionnaire, it is therefore the hostility of Heidegger toward Catholicism that is retained as the most positive point, particularly in the context of Freiburg. Moreover, there is no allusion to his teaching that would lead one to suspect that he expressed the slightest criticism of the regime in power in his classes. More generally, there is not a thing in this report from the SD that would indicate the existence of opposition to National Socialism on Heidegger's part.

The file contains no item for the period between 1938 and 1941, and more specifically there is no trace of any banning of a seminar on Jünger in 1940, contrary to what Heidegger claimed in 1945. On 29 July 1941, a letter from the Ministry of Foreign Affairs in Berlin addressed to the management of the Baden *Gau* of the NSDAP requests a political opinion on Martin Heidegger as well as on a certain Miss Brückler, a doctoral student in geography (item 21), a request possibly related to the fact that he accepted several invitations at that time to conferences in Spain and Portugal that he was forced to cancel due to the turn taken by the war. Shortly thereafter, on 6 August 1941, there is a letter from the NSDAP of Karlsruhe to the NSDAP of Freiburg requesting an immediate political evaluation of Heidegger (item 20), probably relaying the request from Berlin. In response, there is a letter on NSDAP, *Gau* Baden of Freiburg letterhead, dated 20 August 1941 and signed by a certain Dr. Glattes (item 19). The latter writes: "I am sending you, attached, a copy of a political evaluation, dated 7 June 1940.[5] As soon as the director of the Union of Professors returns from vacation, I will have another interview with him, since the present evaluation of Professor Heidegger is not entirely equitable."[6]

The political evaluation in question does not appear in the file kept at Colmar. But the reason for Dr. Glattes's obvious discomfiture and his concern to protect Heidegger as much as possible is explained by what follows. After another exchange of letters, we find the following letter sent by the Freiburg NSDAP on 29 September 1941 (item no. 15): "I inform you that I sent on 12 September 1941 various expert opinions that had been made available to me by the head of the Union of Professors. These expert opinions are also in keeping with the evaluation produced by the head of the Union of Professors. Additionally, I would like to draw your attention to the fact that fellow party member Dr. Krieck is an irreconcilable adversary of fellow party member Heidegger, whose person and scholarship he totally rejects. Heil Hitler! The Central Services Regional Director."[7]

Again, we do not have the text of these expert opinions. But the letter from the local responsible party of the NSDAP reveals several important things, in assessing the play of forces between Heidegger and his main adversary at the heart of Nazism. In 1941, the head of the Union of Professors (*Dozentenbundsführer*) for Baden is none other than Ernst Krieck. The "expert opinions" he was able to supply are surely unfavorable to Heidegger. But the bureaucrats of the NSDAP protect Heidegger by pointing out on each occasion Krieck's personal hostility toward him.

In the file at Colmar, we find but one long "expert opinion" on Heidegger typed by Krieck, dated 14 October 1943. It is accompanied by a letter dated 23 October 1943, sent by the regional Führer of students (*Gaustudentenführer*) to Schuppel, the head of the regional cabinet, in Strasbourg. It reads as follows: "I send you, attached, an evaluation of Professor Heidegger of Freiburg, written by Professor Krieck of Heidelberg. Although this evaluation is very partial and even partially polemic and does not constitute, therefore, a totally serviceable document, it does contain useful details that may interest you concerning Professor Heidegger's career. Heil Hitler! Angst, delegate for the South."[8]

We see that this Führer of students (who answers to the name of Angst) also emphasizes, just as district head Glattes had done earlier, Krieck's personal and clearly well-known hostility. It is therefore confirmation of the fact that Krieck, despite his position as "head of the Union of Professors" for Baden, was scarcely credible, and his power was probably very limited at the beginning of the 1940s, as he was presented in this way in several official letters. As for his expert opinion, it contains hateful assertions, reminiscent of the report in which Heidegger brought up Baumgarten's frequentation of the "Jew Fraenkel" to discredit him in the eyes of the

Nazi authorities. Krieck asserts that "at Marburg, Heidegger was in the closest contact with Jews."[9] Moreover, he criticizes him for practicing a philosophy analogous to the spiritual exercises of the Jesuits and for setting up his domination in an empire in which he himself was "the sovereign, the pope, and the mystagogue."[10] Krieck also notes analogies between Heidegger's teaching and Rudolph Steiner's anthroposophy, as well as the Stefan George circle.

One point about that "expert opinion" is worth remembering: If Krieck means to discredit Heidegger's teaching by presenting the latter as the master of a secret cenacle, he does not challenge his political trustworthiness. Thus, in all the items contained in the "Heidegger dossier" of Karlsruhe, kept presently in Colmar, there is no sign of a negative evaluation having been kept with respect to his political attitude. And it may be assumed that Krieck, in view of what he has written, would not have spared Heidegger if he had been able to keep something credible that went against him.

Heidegger's service record prepared by the Ministry of Education of the Reich and kept in the Bundesarchiv of Berlin confirms this state of affairs. In 1943, we read: "Papiereingabe vom 30/6/43 für Heidegger'sche Schriften, Verlag Klostermann." In the middle of a world war, the Ministry of the Reich orders a delivery of paper to Klostermann Press to print Heidegger, several of whose lectures are to be published. In that same year of 1943, he is authorized to take a vacation in Strasbourg from 9 to 21 October. It is reasonable to assume that he visited the Nazi jurist Ernst Rudolph Huber, who was part of the small circle of intimates and taught *völkisch* law at the University of Strasbourg. All these elements prove that Heidegger continued to be well viewed by the Nazi regime in 1943.

Appendix B
Excerpt from Heidegger's Rectorship Address, Published
Alongside the Anti-Semitic Theses of the Deutsche
Studentenschaft in 1938 by Ernst Forsthoff

4. Unser gefährlichster Widersacher ist der Jude und der, der ihm hörig ist.

5. Der Jude kann nur jüdisch denken. Schreibt er deutsch, dann lügt er. Der Deutsche, der deutsch schreibt, aber jüdisch denkt, ist ein Verräter. Der Student, der undeutsch spricht und schreibt, ist außerdem gedankenlos und wird seiner Aufgabe untreu.

6. Wir wollen die Lüge ausmerzen, wir wollen den Verrat brandmarken, wir wollen für den Studenten nicht Stätten der Gedankenlosigkeit, sondern der Zucht und der politischen Erziehung.

7. Wir wollen den Juden als Fremdling achten, und wir wollen das Volkstum ernst nehmen.
   Wir fordern deshalb von der Zensur:
   Jüdische Werke erscheinen in hebräischer Sprache.
   Erscheinen sie in Deutsch, sind sie als Übersetzung zu kennzeichnen.
   Schärfstes Einschreiten gegen den Mißbrauch der deutschen Schrift.
   Deutsche Schrift steht nur dem Deutschen zur Verfügung. Der undeutsche Geist wird aus öffentlichen Büchereien ausgemerzt.

8. Wir fordern vom deutschen Studenten Wille und Fähigkeit zur selbständigen Erkenntnis und Entscheidung.

9. Wir fordern vom deutschen Studenten den Willen und die Fähigkeit zur Reinerhaltung der deutschen Sprache.

10. Wir fordern vom deutschen Studenten den Willen und die Fähigkeit zur Überwindung des jüdischen Intellektualismus und der damit verbundenen liberalen Verfallserscheinungen im deutschen Geistesleben.

11. Wir fordern die Auslese von Studenten und Professoren nach der Sicherheit des Denkens im deutschen Geiste.

12. Wir fordern die deutsche Hochschule als Hort des deutschen Volkstums und als Kampfstätte aus der Kraft des deutschen Geistes.
    Die Deutsche Studentenschaft.

Sich selbst das Gesetz geben, ist höchste Freiheit. Die viel be-
sungene „akademische Freiheit" wird aus der deutschen Universität verstoßen; denn diese Freiheit war unecht, weil nur ver-
neinend. Sie bedeutete vorwiegend Unbekümmertheit, Belie-
bigkeit der Absichten und Neigungen, Ungebundenheit im Tun
und Lassen. Der Begriff der Freiheit des deutschen Studenten
wird jetzt zu seiner Wahrheit zurückgebracht. Aus ihr entfalten
sich künftig Bindung und Dienst der deutschen Studentenschaft.

Die erste Bindung ist die in die Volksgemeinschaft. Sie ver-
pflichtet zum mittragenden und mithandelnden Teilhaben am
Mühen, Trachten und Können aller Stände und Glieder des
Volkes. Diese Bindung wird fortan festgemacht und in das
studentische Dasein eingewurzelt durch den Arbeitsdienst.

Die zweite Bindung ist die an die Ehre und an das Geschick
der Nation inmitten der anderen Völker. Sie verlangt die in
Wissen und Können gesicherte und durch Zucht gestraffte Bereitschaft zum Einsatz bis ins Letzte. Diese Bindung umgreift
und durchdringt künftig das ganze studentische Dasein als
Wehrdienst.

Die dritte Bindung der Studentenschaft ist die an den geistigen Auftrag des deutschen Volkes. Dieses Volk wird an seinem Schicksal, indem es seine Geschichte in die Offenbarkeit
der Übermacht aller weltbildenden Mächte des menschlichen
Daseins hineinstellt und sich seine geistige Welt immer neu erkämpft, so ausgesetzt in die äußerste Fragwürdigkeit des eigenen Daseins, will dies Volk ein geistiges Volk sein. Es for-
dert von sich und für sich in seinen Führern und Hütern die
härteste Klarheit des höchsten, weitesten und reichsten Wissens. Eine studentische Jugend, die früh sich in die Mannheit
hineinwagt und ihr Wollen über das künftige Geschick der
Nation ausspannt, zwingt sich von Grund aus zum Dienst an
diesem Wissen. Hier wird der Wissensdienst nicht mehr sein
dürfen die dumpfe und schnelle Abrichtung zu einem „vor-
nehmen" Beruf. Weil der Staatsmann und Lehrer, der Arzt
und Richter, der Pfarrer und der Baumeister, das völkisch-
staatliche Dasein führen und in seinen Grundbezügen zu den

Notes

Foreword to the English Edition

1. Hans-Georg Gadamer, "Superficiality and Ignorance: On Farías' Publication," in *Martin Heidegger and National Socialism: Questions and Answers,* ed. E. Kettering and G. Neske (New York: Paragon House, 1990), 142.

2. See Karl Löwith, *My Life in Germany Before and After 1933: A Report,* trans. Elizabeth King (Urbana: University of Illinois Press, 1994).

3. See Karl Löwith, "Les implications politiques de la philosophie de l'existence chez Heidegger," in *Les Temps modernes* 2, no. 14 (November 1946): 343–360.

4. See Georg Lukács, *Existentialisme ou Marxisme?* trans. E. Kelemen (Paris: Les Editions Nagel, 1961).

5. See Palmier, *Les Écrits politiques de Heidegger.*

6. See Robert Faurisson, *Écrits révisionnistes (1974–1998),* 4 vols. (privately published, 1999). Faurisson was associated with other French historical revisionists who denied the existence of the Holocaust, such as Paul Rassinier and Maurice Bardèche.

7. Bekenntnis zu Adolf Hitler und die Nationalsozialistischen Staat, dated 11 November 1933.

8. See Farías, *Heidegger et le nazisme.*

9. Ibid., 14.

10. Hugo Ott, "Wege und Abwege: Zu Victor Farías' kritischer Heidegger-Studie," *Neue Zürcher Zeitung,* no. 275 (27 November 1987): 67.

11. See Bourdieu, *L'Ontologie politique de Martin Heidegger*; Jean-François Lyotard, *Heidegger et "les juifs"* (Paris: Editions Galilée, 1988); Fédier, *Heidegger: Anatomie d'un*

scandale; Lacoue-Labarthe, *La Fiction du politique*; Derrida, *De l'esprit: Heidegger et la question*; Dominique Janicaud, *L'Ombre de cette pensée: Heidegger et la question politique* (Grenoble: Jérôme Millon, 1990); Alain Renaut and Luc Ferry, *Heidegger et les modernes* (Paris: Grasset, 1988).

12. "Je crois à la nécessité d'exhiber, si possible sans limites, les adhérences profondes du texte heideggérien (écrits et actes) à la possibilité et à la réalité de tous les nazismes." (Jacques Derrida, "Heidegger, l'enfer des philosophes," *Le Nouvel Observateur*, 6–12 November 1987, 170–174.)

13. See Janicaud, *Heidegger en France.*

14. See Tilitzki, *Die deutsche Universitätsphilosophie.*

15. See Marion Heinz and Goran Gretić, *Philosophie und Zeitgeist im Nationalsozialismus* (Würzburg: Königshausen und Neumann, 2006).

16. See Antonia Grunenberg, *Hannah Arendt und Martin Heidegger: Geschichte einer Liebe* (Munich: Piper Verlag, 2006).

17. See Yves-Charles Zarka, *Un détail nazi dans la pensée de Carl Schmitt* (Paris: Presses Universitaires de France, 2005).

18. See *Le Monde des livres,* 14 October 1987.

19. See Sluga, *Heidegger's Crisis.*

20. Flasch was extremely positive. See Kurt Flasch, "Er war ein nationalsozialistischer Philosoph; Mit Emmanuel Fayes Buch gibt es eine neue, notwendige Debatte über den braunen Faden in Martin Heideggers Denken," *Süddeutsche Zeitung,* 14 June 2005.

21. See Roger-Pol Droit, "Les crimes d'idées de Schmitt et Heidegger," *Le Monde,* 25 March 2005.

22. See Jean Birnbaum, "Pour la jeune garde heideggérienne, l'oeuvre est indemne de toute impregnation nazie," *Le Monde,* 25 March 2005.

23. See Maxence Caron, *Heidegger: Pensée de l'être et origine de la subjectivité* (Paris: Le Cerf, 2005).

24. See Birnbaum, "Pour la jeune garde heideggérienne."

25. Action Française is a royalist political movement concerned with the restoration of the French monarchy. It is linked to the extreme right-wing political ideas of Joseph de Maistre.

26. See François Fédier, *Heidegger: A plus forte raison* (Paris: Fayard, 2007).

27. See Chapter 7, "György Lukács: Reason in the Service of Dogma," in Leszek Kolakowski, *Main Currents of Marxism,* trans. P. S. Falla (Oxford: Clarendon Press, 1978), 253–307.

28. See Edmund Husserl, *The Crisis of European Sciences and Transcendental Phenomenology: An Introduction to Transcendental Phenomenology,* trans. David Carr (Evanston, Ill.: Northwestern University Press, 1970), 12.

29. See Martin Heidegger, *Being and Time,* trans. John Macquarrie and Edward Robinson (Evanston, Ill.: Harper and Row, 1962), paras. 1–4, pp. 2–35.

30. "Letter on Humanism," in Martin Heidegger, *Basic Writings,* trans. David Farrell Krell (New York: Harper and Row, 1977), 218.

31. Ibid., 219.

32. Ibid., 222.

33. See "Philosophy as Rigorous Science," in Edmund Husserl, *Phenomenology and the Crisis of Philosophy,* trans. Quentin Lauer (New York: Harper and Row, 1965), 71–148.

Chapter 1: Before 1933

1. Heidegger's project of a fundamental ontology bears traces of the influence of his first teacher, Carl Braig, the author of *Vom Sein: Abriß der Ontologie*. In this work, ontology is conceived as "fundamental knowledge" (p. 6), and there is a section on "the ontological meaning of the concept of time." This is, then, an important source of what has survived of a neo-scholastic core in Heidegger's work. Konrad Gröber, who became the archbishop of Freiburg, was one of the main architects of the Concordat between the Catholic Church and Hitler in 1933. He then entered the SA and the SS, where he remained until 1939. In 1945 Gröber protected Hitler during the de-Nazification process.

2. Karl Löwith, "Les Implications politiques de la philosophie de l'existence de Martin Heidegger," *Les Temps modernes*, no. 4 (November 1946): 346, 353.

3. Löwith, "Der okkasionelle Dezisionismus von C. Schmitt," 61–71.

4. Löwith, "Les Implications politiques," 347.

5. See Farías, *Heidegger and Nazism*, 35.

6. "einen bestimmten Kreis" (*Martin Heidegger/Karl Jaspers*, 17); "Dabei merken sie nicht, wie scharf ich sie in der Kontrolle habe" (ibid.); "Schwarmgeister (Theosophen . . .) Georgeaner und ähnl" (ibid., 19).

7. *Heidegger/Jaspers*, 14 July 1923, 41.

8. "die Schar der Heideggerschen Elite die ihn begleitete" (Toni Cassirer, *Aus meinem Leben mit Ernst Cassirer*, 165–167; quoted in Schneeberger, *Nachlese zu Heidegger*, 8).

9. "je organischer und konkreter und unauffälliger der Umsturz sich vollzieht, um so nachhaltiger und sicherer wird er sein" (*Heidegger/Jaspers*, 42); "einer unsichtbaren Gemeinschaft" (ibid.).

10. Martin Heidegger to Karl Löwith, 19 August 1921, quoted in Barash, *Heidegger et son siècle*, 80n3.

11. *Heidegger/Jaspers*, 221. Today we can assess the considerable importance of Spengler's influence on Heidegger's conception of politics: see Chapter 9, 260–262.

12. Dilthey, *Briefwechsel zwischen Wilhelm Dilthey und dem Grafen Paul Yorck*.

13. Ibid., 254.

14. Heidegger, *Les Conférences de Cassel*, 177.

15. Ibid., 154.

16. Clauß, *Die nordische Seele*.

17. Heidegger, *Les Conférences de Cassel*, 179.

18. See Heidegger's letter to Rothacker, 11 August 1934, in Theodore Kisiel, "Martin Heidegger und die Deutsche Vierteljahrschrift," *Dilthey-Jahrbuch* 8 (1993): 223. An excerpt from this text appears later in the present work.

19. Rothacker, *Geschichtsphilosophie*, 86, 108–109.

20. "we find" (Heidegger, *Les Conférences de Cassel*, 204–206); "the future that we" (ibid., 206); "the existence of our nation" (ibid., 202); "loss of history" (ibid., 148).

21. *Sein und Zeit*, 10, p. 46. (While Emmanuel Martineau's out-of-print and unobtainable translation, published in 1985, remains the most readable, no complete French translation of *Being and Time* succeeds in avoiding the use of many neologisms, even when Heidegger himself uses current terms. My quotations are therefore retranslated from the German.)

22. Ibid., 25, pp. 116, 118.

23. "Die Selbigkeit des eigentlich existierenden Selbst ist . . . ontologisch durch eine Kluft getrennt von der Identität des . . . Ich" (ibid., 130; Heidegger's ellipses).

24. "Das Geschick setzt sich nicht aus einzelnen Schicksalen zusammen, sowenig als das Miteinandersein als ein Zusammenvorkommen mehrerer Subjekte begriffen werden kann" (ibid., 74, p. 384).

25. Ibid., 197.

26. Tilitzki, *Die deutsche Universitätsphilosophie in der Weimarer Republik und im Dritten Reich,* 1054. This work is quoted for certain factual information it conveys; I do not in the least approve its manner of interpretation, which is openly revisionist, explicitly taken from Heidegger and Ernst Nolte; it will become the subject of a necessary discussion at the appropriate time. (See below, pp. 313–315.)

27. See GA 90, 44, 187.

28. Heidegger, *Sein und Zeit,* 7, p. 38.

29. Ibid., 8, p. 40.

30. Habermas, *Martin Heidegger,* 21.

31. "der Ansatz eines zunächst gegebenen Ich und Subjekts den phänomenalen Bestand des Daseins von Grund aus verfehlt" (*Sein und Zeit,* 10, p. 46).

32. Ibid., 18, p. 89.

33. "Die Weisheit etwa eines Heidegger: 'Was ich denke, das sage ich, wenn ich Ordinarius bin,' hat mir in der Jugend gefehlt, und heute ist es zu spät." Letter of 1 December 1954 from Ludwig Ferdinand Clauß to Erich Rothacker, Rothacker Collection, Bonn, quoted in Böhnigk, *Kulturanthropologie als Rassenlehre,* 131.

34. "Zusammen mit dem Husserl-Schüler L. F. Clauß beschäftigte Becker sich früh mit der Rassenlehre" (Tilitzki, *Die deutsche Universitätsphilosophie,* 268–269).

35. "Er sei dann gottgläubig 'im Sinne Goethes und Hölderlins' geworden" (ibid.). The manner in which Tilitzki associates Goethe and Hölderlin seems problematic, considering how much Heidegger and the German extreme right disassociate them. (See below, pp. 300–301.)

36. Heidegger did, however, as he amply emphasized after 1945, keep his more discreet note on Husserl on page 38.

37. "entscheidende Ruf des Schicksals" (Clauß, *Die nordische Seele,* 121–122).

38. Ibid., 122.

39. "einen Boden zu finden, auf dem sich eine neue Gemeinschaft des Verstehens gründen läßt" (ibid., 124).

40. Ibid., 146.

41. Ibid., 216.

42. Ibid., 234.

43. "in artlicher Verbundenheit mit ihrem Ausdrucksfeld, dem Leibe" (ibid., 147).

44. Édouard Conte and Cornelia Essner, *La Quête de la race, une anthropologie du nazisme* (Paris: Hachette, 1995), 77.

45. See below, p. 269.

46. See Rothacker, *Gedanken über Martin Heidegger.*

47. Heidegger, *Sein und Zeit,* 197.

48. Tilitzki, *Die deutsche Universitätsphilosophie,* 931–932.

49. Rothacker, *Geschichtsphilosophie,* 86.

50. "die Welt, in der ein Mensch lebt, steht in einer strengen Wechselbeziehung zu seinem Sein" (ibid., 108).

51. "Eben hierüber entbrennen Lebenskämpfe. Wir haben nicht je unsere Welt, wir behaupten unsere Welten" (ibid., 109).

52. "Die existentielle Reduktion. Rasse und Volksgeist" (ibid., 132).

53. "Der letzte Motor des geschichtlichen Lebens ist ein existentieller: er ist nicht denkbar ohne den Antrieb der emotionalen Kräfte, sei es der Dranghaft und spontan aus der Tiefe des Seins quellenden, sei es der reaktiven der Angst und bloßen Lebensbehauptung" (ibid., 133).

54. "Auf gar keinen Fall darf die gute Rasse zum Faulbett selbstzufriedener Langköpfe werden und zu einer Unterschätzung der Zucht menschlicher Haltung und Erziehung. Gute Rasse ist historisch wie persönlich eine höchst verantwortungsvolle Aufgabe, deren Lösung auch verfehlt werden kann. Unsere heute reichlich verklärten germanischen Vorfahren wurden durch den relativ größeren Prozentsatz nordischen Blutes, durch das sie sich vor dem heutigen deutschen Durchschnitt auszeichnen, nur wenig vor den Gefahren der Trunksucht, des Spiels, und vor allem ständiger innerer Uneinigkeit bewahrt. Die entscheidenden Schritte zur deutschen Einheit sind offensichtlich nicht der nordischen Rasse, die in Skandinavien reiner ist, sondern dem 'Preußischen Geiste' und dem Geist der NSDAP zu verdanken, d.h. beide Male erkämpften Lebensstilen, Erziehungsprodukten, die, freilich aus dem Geiste nordischer Überlieferungen gezeugt, dennoch aus einem, mit Güntherschen Maßstäben gemessen, rassisch sehr fragwürdigem Rohstoff geformt waren" (ibid., 138).

55. In the bible of Nazi racial doctrine, the Jews are called the *langköpfige Rasse.* See Böhnigk, *Kulturanthropologie als Rassenlehre,* 52, 135.

56. See Essner, "Le dogme nordique des races," 106.

57. On the racial meaning of "bearing" in Rothacker, see the decisive analyses of Böhnigk, *Kulturanthropologie als Rassenlehre,* 47–49.

58. "Inzwischen hat der Sieg der nationalen Revolution mit der Aufrichtung des dritten Reiches zugleich ein neues Bild des Menschen aufgerichtet. Die Vollendung und Verwirklichung dieses Bildes ist die weltgeschichtliche Aufgabe des deutschen Volkes.—Was dem Mitlebenden aber einen Ruf zur Tat bedeutet, muß dem Geschichtsphilosophen zur Probe aufs Exempel dienen. Die Grundbegriffe müssen am jüngsten Geschehen dieselbe Bestätigung finden, wie am vergangenen: eine neue Haltung zur Welt als der tragende Kern eines neuen Geschehens; aus dem Blickpunkt der neuen Haltung neu sich erschließende Bedeutsamkeiten; gerundet zu einer neuen 'Welt' und ihrem Korrelat, einem neuen Lebensideal; dies Ideal, lebensgeboren als Ausdruck einer Stellungnahme zur Welt, lebensbezogen; solche neue Haltung, nicht 'von selbst' entstanden, verwirklicht wie durch Naturereignisse, kein 'organisches' Geschehen und keine utopische Konstruktion, sondern aus einer bestimmten geschichtlichen Lage geboren und unter Opfern errungen und erkämpft, innerlich und äußerlich; durch Gesetz gegen Widerstände, feindliche Haltungen und absterbende Welten" (Rothacker, *Geschichtsphilosophie,* 145).

59. "Liegt in dieser Sammlung alles Geschehens in der Mitte eines neuen Lebensstils und Lebensideals die Bestätigung unserer geschichtsphilosophischen Grundauffassung, so mögen zuletzt noch die hauptsächlichsten, im Rahmen dieses Lebensstils um Rang und

Anteil ringenden Leitgedanken unserer Staat und Volk erneuernden Bewegung nach ihrem Beitrag zur theoretischen Auffassung des geschichtlichen Lebens befragt werden. Da ist zunächst die neue Wertung des Staatsgedankens, politisch stärkstens zu betonen in einem so spät staatlich geeinten und staatlich so wenig disziplinierten Volke wie dem deutschen zumal des Westens. Leitgedanke und also Verpflichtung zu langjähriger 'politischer Erziehung,' Bildung und Schulung der jungen Generation; als Gegenspiel tief verankerter liberalistischer Läßlichkeiten völlig unentbehrlich und unbedingt stark zu halten; um der stilistischen Formung und Straffung willen, im Hegelschen wie im antiken Sinne mit größtem Pathos zu beseelen" (ibid., 145–146).

60. On "style," see GA 16, 201; on "bearing," see GA 16, 208, and my analyses, below, pp. 73 and 78.

61. Rothacker, *Geschichtsphilosophie*, 137.

62. The racial significance of the word *Eigenart* is undeniable in the context of Rothacker's text, in which "national education" is subordinated to "the idea of the race."

63. "Woraus mit der Instinktsicherheit des großen Staatsmanns Adolf Hitler die Folgerung gezogen hat, indem sein Lebensbuch der Idee der Volksgemeinschaft die erste Stelle in der Reihenfolge der politischen Werte anweist. Dem Volke in dem zweifachen Sinne, der schon im Volksbegriffe Herders angelegt war: Volk als tragender Grund einer echten nationalen Gemeinschaft und dem Geiste nationaler Eigenart. Also national-sozialistisch, wenn national deutsch, und wenn Sozialismus Volksverbundenheit bedeutet. Wenn dieser soziale Gesichtspunkt heute aus vielen Gründen im Vordergrunde der praktischen Innenpolitik und ihrer Ideologie steht, oft bis hart an die Grenze der Jüngerschen Apotheose des 'Arbeiters' als der einziger volks- und staatsbildenden Schicht, so wäre eine betont 'nationale Erziehung' berufen, neben der 'politischen Erziehung' und 'sozialen Erziehung' einer bewußten Kulturpolitik den dritten unentbehrlichen Leitgedanken zu stellen" (Rothacker, *Geschichtsphilosophie*, 146).

64. "Neben Staatsgedanke, Deutschtumsgedanke, Volksgedanke steht als wesentlicher Bestandteil aller zugleich der Rassegedanke" (ibid).

65. Here Rothacker refers in a footnote to the *Völkischer Beobachter*, no. 245, of Saturday, 2 September 1933.

66. "Zunächst fällt die Spannung der Rasseidee zur Idee des Staates ins Auge, dessen Rahmen durch eine Normierung des Handelns an einem Gemeinschaftsbewußtsein, das noch die Volks, Sprach, Sitte-und Geschichtsgemeinschaft hinausreicht, vollends gesprengt zu werden droht. Das eigentliche Gewicht der übrigen politischen Konsequenzen des Rassegedankens liegt aber vor allem in seinem unzerstörbar aristokratischen Charakter. Daß dieser Zug zunächst mit dem Führergedanken in besonders glücklichem Einklang steht, bedarf kaum näherer Begründung. Und ebenso zu dem von A. Rosenberg besonders verdienstlich betonten und mit dem Rassebewußtsein verknüpften Prinzip der Ehre. In tiefgreifenden Spannungen aber befinden sich beide im Rassegedanken vereinten Ideen reinrassiger Abstammung (Gobineau) 'wie gute Rasse' im Sinne der hochqualifizierten Zuchtrasse (H. St. Chamberlain) mit allen Verkleidungsformen der Demokratie und Massenherrschaft, als unvermeidlicher Begünstigungen eines rassisches Erbgutes, dessen Durchschnittsniveau mit der Zunahme der Zahl stetig sinken muß. Nach den streng biologischen Kriterien der Rassenlehre selbst ist eben im Mittel das nordischfälische Blut einerseits, das ostische anderseits sozial ebenso ungleich verteilt wie die

Ergebnisse sozial wertvoller Züchtungen erblicher Begabungen. In diesem Sinne beseitigt die von Adolf Hitler in Nürnberg stark unterstrichene Verlegung des Edelrassigen aus dem ausschließlich somatischen in die dem nordischen Erbanteil entsprechende heroische 'Gesinnung' und Weltanschauung ebenso eine gewisse politische Verlegenheit, wie das baltische Pathos des 'Charakters' und der 'Persönlichkeit' in A. Rosenbergs 'Mythus des 20. Jahrhunderts.' Hier wären zugleich Beispiele dafür zu finden, wie divergierende Ideen als solche in praktisch ergriffenen neuen Idealbildern einen fruchtbaren Ausgleich zu finden vermögen. Wobei allerdings vor allem der ganze Inbegriff aller Maßnahmen und Ideen zur 'Nationalpolitischen Erziehung' mit Bewußtsein in das denkbar engste Ergänzungsverhältnis zur Rasseidee gebracht werden müssen. Ein rassisch befriedigender Bevölkerungsdurchschnitt ist in dem Rassegemisch einzelner deutscher Stämme erreichbar nur durch die energischste Unterstützung aller eugenischen Maßnahmen durch Formung und Zucht des im äußeren und inneren noch knetbaren jugendlichen Menschenmaterials im Geiste der rassisch besten Bestandteile seiner Erbmassen. Man kann den ererbten Prozentsatz nordischen und fälischen Blutes durch bewußte erzieherische Zucht im nordisch-fälischen Geiste in seiner phänotypischen Auswirkung ganz offensichtlich fördern . . ." (Rothacker, *Geschichtsphilosophie*, 147–148).

67. See Essner, "Le dogme nordique des races," ch. 2.

68. "Indem der Nationalsozialismus die ihrer Veranlagung nach dieser Weltanschauung gehörenden Menschen erfaßt und in eine organische Gemeinschaft bringt, wird er zur Partei derjenigen, die eigentlich ihrem Wesen nach einer bestimmten Rasse zuzusprechen sind. Nationalsozialismus ist heroische Weltanschauung" (Adolf Hitler, "Aus der großen Rede des Führers am Nürnberger Parteitag 1933," in Charlotte Köhn-Behrens, *Was ist Rasse? Gespräche mit den grossten deutschen Forschern der Gegenwart* [Munich: F. Eher Nachd., 1934], 17).

69. "Sehr geehrter Herr Rothacker! Für Ihre freudliche Aufforderung zu einem Vortrag danke ich Ihnen sehr. Wir haben jedoch vom 26 Oktober im Schwarzwald ein Lager für die philologischen und naturwissenschaftlichen Fachschaften, dessen Leitung ich übernommen habe. . . . Für die Übersendung Ihrer '*Geschichtsphilosophie*' danke ich Ihnen vielmals. Soweit ich jetzt sehe, machen Sie für den Aufbau des Ganzen einen fruchtbaren Ansatz. Die 'Haltung' trifft eine wesentliche Mitte geschichtlichen Seins, wenn sie nicht 'psychologisch' mißdeutet wird. Es ist schade, daß ihre Arbeit zu sehr im Rahmen des Handbuches versteckt bleibt. Meine Rundfunkrede '*Warum bleiben wir in der Provinz?*' lasse ich demnächst privatim noch einmal drucken; Sie sind für ein Exemplar bereits vorgemerkt. Mit Interesse höre ich von den '*Neuen Deutschen Forschungen.*' Ich hätte dafür gleich zwei Arbeiten. . . . Besteht eine Möglichkeit, diese Arbeiten in der Sammlung unterzubringen? Oder ist das Ganze noch nicht so weit? Heil Hitler! Ihr Heidegger." (*Dilthey-Jahrbuch*, no. 8 [1993]: 223–224.)

70. "die Verwurzelung der Existenz in der Behauptung völkischen Lebens auf dieser Erde" (Rothacker, *Geschichtsphilosophie*, 149).

71. "Ob sie wohl kämen? Ich würde mich sehr freuen" (*Dilthey-Jahrbuch*, no. 8, p. 225).

72. Anders, *Et si je suis désespéré que voulez-vous que j'y fasse?*, 18–20.

73. "Da kam natürlich das Verhältnis zum Volkstum, zur Natur, aber auch zur Jugendbewegung zum Ausdruck. Das Wort 'völkisch' stand ihm sehr nahe. . . . Ein Roman-

tizismus hielt ihn an 'Blut und Boden' fest" ("Ein Gespräch mit Max Müller," in Schramm and Martin, eds., *Martin Heidegger*, 81, 85).

74. Gadamer, "Entretien de Hans-Georg Gadamer," 237.

75. This page from Hermann Mörchen's diary was made public by a radio program broadcast on 22 January 1989, and this testimony was related by O. Pöggeler in "Praktische Philosophie als Antwort an Heidegger," in Martin, ed., *Martin Heidegger und das Dritte Reich*, 84.

76. See Kisiel, "In the Middle of Heidegger's Three Concepts of the Political," 143.

77. GA 16, 835.

78. GA 16, 839.

79. Letter from Martin Heidegger to Elisabeth Blochmann, 30 March 1933, 60.

80. "Wir wissen, daß Martin Heidegger in seinem hohen Verantwortungsbewußtsein, in seiner Sorge um das Schicksal und die Zukunft des deutschen Menschen mitten im Herzen unserer herrlichen Bewegung stand, wir wissen auch, daß er aus seiner deutschen Gesinnung niemals ein Hehl machte und daß er seit Jahren die Partei Adolf Hitlers in ihrem schweren Ringen um Sein und Macht aufs wirksamste unterstürtzte, daß er stets bereit war, für Deutschlands heilige Sache Opfer zu bringen, und daß ein National-sozialist niemals vergebens bei ihm anpochte" (*Der Alemanne: Kampfblatt der Nationalsozialisten Oberbadens*, 3 May 1933, 2; quoted in Schneeberger, *Nachlese zu Heidegger*, 23).

81. Tilitzki, *Die deutsche Universitätsphilosophie*, 191–192.

82. *Martin Heidegger/Elisabeth Blochmann*, 25 May 1932, 50.

83. Letter from Heidegger to Baeumler, referred to by the latter in Baeumler, Brunträger, and Kurzke, *Thomas Mann und Alfred Baeumler*, 242.

84. *Martin Heidegger/Karl Jaspers*, 14 July 1923, 41.

85. "Er war äußerst freundlich und landsmannschaftlich" (*Heidegger/Jaspers*, 6 March 1928, 90).

86. "Was ich in meinem Zeugnis nur indirekt andeuten konnte, darf ich hier deutlicher sagen. Es geht um nichts Geringeres als um die unaufschiebbare Besinnung darauf, daß wir vor der Wahl stehen, unserem deutschen Geistesleben wieder echte bodenständige Kräfte und Erzieher zuzuführen oder es der wachsenden Verjudung im weiteren und engeren Sinne endgültig auszuliefern. Wir werden den Weg nur zurückfinden, wenn wir imstande sind, ohne Hetze und unfruchtbare Auseinandersetzung frischen Kräfte zur Entfaltung zu verhelfen" (Martin Heidegger to Viktor Schwoerer, in Sieg, "Die Verjudung des deutschen Geistes," 50). This passage is also partially quoted and commented on in the remarkable work by Ott, *Laubhüttenfest 1940*, 33, in which the Freiburg historian revisits the theme of Heidegger's anti-Semitism. The letter to Schwoerer is translated in its entirety by Tertulian in "Histoire de l'être et révolution politique," 124–125.

87. Hitler, *Mein Kampf*, 184; English translation, 167–168.

88. "der geistige Kampf gegen die Judaïsierung der abendländischen Welt" (Heyse, *Idee und Existenz*, 112).

89. GA 16, 68.

90. See Kapferer, *Die Nazifizierung der Philosophie an der Universität Breslau*, 28–30.

91. "Das Buch soll eben, wie das Vorwort ausdrücklich sagt, eine 'Einführung in die Philosophie der Gegenwart' sein. Dergleichen Unternehmen, die jetzt aus dem Boden schießen, sind mehr rein literarischer und verlegerischer Natur—aber keine ernsthaften

wissenschaftlichen Notwendigkeiten und Aufgaben. Und so fehlt denn diesem Buch, ebenso wie dem gleichgearteten des Frankfurter Privatdozenten Heinemann, jede Substanz und alles Schwergewicht. . . . Es erübrigt sich, daß ich weiter auf das Buch hier eingehe, weil es überhaupt nicht in die Klasse der Veröffentlichungen gehört, die als Qualifikationbeweis für eine Professur in Frage kommen" (ibid., 29).

92. See clarification in Chapter 6, 165–166.

93. "Solche Literatur kommt für eine ernsthafte Auseinandersetzung nicht in Frage. M. wird immer geschickt über das gerade Moderne zu reden wissen, er wird aber nie das Schwergewicht aufbringen, mit wirklichen Fragen in die Aufgaben der Philosophie einzugreifen. Diese Art von Philosophiedozenten ist unser Ruin" (Kapferer, *Die Nazifizierung*, 30).

94. We have seen in our discussion of the debate over his letter to Schwoerer that Heidegger takes care not to express his anti-Semitism explicitly prior to 1933.

95. *Martin Heidegger/Elisabeth Blochmann*, 25 May 1932, 50.

96. "Freiburg, den 25 Juni 1933. Sehr verehrte Herr Einhauser! Ich entspreche gern Ihrem Wunsche und gebe Ihnen im Folgenden mein Urteil. Hönigswald kommt aus der Schule des Neukantianismus, der eine Philosophie vertreten hat, die dem Liberalismus auf den Leib zugeschnitten ist. Das Wesen des Menschen wurde da aufgelöst in ein freischwebendes Bewußtsein überhaupt und dieses schließlich verdünnt zu einer allgemein logischen Weltvernunft. Auf diesem Weg wurde unter scheinbar streng wissenschaftlicher philosophischer Begründung der Blick abgelenkt vom Menschen in seiner geschichtlichen Verwurzelung und in seiner volkhaften Überlieferung seiner Herkunft aus Boden und Blut. Damit zusammen ging eine bewußte Zurückdrängung jedes metaphysischen Fragens, und der Mensch galt nur noch als Diener einer indifferenten, allgemeinen Weltkultur. Aus dieser Grundeinstellung sind die Schriften und offensichtlich auch die ganze Vorlesungstätigkeit Hönigswalds erwachsen. Es kommt aber hinzu, daß nun gerade Hönigswald die Gedanken des Neukantianismus mit einem besonders gefährlichen Scharfsinn und einer leerlaufenden Dialektik verficht. Die Gefahr besteht vor allem darin, daß dieses Treiben den Eindruck höchster Sachlichkeit und strenger Wissenschaft erweckt und bereits viele junge Menschen getäuscht und irregeführrt hat. Ich muß auch heute noch die Berufung dieses Mannes an die Universität München als einen Skandal bezeichnen, der nur darin seine Erklärung findet, daß das katholische System solche Leute, die scheinbar weltanschaulich indifferent sind, mit Vorliebe bevorzugt, weil sie gegenüber den eigenen Bestrebungen ungefährlich und in der bekannten Weise 'objektivliberal' sind. . . . Heil Hitler! Ihr sehr ergebener. Heidegger." The letter from Heidegger was published by Claudia Schorcht, *Philosophie an den bayerischen Universitäten*, 161; reprinted in GA 16, 132–133.

97. Heidegger, *Les Conférences de Cassel*, 208–209; *Sein und Zeit*, 401.

98. "Gleichzeitig bohrt München, dort ist ein Ordinariat frei. Es hätte den Vorteil des großen Wirkungskreises und wäre nicht so abgelegen wie es heute Freiburg ist. Die Möglichkeit, an Hitler heranzukommen und dgl." (*Heidegger/Blochmann*, 19 September 1933, 74.)

99. "die Grundmöglichkeiten des urgermanischen Stammeswesen" (GA 36/37, 89).

Chapter 2: Heidegger, the "Bringing into Line," and the New Student Law

1. "Im Zuge der allgemeinen Gleichschaltung wurde Professor Dr. Martin Heidegger am 21. April 1933 zum Rektor der Universität Freiburg im Breisgau gewält." The photograph with its inscription was reproduced in Martin, ed., *Martin Heidegger und das Dritte Reich*, 232. See Figure 1.

2. See below, pp. 152–154.

3. "out of 93 teachers, 13 were suspended as being Jewish according to the decree A 7642" (Ott, "Martin Heidegger als Rektor der Universität Freiburg i. Br. 1933/34, Teil I," 132).

4. Karl Jaspers, who had recommended Brock to Heidegger to replace Oskar Becker as an assistant, specifies that "this fact [that Dr. Brock was Jewish] was not known by Heidegger at the time of the recruitment" (*Martin Heidegger/Karl Jaspers*, 271).

5. "zugleich im Namen meines Mannes." The letter was published by Hugo Ott in the postscript to the German second edition of *Martin Heidegger: Unterwegs zu seiner Biographie*, 353–354.

6. "Zu all dem kommt aber noch die tiefe Dankbarkeit gegen die Opferbereitschaft Ihrer Söhne, und es ist ja nur im Sinne dieses neuen (harten, vom deutschen Standpunkt vernünftigen) Gesetzes, wenn wir uns bedingungslos und in aufrichtiger Ehrfurcht zu denen bekennen, die sich in der Stunde der höchsten Not auch durch die Tat zu unserem deutschen Volk bekannt haben" (ibid.).

7. The copy had been communicated to Hugo Ott by Jean-Michel Palmier, the author of the postscript of the French edition of his monograph.

8. "Der in Klammern stehende Text ist ziemlich stark durchgestrichen, wohl von Frau Heidegger selbst, die gerade diese Passage im Herbst 1945 nicht mehr für opportun angesehen hat" (Ott, *Martin Heidegger: Unterwegs zu seiner Biographie*, 353).

9. GA 16, 787.

10. The letter itself was burned in 1940 in the port of Antwerp with other papers concerning Husserl.

11. GA 16, 774. Hermann Heidegger publishes this report only at the end of the volume, as if to put in doubt the authenticity of the text, although this text is known to us by two different sources, and the reference to the "Jew Fraenkel" appears in both copies.

12. "so tue ich das im vollen Bewußtsein von der Notwendigkeit der unabdingbaren Ausführung des Gesetzes zur Wiedereinstellung des Berufsbeamtentums" (GA 16, 140).

13. "mit einem kampfverbundenen Sieg Heil" (GA 16, 99).

14. See GA 16, 107, 116, and GA 16, 113.

15. GA 16, 761.

16. See Ott, "Martin Heidegger als Rektor der Universität Freiburg i. Br. 1933/34, Teil II, 112.

17. "Das war Heideggers Werk. '*Finis universitatum!*' " (Diary of Josef Sauer, 22 August 1933, quoted in Ott, ibid.).

18. See Bernd Martin,"Heidegger und die Reform der deutschen Universität 1933," in Schramm and Martin, eds., *Martin Heidegger*, 181.

19. "An sämtliche deutsche Hochschulen. Der Herr Minister des Kultus, des Unterrichts und der Justiz hat mich mit Erlaß vom 27. Juli 1933 ermächtigt, für die Dauer

meines Rektorates aus der Dozentenschaft der Universität zu meiner Unterstützung einen Kanzler zu ernennen. Die Bestimmung des Aufgabenbereiches des Kanzlers ist mir überlassen worden. Der Kanzler hat innerhalb seiner Aufgaben 'im Auftrage' des Rektors zu zeichnen, meine Verantwortlichkeit für die Führung der Rektoratsgeschäfte bleibt hierdurch unberührt" (ibid., 167).

20. "Es ist damit die erste Grundlage geschaffen für den inneren Ausbau der Universität entsprechend den neuen Gesamtaufgaben der wissenschaftlichen Erziehung" (ibid., 180).

21. "Die völlige Erneuerung der deutschen Hochschulen kann nur erreicht werden, wenn die Hochschulreform einheitlich und umfassend im ganzen Reiche vorgenommen wird" (ibid.).

22. "Die Berufung Heideggers steht im Zusammenhang mit der Durchführung der Hochschulreform und war aus staatspolitischen Erwägungen heraus erforderlich" (Farías, *Heidegger et le nazisme,* 226; English translation, 162).

23. "Gestern bekam ich einen Ruf nach Berlin—verbunden mit einem politischen Auftrag" (*Heidegger/Blochmann,* 71).

24. "Ich werde nicht nach Berlin gehen, sondern an unserer Universität versuchen, die durch die vorläufige neue Verfassungsregelung in Baden gegebenen Möglichkeiten zu einer echten und erprobten Wirklichkeit zu gestalten, und damit den einheitlichen Aufbau der künftigen gesamtdeutschen Hochschulverfassung vorzubereiten. Auf Wunsch der Berliner Regierungsstellen werde ich auch fernerhin engste Fühlung mit der dortigen Arbeit behalten" (Ott, "Martin Heidegger als Rektor der Universität Freiburg i. Br. 1933/34, Teil II," 113).

25. *Warum bleiben wir in der Provinz?* Schneeberger, *Nachlese zu Heidegger,* 216–218; GA 13, 9–11.

26. "Ich soll die preußische Dozentenschaft 'führen' " (*Heidegger/Blochmann,* 19 September 1933, 73).

27. *Heidegger/Blochmann,* 16 October 1933, 76 (Heidegger's emphasis).

28. In the terms used in the letter from Martin Heidegger to Elisabeth Blochmann, *Heidegger/Blochmann,* 30 August 1933, 69.

29. See Chapter 5.

30. The determinative discussions of Minister Schemm with Heidegger are referred to in a letter from the ministerial counselor Müller of Munich and his colleague Fehrle from the ministry of Karlsruhe. Farías, *Heidegger and Nazism,* 164; German ed., 228.

31. "Dieser sowohl als Philosoph als auch als Vorkämpfer für den Nationalsozialismus einen Namen habe" (Claudia Schorcht, *Philosophie an den bayerischen Universitäten,* 235).

32. "Ich bin noch nicht gebunden, nur das weiß ich, daß ich unter Zurückstellung alles Persönlichen mich für die Aufgabe entscheiden muß, durch deren Erfüllung ich dem Werke Adolf Hitlers am besten diene." Quoted in Schorcht, *Philosophie an den bayerischen Universitäten,* 238.

33. "Die Fakultät möchte auch das Bedenken nicht unterdrücken, daß die schulende Wirkung seiner Philosophie geringer sein könnte als die inspirierende, und daß besonders junge Studenten sich leichter an der ekstatischen Sprache berauschen als an den tiefen und nicht leicht fassbaren Inhalten derselben bilden würden" (Letter of 27 September 1933 to the Bavarian Ministry of Culture, quoted in ibid., 237).

34. "Er sei für die Fakultät politisch zu extrem" und "mit solchen Phrasen könne den Studenten keine Philosophie geboten werden" (Minutes of the Full Professor Session, 26 September 1933, quoted in ibid., 237).

35. Ernst Krieck, rector of Frankfurt; Friedrich Neumann, rector of Göttingen; and Lothar Wolf, rector of Kiel.

36. See, e.g., Ott, "Martin Heidegger als Rektor der Universität Freiburg i. Br. 1933/34, Teil II," 190.

37. Also at stake is the neutralization of the independence of the *Länder,* but that does not concern the universities directly.

38. "Im Hinblick auf die fast vollständige Verjudung der deutschen Hochschulen hat der Bundesführer des Nationalsozialistischen Deutschen Studentenbundes zusammen mit dem Vorsitzer der Deutschen Studentenschaft bei den zuständigen Behörden des Reiches und der Länder die Einführung des numerus clausus für Juden, wie auch die restlose Entfernung sämtlicher jüdischer Dozenten und Assistenten von den deutschen Hochschulen als die erste Voraussetzung für die Umgestaltung der deutschen Hochschule gefordert. Weiterhin ergeht im Zusammenhang mit den Abwehrmaßnahmen der Reichsparteileitung und im Einverständnis mit dem Zentralkomitee folgende Anordnung: Ab 1. April 1933 stehen vor den Hörsalen und Seminaren der jüdischen Professoren und Dozenten Posten der Studentenschaft, die die Aufgabe haben, die deutschen Studenten vor dem Besuch solcher Vorlesungen und Seminare zu warnen, mit dem Hinweis, daß der betreffende Dozent als Jude von allen anständigen Deutschen berechtigt boykottiert wird. Für die Durchführung dieser Anordnung sorgen die einzelnen Hochschulgruppenführer zusammen mit den studentischen S.A.-und S.S.-Männern im Einvernehmen mit dem örtlichen Aktionskomitee" (*Völkischer Beobachter, Herausgeber Adolf Hitler. Kampfblatt der national-sozialistischen Bewegung Großdeutschlands,* Munich, 1/2 April 1933, 1; quoted in Schneeberger, *Nachlese zu Heidegger,* 13).

39. These are the terms used by Hugo Ott in the French version of his monograph, *Martin Heidegger: éléments pour une biographie* (Paris: Payot, 1990), 195. It was in the unsorted archives of the Deutsche Studentenschaft preserved in Würzburg that Hugo Ott found, during his initial research, proof of the friendship between Heidegger and Gerhard Krüger, not to be confused with the philosopher and student of Heidegger of the same name. (Conversation of the author with Hugo Ott.)

40. See Farías, *Heidegger and Nazism,* 177–178; German ed., 149. Farías seems to be mistaken in making Stäbel the head of the DSt at that date, whereas he is still no more than the *Bundesführer* of the NSDStB.

41. Löwith, *Mein Leben in Deutschland,* 75.

42. "Die Dozenten der Universität Freiburg wählten anstelle von Herrn Prof. Von Möllendorf zum Rektor unserer Hochschule Prof. Dr. Heidegger. Diese Wahl erfolgte im Zuge der allgemeinen Gleichschaltung. Sie soll eine möglichst vertrauensvolle und enge Zusammenarbeit aller leitenden Stellen gewährleisten. . . . Wir sind überzeugt, daß der neue Rektor die Arbeit der Studentenschaft, die das neue Studentenrecht organisch in den Aufbau der Universität eingliedert, unterstützen und fördern wird. Die Studentenschaft verspricht dem Rektor als dem *Führer* der Universität ihrerseits gemäßt ihrer Aufgabe Gefolgschaft und Mitarbeit. Der aussscheidende Rektor hat sein Amt zur Verfügung gestellt, um ein engeres Zusammenwirken der führenden Stellen zu ermöglichen. Dieses

Opfer und seine Notwendigkeit wissen wir zu würdigen. . . . Die Studentenschaft der Universität Freiburg i. Breisgau" (*Der Alemanne*, 24 April 1933, 5; quoted in Schneeberger, *Nachlese zu Heidegger*, 16).

43. "The fire was crackling in front of the university library" (Ernesto Grassi, quoted in Ott, "Martin Heidegger als Rektor," 182).

44. "Die *große Masse* der Bücher wurde schon auf dem Exerzierplatz verbrannt." *Der Alemanne*, 20 June 1933, 12, quoted in Schneeberger, *Nachlese zu Heidegger*, 66.

45. "Die Studentenschaft der Universität Freiburg erläßt folgenden *Aufruf*: 'Die deutsche Studentenschaft ist entschlossen, den geistigen Kampf gegen die jüdischmarxistische Zersetzung des deutschen Volkes bis zur völligen Vernichtung durchzuführen. Als Sinnbild dieses Kampfes gelte *die öffentliche Verbrennung* des jüdischmarxistischen Schrifttums am 10. Mai 1933. Deutsche, sammelt euch zu diesem Kampf! Bekundet die Kampfgemeinschaft auch öffentlich. . . . Das Feuer der Vernichtung wird uns zugleich zur lodernden Flamme des begeisterten Ringens um den deutschen Geist, die deutsche Sitte und den deutschen Brauch. Die Studentenschaft der Universität Freiburg. Der Kampfbund für deutsche Kultur.' " (*Breisgauer Zeitung*, 8 May 1933, 3; quoted in Schneeberger, *Nachlese zu Heidegger*, 29–30.)

46. Ibid.

47. The announcements and corrections by the League of Combat that appeared in *Der Alemanne* and the *Freiburger Zeitung*, and quoted in Schneeberger, *Nachlese zu Heidegger*, 66, 69, prove definitively that the ceremony of 24 June coincides with the postponed symbolic auto-da-fé originally planned for 17, then 21, June.

48. "Wider den undeutschen Geist. 1. Sprache und Schrifttum wurzeln im Volke. Das deutsche Volk trägt die Verantwortung dafür, daß seine Sprache und sein Schrifttum reiner und unverfälschter Ausdruck seines Volkstums sind. 2. Es klafft heute ein Widerspruch zwischen Schrifttum und deutschen Volkstum. Dieser Zustand ist eine Schmach! 3. Reinheit von Sprache und Schrifttum liegt an Dir! Dein Volk hat Dir die Sprache zur treuen Bewahrung übergeben. 4. Unser gefährlichster Widersacher ist der Jude und der, der ihm hörig ist. 5. Der Jude kann nur jüdisch denken. Schreibt er Deutsch, dann lügt er. Der Deutsche, der Deutsch schreibt, aber jüdisch denkt, ist ein Verräter. Der Student, der undeutsch spricht und schreibt, ist außerdem gedankenlos und wird seiner Aufgabe untreu. 6. *Wir wollen die Lüge ausmerzen, wir wollen den Verrat brandmarken, wir wollen für den Studenten nicht Stätten der Gedankenlosigkeit, sondern der Zucht und der politischen Erziehung.* 7. Wir wollen den Juden als Fremdling achten, und wir wollen das Volkstum ernst nehmen. Wir *fordern* deshalb von der Zensur: Jüdische Werke erscheinen in hebräischer Sprache. Erscheinen sie in Deutsch, sind sie als Übersetzung zu kennzeichnen. Schärfstes Einschreiten gegen den Mißbrauch der deutschen Schrift. Deutsche Schrift steht nun den Deutschen zur Verfügung. Der undeutsche Geist wird aus öffentlichen Büchereien ausgemerzt. 8. Wir *fordern* vom deutschen Studenten Wille und Fähigkeit zur selbstständigen Erkenntnis und Entscheidung. 9. Wir *fordern* vom deutschen Studenten den Willen und die Fähigkeit zur Reinerhaltung der deutschen Sprache. 10. Wir *fordern* vom deutschen Studenten den Willen und die Fähigkeit zur Überwindung des jüdischen Intellektualismus und der damit verbundenen liberalen Verfallserscheinungen im deutschen Geistesleben. 11. *Wir fordern die Auslese von Studenten und Professoren nach der Sicherheit des Denkens im deutschen Geiste.* 12. *Wir fordern die deutsche*

Hochschule als Hort des deutschen Volkstums und als Kampfstätte aus der Kraft des deutschen Geistes. Die Deutsche Studentenschaft." Trans. Dr. Ronald Richter, slightly modified (www.library.arizona.edu/exhibits/burnedbooks).

49. GA 16, 113.

50. GA 16, 112–113.

51. "Gesetz gegen die Überfüllung der deutschen Schulen und Hochschulen": Section 4 of the law consists of an anti-Semitic *numerus clausus* that draws its authority from the law of 7 April on "the reconstruction of the Civil Service." The other key law to which the "New Student Law" is related is the "Gesetzt über die Bildung von Studentenschaften an den wissenschaftlichen Hochschulen" of 22 April 1933, which reserves access to student associations for students said to be "of German stock" (*deutscher Abstammung*).

52. "Das Akademische Rektorat der Universität Freiburg i. Br. gibt bekannt: Die an den preußischen Hochschulen auf den 1. Mai angesetzte feierliche Verkündigung des neuen Studentenrechtes wird an unserer Universität, bei der der Rektoratswechsel in den Beginn des Sommersemester fällt, in angemessener Weise in die *Feier der Rektorat-sübergabe* eingefügt" (*Der Alemanne. Kampfblatt der Nationalsozialisten Oberbadens*, 30 April–1 May 1933, 9).

53. "Die jüdische Verbindung 'Neo-Friburgia' teilt in einem Schreiben an die Studenten mit, daß sie sich *aufgelöst* hat" (*Der Alemanne*, 27 April 1933, 6; quoted in Schneeberger, *Nachlese zu Heidegger*, 16).

54. "Das badische Staatsministerium hat soeben eine Studentenrechtsverordnung erlassen, die in 1 bestimmt, daß die Studenten bei der Immatrikulation eine ehrenwört-liche Erklärung darüber abzugeben haben, ob ihre Eltern und Großeltern deutscher Ab-stammung sind" (*Breisgauer Zeitung* [12 June 1933]: 3; quoted in Schneeerger, *Nachlese zu Heidegger*, 60).

55. "Darin steht der abendländische Mensch aus einem Volkstum und Kraft seiner Sprache erstmals auf gegen das *Seiende im Ganzen* " (GA 16, 108–109).

56. GA 16, 97.

57. Heidegger's speech was supposed to appear in the series *Freiburger Universitäts-reden*, Fr. Wagnersche Universitätsbuchhandlung, as Notebook 11. Instead, Heidegger chose to publish it with Wilh. Gottl. Korn, of Breslau, who republished an entire set of books that same year by Moeller van den Bruck, the author of *The Third Reich*.

58. *Heidegger/Blochmann*, 22 December 1932, 56.

59. Kapferer, *Die Nazifizierung*, 130.

60. See Ott, "Martin Heidegger als Rektor," 182. Ott shows that Heidegger could not have been unaware of the role Leistritz played in the Berlin book-burning, a "fact that was reported at the time in all the newspapers." Besides, as I will show, Heidegger was a subscriber to the party press — i.e., he had the *Völkischer Beobachter* delivered to his home every morning.

Chapter 3: Work Camps, the Health of the People, and the Hard Race in the Lectures and Speeches of 1933–1934

1. "Du darfst die ganze Bewegung nicht von unten her betrachten, sondern vom Führer aus und seinen großen Zielen . . . man darf jetzt nicht mehr an sich selbst denken,

sondern nur an das Ganze und das Schicksal des deutschen Volkes" (Martin Heidegger to Fritz Heidegger, 4 May 1933, GA 16, 93).

2. *Zur Immatrikulation,* GA 16, 95.

3. GA 16, 98.

4. "Volkstum — Wurzel des Geistes" (GA 16, 97).

5. GA 16, 98.

6. "Ich bitte ergebenst um Verschiebung des geplanten Empfanges des Vorstandes des Verbandes der deutschen Hochschulen bis zu dem Zeitpunkt, in dem die Leitung des Hochschulverbandes im Sinne der gerade hier besonders notwendigen Gleichschaltung vollzogen ist" (GA 16, 105).

7. AOR 16/a, Oral Archives, Ministère des affaires étrangères [Ministry of Foreign Affairs], Colmar, France.

8. Hitler, *Mein Kampf,* 317; English translation, 290. See on this point Denis Trierweiler, "*Polla ta deina,* ou comment dire l'innommable. Une lecture d'*Arbeit am Mythos,*" *Archives de philosophie,* 67 (2004): 253.

9. "die innerst bestimmende Mitte des ganzen volklich-staatlichen Daseins" (GA 16, 110).

10. See GA 16, 112, 132, 151, and GA 36/37, 263.

11. "auch den Sieg des Gedankens der schaffenden Arbeit, die selbst ewig antisemitisch war und antisemitisch sein wird" (Hitler, *Mein Kampf,* 557; English translation, 497).

12. Adorno, *Le Jargon de l'authenticité,* 44.

13. Ibid., 43.

14. It is hardly possible to count among the number of translations worthy of the name the revisionist rewriting of François Fédier, which appeared in 1995, with the title *Écrits politiques* by Heidegger. To give only three examples among dozens: When Heidegger praises the NSDAP, referring to the "nationalsozialistische deutsche *Arbeiterpartei*" — i.e., the "National Socialist German Workers' Party," the "translation" revised the text in such a way as to give the illusion of an entirely different political tonality than that of the NSDAP and speaks of the "*workers' party* that German national socialism is" (143). The *Gleichschaltung* called for by Heidegger in his telegram to Hitler, which begins with the dismissal of all Jewish professors, is translated as the "putting in harmony" (313). As for the title of the rectoral address, "Die Selbstbehauptung der deutschen Universität" — i.e., "The Self-Affirmation of the German University," it is translated as "The German University in the Face of All Opposition" (97) in order to make the reader believe that this speech, which recommends the introduction of the Führer principle into the university and the incorporation of the university into the state, is somehow an act of resistance.

15. Martin Heidegger, *Arbeitsdienst und Universität,* GA 16, 125–126.

16. "Das Ziel wird durch Fußmarsch erreicht . . . *S.A.*-oder *S.S.*-Dienstanzug, eventuell Stahlhelmuniform mit Armbinde" (quoted in Ott, *Martin Heidegger,* 218).

17. "Die im Jahre 1933 in Freiburg verkaufte Ansichtpostkarte: der von der Partei ein Gesetzte Rektor der Universität Freiburg an der Spitze der Freiburger S.A. [*In a note:* In meinem Besitz] zeigt die Macht des Geistes als Vorspann für den Geist der Macht." (*Die Neue Rundschau,* Stockholm, October 1946; included in Schneeberger, *Nachlese zu Heidegger,* 266.) In his *Glossarium,* under the date 15 March 1949 (241), Carl Schmitt rejoices maliciously over that detail given by Günther Anders: "in my possession" (*in*

meinem Besitz), which should cause problems for Heidegger, opines Schmitt, with the authorities of the occupying forces.

18. AOR 16/1a, Oral Archives, Ministère des affaires étrangères [Ministry of Foreign Affairs], Colmar, France.

19. What comes to mind in particular is a series of articles that appeared in *France Observateur* during the winter of 1963–1964, following a remark by René Étiemble in an article of 28 November and a brief letter from Dominique Janicaud on 5 December 1963. This controversy was not brought up by Janicaud in *Heidegger en France*.

20. "Das Lager war für jeden eine gefährliche Luft. Es wurde für die, die blieben, und für die, die gingen, gleicherweise eine Probe " (GA 16, 174).

21. "Vor acht Tagen hatte ich in Todtnauberg das erste Lager — ich habe *viel* gelernt. In der Mitte der Lagerzeit mußte ich aber 20 Leute entlassen — die nicht dahin paßten. So ein Lager ist eine *große Probe* — für jeden — und gefährlich — " (GA 16, 178).

22. GA 16, 761–763.

23. "die Universität muß . . . *wieder in die Volksgemeinschaft eingegliedert* und mit dem *Staat verbunden* werden" (GA 16, 761).

24. "ein scharfer Kampf zu führen im nationalsozialistischen Geist, der nicht ersticken darf durch humanisierende, christliche Vorstellungen, die seine Unbedingtheit nieder-halten" (GA 16, 762).

25. "Von der *Arbeit* für *den Staat* kommt *keine Gefahr,* nur von Gleichgültigkeit und Widerstand" (ibid.).

26. "ihre Verwurzelung im Volk und ihre Bindung an den Staat" (GA 16, 763).

27. "Es wird gekämpft aus den Kräften des neuen Reichs, das der Volkskanzler Hitler zur Wirklichkeit bringen wird" (ibid.).

28. "Das harte Geschlecht von heute ist Bürge der Zukunft — der besseren Zukunft" (Forsthoff, *Der Totale Staat*).

29. See GA 16, 772: "Wir sind nur ein Übergang, nur ein Opfer. Als Kämpfer dieses Kampfes müssen wir ein hartes Geschlecht haben, das an nichts Eigenem mehr hängt, das sich festlegt auf den Grund des Volkes."

30. "das kommende deutsche Geschlecht" (GA 16, 251).

31. "*unser Geschlecht* ist der *Übergang* und die *Brücke*" (GA 16, 282).

32. "Da sprach ein leidenschaftlicher Nationalsozialist ohne Weisheit, ohne politisches Verantwortungsgefühl, ohne Willen zu gerechter Differenzierung. Und es blieb ja 1933 nicht bei Reden. Man muß wissen, wie viele sich in diesem Sommer dem Nationalsozialis-mus anzupassen versuchten, um die Gefährlichkeit der provozierenden Frage zu ver-stehen: 'Ist Revolution auch auf der Universität? Nein!' Tausende von denen, auf die ich gebaut hatte, fielen unter Heideggers Einfluß um." (*Martin Heidegger und das "Dritte Reich." Ein Kompendium,* ed. Bernd Martin [Darmstadt: Wissenschaftliche Buchgesell-schaft, 1989], 160.)

33. "Das Entscheidende und Überraschende ist nun, daß das Wesen der Gesundheit keinesfalls zu jeder Zeit und bei jedem Volk in demselben Sinne bestimmt wurde" (GA 16, 150).

34. "Für die Griechen z. B. bedeutet 'gesund' soviel wie bereit und stark sein zum Handeln im Staat. Wer den Bedingungen dieses Handelns nicht mehr genügte, zu dem durfte der Arzt auch im Falle der 'Krankheit' nicht mehr kommen" (ibid.).

35. "Was gesund und krank ist, dafür gibt sich ein Volk und ein Zeitalter je nach der inneren Größe und Weite seines Daseins selbst das Gesetz. Das deutsche Volk ist jetzt dabei, sein eigenes Wesen wieder zu finden und sich würdig zu machen seines großen Schicksals. Adolf Hitler, unser großer Führer und Kanzler, hat durch die nationalsozialistische Revolution einen neuen Staat geschaffen, durch den das Volk sich wieder eine Dauer und Stetigkeit seiner Geschichte sichern soll. . . . Jedes Volk hat die erste Gewähr seiner Echtheit und Größe in seinem Blut, seinem Boden und seinem leiblichen Wachstum. Wenn es dieses Gutes verlustig geht oder auch nur weitgehend geschwächt wird, bleibt jede staatspolitische Anstrengung, alles wirtschaftliche und technische Können, alles geistige Wirken auf die Dauer nutz-und ziellos" (GA 16, 151).

36. "ein Wort wie 'Gesundheit,' worin hinzukommend mitempfinden wird nur noch das Band der Bluts- und Stammeseinheit, der Rasse" (Heidegger, unpublished seminar of winter semester 1933–1934, *Über Wesen und Begriff*, end of the sixth session; see below, Chapter 5, 118–119).

37. GA 16, 269.

38. "Nationalsozialistische Weltanschauung und Rassegedanke," in Seidler, "Die Medizinische Fakultät zwischen 1926 und 1948," 84.

39. See on this point Münster, *Heidegger, la "Science allemande,"* 29.

40. On Heidegger's visits to Eugen Fischer after 1945, see the testimony of Gertrude Fischer, in Müller-Hill, *Murderous Science,* 108.

41. "bitte ich . . . daß der Gesamtcharakter dieser Lehrstelle umgewandelt werden muß im Sinne einer Lehrtätigkeit über das Gesamtgebiet der politischen Pädagogik" (GA 16, 186).

42. See Chapter 4, 100, 101.

43. "Der Führer selbst und allein *ist* die heutige und künftige Wirklichkeit und ihr Gesetz." (Address to the Students, 3 November 1933, GA 16, 184.)

44. "Kraft dieses Grundgesetzes der Ehre bewahrt das deutsche Volk die Würde und Entschiedenheit seines Wesens." (Leipzig Speech of 11 November 1933, GA 16, 190.) The text published by Schneeberger has *"seines Lebens"* instead of *"seines Wesens"* (Schneeberger, *Nachlese zu Heidegger,* 148.)

45. "Wir haben uns losgesagt von der Vergötzung eines boden-und machtlosen Denkens. Wir sehen das Ende der ihm dienstbaren Philosophie." (GA 16, 192.)

46. See Chapter 5 for the unpublished seminar of winter 1933–1934.

47. "Einladung zur Feierlichen Immatrikulation verbunden mit Langemarckgedächtnis." The plan for the ceremony was published in GA 16, 196–197.

48. "Reihenfolge: SA, SS, Stahlhelm, Universitätsfahnen . . ." (ibid., 197).

49. "Dann wird ja auch das *Sein* des deutschen Studenten ein anderes. Dann ändert auch die Immatrikulation ihren Sinn" (ibid., 199).

50. "Der deutsche Student geht jetzt durch den Arbeitsdienst; er steht bei der *S.A.* . . . Das ist neu" (ibid.).

51. "Dieses Wissen aber verwirklicht sich *in* der Staat-werdung des Volkes, dieses Wissen ist der *Staat"* (ibid., 200).

52. "So wird z. B. die *Natur* offenbar als Raum eines Volk, als Landschaft und Heimat, als Grund und Boden. Die Natur wird frei als Macht und Gesetz jener verborgenen Überlieferung der *Vererbung* wesentlicher Anlagen und Triebrichtungen. Die Natur wird

maßsetzende Regel als Gesundheit. Je befreiter die Natur waltet, um so großartiger und gebändigter ist die gestaltende Macht der echten *Technik* ihr dienstbar zu machen. In die Natur gebunden, von ihr getragen und überwölbt, durch sie befeuert und begrenzt, verwirklicht sich die *Geschichte* des Volkes. Im Kampf, dem eigenen Wesen die *Bahn* zu schaffen und die *Dauer* zu sichern, erfaßt das Volk sein Selbst in der wachsenden Staatsverfassung. Im Kampf, das Vermögen zu seiner Größe und Bestimmung sich als wesentliche Wahrheit vorzubilden, stellt es sich maßgebend dar in der *Kunst.* Diese kommt nur so zum großen Stil, daß sie das ganze Dasein des Volkes in die Prägung seines Wesens nimmt" (GA 16, 200–201).

53. "Was geschieht also in der Staatwerdung des Volkes? Jene Mächte, die Natur, die Geschichte, die Kunst, die Technik, der Staat selbst werden *durch* Gesetz und in der Durchsetzung in ihre Grenzen *gebannt.* Und so wird *das* offenbar, was ein Volk sicher, hell und stark macht. Die Offenbarkeit dieser Mächte aber ist das Wesen der *Wahrheit.* In der Durchsetzung jener Mächte versetzt der werdende Staat das Volk in seine wirkliche *Wahrheit* zurück" (GA 16, 201).

54. The word "bearing" (*Haltung*), of such major importance in the racial doctrine of Rothacker, and its approval by Heidegger — as we saw above, p. 23ff — is the final notion expressed at the end of Heidegger's enrollment address. See ibid., 208.

55. "Aus dieser Wahrheit erhebt sich das echte Wissenkönnen, Wissenmüssen und Wissenwollen. Wissen aber heißt *des Wesens der Dinge in Klarheit mächtig und kraft dieser Macht zur Tat entschlossen sein.*"

56. Klemperer, *The Language of the Third Reich.*

57. "bei der deutschen *Jugend. Sie* hat keine Wahl. Sie *muß*" (GA 16, 202).

58. "Der Student greift uns an und fragt uns: Wie hältst Du es mit dem *Staat?*" (Ibid., 203.)

59. " 'primitiv' allerdings und glücklicherweise" (ibid., 202).

60. "In dieser Angriffsbewegung hat sich der Wille der Jugend den staatsgestaltenden Mächten *geöffnet.* Im Angriff *folgt* sie der Führung ihres sicheren Wollens. In dieser Gefolgschaft nimmt der Einzelne sich nicht mehr als vereinzelten — er hat den Eigenwillen weggegeben an die Mächte" (ibid., 203–204).

61. "*Gefolgschaft* erwirkt Kameradschaft — nicht umgekehrt. Solche Kameradschaft erzieht jene namenlosen und nicht-beamteten Führer, die mehr *tun,* weil sie mehr ertragen und opfern. Die Kameradschaft prägt den Einzelnen über sich hinaus und schlägt ihn in das Gepräge eines ganz eigenen Schlages der Jungmannschaft. Wir kennen die Festigkeit ihrer Gesichtszüge, die gestraffte Klarheit ihres Blicks, die Entschiedenheit ihres Händedrucks, die Rücksichtslosigkeit ihrer Rede. Der eigenbrödlerische Einzelne ebenso wie die zucht-und richtungslose Masse werden zerschlagen von der Schlagkraft dieses Schlages junger Menschen. Dieser Schlag von Studenten 'studiert' nicht mehr, d. h. er bleibt nicht irgendwohin geborgen *sitzen,* um von dort aus im Sitzen irgendwohin nur zu 'streben.' Dieser neue Schlag der Wissenwollenden ist jederzeit unterwegs. Dieser Student aber wird zum *Arbeiter*" (ibid., 204).

62. "Oder hat sich mit der neuen deutschen Wirklichkeit *auch* und gerade das *Wesen der Arbeit und des Arbeiters gewandelt?*" (ibid., 204.)

63. "Das so verstandene Wesen der Arbeit bestimmt jetzt *von Grund aus* das *Dasein* des Menschen" (ibid., 205).

64. "Unser Dasein beginnt, sich in eine andere Seinsart zu verlagern, deren Charakter ich vor Jahren als die *Sorge* herausstellte" (ibid.).

65. "Die Arbeit versetzt und fügt das Volk in das Wirkungsfeld aller wesentlichen Mächte des Seins. Das *in* der Arbeit und *als* Arbeit sich gestaltende Gefüge des völkischen Daseins ist der *Staat*. Der nationalsozialistische Staat ist der Arbeitsstaat" (ibid., 205–206).

66. "Der neue Student aber rückt ein in die neue Ordnung des staatlichen Daseins und seines völkischen Wissens, derart, dass er selbst an seinem Teil diese neue Ordnung mitgestalten muß" (ibid., 207).

67. "Der neue deutsche Student *ist Arbeiter*. Aber wo finden wir diesen Studenten? Vielleicht sind es an jeder Hochschule ein *halbes Dutzend*, vielleicht *noch* weniger und im Ganzen nicht einmal jene *Sieben*, mit denen der Führer einst *sein* Werk begann" (ibid., 206).

68. "So meldete ich mich als Mitglied der Deutschen Arbeiterpartei an und erhielt einen provisorischen Mitgliedsschein mit der Nummer: sieben" (Hitler, *Mein Kampf*, 244).

69. "Es war der entscheidendste Entschluß meines Lebens" (ibid.).

70. Maser, *Mein Kampf d'Adolf Hitler*, 158–159.

71. "Das Examen steht für den neuen Studenten nicht am *Ende* der Studienzeit, sondern am Anfang" (GA 16, 207).

72. "Ich verpflichte Euch auf den Willen und das Werk unseres Führers Adolf Hitler. Ich binde Euch an das Gesetz des Daseins des neuen deutschen Studenten. Ich fordere von Euch Zucht und Ernst und Härte gegen Euch selbst. Ich verlange von Euch Opfermut und Vorbildlichkeit der Haltung gegenüber allen deutschen Volksgenossen. Heil Hilter!" (Ibid., 208.)

73. "einer der stärksten nationalsozialistischen Vorkämpfer unter den deutschen Gelehrten, der derzeitige Rektor der Universität Freiburg, *Professor Dr. Heidegger*" (ibid., 765).

74. "die neue Universität ein Stück des nationalsozialistischen Staates darstellen werde" (ibid.).

75. "Es bedarf keines besonderen Hinweises, daß Nichtarier auf dem Unterschriftenblatt nicht erscheinen sollen" (*Martin Heidegger und das Dritte Reich*, 185; included in GA 16, 217, but without the *Abschrift* published by Bernd Martin in the work cited).

76. *Bekenntnis der Professoren an den deutschen Universitäten*, 83–84, for the French. See pp. 36–37 for the English translation of Heidegger's speech.

77. Letter to Stadelmann of 20 July 1945, GA 16, 371, and letter to Stadelmann of 1 September 1945, GA 16, 395.

78. "der Führer unseres neuen Staates" (GA 16, 232).

79. Ibid., 234.

80. "Das Ziel ist: stark zu werden zu einem vollgültigen Dasein als Volksgenosse in der deutschen Volksgemeinschaft" (ibid., 233).

81. "wissen, was die künftige Gesundung des Volkskörpers bedeutet . . . was in der Tatsache liegt, daß 18 Millionen Deutsche zwar zum Volk, aber, weil Außerhalb der Reichsgrenzen lebend, doch nicht zum Reich gehören" (ibid., 233).

82. "Arbeiter und Arbeit, wie der Nationalsozialismus diese Worte versteht . . ." (GA 16, 236).

83. "Es gibt nur *einen einzigen* deutschen 'Lebensstand.' Das ist der in den tragenden Grund des Volkes gewurzelte und in den geschichtlichen Willen des Staates frei gefügte *Arbeitsstand,* dessen Prägung in der Bewegung der nationalsozialistischen deutschen *Arbeiterpartei* vorgeformt wird" (*Der Ruf zum Arbeitsdienst, GA* 16, 239).

84. See Chapter 1, 23.

85. "Freiheit . . . heißt: *Bindung an das innerste Gesetz* und die Ordnungen unseres Wesens" (GA 16, 281).

86. "Der Aufbruch unserer, der zwei Millionen Toten aus den endlosen Gräbern, die wie ein geheimnisvoller Kranz sich um die Grenzen des Reiches und Deutsch-Osterreichs ziehen, beginnt erst" (ibid., 280).

87. Ibid., 282, 284.

88. See Chapter 6.

89. "Das Wort *polemos* . . . bedeutet nicht 'Krieg' . . . Wir dürfen nicht nur *polemos* nicht als Krieg denken" (*Das Rektorat 1933/34, GA* 16, 379).

90. "der große Krieg kommt *jetzt erst* über uns" (ibid., 280).

91. "Der große Krieg muß von uns *geistig* erobert werden, d.h. der *Kampf* wird zum *innersten Gesetz* unseres Daseins" (ibid., 283).

92. "Für den wesentlichen Menschen ist der Kampf die *große Prüfung* alles Seins: in der sich entscheidet, ob wir Knechte sind vor uns selbst oder Herren. . . . Unser Geschlecht — wir in der geheimnisvollen Kameradschaft mit den toten Kameraden — ist die Brücke zur geistigen geschichtlichen Eroberung des großen Krieges" (ibid., 283–284).

93. See Chapter 9.

94. "Der Krieg hat ja in seinem unmittelbaren Ende noch keine Entscheidung gebracht" (GA 16, 281).

95. "This world war has decided nothing" (*What Is Called Thinking?* 66). See on this point Barash, *Heidegger et son siècle,* 176.

96. *Das Rektorat 1933/34, GA* 16, 389.

97. "Wer nach dieser Zeit noch ein Amt in der Leitung des Universität übernahm, konnte eindeutig wissen, mit wem er sich einließ" (GA 16, 390).

98. Hermann Heidegger has republished the text discovered by Victor Farías, but without the text of the letter from Heidegger to Wilhelm Stuckart of 28 August 1934. See GA 16, 308 and 801, and Farías, *Heidegger and Nazism,* 197. I will not analyze Heidegger's project, which has already been commented on by Farías.

99. "Unsere deutsche Gegenwart aber ist erfüllt von einer großen Umwälzung, die durch das ganze geschichtliche Dasein unseres Volkes hindurchgreift. Den Beginn dieser Umwälzung sehen wir in der nationalsozialistischen Revolution" (GA 16, 285–286).

100. Ibid., 285.

101. "Die tragende und bestimmende Mitte der neuen Universität wurde die philosophische Fakultät" (ibid., 292).

102. See outline reproduced in ibid., 304.

103. Heidegger speaks of "ein stark besuchtes Seminar über 'Volk und Wissenschaft' " (ibid., 373). It appears from the dates (winter semester 1933–1934) that it could only be the unpublished seminar that we will study in Chapter 5.

104. "Wir sprechen vom 'Arbeiter der Faust' und vom 'Arbeiter der Stirn' und ihrer Zusammengehörigkeit" (GA 16, 303).

105. See, for example, the *Völkischer Beobachter* of 5 July 1921.

106. "alle Stände sind in ihrer Arbeit getragen und geführt von der Sorge um die geschichtliche Bestimmung des Volkes. Diese bleibt ein Geheimnis. So verborgen dieses Geheimnis bleibt, so offen ist die Gesinnung und Stimmung, in der das Volk dieses Geheimnis bewahrt: es ist die *Ehrfucht* — die Sorge um die Würde und Entschiedenheit seines Wesens" (GA 16, 303).

107. The expression occurs at the beginning of the lecture (ibid., 290), and the theme of the secret (*Geheimnis*) then becomes recurrent; see ibid., 298, 303.

108. Ibid., 298, 302.

109. "Das naturhafte und geschichtliche Wesen des *Volksgeistes,* nicht die Regeln eines bloßen Verstandes und nicht die Berechnungen einer freischwebenden Weltvernunft, bestimmte das Wesen des Menschen. Damals entstand auch und nicht zufällig das Wort *Volkstum.* Dieses neue Wissen und Wollen erstreckte sich notwendig auch auf den Staat . . . der Staat wurde geahnt als eine lebendige Ordnung und ein Gesetz, darin und dadurch das Volk selbst seine Einheit und die Sicherheit seiner Dauer gewinnt" (ibid., 291).

110. See Chapter 8.

111. Both lectures constitute in this sense the "doctrinal" justification of the project sent that same month of August 1934 to Wilhelm Stuckart for the forming of an Academy of Professors of the Reich.

112. "vielleicht in 50 Jahren" (GA 16, 306).

113. "Wer das Große wirklich sehen will, muß selbst Größe haben" (ibid., 307).

114. "*Erziehung des Volkes durch den Staat zum Volk* — das ist der Sinn der national-sozialistischen Bewegung, das ist das Wesen der neuen Staatsbildung. *Solche* Erziehung zum höchsten Wissen ist die Aufgabe der neuen Universität" (ibid.).

115. "Ein Staat *ist* nur, indem er *wird, wird* zum *geschichtlichen Sein* des Seienden, das *Volk* heißt" (ibid., 333).

116. Ibid., 333–334.

117. Ibid., 318.

118. Hitler concludes *Mein Kampf* by adding the name of his mentor and friend Dietrich Eckart to the list of the eighteen "heroes" who died on 9 November 1923 during the failed coup d'état of Munich. He does so in these words: "And I want to place among them, as one of the best, the man who devoted his life to wakening his people, our people, by poetry and thought, and finally by action [*im Dichten und im Denken und am Ende in der Tat*]." *Mein Kampf,* 781.

Chapter 4: The Courses of 1933–1935

1. In this chapter we will approach the four courses taught by Heidegger from May 1933 to February 1935. The first three have only recently appeared in Germany and are still unpublished in French. Only after having examined the unpublished seminars of the winter semesters 1933–1934 and 1934–1935, and Heidegger's conception of the *polemos* in its relation to Carl Schmitt and Alfred Baeumler, will we turn, in Chapter 9, to the course of the summer semester of 1935, *Introduction to Metaphysics,* which is later than those two seminars.

2. The course from the summer semester of 1934 was published first. Announced by

Heidegger in 1934 with the title *The State and Knowledge* (*Der Staat und die Wissenschaft*), it was reedited and published in 1998 with the title *Logik als Frage nach dem Wesen der Sprache* (GA 38), even though the question of the state remains on the horizon of the course (see section 28, e: "Der Staat as das geschichtliche Sein des Volkes"). A first edition of the course appeared in 1991 in Barcelona, titled *Logica. Lecciones de M. Heidegger* (*semestre verano 1934*) *en el legado de Helene Weiss,* translated, and with an introduction, by Victor Farías. That edition is not to be found, as far as I have been able to establish, in any library in France, nor is it reviewed or commented upon, although it was published twelve years ago. Moreover, the courses of the summer semester of 1933 and the winter semester of 1933–1934 appeared in 2001 in GA 36/37.

3. "die *große Wandlung des Daseins des Menschen*" (GA 36/37, 119; the italics are the author's).

4. "Wenn heute der Führer immer wieder spricht von der Umerziehung zur nationalsozialistischen Weltanschauung, heißt das nicht: irgendwelche Schlagworte beibringen, sondern einen *Gesamtwandel* hervorbringen, einen *Weltentwurf,* aus dessen Grund heraus er das ganze Volk erzieht" (GA 36/37, 225).

5. *Der deutsche Idealismus (Fichte, Schelling, Hegel) und die philosophische Problemlage der Gegenwart,* GA 28, 2.

6. To appear in GA 80.

7. *Kant and the Problem of Metaphysics,* 44, pp. 164–165.

8. "Das deutsche Volk im Ganzen kommt zu sich selbst, d.h. findet seine Führung" (*Die Grundfrage der Philosophie,* GA 36/37, 3).

9. "die heutige politische Lage des deutschen Volkes zur Kenntnis nehmen" (ibid., 4).

10. "Wir fassen zusammen: 1. Philosophie ist der unausgesetzte fragende Kampf um das Wesen und Sein des Seienden. 2. Dieses Fragen ist in sich geschichtlich, d.h. es ist das Fordern, Hadern und Verehren eines Volkes um der Härte und Klarheit seines Schicksals willen" (ibid., 12).

11. "Der neue deutsche Staat ist noch nicht da . . . aber wir wollen und werden ihn schaffen" (ibid., 79).

12. "Wir sind ein Volk, das seine Metaphysik *erst gewinnen* muß und gewinnen *wird,* d.h. wir sind ein Volk, das noch *ein Schicksal* hat" (ibid., 80; the italics are those of the author).

13. "*Dieses Fragen,* darin unser Volk sein geschichtliches Dasein aushält, durchhält durch die Gefahr, hinaushält in die Größe seines Auftrags, dieses Fragen *ist sein Philosophieren, seine Philosophie*" (ibid., 4).

14. "Die Philosophie ist die Frage nach dem Gesetz und Gefüge unseres Seins." (Ibid.)

15. "Und das ist wenig genug, ja ein Nichts angesichts der Härte und Dunkelheit unseres deutschen Schicksals und der deutschen Berufung" (ibid., 6).

16. "Dieser . . . Descartes mit seinem allgemeinen Zweifel und gleichzeitiger 'Betonung' des Ich ist der beliebteste und üblichste Gegenstand für philosophisch genannte Prüfungen und Prüfungsarbeiten an den deutschen Universitäten. Dieser seit Jahrzehnten bestehende Brauch ist nur ein, aber ein unmißverständliches Zeichen für die Gedankenlosigkeit und Verantwortungslosigkeit, die sich da breit gemacht hat. Zu dieser geistigen Verlotterung der Studierenden und des Prüfungswesens wäre es nicht gekommen, wenn die Lehrer sie nicht selbst betrieben und zugelassen hätten" (ibid., 10, pp. 38–39).

17. *Einführung in die Phänomenologie im Anschluss an Descartes.*

18. *Phänomenologische Übungen für Anfänger im Anschluss an Descartes* Méditations.

19. *Über Gewissheit und Wahrheit im Anschluss an Descartes und Leibniz.*

20. I have tried to find out whether the inclusion of these seminars was planned in the so-called complete edition (*Gesamtausgabe*). I consulted F.-W. V. Hermann, who said that unfortunately the manuscripts of the seminars on Descartes were missing (personal correspondence, 2 May 2002). Yet I was able to verify, during my research at the Deutsches Literatur Archiv of Marbach, where the Heidegger collection is located, that there was a handwritten transcript for at least two of those seminars, but that the two manuscripts were *gesperrt* — i.e., not consultable without the express agreement of Hermann Heidegger. The fact of not having programmed, in the edition wrongly titled complete, the publication of these two seminars on Descartes is the result not of a material impossibility but of a deliberate exclusion.

21. "behaupte ich: 1. Der Radikalismus des Descartesschen Zweifels und die Strenge der neuen Grundlegung der Philosophie und des Wissens überhaupt ist ein Schein und somit die Quelle verhängnisvoller, auch heute noch nur schwer ausrottbarer Täuschungen. 2. Dieser angebliche Neuanfang der neuzeitlichen Philosophie mit Descartes besteht nicht nur nicht, sondern ist in Wahrheit der Beginn eines weiteren wesentlichen Verfalls der Philosophie. Descartes bringt die Philosophie nicht zu sich selbst zurück und auf ihren Grund und Boden, sondern drängt sie noch weiter vom Fragen ihrer Grundfrage ab" (ibid., p. 39).

22. "Réponses aux secondes objections" (Descartes, René, Charles Adam, and Paul Tannery, *Oeuvres de Descartes/Publiées Par Charles Adam and Paul Tannery* [Paris: J. Vrin, 1957], IX-1, 121; hereafter AT).

23. "der Geist ist seit langem: der Hauch, der Wind, der Sturm, der Einsatz und die Entschlossenheit. Wir brauchen nicht die große Bewegung unseres Volkes heute zu vergeistigen. Der Geist ist schon da." (Course taken in note form by Helene Weiß and published in part in Farías, *Heidegger and Nazism,* 135, English translation slightly modified.) In the so-called complete works, the published course is a very different version and without the editor, Harmut Tietjen, giving any explanation or pointing out the existence of variants. It reads "breath, wind, astonishment, incentive, commitment [*Hauch, Wehen, Staunen, Antrieb, Einsatz*]" (GA 36/37, 7). To read *Staunen* in place of *Sturm*, however, seems dubious, breaking as it does the progression conceived by Heidegger in the metaphorical progression of the vocabulary: *der Hauch, der Wind, der Sturm,* which prepares the voluntarism of the two last terms.

24. "All greatness is contained in the attack [*Alles großes steht im Sturm*]" (*Die Selbstbehauptung der deutschen Universität,* GA 16, 117).

25. See Jacques Derrida, *Of Spirit,* 40; *De l'esprit,* 54.

26. *Of Spirit,* 39; *De l'esprit,* 52.

27. GA 36/37, 7–8.

28. Ibid., 45.

29. Let us specify that there are, in the *Meditations,* two occurrences of the word *subjectum:* in the expression *calor in subjectum* (AT VII, 41), in which the meaning of the word is clearly objectified, and in a more ambiguous passage, which would merit a

separate analysis, in which Descartes writes: "cum volo, cum timeo, cum affirmo, cum nego, semper quidem aliquam rem ut subjectum meæ cogitationis apprehendo . . ." (AT VII, 37). Whatever the case may be, Heidegger does not look that closely at Descartes's text, and he bases his arguments on words or expressions that have been vulgarized by the commentarism that he introduces himself, without truly paying attention to *the actual occurrence* of the terms.

30. "non possumus concipere actum quemcumque sine subjecto sui, veluti saltare sine saltante, scire sine sciente, cogitare sine cogitante" (Hobbes, *Objectiones tertiæ cum responsionibus auctoris,* AT VII, 173). On the objectified use of the word *subjectum* by Hobbes, see Foisneau, *Hobbes et la toute-puissance de Dieu,* 85.

31. "Fateor autem ultro me ad rem, sive substantiam, quam volebam exuere omnibus iis quæ ad ipsam non pertinent, significandam, usum fuisse verbis quammaxime potui abstractis, ut contra hic Philosophus utitur vocibus quammaxime concretis, nempe sub-jecti, materiæ, et corporis, ad istam rem cogitantem significandam, ne patiatur ipsam a corpore div*elli* " (Descartes, in ibid., AT VII, 174).

32. GA 36/37, 216.

33. Ibid., 217–218; see also 173.

34. "*die große Wandlung des Daseins des Menschen*" (ibid., 119).

35. Ibid.

36. See Ernst Jünger, *Über Nationalismus und Judenfrage, Politische Publizistik 1919–1933,* ed. Sven Olaf Berggötz (Stuttgart, 2002), 591; and the essay by Jean-Luc Évard, "Ernst Jünger et les Juifs," *Les Temps modernes,* no. 589 (August–September 1996): 102–130.

37. "Die Erkenntnis und Verwirklichung der eigentümlichen deutschen Gestalt schei-det die Gestalt des Juden ebenso sichtbar und deutlich von sich ab, wie das klare und unbewegte Wasser das Öl als eine besondere Schicht sichtbar macht." (Jünger, *Über Nationalismus und Judenfrage,* 592.) In his remarkable essay *Laubhüttenfest 1940,* Hugo Ott compares Jünger's anti-Semitic declarations to remarks made by Heidegger, especially in the almost contemporaneous letter of 2 October 1929 to Schwoerer, in which the former, having just taken over from Husserl in Freiburg, attacks what he calls "the progressive Jewification" (*der wachsenden Verjudung*) "in the broad and the narrow sense," which would threaten "our German spiritual life."

38. "Wenn heute der Führer immer wieder spricht von der Umerziehung zur national-sozialistischen Weltanschauung, heißt das nicht irgendwelche Schlagworte beibringen, sondern einen *Gesamtwandel* hervorbringen, einen *Weltentwurf,* aus dessen Grund heraus er das ganze Volk erzieht. Der Nationalsozialismus ist nicht irgendwelche Lehre, sondern der Wandel von Grund aus der deutschen und, wie wir glauben, auch der eu-ropäischen Welt" (GA 36/37, 225).

39. "Die Philosophie hat nicht die Aufgabe, Weltanschauung zu geben, wohl aber ist Weltanschauung die Voraussetzung des Philosophierens." (Heidegger, "Davoser Dis-putation," in *Kant und das Problem der Metaphysik,* 284; "Davos Disputation Between Cassirer and Heidegger," in Appendix 3 of *Kant and the Problem of Metaphysics,* 200; translation modified.)

40. "die Leiblichkeit muß in die Existenz des Menschen versetzt werden . . . auch Rasse

und Geschlecht sind hierher zu verstehen und nicht von einer veralteten liberalistischen Biologie darzustellen" (GA 36/37, 89).

41. GA 65, 53.

42. "der liberalen Auffassung des Menschen und der menschlichen Gesellschaft."

43. See GA 36/37, 250.

44. See Chapter 1, 20.

45. "Grundsätzlich unterscheidet sich diese Denkart in nichts von der Psychoanalyse von Freud und Konsorten. Grundsätzlich auch nicht vom Marxismus . . ." (GA 36/37, 211). In these pages, Heidegger lashes out at Guido Kolbenheyer, not indeed for being, as Heidegger says without the least suggestion of criticism, *ein völkischer Mensch,* but on the contrary for supposedly having remained a prisoner of the "biological liberalism" emanating from the Darwinian doctrine of life and nineteenth-century British positivism. The attack on Freud in this context is no doubt linked to the fact that Kolbenheyer was formed in the Vienna of the 1900s.

46. See on this point GA 38, 32.

47. See especially GA 16, 251, 282, 284, 772.

48. See especially ibid., 112, 132, 151.

49. GA 36/37, 263.

50. "die Grundmöglichkeiten des urgermanischen Stammeswesens" (GA 16, 89).

51. "die Deutschen" (GA 38, 170).

52. "Jetzt sei Wir-Zeit" (ibid., 51).

53. See ibid., 13, pp. 56–60.

54. "unser Selbstsein ist das Volk" (ibid., 57).

55. Ibid., 61.

56. "Die völkische Bewegung will das Volk zur Reinheit seiner Stammesart zurückbringen." Ibid.

57. GA 38, 62.

58. "Am 12. November 1933 wurde das Volk befragt" (ibid.).

59. "Bei der Volksbefragung an 12. November 1933 ist das ganze Volk befragt worden" (ibid.).

60. Ibid., 63.

61. "eingefügt in die Ordnung und den Willen eines Staates. Wir sind *da,* eingefügt in dieses Geschehen heute, wir sind *da* in der Zugehörigkeit zu diesem *Volk,* wir sind dieses Volk selbst" (ibid.).

62. "die Zugehörigkeit zum Volk [ist] entscheidungshaft" (ibid., 65).

63. Ibid.

64. "Anderseits können auch solche mitgezählt werden, die völkisch genommen, stammesfremd sind, zum Volk nicht gehören." Ibid.

65. "Volkszählung ist also nur Einwohnerzählung." Ibid.

66. "Oft brauchen wir das Wort 'Volk' auch im Sinne von 'Rasse' (z. B. auch in der Wendung 'völkische Bewegung')." Ibid.

67. "Was wir "Rasse" nennen, hat einen Bezug auf den leiblichen, blutmäßigen Zusammenhang der Volksglieder, ihrer Geschlechter." Ibid.

68. GA 38, 48.

69. "Also auch hier dürfen wir nicht fragen: 'Was ist ein Volk?', um zu einer Aller-weltsdefinition zu kommen, sondern: 'Wer ist dies Volk, das wir selbst sind?'" (ibid., 69).

70. "Menschen, und Menschengruppen . . . die keine Geschichte haben" (GA 38, 81).

71. "Neger wie zum Beispiel Kaffern" (ibid.).

72. See Heidegger, *Les Conférences de Cassel,* 142–143.

73. "Wenn das Flugzeug freilich den Führer von München zu Mussolini nach Venedig bringt, dann geschieht Geschichte" (GA 38, 83).

74. Ibid., 153.

75. GA 36/37, 147.

76. See Chapter 6.

77. Hellingrath, *Hölderlin.*

78. See ibid., 16–17, and Bambach, *Heidegger's Roots,* 242.

79. See Kommerell, *Briefe und Aufzeichnungen, 1919–1944* and *Der Dichter als Füh-rer in der deutschen Klassik;* and Hildebrandt, *Hölderlin.*

80. In the dedication to "Norbert von Hellingrath, fallen on 14 December 1916," the name Hellingrath is capitalized and takes up as much room as the title of the lecture. See Heidegger, *Erläuterungen zu Hölderlins Dichtung,* 33.

81. "The original interpretation of the stanza [IX on the *Rhine*] must be kept free from [*freigehalten*] the reference to Rousseau" (GA 39, 278).

82. "den Anfang einer Anderen Geschichte mit dem Kampf um die Entscheidung über Ankunft oder Flucht des Gottes." (GA 39, 1.)

83. "Das sind jene Dichter, die in ihrem Sagen das künftige Seyn eines Volkes in seiner Geschichte voraussprechen" (ibid., 146).

84. "Geschichte aber ist immer einzige Geschichte je dieses Volkes, hier des Volkes dieses Dichters, die Geschichte Germaniens" (ibid., 288).

85. Ibid., 56.

86. "Wer wir sind, wissen wir nicht, solange wir nicht unsere Zeit wissen. Unsere Zeit ist aber die des Volkes zwischen den Völkern" (ibid.).

87. "*Das 'Vaterland' ist das Seyn selbst*" (ibid.).

88. "ins Wort gehüllt, das so enthüllte Seyn in die Wahrheit des Volkes . . . hineinzu-stellen" (ibid., 173).

89. "Wir müssen lernen, dieses wesentliche deutsche Wort als Nennung eines wesent-lichen Seyns in seinem wahren deutschen Gehalt wesentlich zu gebrauchen, und das heißt auch: selten."

90. "Dieses unser Sein ist aber nicht das eines vereinzelten Subjekts, sondern . . . geschichtliches Miteinandersein als Sein in einer Welt." GA 39, 174.

91. "Daß solches Sein des Menschen je das meine ist, bedeutet nicht, dieses Sein werde 'subjektiviert,' auf den abgelösten Einzelnen beschränkt und von ihm aus bestimmt." Ibid.

92. "Weil Hölderlin dieses Verborgene und Schwere ist, Dichter des Dichters als Dich-ter des Deutschen, deshalb ist er noch nicht die Macht in der Geschichte unseres Volkes geworden" (ibid., 214).

93. "Hierbei mitzuhalten ist 'Politik' im höchsten und eigentlichen Sinne" (ibid.).

94. Ibid., 210.

95. "So spricht man auch heute auf den Kanzeln von Christus als dem Führer, was nicht nur Unwahrheit, sondern was noch schlimmer ist, Christus gegenüber eine Blasphémie" (ibid.).

96. "Goering considers the frequent exclamation in Catholic milieus of 'Long live our celestial Führer Jesus Christ!' blasphemous toward Hitler" (Hermant, *Hitlérisme et humanisme,* 22).

97. Ibid.

98. "Der wahre und je einzige Führer weist in seinem Seyn allerdings in der Bereich der Halbgötter. Führersein ist ein Schicksal und daher endliches Seyn" (GA 39, 210).

99. Rosenberg writes that "the figure is always plastically limited," in *Der Mythus des 20. Jahrhunderts,* 529. This point is brought to bear by Philippe Lacoue-Labarthe and Jean-Luc Nancy in *Le Mythe nazi,* 56.

100. See GA 39, 274–275.

101. See above, pp. 76–77.

102. Rosenberg, *Der Mythus des 20. Jahrhunderts.*

103. See the letter from Heidegger to Oskar Stäbel, *Reichsfürer der Deutschen Studentenschaft,* of 6 February 1934, in Schneeberger, *Nachlese zu Heidegger,* 205–206.

104. "Als Katholik müssen Sie wissen, daß man die Wahrheit sagen muß." Martin, "Ein Gespräch mit Max Müller," in Schramm and Martin, eds., *Martin Heidegger,* 103.

105. See, on this point, the article by Jean-Luc Évard, "La croix gammée chez les poètes," 310.

106. "Die Angel, in der sich gleichsam die ganze Dichtung dreht, haben wir im Beginn der Strophe X in den ersten vier Versen zu suchen" (GA 39, 163).

107. "Mit diesem Wort treffen wir auf die Angel, in der sich das ganze Gedicht dreht" (ibid., 225).

108. Ibid., 226.

109. Ibid.

110. "Der Lichtstrahl ist der Blitz" (ibid., 242).

111. The figure sketched by Heidegger is reproduced in ibid., 245. The form of the cross is less visible in the French edition, which is not identical to the German edition (French translation, 226).

112. GA 39, 245.

113. See, on this point, Wilfried Daim, *Der Mann,* 78.

114. Ibid.

115. See Oskar Becker, "Transzendenz und Paratranszendenz." On Oskar Becker and Heidegger, see below, pp. 262–266.

116. See Chapter 9.

117. GA 39, 242–248.

118. "Daß Hölderlins Gedichte esoterisch sind, ist mir klar. . . . Sie haben aber als Ausleger Hölderlins Esoterik nicht in die öffentliche Sprache übersetzt . . . sondern in eine neue Esoterik." (Kommerell, *Briefe und Aufzeichnungen,* 396.)

119. GA 39, 205.

120. "Der Name Heraklit ist nicht der Titel für eine längst verflossene Philosophie der Griechen. Er ist ebensowenig die Formel für das Denken einer Allerweltsmenschheit an

sich. Wohl aber ist es der Name einer Urmacht des abendländisch-germanischen geschichtlichen Daseins, und zwar in ihrer ersten Auseinandersetzung mit dem Asiatischen"
(GA 39, 134).

121. "des alten nordischen Denkers aus frühgriechischer Zeit," quoted in Karl Löwith,
Mein Leben in Deutschland, 52.

122. On "surpassing" the "Asiatic" destiny, see GA 39, 173, and Löwith, *Mein Leben
in Deutschland.*

123. "Die wahre geschichtliche Freiheit der Völker Europas aber ist die *Voraussetzung*
dafür, daß das Abendland noch einmal geistig-geschichtlich *zu sich selbst* kommt und
sein Schicksal in der großen Entscheidung der Erde gegen das *Asiatische* sicher stellt" (GA
16, 333). See also GA 36/37, 92.

124. This rejection by Heidegger of the identification of the Hitlerian state with a
"work of art" is important. It shows that Hans Jürgen Syberberg's interpretation of the
Nazi state as "total work of art" (*Hitler un film d'Allemagne*), echoed in what Philippe
Lacoue-Labarthe has called "national-esthétisme" (*La Fiction du politique,* ch. 7), falls
short of Heidegger's far more trenchant and brutal comprehension, which as early as
1934 alludes to the domination of the peoples of Europe by Hitler's Reich and to the total
war that will necessarily be brought on by the "decision" against the Asiatic.

125. "Diese wahre geschichtliche Freiheit . . . bedarf nicht der organisierten Scheinge-
meinschaft einer 'Liga der Nationen.' Die Befreiung eines Volkes zu sich selbst aber
geschieht durch den Staat. Der Staat nicht als Apparat, nicht als Kunstwerk, nicht als
Beschränkung der Freiheit—sondern als Entschränkung zur inneren Freiheit aller wesentlichen Mächte des Volkes gemäß dem Gesetz ihrer inneren Rangordnung" (GA 16, 333).

126. "so gipfelt der Auftrag und die Kunde des Adlers" (GA 39, 289).

127. The insignia of the NSDAP is always carried on Heidegger's lapel during this time,
as evidenced by a photograph often reproduced of the Rector-Führer, as well as by the
testimony of Löwith on Heidegger in Rome in 1936.

128. "Da offenbart die Richtungsgestalt des Stromes etwas Entscheidendes. Die Richtung, anfänglich nach Osten weisend, wird plötzlich . . . umgebrochen in die Richtung
nach Norden auf das deutsche Land zu" (GA 39, 204).

129. "Seele aber bedeutet Rasse von innen gesehen" (Rosenberg, *Der Mythus,* 2;
quoted in Bärsch, *Die politische Religion,* 207).

130. "einem großen Strom der deutsch-nordischen Wiedergeburt" (Rosenberg, *Der
Mythus,* 459; quoted in Bärsch, *Die politische Religion,* 205).

131. See GA 39, 250ff.

132. On the true nature of this "battle," see Chapter 6.

133. "dieser sich überkreuzenden Gegenstrebigkeit" (GA 39, 245 and 248).

Chapter 5: Heidegger's Hitlerism in the Seminar On the Essence and
Concepts of Nature, History, and State

1. Heidegger, *Über Wesen und Begriff von Natur, Geschichte und Staat,* WS 1933–
1934. The course outline of the seminar has been preserved in the DLA of Marbach.

2. Heidegger, *Das Rektorat 1933/34. Tatsachen und Gedanken* (1945), GA 16, 372–
394.

3. "Diese Vorlesung [his course on the cave allegory of winter semester 1931–1932] wurde während meines Rektorats im Wintersemester 1933/34 wiederholt und durch ein stark besuchtes Seminar über 'Volk und Wissenschaft' ergänzt" (GA 16, 373).

4. The courses, both titled *The Essence of the Truth*, are published in GA 34 and GA 36/37, respectively.

5. See Kisiel, "In the Middle of Heidegger's Three Concepts of the Political," 145–152. Kisiel's English summary follows the German text rather closely but is selective and therefore incomplete.

6. Kisiel, "Heidegger als politischer Erzieher," 71–87. The excerpts from the seventh meeting are given in an annex, 83–87, not in the order of the text but distributed according to three questions formulated by the author of the article.

7. "Nicht als Rahmen verstanden wir die Zeit, sondern als die eigentliche Grundverfassung des Menschen" (Heidegger, *Über Wesen und Begriff von Natur, Geschichte und Staat*, 5th session, 12 January 1934, taken in notes by Heinrich Buhr).

8. "Wenn wir jetzt nach dem Staat fragen, dann fragen wir nach uns" (ibid.).

9. "So verstehen wir dann unter 'Staat' eine Weise des Seins, in der Mensch ist" (ibid.).

10. "Welches Seiende gehört nun zu diesem Staat? 'Das Volk'?" Ibid.

11. "Was verstehen wir unter 'Volk' mußten wir weiter fragen, denn in der franz. Revolution wurde ebenso geantwortet: das Volk" (ibid.).

12. "Diese Antwort ist nur möglich auf Grund einer Entscheidung zu einem Staat. Die Bestimmung des Volkes hängt davon ab, wie es in seinem Staat ist" (ibid.).

13. "Zunächst stellten wir formal fest, daß das Volk das Seiende ist, das in der Art und Weise des Staates ist, das Staat ist oder sein kann. Formal fragten wir dann weiter. Welche Prägung und Gestalt gibt sich das Volk im Staat, der Staat dem Volk?. . . . Die der Ordnung? Das ist so zu allgemein, denn ich kann alles ordnen, Steine, Bücher und so weiter. Wohl aber trifft eine Ordnung im Sinn von Herrschaft, Rang, Führung und Gefolgschaft die Sache" (ibid.).

14. "Wer regiert, wer darf regieren?" (Ibid.)

15. "insofern Menschsein heißt: in sich die Möglichkeit und Notwendigkeit tragen, in einer Gemeinschaft sein eigenes Sein und das der Gemeinschaft zu gestalten und zu vollenden" (Heidegger, *Über Wesen und Begriff*, 6th session, 19 January 1934, taken in notes by Itel Gelzer).

16. "Diese Entwicklung begann in der Renaissance, als zum Ziel alles Seins erhoben wurde der Einzelmensch als Person, der große Mensch, in den beiden Idealen des *homo universalis* und des Spezialisten. Dieser neue Wille zur Entfaltung der Persönlichkeit war es, was jene vollständige Wandlung zustande brachte, nach welcher fortan alles nur noch für den großen Einzelnen da sein sollte. Alles und also auch die Politik wird nun in eine Sphäre gerückt, innert derer der Mensch sich auszuleben vermag und gewillt ist. So sinken Politik, Kunst, Wissenschaft und all die andern herab zu Gebieten individuellen Entfaltungswillens, und das um so ausgesprochener, je mehr sie durch gewaltige Leistungen erweitert und somit eben spezialisiert werden. In den Folgezeiten aber ließ man die sämtlichen Kulturgebiete nur immer weiter ins unübersehbare auseinanderwachsen bis in unsere Tage, wo die Gefährlichkeit solchen Treibens sich im Zerfall unseres Staates mit elementarer Deutlichkeit zeigte. Als dringende Aufgabe unserer Zeit erkannten wir deshalb, dieser Gefahr zu begegnen, indem wir die *Politik* ihren gehörigen Rang wieder

zu geben versuchen, sie wieder zu sehen lehren als Grundcharakter des in der Geschichte philosophierenden Menschen und als das Sein, in dem der *Staat* sich entfaltet, sodaß dieselbe wahrhaft die Seinsart eines Volkes genannt werden kann" (ibid.).

17. Such is the situation described, for example, by Schmitt in chap. 6 of his *Leviathan.* See Schmitt, *The Leviathan in the State Theory of Thomas Hobbes,* 73–74.

18. "das Seiende des Staates, seine Substanz, seinen tragenden Grund: *das Volk*" (Heidegger, *Über Wesen und Begriff,* 6th session).

19. "Nahe damit verwandt aber ist ein Wort wie 'Volksgesundheit,' worin hinzukommend mitempfunden wird nur noch das Band der Bluts-und Stammeseinheit, der Rasse" (ibid., conclusion of the sixth session). This conclusion, pivotal in grasping the racial dimension of the Heideggerian conception of the people, is unpublished.

20. See Chapter 3, 67–70.

21. "Aber am umfassendsten endlich brauchen wir Volk, wenn wir etwa reden von 'Volk in Waffen': indem wir darunter ja keineswegs etwa nur die verstehen, welche den Stellungsbefehl erhalten, und auch etwas anderes als die bloße Summe der Staatsangehörigen, ja etwas noch stärker Verbindendes sogar als Stammesgemeinschaft und Rasse: nämlich die Nation, und das heißt eine unter gemeinsame Schicksal gewordene und innerhalb *eines* Staates ausgeprägte Seinsart" (ibid.).

22. "das granitene Fundament zu schaffen, auf dem dereinst ein Staat bestehen kann, der nicht einen volksfremden Mechanismus . . . , sondern einen völkischen Organismus darstellt: *Einen germanischen Staat deutscher Nation*" (Hitler, *Mein Kampf,* 361–362; English translation, 329).

23. "Das Politische als Grundmöglichkeit und ausgezeichnete Seinsweise des Menschen ist — wie wir sagten, — der Grund, auf dem der Staat ist. Das Sein des Staates liegt verankert im politischen Sein der Menschen, die als Volk diesen Staat tragen, die sich für ihn entscheiden. Zu dieser politischen, d.h. geschichtlich schicksalhaften Entscheidung bedarf es der Klärung des ursprünglichen Wesenzusammenhangs von Volk und Staat. Es ist ein Verstehen und Wissen vom Wesen des Staates und Volkes nötig für jeden Menschen. Dieses Wissen, die Begriffe und Erkenntnisse gehören zur politischen Erziehung, d.h. zur Hineinführung in unser eigenes politisches Sein." (Heidegger, *Über Wesen und Begriff,* 7th session, taken in notes by Ingeborg Schroth, beginning of 1.) Theodore Kisiel quotes only a few sentences from this paragraph, mixed with other quotations ("Heidegger als politischer Erzieher," 83–84). This is the session with the most careful notes (even though the syntax is as problematic as it is in all Heidegger's courses). I. Schroth distinguishes thirteen sections, and I will indicate in my notes the section from which the quotes are taken, so that the reader can better follow the progress of the session. I will also give references to Theodore Kisiel's study, whenever there is a paragraph that has been partially or fully included by him.

24. "es heißt aber nicht, daß nun jeder, der sich dieses Wissen aneignet, politisch handeln kann und darf als Staatsmann oder *Führer*. Denn der Ursprung alles staatlichen Handelns und Führens liegt nicht im Wissen, sondern im Sein. Jeder *Führer ist Führer, muß* der geprägten Form seines Seins nach *Führer* sein, und versteht und bedenkt u. erwirkt in der lebendigen Entfaltung seines eigenen Wesens zugleich, was Volk und Staat ist" (Heidegger, *Über Wesen und Begriff,* 7th session, end of 1; see Kisiel, "Heidegger als politischer Erzieher," 84).

25. See Darré, *Neuadel aus Blut und Boden*, and the article "Adel" in Schmitz-Berning, *Vokabular des Nationalsozialismus*, 10.

26. "Ein *Führer* braucht nicht politisch erzogen zu werden, wohl aber eine Hüterschar im Volk, die die Verantwortung für den Staat mit tragen hilft. Denn jeder Staat und jedes Wissen um den Staat wächst in einer politischen Tradition. Wo dieser nährende, sichernde Boden fehlt, kann die beste Staatsidee nicht Wurzel fassen und aus dem tragenden Schoss des Volkes hervorwachsen und sich entfalten. Otto der Grosse gründete sein Reich auf die geistlichen Fürsten, indem er sie zu politischem und militärischem Dienst und Wissen verpflichtete. Und Friedrich der Große erzog den preußischen Adel zu Hütern seines Staates. Bismarck übersah diese Verwurzelung seiner Staatsidee in den festen, kräftigen Boden des politischen Adels, und als sein stützender Arm losliess, sank das zweite Reich haltlos zusammen. Wir dürfen die Gründung einer politischen Tradition und Erziehung eines politischen Adels jetzt nicht übersehen" (Heidegger, *Über Wesen und Begriff*, 7th session, beginning of 2; see Kisiel, "Heidegger als politischer Erzieher," 84–85).

27. Schmitt, *Der Hüter der Verfassung*, 91.

28. "Vielmehr hat jeder Einzelne sich jetzt zu besinnen, um zu dem Wissen von Volk und Staat und zu eigener Verantwortung zu kommen. Auf unserer Wachheit und Bereitschaft und unserem Leben ruht der Staat. Die Art und Weise unseres Seins prägt das Sein unseres Staates. Jedes Volk nimmt so Stellung zum Staat und keinem Volk fehlt der Drang zum Staat. Das Volk, das den Staat ablehnt, das staatenlos ist, hat nur die Sammlung seines Wesens noch nicht gefunden; es fehlt ihm noch Gefaßtheit und Kraft zur Verpflichtung an sein *völkisch*es Schicksal" (Heidegger, *Über Wesen und Begriff*, 7th session, end of 2; see Kisiel, "Heidegger als politischer Erzieher," 85).

29. Der hohe Meißner, altitude 2,457 feet, is located in the forest-covered mountain range of Hessen, southeast of Kassel.

30. "Privatdozent Dr. Stadelmann trat sodann vor und hielt einen Ansprache. Die Jugend stände an diesem Tage überall vor den Flammen, um Sonnenwende zu begehen. Er sprach vom Sinn der Sonnenwende, von den Vorkriegsjahren, als damals die deutsche Jugend auf dem Hohen Meißner die Wende beging, von den Schicksalstagen des deutschen Volkes und von den Tagen des Jahres 1933, wo eine neue Generation bereit stände, um ihren treudeutschen Willen kundzutun. Und in solcher Stunde gedenke man besonders jener Baumeister am Volk, die Großes für dieses geschaffen hätten. Einer von ihnen sei unser Altkanzler Bismarck, dem diese Huldigung besonders gewidmet sei. Der Geist Bismarcks sei Ritterlichkeit, Selbstgenügsamkeit, und dieser Geist müsse sich auch bei der akademischen Jugend durchsetzen. Bismarck solle Wegweiser sein für das neue Deutschland. Die Jugend, die jetzt am brennenden Holzstoß stände, müsse danach streben, ein geeinigtes Volk zu bilden, müsse Bismarcks Worte beherzigen: 'Ich würde keine Freunde haben, wenn ich keine Feinde hätte.' Absolute Ritterlichkeit sei dem Starken vorbehalten. Der Grundzug des germanischen Charakters liege in der Befriedigung des eigenen Bedürfnisses. Unser Kampf müsse sich einsetzen für Gottheit, Freiheit, Vaterland, Jugend, Volk!" (*Freiburger Zeitung*, 26 June 1933, p. 7; quoted in Schneeberger, *Nachlese zu Heidegger*, 70.)

31. "Ich würde keine Freunde haben, wenn ich keine Feinde hätte" (ibid.).

32. See Chapter 2, 165.

33. GA 16, 170–171.

34. GA 16, 174.

35. Rudolf Stadelmann to Martin Heidegger, 16 October 1933, quoted in Farías, *Heidegger and Nazism*, 130–131.

36. "Das Wirtschaftsleben der Gegenwart in geschichtlicher und politischer Betrachtung (Liberalismus, Faschismus, Sozialismus)"; "Rassenhygiene und ihre Bedeutung für die Bevölkerungspolitik"; "Vom Arbeitslager zum Arbeitsdienst"; Die Heimatlehre vom nationalen Deutschtum"; "Soziale Hygiene und Bevölkerungspolitik"; "Deutsche Heimatlehre (Rasse, Volkstum, Heimat)."

37. In memory of the failed military coup of Munich. Hitler begins *Mein Kampf* by evoking the event and listing the dead.

38. Stadelmann, *Das geschichtliche Selbstbewußtsein der Nation*. Rede, gehalten am 9. November 1933 vor Rektor, Dozenten und Studenten der Universität Freiburg i. Br.

39. Ibid., 14.

40. "Daraus ergibt sich für Mensch und Volk ein Selbstbewußtsein, das ohne Selbstreflexion ist. . . . Selbstbewußtsein in diesem höchsten Sinn ist Selbsterfahrung, und erst durch sie vermag der Einzelne oder die Nation sich in die Hand zu bekommen und dadurch den Schritt vom Ich zum Selbst zu tun. Erst auf dieser Stufe sprechen wir von *geschichtlichem Selbstbewußtsein* im engeren Verstand des Worts" (ibid.).

41. "das geschichtliche Dasein als ein schicksalhaftes" (ibid., 15).

42. "wozu noch Schulen, wenn die Männer groß werden in Lagern und Stürmen, wozu Besinnung, wenn die Not eines Volkes nach Taten ruft?" (ibid., 4).

43. "wir müssen uns . . . stark machen gegen die Versuchung, auszubrechen aus der Zucht des Geistes, um den Weg zur Tat zu verkürzen" (ibid., 5).

44. "Die Außenpolitik des Reichsführers, zu der sich das deutsche Volk am kommenden Sonntag bekennen wird, ist der Ausdruck dieses zugleich mutigen und verbindlichen Selbstbewußtseins, das auf der Basis der Selbstachtung von den Andern Achtung verlangt" (ibid., 11).

45. "kämpfen kann ich nur für etwas, das ich liebe" (ibid.). Stadelmann refers in the note to "Adolf Hitler, *Mein Kampf,* 9th ed, Munich, 1932, 32ff."

46. Ibid., 11.

47. "Nicht in der Geschichte, sondern im Mythos erkennt sich der Genius der Nation" (ibid., 12).

48. Ibid., 14.

49. "Hegel hat in einem Großartigen Abschnitt seiner 'Philosophie der Weltgeschichte' die 'Gemütlichkeit" definiert und Gemütlichkeit in einer genialen Auslegung philosophisch als 'Empfindung der natürlichen Totalität' präzisiert. Wilhelm Dilthey und auf seinen Spuren neuerdings Ernst Krieck haben als Grundzug des deutschen Geistes die Objektivität herausgehoben: die Hingabe an die Unendlichkeit des Lebens und den Sinn für die Kraftäußerung um ihrer selbst willen" (ibid., 13).

50. "Wissen von einer Ur-geschichte ist . . . Mythologie" (Heidegger, *Einführung in die Metaphysik,* 119; English translation, 155. The difference between Heidegger and Krieck on this point is that the former does not oppose mythos to logos, as the latter does.

51. Stadelmann, *Das Geschichtliche Selbstbewußtsein der Nation,* 18.

52. Ibid., 19.

53. Ibid., 23.

54. "Eine Stunde, vordem Ihr Brief kam, sann ich über das geschichtliche Selbstbewußtsein . . . und dachte dabei lebhaft an Sie" (GA 16, 370).

55. "Wir müssen darum mit besonderer Bereitschaft versuchen, das Wesen von Volk und Staat weiterhin zu klären. Wiederum gehen wir dabei von der Klärung des Politischen als Seinsart des Menschen und Ermöglichung des Staates aus. Dieser Auffassung stehen noch andere Begriffe des Politischen entgegen, z.B. der Begriff des Freund-Feidverhältnisses, der auf Carl Schmitt zurückgeht. Dieser Begriff von Politik als Freund-Feindverhältnis ist gegründet in der Anschauung, daß Kampf, d.h. die reale Möglichkeit des Krieges, Voraussetzung des politischen Verhaltens sei, daß eben die Möglichkeit des Entscheidungskampfes, der auch ohne militärische Mittel ausgefochten werden kann, vorhandene Gegensätze, sie seien moralische, konfessionelle oder wirtschaftliche, verschärft bis zur radikalen Einheit als Freund und Feind. In der Einheit und Totalität dieses Gegensatzes von Freund-Feind ruht alle politische Existenz. Entscheidend für diese Anschauung ist aber, daß die politische Einheit nicht identisch sein muß mit Staat und Volk" (Heidegger, *Über Wesen und Begriff*, 7th session, 3; see Kisiel, "Heidegger als politischer Erzieher," 86).

56. See Chapter 8.

57. The speech is quoted in *Hitlers Zweites Buch. Ein Dokument aus dem Jahr 1928* (Stuttgart, 1961), 27.

58. "Eine andere Fassung des Politischen spricht sich in Bismarcks Worten aus: 'Politik ist die Kunst des Möglichen.' Mit Möglichkeit ist hier nicht eine beliebige, zufällig ausdenkbare gemeint, sondern das Einzig-Mögliche, Nur-Mögliche. Politik ist für Bismarck das Vermögen, das zu sehen und zu erwirken, was wesensnotwendig aus einer geschichtlichen Situation entspringen muß, und zugleich die *teknè*, die Geschicklichkeit, das Erkannte zu verwirklichen. Damit wird Politik zum schöpferischen Entwurf des großen Staatsmannes, der das Gesamtgeschehen der Geschichte, nicht etwa nur der Gegenwart, überblickt, der sich in seiner Staatsidee ein Ziel setzt, das er trotz allen zufälligen Wandlungen der Situation fest im Auge behält. Diese Anschauung von Politik und Staat ist eng an die Person des genialen Staatsmannes gebunden, von dessen Wesensblick und Kraft und Haltung ist das Sein des Staates abhängig, wo dessen Macht und Leben aufhört, beginnt auch die Ohnmacht des Staates" (Heidegger, *Über Wesen und Begriff*, 7th session, 4; see Kisiel, "Heidegger als politischer Erzieher," 86–87).

59. In that "based on the people" no longer has anything democratic about it, and takes on a racial meaning.

60. Schmitt, *Staat, Bewegung, Volk,* 35; French translation, 51.

61. "Das Volk, das Seiende hat ein ganz bestimmtes Verhältnis zu seinem Sein, zum Staat" (Heidegger, *Über Wesen und Begriff*, 7th session, excerpt from 5; see Kisiel, "Heidegger als politischer Erzieher," 87).

62. "Ein Staat *ist* nur, indem er *wird, wird* zum *geschichtlichen Sein* des Seienden, das *Volk* heißt" (Heidegger, *Die gegenwärtige Lage und die künftige Aufgabe der deutschen Philosophie*, GA 16, 333).

63. "Der Mensch, der seinem Wesen nach fragen muß, der muß sich der Gefahr des Nichts, des Nihilismus aussetzen, um aus dessen Überwindung den Sinn seines Seins zu erfassen" (Heidegger, *Über Wesen und Begriff*, 7th session, end of 7, unpublished).

64. See Kershaw, *Hitler 1889–1936: Hubris*, xxvi–xxvii, and the entire chapter 13, esp. 529–531.

65. These are the expressions used by Heidegger in 13 of the seventh session, which we quote in their entirety below, pp. 139–140.

66. "Ohne das Bewußtsein, das Wissen und Sorgen um Höhe und Tiefe, Größe und Ohnmacht seines Seins im Ganzen der Welt ist er nicht mehr als Mensch" (Heidegger, *Über Wesen und Begriff*, 7th session, excerpt from 10, unpublished).

67. "so will und liebt das Volk den Staat als seine Art und Weise, als Volk zu sein. Das Volk ist beherrscht vom Drang, vom *eros* zum Staat" (Heidegger, *Über Wesen und Begriff*, 7th session, excerpt from 11; see Kisiel, "Heidegger als politischer Erzieher," 85). Kisiel puts *ethos* where the transcription has *eros*, which corresponds, moreover, unarguably with Heidegger's intent.

68. "So ist denn auch die Form, die Verfassung des Staates wesentlicher Ausdruck dessen, was das Volk sich als Sinn setzt für sein Sein. Die Verfassung ist nicht ein rationaler Vertrag, eine Rechtsordnung, politische Logik oder sonst etwas Beliebiges, Absolutes, sondern Verfassung und Recht sind Verwirklichung unserer Entscheidung zum Staat, sind die faktischen Zeugen für das, was wir für unsere geschichtliche, *völkische* Aufgabe halten und zu leben versuchen" (Heidegger, *Über Wesen und Begriff*, 7th session, excerpt from 12; see Kisiel, "Heidegger als politischer Erzieher," 85).

69. "So ist denn auch das Wissen um Verfassung und Recht nichts, was nur sogenannte 'Politiker' und Juristen angeht, sondern gehört als Staatsdenken-und-Bewußtsein in das Dasein jedes einzelnen Menschen, der den Kampf um Verantwortung für sein Volk auf sich nimmt. Zu unserer Aufgabe in diesem geschichtlichen Augenblick gehört die klare Aus- und Umbildung des Staatsdenkens. Es muß jeder Mann und jeder Frau, wenn auch nur dumpf und unklar wissen lernen, daß ihr einzelnes Leben das Schicksal des Volkes und Staates entscheidet, es trägt oder verwirft" (Heidegger, *Über Wesen und Begriff*, 7th session, excerpt from 12; see Kisiel, "Heidegger als politscher Erzieher," 85–86).

70. Heidegger, *Sein und Zeit*, 384.

71. That is what Richard Wolin has shown in a particularly revealing way in his article "Carl Schmitt, l'existentialisme, et l'État total," *Les Temps modernes* (February 1990): 50–88.

72. Schmitt, *Les Trois Types de pensée juridique*, 71.

73. "Der Nationalsozialismus . . . sichert und pflegt jede echte Volkssubstanz, wo er sie trifft, in Landschaft, Stamm oder Stand. Er hat das bäuerliche Erbhofrecht geschaffen; das Bauerntum gerettet; das deutsche Beamtentum von fremdgearteten Elementen gereinigt und dadurch als Stand wiederhergestellt. Er hat den Mut, Ungleiches ungleich zu behandeln und notwendige Differenzierungen durchzusetzen" (*Staat, Bewegung, Volk*, 32; French translation, 48).

74. "Ohne den Grundsatz der Artgleichheit könnte der nationalsozialistische Staat nicht bestehen und wäre sein Rechtsleben nicht denkbar" (ibid., 42; French translation, 59).

75. "Dieser Begriff von Führung stammt ganz aus dem konkreten, substanzhaften Denken der nationalsozialistischen Bewegung. . . . Er stammt weder aus barocken Allegorien und Repräsentationen, noch aus einer cartesianischen *idée générale*. Er ist ein Begriff unmittelbarer Gegenwart und realer *Präsenz*. Aus diesem Grunde schließt er auch,

als positives Erfordernis, eine *unbedingte Artgleichheit zwischen Führer und* Gefolgschaft in sich ein" (ibid., 42; French translation, 58–59).

76. Here our reading concurs with that of Richard Wolin: "This position means the final union of the two parallel aspects of his thought, decisionism and *Ordnungsdenken.* The concrete racial life of the Volk (*Artgleichheit*) furnishes henceforth the existential basis of the decision" ("Carl Schmitt, l'existentialisme, et l'État total," 87).

77. "das Seiende des Staates, seine Substanz, seinen tragenden Grund: *das Volk.*"

78. See, for example, Heidegger's rejection of the "ontological interpretation of the substantiality of the subject" (*Sein und Zeit,* 8, p. 22), and his development on the "inadequate ontology of the substantial" apropos of the Kantian "I think" and its critique by Heinz Heimsoeth (ibid., 64, pp. 317–321).

79. See Heidegger, *Sein und Zeit,* 117, 212, 303, 314.

80. "Führertum und Artgleichheit als Grundbegriffe des nationalsozialistischen Rechts" (Schmitt, *Staat, Bewegung, Volk,* 32).

81. GA 36/37, 80, 119, 225.

82. "die *Leiblichkeit* muß *in die Existenz* des Menschen versetzt werden . . . auch Rasse und Geschlecht sind hierher zu verstehen und nicht von einer veralteten liberalistischen Biologie darzustellen" (GA 36/37, 178).

83. GA 36/37, 225.

84. "Zu diesem Wissen gehört auch die Bindung an die Ordnung des Staates. Ordnung ist die Seinsweise des Menschen und somit auch des Volkes. Die Ordnung des Staates äußert sich im abgegrenzten Aufgabengebiet der einzelnen Menschen und Menschengruppen. Diese Ordnung ist nichts bloß Organisches, wie man nach der Fabel des Menenius Agrippa annehmen könnte und annahm, sondern sie ist etwas Geistig-Menschliches, d.h. zugleich Freiwilliges. Sie gründet im Herrschafts- und Dienstschaftsverhältnis der Menschen zueinander. Wie die mittelalterliche Lebensordnung, so ist auch heute die Ordnung des Staates getragen von dem freien, reinen Willen zu Gefolgschaft und Führerschaft, d.h. zu Kampf und Treue. Denn wenn wir fragen: 'Was ist Herrschaft? Worin gründet sie?' Dann erfahren wir in einer wahren, wesentlichen Antwort nichts von Macht, Knechtschaft, Unterdrückung, Zwang. Wir erfahren vielmehr, daß Herrschaft, Autorität und Dienst, Unterordnung in einer gemeinsamen Aufgabe gründen. Nur wo Führer und Geführte gemeinsam in *ein* Schicksal sich binden und für die Verwirklichung *einer* Idee kämpfen, erwächst wahre Ordnung. Dann wirkt sich die geistige Überlegenheit und Freiheit aus als tiefe Hingabe aller Kräfte an das Volk, den Staat, als strengste Zucht, als Einsatz, Standhalten, Einsamkeit und Liebe. Dann ist die Existenz und Überlegenheit des Führers eingesenkt in das Sein, in die Seele des Volkes und bindet es so mit Ursprünglichkeit und Leidenschaft an die Aufgabe. Und wenn das Volk diese Hingabe spürt, wird es sich in den Kampf führen lassen und den Kampf wollen und lieben. Es wird seine Kräfte entfalten und ausharren, treu sein und sich opfern. In jedem neuen Augenblick werden sich Führer und Volk enger verbinden, um das Wesen ihres Staates, also ihres Seins zu erwirken; aneinander wachsend werden sie den beiden bedrohenden Mächten Tod und Teufel, d.h. Vergänglichkeit und Abfall vom eigenen Wesen, ihr sinnvolles, geschichtliches Sein und Wollen entgegensetzen" (Heidegger, *Über Wesen und Begriff,* 7th session, 13, unpublished).

85. "sich niemand zu wundern braucht, wenn in unserem Volke die Personifikation des

Teufels als Sinnbild alles Bösen die leibhaftige Gestalt des Juden annimmt" (Hitler, *Mein Kampf*, 355; English translation, 324).

86. Carl Schmitt, "La science allemande du droit dans sa lutte contre l'esprit juif," 180.

87. Ibid., 70.

88. Hitler, *Mein Kampf*, 336; English translation, 307. There is little need to point out that the racist interpretation of the temple scene is a sordid invention of Hitler's.

89. "Des Weiteren hatten wir noch etwas nachzutragen über die inneren Gründe des Scheiterns der Bismarckschen Politik. Wir haben gehört, das ein Volk neben der Notwendigkeit eines Führers noch die einer Überlieferung habe, deren Träger ein politischer Adel sei. Daß das Zweite Reich nach dem Tode Bismarcks einem rettungslosen Zerfall ausgeliefert war, hat seinen Grund nicht nur darin, daß es Bismarck nicht gelang, diesen politischen Adel zu schaffen. Er brachte es auch nicht fertig, das Proletariat als eine in sich berechtigte Erscheinung zu betrachten und es mit verständnisvollem Entgegenkommen in den Staat zurückzuführen. Der Hauptgrund ist aber wohl der, daß sich der völkische Charakter des zweiten Reiches in dem erschöpfte, was wir Patriotismus und Vaterland nennen. Diese Elemente des Zusammenschlusses von 1870–71 sind an sich nicht negativ zu bewerten, sie sind aber völlig unzureichend für einen wahrhaft völkischen Staat. Sie hatten auch nicht die letzte Verwurzelheit im Volk."

90. "Er [der völkische Staat] hat die Rasse in den Mittelpunkt des allgemeinen Lebens zu setzen" (Hitler, *Mein Kampf*, 446; English translation, 403).

91. "Indem das alte Reich an der Frage der Erhaltung der rassischen Grundlagen unseres Volkstums achtlos vorüberging, mißachtete es auch das alleinige Recht, das auf dieser Welt Leben gibt" (ibid., 359; English translation, 327).

92. "in seinem Blute wurzelnden Eigenschaften seines Wesens" (ibid., English translation slightly modified).

93. "Wenn wir nach dem Volk im Raum fragen, so müssen wir zuvor zwei irrige Vorstellungen beseitigen. Hören wir diese beiden Worte, so denken wir zunächst an ein zeitgenössisches Schlagwort, an 'Volk ohne Raum.' Wenn wir darunter Lebensraum verstehen, so ist damit zweifellos zuviel gesagt. Man könnte vielleicht sagen: Volk ohne genügenden, ohne ausreichenden Lebensraum zu seiner positiven Entfaltung. Wir müssen immer wissen, daß zum Volk in seinem Konkretsein notwendig der Raum hinzugehört, daß es ein 'Volk ohne Raum' im wörtlichsten Sinne gar nicht gibt" (Heidegger, *Über Wesen und Begriff*, end of 8th session; see English summary by Kisiel, "In the Middle," 148).

94. Grimm, *Volk ohne Raum* (Munich, 1926).

95. See Vermeil, *Doctrinaires de la révolution allemande*, 289.

96. He is indeed speaking here of an "Im-Raum-Sein eines Volkes."

97. "Die Geschiche lehrt uns, daß Nomaden nicht von der Trostlosigkeit der Wüste und der Steppe zu solchen geprägt wurden, sondern daß sie auch vielfach Wüste hinterließen, wo sie fruchtbares und kultiviertes Land vorfanden, und daß bodenständige Menschen auch in der Wildnis sich eine Heimat zu schaffen wussten" (Heidegger, *Über Wesen und Begriff*, 8th session [unpublished]).

98. "Einem slawischen Volke würde die Natur unseres deutschen Raumes bestimmt anders offenbar werden als uns, dem semitischen Nomaden wird sie vielleicht überhaupt nie offenbar" (ibid.).

99. Heidegger nominalizes the adjective *völkisch,* which refers to the people understood as a race, in speaking of the "spezifischen Völkischen" at the end of the eighth session.

100. "Führer hat es mit Volkswillen zu tun, dieser ist nicht Summe der Einzelwillen, sondern ein Ganzes von ursprünglicher Eigentümlichkeit. Die Frage nach dem Willensbewußtsein der Gemeinschaft ist ein Problem in allen Demokratien, das freilich aber erst dann fruchtbar werden kann, wenn Führerwille und Volkswille in ihrer Wesenheit erkannt sind. Heute gilt es, das Grundverhältnis unseres gemeinsamen Seins auf diese Wirklichkeit von Volk und Führer einzurichten, wobei beide als eine Wirklichkeit nicht zu trennen sind. Erst dann, wenn dieses Grundschema durch Anwandlung im Wesentlichen erfolgt ist, ist eine wahre Führerschaft möglich" (Heidegger, *Über Wesen und Begriff,* 8th session, conclusion unpublished in German; see English summary by Kisiel, "In the Middle," 150–151). Kisiel translates the *wahre Führerschaft* as "a true schooling of leaders," which is questionable, since Heidegger maintains that one cannot learn to become a Führer.

101. "Zur Herrschaft gehört Macht, die eine Rangordnung schafft durch die Willensdurchsetzung des Herrschenden, sofern er wirklich mächtig ist, d.h. Wege und Ziele weist den Beherrschten . . ." (Heidegger, *Über Wesen und Begriff,* excerpt from the 9th session, 23 February 1934, taken in note form by Emil Schilt—the entirety of the ninth session is unpublished; for the English summary of Kisiel, see "In the Middle," 151–152).

102. "Arten der Willensdurchsetzung: a) Überzeugung durch Rede b) Zwang durch Tat. In unseren Tagen überzeugt der Führer durch Reden" (Heidegger, *Über Wesen und Begriff,* excerpt from 9th session).

103. The only knowledge I have been able to obtain of this passage from the ninth session is through the English summary of Kisiel, "In the Middle," 151.

104. "Der wirkende Wille überzeugt aber am eindringlichsten durch Taten. Der große Täter und Wirker ist zugleich der Mächtige, der Herrscher, dessen Dasein und Wille bestimmend wird durch Überzeugung, d.h. durch Erkennung und Anerkennung des höher waltenden Willens des Führers" (Heidegger, *Über Wesen und Begriff,* 9th session).

105. "Gegenwärtige politische Erziehung = Schaffung einer neuen Grundhaltung willensmäßiger Art" (ibid.).

106. "Eine Umwandlung unseres ganzen Daseins ist notwendig . . ." (GA 36/37, 161).

107. "die *große Wandlung des Daseins des Menschen*" (GA 36/37, 119).

108. "Der Nationalsozialismus ist nicht irgendwelche Lehre, sondern der Wandel von Grund aus der deutschen . . . Welt" (GA 36/37, 225).

109. "Der Führerwillen schafft allererst die anderen zu einer Gefolgschaft um, aus der die Gemeinschaft entspringt. Aus dieser lebendigen Verbundenheit geht ihr Opfer und Dienst hervor nicht aus Gehorsam und Zwang von Institutionen" (Heidegger, *Über das Wesen und Begriff,* 9th session).

110. Farías, *Heidegger and Nazism,* 4. In the later German version of the book (40–41), Farías carries that thesis even further, doubtless to defend himself, but at the risk of giving it an importance I consider excessive.

111. "Denkschrift über die inneren Gründe für die Verfügungen zur Herstellung einer erhöhten Schlagkraft der Bewegung."

112. See Kershaw, *Hitler 1889–1936,* 718n152.

113. "Das *Fundament* der politischen Organisation ist die Treue. In ihr offenbart sich als edelster Gefühlsausdruck die Erkenntnis der Notwendigkeit des *Gehorsams* als *Voraussetzung* für den Aufbau jeder menschlichen Gemeinschaft. Die Treue in Gehorsam kann *niemals* ersetzt werden durch formale technische Maßnahmen und Einrichtungen, gleich welcher Art. Der Zweck der politischen Organisation ist die Ermöglichung weitester Verbreitung einer für die Lebensbehauptung der Nation notwendig angesehen Erkenntnis sowie des ihr dienenden Willens. Der Endzweck ist damit die Erfassung der Nation für diese Idee. Der *Sieg* der nationalsozialistischen *Idee* ist das *Ziel* unseres Kampfes. Die Organisation unserer Partei ein Mittel zur Erreichung dieses Ziel" (Kershaw, *Hitler 1889–1936*, 500; English translation, 403).

114. "Bedenklich schien ihm bloß das maßlose Organisieren auf Kosten der lebendigen Kräfte" (Löwith, *Mein Leben in Deutschland*, 57; French translation, 78).

115. We have seen Heidegger affirm, in the seventh session, that "it is only when the *Führer* and those he leads bind themselves in one *sole* destiny and struggle for the realization of *one* idea, that true order can grow."

116. Indeed, Heidegger affirms in his seminar that "the order of the state is today borne by the free and pure will to obey and be led, that is, for combat and loyalty." It is true that we observe a difference, in that obedience (*Gehorsam*) is placed, in the *Denkschrift*, alongside loyalty, while in the seminar it is placed next to institutional constraint. But the basis of the doctrine remains the same: all that matters is unconditional loyalty to the Führer and doing battle for the same "idea."

117. "Der Staat . . . ist die wirklichste Wirklichkeit, die in einem neuen, ursprünglichen Sinn dem ganzen Sein einen neuen Sinn geben muß. Die höchste Verwirklichung menschlichen Seins geschieht im Staat" (Heidegger, *Über Wesen und Begriff*, end of 9th session).

118. "Der Führerstaat — wie wir ihn haben — bedeutet die Vollendung der geschichtlichen Entwicklung: die Verwirklichung des Volkes im Führer. Der preußische Staat, wie er sich vollendete unter Bildung des preußischen Adels, ist die Vorform des heutigen. Dieses Verhältnis bezeugt die Wahlverwandtschaft, die zwischen dem Preußentum und dem Führer besteht. Aus dieser großen Tradition stammt und in ihm stehen wir, wenn wir uns zu seinem Sinn bekennen, das Wort des großen Kurfürsten aus lutherischem Geiste: *Sic gesturus sum principatum, ut sciam rem esse populi, non meam*" (ibid.).

Chapter 6: Heidegger, Carl Schmitt, and Alfred Baeumler

1. See Chapter 2, 53–55 and 57.

2. *Erik Wolf Nachlaß*, C 130.

3. "Zur Demokratie gehört also notwendig erstens Homogeneität und zweitens — nötigenfalls — die Ausscheidung oder Vernichtung des Heterogenen" (Carl Schmitt, *Die geistesgeschichtliche Lage des heutigen Parlementarismus*, 2nd ed. [Munich, 1926], 14; quoted by in Manfred Gangl, "Gesellschaftliche Pluralität und politische Einheit," 109).

4. "Das deutsche Recht und der deutsche Staat beruhen von jetzt ab nicht mehr auf einer leeren und formalen 'Gleichheit Aller vor dem Gesetz' oder dem irreführenden 'Gleichheit alles dessen, was Menschenantlitz trägt,' sondern auf der sachlichen und substanzhaften Gleichartigkeit des ganzen, in sich einheitlichen und gleichartigen deutschen

Volkes. Gleichartigkeit ist mehr und etwas Tieferes als Gleichschaltung, die nur ein Mittel und Werkzeug der Gleichartigkeit ist. . . . Die Bestimmungen über Beamte, Ärzte und Anwälte reinigen das öffentliche Leben von nichtarischen fremdgearteten Elementen" (Schmitt, "Das gute Recht der deutschen Revolution"; see Gangl, "Gesellschaftliche," 118–119).

5. See Heidegger, *Die Grundbegriffe der Metaphysik,* GA 29/30, 243–245; French translation, 245–247.

6. See the letter from Karl Vossler to Benedetto Croce of 25 August 1933, presenting Heidegger and Schmitt as "the two intellectual disasters of the New Germany" (quoted by Schneeberger, *Ergänzungen,* 110–111); and Jaspers's judgment of 22 December 1945 (quoted in *Martin Heidegger/Karl Jaspers,* 272; French translation, 421).

7. According to the expression used by Derrida in "Heidegger's Ear," in *Reading Heidegger: Commemorations,* 204; and in *Politiques de l'amitié* (Paris: Galilée, 1994), 403.

8. "Sehr verehrte Herr Schmitt! Ich danke Ihnen für die Übersendung Ihrer Schrift, die ich in der zweiten Auflage schon kenne und die einen Ansatz von der größten Tragweite enthält. Ich wünsche sehr, mit Ihnen darüber einmal mündlich sprechen zu können. An Ihrem Zitat von Heraklit hat mich ganz besonders gefreut, daß sie den *basileus* nicht vergessen haben, der dem ganzen Spruch erst seinen vollen Gehalt gibt, wenn man ihn ganz auslegt. Seit Jahren habe ich eine solche Auslegung mit Bezug auf den Wahrheitsbegriff bereit liegen — das *edeixe* und *epoiese,* die im Fragment 53 vorkommen. Aber nun stehe ich selbst mitten im *polemos* und Literarisches muß zurücktreten. Heute möchte ich Ihnen nur sagen, daß ich sehr auf Ihre entscheidende Mitarbeit hoffe, wenn es gilt, die Juristische Fakultät im Ganzen nach ihrer wissenschaftlichen und erzieherischen Ausrichtung von Innen her neu aufzubauen. Hier ist es leider sehr trostlos. Die Sammlung der geistigen Kräfte, die das Kommende heraufführen sollen, wird immer dringender. Für heute schließe ich mit freundlichen Grüßen. Heil Hitler! Ihr Heidegger" (published in *Telos,* 72 [summer 1987]: 132 [*Special Issue: Carl Schmitt: Enemy or Foe?*]; included in GA 16, 156).

9. Farías, *Heidegger and Nazism,* 138; German translation, 199.

10. Since Farías, the existence of that invitation to join the Nazi party seems to have been accepted (see, for example, D. Séglard's presentation of Schmitt in *Les Trois Types de pensée juridique,* 26).

11. The *Nachlaß Schmitt* in Düsseldof does mention (p. 75) the existence of two letters from Heidegger, but upon verification, it turns out to have been an error: one of these two letters was only a copy of the one from 22 August 1933.

12. Schmitt, *Les Trois Types,* 81.

13. Ibid., 72.

14. Ibid., 74.

15. Hölderlin, *Sämtliche Werke,* Berlin, 1923, vol. VI, p. 9; quoted by Schmitt, *Les Trois Types,* 75.

16. Ibid., 102.

17. GA 16, 105; see Chapter 3, 61–62.

18. GA 16, 157; see Chapter 2, 45.

19. Martin Heidegger to Elisabeth Blochmann, 30 August 1933, 69; French translation, 292.

20. See the letter from Carl Schmitt to the rector of the University of Freiburg of 25 January 1935, quoted by Seemann, *Die politischen Säuberungen*, 100.

21. "Die eigentlich *politische* Unterscheidung ist die Unterscheidung von *Freund* und *Feind*" (Schmitt, *Der Begriff des Politischen*, 7).

22. "Die Möglichkeit spezifisch politischer Beziehungen ist dadurch gegeben, daß es nicht nur Freunde — Gleichgeartete und Verbündete — sondern auch Feinde gibt" (ibid., 8).

23. "Der Feind ist in einem besonders intensiven Sinne *existenziell* ein Anderer und Fremder, mit dem im extremen Fall *existenzielle Konflikte* möglich sind" (ibid.).

24. "Weder die Frage, ob der 'äußerste Fall' gegeben ist, noch die weitere Frage, was als 'äußerstes Mittel,' lebensnotwendig wird, um die eigene Existenz zu verteidigen und das eigene Sein zu wahren — *in suo esse perseverare* — könnte ein Fremder entscheiden. Der Fremde und Andersgeartete mag sich streng 'kritisch,' 'objektiv,' 'neutral,' 'rein wissenschaftlich' geben und unter ähnlichen Verschleierungen sein fremdes Urteil einmischen. Seine 'Objektivität' ist entweder nur eine politische *Verschleierung* oder aber die völlige, alles Wesentliche verfehlende *Beziehungslosigkeit*. Bei politischen Entscheidungen beruht selbst die bloße Möglichkeit richtigen Erkennens und Verstehens und damit auch die Befugnis mitzusprechen und zu urteilen nur auf dem existenziellen *Teilhaben* und Teilnehmen, nur auf der echten *participatio*. Den extremen Konfliktsfall können daher nur die Beteiligten *selbst* unter sich ausmachen; insbesondere kann jeder von ihnen nur *selbst* entscheiden, ob das Anderssein des Fremden im konkret vorliegenden Konfliktsfall die Negation der eigenen Art Existenz bedeutet und deshalb abgewehrt oder bekämpft werden muß, um die eigene, seinsmäßige Art von Leben zu retten" (ibid.).

25. See Chapter 9, 289–300.

26. "Das Bewußtsein der Artgleichheit und völkischen Zusammengehörigkeit aktualisiert sich vor allem in der Fähigkeit, die Artverschiedenheit zu erkennen und den Freund vom Feind unterscheiden. Und zwar kommt es darauf an, die Artverschiedenheit dort zu erkennen, wo sie nicht durch die Zugehörigkeit zu einer fremden Nation ohne weiteres sichtbar ist, etwa in dem Juden, der durch eine aktive Beteiligung an dem kulturellen und wirtschaftlichen Leben die Illusion einer Artgleichheit und einer Zugehörigkeit zum Volke zu erwecken suchte und zu erwecken verstand." (Ernst Forsthoff, *Der Totale Staat*, 38; quoted in Gross, *Carl Schmitt und die Juden*, 65.)

27. "A. Baeumler deutet Nietzsches und Heraklits Kampfbegriff ganz ins Agonale. Frage: woher kommen in Walhall die Feinde? H. Schaefer, *Staatsform und Politik* (1932), weist auf den 'agonalen Grundcharakter' des griechischen Lebens hin; auch bei blutigen Zusammenstößen von Griechen mit Griechen war der Kampf nur 'Agon,' der Gegner nur 'Antagonist,' Gegenspieler oder Gegenringer, nicht Feind, und die Beendigung des Wettringens infolgedessen auch kein Friedensschluß (*eirenè*). Das hört erst mit dem peloponnesischen Kriege auf, als die politische Einheit des Hellenentums zerbrach. Der große metaphysische Gegensatz *agonalen* und *politischen* Denkens tritt in jeder tieferen Erörterung des Krieges zutage. Aus neuester Zeit möchte ich hier das großartige Streitgespräch zwischen Ernst Jünger und Paul Adams (Deutschland-Sender, 1. Februar 1933) nennen, das hoffentlich bald auch gedruckt zu lesen ist. Hier vertrat Ernst Jünger das agonale Prinzip ('der Mensch ist nicht auf den Frieden angelegt') während Paul Adams den Sinn des Krieges in der Herbeiführung von Herrschaft, Ordnung und Frieden sah" (Schmitt, *Der Begriff des Politischen*, 10n1).

28. Jünger, *Briefe 1930–1983 Ernst Jünger, Carl Schmitt,* ed. Helmut Kiesel, Stuttgart, 1999, 49.

29. "Ungleichheit und Kampf sind die Voraussetzungen der Gerechtigkeit. Diese Gerechtigkeit waltet nicht über der Welt, nicht über dem Gewühl der Streitenden, sie kennt keine Schuld und keine Verantwortung, kein Gerichtsverfahren und keinen Urteilsspruch: sie ist dem Kampfe immanent. Deshalb ist sie in einer Friedenswelt nicht möglich. Gerechtigkeit kann nur sein, wo Kräfte in Freiheit sich miteinander messen. Unter einer absoluten Autorität, in einer Ordnung der Dinge, die einen göttlichen Herrn kennt, im Bereich der *Pax Romana*, da ist keine Gerechtigkeit mehr, denn da ist kein Kampf mehr. Da erstarrt die Welt in einer konventionellen Form. Nietzsche dagegen steht: aus dem Kampfe selber gebiert sich in jedem Augenblick die Gerechtigkeit neu, der Kampf ist der Vater aller Dinge, er macht den Herrn zum Herrn und den Sklaven zum Sklaven. So spricht Heraklit von Ephesus. Das ist aber auch urgermanische Anschauung: im Kampfe erweist sich, wer edel ist und wer nicht; durch den eingeborenen Mut wird der Herr zum Herrn, und durch seine Feigheit wird der Sklave zum Sklaven. Eben darin äußert sich auch die ewige Gerechtigkeit: sie gliedert und trennt, sie schafft die Ordnung der Welt, sie ist die Urheberin jedes Ranges. So entspringt aus dem Kerngedanken der griechischgermanischen Metaphysik Nietzsches seine große Lehre: daß es nicht eine Moral gibt, sondern nur eine Moral der Herren und eine Moral der Sklaven" (Baeumler, *Nietzsche,* 67).

30. Ibid., 68.

31. "Nietzsche bis in die Instinkte hinein Krieger ist" (ibid.).

32. It would certainly be most enlightening, in order to gauge the extent of their Nazi extremism in 1932–1933, to be able to read the correspondence between Heidegger and Baeumler some day, if it has not been destroyed. The Baeumler archive has been kept in Munich, and its accessibility depends upon the good will of his widow, Marianne Baeumler. According to the latter, the letters from Heidegger to Baeumler have been lost, with the exception of one, dated 19 August 1932 (see Baeumler, *Thomas Mann und Alfred Baeumler,* 242).

33. *Karlsruher Zeitung,* 16 June 1930, p. 2; quoted in Schneeberger, *Ergänzungen,* 12. Schneeberger points out that in his 1943 edition of the text (therefore at a time when the Nazi defeat was considered inevitable), Heidegger took care not to recall that that lecture had first been given during the Karlsruhe convention.

34. Bambach, *Heidegger's Roots,* 41.

35. See Ott, *Martin Heidegger. Unterwegs,* 272.

36. According to the testimony of one listener: "Wahrheit und Wirklichkeit trafen sich auf dem Boden der Heimat." (Heinrich Berl, *Gespräche mit berühmten Zeitgenossen,* 67; quoted in Schneeberger, *Ergänzungen,* 2.)

37. "die Urgesetze unseres germanischen Menschenstammes" (GA 36/37, 89).

38. "die Grundmöglichkeiten des urgermanischen Stammeswesens" (ibid.).

39. GA 39, 134: see Chapter 4, 110.

40. Heidegger insists on pointing out here in a note that Heraclitus "was descended from a race of noble sovereigns" (*er stammte aus adligem Herrschergeschlecht*).

41. "Groß und einfach steht am Beginn des Spruches: *polemos,* Krieg. Gemeint ist dabei nicht das äußere Vorkommnis und die Voraustellung des 'Militärischen,' sondern das Entscheidende: das Stehen gegen den Feind. Wir haben mit 'Kampf' übersetzt, um das

Wesentliche festzuhalten; aber anderseits ist wichtig zu bedenken: es heißt nicht *agon,* Wettkampf, in dem zwei freundliche Gegner ihre Kräfte messen, sondern Kampf des *polemos,* Krieg, d.h. es gilt Ernst in dem Kampf, der Gegner ist nicht ein Partner, sondern Feind. Der Kampf als Stehen gegen den Feind, deutlicher: das Durchstehen in der Auseinandersetzung" (Heidegger, GA 36/37, 90).

42. See the conclusions of the unpublished seminar, *Hegel, on the State,* analyzed in Chapter 8, p. 158ff.

43. See above, pp. 81–82.

44. See this passage of major importance in GA 16, 283.

45. "Der Weltkrieg ist für *jedes* Volk die große Erprobung darüber, ob es imstande sein wird, dieses Geschehnis in sich geistiggeschichtlich zu verwandeln. Der Weltkrieg ist die Frage an die einzelnen Völker, ob sie an diesem Geschehnis sich verjüngen oder alt werden wollen" (GA 16, 299).

46. See *Das Rektorat 1933–34,* GA 16, 379.

47. "Feind ist derjenige und jeder, von dem eine wesentliche Bedrohung des Daseins des Volkes und seiner Einzelnen ausgeht. Der Feind braucht nicht der äußere zu sein, und der äußere ist nicht einmal immer der gefährlichere. Und es kann so aussehen, als sei kein Feind da. Dann ist Grunderfordernis, den Feind zu finden, ins Licht zu stellen oder gar erst zu schaffen, damit dieses Stehen gegen den Feind geschehe und das Dasein nicht stumpf werde. Der Feind kann in der innersten Wurzel des Daseins eines Volkes sich festgesetzt haben und dessen eigenem Wesen sich entgegenstellen und zuwiderhandeln. Um so schärfer und härter und schwerer ist der Kampf, denn dieser besteht ja nur zum geringsten Teil im Gegeneinanderschlagen; oft weit schwieriger und langwieriger ist es, den Feind als solchen zu erspähen, ihn zur Entfaltung zu bringen, ihm gegenüber sich nichts vorzumachen, sich angriffsfertig zu halten, die ständige Bereitschaft zu pflegen und zu steigern und den Angriff auf weite Sicht mit dem Ziel der völligen Vernichtung anzusetzen" (Heidegger, GA 36/37, 90–91).

48. "Das Wesen des Seins ist Kampf; jedes Sein geht durch Entscheidung, Sieg und Niederlage hindurch. Man ist nicht einfach nur Gott oder eben Mensch, sondern mit dem Sein ist je eine kämpferische Entscheidung gefallen und damit der Kampf in das Sein versetzt; man ist nicht Knecht, weil es so etwas unter vielen anderen auch gibt, sondern weil dieses Sein in sich eine Niederlage, ein Versagen, ein Ungenügen, eine Feigheit, ja vielleicht ein Gering- und Niedrigseinwollen birgt. Daraus wird deutlich: der Kampf stellt ins Sein und hält darin; er macht das Wesen des Seins aus, und zwar derart, daß er alles Seiende mit *Entscheidungscharakter durchsetzt,* jener ständigen Schärfe des Entweder-Oder; entweder die oder ich; entweder stehen oder fallen. Dieser kämpferische Entscheidungscharakter alles Seins bringt in das Seiende eine *Grundstimmung,* die sieghafter Jubel und Wille, Furchtbarkeit des ungebändigten Andrangs (Widerstandes) zugleich ist, Erhabenheit und Grimm in einem — was wir in einem Wort nicht zu sagen vermögen, wofür aber die Griechen ein Wort haben, das in der großen Dichtung der Tragiker wiederkehrt: *to deinon*" (GA 36/37, 94–95).

49. "Der Krieg ist es, der die Menschen und ihre Zeiten zu dem machte, was sie sind. Ein Geschlecht wie das unsere ist noch nie in die Arena der Erde geschritten, um unter sich die Macht über sein Zeitalter auszuringen. . . . Der Krieg, aller Dinge Vater, ist auch der unsere; er hat uns gehämmert, gemeißelt und gehärtet, zu dem, was wir sind. Und

immer, solange des Lebens schwingendes Rad noch in uns kreist, wird dieser Krieg die Achse sein, um die es schwirrt. Er hat uns erzogen zum Kampf, und Kämpfer werden wir bleiben, solange wir sind" (Jünger, *Der Kampf als inneres Erlebnis,* 13–14).

50. "als das Unbändige, Zügellose, Rauschhafte und Wilde, Rasende, Asiatische" (GA 36/37, 92).

51. Ibid.

52. "in der großen Entscheidung der Erde gegen das *Asiatische*" (GA 16, 333).

53. GA 39, 134.

54. "die Bewahrung der europäischen Völker vor dem Asiatischen" (Heidegger, "Europa und die deutsche Philosophie," 31).

55. Derrida, *Reading Heidegger: Commemorations,* 214, translation modified; *Politiques de l'amitié,* 417.

56. Ibid., 204. See also 208, 214, etc.; French translation, 403–404. See also 409, 416, etc.

57. Ibid., 211; French translation, 412.

58. Ibid., 211; French translation, 413.

59. See Chapter 4, 110.

Chapter 7: Law and Race

1. Ott, *Martin Heidegger. Unterwegs,* 228. Moreover, Hugo Ott, who, in the early 1950s followed Erik Wolf's teaching (a seminar on Feuerbach) and therefore knew him personally, is of the opinion that his commitment to the Confessing Church constituted only one part (*nur ein Teil*) of the man (conversation with the author).

2. "Die Rechtsidee des Nationalsozialismus," "Die Verbrechensbekämpfung im Nationalsozialistischen Staat." *Vorlesungsverzeichnis der Universität Freiburg,* Sommersemester 1934, 18ff.; quoted in Seemann, *Die politischen Säuberungen,* 29.

3. "Recht gehört zum ursprünglichen Wesen des Menschen selbst, denn das Wesen des Menschen erkennen wir mit daran, daß es eine Welt des Rechtes hat. Unabwendbar ist dieses Inder-Welt-des-Rechts-sein und unabweisbar folgt aus ihm das Fragen nach dem richtigen Recht. Es ist kein Ergebnis neutzeitlichen Grübelns und meint nichts auf Papier geschriebenes. Es ist etwas im Blute lebendes" (Wolf, *Richtiges Recht im nationalsozialistischen Staate,* 3).

4. Ibid., 4–7.

5. "das Schicksal der deutschen Volksgemeinschaft" (ibid., 9).

6. "unser wirkliches Recht kann . . . nur das Recht des Nationalsozialismus im Dritten Reich sein" (ibid., 10).

7. "Denn dieser stellt, wie es der Führer mehrfach ausgesprochen hat, das Volk vor den Staat, er will Volksrecht, nicht Behördenrecht. Der Staat ist ihm nur Mittel zum Zweck der restlosen Verwirklichung der Volksgemeinschaft" (ibid., 12).

8. "Es sind vor allem zwei Tatsachen des natürlichgeschichtlichen Lebens: Volk und Rasse. Aus ihnen erheben sich zwei Forderungen an jedes Einzelleben: Gemeinnützigkeit und Opfersinn. Und zwei Werte wollen diese Forderungen verwirklichen: Einheit der Nation und soziale Gemeinschaft. Die Lebensganzheit, in der das geschieht, heißt Staat, totaler Staat. In ihm muß der Aufbau des neuen Rechts sich vollziehen" (ibid., 13).

9. "Der Einzelne, wo er auch stehe, gilt nichts. Das Schicksal unseres Volkes in seinem Staat gilt alles." (Quoted in Ott, *Martin Heidegger. Unterwegs*, 229.) This essential letter was not published by Hermann Heidegger in vol. 16 of the so-called complete works.

10. "Volk im national-sozialistischen Sinne deckt sich aber auch nicht mit der Bevölkerung innerhalb der Reichsgrenzen, es umfaßt in einem weiteren Sinne auch die Deutschstämmigen auf anderen Territorien. Der Volksorganismus ist für den Nationalsozialisten keine Anhäufung massenhaft auftretender Einzelner, sondern gegliederte Einheit berufsständischer Volksgruppen. Die Ständeordnung ruht auf den natürlichen Volksordnungen der Ehe und Familie, der Gemeinde und des Stammes, endlich des Staates" (Wolf, *Richtiges Recht im nationalsozialistischen Staate*, 13–14).

11. "Und vor allem, vergessen wir nicht: Volksrecht aus dem Volksgeist ist auch gegenwärtig wachsend. Wo echtes Volksleben der Gegenwart ist, da sind Ansätze zu neuem Recht. Im ungeschriebenen Kameradschaftsgesetz der S.A. und S.S., in den neuen Lebensformen der Hitlerjugend, in manchem echt gewachsenen Lebensformen der Hitlerjugend, in manchem echt gewachsenen berufständischen Verband, in NSBO und Arbeitsfront ist lebendiges Recht in Uebung, dem Kraft zu verallgemeinerter Geltung innewohnt" (ibid., 15).

12. "Das neue Volksleben versteht sich und seine Geschichte von einem neuen Erlebnis der *Rasse* her. Dabei liegt der Kern des Erlebens weniger in einer Besinnung auf den biologischen Ursprung der Völkerentwicklung, als in der lebendigen Erfahrung des rassischen Eigenseins der Deutschen, deren Kulturaufbau in tausendjähriger Entwicklung ohne wesentliche Mitwirkung Fremdstämmiger erfolgt ist. Fremdstämmig heißt: nicht zugehörig zu einer der vier unter einander vermischten deutschen Rassen, der nordischen, fälischen, dinarischen und alpinen, die auf den indogermanischen oder arischen Wurzelstamm zurückgeführt werden. Im Gegensatz zur Theorie des imperialistischen Nationalismus, der nur die Wirtschafts- und Kulturgemeinschaft einer staatlich regierbaren Menschenmasse über den Begriff 'Volk' entscheiden läßt, ist für den Nationalsozialismus Grundlage der Volksgemeinschaft die Rassen-und Sprachgemeinschaft; ihr spricht er und keineswegs bloß aufgrund biologischer Erwägungen, den Vorrang zu. Er stützt sich nicht allein auf jenes Ergebnis der modernen Anthropologie, demzufolge, um ein Wort Eugen Fischer zu gebrauchen, 'die Schicksale der Völker und Staaten aufs stärkste und entscheidendste von der rassischen Natur ihrer Träger beeinflußt' sind. Vielmehr hat er in einer zuvor kaum in Ansätzen vorhandenen Weise vermocht, die Rassenzugehörigkeit zum geistigen und politischen Erlebnis weiter Volksteile zu machen. Es handelt sich hier um ein sehr vielschichtiges Gemeinschaftserlebnis. Es hat keineswegs nur oder auch nur wesentlich naturkundlich zu erfassende Grundlagen. Im Rassenerlebnis schwingen geistige Dinge, wie Ueberlieferung, Familie, Adel, Haltung und Gesinnung mit. Folgerichtig wirkt dieses neue Erlebnis sich auch im Rechtsgedanken aus" (ibid., 15–16).

13. This is a transparent reference to the "law of the Reich on heritable farmland" of 29 September 1933, the work of the "Reich peasant leader," Walter Darré. Only those of German blood or related stock since 1800 could be farmers; thus all "eighth-part Jews" or "eighth-part Blacks" were excluded from the future order of landowners. See Conte and Essner, *La Quête de la race*, 214–215.

14. "Es wächst die Einsicht, daß ein Volksrecht die Tatsache des rassischen Volksursprungs nicht übersehen darf. Dabei sollte die Frage des Anteils der verschiedenen arischen Rassen am Aufbau unseres Volkstums nicht in den Vordergrund treten. Sie dürfte leicht zu

einem einheitsgefährdenden Rangstreit führen. Am Rechtsaufbau des nationalsozialistischen Staates müssen alle deutschen Stämme teilnehmen und teilhaben. Die juristische Bedeutung des Rassegedankens kann nicht in einer rechtlichen Bevorzugung nordischer Rassetypen gegenüber den andern liegen. Sie beruht in den Maßnahmen zur Erhaltung des heutigen deutschen Rassenbestandes, wozu der Schutz vor Ueberfremdung durch Ausschluß Fremdstämmiger von der Erwerbung ländlichen Grundbesitzes, Erschwerung ihrer Einbürgerung, Verminderung ihres unmittelbaren Einflusses auf Erziehung, Rechtsprechung, Staatsführung, Schrifttum gehört. Zur Verhütung einer weiteren Rassenverschlechterung innerhalb der Deutschstämmigen dienen Vorschriften sozial-eugenischer Art, Zwangssterilisierung von Berufsverbrechern und schwer Erbkranken, endlich Auswanderungshemmung." (Wolf, *Richtiges Recht im nationalsozialistischen Staate*, 16.)

15. On the great raciological debate between the "German race" and the "Nordic race," see the indispensable study by Cornelia Essner, "Le dogme nordique des races," 65–116.

16. "körperliche und geistige Unterschiede" (Fischer, *Der Begriff des völkischen Staates*, 14).

17. "Im totalen nationalsozialistischen Staat erscheint das Verbrechen in erster Linie als Ungehorsam und Auflehnung, im Verbrecher wird der Feind des Staates getroffen" (Wolf, *Richtiges Recht im nationalsozialistischen Staate*, 23). This passage is reprinted in Wolf, "Das Rechtsideal des nationalsozialistischen Staates."

18. "Der Anspruch des nationalsozialistischen Staates ergreift das irdische Dasein des Menschen in umfassender Weise. Er findet seine Grenze weder an geschichtlichen Traditionen noch an gewissen Grundrechten oder Menschenrechten. Diese Vorstellung vom totalen Staat darf man, wie Ernst Forsthoff einleuchtend gezeigt hat, nicht mechanistisch verstehen, als gelte es nun, mit dem Behördenapparat des Staates alle übrigen Lebensgebiete zu organisieren und zu schematisieren. Der totale Staat ist keine mechanische, sondern eine organische Einheit, er schematisiert nicht, er gliedert. Er drängt in diesem Gegliedertsein zu einer aristokratischen Herrschaftsordnung, die im persönlichen Führer gipfelt und hierarchisch in einer Stufenfolge von Rangordnungen und Aemtern sich aufbaut" (Wolf, *Richtiges Recht im nationalsozialistischen Staate*, 23–24). The text is reprinted in his "Das Rechtsideal," 355–356.

19. "diese Impflichtnahme hebt den privaten Charakter der Einzelexistenz auf" (Wolf, *Richtiges Recht im nationalsozialistischen Staate*, 25).

20. Jean Cavaillès was worried about the relations between German Protestantism and Hitlerism in 1933. He carried out research in Germany and published three articles on the topic: "Protestantisme et Hitlerisme. La crise du protestantisme allemande," *Esprit* (November 1933): 305–316; "Les conflits à l'intérieur du protestantisme allemand," *Politique* 2 (1934): 179–183; and "La crise de l'Église protestante allemande," *Politique* 12 (1934): 1036–1042.

21. "die wesensnotwendige Verbindung von Nationalsozialismus und Christentum " (Wolf, *Richtiges Recht im nationalsozialistischen Staate*, 26).

22. See Max Müller, "Neudeutsche Jugend und neuer Staat," 182–186.

23. The work by Carl Schmitt is quoted by Wolf, "Das Rechtsideal," 356. I pointed out this article by Erik Wolf to Alexander Hollerbach, in refuting the latter's contention that Wolf had always opposed Carl Schmitt (conversation with the author).

24. "Es gehört . . . zu den Kennzeichen der Echtheit der nationalsozialistischen Revolution, daß die Bewegung eine zuvor versiegte Rechtsquelle: das Volkstum, wieder entdeckt und eine neue: das Führertum, erschlossen hat. . . . Es ist nicht mehr das herkömmliche Ideal formaler Gleichheit der abstrakten Rechtssubjekte, es ist der Gedanke ständisch gestufter Ehre der völkischen Rechtsgenossen. Auf diese Art wird die Ehre, von der ein Führer der Bewegung sagte, daß deutsches Rechtsleben seit jeher auf ihr beruht habe, der allumfassende Grundwert unserer neuen Rechtsordnung, das Rechtsideal des Nationalsozialismus" (Wolf, "Das Rechtsideal," 348–349). Erik Wolf, as if to show that he has read Rosenberg's work carefully, refers in his notes to several pages of *The Myth of the Twentieth Century*: 145ff., 204, 563, and others.

25. "Im obersten *Führer* selbst als die Verkörperung der Volksehre ist dann eine zentrale Rechtsmacht vorhanden" (Wolf, "Das Rechtsideal," 362).

26. "Im Kampf mit den üblen Auswüchsen des liberalistischen Zeitalters gilt es zwar unsozialen Egoismus und eigenbrötlerische Volksfremdheit rücksichtslos zu beseitigen, aber andererseits auch die sittliche, geistige und rechtliche Freiheit der Rechtsgenossen zu pflegen, denn hier liegen die lebenspendenden Wurzeln echten Führer-und Heldentums, auch auf dem Felde völkischer Rechtserneuerung" (ibid., 353).

27. "Der Anspruch des nationalsozialistischen Staates ergreift das irdische Dasein des Menschen in umfassender Weise. . . . Diesen neuen Staat darf man nicht mechanistisch verstehen, als gelte es nun mit dem Behördenapparat alle übrigen Gebiete des Lebens: Kirche, Kunst, Wissenschaft, zu organisieren. . . . Soziologischwestliches Denken erkennt ihn nur als Apparat, deutscher Sinn auf der Stufe höchster Entfaltung hat in ihm die Wirklichkeit der sittlichen Idee erblickt. Der Staat darf niemals losgelöst vom Volk betrachtet werden, denn er ist ja die politische Einheit selbst, die bald als Volk, bald als Staat, bald als politische Bewegung sichtbar wird" (ibid., 355–356).

28. "Die ehrbegründeten Wesensmerkmale des Volks sind zugleich die Wesensmerkmale seines Rechts. Diese Merkmale sind Blut, Stand und Überlieferung. Mit ihnen stoßen wir zu den Inhalten des neuen Rechtsideals der Ehre vor. Es besteht aus völkischen, ständischen und geschichtlichen Werten. Davon ist jetzt ein Näheres zu sagen. 1. Der Gedanke der Blut- oder Artgleichheit des Volkstums meint jene auf dem Naturgrund rassischen Erbgutes erwachsene, vielgliedrige Einheit der deutschen Stämme in ihrem innersten Wesen, das mit den Worten Volksgeist oder Volksseele umschrieben wird. Eine Rechtsidee, die im Volksgeist die Wurzel des Rechtes sieht und im Dienst am Volkstum sein Ziel, muß demnach fordern, daß den arteigenen Volksgenossen (die nicht das gleiche sind, wie juristische 'Staatsbürger'!) gewisse, für den Aufbau der Volksgemeinschaft besonders wichtige Funktionen vorbehalten bleiben, weil Ausländern oder Staatsbürgern fremdrassiger Artung hierfür die völkischen Voraussetzungen fehlen" (ibid., 357).

29. "Zu den nichtartgleichen Volksgästen, denen keine Rechtsstandschaft zukommt, gehören rassisch fremdstämmige und Ausländer" (ibid., 360).

30. "Eine völkische Rechtsordnung kann sog. 'sujets mixtes' im Sinne des bisherigen Völkerrechts nicht anerkennen" (ibid., 361).

31. I have in mind the afterword he wrote for the French edition of Hugo Ott's monograph.

32. Palmier, *Les Écrits politiques de Heidegger*, 74.

33. Kern, *Die Überleitung der Justiz auf das Reich*, 36.

34. "Prof. Dr. Eduard Kern. Tübingen. Gustav-Schabstrasse 6," letter to Vittorio Klostermann of 24 [?] 1941 (coll. V. Klostermann, DLA, Marbach). We learn from a letter dated 11 January 1941 to V. Klostermann that it was at Heidegger's recommendation that Erik Wolf contacted Klostermann, who henceforth became his publisher.

35. The typewritten list was sent to Vittorio Klostermann on 22 February 1948 (coll. V. Klostermann, DLA, Marbach).

36. The letters of 22 November 1945, 3 December 1946, and 22 August 1947.

37. Letter from the Office of Military Government for Hesse to Vittorio Klostermann, 19 August 1957 (coll. V. Klostermann, DLA, Marbach).

38. "Es muß die Gewähr gegeben sein, daß der Verfasser weder in Wort noch Schrift für den Nationalsozialismus oder seine Ziele eingetreten ist." (Vittorio Klostermann to Erik Wolf, 3 December 1946; coll. V. Klostermann, DLA, Marbach).

39. *Quaestiones et Responsa. Ein rechtsphilosophisches Gespräch für Erik Wolf zum 65. Geburtstag,* Vittorio Klostermann, Frankfurt, 1968. Heidegger is among the 21 participants of the colloquium listed on p. 43.

40. "Wolf spielte in Freiburg . . . die Rolle dessen, der den Studenten das geistige Korsett eines menschlichen, demokratischen und ethischen Grundsätzen orientierten Rechts vorzog" (Hanno Kühnert, "Das Recht und die Nähe der Theologie, Zum Tode von Erik Wolf," *FAZ,* 20 October 1977, no. 244, p. 25).

41. Palmier, *Les Écrits politiques de Heidegger,* 332.

42. "in einer zur Rehabilitation Martin Heideggers verfassten Broschüre eines jungen Franzosen" (cited in Alexander Hollerbach, "Im Schatten des Jahres 1933: Erik Wolf und Martin Heidegger," in Schramm and Martin, eds., *Martin Heidegger. Ein Philosoph und die Politik,* 138).

43. There is no need to go to a German library to read the main Nazi writings of Erik Wolf, which are available both at the Bibliothèque Nationale de Paris and at the BNU at Strasbourg.

44. See Schwan, *Politische Philosophie im Denken Heideggers.*

45. Palmier, *Les Écrits politiques de Heidegger,* 159. At the end of the italicized passage (my italics), one would expect the conditional "would be"; the indicative "is" may be a revealing lapsus.

46. Jean-Michel Palmier, in his chapter on Heidegger's rectorship (73), says his information is based on "the various essays of François Fédier."

47. Ibid., 72.

48. Ibid., 75.

49. Ibid., 81.

50. See Chapter 2, 49ff.

51. Reinhard Brandt, "Martin Heidegger: 'Die Selbstbehauptung der deutschen Universität,'" published as appendix to *Universität zwischen Selbst- und Fremdbestimmung. Kants "Streit der Fakultäten"* (Berlin: Academie Verlag, 2003), 169–170, 179. In reality, Brandt's study leaves a contrasting impression. On the one hand, the author develops judicious critiques of Heidegger's address, showing the degree to which he is destructive to both law and philology; but on the other hand he speaks of seeking "the properly philosophical meaning of the academic and *völkisch* self-affirmation" and compares the situation of the rectoral address in Heidegger's "philosophy" to that of the *Conflict of the*

Faculties in Kant's metaphysics. The author does not seem to have sufficiently perceived that Heidegger's speech is not only destructive of law and philology but, by reducing "the spirit" to the forces of earth and blood, of philosophical thought itself.

52. "Recht und Sitte ist das Höchste der Welt, und wie nach meiner Meinung das deutsche Volk das erste an Geist und Seele ist, wollte es stets an der Spitze stehen von Recht und Sitte" (Adalbert Stifter, quoted by Erik Wolf).

53. Erik Wolf, *Vom Wesen des Rechts in deutscher Dichtung. Hölderlin-Stifter-Hebbel-Droste* (Frankfurt-am-Main: Klostermann, 1946), 160.

54. "Recht . . . verwirklicht sich zwar in jedem menschlichen Dasein, aber nicht in jedem auf gleiche Art" (ibid., 163).

55. Ibid., 164–165.

56. "Nur der wesentliche Mensch hat wirkliches Recht. Er ist im Recht, bleibt im Recht und setzt ins Recht. Kein Unwesen kann Recht behalten" (ibid., 166).

57. "die Urordnungen der Familie, des Stammes und Volkes, der Stadt als wirklicher Lebensgemeinschaft, des Vaterlandes" (ibid., 33).

58. "Nicht nur ist das Recht etwas Ursprüngliches . . . es ist etwas *Schicksalhaftes*. . . . Die Manifestationen des Rechts in Natur, Heros, Volk sind ja selbst Manifestationen des Schicksals" (ibid., 37).

59. "Mit Heraklit verwandt erscheint seine Idee des Schicksalsrechts, seine Bejahung des Krieges, sein heroisches Fordern des Einsatzes aller Volkskräfte für den Kampf um das Vaterland" (ibid., 39).

60. Ibid., 44.

61. "Sein Staat ist Gemeinde, Gemeinschaft, Korporation, Polis, aber nicht Leviathan, Gesellschaft oder gar bloßer Behördenapparat" (ibid., 49).

62. Ibid.

63. Ibid., 52.

64. *Erik Wolf Nachlaß*, C 130.

65. "Nicht aus 'Konjunktur' . . . sondern um meinen guten sozialen Willen zu zeigen, bin ich im Sommer 1933 dem NSJuristenbund beigetreten und habe für den sog. 'Opfer-ring' der Partei einen monatlichen Beitrag bezahlt, in der Meinung, das Geld werde sozialen Zwecken zugeführt" (Erik Wolf, Oral Archives, Ministère des affaires étrangères [Ministry of Foreign Affairs], Colmar, France; hereafter MAE).

66. "Seit 1929 stand ich unter dem tiefen Eindruck der Existentielphilosophie Martin Hei-deggers, zu der ich über den Neukantianismus, die Phänomenologie Husserls und Lektüre Kierkegaards gekommen war. Stark beeinflusst hatte mich auch 1924/27 die Dichtung und Forschung des Kreises um Stefan George, vor allem mein persönlicher Verkehr mit Gundolf, der mich in Platons Idee des philosophischen Herrschers einführte und von einem 'großen Menschen' das Heil der deutschen Zukunft erwartete" (Erik Wolf, MAE).

67. "In allendem habe ich mich bemüht, den Irrtum wieder gut zu machen, dem ich 1933 unter dem suggestiven Einfluss eines bedeutenden Denkers [Heidegger, quoted immediately following] erlegen war. Dieser Irrtum war, daß ich an die Möglichkeit ge-glaubt habe, es lasse sich auch unter der Herrschaft des Nationalsozialismus das Ideal sozialer Gerechtigkeit verwirklichen" (Erik Wolf, MAE).

68. "Die Aufgaben der evangelisch-christlichen Jugendbewegung im dritten Reich" (*Wort und Tat. Zeitschrift für Weltanschauung und Geisteskampf*, January 1934, 21.

69. "So geht es jetzt darum, unser Christsein, Bündischsein, Deutschsein, dessen wir in den drei großen Erlebnissen des Evangeliums, der Jugendbewegung, des Nationalsozialismus innegeworden sind, wirklich durchzuhalten. Deshalb ist nicht die Zerlegung dieser Erlebnisse in ihre jeweilige Besonderheit und Unterschiedenheit wichtig, sondern die Einsicht in ihre unauflösliche Einheit in unserem Leben selbst. Wir wissen, daß wir als evangelische Jugend in der Gemeinde leben und in Treue zu unserer Kirche stehen; wir wissen, daß wir als bündische Jugend Bundesleben führen und für unseren Bund einstehen; wir wissen, daß wir als deutsche Jugend unser Volkstum bewahren und hinter unserem Führer Adolf Hitler stehen. Aber das ist eben kein Nebeneinander, sondern ein Ineinander, und die Besonderheit unseres Lebens liegt nicht darin, wie manche meinen, als gute Christen schlechte Volksgenossen, als gute Bündische schlechte Kirchengemeidegleider, als gute Volksgenossen lässige Christen zu sein — sondern darin, diese dreifache Entfaltung unseres Wesens zu einer lebendigen Einheit zu gestalten, aus der dann Kirche, Volk, Staat und Bund neue Kräfte zuwachsen" (ibid., 22).

70. Künneth, *Die völkische Religion der Gegenwart,* 7.

71. Ibid., 8.

72. See Wolf, "Richtiges Recht und evangelischer Glaube," 243–374.

73. Ibid., 3rd ed., 254.

74. See ibid., 3rd ed., 241; and 5th ed., 243.

75. Ibid, 3rd ed., 256.

76. Ibid., 248.

77. "Die wesensnotwendige Verbindung von Nationalsozialismus und Christentum" (ibid., 249).

78. The attack on the racial doctrine exposited by Erik Wolf is found in Helmut Metzdorf, "Gegen die Verfälschung des Rassebegriffes," *Der Alemanne,* 27 October 1935; quoted by Alexander Hollerbach, "Zu Leben und Werk Erik Wolfs," appended to Erik Wolf's *Studien zur Geschichte des Rechtsdenkens,* Ausgewählte Schriften Band 3 (Frankfurt am Main: Klostermann, 1982), 249n51.

79. "Vielmehr erleben und erkennen wir im Recht einen Teil unserer Welt, eine Daseinsqualität, die unserer bestimmten Seinsstruktur eigen ist. Diese Seinsstruktur ist die Struktur der Gemeinschaft, in der wir sind und die uns das Recht als ein Moment dieses besonderen Daseins überhaupt erst offenbar macht" (Erik Wolf, "Richtiges Recht und evangelischer Glaube," 5th ed., 248).

80. "das richtige Recht der deutschen Gegenwart" (ibid., p. 249).

81. "das politisch-kulturelle Ganze der deutschen Volksgemeinschaft" (ibid.).

82. "Das Stück Leben, worin heute allenthalben die Wirklichkeit des Rechts als Einheit geschaut wird, ist die *politische Existenz einer Volksgemeinschaft*" (ibid., 252).

83. "Das Recht wird als Ordnung einer konkreten Gemeinschaft gewürdigt" (ibid.).

84. "Das Recht wird . . . begriffen . . . als ein geistesgeschichtlicher Tatbestand, der nur vom Boden einer existentiellen Gemeinschaftszugehörigkeit aus richtig erfaßt und erlebt werden kann" (ibid.).

85. Ibid., 256.

86. Ibid., 270.

87. Ibid., 268.

88. Ibid., 269.

89. "Die grundlegende Neugestaltung des politischen Selbstbewusstseins des deutschen Volkes im Nationalsozialismus" (ibid., 259).

90. "Die Kirche steht aber auch in der Welt des Rechts der Volksgemeinschaft, innerhalb derer, sie ihre Gemeinde sammelt" (ibid., 263).

91. " . . . in der Volksgemeinschaft Adolf Hitlers sich ankündigende Völkerreich des 20. Jahrhunderts." See the review of the work of Hans K. E. L. Keller, *Das rechtliche Weltbild*, Erster Band, *Gegenreich Frankreich, Geschichte des westlichen Internationalismus* (Berlin: Batschari Verlag, 1935), reviewed by Erik Wolf in *Historische Zeitschrift* 156 (1937): 106–108.

92. "Politisch betrachtet wirft K.s Buch ein neues Schlaglicht auf die gegenwärtige europäische Situation" (ibid., 108).

93. See review of the work of Hans-Helmut Dietze, *Naturrecht in der Gegenwart* (Bonn: L. Röhrscheid, 1936), reviewed by Erik Wolf in *Historische Zeitschrift* 156 (1937): 108–110.

94. On the Academy for German Law to which Heidegger will belong, see Chapter 8, 205–207.

95. Erik Wolf, "Das Rechtsideal des nationalsozialistischen Staates," *Archiv für Rechts-und Sozialphilosophie*, 28 (1934–1935), 170.

96. "bestimmte Werte und Schutzgedanken wie: Rasse, Volk, Vaterland, Ehre, Treue, Wehrkraft . . . , in denen der Geist der nationalsozialistischen Strafrechtserneuerung sich ausspricht" (ibid., 172).

97. Ibid., 174.

98. Ibid., 179.

99. "Politische Gemeinschaftsordnung. Ein Versuch zur Selbstbesinnung des christlichen Gewissens in den politischen Nöten unserer Zeit."

100. "Es wird ein bis in einzelne gehendes internationales Judenstatus festgelegt, das etwa folgenden Inhalt haben könnte: . . . Die Juden haben in allen Staaten, in denen sie beheimatet sind, die Stellung von Ausländern." (Quoted by Silke Seemann, who stresses the "nationalist and tendentiously anti-Semitic" character of the memorandum, in *Die politischen Säuberungen . . .*, 230–231). The section of the memorandum on the "Jewish question" (*Judenfrage*) is quoted and commented on at greater length by Hugo Ott, in "Der 'Freiburger Kreis,'" *Mitverschwörer-Mitgestalter. Der 20. Juni im deutschen Südwesten*, ed. Klaus Eisele and Rolf-Ulrich Kunze (Constance: UVK, 2004), 121–124.

101. During his stay in Paris, Erik Wolf received a long phone call from Ernst Jünger, who knew of him by having read his study on Adalbert Stifter and their shared liking for the study of coleopterans (see Alexander Hollerbach, "Erinnerung an Erik Wolf," *Freiburger Universitätsblätter*, December 2002, p. 99.) There is a correspondence, part of which I have consulted, between Erik Wolf and the Jünger brothers; some of it has been kept in Marbach (Wolf's letters) and some in the *Nachlaß Wolf* of the University of Freiburg (letters received by Wolf).

102. Silke Seemann affirms that Theodor Maunz had belonged to the NSDAP "since 1933" (*Die politischen Säuberungen . . .*, 99). In reality, I was able to verify in the archives of the Ministère des affaires étrangères in Colmar that Maunz had also joined the Nazi Party on 1 May 1937.

103. Seemann, *Die politischen Säuberungen,* 108.

104. "bereits drei Juden wieder in der Fakultät säßen" (quoted in Seemann, *Die politischen Säuberungen,* 111).

105. "Insbesondere Theodor Maunz und Erik Wolf drängten als Vertreter der Rechts- und Staatswissenschaftlichen Fakultät im Senat auf eine schnelle Entscheidung im Fall Müllers" (ibid., 304).

106. Ibid., 305.

107. See, e.g., Ernst Rudolf Huber's compilation of Nazi *völkisch* law, titled *Verfassungsrecht des Großdeutschen Reiches,* 2nd ed. (Hamburg, 1939), in which the author quotes in detail and comments on the uninterrupted flow of anti-Semitic laws and decrees from 1933 to November 1938 ("Die Stellung der Juden," 181–185).

108. Seemann, *Die politischen Säuberungen,* 320–322.

109. In the words of Max Müller, in Schramm and Martin, eds., *Martin Heidegger. Ein Philosoph und die Politik,* 106.

110. Ernst Rudolf Huber, *Idee und Ordnung des Reiches* (Hamburg, 1943).

111. Maunz, "Gestalt und Recht der Polizei."

112. "Polizei — S.S. — Wehrmacht" (ibid., 28–36).

113. See Seemann, *Die politischen Säuberungen,* 99.

114. "echtes Sein sei sich selbst 'nomos'" (Hollerbach, "Im Schatten des Jahres 1933," 146, who refers in this connection to Walter Henemann, *Die Relevanz der Philosophie Martin Heideggers für das Rechtsdenken,* Diss. Jur., Freiburg, 1970).

115. "Dike als Fügung des Seins für alles Seiende bedeutet aber auch Einheit und Selbstbehauptung des wesenhaften Seins in allem Seienden" (Erik Wolf, *Griechische Rechtsdenken,* 1950–1970, vol. I [Parmenides], 293; quoted in Schneider, "Recht und Denken." The article by H.-P. Schneider omits the texts of the years 1933–1944 completely and treats the relations between Heidegger and Wolf only in reference to the writings of 1950–1970, which makes it impossible to see the Nazi basis that continued to spread in depth, below the seemingly innocuous usage of the most general terms.

116. See Chapter 8, 239.

117. See, e.g., the 1950 article in homage to Heidegger: Erik Wolf, "ΑΝΗΡ ΔΙΚΑΙΟΣ," 80–105.

Chapter 8: Heidegger and the Longevity of the Nazi State in the Unpublished Seminar on Hegel and the State

Epigraph from "Man hat gesagt, 1933 ist Hegel gestorben; im Gegenteil: er hat erst angefangen zu leben." (Heidegger, *Hegel, über den Staat,* Winterseminar 1934–1935, Deutsches Literaturarchiv, Marbach am Neckar, beginning of the eighth session, 23 January 1935, *reportatio* by Wilhelm Hallwachs, f. 75 v°.)

1. "der Staat auch noch nach 50 oder 100 Jahren existieren soll" (ibid., f. 1 r°).

2. Quoted by Schneeberger, *Nachlese,* 255.

3. "Der Durchbruch der Rechtsphilosophie heißt daher: Feierlich Abschied nehmen von der Entwicklung einer Knechtsphilosophie im Dienste undeutscher Dogmen. Lebensrecht und nicht Formalrecht soll unser Ziel sein. . . . es soll aber ein Herrenrecht und nicht

Sklavenrecht sein. Der Staatsbegriff des Nationalsozialismus wird von uns neugebaut auf Einheit und Reinheit des deutschen Menschentums, formuliert und verwirklicht im Recht und im Führerprinzip." (Hans Frank, *Frankfurter Zeitung*, 5 May 1934; quoted in Farías, *Heidegger and Nazism*, 206; German translation, 278).

4. "das Fundament unserer Gesetzgebung die Erhaltung der rassischen Wertsubstanz unseres Volkes ist" (Hans Frank, ed., *Akademie für Deutsches Recht, Jahrbuch 1, 1933/34*, p. 177; quoted in Farías, *Heidegger und der Nationalsozialismus*, 279; this quotation is not included in the English edition).

5. "Warum sich Hitler nicht von diesem Kerl befreie, das verstünde er nicht" (Löwith, *Mein Leben in Deutschland*, 58).

6. "Er ließ auch keinen Zweifel über seinen Glauben an Hitler" (ibid., 57).

7. See Barash, *Heidegger et son siècle. Temps et l'Être, temps de l'histoire*, 131–134. The author had already spoken about this seminar in "Martin Heidegger in the Perspective of the 20th Century," *Journal of Modern History*, 64, no. 1 (March 1992): 52–78. He brings it up again more briefly in *Martin Heidegger and the Problem of Historical Meaning*, 2nd ed. (New York: Fordham University Press, 2003), 224–225.

8. See Heinz and Kisiel, "Heideggers Beziehungen zum Nietzsche-Archiv," 110.

9. Fistetti, *Heidegger e l'Utopia della Polis*, 31–36.

10. "Als Hegel Heidelberg verließ, brachte er in einem Abschiedsschreiben zum Ausdruck, daß er nicht in philosophischen Absichten nach Berlin gehe, sondern in politischen: die Staatsphilosophie sei fertig. Er hoffe auf politische Wirksamkeit, am bloßen Dozieren habe er keinen Geschmack. Seine Philosophie gewann höchstmerkwürdigen Einfluß auf die Staatsgesinnung" (Heidegger, GA 36/37, 19).

11. ". . . der eigenen Konkreten Volkseinheit, der deutschen" (Haering, "Der werdende Hegel," 26). Haering will subsequently publish *Hegel, sein Wollen und sein Werk*, in which his *völkisch* reading of Hegel is even more explicit. And he will also publish, in 1942, a collective work of Nazi inspiration titled *Das Deutsche in der deutschen Philosophie*.

12. "Die Absicht der Übung ist die *philosophische Besinnung über den Staat.* Durchzuführen an der Hand von Hegel. Die philosophische Besinnung über den Staat könnte man heute für unzeitgemäß halten, da man ja heute sagt, daß der heutige Staat nicht durch Bücher entstanden sei, sondern durch Kampf. Einer solchen Behauptung liegt die Vorstellung zu Grund, daß das Geistige nur in Büchern steht. Man vergisst dabei, daß der Staat auch noch nach 50 oder 100 Jahren existieren soll. Dann muß er aber etwas haben, *wovon* er existiert. Er kann nur dauern durch den Geist. Der Geist aber wird getragen durch die Menschen. Die Menschen aber müssen erzogen werden" (Heidegger, *Hegel, über den Staat, op. cit.*, f. 1 r°).

13. See Heidegger, GA 36/37, 7, and above, Chapter 4, 94–95.

14. "der Wirkung nach innen wie nach außen willen muß erneut die Einheit und Geschlossenheit des deutschen Volkes und seines Willens zu Freiheit und Ehre durch das Bekenntnis zur Führerschaft Adolf Hitlers zum Ausdruck gebracht werden" (Farías, *Heidegger and Nazism*, 192; German ed., 262).

15. "Unser Staat wird in 60 Jahren bestimmt nicht mehr vom Führer getragen, was *dann* aber wird, steht bei *uns*." (Heidegger, *Hegel, über den Staat*, f. 16 v°.)

16. "Warum haben wir gerade Hegel gewählt für diese Arbeit?, da doch auch andere Philosophen, z.B. Plato, Kant, Fichte über den Staat gedacht haben. Darum, weil 1)

Hegels Philosophie keine beliebige ist, sondern weil wir vielmehr in dieser Philosophie sehen müssen die Vollendung der gesamten abendländischen Philosophie, Vollendung im großen Ansatz in Richtung auf die Aufhebung des antiken und des christlichen Denkens in *einem* großen System. Hegel hatte davon das klare Bewußtsein, er hatte die Überzeugung, daß mit ihm die Philosophie ans Ende gekommen wäre. Das ist auch richtig. Was nach Hegel kommt, ist keine Philosophie mehr. Auch nicht Kierkegaard oder Nietzsche. Diese beiden sind keine Philosophen, sondern Menschen ohne Kategorie, die erst spätere Zeiten begreifen werden. Bis zu Hegel gibt es Philosophie, die er wie gesagt abschließt" (ibid., f. 1 r°–1 v°).

17. See Heidegger, GA 36/37, 72 and 15.

18. "Deshalb ist die Besinnung auf Hegels Philosophieren über den Staat gleichzusetzen der Besinnung auf den Grundansatz und die Grundrichtung des abendländischen Staatsdenkens überhaupt. Zweiter Grund ist, weil Hegels Staatslehre nach vorne (für die Zeit *nach* ihm) sowohl unmittelbar wie mittelbar entscheidend war und zwar sowohl im positiven wie im negativen Sinne. So geht im negativen Sinn Karl Marx auf ihn zurück. Aber auch den Liberalismus des Neunzehnten Jahrhunderts lernt man nur begreifen, wenn man das Hegel'sche Staatsdenken begriffen hat. So also ist diese Übung zu denken. Es soll eine Übung für Anfänger sein. D.h. es wird nichts vorausgesetzt, im negativen Sinn sofern die Beherrschung des philosophischen Handwerkszeugs nicht unmittelbar verlangt wird. Das besagt nicht, daß wir uns nicht im Verlauf der Übung einiges aneignen werden. Es wird auch nicht vorausgesetzt ein *festes* Wissen über den Gegenstand. Solches Wissen können Sie ruhig zu Hause lassen. Um so mehr ist vorausgesetzt wirklicher *Wille* zu einem echten Wissen. Darin liegt das Wissenwollen um das *Wesen* dessen, wovon wir handeln, das Fordern der *begrifflichen Klarheit,* der Anspruch der *ursprünglichen Begründung* dieses Wissens. Dies sind die drei Grundvoraussetzungen" (Heidegger, *Hegel, über den Staat,* 2r°–3r°).

19. Indeed we find in Heidegger's work no precise, deep analysis of classical, medieval, or modern doctrines about the state. And his elementary considerations on the Greek *polis* do not stand comparison with the richness of the investigations found in Aristotle's *Politics.*

20. "Heidegger's way of thinking, which seems to me essentially un-free, dictatorial, incommunicative, would be disastrous in teaching today" (quoted in Heidegger, *Correspondance avec Karl Jaspers,* 420).

21. See on this point Bouveresse, "Heidegger, la politique et l'intelligentsia française," *Essais IV. Pourquoi pas des philosophes?* (Marseille: Agone, 2004), 131.

22. Kroner, "Rede zur Eröffnung des II. Internationalen Hegelkongresses," 13–15.

23. "Aus dem neuen Verhältnis, das unsere Zeit zur Gemeinschaft und zu den ewigen Kräften des Volkstums gewonnen hat, wird auch ein neues Verständnis der Kultur und der Geschichte sowie des Rechtes, des Staates und der Wirtschaft erwachsen. Stärker als früher werden die sogenannten Geisteswissenschaften über die Isolierung der Fächer hinausstreben und in der philosophischen Durchdringung aller Formen des Gemeinschaftslebens einen Mittelpunkt suchen. Diese neue Haltung der Geisteswissenschaften bestimmt die neue Richtung der Zeitschrift. Unser Wille kommt in dem neuen Titel zum Ausdruck. Aus einer 'Internationalen Zeitschrift für Philosophie der Kultur' ist eine 'Zeitschrift für Deutsche Kulturphilosophie' geworden. Aber wir wollen damit uns nicht von dem geistigen Austausch mit anderen Völkern abschließen. Mit der gleichen Entschieden-

heit, mit der wir das fahle Gespenst einer internationalen Kulturphilosophie ablehnen, begrüßen wir jede philosophische Berührung mit dem Geiste anderer Nationen auf dem einzig fruchtbaren und lebenspendenden Boden völkischer Eigentümlichkeit" (Glockner and Larenz, "Zur Einführung," 1–2. It was at this time that the journal was "brought into line," since it did not come out in 1934).

24. Heidegger, *Hegel, über den Staat,* f. 3 v°.

25. "Der Text [ist] uns zunächst mehr oder weniger unverständlich. Wie sollen wir seiner Herr werden? Es gibt 2 Wege. 1) Uns klar werden über das *hegelsche Philoso-phieren.* . . . 2) *unabhängig* von Hegel uns darauf besinnen, wo so etwas überhaupt hingehört: Staat, in welchen Bereich es gehört, uns gewissermaßen eine Vorübung ver-schaffen" (ibid., f. 3 v°–4 r°).

26. Heidegger, *Sein und Zeit,* 15, pp. 69–70ff.

27. "das Werkzeug hat wesentlich 1) den Charakter des *Passiven* u[nd] 2) gleichzeitig den Charakter der *Aktivität*" (Heidegger, *Hegel, über den Staat,* f. 8 v°).

28. *Ibid.,* f. 9 r°.

29. Ibid., f. 10 r°.

30. "Eigentliche Nihilisten sind diejenigen, die nicht einsehen, daß wir Sein gar nicht begreifen können, wenn es nicht das Nichts wäre" (ibid., f. 11 v°).

31. "Der Vertrag von Versailles ist wirklich, aber doch nicht vernünftig" (ibid., f. 13 r°).

32. "Wir wollen jetzt noch einige Ergänzungen und Erklärungen geben zu dem, was in der vorigen Stunde besprochen wurde, zuvor ist aber noch eine weitere Vorfrage zu erledigen: Verschiedene Hörer sind mit der Bemerkung an mich herangetreten, das Thema unserer Übung läge ihnen zu fern, sie könnten die geplanten Erörterungen ja zu nichts 'gebrauchen.' Das charakterisiert ja meine Seminarübungen ganz vortrefflich. Zur Illustrierung will ich eine kleine Geschichte erzählen.Ich machte neulich Besuch in einer hiesigen Familie, dem Mädchen, welches mich anmeldete, entfuhr es dabei: Heidegger! ist das der, bei dem die Studenten nichts lernen? Das Mädchen hatte kurz zuvor noch bei einem Chemieprofessor gedient. Dies war die allerbeste Definition für meine Lehrtätig-keit. Sie lernen praktisch hier nichts! Die Frage, ob man Philosophie brauchen kann, ist von vornherein nicht zu entscheiden. Vielleicht merken Sie es nach 4 Jahren, wenn Sie fertig studiert haben, oder vielleicht erst im 40ten Lebensjahr, dann ist es aber zu spät. Um ein Automobil oder ein Fahrrad herzustellen, braucht man allerdings keine Philosophie, aber doch Mechanik, d.h. dann aber Physik d.h. wie sie durch Galilei begründet wird. Wir hätten aber keinen Galilei und Newton, wenn es keinen Aristoteles gegeben hätte. Aristoteles philosophiert aber nicht in der Voraussicht, daß man seine Philosophie zum Automobilbau gebrauchen kann. Es handelt sich jetzt nicht um Automobile sondern um den Staat. Der Staat steht nicht an der Wand herum, so daß wir ihn hernehmen und betrachten könnten, sondern wir wissen ja gar nicht, was der Staat ist, wir wissen nur, daß so etwas wie Staat im Werden ist. Unser Staat wird in 60 Jahren bestimmt nicht mehr vom Führer getragen, was *dann* aber wird, steht bei *uns.* Deshalb müssen wir philoso-phieren" (ibid., second session, f. 15 v°–16 v°).

33. "Selbst auf die Gefahr hin daß von Hegel's Staatslehre kein Stein auf dem anderen bleiben sollte, müssen wir uns mit ihm auseinandersetzen, weil eben Hegels Philosophie die *einzige* bisherige Philosophie über den Staat ist" (ibid., f. 23 v°).

34. "er hat die geistige Kraft, die begriffliche Sicherheit und Tiefe aus Hegels Philosophie" (ibid., f. 23 r°).

35. "Dialektik an sich ist eine Fürchterlichkeit des Denkens. Mit Hegel kann man *alles*" (ibid., f. 23 r°).

36. "Wir wollen nun von der anderen Seite her von dem Staat sprechen, von *uns* her, so aus dem Handgelenk. Wo ist nun der Staat heute? 'Der Staat,' der Ausdruck ist von vornherein *vieldeutig. Ist es unser Staat? das was jetzt wird? oder meinen wir 'den Staat überhaupt'? jeden Staat, sofern der Staat geschichtlich ist? reden wir von den verschiedenen Staaten und Staatsformen? Der Staat, was heißt das allgemein? Wir sehen, schon die Frage nach dem Staat ist an sich unklar und verworren. Fragen wir nach unserem Staat, wo ist er denn? . . . Heute weiß noch niemand, wer der Staat ist. Ein Staat wird, d.h. wir glauben daran, daß er wird, der ein Staat dieses Volkes ist, so daß jeder in seiner Weise wirklich weiß, was der Staat ist. . . . Was aber heißt hier Sein (der Staat ist)? Uns fehlen vollkommen die Begriffe, alles ist wirr*" (ibid., f. 23 v°–24 v°).

37. "Man hat gesagt, 1933 ist Hegel gestorben; im Gegenteil: er hat erst angefangen zu leben" (ibid., beginning of the eighth session, f. 75 v°).

38. ". . . also ist Recht gar nicht im Sinn des juristischen Rechts . . . genommen, sondern es hat metaphysischen Sinn" (fourth session, 28 November 1934, f. 30 r°–v°).

39. "Wissen *gehört* zum Willen" (ibid., f. 38 v°).

40. "Bloßes Wissen, das nicht will, ist bloße Kenntnis und nicht Wissen im Sinne des Seins und des Seins in der Sache stehen" (ibid.).

41. "Wir sagen z.B. . . . 'ich weiß mich entschieden' so ist Wissen nicht im Sinne der Kenntnis genommen, sondern 'ich *weiß* [mich] dazu *entschlossen*, ich *bin* es' " (ibid.).

42. "was Hegel unter Freiheit versteht, wir nicht begreifen können, wenn wir es als Wesensbestimmung eines *einzelnen* Ich nehmen. . . . Freiheit nur wirklich ist, wo eine Gemeinschaft von Ichen, Subjekten da ist" (ibid., f. 39 v°–40 r°).

43. "Die vollendete Wirklichkeit der Anerkennung ist der *Staat*. Im Staat kommt das Volk zu sich selbst, gesetzt, daß der Staat = der Staat des Volkes ist" (ibid., f. 40 r°).

44. "Wir wollen in der nächsten Stunde sehen, wie das Recht sich von der *Rechtswissenschaft* ausnimmt und wie andererseits *metaphysisch* die Wirklichkeit des Rechts und Staats sich *uns* offenbart" (ibid., f. 41 v°).

45. "Wenn wir *selbst* fragen wollen, stehen wir dem Recht gegenüber als einem *Teil* unserer selbst, bei der Frage *nach uns selbst?*" (Ibid., f. 48 r°.)

46. Ibid., f. 48 r°–v°.

47. "Das Gesetz hängt mit dem Sich-selbst-wissen zusammen. Das Sich-selbst-wissen ist aber nicht ein bloßes Kennen und Unterrichtet-sein über Zustände, sondern das Sich-selbst-wissen ist Grund des Seins. Ganz bestimmte Form = Macht des Seins ist es, in der *staatliches* Sein sich verwirklicht" (ibid., f. 49 v°).

48. "Aus diesen 3 Entscheidungen ist zu entnehmen, daß wir in der Zeit, in die diese Entscheidungen fallen, keinen Staat hatten. Wo wirklich ein Staat *da* ist, sind solche Entscheidungen unmöglich" (ibid., 6th session, 12 December 1934, f. 50 r°–v°).

49. "die geschichtliche Wirklichkeit des Volkes und Staates" (ibid., f. 49v°).

50. "Der Staat ist die absolute Macht auf Erden" (ibid., seventh session, 9 January 1935, f. 69 v°).

51. On that last equivalence, see below, 236–241.

52. "Die Verfassung ist nicht anderes als dasjenige, worin der Staat sich selbst *faßt*" (ibid., f. 63 v°).

53. Letter from Ernst Forsthoff to Jean-Pierre Faye, 31 August 1963, quoted in *Théorie du récit* (Paris: Hermann, 1973), 49.

54. "das innere Sich-gestalten des Staates als *Organismus*" (Heidegger, *Hegel, über den Staat,* f. 64 r°).

55. Ibid., f. 64 v°–65 r°.

56. Ibid, f. 65 r°.

57. See above, Chapter 4, 87–89 and 97–99.

58. "Hier ist *Organismus* weder biologisch noch allgemein metaphysisch, als System, gemeint, sondern daß dieses Zusammenwirkende nicht nur funktioniert, sondern in der *Regierung* sich selbst weiß, bei *sich selbst ist*" (ibid., f. 65 r°).

59. Ibid., f. 66 v°.

60. "Indem er Staat er selbst wird, wird er notwendig in diesem Sich-selbst-behaupten = ein Sich-absetzen gegen einen anderen. . . . Der Staat ist das Treibende im Geschehen der Völker, sofern Staat nichts anderes ist als der Geist des Volkes" (ibid., f. 72 r°–72 v°).

61. "Liberalismus ist immer eine besondere Art der . . . Mißdeutung der Freiheit" (ibid., f. 73 v°).

62. "Welches ist nun die *heutige* Staatsauffassung?" Ibid., 8th session, 23 January 1935, f. 75 v°.

63. "Wir sprechen wohl vom *totalen* Staat. Er sei nicht ein besonderer *Bereich* (neben anderen), keine Apparatur, dazu da, die Gesellschaft zu schützen (vor dem Staat *selbst*), ein Bereich, mit dem nur bestimmte Leute sich abzugeben hätten. Aber was ist politisch der 'totale Staat'? Wie ist es in ihm zum Beispiel mit der Universität beschaffen? Die Beziehung von Universität zum Staat sei früher nur so gewesen, daß der Staat sie unterhält, und sie ihre Wege geht. Wie ist es denn jetzt?" Ibid., f. 75 v°–75 r°.

64. "Heute spricht man vom 'totalen' Staat und vom völkischen Staat" (Heinz and Kiesel, "Heideggers Beziehungen," 110).

65. "An diesem Tage ist demnach, so kann man sagen, 'Hegel gestorben'" (Schmitt, *Staat, Bewegung, Volk,* 32).

66. Richard Wolin, *The Politics of Being: The Political Thought of Martin Heidegger* (New York: Columbia University Press, 1992), 106; Domenico Losurdo, *Hegel et la catastrophe allemande* (Paris: Albin Michel, 1994), 129; Jean-François Kervégan, *Hegel, Carl Schmitt. Le politique entre spéculation et positivité* (Paris: Presses Universitaires de France, 1992), 323; and André Stanguennec, "À l'origine de l'idée allemande de nation: la philosophie romantique et la philosophie hégélienne de l'État" (*Revue française d'histoire des idées politiques,* no. 14, 2001), 350.

67. "Das bedeutet aber nicht, daß das große Werk des deutschen Staatsphilosophen bedeutungslos geworden und der Gedanke einer über dem Egoismus gesellschaftlicher Interessen stehenden politischen Führung preisgegeben wäre. Was an Hegels mächtigem Geistesbau überzeitlich groß und deutsch ist, bleibt auch in der neuen Gestalt weiter wirksam" (Schmitt, *Staat, Bewegung, Volk,* 32).

68. "Nur die der innerstaatlichen Lage des 19. Jahrhunderts entsprechenden Formen

des hegelischen Beamtenstaates sind beseitigt und durch andere, unserer heutigen Wirklichkeit entsprechende Gestaltungen ersetzt" (ibid.).

69. "Das deutsche Berufsbeamtentum ist aus einer unklar und unhaltbar gewordenen Zwitterstellung befreit . . ." (ibid.).

70. "Der Nationalsozialismus . . . sichert und pflegt jede echte Volkssubstanz, wo er sie trifft, in Landschaft, Stamm oder Stand. Er hat . . . das deutsche Beamtentum von fremdgearteten Elementen gereinigt und dadurch als Stand wiederhergestellt. Er hat den Mut, Ungleiches ungleich zu behandeln und notwendige Differenzierungen durchzusetzen" (ibid., 32.)

71. " . . . für bestimmte Organisationen der Partei, wie SA und SS." (ibid, p. 33.)

72. "Daher könne auch die Gesichtspunkte der Haftung, insbesondere die der Körperschaftshaftung für Amtsmißbrauch . . . nicht auf die Partei oder die SA übertragen werden" (ibid., 22).

73. "Der dreigliederige Aufbau . . . entspricht auch den großen, durch Hegel begründeten Überlieferungen deutschen Staatsdenkens" (ibid., 13).

74. "Erst in der zweiten Hälfte des 19. Jahrhunderts ist er unter dem Einfluß liberaler und artfremder Theoretiker und Schriftsteller aus dem Bewußtsein des deutschen Volkes verdrängt worden" (ibid.).

75. "L'état total n'est pas une unité mécanique, mais organique, il ne schématise pas, il structure. À travers cet être-structuré, il tend à un ordre de domination aristocratique, qui culmine dans le *Führer* personnel et s'édifie sur une suite de hiérarchies et de fonctions." [The total state is not a *mechanical,* but an organic unity; it does not schematize, it structures. Through that structured-being, it tends toward an order of aristocratic domination, which culminates in the personal *Führer* and is built on a series of hierarchies and functions.] (Wolf, *Richtiges Recht,* 23–24. The text was republished in 1935 in *Das Rechtsideal,* 355–356).

76. Wolf, "Richtiges Recht und evangelischer Glaube," 248.

77. "die Universität muß . . . *wieder in die Volksgemeinschaft eingegliedert* und mit dem *Staat verbunden* werden" (Heidegger, "Die Universität im neuen Reich," GA 16, 761).

78. "Mit solchen Fragen und Überlegungen kommen wir nicht durch, sondern nur durch *wesentliche* Besinnung *metaphysischer Art.* Die Bedeutung der Auseinandersetzung mit Hegels Staatsphilosophie und zunächst der Besinnung auf sie liegt darin, zu lernen, *wie* ein metaphysisches Denken und Durchdenken des Staates aussieht. Es handelt sich um die *Form* des Staatsdenkens. Es ist sicher, daß unser neues Ringen um den Staat aus der *soziologischen* Fragestellung *heraus* ist, wenn es auch immer wieder in sie zurückfällt. Diese .., vor allem 262 ff. sind es, an denen *Marx* mit seiner Kritik einsetzt, er stellt dabei Hegel auf den Kopf. Dieser Zusammenhang zwischen Allgemeinem und Einzelne als Geschehen in der Wirklichkeit des Staates verankert, gehört *mit* hier herein. Aber dies ist doch nur eine ganz *allgemeine* Bestimmung. In diesen .. (d.h. im letzten, spricht Hegel zum ersten Male vom 'politischen' (267): 'Die Notwendigkeit der Idealität . . . u.s.w.,' '*Der politische Staat.'* Was heißt hier *politisch?* Gibt es einen Staat, der *nicht* politisch ist? Zum Unterschied gibt es bei Hegel den *äußeren* Staat, oder den *Not-staat,* oder *Verstandesstaat.* Dieser *äußere* Staat ist das ganze System der bürgerlichen Gesellschaft, der Regelung ihrer Bedürfnisse, der Gliederung der Stände, dieses ganze Ineinander, das die Bedürfnisse

der Einzelnen und der einzelnen Gruppen regelt. 3) spricht Hegel vom *geistigen* Staat; es ist das gesamte Geschehen der Weltgeschichte, des Prozesses des zu sich selbst Kommens des Staates, *im* Auf-und Unter-gehen der einzelnen Staaten, dieses gesamten Kosmos. Also Hegel faßt den Begriff Staat auch in einem weiten Sinn, der sich mit *politisch nicht* deckt. Der politische Staat ist *mehr* Staat, ist der eigentliche *staatliche* Staat" (Heidegger, *Hegel, über den Staat,* f. 76 r°–77 v°).

79. See Chapter 7, 182.

80. "Was heißt politisch? auf die *polis* bezogen, *politisch* ist eine besondere Eigenschaft der *politeia*, geht mit der *polis* zusammen, kommt an einer *polis* vor. Man kann aber auch so verstehen: das Politische ist das, was das *Wesen* des Staates (der *polis*) gerade *ausmacht.* Also 1) als Eigenschaft 2) als Wesensgrund. Je nach der einen oder anderen Auffassung hat der Satz Richtigkeit oder nicht, wenn wir sagen: 'Das Wesen des Staates muß aus dem Politischen bestimmt werden.' *Richtig* ist der Satz, wenn er auf einen *Un*staat angewendet wird, unsinnig (tautologisch) wenn der Staat schon wirklicher Staat ist. Für die Bestimmung des Wesens des Politischen ist der Rückgang auf das Wesen des Staates das Allererste" (ibid., f. 77 v°–78 r°).

81. "Der Begriff des Staates setzt den Begriff des Politischen voraus" (Schmitt, *Der Begriff des Politischen*, 1933, 20).

82. "*Heute kann das Politische nicht mehr vom Staate her, sondern muß der Staat vom Politischen her bestimmt werden*" (Schmitt, *Staat, Bewegung, Volk,* 15).

83. See Chapter 6, 158.

84. "Was heißt *polis?* Status heißt *Zustand,* status rei publicae = Zustand der öffentlichen Dinge (zuerst moderner Gebrauch im Italienischen stato). *Dieser Staat* hat mit polis gar nichts zu tun. *polis* ist auch *nicht* die Gemeinschaft der *politeia.* Was *polis* ist, erfahren wir schon aus *Homer,* Odyssee, VI. Buch, Vers 9 ff. 'Um die *polis* herum zog er (fuhr er) mit einer Mauer, und baute Häuser und Tempel der Götter und teilte aus das Ackerland.' *Polis* ist so die eigentliche *Mitte* des Daseinsbereiches. Diese Mitte ist eigentlich der Tempel und der *Markt,* auf dem die Versammlung der *politeia* stattfindet, *polis* ist die eigentlich bestimmende Mitte des geschichtlichen Daseins eines Volkes, eines Stammes, einer Sippe; das, worum sich das Leben abspielt; die Mitte, auf die alles bezogen ist, um dessen Schutz als Selbstbehauptung es geht. Das Wesentliche des Daseins ist Selbstbehauptung. Mauer, Haus, Land, Götter. Von hier aus ist das Wesen des Politischen zu begreifen" (Heidegger, *Hegel, über den Staat,* f. 78 v°).

85. "der Status schlechthin" (Schmitt, *Der Begriff des Politischen,* 1933, 20).

86. Martin Heidegger, "Der Ursprung des Kunstwerks: Erste Ausarbeitung," ed. Hermann Heidegger, *Heidegger Studies* 5 (1989): 5–22. The text is either an initial version of the lecture that was never given as such, or the text of the lecture as it was actually given, in which case the text published by Emmanuel Martineau might be that of the lecture as delivered two months later in Zurich. Whatever the case may be, it is not credible that that first version was composed in 1931–1932, as asserted by Friedrich-Wilhelm von Hermann (*Heidegger Studies* 8 [1992]: 5). A French translation of the lecture by Nicolas Rialland has been put on the Internet. Available at nicolas.rialland.free.fr/heidegger and http://www.scribd.com/doc/6074398/Heidegger-De-lOrigine-de-lOeuvre-dArt.

87. "Ein Bauwerk, ein griechischer Tempel . . ." (Heidegger, *Holzwege,* 30).

88. In that first version, we read: "Das Bauwerk, der als Tempel die Gestalt des Gottes einbehält" (*Heidegger Studies* 5 [1989]: 12).

89. "eröffnet der Tempel das Da, worin ein Volk zu sich selbst, d.h. in die fügende Macht seines Gottes kommt" (ibid.).

90. " . . . die ausbreitsame und gewurzelte Mitte, in der und aus der ein Volk sein geschichtliches Wohnen gründet" (ibid., 13).

91. Heidegger affirms that "for the Germans," in Hölderlin's poetry, "the yet unexplored milieu of their world and land is preserved and important decisions are being prepared" (ibid., 15). Numerous other texts, among which are the recently published texts *On Ernst Jünger* (GA 90), show that these "important decisions" refer to the future World War II.

92. Kershaw, *Hitler, 1889–1936: Hubris*, 453.

93. "Die politische Tat, das Werk der Kunst, die Gliederung der Volksordnung" ("Europa und die deutsche Philosophie," *Europa und die Philosophie*, ed. Hans-Helmut Gander [Frankfurt am Main: Klostermann, 1992], 31).

94. See Chapter 9, 260.

95. "Der Kampf des Führers gegen Versailles war der Kampf gegen den jüdisch-demokratischen Mythus. Es war Rosenbergs Aufgabe, diesen Kampf in der Ebene des Grundsätzlichen zu Ende zu führen. Der Mitkämpfer des Führers löste die Aufgabe durch den Nachweis, daß die Weltgeschichte nicht als eine imaginäre 'Entwicklung' zu einem imaginären Ziele verstanden werden kann, sondern die Selbstbehauptung und der Kampf seinsgestaltender Mythen gegeneinander ist" (Baeumler, *Alfred Rosenberg*, 69–70. See Bambach, *Heidegger's Roots*, 278–280.)

96. "Neuerdings ist das *Freund-Feindverhältnis* aufgetaucht als Wesen des Politischen. Es setzt die *Selbstbehauptung voraus*, ist also Wesens*folge* des Politischen. Freund und Feind gibt es nur, wo Selbstbehauptung ist. Selbstbehauptung in diesem Sinn verlangt eine bestimmte Auffassung des geschichtlichen Seins des Volkes und des Staates selbst. Weil der Staat diese Selbstbehauptung des geschichtlichen Seins eines Volkes ist *und* weil man Staat *polis* nennen kann, zeigt sich demzufolge das Politische als Freund-Feindverhältnis; aber nicht *ist* dieses Verhältnis *das* Politische" (Heidegger, *Hegel über den Staat*, f. 78 v°–79r°).

97. "Neuerdings ist das Freund-Feind Verhältnis aufgetaucht als Wesen des Politischen. Vgl. Dazu das Freund-Feindverhältnis als das Politische von Carl Schmitt. Dieses setzt die Selbstbehauptung voraus; aber [das] Freund-Feind Verhältnis trifft nicht das Politische, sondern die Selbstbehauptung, die eine geschichtliche ist. Sofern der Staat diese Selbstbehauptung des geschichtlichen Seins eines Volkes ist, zeigt sich die *polis* in ihrem Geschehen im Freund-Feind Verhältnis, dieses ist nicht das Politische" (ibid., *reportatio* by Siegfried Bröse, DLA Marbach).

98. Heidegger never broke with Carl Schmitt. In 1944, when he was in Berlin with his wife, he telephoned Carl Schmitt and had lunch with him. All they talked about was the war. See Gary Ulmen, "Between the Weimar Republic and the Third Reich: Continuity in Carl Schmitt's Thought," *Telos*, no. 119 (Spring 2001): 29.

99. Heidegger, *"Spiegel-Gespräch,"* 105. In the entire conversation, there is not a word on the Nazi enterprise of extermination and the Shoah. The only reservation expressed by Heidegger is about the indigence of "thought" on the part of the directors of the movement.

Chapter 9: *From the Justification of Racial Selection to the Ontological Negationism of the* Bremen Lectures

Epigraph from Martin Heidegger, *Nietzsches Metaphysik,* written for winter semester 1941/1942 but not delivered, GA 50, 56–57.

1. From GA 40 to GA 55.

2. GA 65: *Beiträge zur Philosophie;* GA 66: *Besinnung;* GA 67: *Metaphysik und Nihilismus;* GA 68: *Hegel;* GA 69: *Die Geschichte des Seyns . . . Koinon;* GA 90: *Zu Ernst Jünger.*

3. Heidegger, *Nietzsche Seminare 1937 und 1944,* GA 87 (published in 2004).

4. Quoted by Max Müller in Schramm and Martin, eds., *Martin Heidegger. Ein Philosoph und die Politik,* 112.

5. See GA 16, 370–371, and below, 307. Rudolf Stadelmann died shortly afterward, and Heidegger's letters have remained in his personal archives.

6. Philipse, *Heidegger's Philosophy of Being,* 251.

7. Heidegger, *Questions I,* trans. Henry Corbin (Paris: Gallimard, 1987), 310.

8. Heidegger, "Letter on Humanism," 243. (Translation modified.)

9. See below, pp. 304–307.

10. "Nicht weniger kläglich war die allgemeine Anbiederung an die politische 'Weltanschauung.' Das neue Vorlesungsverzeichnis wimmelte von Titeln, die den 'Staat' angehängt hatten: 'Die Physik und der Staat,' 'Kunst und Staat,' 'Philosophie und Politik,' 'Plato und der Nationalsozialismus' usw. Die Folge war, daß im nächsten Semester vom Minister ein Schreiben kam, welches den Dozenten die politischen Themen verbot, soweit sie ihrem Fach nach nicht dafür zuständig waren. Zwei Jahre später war die Entwicklung soweit gediehen, daß der Minister auf Grund der miserablen Prüfungsergebnisse erklärte, er werde keine politisierenden Professoren mehr dulden. Die Resultate der 'volksnahen' Wissenschaft führten zu einer Entpolitisierung, und zwar aus politischen Gründen, und der totale Staat wurde paradoxer Weise wieder zum Befürworter der Neutralität in geistigen Dingen!" (Löwith, *Mein Leben in Deutschland,* 76).

11. "I am convinced that the course lecture fully supports the sentences alluded to" (. . . *bin ich überzeugt, daß die Vorlesung die erwähnte Sätze durchaus verträgt*), Heidegger to *Die Zeit,* 24 September 1953.

12. Heidegger, *Einführung in die Metaphysik,* 2nd ed., 152; *Martin Heidegger: An Introduction to Metaphysics,* trans. Ralph Manheim (New Haven and London: Yale University Press, 1987 [1959]), 199.

13. Joachim Haupt devoted an entire brochure to exposing the racist meaning of the "new student law." It is titled *Neuordnung im Schulwesen und Hochschulwesen.* He concludes (p. 24) on a presentation of the "Napolas," where the students wear the *Hitleruniform* and the "young combatants for the Revolution" are educated by the "older combatants" under the aegis of the "*völkisch* idea."

14. See Winfried (pseudonym for Joachim Haupt), *Sinnwandel der formalen Bildung* (Leipzig, 1935), and the factual information gathered in Franck H. W. Edler, "Heidegger and Ernst Krieck: To What Extent Did They Collaborate?" Available at http://commhum .mccneb.edu/PHILOS/krieck.htm.

15. In 1935, Reinhard Hoehn was responsible in the SD for "seeking out the adver-

sary" (*Gegnerforschung*). In 1937 he was himself harassed, and it seems that after 1938 Krieck lost much of his power. The latter hounded Heidegger, however, to the end (see Appendix A).

16. "Ein Staat—er *ist.* Worin besteht dessen Sein? Darin, dass die Staatspolizei einen Verdächtigen verhaftet" (Heidegger, *Einführung,* 27; English translation, 35, slightly modified.)

17. "mag es gut sein, künftig auf den Gebrauch des Titels 'Ontologie,' 'ontologisch' zu verzichten" (ibid., 31; English translation, 41).

18. "Es gilt, das geschichtliche Dasein des Menschen und d.h. immer zugleich unser eigenstes künftiges, im Ganzen der uns bestimmten Geschichte in die Macht des ursprünglich zu eröffnenden Seins zurückzufügen. . . . Deshalb brachten wir die Frage nach dem Sein in den Zusammenhang mit dem Schicksal Europas, worin das Schicksal der Erde entscheiden wird, wobei für Europa selbst unser geschichtliches Dasein sich als die Mitte erweist" (ibid., 32; English translation, 41–42, modified).

19. See ibid., 29; English translation, 38.

20. " . . . den Anfang unseres geschichtlich-geistigen Daseins wiederholen, um ihn in den anderen Anfang zu verwandeln" (ibid.).

21. Ibid., 30; English translation, 39.

22. Ibid., 28, 35; English translation, 37, 45.

23. Ibid., 36.

24. Heidegger, *Kant and the Problem of Metaphysics,* 173 (translation slightly modified); *Kant und das Problem der Metaphysik,* 246.

25. GA 36/37, 119.

26. Heidegger, "Davos Disputation," *Kant and the Problem of Metaphysics,* 200 (translation modified); *Kant und das Problem der Metaphysik,* 284.

27. See Chapter 8, 205–207.

28. See Heinz and Kisiel, "Heideggers Beziehungen zum Nietzsche-Archiv," 109.

29. Ibid., 107.

30. "während er in Wirklichkeit damit das Schlechte mit seinem guten Namen deckt" (Löwith, *Mein Leben in Deutschland,* 142.)

31. Heinz and Kisiel, "Heideggers Beziehungen," 111.

32. Jambet, *Henry Corbin, L'Herne,* 319.

33. "Eine weltanschauliche Überprüfung des heute neu erscheinenden deutschen Schrifttums ist politisch notwendig und steht hier nicht zur Erörterung" (Heinz and Kisiel, "Heideggers Beziehungen," 121).

34. In his 1961 preface, Heidegger speaks only of formal corrections and does not mention that many of the omissions and modifications affect the very basis of his doctrine. See *Nietzsche I,* 10.

35. Heidegger refers in his class to "the beautiful book" (*"das schöne Buch"*) by Hildebrandt on Nietzsche and Wagner (GA 43, 105), praise that he *removes* in 1961 (*Nietzsche I,* 106).

36. "einem verständigen Nachwort" (Heidegger, *Nietzsche: der Wille zur Macht als Kunst,* GA 43, 13 [*Nietzsche I,* 19]).

37. Alfred Baeumler, *Nietzsche, Der Wille zur Macht, Versuch einer Umwertung aller Werte,* mit einem Nachwort von Alfred Baeumler (Stuttgart: Alfred Kröner, 1930), 699.

38. "hier spricht der Gesetzgeber einer bestimmten Epoche der abendländischen Geschichte, Diktator der Zukunft" (ibid., 703).

39. In 1936, Heidegger reused this expression for his praise of Mussolini and Hitler (see GA 42, 40–41).

40. "Es soll die Gegenbewegung gegen den europäischen Nihilismus zum Ausdruck bringen, es soll die morsch gewordenen Grundlagen der christlichen Kultur aus der Erkenntnis dessen heraus, was das Wesen des Lebens ausmacht, durch neue Grundlagen, in Wahrheit ältere, ersetzen" (Baeumler, *Nietzsche*, 704).

41. "Wer erziehen will, das ist seine Einsicht, der muß auf den Grund des Lebens hinabsteigen. Er muß beim Leibe und bei der leiblichen Zeugung beginnen. So dachten die Griechen, und auf diesen griechischen Begriff von Erziehung weist der Titel des vierten Buches hin Zucht und Züchtung" (ibid., 705). Baeumler gives no explanation about the "Greek" character of this concept.

42. Ibid., 706.

43. "Instinkte und Affekte drücken bei jeder Rasse und bei jedem Stande etwas von ihren Existenzbedingungen aus; verlangen, daß diese Affekte der 'Tugend' weichen sollen, heißt fordern, daß jene Rassen oder Stände zugrunde gehen sollen" (ibid., 707).

44. "Es folgt die Kritik der Philosophie, wobei sich Nietzsche außer mit den Griechen nur mit den Deutschen auseinandersetzt" (ibid.).

45. "Er zeichnet das Bild des Herrn der Erde, des heroischen Menschen, der sich als ein Schicksal weiß. Mit Hohn tut er die liberale Phrase vom Adel des Geistes ab: es gibt keinen rechten Geist ohne den rechten Leib, erst das Geblüt adelt den Geist" (ibid., 709).

46. GA 50, 56–57; *Nietzsche II*, 309.

47. On this point, see below, pp. 258–262.

48. "Baeumler sonst zu den ganz Wenigen gehört, die gegen die psychologisch-biologistische Deutung Nietzsches durch Klages angehen" (GA 43, 26); cf. *Nietzsche I*, 31, in which the *ganz* became *sehr*.

49. See, for example, Charles Bambach, who despite important developments on the multiple affinities between Baeumler and Heidegger in their reading of Nietzsche believes it is Baeumler who is targeted in the Heideggerian critique of "biologism." Bambach, *Heidegger's Roots*, 283–286.

50. See GA 36/37, 263. On the opposition between Baeumler and Klages within National Socialism, which sheds light on the reasons for Heidegger's hostility toward Klages, see the article in the *Völkischer Beobachter:* "Gegenpole innerhalb der völkischen Idee. Klages und Baeumler," and the article by Tobias Schneider, "Ideologische Grabenkämpfe. Der Philosoph Ludwig Klages und der nationalsozialismus 1933–38," *Vierteljahrshefte für Zeitgeschichte* (April 2001): 275–294.

51. Bärsch, *Die politische Religion des Nationalsozialismus*, 332, 336.

52. "Die Lehre Nietzsches von der ewigen Wiederkehr paßt Baeumler nicht in seine Politik, oder er meint mindestens, sie passe nicht dazu" (GA 43, 26).

53. "Die Lehre Nietzsches von der ewigen Wiederkehr widerderstreitet Baeumlers Auffassung von der Politik" (*Nietzsche I*, 31).

54. GA 43, 26.

55. See GA 47, 68–95.

56. "Bildberichte über die Akropolis neben solchen von einem Negerkral . . . stehen" (GA 47, 70).

57. See GA 38, 81 and above, Chapter 4, 102.

58. See especially the article by Hans Zehrer, "Die Revolution von Rechts," in which the author, basing his view on Jünger's "total mobilization" and Carl Schmitt's "transformation of quantity into quality" hails, not a true revolution, but in fact the "subsumption" (Einordnung) "of the NSDAP into the State" (*Die Tat* [April 1933]: 1–16).

59. "sie ist aus einem Aufbruch deutschester Menschen zu einem amerikanischen Magazin etwas gehobener Art geworden" (GA 47, 71).

60. GA 47, 74–76.

61. "als einen pessimistischen Prediger einer schwachen und hoffnungslosen Untergangsstimmung" (GA 47, 75).

62. "Aufgrund einer biologischen Deutung des 'Willens zur Macht' wurde er zu einem der ersten und wesentlichen politischen Erzieher in dem Jahrzehnt zwischen 1920 und 30, indem er versuchte, Geschichte für den Staatsmann zu schreiben und die Kunst der Staatsmannes geschichtlich zu entwickeln" (GA 47, 75).

63. "Im Vorwort zu seiner Schrift 'Der Staat' (1924), in dem er die philosophischen Grundgedanken des 'Untergangs des Abendlandes' (1917) zusammenfaßt, finden wir die Sätze: 'wo wir heute stehen: am Übergang vom Parlamentarismus zum Cesarismus. Wir leben in einer großen Zeit. . . . Das Schicksal Deutschlands hängt von dem Einfluß ab, welchen sich die Männer erobern, die diese Lage begriffen haben und ihr gewachsen sind' (Vorwort S. IV). 'Englische Erfolge sind stets durch Mißerfolge eingeleitet und nur durch Zähigkeit im Endkampf gesichert worden' (Vorwort S. III)" (Oswald Spengler, *Der Staat,* Munich, 1924; quoted by Heidegger, GA 47, 75).

64. " 'Politisch begabte Völker gibt es nicht. Es gibt nur Völker, die fest in der Hand einer regierenden Minderheit sind und die sich deshalb gut in Verfassung fühlen. Die Engländer sind als Volk ebenso urteilslos, eng und unpraktisch in politischen Dingen wie irgend eine andere Nation, aber sie besitzen eine *Tradition des Vertrauens,* bei allem Geschmack an öffentlichen Debatten. . . . Vertrauen, das heißt unwillkürlicher Verzicht auf Kritik. . . . *Politische Begabung einer Menge ist nichts als Vertrauen auf die Führung.* Aber sie will erworben werden, sie will langsam reifen, durch Erfolge bewährt und zur Tradition geworden sein' (S. 147)" (quoted by Heidegger, ibid.).

65. "Das Grundsätzliche und Wesentliche über Politik, aus welcher Auffassung Spenglers politische Haltung und Geschichtsbetrachtung entspringt, zeigt sich in folgenden Sätzen, die oft wörtlich an Nietzsche erinnern: 'Politik ist die Art und Weise, in der sich das menschlich strömende Dasein behauptet, *wächst,* über andere Lebensströme triumphiert. *Das ganze Leben ist Politik,* in jedem triebhaften Zuge, bis ins innerste Mark. Was wir heute gerne als Lebensenergie (Vitalität) bezeichnen, jenes "es" in uns, das vorwärts und aufwärts will um jeden Preis, der blinde, kosmische, sehnsüchtige Drang nach Geltung und Macht, der pflanzenhaft und rassehaft mit der Erde, der "Heimat" verbunden bleibt, das Gerichtetsein und Wirkenmüssen ist es, was überall unter höheren Menschen als politisches Leben die großen Entscheidungen sucht und suchen muß, um ein Schicksal entweder zu sein oder zu erleiden. Denn man wächst oder stirbt ab. Es gibt keine dritte Möglichkeit' (S. 145)" (quoted by Heidegger, GA 47, 76).

66. "Politik ist die Art und Weise, in der dieses strömende Dasein sich behauptet, wächst, über andere Lebensströme triumphiert." In this instance I quote the exact sentence from Spengler, which Heidegger modified slightly in order to take into account the preceding one, which he does not quote.

67. GA 36/37, 263.

68. "Die menschlichen Daseinsströme nennen wir Geschichte, sobald wir sie als Bewegung: Geschlecht, Stand, Volk, Nation betrachten" (Spengler, *Der Staat,* 145).

69. "Deshalb ist der Adel als Ausdruck einer starken Rasse der eigentlich politische Stand, und Zucht, nicht Bildung, die eigentlich politische Art der Erziehung" (ibid.).

70. GA 47, 91.

71. GA 38, 75.

72. GA 36/37, 89.

73. Becker, "Transzendenz und Paratranszendenz ," *Travaux du IXe congrès international de philosophie. Congrès Descartes,* vol. 8, part I, p. 97.

74. Reinhard Mehring, "Der sozialdemokratische Strafrechtsdiskurs in Weimar und seine Kritik. Gustav Radbruch, Erik Wolf und Karl Larenz," *Linke Juristen in der Weimarer Republik,* ed. Manfred Gangl (Berlin: Peter Lang, 2003), 169–187.

75. "Hier ist der Ort, wo Grunderfahrungen, wie die Zugehörigkeit zu einem bestimmten Volkstum, einer bestimmten Rasse und der heimatlichen Landschaft ihren Platz haben. Was in diesen Grunderfahrungen sichtbar wird, sind die alten mütterlichen Mächte des Blutes und der Erde, von jeher mythisch verwandt" (Becker, "Transzendenz," 102).

76. See below, p. 264.

77. Becker, "Nordische Metaphysik," 81–92.

78. Löwith, *Mein Leben in Deutschland,* 51–52. Sluga, *Heidegger's Crisis,* 219–223.

79. "Das Wesen des Menschen angehörig ist . . . der Geborgenheit in seiner Rasse" (Becker, "Nordische Metaphysik," 91).

80. See below, p. 492.

81. Sluga, *Heidegger's Crisis,* 222.

82. Becker, *Gedanken Friedrich Nietzsches über Rangordnung, Zucht und Züchtung.*

83. Löwith, *Nietzsches Philosophie der ewigen Wiederkunft des Gleichen.*

84. "unseres jüngst verstorbenen hoch geschätzten Freundes Oskar Becker" (Heidegger, GA 29/30, 532).

85. Becker, *Dasein und Dawesen.* See Sluga, *Heidegger's Crisis,* 280.

86. Otto Pöggeler, ed., *Heidegger. Perspektiven zur Deutung seines Werks* (Cologne: Kiepenheuer & Witsch, 1970).

87. See Heidegger, GA 17, *Einführung in die phänomenologische Forschung.*

88. Heidegger, *Nietzsche II,* 142, 179, etc.

89. Let us recall in this connection that he who, in France, explicitly conceived of man's power of knowing as a *subjectum* was not Descartes but, as early as during the Renaissance, Charles de Bovelles, who, in 1511, in chapter 8, proposition 7, of his *Livre de l'intellect,* posited the equivalence *subjectum sive cognitrix potestas et spectatrix facultas.*

90. "die 'Betrachtungen' bezeichnen sich selbst als 'Mediationes de prima philosophia,' als solche also, die sich im Umkreis der Frage nach dem ens qua ens halten" (Heidegger, *Nietzsche* II, 433).

91. "Jetzt heißt Freisein, daß der Mensch an die Stelle der für alle Wahrheit maßge-

benden Heilsgewißheit eine solche Gewissheit setzt, kraft derer er und in der er sich seiner selbst gewiß wird als des Seienden, das dergestalt sich selbst auf sich stellt" (ibid., 145). See also the development in the 1941 course titled "Der Wandel der Wahrheit zur Gewißheit" (ibid., 421–429).

92. In his supplementary notes to the course on *Nietzsche's Metaphysics* written for the WS 1941–1942, Heidegger writes: "Neuzeit, Beginn. Subjektivität und certitudo: Descartes. . . . Justification, iustitia — Luther" (GA 50, 83). There is, however, no explication of this parallel, nor any realization of the fact that the conception of man in the Reformation and in the philosophy of Descartes are without common measure.

93. *"illa, quae divinitus revelata sunt, omni cognitione certiora credamus, cum illorum fides, quaecumque est de obscuris, non ingenii actio sit, sed voluntatis"* (Descartes, *Regulae ad directionem ingenii*, Reg. III, AT X, 370).

94. See especially the development of 1949, titled "Die Herrschaft des Subjects in der Neuzeit," in Heidegger, *Nietzsche II*, 141–147.

95. AT VI, 62.

96. "Wenn ein Mensch sich opfert, kann er das nur, sofern er ganz er selbst ist — aus der Selbstheit unter Dahingabe seiner Einzelheit. . . . Die Subjekivität kann niemals von der Ichheit her bestimmt und auf diese gegründet werden. Doch wir bringen den falschen Ton des 'Individualistischen' nur schwer aus dem Ohr, wenn wir das Wort 'Subjekt' und 'Subjektiv' hören, gilt es einzuschärfen: Je mehr und allseitiger der Mensch als geschichtliches Menschentum (Volk, Nation) sich auf sich selbst stellt, um so 'subjektiver' wird der Mensch im metaphysischen Sinne. Die Betonung der Gemeinschaft gegenüber der Eigensucht des Einzelnen ist, metaphysisch gedacht, nicht Überwindung des Subjektivismus, sondern erst seine Erfüllung, denn der Mensch — nicht der abgesonderte Einzelne, sondern der Mensch in seinem *Wesen* — kommt jetzt in die Bahn: Alles, was ist, was gewirkt und geschaffen, gelitten und erstritten wird, auf sich selbst zu stellen und in seine Herrschaft einzubeziehen" (GA 48, 211–212).

97. *Beiträge*, GA 65, 54.

98. "In diesen Tagen sind wir selbst die Zeugen eines geheimnisvollen Gesetzes der Geschichte, daß ein Volk eines Tages der Metaphysik, die aus seiner eigenen Geschichte entsprungen, nicht mehr gewachsen ist und dies gerade in dem Augenblick, da diese Metaphysik sich in das Unbedingte gewandelt hat" (Heidegger, *Nietzsche II*, 165.) See also GA 48, 205.

99. See Silvio Vietta, *Heidegger critique du national socialisme et de la technique* (Puiseaux: Pardès, 1989, 117. In addition to his mistaken interpretation of the passage on the invasion of France, the author feels obliged, in order to lend credibility his thesis of a critique of Nazism in 1940, to comment on the 1940 courses with the help of the lectures from the 1950s (ibid., 118–119).

100. "In Wahrheit ist dies ['Motorisierung' der Wehrmacht] ein metaphysischer Akt" (GA 48, 333); for the suppression of that conclusion in 1961, see *Nietzsche II*, 256.

101. Klemperer, *Language of the Third Reich*, 73–74.

102. Heidegger maintains, both in his *Nietzsche* and in the *Letter on Humanism*, that "the interpretation that has been the commonly accepted one until now, i.e. the metaphysical interpretation of man" (*die bisherige, d.h. metaphysische Auslegung des Menschen*), was that of man as *animal rationale* (*Nietzsche II*, 193; *Über den Humanismus*

[Frankfurt am Main: Klostermann, 2000], 13). Now, we know that on the contrary the scholastic definition of man as *animal rationale* was explicitly rejected by Montaigne (*Essais,* livre III, chap. xiii, 1069), then by Descartes himself in *Méditation seconde* and *Recherche de la vérité* (AT VII, 25, and AT X, 515–16). The modernity of the philosophical thought of man, in Descartes, is to be seen in his refusal to bring thought to a halt by a ready-made definition that would spare us further investigative efforts.

103. GA 48, 267; *Nietzsche II,* 200. Without denying the fact that many things are highly problematical in Nietzsche, beginning with the first dissertation of *The Genealogy of Morals,* the Heideggerian interpretation of Nietzsche also needs to be called into question.

104. "Europa will sich immer noch an die 'Demokratie' klammern und will nicht sehen lernen, daß diese sein geschichtlicher Tod würde" (GA 43, 193).

105. GA 50, 56–57; *Nietzsche II,* 309.

106. Heidegger, *Was heißt Denken?,* 65.

107. In France, it was announced that the translation of the *Beiträge* was to be carried out by Heidegger's authorized person in France, François Fédier. But nearly fifteen years since that that announcement, the translation still has not appeared. An American translation was published in 1999.

108. Tertulian, "Histoire de l'être," 109–136; and "Qui a peur du débat?," *Les Temps modernes,* 529–530 (August–September 1990): 214–240.

109. Vietta, *Heidegger critique du national socialisme et de la technique,* 125. The French translation was published by the far right press Pardès in the collection "Révolution conservatrice" (which also includes Carl Schmitt, Werner Sombart and Armin Mohler), directed by Alain de Benoist.

110. Ibid., 86.

111. Heidegger allegedly told the educationist Heribert Heinrich that he had distanced himself from Hitler and National Socialism not after Stalingrad, as did all the Germans, but in 1938. In reality, his writings during the years 1938–1942 show that there is no truth to this, and that his Nazism took on a sharp increase in virulence at the beginning of the 1940s.

112. See, for example, GA 65, 13.

113. "einem Wesenwandel des Menschen aus dem 'vernünftigen Tier' (animal rationale) in das Da-sein" (Heidegger, *Beiträge,* GA 65, 3).

114. GA 36/37, 119.

115. "der Wandel von Grund aus der deutschen . . . Welt" (GA 36/37, 225).

116. See above, p. 146.

117. "Der Führerwillen schafft allererst die anderen zu einer Gefolgschaft um, aus der die Gemeinschaft entspringt" (Heidegger, *Über das Wesen und Begriff,* 9th session).

118. "Die Besinnung auf das Volkhafte ist ein wesentlicher Durchgang. So wenig wir dies verkennen dürfen, so sehr gilt es zu wissen, daß ein höchster Rang des Seyns errungen sein muß, wenn ein 'völkisches Prinzip' als maßgebend für das geschichtliche Da-sein gemeistert ins Spiel gebracht werden soll" (Heidegger, *Beiträge,* GA 65, 42).

119. See GA 65, 55.

120. See, for the reference to the rectoral address, GA 65, 48; for the reference to the 1934 summer semester course, see GA 65, 48 and 79.

121. GA 9, 316.

122. GA, 65, 19.

123. GA 65, 24–25.

124. GA 65, 40.

125. GA 65, 42.

126. "Hier ist in der Tat das Fragen der Frage: wer wir sind, *gefährlicher* als jede andere Gegnerschaft, die einem je auf derselben Ebene einer Gewißheit über den Menschen begegnet (die Endform des Marxismus, die wesentlich weder mit Judentum noch gar mit dem Russentum etwas zu tun hat; wenn irgendwo noch ein unentfalteter Spiritualismus schlummert, dann im russischen Volk; der Bolschewismus ist ursprünglich westlich, europäische Möglichkeit: das Heraufkommen der Massen, die Industrie, Technik, das Absterben des Christentums; sofern aber die Vernunftherrschaft als Gleichsetzung aller nur die Folge des Christentums ist und dieses im Grunde jüdischen Ursprungs [vgl. Nietzsches Gedanke vom Sklavenaufstand der Moral], ist der Bolschewismus in der Tat jüdisch; aber dann ist auch das Christentum im Grunde bolschewistisch! Und welche Entscheidungen werden von hier aus notwendig?). Aber die Gefährlichkeit der Frage, wer wir sind, ist zugleich, wenn Gefahr das Höchste ernötigen kann, der einzige Weg, um zu uns selbst zu kommen und damit die ursprüngliche Rettung, d.h. Rechtfertigung des Abendlandes aus seiner Geschichte, anzubahnen. Die Gefährlichkeit dieser Frage ist so wesentlich in sich für uns, daß sie den Anschein der Gegnerschaft zum neuen deutschen Willen verliert" (Heidegger, *Beiträge,* GA 65, 54).

127. Heidegger anticipates what Hitler would maintain in 1941. See Wistrich, *Hitler and the Holocaust,* 133–134.

128. We must also recall in this connection his letter of 22 June 1932 to Elisabeth Blochmann, in which he qualifies the Catholic *Zentrum* as "diabolical" (*teuflisch*), in Heidegger/Blochmann, 52.

129. GA 65, 142.

130. "Das Wesen des Volkes aber ist seine 'Stimme'" (Heidegger, *Beiträge,* GA 65, 319).

131. "Die *Stimme* des Volkes spricht selten und nur in Wenigen" (ibid.).

132. See above, p. 279.

133. GA 65, 398.

134. "Das Wesen des Volkes gründet in der Geschichtlichkeit der *Sich*gehörenden *aus* der Zugehörigkeit zu dem Gott. Aus dem Ereignis, worin diese Zugehörigkeit geschichtlich sich gründet, entspringt erst die Begründung, warum 'Leben' und Leib, Zeugung und Geschlecht, Stamm, im Grundwort gesagt: die Erde, zur Geschichte gehören . . ." (Heidegger, *Beiträge,* GA 65, 399).

135. See Jean-Luc Évard, *Ernst Jünger. Autorité et domination,* 253. On Jünger and the Artamanen, see below, p. 297.

136. Tertulian, "Histoire de l'être et révolution politique," 128.

137. "Dieses Volk ist in seinem Ursprung und seiner Bestimmung einzig gemäß der Einzigkeit des Seyns selbst, dessen Wahrheit es einmalig an einer einzigen Stätte in einem einzigen Augenblick zu gründen hat" (Heidegger, *Beiträge,* GA 65, 97).

138. "*Ranggeben ist die totale Repräsentation der totalen Mobilmachung.* (für passive, aktive und diktatorische Typen) (die Vielen, die Wenigen, die Einzigen)" (Heidegger, *Zu Ernst Jünger,* GA 90, 59).

1 3 9. What sort of *Bund* does Heidegger have in mind in the *Beiträge* and in his writings on Jünger? Jünger's praise of the Artamanen *Bund* may be part of the answer. See below, p. 297.

1 4 0. GA 69, 46–47.

1 4 1. "*[Das Machen] Die Mache — Machenschaft.* . . . Einigen von ihnen dürfte bekannt sein, was und wer hier am Werk ist. Es gibt auch das. Es ist eine *literarische* Spielart des Infamen, also des auf eine besonders monströse — weil [mit Worten] zusammengereimte — Weise Namenlosen" (Paul Celan, *Werke,* 1 5 4); the text is translated into French by Denis Trierweiler in "*Polla ta deina,* ou comment dire l'innommable . . . ," 263.

1 4 2. "Die *jüdisch-christliche* Herrschaft treibt . . . ihrer Art gemäß ein Doppelspiel und steht zugleich auf der Seite der 'Diktatur des Proletariats' und auf der Seite der liberal-demokratischen Kulturbeflissenheit; dieses Doppelspiel verschleiert noch eine Zeitlang die schon bestehende Entwurzelung und Unkraft zu wesentlichen Entscheidungen" (Heidegger, *Besinnung,* GA 66, 59).

1 4 3. "Es gibt doch eine gefährliche internationale Verbindung der Juden" (Karl Jaspers, *Philosophische Autobiographie* [Munich: Piper, 1 9 7 7], 1 0 1).

1 4 4. "Es gibt keine Haltung, die ihre letzte Rechtfertigung nicht in dem aus ihr entspringenden Nutzen für die Gesamtheit finden könnte" (Hitler, quoted by Heidegger, *Besinnung,* GA 66, 1 2 2). The reference given in the note is as follows: "Rede des Führers vor dem 1. Großdeutschen Reichstag am 3 0 Januar 1 9 3 9. Druckerei der Reichsbank Berlin 1 9 3 9, S. 1 9."

1 4 5. "Liegt in diesem Begriff Haltung nicht schon der Verzicht auf jede wesentliche Fraglichkeit des Menschenwesens hinsichtlich seines verborgenen Bezugs zum Seyn?" (ibid.).

1 4 6. *Rassengedanke* is a major term in the racial vocabulary of Nazism, but the underlining of the word *Gedanke* is Heidegger's initiative, as if to show that racism could be raised to the level of "thought."

1 4 7. "Der *Gedanke* der Rasse, das will sagen, das Rechnen mit der Rasse entspringt der Erfahrung des Seins als Subjektivität und ist nicht ein 'Politikum.' Rasse-züchtung ist ein Weg der Selbstbehauptung für die Herrschaft. Diesem Gedanken kommt entgegen die Auslegung des Seins als 'Leben,' d.h. als 'Dynamik' " (Heidegger, *Koinon,* GA 69, 70).

1 4 8. "Rassen-pflege ist eine machtmäßige Maßnahme. Sie kann daher bald eingeschaltet bald zurückgestellt werden. Sir hängt in ihrer Handhabung und Verkündung ab von der jeweiligen Herrschafts-und Machtlage. Sie ist keineswegs ein 'Ideal' an sich, denn sie müßte dann zum Verzicht auf Machtansprüche führen und ein Geltenlassen jeder 'biologischen' Veranlagung betreiben. Daher ist streng gesehen in jeder Rassenlehre bereits der Gedanke eines Rasse*vorrangs* eingeschlossen. Der Vorrang gründet sich verschiedenartig, aber immer auf solches, was die 'Rasse' geleistet hat, welche Leistung den Maßstäben der 'Kultur' und dgl. untersteht. Wie aber, wenn diese und zwar aus dem engen Gesichtskreis des Rassedenkens her gerechnet nur Rasseprodukt überhaupt ist? (Der Zirkel der Subjektivität.) Hier kommt der selbstvergessene Zirkel aller Subjektivität zum Vorschein, der nicht eine metaphysische Bestimmung des Ich, sondern des ganzen Menschenwesens in seiner Beziehung zum Seienden und zu sich selbst enthält. Der metaphysische Grund des Rassedenkens ist nicht der Biologismus, sondern die metaphysisch zu denkende Subjektivität alles Seins von Seiendem (die Tragweite der Überwindung des Wesens der Meta-

physik und der neuzeitlichen Metaphysik im besonderen). (Zu grobes Denken in allen Widerlegungen des Biologismus: daher vergeblich.)" GA 69, 70–71.

149. See below, pp. 308–315.

150. "gerade der ehrlichste Kampf für die Rettung von Freiheit und Sittlichkeit nur der Erhaltung und Mehrung eines Machtbesitzes gilt, dessen Mächtigkeit deshalb keine Befragung duldet, weil der Vordrang der Macht als Sein des Seienden sich bereits der Moralität und ihrer Verteidigung als wesentliches Machtmittel bemächtigt hat" (GA 69, 183).

151. "Und man verfiele einer törichten Verkleinerung dessen, was an wirksamen Strebungen ins Spiel gebracht wird, wollte man die Rettung der Volkstümer und die Sicherung seines 'ewigen' rassischen Bestandes nicht als höchste Ziele anerkennen" (ibid.).

152. Here Heidegger refers in a note to the development already quoted on "power and race."

153. "Erst dadurch empfängt der Eintritt in den Kampf um den Weltmachtbesitz seine Tragweite und Schärfe, weil auch diese Zielsetzung ein Mittel ist, das durch den Vordrang der Macht auf die Bahn gebracht wird. Diese Arten von Zielsetzung und die Weisen ihrer Veröffentlichung und Einprägung sind in den Weltmachtkämpfen unentbehrlich; denn die Verteidigung der 'geistigen' Güter der Menschheit und die Rettung der 'leiblichen' 'Substanz' der Menschentümer müssen überall als Aufgaben festgehalten und neu gestellt sein, wo das Seiende vom Grundgefüge der 'Metaphysik' durchherrscht ist, demgemäß geistige 'Ideale' verwirklicht werden sollen und ihre Verwirklichung der ungebrochenen leiblichseelischen Lebenskraft bedarf. Dasselbe Gefüge der Metaphysik ist aber der geschichtliche Grund dafür, daß über die Auslegung des Seins als der Wirklichkeit und Wirksamkeit schließlich das Wesen des Seins als Macht sich vordrängt. Jene Zielsetzungen sind metaphysisch notwendig und nicht als zufällige Wünschbarkeiten und 'Interessen' ausgedacht und vorgebracht" (GA 69, 182–184).

154. GA 69, 191.

155. GA 69, 195. One this one occasion, I ask the reader's forgiveness for not translating this prose, which is, properly speaking, to borrow the very accurate term of Paul Celan, *unnamable.*

156. GA 69, 210.

157. See Heidegger, *Zu Ernst Jünger,* GA 90, 230–231.

158. See especially GA 69, 181.

159. "Die bürgerlich-christliche Form des englischen 'Bolschewismus' ist die gefährlichste. Ohne die Vernichtung dieser bleibt die Neuzeit weiter erhalten" (Heidegger, *Koinon,* GA 69, 208–209).

160. Heidegger, *Zu Ernst Jünger,* GA 90.

161. The text was published in GA 90, 213–266.

162. See GA 90, 469.

163. GA 90, 218.

164. GA 90, 222.

165. Jünger, *Der Arbeiter,* 292.

166. "sich durch Bedürfnislosigkeit auszeichnend, die *höhere Kaste:* also ärmer und einfacher, doch im Besitz der Macht" (Nietzsche, *Der Wille zur Macht, Versuch einer Umwertung aller Werte* [Stuttgart: Alfred Kröner, 1930], 764, p. 506).

167. GA 90, 219.

168. "der Arbeiter ist soldatisch-kriegerisch gedacht und nach der *Art* — d.h. als Typus (zu Deutsch: Schlag) gewertet" (Heidegger, *Zu Ernst Jünger,* GA 90, 220).

169. "Die Westmächte waren zur höchsten Klarheit und Schärfe ihres bisherigen Willens vorgedrungen, im Sinne der nationalen Demokratien die Weltmacht im Besitz zu halten. Bei uns war erst nur in den Ahnungen weniger wesentlicher Krieger die Ahnung zur Gewißheit geworden, daß ein Wandel in der Art der Weltmachthaberschaft sich vorbereite. Die Westmächte kämpfen um die Rettung des Bisherigen, wir kämpfen um die Gestaltung eines Künftigen" (GA 90, 221).

170. "Die Frage, wer die 80 Millionen *sind,* beantwortet sich auch nicht nach dem, was ihre Vorfahren geschaffen haben, sondern nach dem, was sie selbst als Auftrag der Zukunft zu wissen und zu wollen vermögen, um daraus erst zu ermessen, ob sie der Berufung auf die Vorfahren würdig sind. Der Kampf geht in der nächsten Zone einzig um die Weltmacht: und zwar nicht so sehr im Sinne des bloßen Machtbesitzes als vielmehr der Fähigkeit, die Macht als Wesen des Wirklichen in der Macht zu erhalten und d.h. hier immer: zu steigern. Die Entscheidung ist zunächst, ob die demokratischen 'Imperien' (England, Amerika) machtfähig bleiben, oder ob die imperiale Diktatur der unbedingten Rüstung um der Rüstung willen machtfähig wird" (GA 90, 221).

171. "Aber diese Entscheidung ist erst eine Vorentscheidung, mag ihr Austrag ein Jahrhundert und mehr für sich fordern. Denn gesetzt, daß der Machtbesitz im Sinne der imperialen Diktatur der unbedingten Rüstung um der Rüstung willen zugleich die wesentliche Möglichkeit der vollständigen Verwüstung des Erdkreises in sich birgt, dann erhebt sich die Frage, ob der höchste Machtbesitz zur höchsten Machthabe fähig wird, die Macht selbst als Wesen der Wirklichkeit zu überwinden und eine neue Wahrheit des Seyns wenn nicht zu stiften, so doch in ihrer Gründung vorzubereiten. Erst wenn dieser Ort solcher Entscheidung erreicht ist, kann das Weltalter der Neuzeit für überwunden gelten. Daß die verborgene und noch ungeläuterte Wesenskraft der Deutschen so weit hinausreicht, daß ist *unser* Glaube. Weil aber die einfachen Entscheidungen über das Wesen des Seins weder gemacht werden können, noch blindlings wachsen, sondern ein Geschenk sind des Seyns selbst oder eine Entbehrung, deshalb dürfen wir Entscheidungszonen nicht überspringen wollen" (GA 90, 222).

172. GA 90, 221.

173. See above, pp. 18–19.

174. See below, p. 304.

175. GA 90, 244.

176. GA 90, 38.

177. "Der Mensch ist nicht weniger Subjekt, sondern wesentlicher, wenn er sich als Nation, als Volk, als Rasse, als ein irgendwie auf sich selbst gestelltes Menschentum begreift" (ibid.).

178. "Aber Rassehaben und Rasse eigens und ausdrücklich als 'Prinzip,' Ausgang und Ziel des Menschseins aufzustellen, ist abgründig verschieden; zumal dann, wenn die Rassezüchtung *nicht nur als eine* Bedingung des Menschseins eigens betrieben wird, sondern wenn dies Rassesein und als diese Rasse Herrschen zum höchsten Ziel erhoben wird" (GA 90, 39).

179. "dann ist der vielgeforderte Vorrang des Gemeinnutzes vor dem Eigennutz nur ein Schein" (ibid.).

180. "Rassenbildung als Prinzip" (GA 90, 66). Heidegger refers to *Der Arbeiter,* 102, where Jünger embraces "that will for a cultivation of race" (*diese Wille zur Rassenbildung*).

181. "Eine organische Konstruktion ist z.B. die SS" (GA 90, 204).

182. We know by the testimony of one of his disciples, Georg Picht, that the Hitlerian seminar was taken by students in SS and SA uniforms: "Im Herbst 1933 ging ich mit zwei Mitgliedern von Heideggers Seminar durch die Kaiserstraße — rechts ein baumlanger SS-Mann, links ein SA-Mann, ich als Zivilist in der Mitte" (Picht, "Die Macht des Denkens," 176).

183. Vermeil, *L'Allemagne contemporaine,* 298.

184. Karl Löwith, "Les implications politiques de la philosophie de l'existence de Martin Heidegger," *Les Temps modernes* (November 1946): 357–358.

185. Armin Mohler, "L'ouvrage *La Révolution conservatrice,* Les implications politiques de la philosophie" 196. The perversity of this individual is seen in the way he uses his artificial opposition between the "conservative revolution," consisting of the "intellectual élite," and "National Socialism," considered solely as a "mass movement," in order to justify his commitment to serve Nazi Germany in 1942 — his contention being that he had had the "naiveté" to assimilate the one to the other.

186. On 7 November 1933, the *Berliner Tageblatt* published a list of poets and artists of the German Academy of Poetry (*Die Deutsche Akademie der Dichtung*) in which Ernst Jünger had accepted membership, who gave their public support to Hitler. Jünger's name appears there, along with those of Gottfried Benn, Hans Grimm, Erwin Guido Kolbenheyer, etc.

187. Paul Noack, *Carl Schmitt. Eine Biographie* (Berlin, Frankfurt am Main: Propyläen, 1993), 160.

188. Jünger, *Entretiens avec Ernst Jünger,* 88.

189. Quoted in Karl-Heinz Weissman, "Maurice Barrès und der 'Nationalismus' im Frühwerk Ernst Jüngers," *Magie der Heiterkeit. Ernst Jünger zum Hundertsten,* ed. Günther Figal and Heimo Schwilk (Stuttgart: Klett-Cotta, 1995), 140.

190. "Die echte Revolution hat noch gar nicht statt gefunden, sie marschiert unaufhaltsam heran . . . ihre Idee ist die völkische, zu bisher nicht gekannter Schärfe geschliffen, ihre Banner das Hakenkreuz, ihre Ausdrucksform die Konzentration des Willens in einem einzigen Punkt — die Diktatur ! . . . Denn nicht das Geld wird in ihr die bewegende Kraft dar stellen, sondern das Blut, das in geheimnisvollen Strömen die Nation verbindet. . . . Das Blut soll . . . die Freiheit des Ganzen unter Opferung des Einzelnen erstehen lassen . . . es soll alle Stoffe ausscheiden, die uns schädlich sind." (*Völkischer Beobachter,* 23/24 September 1923); see Gilbert Merlio, "Ernst Jünger, la tentation de l'idéologie," *Les Frères Jünger et la "révolution conservatrice" allemande,* in *Les Carnets Ernst Jünger* 6 (2001): 51.

191. See Jünger, *Politische Publizistik,* 721.

192. "Herr Dr. Merkenschlager ist mir durch seine Veröffentlichungen über die Rassenfrage bekannt. Da ich diese Veröffentlichung für bedeutend halte, habe ich mit ihm einen Briefwechsel geführt und ihn auch einmal in der Biologischen Reichsanstalt aufgesucht" (Jünger, *Briefe 1930–1983, Ernst Jünger, Carl Schmitt,* 34–35).

193. "der Arbeiter . . . seine Tätigkeit als eine Form zu erkennen, in der das Gesetz der Rasse zum Ausdruck kommt" (ibid., 35).

194. See Chapter 3, p. 83, and Farías, *Heidegger and Nazism,* 194–195.

195. "Das künftige Denken ist nicht mehr Philosophie . . ." (Heidegger, "Letter on Humanism," 265, trans. modified).

196. "Deutschland hat nur einen Dichter hervorgebracht, außer Goethe: das ist Heinrich Heine — und der noch dazu ein Jude . . . Dieses Wort wirft ein seltsames Licht auf den Dichter Goethe. Goethe — Heine, 'der' Dichter Deutschlands. Wo bleibt Hölderlin . . . ?" (Heidegger, *Denken und Dichten,* GA 50, 150–151).

197. "die starken Rassen der nördlichen Europa," GA 50, 108.

198. "Tragik des j. Assimilantentums seit 1900: sie konnten, als ganzes, den großen Schritt von Goethe bis Hölderlin nicht mitmachen, sondern blieben in der alten Bildung, mit der sie jetzt die neue kritisierten, aus einem aufreizend ahnungslosen Überlegenheitsgefühl heraus. Sie begriffen nicht den Schritt vom Begriff zur Gestalt und was im deutschen Geist damit gemeint war. Oder sie begriffen zuviel, wie Gundolf" (Carl Schmitt, *Glossarium,* 153).

199. "Das . . . Denken Hölderlins . . . ist darum wesentlich anfänglicher und deshalb zukünftiger als das blosse Weltbürgertum Goethes" (Heidegger, "Letter on Humanism," 242–243).

200. "Ein Philosoph kann sich im Politischen täuschen — dann wird er seinen Irrtum offen darlegen. Aber er kann sich nicht täuschen über ein Regime, das Millionen von Juden umgebracht hat — bloß weil sie Juden waren, das den Terror zum Normalzustand gemacht hat und alles, was je wirklich mit dem Begriff Geist und Freiheit und Wahrheit verbunden war, in sein blutiges Gegenteil verkehrt hat" (letter from Herbert Marcuse to Martin Heidegger, 28 August 1947, "Herbert Marcuse/Martin Heidegger Briefwechsel," 135.

201. "Der 'Historikerstreit' des Jahres 1986 ist von Heidegger vorweggenommen!" Ott, *Martin Heidegger: Unterwegs,* 186. The revisionist historian Ernst Nolte quotes this expression in his *Heidegger. Politik und Geschichte im Leben und Denken,* 220.

202. "Stehen Sie nicht mit diesem Satz außerhalb der Dimension, in der überhaupt noch ein Gespräch zwischen Menschen möglich ist — außerhalb des Logos?" (Herbert Marcuse to Martin Heidegger, 13 May 1948, "Herbert Marcuse/Martin Heidegger Briefwechsel," 138–139).

203. Heidegger, *Die Technik und die Kehre.* Philippe Lacoue-Labarthe, who was the first to publish the sentence in French in *La Fiction du politique* (p. 58), errs in placing it in the sole lecture that was "left unpublished" (*La Fiction,* 57). Indeed, the passage provisionally left out by Heidegger in 1962, then restored in 1964, belongs not to the lecture "The Danger," which remained unpublished until 1994, but to the one titled "The Frame."

204. Schirmacher, *Technik und Gelassenheit,* 25.

205. "Ackerbau ist jetzt motorisierte Ernährungsindustrie, im Wesen das Selbe wie die Fabrikation von Leichen in Gaskammern und Vernichtungslagern, das Selbe wie die Blokade und Aushungerung von Ländern, das Selbe wie die Fabrikation von Wasserstoffbomben" (quoted in ibid., 25, and included in GA 79, 27).

206. See Heinrich Wiegand Petzet, *Auf einen Stern zugehen, Begegnungen mit Martin Heidegger, 1929 bis 1976* (Frankfurt: Societät, 1983), 61.

207. "Hunderttausende sterben in Masse. Sterben sie? Sie kommen um. Sie werden

umgelegt. Sterben sie? Sie werden Bestandstücke eines Bestandes der Fabrikation von Leichen. Sterben sie? Sie werden in Vernichtungslagern unauffällig liquidiert. Und auch ohne Solches — Millionen verelenden jetzt in China durch den Hunger in ein Verenden. Sterben aber heißt, den Tod in sein Wesen austragen. Sterben können heißt, diesen Austrag vermögen. Wir vermögen es nur, wenn unser Wesen das Wesen des Todes mag. Doch inmitten der ungezählten Tode bleibt das Wesen des Todes verstellt. Der Tod ist weder das leere Nichts, noch ist er nur der Übergang von einem Seienden zu einem anderen. *Der Tod gehört in das aus dem Wesen des Seyns ereignete Dasein des Menschen.* So birgt er das Wesen des Seyns. Der Tod ist das höchste Gebirg der Wahrheit des Seyns selbst, das Gebirg, das in sich die Verborgenheit des Wesens des Seyns birgt und die Bergung seines Wesens versammelt. Darum vermag der Mensch den Tod nur und erst, wenn das Seyn selber aus der Wahrheit seines Wesens das Wesen des Menschen in das Wesen des Seyns vereignet. Der Tod ist das Gebirg des Seyns im Gedicht der Welt. Den Tod in seinem Wesen vermögen, heißt: sterben können. Diejenigen, die sterben können, sind erst die Sterblichen im tragenden Sinn dieses Wortes" (Heidegger, *Bremer und Freiburger Vorträge*, GA 79, 56).

208. These critical analyses from the 1949 *Bremen Lectures* are completed and rendered more specific by a lecture given at the University of Bremen on 30 November 2007, published since then. See E. Faye, "Der Nationalsozialismus in der Philosophie," 53–73.

209. Jean Bollack intuited this. See his essential study and his perception of the walk in the marsh taken by Celan and Heidegger: "Le mont de la mort: le sens d'une rencontre entre Celan et Heidegger," 349–376.

210. "the half-/trod log-/trails on the highmoor" (Paul Celan, "Todtnauberg," translated by Pierre Joris, available at http://wings.buffalo.edu/epc/authors/joris/todtnauberg .html)

211. "Ich kenne alles von ihm." See Gerhart Baumann, *Erinnerungen an Paul Celan* (Frankfurt am Main: Suhrkamp, 1986), 59.

212. "Ins Hüttenbuch, mit dem Blick auf den Brunnenstern, mit einer Hoffnung auf ein kommendes Wort im Herzen." See Bollack, "Le mont de la mort," 370.

213. "Und meine Wünsche? Daß Sie zu gegebener Stunde die Sprach hören, in der sich Ihnen das zu Dichtende zusagt" (ibid.).

214. Heidegger, *Feldweg Gespräche*, GA 77, 20–21 and 245. In these texts written in 1945, Heidegger also asserts that "war decides nothing" (*Der Krieg entscheidet nichts*), 244. That is not what he said in June 1940! But on the basics Heidegger has not changed: just as in 1935, he still considers the Germans as the middle of the heart (*Herzmitte*) of the West (ibid.).

215. "Wir Deutschen können . . . nicht untergehen, weil wir noch gar nicht aufgegangen sind und erst durch die Nacht hindurchmüssen" (Martin Heidegger to Rudolf Stadelmann, 20 June 1945, GA 16, 371).

216. Rickey, *Revolutionary Saints*, 3.

217. Ibid.

218. Antonio Gnoli. "Il Sessantotto? Lo invento Heidegger," conversation with Ernst Nolte, *La Repubblica* (Rome), 11 September 1992, 31; the anecdote is quoted by Thomas Sheehan in an excellent article on Nolte and Heidegger: "A Normal Nazi," *New York Review of Books*, 40, nos. 1–2, 14 January 1993, 30–35.

219. "im historischen Recht" (Nolte, *Heidegger. Politik und Geschichte,* 296).

220. "Ein Historiker oder Geschichtsdenker . . ." (Nolte, *Historische Existenz,* 11).

221. "Zu diesen Existenzialen gehören z.B. Religion, Staat, Adel, Krieg . . ." (ibid., 10).

222. "Wenn er dasjenige Phänomen war, in dem die historische Existenz sich als gefähr- dete ihrer selbst bewußt wurde und einen politischen Endkampf führte . . ." (ibid., 14).

223. But Dominique Janicaud does not mention the controversy in his *Heidegger en France.*

224. Jean Beaufret presents Heidegger's unconditional and enthusiastic allegiance, as is proven, for example, by the letter to his brother Fritz (see above, p. 61), as a "temporary" and conditional "acceptance." This is the legend Beaufret spread in France for more than thirty years.

225. Maurice Bardèche is the brother-in-law of Robert Brasillach, and very soon after World War II he undertook the revision of "the Nuremberg trial in a series of works." Beaufret points out that he does not share Bardèche's "doctrine," but this does not diminish his friendship for the author who devoted himself to the rehabilitation of the "collaboration" with Nazism.

226. Beaufret, "Jean Beaufret à Robert Faurisson," 204–205.

227. Faurisson, "Les révisionnistes proposent un débat public," 9.

228. In the preface to his monograph on Heidegger, Hugo Ott had mentioned the convergence between Beaufret and Faurisson, whom he aptly described as "the unquali- fiable propagandist of the lie" about the reality of Auschwitz.

229. François Fédier, "Lettre au professeur H. Ott," *Regarder voir* (Paris: Belles Let- tres, 1995), 245–252. François Fédier uses the same technique as in his *Anatomie d'un scandale,* in which he claims Heidegger could not have known during his lifetime who the eugenicist and raciologist Eugen Fischer (the main medical authority for the Nuremberg Laws on the "safeguard of German blood") truly was, and with whom he maintained friendly relations until the end. Yet the only thing required was a casual glance at Fischer's racist and radically anti-Semitic publications, quoted by and commented on by Erik Wolf on 7 December 1933, in a lecture attended by Rector Heidegger.

230. Fédier, "Critique et soupçon," ibid., 287.

231. Massimo Amato, "Présentation," in Ernst Nolte, *Les Fondements historiques du national-socialisme,* 16.

232. "Perspektiven für eine Historisierung der neueren Philosophiegeschichtsschrei- bung" (Tilitzki, *Die deutsche Universitätsphilosophie,* 15).

233. "Wer die deutschen Positionen als politisch legitime in einem Weltbürgerkrieg akzeptiert . . ." (ibid., 28).

234. Ibid., 29.

235. "die Particularität 'völkischer Existenz' gegen alle Universalismen" (ibid., 30).

236. Ibid.

237. See "Die Kommentierung der NS-Rassenideologie und Rassenpolitik" in Tilitzki, *Die deutsche Universitätsphilosophie,* 1041–1074.

238. Ibid., 1068–1069.

239. "Ein Fallbeispiel: Heidegger und der deutsche Austritt aus dem Völkerbund" (ibid., 24–28).

Conclusion

1. "Auch in die Logik kann man die Gestalt des Führers hineinbringen." This remark is reported by Max Müller in Schramm and Martin, eds., *Martin Heidegger. Ein Philosoph und die Politik*, 106.

2. See *Junge Freiheit*, 1 November 2002, p. 10. Hermann Heidegger says in the interview that he entered the *Hitlerjugend* in 1933 and that he soon became an enthusiastic *Jungvolkführer*.

3. His past as an anti-Semitic collaborator in Belgium was not discovered until after his death.

Appendix A: The Political Trustworthiness of the Parteigenosse
Heidegger According to the Secret Reports of the SD

1. There is a large inventory on this file by Jacques Le Rider, "Le dossier Heidegger des archives du ministère des Affaires étrangères," *Allemagnes d'aujourd'hui*, no. 107 (Jan.–March 1989): 97–109. My analysis contains some supplementary information and quoted material, and it seems to me important to draw attention to this file, the content of which contradicts Heidegger's assertions in 1945, according to which he allegedly manifested "mental resistance" to the regime.

2. "Etwas verschlossener Charakter, nicht sehr volksnahe, lebt nur für seine Wissenschaft. Steht nicht immer auf dem Boden der Wirklichkeit" (Oral Archives, Ministère des affaires étrangères [Ministry of Foreign Affairs], Colmar, France; hereafter MAE).

3. "[Er] legte aber 1934 sein Amt nieder, da er nicht die notwendigen taktischen Fähigkeiten zu einer solchen Amstführung besaß" (MAE).

4. "Er kam, ausgehend von den Kirckegaard'schen *[sic]* Auseinandersetzungen mit der Kirche und Husserl'schen Phänomenologie in einer selbstständigen Weiterentwicklung, immer mehr in einen Gegensatz zur Kirche und zum Christentum überhaupt. . . . Zusammenfassend kann man sagen, daß H. im Rahmen der Freiburger Universität wegen seiner klaren Haltung katholischen und anderen christlichen Mächtegruppen gegenüber eine positive Kraft bedeutet" (MAE).

5. It appears that 1941 was the intended date, since item 17 mentions a report dated 7 June 1941.

6. "In der Anlage übersende ich Ihnen Abschrift einer politischen Beurteilung vom 7. Juni 1940. Sobald der Dozentenbundführer aus seinem Urlaub zurück ist, werde ich mich mit ihm noch besprechen, da die vorliegende Beurteilung Prof. Heidegger nicht völlig gerecht wird" (MAE).

7. "Zu Ihrer Unterrichtung teile ich Ihnen mit, daß ich Ihnen am 12. September 1941 verschiedene Gutachten übersandt habe, die mir der Dozentenbundsführer zur Verfügung stellte. Diese Gutachten entsprechen auch der Beurteilung durch den Dozentenbundsführer. Nachträglich möchte ich Sie noch darauf aufmerksam machen, daß Parteigenosse Heidegger in Parteigenosse Prof. Dr. Krieck einen unversöhnlichen Gegner bezitzt, der ihn und seine Wissenschaft völlig ablehnt" (MAE).

8. "In der Anlage übersende ich Ihnen eine Beurteilung des Prof. Heidegger, Freiburg, die von Prof. Krieck, Heidelberg, angefertigt wurde. Wenn auch die Beurteilung stark

einseitig und zum Teil sogar polemisch ist und somit keine voll brauchbare Unterlage darstellt, sind darin doch interessante Einzelheiten über den Werdegang von Prof. Heidegger enthalten, die dort interessieren dürften. Heil Hitler! Angst Beauftragter Süd-" (MAE).

9. "In Marburg stand H. in engster Fühlung mit Juden" (MAE).

10. "Es war ihm vielmehr darum zu tun, seine eigene Herrschaft in einem eigenen Reich zu errichten, ein Reich, in dem der Philosoph selbst Herrscher, Papst, Mystagoge ist" (Ernst Krieck, MAE).

Bibliography

Works by Heidegger Cited in Text

The titles of the 102 volumes of the so-called complete works (*Gesamtausgabe;* hereafter GA) may be found in Dieter Thomä, *Heidegger Handbuch: Leben — Werk — Wirkung* (Stuttgart, Weimar: J. B. Metzler, 2003), 542–543. After the list of volumes of the GA most directly relevant to the present work, I will mention (in chronological order of their composition, as far as possible) the writings of Heidegger I reference that were published prior to the GA, as well as correspondence published elsewhere than in the GA.

For an extensive bibliography of publications in French, see Dominique Janicaud, *Heidegger en France*, I, *Récit* (Paris: Albin Michel, 2001), 544–552.

Gesamtausgabe (Frankfurt am Main: Vittorio Klostermann, 1975 *et seq.*):

GA 9 *Abteilung 1, Veröffentlichte Schriften 1914–1970, Wegmarken,* ed. Friedrich-Wilhelm von Herrmann, 1976.

GA 16 *Reden und andere Zeugnisse eines Lebensweges,* ed. Hermann Heidegger, 2000.

GA 17 *Einführung in die phänomenologische Forschung,* ed. Friedrich-Wilhelm von Herrmann (Winter semester 1923–1924), 1994.

GA 29/30 *Die Grundbegriffe der Metaphysik. Welt — Endlichkeit — Einsamkeit* (Winter semester 1929–1930), ed. Friedrich-Wilhelm von Herrmann, 1983; French trans., Daniel Panis, 1992.

GA 36/37 *Sein und Wahrheit:*

1. *Die Grundfrage der Philosophie* (Summer semester 1933).

2. *Vom Wesen der Wahrheit* (Winter semester 1933–1934), ed. Hartmut Tietjen, 2001.

GA 38 *Logik als die Frage nach dem Wesen der Sprache* (Summer semester 1934), ed. Günther Seubold, 1998.

GA 39 *Hölderlins Hymnen "Germanien" und "Der Rhein"* (Winter semester 1934–1935), ed. Suzanne Ziegler, 1980; French translation by Julien Hervier and François Fédier, 1988.

GA 41 *Die Frage nach dem Ding: Zu Kants Lehre von den transzendentalen Grundsätzen* (Winter semester 1935–1936), ed. Petra Jaeger, 1984.

GA 42 *Schelling: Vom Wesen der menschlichen Freiheit* (Summer semester 1936), ed. Ingrid Schüßler, 1988.

GA 43 *Nietzsche: der Wille zur Macht als Kunst* (Winter semester 1936–1937), ed. Bernd Heimbüchel, 1985.

GA 44 *Nietzsches metaphysische Grundstellung im abendländischen Denken: Die ewige Wiederkehr des Gleichen* (Summer semester 1937), ed. Marion Heinz, 1986.

GA 47 *Nietzsches Lehre vom Willen zur Macht als Erkenntnis* (Summer semester 1939), ed. Eberhard Hanser, 1989.

GA 48 *Nietzsche: Der europäische Nihilismus* (2nd trimester 1940), ed. Petra Jaeger, 1986.

GA 50 1. *Nietzsches Metaphysik* (for the winter semester 1941–1942; not taught). 2. *Einleitung in die Philosophie—Denken und Dichten* (Winter semester 1944–1945), ed. Petra Jaeger, 1990.

GA 65 *Beiträge zur Philosophie (Vom Ereignis)*, ed. Friedrich-Wilhelm von Herrmann, 1989.

GA 66 *Besinnung*, ed. Friedrich-Wilhelm von Herrmann, 1997.

GA 67 *Metaphysik und Nihilimus: 1. Die Überwindung des Nihilismus. 2. Das Wesen des Nihilismus*, ed. Hans-Joachim Friedrich, 1999.

GA 69 *Die Geschichte des Seyns: 1. Die Geschichte des Seyns (1938–1940). 2. Koinon: Aus der Geschichte des Seyns (1939–1940)*, ed. Peter Trawny, 1998.

GA 77 *Feldweg Gespräche*, ed. Ingrid Schüßler, 1995.

GA 79 *Bremer und Freiburger Vorträge*, ed. Petra Jaeger, 1994.

GA 87 *Nietzsche. Seminare 1937 und 1944,* ed. Peter v. Ruckteschell, 2004.

GA 90 *Zu Ernst Jünger*, ed. Peter Trawny, 2004.

Ernst Cassirer and Martin Heidegger. *Débat sur le kantisme et la philosophie (Davos, mars 1929) et autres textes de 1929–1931*. Paris: Beauchesne, 1972.

Les Conférences de Cassel (1925). German text and French translation by Jean-Claude Gens. Paris: Vrin, 2003.

Sein und Zeit, 8th ed. Tübingen: Max Niemeyer, 1957 [included in GA 2].

Kant und das Problem der Metaphysik, 5th ed. Frankfurt am Main: Vittorio Klostermann, 1991 [included in GA 3]; *Kant and the Problem of Metaphysics*, 5th ed. Trans. Richard Taft. Bloomington: Indiana University Press, 1997.

Die Selbstbehauptung der deutschen Universität: Das Rektorat, 1933–1934. Ed. Hermann Heidegger. Frankfurt am Main: Vittorio Klostermann, 1983.

Bekenntnis der Professoren an den deutschen Universitäten und Hochschulen zu Adolf Hitler und dem nationalsozialistischen Staat. Überreicht vom Nationalsozialistischen Lehrerbund, Deutschland/Sachsen, Dresde (n.d.) [1934]. Contains Martin Heidegger's "Profession of Faith in Adolf Hitler" of 11 November 1933, translated into four languages.

"Wege zur Aussprache." *Alemannenland: Ein Buch von Volkstum und Sendung.* Ed. Franz Kerber. Stuttgart: J. Engelhorns Nachf., 1937. 135–139.

Einführung in die Metaphysik. Tübingen: Max Niemeyer, 1953; 2nd ed. 1958 [included in GA 40]; *Martin Heidegger: An Introduction to Metaphysics.* Trans. Ralph Manheim. New Haven: Yale University Press, 1959.

"Der Ursprung des Kunstwerks: Erste Ausarbeitung." *Heidegger Studies* 5 (1989): 5–22.

"Europa und die deutsche Philosophie." Vortrag im Kaiser-Wilhelm-Institut, Bibliotheca Herziana Rom, 8 April 1936, *Europa und die Philosophie.* Ed. Hans-Helmut Gander. Frankfurt am Main: Vittorio Klostermann, 1993. 31–41.

"Letter on Humanism." In *Basic Writings: From Being and Time (1927) to The Task of Thinking.* Trans. David Farrell Krell. New York: Harper Perennial Modern Thought, 2008.

Holzwege. Frankfurt am Main: Vittorio Klostermann, 1949 [included in GA 5]; *Chemins qui ne mènent nulle part.* French translation by Wolfgang Brokmeier. Paris: Gallimard, 1962.

Erläuterungen zu Hölderlins Dichtung. Frankfurt am Main: Vittorio Klostermann, 1951 [included in GA 4].

Nietzsche I and II. Pfullingen: Günther Neske, 1961 [included in GA 6]. French translation by Pierre Klossowski. Paris: Gallimard, 1971.

Was heißt Denken? Tübingen: Max Niemeyer, 1971 [included in GA 8]; *What Is Called Thinking?* Trans. J. Glenn Gray. New York: Harper & Row, 1968.

Die Technik und die Kehre. Pfullingen: Günther Neske, 1962.

"*Spiegel-Gespräch*": *Antwort, Martin Heidegger im Gespräch.* Ed. Günther Neske and Emil Kettering. Pfullingen: Günther Neske, 1988.

"Drei Briefe Martin Heideggers an Löwith." *Zur philosophischen Aktualität Heideggers.* Ed. Dietrich Papenfuss and Otto Pöggeler, t. 2. Frankfurt am Main: Vittorio Klostermann, 1990. 27–39.

Heidegger's correspondence with Erich Rothacker. In "Martin Heidegger und die Anfänge der *Deutschen Vierteljahrsschrift für Literaturwissenschaft und Geistesgeschichte:* Eine Dokumentation." Ed. Joachim W. Storck and Theodore Kisiel. *Dilthey-Jahrbuch für Philosophie und Geschichte der Geisteswissenschaften.* 1992–1993. 8:187–225.

Martin Heidegger/Elisabeth Blochmann: Briefwechsel, 1918–1969. Ed. J. W. Storck. Marbach am Neckar: Deutsche Schillergesellschaft, 1989. [Heidegger/Blochmann Correspondence]

Martin Heidegger/Karl Jaspers: Briefwechsel, 1920–1963. Ed. Walter Biemel et Hans Saner. Frankfurt am Main: Vittorio Klostermann; Munich, Zurich: Piper, 1990. [Heidegger/Jaspers Correspondence]

Correspondance avec Karl Jaspers, followed by *Correspondance avec Elisabeth Blochmann.* Trans. Pascal David. Paris: Gallimard, 1996.

"*Mein liebes Seelchen!*" *Briefe Martin Heideggers an seine Frau Elfride 1919–1970.* Ed. Gertrude Heidegger. Munich: Dt. Verl.-Anst, 2005.

Works by Other National Socialist and Völkisch *Authors*

Baeumler, Alfred. *Alfred Rosenberg und der Mythus des 20. Jahrhunderts.* Munich: Hoheneichen, 1943.

———. "Nachwort." In Nietzsche, *Der Wille zur Macht: Versuch einer Umwertung aller Werte.* Stuttgart: Alfred Kröner, 1930. 699–709.

———. *Nietzsche: Der Philosoph und Politiker.* Leipzig: Reklam, 1931.

Bannes, Joachim. *Hitlers Kampf und Platos Staat: Studie über den ideologischen Aufbau der nationalsozialistischen Freiheitsbewegung.* Berlin and Leipzig: Walter de Gruyter and Co., 1933.

Becker, Oskar. *Dasein und Dawesen: Gesammelte Philosophische Aufsätze.* Pfullingen: Günther Neske, 1963.

———. *Gedanken Friedrich Nietzsches über Rangordnung, Zucht und Züchtung.* Kriegsvorträge der Rheinischen Friedrich-Wilhelms-Universität Bonn a. Rh., Aus der Vortragsreihe: "Führungsformen der Völker." Bonn: Gehr. Scheur, 1942.

———. "Nordische Metaphysik." *Rasse, Monatschrift der Nordischen Bewegung,* 5. Leipzig and Berlin: 1938. 81–92.

———. "Para-Existenz. Menschliches Dasein und Dawesen." *Heidegger: Perspektiven zur Deutung seines Werks.* Ed. Otto Pöggeler. Cologne and Berlin: Kiepenheuer und Witsch, 1970. 261–285.

———. "Transzendenz und Paratranszendenz." *Travaux du IXe congrès international de philosophie. Congrès Descartes,* t. VIII. *Analyse réflexive et transcendance.* Paris: Hermann, 1937. 97–104.

Bertram, Ernst. *Nietzsche, Versuch einer Mythologie,* "Blätter für die Kunst," 3rd ed. Berlin: Georg Bondi, 1919.

Böhm, Franz. *Anti-Cartesianismus: Deutsche philosophie im Widerstand.* Leipzig: Felix Meiner, 1938.

Clauß, Ludwig Ferdinand. *Die nordische Seele: Artung, Prägung, Ausdruck.* Halle am Donau: Max Niemeyer, 1923.

———. *Die nordische Seele: Eine Einführung in die Rassenseelenkunde.* Munich and Berlin: J. S. Lehmanns, 1940.

Darré, Walther. *Neuadel aus Blut und Boden.* Munich: J. S. Lehmanns, 1930.

Fischer, Eugen. *Das antike Weltjudentum. Tatsachen, Texte, Bilder.* Forschungen zur Judenfrage, Bd. 7, von Eugen Fischer und Gerhard Kittel. Hamburg: Hanseatische Verlagsanstalt, 1943.

———. *Das völkische Staat, biologisch gesehen.* Berlin: Junker u. Dünnhaupt, 1933.

———. *Der Begriff des völkischen Staates, biologisch betrachtet: Rede bei der Feier der Erinnerung an den Stifter der Berliner Universität, König Friedrich Wilhelm III, in der Alten Aula am 29. Juli 1933.* Berlin: Preußischer Druckerei- und Verlags-Aktiengesellschaft, 1933.

Forsthoff, Ernst. *Der Totale Staat.* Hamburg: Hanseatische Verlagsanstalt, 1933.

———. *Deutsche Geschichte seit 1918 in Dokumente,* 2nd ed. Stuttgart: A. Kröner, 1938.

———. *Deutsche Geschichte von 1918 bis 1938 in Dokumente,* 2nd ed. Stuttgart: A. Kröner, 1943.

Frank, Hans. *Akademie für Deutsches Recht, Jahrbuch 1, 1933–1934.* Munich: J. Schweizer, 1933–1934.

Glockner, Hermann, and Karl Larenz. "Zur Einführung." *Zeitschrift für deutsche Kulturphilosophie: Neue Folge des Logos*, t. 1, 1935. 1–2.

Grimm, Hans. *Volk ohne Raum*. Munich: A. Langen, G. Müller, 1926.

Günther, Hans F. K. *Platon als Hüter des Lebens*. Munich: J. F. Lehmann, 1928. French translation by Elfrida Popelier. Puiseaux: Pardès, 1987.

Haering, Theodor. *Das Deutsche in der deutschen Philosophie*. Stuttgart, Berlin: W. Kohlhammer, 1942.

——. "Der werdende Hegel." *Verhandlungen des Zweiten Hegelkongresses*. Ed. B. Wigersma. Tübingen/Haarlem: Mohr/Tjeenk Willink, 1932. 19–39.

——. *Hegel, sein Wollen und sein Werk, eine chronologische Entwicklungsgeschichte der Gedanken und der Sprache Hegels*. Vol. 2. Leipzig: Teubner, 1938.

Haupt, Joachim. *Neuordnung im Schulwesen und Hochschulwesen*. Das Recht der nationalen Revolution, Heft 5. Berlin: C. Heymann, 1935.

—— [under pseudonym Winfried]. *Sinnwandel der formalen Bildung*. Leipzig: Armanen Verlag, 1935.

Heyse, Hans. *Idee und Existenz*. Hamburg: Hanseatische Verlagsanstalt, 1935.

Hildebrandt, Kurt. *Hölderlin: Philosophie und Dichtung*. Stuttgart: Kohlhammer, 1939.

——. *Norm, Entartung, Verfall: Bezogen auf den Einzelnen, die Rasse, den Staat*. Berlin: Die Runde, 1934.

Hitler, Adolf. *Hitlers Zweites Buch. Ein Dokument aus dem Jahr 1928*. Stuttgart: Deutsche Verlags-Anstalt, 1961.

——. *Mein Kampf*. Munich: Verlag Franz Eher Nachfolger, 1932. *Mein Kampf* [My Struggle]. Trans. Ralph Manheim, introduction by Abraham Foxman (2001). Boston and New York: Houghton Mifflin, 1971.

Hoffmeister, Johannes, and Hans Fegers. *Friedrich Hölderlin: En commémoration du centenaire de sa mort le 7 juin 1843*. Textes réunis et présentés sur l'initiative de l'Institut allemand. Paris: Sorlot, 1943.

Huber, Ernst Rudolf. *Verfassungsrecht des Großdeutschen Reiches*, 2nd ed. Hamburg: Hanseatische Verlagsanstalt, 1939.

Jünger, Ernst. *Briefe, 1930–1983, Ernst Jünger, Carl Schmitt*. Ed. Helmut Kiesel. Stuttgart: Klett-Cotta, 1999.

——. *Der Arbeiter: Herrschaft und Gestalt*, 3rd ed. Hamburg: Hanseatische Verlagsanstalt, 1932; French translation by Julien Hervier. Paris: Christian Bourgois, 1989.

——. *Der Kampf als inneres Erlebnis, Werke, Essays I*. Stuttgart: Kiett, n.d. 13–14.

——. *Entretiens avec Ernst Jünger*. Ed. Julien Hervier. Paris: Gallimard, 1986.

——. *Politische Publizistik, 1919 bis 1933*. Ed. Sven Olaf Berggötz. Stuttgart: Klett-Cotta, 2001.

Kern, Eduard. *Das Führertum in der Rechtspflege*. Freiburg im Breisgau: Wagner, 1935.

——. *Die Überleitung der Justiz auf das Reich*. Freiburg im Breisgau: Wagner, 1934.

Krebs, Engelber. *Jesuitischer und deutscher Geist: Geschichtliche Abhängigkeiten und gemeinsame Wesenszüge*. Freiburg im Breisgau: Waibel, 1934.

Krieck, Ernst. *Völkisch-politische Anthropologie*. 3 vols. Leipzig: Armanen Verlag, 1936–1938.

Künneth, Walter. *Die völkische Religion der Gegenwart*. Berlin: Wichern, 1931.

Kunz, Willi. *Ernst Krieck: Leben und Werk*. Leipzig: Armanen Verlag, 1942.

Maunz, Theodor. "Gestalt und Recht der Polizei." In *Idee und Ordnung des Reiches*. Ed. Ernst Rudolph Huber. Vol. 2. Hamburg: Hanseatische Verlagsanstalt, 1943. 5–104.

Merkenschlager, Friedrich and Saller, Karl. *Ofnet: Wanderungen zu den Mälern am Weg der deutschen Rasse*. Berlin: K. Wolf, 1934.

Müller, Max. "Neudeutsche Jugend und neuer Staat." *Leuchtturm*. September 1933. Reprinted in Hans Müller, ed., *Katholische Kirche und Nationalsozialismus*. Munich: Deutsche Taschenbuch, 1965. 182–186.

Otto, Hermann, and Werne Stachowitz. *Abriß der Vererbungslehre und Rassenkunde, einschließlich der Familienkunde, Rassenhygiene und Bevölkerungspolitik*, 13th ed. Frankfurt am Main: Moritz Dieterweg, 1941.

Rosenberg, Alfred. *Der Mythus des 20. Jahrhunderts: Eine Wertung der seelisch-geistigen Gestaltungskämpfe unserer Zeit*, 3rd ed. Munich: Hoheneichen, 1935.

Rothacker, Erich. *Gedanken über Martin Heidegger*. Bonn: Bouvier, 1973.

———. *Geschichtsphilosophie*. In *Handbuch der Philosophie: IV, Staat und Geschichte*. Ed. Alfred Baeumler and Manfred Schröter. Munich and Berlin: R. Oldenbourg, 1934.

———. *Logik und Systematik des Geisteswissenschaft*. In *Handbuch der Philosophie: II, Natur, Geist, Gott*. Ed. Alfred Baeumler and Manfred Schröter. Munich and Berlin: R. Oldenbourg, 1927.

Schadewald, Wolfgang. "Der neue deutsche Student." *Freiburger Studentenzeitung*, 27 July 1933.

Schmitt, Carl. "Das gute Recht der deutschen Revolution." *Westdeutscher Beobachter*, 12 May 1933.

———. *Der Begriff des Politischen*. Hamburg: Hanseatische Verlagsanstalt, 1933.

———. *Der Begriff des Politischen*. Text von 1932 mit einem Vorwort und drei Corollarien. Berlin: Duncker & Humblot, 1963; *La Notion de politique. Théorie du partisan* [French translation]. Trans. Marie-Louise Steinhauser. Paris: Calmann-Lévy, 1972.

———. "Der deutsche Staat der Gegenwart." *Staat, Bewegung, Volk*. Heft 1, Herausgegeber: Prof. Dr. Carl Schmitt, Preußischer Staatsrat, Mitglied der Akademie für Deutsches Recht. Hamburg: Hanseatische Verlagsanstalt, 1933; *État, Mouvement, Peuple, l'organisation triadique de l'unité politique*. Trans. Agnès Pilleul. Paris: Kimé, 1997.

———. *Der Hüter der Verfassung*. Tübingen: J. B. C. Mohr, 1931.

———. *Die geistesgeschichtliche Lage des heutigen Parlementarismus*, 2nd ed. Munich: Duncker & Humblot, 1926.

———. *Glossarium*. Ed. Eberhard Freiherr von Medem. Berlin: Duncker & Humblot, 1991.

———. "La science allemande du droit dans sa lutte contre l'esprit juif." French trans. Mina Köller and Dominique Séglard. *Cités* 14 (2003): 173–180.

———. *Les Trois Types de pensée juridique*. Trans. Dominique Séglard. Paris: Presses Universitaires de France, 1995.

———. *The Leviathan in the State Theory of Thomas Hobbes*. Trans. George Schwab and Erna Hilfstein. Westport, Conn.: Greenwood Press, 1996.

Spengler, Oswald. *Der Staat, Das Problem der Stände, Staat und Geschichte, Philosophie der Politik*. Sonderdrück aus "Der Untergang des Abendlandes," II Band, Munich: C. H. Beck, 1924.

———. *Jahre der Entscheidung, Erster Teil, Deutschland und die Weltgeschichtliche Entwicklung.* Munich: C. H. Beck, 1933.

Stadelmann, Rudolf. *Das geschichtliche Selbstbewußtsein der Nation.* Tübingen: J. C. B. Mohr, 1934.

———. *Das Jahr 1865 und das Problem von Bismarcks deutscher Politik.* Munich and Berlin: R. Oldenburg, 1933.

———. *Vom Erbe der Neuzeit,* Bd. 1. Leipzig: Koehler & Amelang, 1942.

———. "Vom geschichtlichen Wesen der deutschen Revolution." *Zeitwende* 10 (1934): 109–116.

Wolf, Erik. "ΑΝΗΡ ΔΙΚΑΙΟΣ. Zur rechtsphilosophischen Interpretation der Tragödie 'Ödipus Rex' von Sophokles." *Anteile. Martin Heidegger zum 60. Geburtstag.* Frankfurt am Main: Vittorio Klostermann, 1950. 80–105.

———. "Die Aufgaben der evangelisch-christlichen Jugendbewegung im dritten Reich." *Wort und Tat. Zeitschrift für Weltanschauung und Geisteskampf* (January 1934): 21–25.

———. "Das Rechtsideal des nationalsozialistischen Staates." *Archiv für Rechts-und Sozialphilosophie* 28 (1934–1935): 348–363.

———. "Der Methodenstreit in der Strafrechtslehre und seine berwindung." *Deutsche Rechtswissenschaft: Vierteljahresschrift der Akademie für deutsches Recht* (April 1939): 168–179.

———. *Griechisches Rechtsdenken, I. Vorsokratiker und frühe Dichter.* Frankfurt am Main: Vittorio Klostermann, 1950.

———. *Richtiges Recht im nationalsozialistischen Staate.* Freiburger Universitätsreden, Heft 13. Friburg-am-Brisgau: Fr. Wagnersche Universitätsbuchhandlung, 1934.

———. "Richtiges Recht und evangelischer Glaube." *Die Nation vor Gott: Zur Botschaft der Kirche im Dritten Reich.* Ed. Walter Künneth and Helmuth Schreiner. Berlin: Im Wichern, 3rd ed., 1934, 241–265; 5th ed., 1937, 243–274.

Zehrer, Hans. "Die Revolution von Rechts." *Die Tat* (April 1933): 1–16.

Apologetic and Revisionist Studies

Baeumler, Marianne, Hubert Brunträger, and Hermann Kurzke. *Thomas Mann und Alfred Baeumler: Eine Dokumentation.* Würzburg: Königshausen & Neumann, 1989.

Beaufret, Jean. "Heidegger et le nazisme." *France-Observateur,* no. 718, 6 February 1964.

———. "Heidegger vu de France." *Die Frage Martin Heideggers: Beiträge zu einem Kollokium mit Heidegger aus Anlass seines 80.Geburtstages.* Heidelberg: Carl Winter, 1969. 9–16.

———. "Jean Beaufret à Robert Faurisson." *Annales d'histoire révisionniste: Historiographie et société,* no. 3 (Autumn–Winter 1987): 204–205.

Faurisson, Robert. "Les révisionnistes proposent un débat public." *Annales d'histoire révisionniste,* no 4 (Spring 1988): 9–24.

Fédier, François. *Heidegger: Anatomie d'un scandale.* Paris: Robert Laffont, 1988.

———. *Heidegger, Écrits politiques, 1933–1966.* Paris: Gallimard, 1995.

———. "Mißtrauen und Kritik." German translation by Ruprecht Paqué. *Weltbürgerkrieg der Ideologien. Antworten an Ernst Nolte. Festschrift zum 70. Geburtstag.* Ed.

Thomas Nipperdey, Anselm Doering-Manteuffel and Hans- Ulrich Thomas. Berlin and Frankfurt am Main: Propyläen, 1993: 277–303.

———. *Regarder voir*. Paris: Les Belles Lettres/Archimbaud, 1995.

Gernhuber, Joachim. "Das völkische Recht. Ein Beitrag zur Rechtstheorie des National-sozialismus." *Tübinger Festschrift für Eduard Kern*. Herausgegeben von der Reichs-wissenschaftlichen Abteilung der Rechts- und Wirtschaftswissenschaftlichen Fakultät der Universität Tübingen. Tübingen: J. C. B. Mohr, 1968. 67–200.

Heidegger, Hermann. "Mein Vater wollte sich nicht gemein machen." *Junge Freiheit*, 1 November 2002, 10.

Mehring, Reinhard. "Der sozialdemokratische Strafrechtsdiskurs in Weimar und seine Kritik: Gustav Radbruch, Erik Wolf und Karl Larenz." In *Linke Juristen in der Weimarer Republik*. Ed. Manfred Gangl. Berlin: Peter Lang, 2003. 169–187.

———. "Rechtsidealismus zwischen Gemeinschaftspathos und kirchlicher Ordnung: Zur Entwicklung von Erik Wolfs Rechtsgedanken." *Zeitschrift für Religion und Geistes-geschichte* 44 (1992): 140–156.

Mohler, Armin. *Die Konservative Revolution in Deutschland 1918–1932: Grundriß ihrer Weltanschauungen*. Stuttgart: Friedrich Vorwerk, 1950.

———. "L'ouvrage *La Révolution conservatrice en Allemagne* trente ans après." *La 'Révolution conservatrice' dans l'Allemagne de Weimar*. Ed. Louis Dupeux. Paris: Kimé, 1992. 195–198.

Nolte, Ernst. *Heidegger: Politik und Geschichte im Leben und Denken*. Berlin and Frank-furt am Main: Propyläen, 1992.

———. *Historische Existenz: Zwischen Anfang und Ende der Geschichte?* Munich and Zurich: Piper, 1998.

———. "Il Sessantotto? Lo invento Heidegger." Entretien rapporté par Antonio Gnoli, *La Repubblica* (Rome), 11 September 1992.

———. *Les Fondements historiques du national-socialisme*. German translation by Jean-Marie Argelès, Italian translation of the presentation and debate by Philippe Baillet. Paris: Éditions du Rocher, 2002.

Palmier, Jean-Michel. *Les Écrits politiques de Heidegger*. Paris: L'Herne, 1968.

Petzet, Heinrich Wiegand. *Auf einen Stern zugehen, Begegnungen mit Martin Heidegger, 1929 bis 1976*. Frankfurt: Societät, 1983.

Schnur, Roman. *Festschrift für Ernst Forsthoff zum 70. Geburtstag,* 2nd ed. Munich: Beck, 1974.

Tietjen, Hartmut. "Martin Heideggers Auseinandersetzung mit der nationalsozialisti-schen Hochschulpolitik und Wissenschaftsidee." *Wege und Irrwege des neueren Um-ganges mit Heideggers Werk: Ein deutsch-ungarisches Symposion*. Ed. Istvan M. Feher. Berlin: Duncker & Humblot, 1991. 109–128.

Tilitzki, Christian. *Die deutsche Universitätsphilosophie in der Weimarer Republik und im Dritten Reich*. 2 vols. Berlin: Akademie Verlag, 2002.

Vietta, Silvio. *Heidegger critique du nationalsocialisme et de la technique*. German trans-lation by Jean Ollivier, collection "Révolution conservatrice." Puiseaux: Pardès, 1989.

Works Critical of Heidegger

Adorno, Theodor. *Dialectique négative*. Paris: Payot et Rivages, 2003.

———. *Jargon der Eigentlichkeit. Zur deutschen Ideologie*. Frankfurt am Main: Suhrkamp, 1965; *Le Jargon de l'authenticité: De l'idéologie allemande*. Trans. Éliane Escoubas. Paris: Payot, 1989.

Anders, Günther. *Et si je suis désespéré que voulez-vous que j'y fasse?* Entretien avec Mathias Greffrath, trans. Catherine Weinzorn. Paris: Allia, 2001.

———. *Sur la pseudo-concrétude de la philosophie de Heidegger*. English translation by Luc Mercier. Paris: Sens et Tonka, 2003.

———. *Über Heidegger*. Munich: Beck, 2001.

Barash, Jeffrey Andrew. *Heidegger et son siècle: Temps de l'Être, temps de l'histoire*. Paris: Presses Universitaires de France, 1995.

———. *Martin Heidegger and the Problem of Historical Meaning*. Revised and expanded edition. New York: Fordham University Press, 2003.

———. "Martin Heidegger in the Perspective of the 20th Century." *Journal of Modern History* 64, no. 1 (March 1992): 52–78.

Bollack, Jean. "Le mont de la mort: le sens d'une rencontre entre Celan et Heidegger." *La Grèce de personne*. Paris: Seuil, 1997. 349–376.

Bourdieu, Pierre. *L'Ontologie politique de Martin Heidegger,* new ed. Paris: Minuit, 1988.

Bouveresse, Jacques. "Heidegger, la politique et l'intelligentsia française." *Essais IV: Pourquoi pas des philosophes?* Marseille: Agone, 2004. 129–161.

Cassirer, Ernst. *Le Mythe de l'État*. French translation by Bertrand Vergely. Paris: Gallimard, 1993.

Delacampagne, Christian. *Histoire de la philosophie au XXe siècle*. Paris: Seuil, 1995.

Farías, Victor. Foreword to the Spanish edition. *The Heidegger Case: On Philosophy and Politics*. Ed. Tom Rockmore and Joseph Margolis. Philadelphia: Temple University Press, 1992. 333–347.

———. *Heidegger et le nazisme.*Trans. from Spanish and German by Myriam Benarroch and Jean-Baptiste Grasset. Paris: Verdier, 1987; *Heidegger and Nazism*. Ed. J. Margolis and T. Rockmore, trans. from French and German by P. Burrell and G. R. Ricci. Philadelphia: Temple University Press, 1989; *Heidegger und der Nationalsozialismus*. Expanded ed. Trans. from Spanish and French by Klaus Laermann. Frankfurt am Main: S. Fischer, 1989.

———. *Logica: Lecciones de M. Heidegger (semestre verano 1934) en el legado de Helene Weiss*. Trans. Victor Farías. Madrid and Barcelona: Anthropos, 1991.

Faye, Emmanuel. "Heidegger, der Nationalsozialismus und die Zerstörung der Philosophie." In *Politische Unschuld? In Sachen Martin Heidegger*. Ed. B. H. F. Taureck. München: Wilhelm Fink, 2007. 45–80.

———. "Heidegger und die Französischen Katholiken." In *Vergangenheitsbewältigung im Französischen Katholizismus und Deutschen Protestantismus*. Ed. Lucia Scherzberg. Padeborn: Ferdinand Schöning, 2008. 121–143.

———. "Der Nationalsozialismus in der Philosophie: Sein, Geschichtlichkeit, Technik und Vernichtung in Heideggers Werk." In *Vergessen? Verdrängt? Errinert? Philosophie im*

Nationalsozialismus. Schriftenreihe der deutschen Abteilung des europäischen Unesco Lehrstuhls für Philosophie (Paris), Bd. 4. Ed. H. J. Sandkühler. Bremen: Universität Bremen, 2008. 53–73.

———. "Nazi Foundations in Heidegger's Work." *South Central Review* 23, no. 1 (2006): 55–66.

———. "Pour un approfondissement des recherches sur le nazisme de Heidegger." *Canadian Philosophical Review: Dialogue* 47, no. 1 (Winter 2008): 167–179.

———. "Résumé de Heidegger, l'introduction du nazisme dans la philosophie, Book Symposium/Tribune du livre." *Canadian Philosophical Review: Dialogue* 47, no. 1 (Winter 2008): 141–144.

Faye, Jean-Pierre. "Heidegger et la 'Révolution.'" *Médiations* (Fall 1961): 151–159.

———. *Langages totalitaires: Critique de la raison et de l'économie narrative*. Expanded ed. Paris: Hermann, 1973.

———. "Martin Heidegger: Discours et proclamations." *Médiations* (Fall 1961): 139–150.

———. *Le Piège: La philosophie heideggérienne et le nazisme*. Paris: Balland, 1994.

Ferry, Luc, and Alain Renaut. *Heidegger et les Modernes*. Paris: Grasset, 1988.

Fried, Gregory. *Heidegger's Polemos: From Being to Politics*. New Haven: Yale University Press, 2000.

Givsan, Hassan. *Eine bestürzende Geschichte: Warum Philosophen sich durch der "Fall Heidegger" Korrumpieren lassen*. Würzburg: Königshausen & Neumann, 1998.

———. *Heidegger: Das Denken der Inhumanität. Eine Ontologische Auseinandersetzung mit Heideggers Denken*. Würzburg: Königshausen & Neumann, 1998.

Goldschmidt, Georges Arthur. "Heidegger, penseur et militant nazi." *Le Matin*, 15 October 1987.

Grosser, Alfred, "Lettre à *France-Observateur*." No. 718, 6 February 1964.

Habermas, Jürgen. *Martin Heidegger, l'oeuvre et l'engagement*. Paris: Cerf, 1988.

Imbach, Ruedi. "Heidegger et la philosophie médiévale: À propos d'un nouvel annuaire philosophique." *Freiburger Zeitschrift für Philosophie und Theologie*. Universitätsverlag Freiburg (Switzerland), vol. 49, course book 3, 2002. 426–435.

Jaspers, Karl. *Notizen zu Martin Heidegger*. Ed. Hans Saner. Munich and Zurich: Piper, 1989.

———. *Philosophische Autobiographie*. Munich: Piper, 1977.

Krockow, Christian Graf von. *Die Entscheidung: Eine Untersuchung über Ernst Jünger, Carl Schmitt, Martin Heidegger*. Stuttgart: Ferdinand Enke, 1958.

Kroner, Richard. "Rede zur Eröffnung des II. Internationalen Hegelkongresses." *Verhandlungen des Zweiten Hegelkongresses vom 18. Sept. bis 2. Okt. 1931 in Berlin*. Ed. B. Wigersma. Tübingen: Mohr, Haarlem, Willink, 1932. 19–39.

Leaman, George R. "Contextual Misreadings: The U.S. Reception of Heidegger's Political Thought." Diss., University of Massachusetts, 1991.

———. *Heidegger im Kontext*. Gesamtüberblick zum NS-Engagement der Universitätsphilosophen. Hamburg: Argument Verlag, 1993.

Linde, Reinhard. *Bin ich, wenn ich nicht denke? Studien zur Enkräftung, Wirkung und Struktur totalitären Denkens*. Herbolzheim: Centaurus Verlag, 2003.

Losurdo, Domenico. *Heidegger et l'idéologie de la guerre*. Trans. from Italian by Jean-Michel Buée. Paris: Presses Universitaires de France, 1998.

Löwith, Karl. "Besprechung des Buches 'Rasse und Seele' von Ludwig Ferdinand Clauß" (1926). *Sämtliche Schriften,* 1. *Mensch und Menschenwelt. Beiträge zur Anthropologie.* Ed. Klaus Stichweh. Stuttgart: J. M. Metzler, 1981. 198–208.

——. "Der okkasionelle Dezisionismus von C. Schmitt." *Sämtliche Schriften,* vol. 8. Stuttgart: M. Metzler, 1984. 61–71.

——. *Mein Leben in Deutschland vor und nach 1933. Ein Bericht.* Stuttgart: J. B. Metzler, 1986; *Ma vie en Allemagne avant et après 1933.* French translation by Monique Lebedel. Paris: Hachette, 1988.

Marcuse, Herbert. "Herbert Marcuse-Martin Heidegger Briefwechsel." *Befreiung Denken — Ein politischer Imperativ. Ein Materialenband zu Herbert Marcuse.* 2nd ed. Ed. Peter-Erwin Jansen. Offenbach: Verlag, 2000. 135–139.

Marten, Rainer. "Heideggers Geist." *Die Heidegger Kontroverse.* Ed. Jürg Altwegg. Frankfurt am Main: Athenäum, 1988. 225–241.

Martin, Bernd, ed. *Martin Heidegger und das Dritte Reich: Ein Kompendium.* Darmstadt: Wissenschaftliche Buchgesellschaft, 1989.

Mascolo, Dionys. *Haine de la philosophie. Heidegger pour modèle.* Paris: Jean-Michel Place, 1993.

Meschonnic, Henri. *Le langage Heidegger.* Paris: Presses Universitaires de France, 1990.

Minder, Robert. *Dichter in der Gesellschaft.* Frankfurt: Insel Verlag, 1983.

Münster, Arno. "Heidegger et le nazisme: Suite d'une polémique." *La Quinzaine littéraire,* no. 812, 16–31 July 2001.

——. *Heidegger, la " science allemande" et le national-socialisme.* Paris: Kimé, 2002.

Ott, Hugo. "Der 'Freiburger Kreis.'" *Mitverschwörer-Mitgestalter. Der 20. Juli im deutschen Südwesten.* Ed. Klaus Eisele et Rolf-Ulrich Kunze. Constance: UVK, 2004. 107–128.

——. *Laubhüttenfest 1940. Warum Therese Loewy einsam sterben mußte.* Freiburg-im-Brisgau, Basel, and Vienna: Herder, 1994.

——. "Martin Heidegger als Rektor der Universität Freiburg i. Br. 1933/34, Teil I: Die Übernahme des Rektorats der Universität Freiburg i. Br. durch Heidegger im April 1933." *Zeitschrift des Breisgau-Geschichtsvereins* ("Schau-ins-Land"), no. 102 (1983). 121–136.

——. "Martin Heidegger als Rektor der Universität Freiburg i. Br. 1933/34, Teil II: Die Zeit des Rektorats von Martin Heidegger (23 April 1933 bis 23 April 1934)." *Zeitschrift des Breisgau-Geschichtsvereins* ("Schau-ins-Land"), no. 103 (1984). 107–130.

——. "Martin Heidegger als Rektor der Universität Freiburg i. Br. 1933–1934." *Zeitschrift für die Geschichte des Oberrheins,* no. 132 (1984): 343–358.

——. "Martin Heidegger als Rektor der Universität Freiburg i. Br. nach 1945. Ein Beispiel für die Auseinandersetzung mit der politischen Vergangenheit." *Historisches Jahrbuch,* no. 105 (1985): 95–128.

——. "Martin Heidegger — Mentalität der Zerrissenheit." *Freiburger Diözesan Archiv* 110 (1990): 427–448.

——. *Martin Heidegger: Unterwegs zu seiner Biographie.* Frankfurt and New York: Campus Verlag, 1988; 2nd ed. 1992.

——. "Zum Verhältnis Husserl-Heidegger: Der eine fehlte, der nicht hätte fehlen dürfen: Heidegger." *Badische Zeitung,* 19 August 1996.

Philipse, Herman. *Heidegger's Philosophy of Being: A Critical Interpretation.* Princeton, N.J.: Princeton University Press, 1998.

Quesada, Julio. *Heidegger, de camino al Holocausto.* Madrid: Biblioteca Nueva, 2008.

Rockmore, Tom. *Heidegger and French Philosophy. Humanism, Antihumanism and Being.* New York: Routledge, 1995.

———. *On Heidegger's Nazism and Philosophy.* Berkeley: University of California Press, 1992.

Rockmore, Tom, and Joseph Margolis, eds. *The Heidegger Case: On Philosophy and Politics.* Philadelphia: Temple University Press, 1992.

Schneeberger, Guido. *Ergänzungen zu einer Heidegger-Bibliographie.* Bern: AG Suhr, 1960.

———. *Nachlese zu Heidegger: Dokumente zu seinem Leben und Denken.* Bern: AG Suhr, 1962.

Schramm, Gottfried, and Bernd Martin, eds. *Martin Heidegger: Ein Philosoph und die Politik.* Freiburg im Breisgau: Rombach, 2001.

Schwan, Alexander. *Politische Philosophie im Denken Heideggers.* Cologne and Opladen: Westdeutscher Verlag, 1965.

Shayegan, Daryush. "Heidegger et l'Iran." *Le Portique,* no. 18, (2nd semester 2006).

Sheehan, Thomas. "Heidegger and the Nazis," *New York Review of Books,* 16 January 1988, 38–47.

———. "A Normal Nazi." *New York Review of Books* 40, no. 1–2 (14 January 1993): 30–35.

Sieg, Ulrich. " 'Die Verjudung des deutschen Geistes.' Ein unbekannter Brief Heideggers." *Die Zeit,* no. 52 (22 December 1989): 50.

Tertulian, Nicolas. "Carl Schmitt entre catholicisme et national-socialisme." *Les Temps modernes,* no. 589 (August–September 1996): 131–157.

———. "Histoire de l'être et révolution politique." *Les Temps modernes,* no. 523 (February 1990): 109–136.

———. "Le concept de *peuple politique* dans la révolution conservatrice." *Penser la souveraineté à l'époque moderne et contemporaine.* Ed. Gian Mario Cazzaniga and Yves-Charles Zarka. Pisa and Paris: Edizioni ETS-Librairie philosophique J. Vrin, 2001. 479–489.

———. "Qui a peur du débat?" *Les Temps modernes,* no. 529–530 (August–September 1990): 214–240.

Tibon-Cornillot, Michel. "Heidegger: le chaînon manquant." *Libération,* 17 February 1988, 41–42.

Trierweiler, Denis. "*Polla ta deina,* ou comment dire l'innommable. Une lecture d'*Arbeit am Mythos.*" *Archives de philosophie* 67 (2004): 249–268.

Ward, James F. *Law, Philosophy and National Socialism: Heidegger, Schmitt, and Radbruch in Context.* Bern and New York: Lang, 1992.

Weil, Éric. "Le cas Heidegger." *Les Temps modernes,* July 1947, 128–138; reprinted in *Philosophie et réalité.* Vol. 2. Paris: Beauchesne, 2003. 255–266.

Wolin, Richard. "Carl Schmitt, l'existentialisme et l'État total." *Les Temps modernes,* February 1990, 50–88.

———. *Heidegger's Children: Hannah Arendt, Karl Löwith, Hans Jonas, and Herbert Marcuse.* Princeton, N.J.: Princeton University Press, 2001.

———. *The Heidegger Controversy: A Critical Reader,* 2nd ed. Cambridge, Mass.: MIT Press, 1993.

———. *The Politics of Being: The Political Thought of Martin Heidegger.* New York: Columbia University Press, 1992.

———. *The Seduction of Unreason: The Intellectual Romance with Fascism from Nietzsche to Postmodernism.* Princeton, N.J.: Princeton University Press, 2004.

Other Works

Adam, Uwe Dietrich. *Hochschule und Nationalsozialismus: Die Universität Tübingen im Dritten Reich.* Tübingen: J. C. B. Mohr, 1977.

Arnold, Claus. *Katholizismus als Kulturmacht: Der Freiburger Theologe Joseph Sauer (1872–1949) und das Erbe des Franz Xaver Kraus.* Padeborn: F. Schöning, 1999.

Bambach, Charles. *Heidegger's Roots: Nietzsche, National Socialism and the Greeks.* Ithaca, N.Y.: Cornell University Press, 2003.

Bärsch, Claus-Ekkehard. *Die politische Religion des Nationalsozialismus. Die religiösen Dimensionen der NS-Ideologie in den Schriften von Dietrich Eckart, Joseph Goebbels, Alfred Rosenberg und Adolf Hitler,* 2nd ed. Munich: Wilhelm Fink, 2002.

Baumann, Gerhart. *Erinnerungen an Paul Celan.* Frankfurt am Main: Suhrkamp, 1986.

Bendersky, Joseph W. *Carl Schmitt: Theorist for the Reich.* Princeton, N.J.: Princeton University Press, 1983.

Benn, Viktor. "Die einstweilige Leitung des Deutschen Evangelischen Kirchenrechts (Juli bis September 1933)." *Zeitschrift für evangelisches Kirchenrecht* 1 (1951): 365–382.

Berl, Heinrich. *Gespräche mit berühmten Zeitgenossen.* Baden-Baden: H. Bühler, Jr., 1946.

Böhnigk, Volker. *Kulturanthropologie als Rassenlehre: Nationalsozialistische Kulturphilosophie aus der Sicht des Philosophen Erich Rothacker.* Würzburg: Königshausen & Neumann, 2002.

Braig, Carl. *Vom Sein: Abriß der Ontologie.* Berlin: Die Runde, 1896.

Brandt, Reinhard. *Universität zwischen Selbst- und Fremdbestimmung. Kants "Streit der Fakultäten." Mit einem Anhang zu Heideggers "Rektoratsrede."* Berlin: Akademie Verlag, 2003.

Bräunche, E. O. , W. Köhler, H. P. Lux, and T. Schnabel, eds., *1933. Machtergreifung in Freiburg und Südbaden.* Freiburg-im-Breisgau: Schillinger, 1983.

Breuer, Stefan. *Anatomie de la révolution conservatrice.* Trans. from German by Olivier Mannoni. Paris: Éd. de la Maison des sciences de l'homme, 1996.

Buchner, Hartmut. *Japan und Heidegger, Gedenkschrift der Stadt Meßkirch zum hundersten Geburtstag Martin Heideggers.* Sigmaringen: Jan Thornbecke, 1989.

Cassirer, Toni. *Aus meinem Leben mit Ernst Cassirer.* New York: 1950; Hamburg: Felix Meiner, 2003.

Cavaillès, Jean. "La crise de l'Église protestante allemande." *Politique,* no. 12 (1934): 1036–1042.

———. "Les conflits à l'intérieur du protestantisme allemand." *Politique,* no. 11 (1934): 179–183.

———. "Protestantisme et hitlérisme. La crise du protestantisme allemand." *Esprit,* November 1933: 305–316.

Celan, Paul. *Gedichte.* Frankfurt am Main: Suhrkamp, 1975.

———. *Werke: Tübinger Ausgabe, Der Meridian: Endfassung, Entwurfe, Materiale*. Ed.
Bernhard Böschenstein and Heino Schmull. Frankfurt am Main: Suhrkamp, 1999.

Conte, Edouard, and Cornelia Essner. *La quête de la race: une anthropologie du nazisme*.
[Paris]: Hachette, 1995.

Daim, Wilfried. *Der Mann, der Hitler die Ideen gab. Von den religiösen Verirrungen eines
Sektierers zum Rassenwahn des Diktators*. Munich: Isar, 1958.

Derrida, Jacques. *De l'esprit: Heidegger et la question*. Paris: Editions Galilée, 1987;
Heidegger et la question: De l'esprit et autres essais, 2nd ed. Paris: Flammarion, 1990;
Of Spirit: Heidegger and the Question. Trans. Geoffrey Bennington and Rachel
Bowlby. Chicago: University of Chicago Press, 1989.

———. *Politiques de l'amitié*. Paris: Galilée, 1984.

———. *Reading Heidegger: Commemorations*. Ed. John Sallis. Trans. John P. Leavey, Jr.
Bloomington: Indiana University Press, 1993.

Detsch, Richard. "The Intersection of Heidegger's Philosophy and His Politics as Reflected in the Views of His Contemporaries at the University of Freiburg." *Journal of
the History of Philosophy* 38, no. 3 (July 2000): 407–428.

Dilthey, Wilhelm. *Briefwechsel zwischen Wilhelm Dilthey und dem Grafen Paul Yorck v.
Wartenburg, 1877–1897*. Ed. Sigrist v. d. Schulenburg. Coll. "Philosophie und Geisteswissenschaften." Ed. Erich Rothacker 1. Band. Halle (Saale): Max Niemeyer, 1923.

———. *Über das Studium der Geschichte, der Wissenschaften vom Menschen, der Gesellschaft und dem Staat (1875)*. Ges. Schriften, vol. 5. Ed. Georg Misch. Stuttgart: B. G.
Teubner, 1924. 36–341.

Domarus, Max. *Hitler, Reden und Proklamationen, 1932–1945. Kommentiert von einem
deutschen Zeitgenossen*. I, *Triumph (1932–1938)*. Neustadt a. d. Aisch: Schmidt, 1962.

Dupeux, Louis, ed. *Aspects du fondamentalisme national en Allemagne de 1890 à 1945*.
Strasbourg: Presses Universitaires de Strasbourg, 2001.

———. *La "Révolution conservatrice" dans l'Allemagne de Weimar*. Paris: Kimé, 1992.

Essner, Cornelia. "Le dogme nordique des races." *La Quête de la race, une anthropologie
du nazisme*. Ed. Edouard Conte and Cornelia Essner. Paris: Fayard, 1995.

Évard, Jean-Luc. *Ernst Jünger: Autorité et domination*. Paris: Éditions de l'Éclat, 2004.

———. "Ernst Jünger et les Juifs." *Les Temps modernes*, no. 589 (August–September
1996): 102–130.

———. "La croix gammée chez les poètes." *La Fascination de l'Inde en Allemagne, 1800–
1933*. Ed. Marc Cluet. Rennes: Presses Universitaires de Rennes, 2004. 299–314.

Figal, Günther, and Heimo Schwilk. *Magie der Heiterkeit: Ernst Jünger zum Hundertsten*. Stuttgart: Klett-Cotta, 1995.

Fistetti, Francesco. *Heidegger e l'Utopia della Polis*. Genova: Marietti, 1999.

———, ed. *La Germania segreta di Heidegger*. Bari: Dedalo, 2001.

Foisneau, Luc. *Hobbes et la toute-puissance de Dieu*. Paris: Presses Universitaires de
France, 2000.

Fritsche, Johannes. *Historical Destiny and National Socialism in Heidegger's Being and
Time*. Berkeley: University of California Press, 1999.

Gadamer, Hans-Georg. "Entretien de Hans-Georg Gadamer avec Philippe Forget et
Jacques Le Rider du 18 avril 1981." *Entretiens avec Le Monde. I. Philosophies*. Paris:
La Découverte-*Le Monde*, 1984.

Gadamer, Hans-Georg, and Silvio Vietta. *Im Gespräch*. Munich: Fink, 2002.

Gangl, Manfred. "Gesellschaftliche Pluralität und politische Einheit." *Intellektuelle im Nationalsozialismus*. Ed. Wolfgang Bialas and Manfred Gangl. Frankfurt am Main: Peter Lang, 2000.

Groh, Ruth. *Arbeit an der Heillosigkeit der Welt: Zur politisch-theologischer Mythologie und Anthropologie Schmitts*. Frankfurt am Main: Suhrkamp, 1998.

Gross, Raphaël. *Carl Schmitt und die Juden. Eine deutsche Rechtslehre*. Frankfurt am Main: Suhrkamp, 2000.

Habermas, Jürgen. *Zwischen Naturalismus und Religion: Philosophische Aufsätze*. Frankfurt am Main: Suhrkamp, 2005.

Hausmann, Frank-Rutger. *Ein Verleger und seine Autoren: Vittorio Klostermann im Gespräch mit Martin Heidegger, Ernst und Friedrich Georg Jünger*. Frankfurt am Main: Vittorio Klostermann, 2002.

Heinemann, Walter. "Die Relevanz der Philosophie Martin Heideggers für das Rechtsdenken." Diss. Jur. Freiburg-am-Brisgau, 1979.

Heinz, Marion, and Theodore Kisiel. "Heideggers Beziehungen zum Nietzsche-Archiv." *Annäherungen an Martin Heidegger. Festschrift für Hugo Ott zum 65. Geburtstag*. Ed. Hermann Schäfer. Frankfurt am Main: Campus, 1996. 103–136.

Hellingrath, Norbert von. *Hölderlin: zwei Vorträge*. Munich: Hugo Bruckmann, 1922.

Hermant, Max. *Hitlérisme et humanisme*. Coulommiers, Paris: Imprimerie Paul Brodard et Ateliers Joseph Taupin réunis, 1936.

Hollerbach, Alexander. "Erinnerung an Erik Wolf." *Freiburger Universitätsblätter*, December 2002, 99–109.

——. "Juristische Lehre und Forschung in Freiburg in der Zeit des National-sozialismus." *Die Freiburger Universität in der Zeit des Nationalsozialismus*. Ed. Eckhard John, Bernd Martin, M. Mück, and Hugo Ott. Würzburg: Ploetz, 1991. 91–113.

——. "Zu Leben und Werk Erik Wolfs." *Erik Wolf: Studien zur Geschichte des Rechtsdenkens*. Ausgewählte Schriften III. Frankfurt am Main: Vittorio Klostermann, 1982. 235–271.

Jambet, Christian, ed. *Henry Corbin, L'Herne*. Paris: L'Herne, 1981.

Janicaud, Dominique. *Heidegger en France*. 2 vols. Paris: Albin Michel, 2001.

——. *La Philosophie française et l'inspiration germanique hier et aujourd'hui. Bulletin de la Société française de philosophie*. Paris: Librairie philosophique J. Vrin, July–August 2002.

Kapferer, Norbert. *Die Nazifizierung der Philosophie an der Universität Breslau, 1933–1945*. Münster, Hamburg, and Berlin: Lit, 2001.

Kershaw, Ian. *Hitler, 1889–1936: Hubris*. New York: W. W. Norton, 1999.

Kervégan, Jean-François. *Hegel, Carl Schmitt: Le politique entre spéculation et positivité*. Paris: Presses Universitaires de France, 1992.

Kisiel, Theodore. "The Essential Flaw in Heidegger's 'Private National Socialism.' " *Philosophie und Zeitgeist im Nationalsozialismus*. Ed. Marion Heinz and Geran Gretić. Würzburg: Königshausen & Neumann, 2006. 291–311. (In this article [p. 311], T. Kisiel gives a transcription of the Latin phrase with which the Hitlerian seminar of 1933–34 closes that differs substantially from the one he proposed in "In the Middle" [p. 152]).

——. "Heidegger als politischer Erzieher: der NSArbeiterstaat als Erziehungsstaat, 1933–34." *Die Zeit Heideggers.* Ed. Norbert Lesniewski. Frankfurt am Main: Lang, 2002. 71–87.

——. "Heidegger's *Gesamtausgabe:* An International Scandal of Scholarship." *Philosophy Today,* 39, no. 1 (1995): 3–15.

——. "In the Middle of Heidegger's Three Concepts of the Political." *Heidegger and Practical Philosophy.* Ed. François Raffoul and David Pettigrew. New York: SUNY Press, 2002. 135–157.

Klemperer, Victor. *The Language of the Third Reich: LTI — Lingua Tertii Imperii/A Philologist's Notebook.* Trans. Martin Brady. London and New Brunswick, N.J.: Athlone, 2000.

Kommerell, Max. *Briefe und Aufzeichnungen, 1919–1944.* Ed. Inge Jens. Freiburg im Breisgau: Olten, 1967.

——. *Der Dichter als Führer in der deutschen Klassik.* Berlin: Bondi, 1928.

Kroner, Richard. *Die Selbstverwirklichung des Geistes: Prolegomena zur Kulturphilosophie.* Tübingen: J. C. B. Mohr, 1928.

Kühnert, Hanno. "Das Recht und die Nähe der Theologie. Zum Tode von Erik Wolf." *FAZ,* 20 October 1977, no. 244, p. 25.

Lacoue-Labarthe, Philippe. *Heidegger, la politique du poème.* Paris: Galilée, 2002.

——. *La Fiction du politique.* Paris: Bourgois, 1987.

Lacoue-Labarthe, Philippe, and Jean-Luc Nancy. *Le Mythe nazi.* La Tour d'Aigues: Éditions de l'Aube, 1991.

Laugstien, Thomas. *Philosophieverhältnisse im deutschen Faschismus.* Hamburg: Argument, 1990.

Le Rider, Jacques. "Le dossier Heidegger des archives du ministère des Affaires étrangères." *Allemagnes d'aujourd'hui,* no. 107 (January–March 1998): 97–117.

Leske, Monika. *Philosophie im "Dritten Reich": Studie zur Hochschul-und Philosophiebetrieb im faschistischen Deutschland.* Berlin (DDR): Dietz, 1990.

Losurdo, Domenico. *Hegel et la catastrophe allemande.* Trans. from Italian by Charles Alunni. Paris: Albin Michel, 1994.

Löwith, Karl. *Nietzsches Philosophie der ewigen Wiederkunft des Gleichen.* Berlin: Die Runde, 1935.

Lusset, Félix. "Note sur l'épithète *völkisch:* problème de traduction ou exigence intellectuelle?" *Allemagne d'aujourd'hui,* nouvelle série no. 7 (March–April 1967): 54–56.

Maser, Werner. *Mein Kampf d'Adolf Hitler.* Paris: Plon, 1966.

Merlio, Gilbert. "Ernst Jünger. La tentation de l'idéologie." *Les Frères Jünger et la "révolution conservatrice" allemande. Les Carnets.* Revue du Centre de recherche et de documentation Ernst Jünger, no. 6 (2001): 47–73.

Milchman, Alan, and Alan Rosenberg. *Martin Heidegger and the Holocaust.* Atlantic Highlands, N.J.: Humanities Press, 1996.

Müller-Hill, Benno. *Tödliche Wissenschaft.* Reinbek bei Hamburg: Aktuel Rororo, Rohwolt, 1984; English translation, *Murderous Science, Elimination by Scientific Selection of Jews, Gypsies, and Others, Germany 1933–1945.* Plainview, N.Y.: Cold Spring Harbor Laboratory Press, 1988; French translation, *Science nazie, science de mort. La ségrégation des Juifs, des Tziganes et des malades mentaux de 1933 à 1945.* Trans. from German by Olivier Mannoni. Paris: Odile Jacob, 1989.

Nachlaß Carl Schmitt. Verzeichnis des Bestandes im Nordrhein-Westfälischen Hauptstaatsarchiv. Bearbeitet von Dirk van Laak und Ingeborg Villinger. Siegburg: Republica, 1993.

Neaman, Elliot Y. *A Dubious Past. Ernst Jünger and the Politics of Literature After Nazism.* Berkeley: University of California Press, 1999.

Noack, Paul. *Carl Schmitt: eine Biographie.* Berlin and Frankfurt am Main: Propyläen, 1993.

Parfait, Nicole. *Une certaine idée de l'Allemagne: L'identité allemande et ses penseurs de Luther à Heidegger.* Paris: Desjonquères, 1999.

"Philosophie im Deutschen Faschismus." Special issue, *Widerspruch, Münchner Zeitschrift für Philosophie,* no. 13 (1987).

Picht, Georg. "Die Macht des Denkens." *Antwort, Martin Heidegger im Gespräch.* Ed. Günther Neske and Emil Kettering. Pfullingen: Günther Neske, 1988. 175–183.

Pöggeler, Otto. "Den Führer zu Führen. Heidegger und kein Ende." *Neue Wege mit Heidegger.* Ed. Otto Pöggeler. Freiburg and Munich: K. Alber, 1992. 203–255.

———. *Phänomenologie und philosophische Forschung bei Oskar Becker.* Bonn: Bouvier, 2000.

Puschner, Uwe. *Die völkische Bewegung im wilhelminischen Kaiserreich: Sprache, Rasse, Religion.* Darmstadt: Wissenschaftliche Buchgesellschaft, 2001.

Rentsch, Thomas. *Martin Heidegger: Das Sein und der Tod.* Munich and Zurich: Piper, 1989.

Rickey, Christopher. *Revolutionary Saints: Heidegger, National Socialism, and Antinomian Politics.* University Park: Pennsylvania State University Press, 2002.

Rother, Ralf. *Wie die Entscheidung lesen? Zu Platon, Heidegger und Carl Schmitt.* Vienna: Turia & Kant, 1993.

Rudloff, Bernhard. "Heidegger and Carl Schmitt: The Historicity of the Political (Part One)." *Heidegger Studies* 20 (2004): 83–99.

Schalow, Frank. *Language and Deed: Rediscovering Politics Through Heidegger's Encounter with German Idealism.* Amsterdam: Rodopi, 1998.

Schärfer, Gunther Hermann. *Die Rechtsontologie Werner Maihofers: Möglichkeiten und Grenzen einer Rechtsphilosophie im Anschluß an Martin Heidegger.* Diss., Universität Tübingen, 2004.

Schirmacher, Wolfgang. *Technik und Gelassenheit. Zeitkritik nach Heidegger.* Freiburg im Breisgau and Munich: K. Alber, 1983.

Schmitz-Berning, Cornelia. *Vokabular des Nationalsozialismus.* Berlin and New York: Walter de Gruyter, 1998.

Schnabel, Thomas. "Von der Splittergruppe zur Staatspartei: Voraussetzungen und Bedigungen des NS Aufstiegs in Freiburg i. Br." *Zeitschrift des Breisgau-Geschichtsvereins.* "Schau-ins-Land," Heft 102, Freiburg: 1983.

Schneider, Hans-Peter. "Recht und Denken. Erinnerungen an Erik Wolf und Martin Heidegger," *Verfassung-Philosophie-Kirche, Festschrift für Alexander Hollerbach zum 70. Geburtstag.* Ed. Joachim Bohnert, Christof Gramm, Urs Kindhäuser, Joachim Lege, Alfred Rinker, and Gerhard Robbers. Berlin: Duncker & Humblot, 2001. 455–483.

Scholder, Klaus. *Die Kirchen und das Dritte Reich.* Tome I. Frankfurt am Main, Berlin, Vienna: Propyläen, 1977.

Schorcht, Claudia. *Philosophie an den bayerischen Universitäten 1933–1945*. Erlangen: H. Fischer, 1990.

Schulze, Winfried, and Otto Gerhard Oexle, eds. *Deutsche Historiker im Nationalsozialismus*. Frankfurt am Main: Fischer Taschenbuch, 1999, 2000.

Seemann, Silke. *Die politischen Säuberungen des Lehrkörpers der Freiburger Universität nach dem Ende des Zweiten Weltkrieges (1945–1957)*. Freiburg im Breisgau: Rombach, 2002.

Seidel, Eugen, and Ingeborg Seidel-Slotty. *Sprachwandel im Dritten Reich. Eine kritische Untersuchung faschistischer Einflüsse*. Halle (Saale): Veb Verlag Sprache und Literatur, 1961.

Seidler, Eduard. "Die Medizinische Fakultät zwischen 1926 und 1948." *Die Freiburger Universität in der Zeit des Nationalsozialismus*. Ed. E. John, B. Martin, M. Mück and H. Ott. Freiburg im Breisgau and Würzburg: Ploetz, 1991.

Semerari, Giuseppe. "Storicità come destino." *Studi Filosofici* 3, 1980.

Sloterdijk, Peter. *Nicht gerettet. Versuche nach Heidegger*. Frankfurt am Main: Suhrkamp, 2001.

Sluga, Hans. *Heidegger's Crisis: Philosophy and Politics in Nazi Germany*. Cambridge, Mass.: Harvard University Press, 1993.

Sontheimer, Kurt. *Antidemokratisches Denken in der Weimarer Republik. Die politischen Ideen des deutschen Nationalismus zwischen 1918 und 1933*. Munich: Nymphenburger, 1962.

Spranger, Eduard. *Rudolf Stadelmann zum Gedächtnis*. Akademische Trauerfeier am 21. Januar 1950 im Festsaal der Universität Tübingen. Tübingen: J. C. B. Mohr, 1950.

Stanguennec, André. "À l'origine de l'idée allemande de nation: la philosophie romantique et la philosophie hégélienne de l'État." *Revue française d'histoire des idées politiques,* no. 14 (2001): 337–350.

Syberberg, Hans Jürgen. *Hitler un film d'Allemagne*. Coll. Change. Paris: Seghers/Laffont, 1978.

Traverso, Enzo. *Le Totalitarisme. Le XXe siècle en débat*. Paris: Seuil, 2001.

Trierweiler, Denis. "Remarques sur la discrimination ami/ennemi et sur le *Juspublicum européen*." *Droits,* no. 40 (November 2004): 195–206.

———. "Une étrange édition: Schmitt expurgé." *Cités,* no. 17 (2004): 173–179.

Ulmen, Gary. "Between the Weimar Republic and the Third Reich: Continuity in Carl Schmitt's Thought." *Telos,* no. 119 (2001): 18–31.

———. "Heidegger and Schmitt: The Bottom Line." *Telos,* no. 72 (Summer 1987): 132.

Vermeil, Edmond. *Doctrinaires de la révolution allemande, 1918–1938*. Paris: Nouvelles Éditions Latines, 1948.

———. *L'Allemagne contemporaine: sociale, politique, culturelle, 1890–1950,* t. II, *La République de Weimar et le Troisième Reich, 1918–1950*. Paris: Aubier Éditions Montaigne, 1958.

Wistrich, Robert S. *Hitler and the Holocaust*. New York: Random House, 2001.

Würtenburger, Thomas, Werner Meihofer, and Alexander Hollerbach. *Existenz und Ordnung. Festschrift für Erik Wolf zum 60. Geburtstag*. Frankfurt am Main: Vittorio Klostermann, 1962.

———. *Questiones & Responsa: ein rechtsphilosophisches Gespräch für Erik Wolf zum 65. Geburtstag, veranstaltet am 15. Juli 1967.* Frankfurt am Main: Vittorio Klostermann, 1968.

Zarka, Yves-Charles. "Carl Schmitt, l'ennemi substantiel et la législation nazie." *Droits,* no. 40 (November 2004): 173–188

Index